D1564262

The United States and the Nuclear Dimension of
European Integration

The United States and the Nuclear Dimension of European Integration

Gunnar Skogmar

D
1065
.U5
S56
2004

© Gunnar Skogmar 2004

All rights reserved. No reproduction, copy or transmission of this
publication may be made without written permission.

No paragraph of this publication may be reproduced, copied or transmitted
save with written permission or in accordance with the provisions of the
Copyright, Designs and Patents Act 1988, or under the terms of any licence
permitting limited copying issued by the Copyright Licensing Agency, 90
Tottenham Court Road, London W1T 4LP.

Any person who does any unauthorised act in relation to this publication
may be liable to criminal prosecution and civil claims for damages.

The author has asserted his right to be identified as the author of this work
in accordance with the Copyright, Designs and Patents Act 1988.

First published 2004 by
PALGRAVE MACMILLAN
Houndmills, Basingstoke, Hampshire RG21 6XS and
175 Fifth Avenue, New York, N.Y. 10010
Companies and representatives throughout the world

PALGRAVE MACMILLAN is the global academic imprint of the Palgrave
Macmillan division of St. Martin's Press, LLC and of Palgrave Macmillan Ltd.
Macmillan® is a registered trademark in the United States, United Kingdom
and other countries. Palgrave is a registered trademark in the European
Union and other countries.

ISBN 1–4039–3899–7

This book is printed on paper suitable for recycling and made from fully
managed and sustained forest sources.

A catalogue record for this book is available from the British Library.

Library of Congress Cataloging-in-Publication Data
Skogmar, Gunnar, 1937–
    The United States and the nuclear dimension of European integration /
Gunnar Skogmar.
       p. cm.
    Includes bibliographical references and index.
    ISBN 1–4039–3899–7
    1. Europe, Western—Foreign relations—United States. 2. United
States—Foreign relations—Europe, Western. 3. Europe—Economic
integration. 4. European federation—History—20th century. 5. Nuclear
arms control—Europe—History—20th century. I. Title.

D1065.U5S56 2004
327.7304′09′045—dc22
                                                    2004046886

10   9   8   7   6   5   4   3   2   1
13   12   11   10   09   08   07   06   05   04

Printed and bound in Great Britain by
Antony Rowe Ltd, Chippenham and Eastbourne

.620807399

55228880

To Lena and our sons
and to the memory of my parents

Contents

Acknowledgements

I would like to express my thanks to friends and colleagues who commented on a draft version of the typescript: Carl-Axel Gemzell, Magnus Jerneck, Göran Skogmar and Torbjörn Vallinder. Their advice, based on great experience in diverse fields, helped me eliminate some questionable things and made me think a second or third time about some propositions. I certainly cannot blame them for any remaining deficiencies.

A grateful thought goes to those who were helpful some years ago when the project was conceived. Håkan Wiberg as Head of the Copenhagen Peace Research Institute supported my research on a closely related subject, which led to the present one. Bertel Heurlin as the driving force behind the Copenhagen Research Project on European Integration gave friendly encouragement and contributed to my decision to undertake some serious work on integration. I also had useful initial discussions with Gérard Bossuat and Johnny Laursen.

Generous financial support for the project was given by the Danish Research Agency. This made possible both the requisite archival research abroad and a concluding period of concentrated research at Roskilde University. I also acknowledge my thanks to friends and colleagues at the Department of Social Sciences there for encouragement and financial support.

I have benefited greatly from linguistic and other judicious advice from Sir David Ratford who corrected and improved my English, which is not my native language, and translated citations from other languages. I also wish to thank Jan Prawitz for checking technical facts, and the staff at Palgrave Macmillan - Luciana O'Flaherty, Daniel Bunyard, Timothy Kapp and Mary Payne - for their friendly cooperation.

The research for the book was assisted by many competent archivists. I would like to thank the staff at: *Archives Nationales*, Paris; *Auswärtiges Amt, Politisches Archiv*, Berlin; *Bundesarchiv*, Koblenz; Dwight D. Eisenhower Library, Abilene, Ks.; Historical Archives of the European Communities, Florence; *Institut Pierre Mendès France*, Paris; *Archives du Ministère des Affaires Etrangères*, Paris; National Archives and Record Administration, College Park, Md.; National Security Archive, Washington, D.C.; *Office universitaire de recherche socialiste*, Paris; Public Record Office, London; Seeley G. Mudd Manuscript Library, Princeton, N.J. *The Centre culturel suédois* and the apartment of the Danish Preetzholm-Aggerholm Foundation provided inspiring milieux for historical studies in Paris.

To all my family I owe the deepest thanks. Lena helped with various aspects of the project and was the emotional base for this and all other activities. Martin, Urban, Klas and Sten cheered me up and gave direly needed computer support when summoned in emergency. At this stage in life I often think of the efforts and support of my parents. I dedicate the book to Lena and our sons, and to the memory of my parents.

Malmö, April 2004   GUNNAR SKOGMAR

List of Abbreviations

For abbreviations in references, *see* Bibliography

ABC	Atomic, Biological and Chemical
AEC	Atomic Energy Commission
CFEP	Council on Foreign Economic Policy
CDU	*Christlich-Demokratische Union*
CEA	*Commissariat à l´énergie atomique*
CIA	Central Intelligence Agency
CM	´Common Market´/European Economic Community
CSU	*Christlich-Soziale Union in Bayern*
DOS	Department of State
ECSC	European Coal and Steel Community
EDC	European Defence Community
EEC	European Economic Community/´Common Market´
EPU	European Payments Union
Euratom	European Atomic Energy Community
F-I-G	French-Italian-German cooperation on arms
FO	British Foreign Office
FOA	Foreign Operations Administration
FRG	Federal Republic of Germany
GATT	General Agreement on Tariffs and Trade
GNP	Gross National Product
HICOG	High Commissioner for Germany
ICA	International Cooperation Administration
IAEA	International Atomic Energy Agency
IMF	International Monetary Fund
JCS	Joint Chiefs of Staff
MP	Member of Parliament
MSA	Mutual Security Agency
NATO	North Atlantic Treaty Organization
NPT	Non-Proliferation Treaty
NSC	National Security Council
OEEC	Organization for European Economic Cooperation
OCB	Operations Coordinating Board
PPS	Policy Planning Staff of the Department of State
SACEUR	NATO´s Supreme Allied Commander Europe
SHAPE	Supreme Headquarters, Allied Powers, Europe
SPD	*Sozialdemokratische Partei Deutschlands*
UKAEA	United Kingdom Atomic Energy Authority
UN	United Nations
WEU	Western European Union

Introduction

The United States supported supranational integration on the European continent in order to contain both the Soviet Union and future independent German power. Another aim was to end Franco-German rivalry as a cause of war in Europe. The unsolved 'German problem' was permanently at the centre of attention in Washington. The Truman Administration had initiated a policy of support for closer cooperation and integration in Western Europe and the Eisenhower Administration pursued this policy even more emphatically. Eisenhower and his Secretary of State, John Foster Dulles, had long experience of both the battlefields and the negotiating tables of Europe; they were both convinced that supranationalism was the key to a viable European security system and economic growth in the region. The new Administration added certain elements which were largely influenced by Eisenhower's own ideas. The first was the 'New Look' strategy, with its emphasis on nuclear weapons as a means of economizing on defence. The strategy was primarily focused on Europe and gradually implemented there. The second was the 'Atoms for Peace' policy. 'Atoms for Peace' was, among other things, a proposal to the Soviet Union to develop jointly with the US a system for preventing the spread of nuclear weapons in the respective spheres of the superpowers. Thus, Washington's emphasis on political and economic integration and the crucial role of nuclear weapons in the rearmament of Western Europe determined much of American policy on European projects for cooperation and integration during the Eisenhower presidency.

The period 1950-57 may be regarded as the foundation period of the present European Union. This study starts in 1953 when the Eisenhower Administration took office. The first project for sectoral integration, the European Coal and Steel Community (ECSC), had been organized between 1950 and 1952 and the European Defence Community (EDC) had been signed in 1952 by the six members of the Coal and Steel Community, but not ratified. After the failure of the EDC in August 1954, when France refused ratification, there followed negotiations about the replacement project, the Western European Union (WEU), which included Britain as a member. The WEU was successfully completed in March 1955. The *relance européenne* that was launched in the spring of 1955 was the final attempt at Six state integration, comprising the twin projects of the Common Market for general economic integration and

1

Euratom for sectoral integration of nuclear energy. In parallel, the British made efforts to develop an alternative framework for both general economic and nuclear cooperation under the auspices of the OEEC. The US did not participate directly in the negotiations about the *relance,* but American policy gave priority to the Six-state supranational model and supported it forcefully but discreetly. The study ends when the Treaties of Rome, on the Common Market and Euratom, were signed and ratified in 1957. The most essential foundation stone - the Common Market - of the present European Union had been laid. Euratom became a step towards comprehensive nuclear arms control. Other hopes placed in that Community later came to nothing.

During these years the negotiations on the various European projects all contained a nuclear dimension. A main problem for the US and the European states was to organize the *Einbindung* of Germany[1] generally and German military power in particular. *Einbindung* was also a goal for several political forces within German society itself who wanted to ensure that in future there would be no material basis for another outburst of aggressive nationalism. The integration of the basis of conventional military power had been achieved through the Coal and Steel Community but the more important nuclear weapons question remained to be solved. Thus, essential parts of the negotiations about the EDC, the WEU and the Common Market/ Euratom focused on finding a model for reliable control of the intertwined civil-military relationships in the nuclear energy sector of the Six.

The German problem was closely related to a ´French problem´. In the short run, France was the obvious candidate for becoming the ´fourth country´. In the European negotiations France insisted constantly, although exposed to a multitude of pressures from the US, the other Five, and to some extent from Britain, that the French nuclear weapons option should not be closed as long as the three nuclear powers continued to increase their arsenals and there was no progress in the disarmament negotiations. French nuclear weapons were highly undesirable from the point of view of American policy on Germany. It was believed in the State Department that if France had nuclear weapons Germany could not be prevented from procuring them in the long run. French nuclear weapons also went against the general aim of non-proliferation that was expressed in ´Atoms for Peace´.

This study treats, then, American policy with respect to the European negotiations 1953-57, with the focus on the nuclear dimension of that policy. It is governed by the questions: What were the American goals for European integration? What means and tactics were used to promote them? What was the effect of the outcomes of the negotiations about the European projects as regards legal and material restrictions on the spread of nuclear weapons? What was the impact of the nuclear dimension on the outcomes? To what extent were the American goals attained? Tentative answers will be given intermittently in the current text and more explicitly in the conclusion of each chapter and in the final section, 'Integration and Non-Proliferation'. The questions are all parts of the general theme of the study: the interaction of the goals of *integration* and *non-proliferation of nuclear weapons* in US European policy. European integration was a general political goal, and a crucial effect of successful integration was that it would contribute to non-proliferation there. Conversely, integration of the nuclear sector was a part of and a stage in the process toward European political and economic integration.

The central argument of the book is that a dominant consideration in the American support of European integration was the wish to prevent, retard or minimize nationally controlled nuclear weapons in Germany and France, and developments toward a European 'Third Force' outside NATO.

The argument refers to the US relationship to different 'options'. Acquisition of nuclear weapons by the Europeans could take place in one of three ways, or combinations of them. They may be called (1) the national option, (2) the transfer option, and (3) the European option. The first possibility was development by a country of a national nuclear force that was independently controlled. There were essentially two levels for such a force, the tactical A-bomb level, and the strategic H-bomb level, each having a different significance for US policy. The second option was to share some of the US nuclear weapons with European allies by transferring possession and control to a country or a supranational organization. The fundamental point was whether 'sharing' would result in complete transfer, or whether an American legal and practical veto on use would remain. The third possibility, the European option, was development of a nuclear force through cooperation between two or more European powers. Several combinations were possible in principle, but the one which was actually developed to a certain level during a short period was a Franco-German-Italian project. The European option might develop into either an 'Atlantic Europe' or a more or less 'neutralist' Third Force, possessing thermonuclear capacity, between the US and the Soviet Union. In the latter case the bipolar structure of the international system would be changed fundamentally. It should be noted that countries could - and did - exploit one of the options tactically, for example in order to obtain resources and nuclear information from the US and Britain, or to promote another option, for example by advancing the European option in order to press the US to approve transfer.

The crucial problem in all three scenarios was Germany. France was a problem in its own right, but it was also important because of its impact on Germany.

The US nuclear sharing policy - perhaps less a 'policy' than a conglomerate of contradictory, diffuse or tactically motivated ideas - developed as a response to the need to counteract other options, to restore confidence among the allies or as a means to other goals held within the Administration and Congress. The doubt about US reliability in all circumstances generated centrifugal forces among the NATO allies and a search in Washington for measures to keep the alliance together. Many policymakers, including the President, believed that if the Europeans were to place their fate in American hands they needed some nuclear forces under their own control. One of the motives for sharing was that it seemed to offer the prospect of withdrawing American troops from Europe within a not too distant future. Paradoxically, however, the very notion of withdrawal had to be kept wholly secret from the Europeans, because if they knew about it the pressure for independence would increase.

From the perspective of political science the approach chosen here is based on certain premises of 'liberal intergovernmentalism'. The most influential recent attempt at explaining European integration in these terms has been made by Andrew Moravcsik.[2] In liberal intergovernmentalism European integration is seen as the outcome of a process of bargaining between states, represented by national leaders who make a series of rational choices. The approach is based on the realist and neorealist traditions in the theory of international relations. However, the process of preference formation is 'liberal' in the sense that the interests of states are not regarded as fixed and given once and for all, but as varying over time in response to pressures from domestic interests whose preferences are aggregated through political institutions. National and transnational coalitions form, and the pressures are expressed in national preferences. The outcome of European integration may be explained, then, through consideration of national preference formation and the strategic interaction of states in the bargaining process. As regards the nuclear dimension, which is in focus here, attention will be given to some transnational coalitions that worked for and against different outcomes, particularly in the case of Euratom. The centre of gravity of the study will lie in security factors in US policy towards European integration but these, just like economic factors, are seen not as fixed and given but as affected by the interplay of interests of different agencies within the Administration, and in Congress. Divergences between the State Department and the Atomic Energy Commission will be given particular attention here. Policy was also strongly influenced by the personal views of Eisenhower and Dulles. Both had strong convictions, they worked closely with one another, and the President often acted decisively as arbiter between domestic interests when defining the goals.

Which were the interacting states and other significant actors involved in bargaining about the projects studied here? Liberal intergovernmentalism departs from the notion that interstate bargaining outcomes are decisively shaped by the relative power of the nation-states which participate.

Moravcsik´s study focuses on the policies of the leading European powers - Germany, France and Britain. In the chapter on the Treaties of Rome, which is the starting point of a study stretching over decades, he also pays some attention to the roles of leading European integrationists like Jean Monnet and Paul-Henri Spaak. Other participating states in the negotiations in Brussels 1955-57 - Italy and the Benelux countries - are largely ignored as their power was much less significant in determining outcomes.

However, the role of the United States in the early stage, the foundation period in the fifties, tends to disappear or be underestimated in this perspective. I will argue that the US had an essential, indeed hegemonic, role in all negotiations about European cooperation and integration in the decade, even if that role diminished or became much less significant in the following decades. The US was sometimes represented directly in the European negotiations in the fifties, sometimes the American standpoints were communicated through a multitude of other channels. American diplomacy was constantly vigilant and active behind the scenes. The negotiating parties kept the Americans informed about the details of the negotiations, asked for US views and sometimes for pressures to be applied to other parties. Particularly in the case of the negotiations about the foundation of the Common Market and Euratom it was a very deliberate US policy to act discreetly in order not to disturb European sensitivities, French sensitivities in particular. It was believed in the State Department that the EDC failure could partly be explained by the fact that too much overt pressure had been applied. It should further be remembered that the main European actors in varying degrees had dependent relationships to the US. For Britain the ´special relationship´ of World War II and earlier was one of the pillars of British foreign policy; Britain also strived for reconstruction of the special relationship in the nuclear field which had largely been dismantled by the US after the war.[3] Post-war Germany has been characterized as a ´penetrated political system´, meaning that national freedom of action was particularly circumscribed by exterior forces.[4] This was of course the consequence of the defeat in World War II. An alliance with America developed and became so strong that it became a ´second *Grundgesetz*´ [basic law]. The alliance was in no small degree also the result of the close personal relationship between two dominant foreign-policy makers in the fifties, the US Secretary of State John Foster Dulles and the Chancellor of the Federal Republic, Konrad Adenauer. Adenauer was the leader of what has been termed a *Kanzlerdemokratie*. His domestic position was strong during these years; the governing coalition commanded a two-thirds majority in Parliament. France was attempting to restore some of the Great Power position that had been lost in the war and was the main carrier of aspirations for greater European autonomy. But France was dependent on American aid because of economic problems and colonial wars, although dependence was decreasing in the middle fifties.

My view is that the essential actors in the European integration game in the period which is in focus here were four: the United States, Germany, France and Britain. Italy and the Benelux countries had minor parts and their preferences normally coincided with American policy. Prominent integrationists like Monnet and Spaak had a mediating and idea-producing role but no significant power base of their own. They worked to further the development toward a supranational and Atlanticist Europe and normally cooperated closely with US policymakers in furthering these goals.

For Moravcsik, as for Milward, the economic factors are primary and the geopolitical/security factors secondary when explaining European integration. However, when the US is conceived as an essential, dominant or hegemonic actor this has, in my view, consequences for the evaluation of the relative weight of security and economic factors in the formation of national preferences.[5] For the US, it is quite evident that the basic motive for promoting and supporting European integration in the fifties was closely related to global security policy. The economic benefits of European integration were seen in the containment perspective as a means of increasing security. The risks of damaging effects on the American economy were seen partly as the necessary price to pay for security, partly as outweighed by the economic benefits that could be expected from integration. Security motives similarly played a very great role in the formation of French preferences. In France, the need for security against Germany was for long a dominant consideration - in the French collective memory the years 1870, 1914 and 1940 were always present. In the second phase of the negotiations about the Common Market, on the other hand, the economic factors were possibly strong enough to ensure sufficient support by French economic interests. The Common Market was perceived by many as the right economic solution then, but economic integration which included Germany at the same time gave increased security. It is, however, by no means certain that the Common Market would have been ratified in France if the nuclear security problem in Euratom had not been solved in a satisfactory manner. In Germany, Adenauer and his close entourage wanted European integration primarily for political reasons, although there were major economic forces in Germany which wanted broader multilateral and intergovernmental solutions. The German parliamentary opposition, the Social-Democrats, initially opposed but eventually adhered to Adenauer´s line, also largely for political reasons.

One purpose of the present study is to draw some conclusions about the interplay of economic motives and security motives in the negotiations about the twin projects Euratom/the Common Market. Therefore, the main issues in the Common Market negotiations are sketched briefly in the treatment of these negotiations, although the major part deals with the negotiations about Euratom (and to some extent the British alternative for nuclear cooperation).

I have used documents from archives in the United States, Germany, France, and the United Kingdom.[6] The major part is diplomatic correspondence, memoranda and other internal material produced in the foreign ministries in connection with the negotiations in Europe. Much of it has not, to my knowledge, been utilized before. Many of the American sources emanate from the National Archives, in which State Department documents are preserved, and the Eisenhower Library also contributed substantially. Three published collections of documents have been used extensively: *Foreign Relations of the United States* (FRUS), *Documents diplomatiques français* (DDF), and a valuable more recent publication, *Die Bundesrepublik Deutschland und Frankreich: Dokumente 1949-1963* (BDF).

The book is based on a relatively larger quantity of unpublished sources from archives with respect to the Euratom/Common Market negotiations 1955-57 than for the negotiations about the EDC and the WEU in the preceding years. This is because the study originally focused on American policy toward Euratom and the Common Market; for the earlier period I planned to give a background account only. However, as work proceeded it became clearer that there was a continuity in American policy with respect to the nuclear dimension in US support of European unity. There is a similar pattern in all the negotiations in the period 1953-57; this finding may in fact be regarded as a major result of the study. Consequently, the treatment of the earlier period was upgraded - but much of the work in archives had been done by then.

Fewer sources from Britain than from the other three main countries have been consulted. The British role - largely outside the negotiations aiming at supranational integration - was given more attention relatively late. I then concentrated the work in the Public Record Office on the periods which I found most important, that is, when Foreign Office consideration of policy on Euratom became more intensive.

One ambition is to use material from different countries covering the same events, in order to illustrate different perspectives and interpretations of a situation. Another is sometimes to give an account of inter-agency conflicts about an issue, and ministerial deliberations that preceded decisions about standpoints that were advanced externally. Policy memoranda, minutes from meetings and briefing material in the State Department and the White House are of particular interest.

Much of the material about nuclear policy is rather technical and located at the level of officials below the level of top decision-makers. However, several of the technical and legal questions have - or were perceived at the time as having - great political importance. I have traced certain disputes about technical matters in considerable detail and tried to relate them to the political and economic issues that were at stake. In particular, the question of access to enriched uranium will be stressed. In the fifties, high-enriched uranium was seen as necessary for H-bombs, medium-enriched as necessary or preferable for nuclear submarines, and low-enriched as important for development of first-generation power reactors (until sufficient plutonium had been produced in the power systems). The complicated enrichment technology was - and is - highly classified. The giant American enrichment production complex, which had been built for arms production, was a strategic asset in the European negotiations.

Secondary archive-based material and memoirs have been used on various points, particularly in cases when there are gaps in the primary sources, and when the secondary material contains illustrative citations. Well-known standard works about the negotiations on the European projects in the fifties have been used to some extent, although some of them were written a couple of decades ago (much material has been released since then), and were based on material mainly from one or two countries.[7] A second group of studies are those treating US policy towards European integration, the importance of the German question in that policy, and the role of leading European integrationists like Jean Monnet.[8] Third, I have used contributions by authors who have studied the integration policy or nuclear policy of one of the major European countries, or the relationship of that country to the US.[9] Finally, there are some studies that have been particularly influential in forming my views about the bases of US foreign policy in the fifties, the role of nuclear weapons and disarmament considerations in that policy, the centrality of the 'German question', and the impact of US strategy on the nuclear ambitions of European countries. The works by Beatrice Heuser, Melvin P. Leffler, Geir Lundestad and Marc Trachtenberg may be mentioned.

The text is organized in the following way. Chapter 1 gives a brief overview of the European policy of the Eisenhower Administration. The most general global goals for security and economic reconstruction are outlined and two converging lines of US European policy which can be related to these goals are identified: the nuclear policy which had both a military and a civil side, and the policy for promoting European integration. In the subsequent chapters the negotiations about the European projects in the 1953-57 period - standpoints, tactics, alliances - are treated in detail. The primary focus is always the role of the US and the importance of the nuclear dimension in the total negotiation context. Chapter 2 deals with the European Defence Community and Chapter 3 with the Western European Union. The negotiations about Euratom and its linkage to the Common Market are divided into two phases, contained in Chapters 4 and 5 respectively. The first phase is the period of preliminary negotiations in the Intergovernmental Committee that ended with the preliminary fixing of standpoints and the decision in Venice in May 1956 to continue the negotiations in the Intergovernmental Conference. The second phase covers essentially the period up to the signature of the Treaties of Rome in March 1957. The chapters contain concluding sections which summarize the main themes and attempt to give answers to some of the questions that were formulated above. Finally, a general conclusion sums up certain earlier results and offers tentative answers to other questions.

1

The European Policy of the Eisenhower Administration

Double Containment and European Integration

The security policy of the Truman Administration has sometimes been called 'double containment'. Two primary threats were identified, the expansion of Soviet power or the spread of Communist ideology, and the resurgence of Germany as an independent, powerful and militarist state. US policy was designed to counter the double threat. A diversified arsenal of military and economic means was developed. The strategy to contain the Soviet Union and Communism aimed at retaining predominance on the Eurasian continent. American defence officials considered the preservation of a favourable balance of power in Eurasia as fundamental to US national security. In the view of the historian Melvin P. Leffler, basing his argument on the massive number of documents about the early years of the Cold War that were declassified in the eighties and early nineties, these officials did not expect a Soviet military attack in the short term, but they were fearful about socio-economic dislocation, revolutionary nationalism, British weakness and Eurasian vacuums of power.[1] The 'German question' was part of the short-term problem of countering the first threat, and a potential long-term threat in its own right. Historically, the Germans had been able to tip the world balance of power by applying *Schaukelpolitik*, that is, allying now with the West, now with the East, according to the current conception of the national interest. With respect to containment of the USSR and Communism it was thus considered vital to keep West Germany firmly anchored in the Western camp. 'Neutralism' was seen by US policy-makers as a dangerous first step to a deal with the East. Germany had a strong incentive to seek a deal in order to obtain the major national objective of unification. Although US officials ritually endorsed the cause of reunification as a means of retaining the loyalty of West Germany, they believed that actual reunification would involve a nightmare deal in which Moscow gave up East Germany in return for Bonn's staying outside the Western alliance. It was equally vital to avoid the danger of independent German power. The inability of Europe to assimilate the united and industrially expanding *Reich* after 1870 was seen by many as the basic cause of the two world wars.

Geir Lundestad concludes, in his illuminating book about the United States and European integration, that Washington´s abiding concern about the role of Germany was perhaps the most striking part of his study. In some respects, Washington also felt that even France and other Western European allies of the US had to be contained. That was the ´triple containment´, or the endeavour to control Europe as part of the American ´empire´.[2] Marc Trachtenberg has a similar view of the centrality of the German problem, and he stresses the significance of containment of Germany to avoid the cold war developing into a real war: ´The basic argument is...quite simple: the claim is that the problem of German power lay at the heart of the cold war...If the western countries could create a political system of their own in which German power was limited, this was something the USSR could live with; if they were unable to do so, there might be very serious trouble indeed.´[3]

Washington´s solution to the contradictions in the perceived threats and the American goals for Europe was to promote and support European integration. The early thinking of the State Department was summarized clearly by the ´containment strategist´ - at that time Director of the Policy Planning Staff - George F. Kennan:

> In the long run there can be only three possibilities for the future of western and central Europe. One is German domination. Another is Russian domination. The third is a federated Europe, into which the parts of Germany are absorbed but in which the influence of the other countries is sufficient to hold Germany in her place. - If there is no real European federation and if Germany is restored as a strong and independent country, we must expect another attempt at German domination. If there is no real European federation and if Germany is *not* restored as a strong and independent country, we invite Russian domination, for an unorganized Western Europe cannot indefinitely oppose an organized Eastern Europe. The only resonably hopeful possibility for avoiding one of these two evils is some form of federation in western and central Europe.[4]

In 1949, the Policy Planning Staff undertook the first in-depth analysis of the problem of European integration and the American attitude towards it. Referring to Britain´s conception of its own world role and reluctant attitude to supranationalism in Europe, the Staff strongly recommended that Britain stay out of any closer European Union. Continental integration was important to the US not so much for economic as for political reasons. The political reasons centred around Germany. Franco-German understanding was the key aim of America´s European policy. A fundamental prerequisite to a closer union of the European continent, it was stressed, was however the continued US military commitment to Europe within the framework of the recently formed Atlantic alliance. American leadership in that alliance would replace merging sovereignties at the military level.[5]

Although the idea that Britain would stay outside European Union had so far been unthinkable, the Secretary of State, Dean Acheson, supported the idea of not building on Britain in America's European policy. He opted for a limited supranational group rather than a wider and looser entity. He insisted that he did not 'wish to see progress ...on the road to integration (including Western Germany)... retarded by British reluctance...France and France alone...can take the decisive leadership in integrating Western Germany into Western Europe'.[6]

The US integration project coincided with the objectives of forces in all the European countries that were also striving towards integration. During the war various groups of European integrationists had already outlined plans for a new European post-war order, to prevent future wars and foster economic growth by dismantling protectionism. The integrationists gained considerable influence after the war, particularly in the disillusioned defeated countries Germany and Italy, in the small countries that had been occupied, and in Christian-Democratic parties everywhere. An important counterforce was the West German Social-Democratic party, representing almost half of the population; until the middle fifties the party opposed US-led integration and strived for East-West détente and reunification on the basis of neutralism. The French Communists and Gaullists were other opposing forces. In Britain, all political strands were united in their resistance to supranationalism. In this pattern, the American superpower allied with the European pro-integration forces in a manner similar to that by which the small states of Germany and Italy had become united under the hegemony and guidance of Prussia and Piedmont in the nineteenth century, to overcome the resistance of those who were against a supranational model for European unification. The US was invited to assume this role.

The integration process went through its well-known stages. The Council of Europe did not move in the direction of supranationalism because of British reluctance. Economic reconstruction was built on the basis of the Marshall Plan and its organizational off-shots, the Organization for European Economic Development (OEEC), and the European Payments Union (EPU). These organizations were also unsuited as vehicles of further integration. The Dunkirk Treaty and the Brussels Pact were subsumed under the Atlantic Pact/NATO in April 1949, whereby a security system for Western Europe under US leadership was established. NATO was a traditional military alliance, and as such basically intergovernmental, even if the integrated command that was built up in the fifties brought some supranational features. The first supranational organization, the European Coal and Steel Community (ECSC), emerged in 1949-50 in cooperation between pioneering European integrationists, notably Jean Monnet, and the Americans. The project was the outcome of a conflict that had been going on for a couple of years about the future of the German coal and steel industry. The French government had worked for a model for internationalisation of the Ruhr under the authority of the Occupation Powers, although with some German representation, that is, a model built on principles similar to those of the Versailles settlement. The Americans did not accept this, but insisted that French production of coal and steel should be included in a comprehensive solution based on Franco-German equality. The Schuman Plan outlined a supranational system for one sector of the economies of France, the Federal Republic, Italy and the Benelux countries, a sector that was economically crucial and militarily important. The plan was a political innovation and a viable compromise that broke the deadlock.[7] There were objections to it in the US on economic grounds; the ECSC was seen by many as a future cartel that was inimical to the interests of US industry, and hard to reconcile with the principles of free trade. The political goal of uniting Europe was however regarded as the overriding interest.

Some planning for German rearmament started in the US as early as 1948-49. It was believed that if Germany were not allowed to rearm, the military vacuum would make Central Europe impossible to defend against Soviet aggression. It was argued that a country that was not permitted to defend itself could not be defended, and the German potential for arms production was needed. After the first Soviet bomb test in 1949, an attack was not seen as probable in the short term, but it was thought that the Kremlin´s capacity to threaten the US with atomic bombs within a couple of years might tempt it to try to conquer Western Europe; it was urgent to use the available time to build up the defence of Western Europe. American officials were worried that the Europeans´ sense of their own military weakness might incline them to opt for neutrality or to fall in with Soviet demands. An additional motive was that a weak position in Europe increased the risk when confronting the adversary in limited wars elsewhere in the world. Acheson´s overall view was that the need to rearm Europe justified the risks inherent in rearmament; it would fully integrate Germany in Western Europe and be the best possible insurance against future aggression. Gradualists within the State Department advocated that the rearmament policy, although the right one in principle, should not be introduced hastily, as this might give the Germans too much bargaining leverage, discourage liberal forces in Germany and restore the militarists to power; it might also ignite a destructive controversy with France, play into the hands of the French Communists and weaken overall strength throughout Europe.[8] However, the project for German rearmament and membership of NATO was submitted to the European allies at the outbreak of the Korean war, after France and Germany had agreed in principle on the Schuman Plan. As expected, the idea was received with very little enthusiasm in the countries that had been liberated from occupation few years earlier, and there were also strong German reservations. To the French, the project was extremely unpalatable.

Both the State Department and the military believed that it was necessary to organize German rearmament within a framework which gave sufficient guarantees against renewed aggression. The priority choice was that Germany would become a member of NATO, but have no Air Force, no Navy and no General Staff. German divisions would be integrated into higher echelons, and German industry would produce only light equipment.[9] The US applied a mix of pressures and promises, but France refused stubbornly to admit German membership of NATO. In October, the French responded by presenting the Pleven Plan for a European Army. The plan foresaw a Supreme Commander, a European Defence Minister, a European Assembly, and a common European defence budget.

Initially, US officials found the plan totally unacceptable. During 1951, the attitude changed. Acheson was convinced that Germany had to be accorded real equality. The occupation regime must be terminated. The supreme authority of the allies should be limited to stationing troops in Germany, maintaining access to Berlin, settling territorial questions and controlling the final peace settlement and the unification issue. These rights would serve to prevent possible German attempts to make a deal with the Soviet Union. It made sense to support military institutions that would hold NATO's forces together after American and British troops had withdrawn from Europe. Acheson's conclusion was that there should be simultaneous progress on the issues of German sovereignty, German rearmament, and a European army. General Eisenhower, Supreme Commander of NATO and stationed in Paris, was converted to these ideas and gave strong support to the concept of a European army. It was feared in the US that the Germans would prolong the ongoing negotiations about the Treaty on the Coal and Steel Community in order to obtain a fully equal status in the European army, and even that the plan for the Community itself might unravel. Leverage was however brought upon German politicians and industrialists, and the Treaty was signed in May 1951.[10]

Thus, support for a European army within a European Defence Community (EDC) became the cornerstone of US policy for European integration.

Nuclear Foreign Policy and Arms Control

The two pillars of the nuclear foreign policy of the Truman Adminstration were the Baruch Plan and a comprehensive system for controlling the Western world's nuclear resources and information.

The Baruch Plan was submitted to the United Nations in early 1946. It was the basis for negotiations with the Soviet Union during the following years about nuclear disarmament and international control of nuclear energy. The Soviet counterproposal, the Gromyko Plan, was delivered shortly thereafter. It was clear from the beginning that the chances of agreement were extremely small. The negotiation machinery however grinded on ritually for years, reflecting the tensions of the cold war. Only minor changes were made in the initial positions; in 1950 the negotiations had come to a halt. Somewhat simplified, the American position was 'first control, then prohibition and abolition of nuclear weapons', and the Soviet position 'first prohibition and abolition, then (or simultaneously) control'. The Baruch Plan outlined a supranational programme for global development and control of atomic energy that was utopian in existing world conditions. The premise of the plan was that the military and civil aspects of atomic energy cannot be separated. An international Authority under the UN would govern the nuclear field. It would have 'managerial control or ownership of all atomic energy activities potentially dangerous to world security', and it would have the power to 'control, inspect, and license all other activities'. Included in the dangerous category were the various stages of the fuel cycle, such as production of raw materials, enrichment of uranium and production of plutonium. A core point of the plan was that sanctions would be decided in case of violation of the rules; no veto against such decisions would be allowed. Thus, the principle of veto rights for the permanent members of the Security Council - the lesson from the League of Nations when constructing the United Nations - would not apply in this field.[11]

The second pillar of US policy was the system for controlling information and resources, which aimed at keeping the atomic monopoly as long as possible. The principles for US post-war nuclear policy were codified in the Atomic Energy Act of 1946, and they were in force until the provisions of the Act were relaxed in August 1954. Most activities were placed under the direct or indirect authority of the Federal Government. The US nuclear programme was a crash programme to maximize armament. The civil aspects of atomic energy were not developed for the time being, although the development of propulsion reactors for submarines and other vessels became the foundation of the dominating technology for power reactors later. The spread of scientific and technical nuclear information to the outside world was restricted to a necessary minimum. It was considered important to control as much as possible of the nuclear raw materials - uranium and thorium - of the Western world in order to secure the supply to the US nuclear plants, and deny access to others. The raw materials were at this time thought scarce, and there were constant worries until the early fifties whether supplies from the Western world would be sufficient for US armaments.[12] The limited war-time cooperation with Britain ceased, except in the raw material field, where British assistance to obtain materials from the British sphere of influence was needed. In the Western world, only France produced substantial quantities of uranium which were not destined for the needs of the US or Britain. Intense prospection was conducted in Metropolitan France and in overseas areas under French control to prepare future independence.[13]

The US-British and French control of the actual uranium production of the Western world provided some guarantee against unobserved

German procurement of uranium. The control of nuclear raw materials was a diminishing asset, however. A situation of diminishing scarcity internationally could be foreseen as new deposits were discovered. German nuclear scientists pressed already in the early fifties for starting prospection efforts in the Federal Republic. It was not at all improbable that there was uranium in the territory of the Federal Republic. Uranium had been discovered in France, and much uranium had already been extracted from East Germany and delivered to the Soviet armament programme.

A very important American asset in a short and medium term perspective - an asset that will be brought to attention repeatedly - was the huge enrichment capacity that had been decided in the forties and early fifties. The investments in enrichment plants were truly gigantic. The technology of enrichment was extremely complicated and everything related to it was kept secret even after the liberalization of the atomic energy legislation in 1954. In the West, only the US and Britain possessed enrichment capacity. The British plant was however small; it was designed to be sufficient for the comparatively limited H-bomb programme and there were technical problems with it. For all practical purposes, the Americans had a monopoly on production and supply of enriched uranium in the West.[14] Enriched uranium was highly strategic from both a non-proliferation and an economic perspective. Access to enriched uranium was necessary for a number of military and civil purposes and the enrichment monopoly was an effective instrument for promoting American foreign policy goals.[15]

With respect to the Soviet orbit the control of nuclear resources was part of the general American embargo policy, that is, the secret policy for restricting Western trade with the Eastern bloc, especially the parts which supported the military sector. All kinds of resources related to nuclear energy were priority items on the embargo lists. For many other strategic goods on the lists there was a balancing problem. If the economic reconstruction of Western Europe was to succeed some established trade patterns and export to the Eastern bloc had to be maintained; otherwise the security of Europe would be weakened.[16] This did not apply to the nuclear sector, however.

For the states defeated in the war special restrictions applied for arms control with respect to nuclear energy and weapon-carriers. Italy was prohibited by its Peace Treaty to possess, construct or experiment with atomic weapons and guided missiles, and similar restrictions applied for the small former allies of the Axis in Europe, and for Japan.[17] The crucial problem was Germany, with which no peace treaty had been concluded. The nuclear activities in the Federal Republic were subjected to very tight restrictions after the war. Before 1949 only nuclear basic research of non-military significance was allowed, as specifically permitted by the zone commanders. In the Occupation Statute which regulated the relationship with the new Federal Republic, the three western Allies, represented by the Allied High Commission and its Military Security Board, retained authority in the arms control area. Commission Law no. 22 defined restrictions and Allied inspection rights in the nuclear field. It prohibited most nuclear activities: construction and possession of reactors, enrichment plants, nuclear raw materials, and so on. The prohibitions could be abrogated by the Board; in this way the research that had been allowed by the zone commanders was permitted to continue. Thus, the establishment of the Federal Republic did not greatly widen the permitted area.[18]

The guiding principle for arms control of the Federal Republic after the Pleven Plan for a European army had been submitted was agreed at the Conference of Foreign Ministers of the three Western Allies in Brussels in December 1950. It was decided that the prohibitions with respect to the most significant weapons would be maintained when Germany entered the Western defence system. The Federal Republic would not be allowed to produce or engage in research on heavy military equipment, on atomic, biological and chemical (ABC) weapons, long-range and guided missiles, warships other than small defensive ones, and military aircraft. The list reflected the essence of strategic military power in the nuclear age, nuclear weapons and their carriers.[19]

Nuclear Foreign Policy and Integration Policy

Double containment continued to be the basic premise of American foreign policy under the Eisenhower Administration. However, the view of the means for achieving this goal changed fundamentally. It was an article of faith for the new Administration that the militarization of the US economy which had taken place under the Truman presidency could not continue at a similar pace. US defence spending had increased from 4.7 per cent of GNP in the last year before the Korean war to an extraordinary 17.8 per cent in 1952-53.[20] The country was engaged in an arms race with the Soviet Union, and it was believed that to continue to increase the proportion of the economy and the Federal budget devoted to this purpose would threaten the functioning of the US economy and ultimately American society and the Western world in general. The US should prepare for a prolonged struggle, a 'long haul', it was concluded. As the Secretary of the Treasury, George M. Humphrey, formulated it, 'the present Administration was engaged in a dual effort to restore a more normal American economy and at the same time to put the nation in a posture of prolonged preparedness, the idea being that this would frustrate Stalin's design of destroying the power of the United States without war through the sapping of its economic health'.[21] A balancing of policies against both military and political-economic threats from the Soviet Union was seen to be necessary. President Eisenhower was personally persuaded of the fundamental importance of balancing military expenditures and the economy in a new way. When entering office

Eisenhower ordered a review of national security policy starting from this premise.

He also held the view - contrary to the military leadership and most former colleagues - that some balancing between the sword and the olive-branch would be required in dealings with the Soviet leadership, even if military security came first and negotiations should be conducted from positions of strength. After the death of Stalin in March 1953 there was a noticeable reduction in tension. The implications of the growing arsenals of nuclear weapons on both sides were clearer to Eisenhower than to many others; it has been observed that 'Eisenhower entered the presidency in January 1953 with a more thorough knowledge of nuclear weapons than any president before or since'. He also thought that it was desirable to convince the allies of the US wish to obtain settlements with the Soviet Union in order to maintain their continued support. Eisenhower took the iniative to explore the possibility of dealing with the new Soviet leaders by diplomatic means. He addressed them in April, in a probing 'Chance for Peace' speech. He talked about the need for a settlement of conflictual issues, an armistice in Korea, a treaty for Austria, and so on. If there were progress in these areas it would be possible to proceed concurrently with reduction of armaments. Eisenhower mentioned a number of possible measures for prohibiting certain weapons and limiting the arsenals, and for non-proliferation of atomic weapons while promoting the use of atomic energy for peaceful purposes. There was no very clear reaction from the Soviet side.[22]

Europe was in the focus of Washington's political and strategic equation. Among other things, bases in Europe were necessary for the effective use of American air power. Eisenhower told his advisers that 'if the Communists succeeded in gaining control of Europe the world balance of power would be hopelessly upset against us. It would be necessary to spend many more billions than we are now spending to redress this balance of power'.[23] Europe was also the locus of the German problem. Germany was rising economically, and the second object of the double containment was becoming more acute. How would independent German power be curbed in the future and its capacity used in the West-East struggle?

From these premises for national security policy, the Eisenhower Administration developed two parallel approaches to nuclear foreign policy during 1953. The first was a revised military strategy, the so-called 'New Look', that was approved on 30 October 1953 (NSC 162/2), and its application to Europe a year later (MC 48). The second was the multifaceted 'Atoms for Peace' campaign that was announced to the world in a speech by the President to the UN General Assembly on 8 December 1953.[24]

Atoms for War

The core of the New Look strategy was 'conventionalization' of nuclear weapons. Eisenhower and Dulles 'were in complete agreement that somehow or other the taboo which surrounds the use of atomic weapons would have to be destroyed'.[25]

The new strategy may be traced back to thoughts within the US military establishment in the autumn of 1951, or to assessments by the British Chiefs of Staff in 1952. According to them, the most likely scenario was no longer a general Soviet attack. The West should prepare for a long drawn-out conflict more likely to take place on a political and economic level – the 'long haul' thesis. In the NSC 162/2 it was recognized that the USSR did not seem likely deliberately to launch a general war against the US during the period covered by the estimates, that is, up to 1955. Worst-case scenarios were however also taken into consideration. The Soviets might provoke the West's reactions and unwittingly unleash general war; they might start an attack on the West with nuclear bombardment of American nuclear forces. It was recognized that it would be too expensive both for the US and the Allies to realize within the planned time span the goals for conventional forces that had been decided in Lisbon in 1952. Deterrence and a forward strategy for Europe – that is, drawing the defence line 'at the Elbe' instead of 'at the Rhine' or at the periphery along the Atlantic coast - had to be based on nuclear weapons, it was argued, to counter Soviet superiority in conventional forces while avoiding economic bankruptcy.[26] New 'tactical' nuclear weapons with smaller yields would uphold the balance; they emerged in large quantities from the huge American production plants from 1952 onwards. A division of labour between the US and the NATO partners in Western Europe was envisaged. The US Strategic Air Command would take care of warfare at the global, strategic level with H-bombs and long range weapon-carriers, and the Europeans were to take most of the responsibility for defending Western Europe on the ground with manpower, tactical A-bombs and short range carriers while waiting for reinforcement from mobile American forces. A partial US disengagement from Europe and other parts of the world would become possible in due time.

A conclusion that was drawn from these premises was that the European allies should also in some way have access to tactical nuclear weapons. The NATO forces in Europe should be organized and equipped according to the same principles. There should be no discrimination between the various national armies. The very principle of functional military integration contributed to the dogma that a nuclearization of Europe was necessary. A war would be nuclear from the beginning; nuclear weapons would be the only important ones. It was recognized that it was impossible to say simultaneously both that they were normal weapons and that the Europeans could not possess them. Such a situation was unhealthy, Eisenhower and

Dulles believed, and NATO could not cope with it.[27] The global division of tasks and the US leadership implied limiting nuclear armament to the A-bomb level. However, Britain was already, without American blessing, on its way to developing the H-bomb independently.

The strategy for the defence of Western Europe in MC 48 was approved by the NATO Council in Paris on 17 December 1954. The significance of MC 48 has been stressed in particular by Trachtenberg; he has described it as one of the great taproots of the Eisenhower nuclear sharing policy. The strategy placed an extraordinarily heavy emphasis on nuclear weapons. Its essence was that there was one and only one way in which the Soviets could be prevented from overrunning Western Europe and that was through massive and very rapid use of nuclear weapons, both tactically and strategically. The tactical weapons would prevent Europe from being overrun during the relatively brief period during which the basic sources of Soviet power would be destroyed by American strategic air power. MC-48 proclaimed that 'it lies within NATO's power to provide an effective deterrent in Europe, and should war come despite the deterrent, to prevent a rapid overrunning of Europe' but only if 'the ability to make immediate use of atomic weapons is ensured... Any delay in their use - even measured in hours - could be fatal'.[28] The demand for very rapid response created a highly dangerous and unstable situation with rules for the use of nuclear weapons that in Trachtenberg's view (some material is still not declassified) were not defined in a completely precise way. The rapid response requirement was supposed to make it necessary to predelegate to NATO's Supreme Commander in Europe (SACEUR), always an American general, the decision to release nuclear weapons and to use them if it was clear that a Soviet attack was imminent. The importance of striking first was emphasized, the strategy was preemptive. Judgment on the point at which it was clear that an attack was imminent and on the decision to start the war was probably placed in the hands of SACEUR. The necessity for rapid action also meant that the weapons that were deployed in European hands would have to be under their effective control for the strategy to work. Thus, the strategy also pulled the US toward a policy of transferring of control of weapons to the Europeans. The US operational posture as it developed during the Eisenhower period, it was stated in a major historical study by the Defense Department, 'strained for rapid (indeed preemptive) and massive response to an imminent attack'.[29]

The European allies accepted the New Look and MC 48 with mixed feelings but without serious objections. The Americans had expected greater opposition. On 12 January 1954, Dulles made his 'massive retaliation' speech, which was mistakenly interpreted as meaning that massive retaliation would be the response to every kind of Soviet attack.

There were *pros* and *cons* in the New Look strategy from the perspective of the Europeans. The advantage of less American pressure for large expenditures for troops and conventional weapons could be seen clearly. It was also realized that a European build-up of conventional forces instead of American nuclear weapons would weaken the American presence in Europe and thus weaken the US nuclear guarantee further. A fundamental question was however always present in the European capitals: Would the US be ready to use nuclear weapons in Europe when the American homeland was increasingly becoming exposed to Soviet nuclear reprisal? In other words, was a deterrence strategy ultimately based on massive retaliation for the sake of Europe credible when America was becoming vulnerable? Would the reliance on nuclear weapons make Europe an atomic battlefield that would annihilate the continent's people and cultural heritage? These fears were of course reinforced by the existence of H-bombs and reports about a developing capacity of long-range bombers presumably capable of round-trip missions against the United States.[30]

Atoms for Peace

Several factors contributed to the development of the Atoms for Peace policy.

A committee on US disarmament policy which had been appointed by the outgoing Administration delivered its report in January 1953. The report gave some hard facts about the positions in the nuclear arms race. It was stated that the stockpiles of fissionable material were increasing on both sides, but there was no proportionality between the size of the stockpiles and the destructive power because of improvements in weapons design, variable requirements for military use and the development of thermonuclear weapons. There was no permanent and important shortage of raw materials for any Great Power. Atomic weapons were cheap compared to other military items. The time when the Russians would have the material to make 1000 atomic bombs might well be only a few years away, and the time when they would have 5000 only a few years further on. 'On the subject of Soviet work in the thermonuclear field we know nothing of any real value, but it would be the height of folly not to expect that in time the Soviet Union will learn what we have learned'. There was to be a time of 'enoughness' for fissionable material, and this time was approaching. When atomic bombs were numbered in the thousands it was no longer their number but the effectiveness of the instruments of delivery which was the primary limitation on the scale of damage that could be done. Both sides would have means of deterrence, no side would have the ability to knock out the other.

The report also contained some comments on the European situation. It was stated that one of the elements in the US position on atomic weapons had always been the determination to retain in the Americans' own hand the authority to take the ultimate decision about the use of the atomic bomb.

It had thus been treated differently from other weapons. In the case of the defence of Europe, where military decisions had been worked out in the councils of a coalition, this had not been true for the atomic bomb. Reliance on atomic weapons to defend Europe was necessary, but the geographic proximity to the Soviet Union meant that a relatively small number of atomic bombs and a relatively simple delivery system would give the Soviet Union a very heavy atomic capability with respect to Western Europe. The report formulated the dilemma inherent in the New Look strategy - the dilemma which would later bring about European demands and American half-promises that the US would transfer nuclear weapons to the Europeans, or in other ways let them in on decisions to use nuclear weapons:

> In such a situation it may be that the American atomic bomb will be useable only at the risk of truly horrible losses in Europe, and while this prospect might not in fact be sufficient to lead the American government to abandon its reliance on such weapons, it can hardly be denied that in a situation of this sort the balance of feeling and action in Europe might be sensibly altered for the worse. Thus in Europe there are at one and the same time powerful factors which tend to recommend an increasing dependence upon atomic weapons, and possible future developments which make that dependence dangerous.

The report recommended that there should be much greater candour as regards the information given to the American public about the dangers inherent in the build-up of nuclear weapons on both sides and that American continental defence should be provided for. Total abolition of nuclear weapons was not possible since the Soviet Union did not admit control. The US should disengage from the disarmament discussions in the UN. A realistic aim might be to communicate with the USSR, and to negotiate reductions and controls that would diminish the possibilities for either side to develop a ´knock-out´ capability.[31]

The President had a high opinion of the report although he queried the conclusion by the committee about disengagement from the disarmament talks.[32] An element of a discussion in the National Security Council in February gives a clue to another factor that determined the policy that was finalized nine months later. The question was whether the enormous expansion of capacity (enrichment plants and plutonium-producing reactors) for producing fissile material for bombs, which had been decided in several steps since the late forties, would actually be needed. Eisenhower said that if the half built expansion program were called off it would ´make us look very silly´ and be a complete loss. He inquired when the ´enoughness´ stage would be achieved and whether it would then be possible to turn the atomic energy programme toward peaceful uses. The Chairman of the Atomic Energy Commission replied that with respect to fissionable material the answer was in the affirmative but that it would be deceiving the American people if they were allowed to believe that the expensive enrichment plants which existed or were being built could ever be exploited for peaceful purposes.[33]

Thus, the problem was: What to do with the gigantic investments in the nuclear military production plants when 'enoughness' had been reached? In a subsequent discussion about 'enoughness' in the NSC the information was given that the Joint Chiefs of Staff estimated that 1959 was the date when the US would have on hand the weapons they believed would be needed.[34] This meant that if production of fuel for civil nuclear power would in due time replace the production of weapons, the time perspective was short.

Work along the lines of the committee report was supported by the President and went on during the first half of 1953; it became known as 'Operation Candor'. The President ordered a reassessment of the premises of the earlier policy toward the Soviet Union, arguing that something positive was needed in order to balance the threat of annihilation caused by the arms race. A policy review called 'Solarium' was initiated. Three teams spent the summer considering what possible alternative policies might be adopted toward the Soviet Union; this study overlapped with 'Operation Candor'.[35]

The Joint Chiefs of Staff and the Department of Defense, who were in the midst of developing the New Look strategy, strongly opposed any discussions related to disarmament. It was feared that moves in this direction would dampen support for the military programme. Instead, the military adopted the position of being in favour of total and complete disarmament as the only way in which to have real peace. This utopian demand would ensure that there were no agreements that might jeopardize the military sector.[36]

There were industry pressures for less restrictive and militarized nuclear legislation. Industrial interests had for some time been urging that the enormous US nuclear advance should be utilized to take the lead in developing the peaceful uses of atomic energy.[37] Many experts argued that atomic power would revolutionize the production of energy in the long run. The State Department gave strong support to the idea of letting industry in on developing atomic power at home, and of promoting the peaceful atom internationally. As early as June Under Secretary Walter Bedell Smith pleaded to Congress that 'atomic energy should, as rapidly as, and to the extent that, security considerations permit, become integrated into the national economy', it was of paramount importance to the US international relationships generally that the US led the development of atomic power:

> It would be very damaging to the position of the United States if another country were to be the first in this field of endeavor. It would be especially damaging if the Soviet Union were to precede us in the development of atomic power. If this were to happen, the Soviet Union would cite their achievement as proof of their propaganda line that the United States

is interested in atomic energy only for destructive purposes while the Soviets are interested in developing it for peaceful purposes.

The prospects for international control were dim, Bedell Smith recognized. However, the US should at all times be prepared to enter into an arrangement, no less effective than the Baruch Plan, for the international control of atomic energy. New legislation designed to foster the development of atomic power in the US 'should include provisions which - recognizing this natural aspiration of foreign countries - would enable the United States to make available, in appropriate cases and under suitable safeguards, information and material to assist them in making progress in this field'.[38]

On 12 August 1953 the first Soviet thermonuclear test was registered. This was a momentous event which sent a signal to the world that West-East strategic parity was approaching earlier than expected, and that Western Europe was becoming extremely vulnerable. There is some evidence that the test actually indicated a Soviet lead in some respects in the H-bomb race, although the technical facts were kept secret. It became more urgent for the US to explore new ways of negotiating about disarmament and arms control, and to find measures that would calm world opinion.

The ongoing planning about 'candor' on nuclear arms, and the promotion of peaceful atomic energy at home and abroad, was supplemented by a concept of an 'atomic pool'. The idea was that both the West and the East would turn over certain amounts of fissionable materials to an international authority, a kind of 'bank', and that this material would be used for peaceful purposes. It seems that Eisenhower himself was the originator of the idea.[39] It was thus a measure for arms control, in the sense of limiting the growth of the arsenals of the nuclear powers. However, the concept also contained an aspect that would favour the US in case limitations on production of fissionable materials were eventually to be agreed. Eisenhower asked the AEC Chairman, Lewis L. Strauss, to 'consider the following proposal, which he did not think anyone had yet thought of. Suppose the United States and the Soviets were each to turn over to the United Nations, for peaceful use, X kilograms of fissionable material. - The amount X could be fixed at a figure which we could handle from our stockpile, but which it would be difficult for the Soviets to match'.[40]

During the autumn of 1953 intensive preparations for the Atoms for Peace plan went on. Many drafts were presented and redrafted; Eisenhower was involved continually. He went on repeating that a positive approach to the nuclear problem was needed. The 'Candor' approach with its stress on the horrifying consequences of the nuclear arms race left no hope for America and the world.

Dulles was critical of the aspects of the planned policy which had a bearing on negotiations with the Soviet Union about disarmament and international control of atomic energy. His main concern was Germany and NATO and his highest priority was to obtain ratifications of the EDC Treaty. When the Atoms for Peace plan was approaching completion Dulles delivered a memorandum to the President in which he developed his views of the conflict between East-West negotiations, and US policy for European integration. He wrote that talks with leading French and German representatives had led him to the conclusion that the US should not seriously seek discussions with the Soviets until decisions had been taken on the EDC. France was expected to act on the EDC in January, he stated. If US-Soviet discussions were started or impending before then,

...Their pendency would almost surely arrest any positive action on EDC or possible alternatives.

...The Soviets would concentrate on breaking up Western defense arrangements rather than on trying to reach a constructive settlement.

I think there may be a fair chance of some settlement with the Russians if we have a firm foundation in Western Europe - but not before.

Thus, Dulles went on, acceptance of an invitation from the Soviets to discuss atomic weapons and bases would have a paralysing effect on the Western European plans, and a refusal would seriously hurt the US standing and influence in friendly countries. A public appeal would in any case not be appropriate. When the time came, the approaches should be primarily private. Dulles finished by proposing that the President might make a more general speech describing the atomic danger, declaring determination to defend against attack and repeating in general terms the US willingness to discuss limitation and control of armaments, and so on.[41]

Notwithstanding Dulles' apprehensions, the Atoms for Peace policy was presented with a maximum of publicity before the EDC project had been finalized. It was the new Administration's first major move on the international scene. Eisenhower's speech contained different and somewhat diffuse elements; it could be - and has been - interpreted in various ways. The general approach was, however, a combination of the start of a propaganda campaign for peaceful atomic energy and an invitation to the Soviet Union to discuss disarmament and arms control on the basis of other premises than the Baruch Plan. The actual state of the art of civil atomic power was extremely exaggerated: 'The United States know that peaceful power from atomic energy is no dream of the future. That capability, already proved, is here - now - today'. Actually, the opinion of most experts at the time was that it would take at least a decade before nuclear power would become competitive with conventional energy sources. Eisenhower also presented the proposal for contributions from the 'governments principally involved' of uranium and fissionable material to an International Atomic Energy Agency under the aegis of the United Nations, that is, a common

West-East atomic pool or 'bank'. The issue of safeguards for making sure that the contributions to the Agency were used for peaceful purposes only was not mentioned explicitly, although it was stated that an advantage of the proposal was that it did not presuppose a completely acceptable system for worldwide inspection and control. In this way it was indicated that the principles that had been upheld since 1946 - the Baruch Plan - might be abandoned. The speech also opened the way for possible West-East discussions about arms control of states which had not yet acquired nuclear weapons, that is - using the term that became customary later - about non-proliferation. It could be interpreted as a signal to the Soviet Union that fundamental problems in East-West relations, Germany and China, might also be discussed in such terms.

Some diplomatic contacts with the Russians were established in parallel just before and immediately after the speech. The first Soviet response was judged 'noticeably free from vituperation', although the reaction to substantive parts of the American move was 'that in Soviet eyes it was probably regarded as means of maintaining superiority of US in military stockpile'.[42]

The first part of the Atoms for Peace policy that was implemented after the speech was preparation for future expansion of civil nuclear power on a large scale. The US Atomic Energy Act was revised on 30 August 1954, to permit greater freedom for industry to launch nuclear power nationally and internationally.[43] Many earlier restrictions on the dissemination of scientific-technical information were removed, although not on such information that was particularly sensitive, such as enrichment technology. A special system of state control for export of nuclear materials and products was constructed. Bilateral agreements for cooperation concerning civil uses of atomic energy of two types - 'research bilaterals' and 'power bilaterals' - were established between the US and a number of states, from the spring of 1955. Within the framework of such agreements contracts between industries were to be concluded. The bilaterals regulated the outflow of information and resources to the receiving countries. They stipulated that the resources received from the US should be subjected to US safeguards to ensure peaceful use. US inspectors had the right to control the whereabouts of the resources exported from the US in the recipient country, and thus to look into that part of the nuclear sector. The control requirement did not encompass the entire nuclear sector, however. It was possible in principle for the recipient country to have another uncontrolled sector in which nuclear weapons could be manufactured. In the US, it was not thought possible to go further for the time being.

An international conference about peaceful uses of atomic energy was arranged in Geneva in September 1955. The initiative was American, but the conference was held under UN auspices. It was the biggest scientific conference ever. It became a successful manifestation for rapid development of nuclear power technology and an arena for West-East competition and propaganda. The US in particular, but also the Soviet Union and other countries, released large amounts of scientific-technical information that had been secret up till then. However, certain parts, like the crucial enrichment technology, remained secret and the question of the interrelationships between civil and military uses of atomic energy was scrupulously avoided. One of the results of the conference was that it became clear that there were two main alternatives for the first generation of power reactors, one based on enriched uranium - sponsored by the US and the USSR - the other on natural uranium - sponsored by Britain, France and Canada.

The second part of the Atoms for Peace policy were contacts and negotiations first with the USSR and then also with other countries about an international Agency. They started after Eisenhower's speech and eventually resulted in unanimous agreement on the Statute for the International Atomic Energy Agency (IAEA) at an 81-nation conference in the autumn of 1956. The Western positions were coordinated under US leadership in eight-state[44] informal discussions between the countries which had advanced nuclear programmes or important uranium deposits.

Already in March 1954 Eisenhower's original proposal was changed on an important point. The US informed the Soviets that the 'pool' or 'bank' concept no longer applied. The Agency would act as a channel - a 'clearing house' or 'broker' - for distribution of fissionable materials, rather than as recipient of the materials. The Soviets however declined to negotiate about the Agency until agreement had been reached on certain disarmament issues, and declared that steering a stream of fissionable material to other countries would mean new military threats. They withdrew from the discussions for a time. During the spring and summer of 1954 the Russians were told that the proposals for the Agency were not intended as disarmament proposals, and that the US would proceed with the plan with or without the participation of the Soviet Union. During the debate in the UN General Assembly in the autumn of 1954 the Soviets opposed approval of international transactions for peaceful purposes by an international Agency, apparently fearing that an organ dominated by the US might become in a position to inspect the Soviet civil programme and transactions between states in the Eastern Bloc. At this point the American delegate made a declaration which changed the negotiation climate:

This is not a correct interpretation of [the American] proposal. The Agency would concern itself only with materials specifically earmarked for Agency projects by the contributing states. It would have no control over the use of any other fissionable material. Any contributing states would remain free to transfer fissionable materials to another state without securing the consent of the Agency.[45]

Thus, the main principles for the Agency, like in the bilateral system, would be voluntariness and incompleteness. The Agency would not, as in the Baruch Plan, have the right of ownership or managerial control of the essential parts of the entire nuclear sector of a country.

The negotiations continued until the Statute was adopted two years later. The US returned to the pool/bank concept as a possibility. It was eventually agreed that the IAEA might assume the functions of either bank or broker if a country decided to make fissile materials or raw materials available to the Agency. If so, control administered by the IAEA, that is, involving inspectors both from the West and the East, would be applied to make sure that these materials were used only for peaceful purposes. IAEA control might also be applied voluntarily to other international transactions, for example in arrangements like the US bilaterals. There was no requirement that the entire nuclear sector of a country, or the essential parts of it, would be subjected to safeguards. Because of this, the control function of the IAEA was not an effective instrument for non-proliferation for the time being but it was a point of departure for developing such an instrument later.

In the American system of civil 'bilaterals' a clause was included in the agreements that would prepare for a possible transformation of the US safeguards to IAEA safeguards in the future. The clause said that the parties would consult if one of them wished the resources under the bilateral to be subjected to IAEA safeguards; mutual consent was required. However, the US had specific means of pressure in such a situation. For example, it was stipulated that if agreement could not be reached unused raw materials and fissile materials should be returned to the US. Obviously, this might be problematic for the recipient country when an industry based on deliveries from the US had been built up.[46]

There was a provision that would prevent international installations which competed with existing national capacities from being built up by the IAEA. The Statute stipulated that the IAEA could acquire or establish any facilities, plant and equipment useful in carrying out its functions, whenever those 'otherwise available to it in the area concerned are inadequate or available only on terms it deems unsatisfactory'.[47] The most important field in which facilities and plants were already available concerned enrichment. As was shown above, the enormous US enrichment plants would become idle when military 'enoughness' had been reached.

There was no demand in the Statute that fissile material should be transferred from military to peaceful uses. The features of potential disarmament or arms control of the existing three nuclear weapon states in Eisenhower's original proposal were abandoned at an early stage. Instead, the IAEA was turned into a potential instrument for arms control of other states, that is, for non-proliferation. The implication was that the US and the Soviet Union might some day agree to keep nuclear order in their respective camps. They might cooperate about non-proliferation, and standards and machinery for this possibility should be prepared.

In addition, there was an immediate motive for the US to organize the IAEA which was related both to economic competition in the West and to East-West competition. When atomic power spread over the world and fissile material became more abundant, the effectiveness of bilateral controls would diminish gradually in the absence of internationally accepted safeguards. Countries would be tempted to relax controls in order to support sales, and the Soviets might offer nuclear aid ´with no strings attached´. The US Secretary of State formulated this dilemma:

...if there is no such organization with a standard system of controls, then you may get into a situation where nations will shop around and buy their materials from the nation which imposes the least controls... and in the end the whole control system would break down.[48]

No one nation can, alone, indefinitely police the spread of nuclear powerplants. In our bilateral agreements we now provide for safeguards, including inspection by our own nationals, to assure against improper use of nuclear material. But this is a short-term solution. Sovereign nations would accept an international system of broad applicability. But they will not long be content to have their electric-power systems under continuous supervison by technicians merely serving another nation.[49]

Support for Political and Economic Integration in Western Europe

Both Eisenhower and Dulles often articulated their conviction about the connection between containment of Communism, the German problem, and European integration. Their personal experiences contributed to the belief that supranational integration based on Franco-German conciliation was a vital part of the solution to the double containment problem.

Eisenhower, when serving as NATO Supreme Commander in Europe, had become convinced about the necessity of a federated Europe. His ideas about the membership varied a little over time but France and West Germany were always included. In June 1951 he wrote in his diary that he could see no satisfactory solution to the European security problem unless there existed ´a U.S. of Europe - to include all countries now in Nato; West Germany & [he thought] Sweden, Spain & Jugoslavia, with Greece definitely in if Jugoslavia [were]´. He seemed to doubt Britain´s willingness to participate: ´If *necessary*, the U.K. could be omitted´. A month later he made a strong public plea for European economic and political integration in an after-dinner speech delivered to the English Speaking Union in Washington. Later, as President, he often referred to this speech as giving the essence of his convictions in the matter. He was willing to listen to and cooperate about the modalities with European integrationists like Monnet – since, he wrote, 'I believe implicitly in the idea'. In November, his list of candidate countries in the diary was shorter and Britain was absent: 'Denmark, Holland, Belgium Luxemburg, France, Italy and western Germany should form one Federated State. To help this America could afford to spend a lot, because we'd get something successful, strong, sturdy'. He wrote to the British Foreign Secretary, Anthony Eden, that it would merely complicate matters if Britain were to attempt to participate directly in the EDC or to join a European political union, and that it was a great benefit to all if Britain continued to carry out world-wide responsibilities. Eisenhower was at that time, after some initial hesitation about whether the project was militarily feasible, strongly in favour of the EDC and he continued to be so when he became President. However, he grew increasingly irritated with the British concentration on the Commonwealth and the special relationship, and the lack of support for supranationalism on the European continent. During the first month of his presidency he commented in the diary:

> Both Foster Dulles and I have pointed out to him [Churchill] that until Europe makes a success of the European Army and the Schuman Plan, we can have little confidence of its future. One of the stumbling blocks to such success is Europe's feeling that Britain is not greatly concerned and will not help them politically, economically and otherwise. It is almost frustrating to attempt to make Winston see how important it is to the welfare of all three regions -- Europe, Britain and the United States -- to exert British *leadership* in bringing about this development.[50]

The President and the Secretary of State were both convinced that support for supranational integration on the European continent was necessary for double containment, and the idea had a strong backing in Congress. There was however an awareness among many American officials that the necessary short-run support for political and economic integration contained the embryo of undesirable Third Force developments and 'neutralism'.

An internal debate about US objectives for Western Europe among officials of the State Departement and the Mutual Security Agency in November-December 1952, that is, immediately before the installation of the Eisenhower Administration, is illustrative. Everybody agreed that the US should continue to promote European unification, but there were two different views about the limits and aims of the support. One was that unification must aim at creating increasing interdependence within the Atlantic framework. The concept of European independence was out-of-date. The Truman Administration had supported European efforts to unite since 1947, but had subsequently concluded that European unity outside NATO was not in the American interest. A proponent of this view posed the basic question: Do we really want Europe to unite? According to the second view, the US need not be too preoccupied about increasing European independence. Too much distrust and measures of precaution would create difficulties. If the US believed in its own statements about the common heritage, attitudes, common objectives of the Atlantic countries, there was no reason to worry about future inability to maintain the basic harmony between the US and a united Europe. The US should accept as an inescapable fact that a united Europe could become a 'Third Force', and that its size and development must lead to independence from American domination and control. The US should have confidence in its own power and wisdom and not worry unduly about such a 'Third Force'.[51]

A secret committee report, the Draper Report, about United States policies with respect to Western Europe, which appeared during the first months of the Eisenhower Administration, provides an example of the first kind of thinking. The point of departure was that the most acute reconstruction of Western Europe had been accomplished, and longer-term policies were needed to promote US general foreign policy goals. The report did not deviate from the axiom that supranationalism should be supported in order to create a strong Europe, but it emphasized that vigilance was required. Europe should be built up, but not to the point of creating a neutral, antagonistic or hostile bloc equipped with the 'most modern weapons'. American leadership within the Atlantic framework should be preserved:

...European support for NATO and NATO objectives would be adversely affected by the development of a Western European 'Third Force' if the latter were neutral, antagonistic or hostile. A strong cooperating power within the Atlantic context would of course be another matter. A kind of integration to be avoided is one that would merely hamper the strong without invigorating the weak. This is a particularly disturbing possibility. A tendency in this direction exists within NATO. It is exemplified by the French attitude toward the developing Franco-German relationship within the Western community, and could attain sizeable proportions. Any such development tends to weaken the fibre and diminish the unity of the Atlantic Community...[US policy] should take account of the need for minimizing the risk either that the new European institutions might be so emasculated as to be too weak for their purpose, or that they might some day be perverted to the service of unconstructive or even hostile purposes. ...The U.S. wants a European defense establishment, complementing that of the U.S., able to support a foreign policy in line with U.S. objectives with respect to the Soviet Bloc. The U.S., however, certainly wants to minimize the possibility that a strong European military power, having the most modern weapons at its disposal and being capable of large scale warfare, might take military action outside the NATO context and out of concert with the U.S. Our record in connection with the linking of NATO and the EDC clearly reflects this desire. An increasingly strong European power bloc, developing along lines inconsistent with the objectives of NATO and the concept of the Atlantic Community, would probably strive for a military position, including the possession of atomic and other novel weapons for mass destruction, comparable to that of the United States and the U.S.S.R. Here again, it is probable that U.S. interests require military development along Atlantic-wide rather than exclusively European-wide lines. The NATO-EDC link emphasizes this point.[52]

Economically, Europe was still in a state of unilateral dependence. Two approaches co-existed in US policy-making. One was the general goal for foreign economic policy of promoting liberalization of trade and payments, and a return to world-wide multilateralism and currency convertibility. The other was the regional approach, aiming at reconstruction based on a liberalized market in Europe, even if it compromised multilateralism.

Although the principles of multilateralism were supported by many domestic economic interests and agencies like the Treasury and the Department of Commerce the regional approach gained the upper hand. Derived from customs union theory it elevated America´s own historical experience to a paradigm of modernization. A liberalized market in Western Europe would give fast economic growth based on scale, specialization, competition and higher productivity. Growth would make possible increased consumption, it would mitigate class conflict and prevent the advance of Communism in Europe. Economic integration was also seen as a stage toward the goal of political unification. It was recognized that it was difficult to establish world-wide multilateralism for the time being. The OEEC had turned out not to be an instrument for political unification, but an intergovernmental forum for liberalization of trade. The liberalization of trade and payments proved to be feasible only on a regional basis. Although Marshall aid had given an enormous impetus to the economic resurgence of Western Europe, a very serious dollar gap still existed. The creation of the European Payments Union (EPU), an offshoot of the Marshall Plan, in 1950 was important for economic recovery. It took place, however, within a framework of limited, rather than worldwide, multilateralism. It was designed to increase the interdependence of European economies in order to reduce their dependence on the US, and it discriminated against dollar imports.[53]

Economic growth in Europe based on these principles fitted well into the economic philosophy of the Republicans and the economic reasoning behind the New Look. The Administration was aiming at tax-cuts, and reduction of US aid to Europe was an important means to this end. Instead of large programmes for aid, private US investments in Europe would eventually take their place. 'Trade not aid' was the aim. This was not seen as possible in the next few years, however. US investments had still attained only a modest volume and American financing was necessary in order to maintain a high level of dollar flows. Even if the termination of economic aid could serve as a unifying force, it could do so only if there were adequate dollar flows at high levels of trade and investment. A balancing was required: 'The task for U.S. statesmanship is to steer the difficult course of helping and guiding the Europeans toward self-reliance in an expanding economy without on the one hand giving so much help that Europeans relax their efforts and without, on the other hand, withholding what is really necessary for enduring improvement'.[54]

The UK in early 1953 asked for a large credit and greater imports to support a move to sterling-dollar convertibility. If the request had been accepted the separation of currency areas might have been overcome. The American response was characterized by delay, and decisions on foreign economic policy evolved slowly during the next year. There was a general consensus within the Administration that eventual general currency convertibility was desirable, but there were deep divisions about how, and at what pace, this would be achieved. A collapse of the EPU, which had been a functioning instrument for allowing growth on the European continent, seemed to be a consequence of the British plan. The State Department's attitude was that support for the British project for convertibility would divide the Europeans, create tensions within the OEEC and sink the EDC project. It insisted on the problems with convertibility and the importance of the US interest in European integration. It did not want to endanger the principles on which US policy for post-war European stability had been built: regional integration, OEEC trade liberalization and dollar discrimination. In August 1953, the first review of foreign economic policy since the Marshall Plan was initiated. A leading businessman, Clarence B. Randall, was appointed Chairman of a bipartisan Commission of Foreign Economic Policy (CFEP). The report by the Commission in early 1954, the Randall Report, outlined a number of compromises that were hardly inconsistent with the general State Department line in favour of economic regionalism. The approach in the report was endorsed by the President in a message to Congress in March 1954. In the Randall Report, currency convertibility was singled out as the main goal, but its attainment was pragmatically postponed to the moment when the persistent world balance of payments problem had been reduced. The role of increased mutual trade rather than aid was stressed, but the issue of lower tariff barriers to the US market to enable the Europeans to gain dollars remained nebulous. The report did not dwell on the issue of regionalism and European integration, but it supported the EPU as a temporary arrangement on the way to full convertibility. Actual decisions about abandoning the current regional framework were *de facto* left to the Europeans themselves.[55]

Reconciling Nuclear Policy and Integration Policy

It may be concluded from the foregoing that a major problem for US policy for European integration during the Eisenhower period was this: How to adapt integration policy to the two-sided nuclear policy which had emerged primarily as a way to cope with the problem of military and economic containment of the Soviet Union? Four considerations were particularly important: First, how to solve a most vital part of the German question, the issue of nuclear arms control of the Federal Republic? Second, what would be the American policy toward France in the nuclear field? Third, how to promote the general goal of preventing proliferation of nationally controlled nuclear weapons, perhaps in cooperation with the Soviet Union? Fourth, how to prepare American military withdrawal from Europe within a foreseeable future?

The attempts to balance between answers to these questions steered US policy on the integration projects which contained the nuclear dimension, the EDC, the WEU and Euratom. The construction of these projects would have effects on the three nuclear options that were identified above: the national option, the transfer option, and the European option.

Both the Administration and Congress were determined adversaries of a fully national option for NATO countries. At the centre of attention was the Federal Republic. Nationally manufactured and controlled German nuclear weapons were a nightmare that should be avoided at any price, and it was clear that this was what the Russians feared most of all. It might trigger a Soviet preemptive attack. However, the possibility of a German national option might be used tactically as a bargaining chip in East-West negotiations. The European countries were similarly united in their resistance to the German national option, and the European integrationists thought, like US officials, that supranational integration was the most suitable means to prevent it. The case of France was complicated. The cooperation of France on integration was absolutely necessary as France was one of the two pillars of the Franco-German reconciliation project on which American European policy was constructed. However, France was divided between opponents and adherents of supranationalism in military matters. The forces behind the French national nuclear option were in the majority, and the French were influenced by the British example which pointed toward the H-bomb level. For the US, the French national option - in any case one aiming at the H-bomb - was undesirable from a general non-proliferation and hegemony perspective, and even more because it might threaten the extremely important goal of preventing the German national option.

The negotiations with the Soviet Union about the IAEA were present, along with the negotiations about the nuclear dimension in the European integration projects, as a reminder that a West-East settlement to try to prevent proliferation of nuclear weapons in general, and to Germany in particular, might be possible.

As early as April 1954 Eisenhower suggested to Dulles that the British and French should be told that ´we were holding a certain number of atomic weapons of varied types for their possible use so as to place upon them a greater degree of responsibility in deciding whether or not in fact such weapons should be used or should not be used´. He often returned to the question of how Europe could be expected to trust the US, if the Americans were unwilling to trust their allies by sharing the most important weapons with them. In his view, it was natural for the European countries to want nuclear forces of their own, as long as the Soviets had them; he stated that it was as ´sure as day follows night that a number of countries would develop nuclear capabilities´. It would be wasteful to duplicate the efforts that the US had already made. The allies should be supplied with the weapons and the technology they needed.[56] Thus, he saw the transfer option as a necessary condition for preventing the national option, for halting proliferation, if a settlement with the Soviets was undesirable or could not be obtained. Eisenhower went far in this direction. In 1957 there was the first talk about America´s sharing nuclear weapons with its allies; perhaps it was only explained at the meeting of the NATO Council in December 1957 - after Sputnik - that the US intended to give NATO allies nuclear carriers but would retain control of the warheads.[57] Congress was much more anxious than the President to keep every single part of the huge nuclear arsenal under ultimate American control, and was also reluctant to accept legislation that would liberalize the transfer of military nuclear information to Allies. Congressional action came only when the atomic energy legislation was modified in 1958 so as to permit release of nuclear weapons information to allies which had made ´substantial progress´ in the field. This condition was interpreted as applying to Britain only.

Eisenhower was also in favour of the European option. His goal was the withdrawal of American troops from Europe. He talked about making Western Europe ´a third great power bloc´. If this was realized, he said, the US would no longer have to bear the enormous burden of the defence of Europe and America could ´sit back and relax somewhat´.[58] Trachtenberg argues that Eisenhower was thinking in terms of a three-stage process and that all the major elements in America´s European policy in the mid- and late 1950s were rooted in this kind of thinking. During an initial emergency period, lasting for perhaps five to ten years, a sizeable American army would be stationed in Europe. There would be a second period when Europe would take over the burden of providing for the ground defence. America would continue to underwrite the defence of Western Europe with its strategic nuclear force. Only a small American ground force would remain on the continent. In a third period, Europe would stand on its own militarily ´while remaining friendly with America´ and would emerge as ´a truly independent´ power mass in world affairs; ´implicit in this policy was the assumption that the Europeans would have a nuclear capability of their own

- that western Europe would not simply remain a strategic protectorate of the United States'.[59]

It should be observed, however, that Eisenhower probably did not envisage a 'Third Force' Europe at the level of the superpowers. Although he was not quite clear on this point, he seemed to envisage a European nuclear capacity mainly at the tactical level, not a European federation equipped with H-bombs and intercontinental carriers and certainly not outside the NATO framework. There was obviously no guarantee that a truly independent power bloc would always remain friendly with America. Eisenhower's perspective may be interpreted as meaning that America's military and economic power would always be sufficient to prevent a European bloc from developing beyond the limits of an 'Atlantic Europe'. Furthermore, whatever his personal views, it is clear that substantial parts of the Administration, including the State Department, and certainly a majority in Congress, saw the European option as a potential danger in the long run.

Some researchers, when discussing the general goals of American policy for European integration, stress the limits of US support for unification. Bossuat, for example, concludes his extensive study of the State Department and European integration 1952-59 by observing: 'But European unity should in no case prepare Europe to act autonomously in world affairs. A French, or Franco-German, deviation in that sense would be questionable'.[60] Eckart Conze's interpretation is that a united Europe was desirable in order to lift the burdens on America and its economy without challenging American hegemony. The goal was to pay a lower price for hegemony, while preventing the emergence of potential rivals.[61]

2

The Nuclear Dimension of the European Defence Community

The Inherited Package: Arms Control in the EDC Treaty 1951-52

The elaboration of the EDC Treaty (the Paris Agreements) was tied to the working out of new contractual arrangements (the Bonn Agreements) giving the Federal Republic sovereignty, within limits, in return for its defence contributions. The contractual arrangements, conditional upon ratification of the EDC, defined areas in which the three Western Allies reserved supreme authority, essentially those related to all-German questions and Berlin. The two lines of action converged in the intricate legal complex that was signed in May 1952. It included the EDC treaty with associated protocols, the contractual arrangements with German letters containing declarations, for example about restrictions on German armament, and mutual security guarantees between members of the EDC and members of NATO.

The principle which Adenauer advanced in the EDC negotiations and other integration negotiations was *égalité des droits* [equality of rights]. The argument was that if the disillusioned and war-tired German people were to rearm, there must be no discrimination against the Federal Republic. Adenauer stated that he would accept any controls that were applied equally to all EDC member states; he also indicated that he would agree to positive allocations of production and restrictions in the EDC treaty on armaments, for example special weapons. There should be no controls on scientific research and industry.[1] Everybody understood that equality could not be complete, the question was to find a compromise that was not too openly discriminatory. The negotiations on arms control dealt with the problem of drawing the line between prohibited and other weapons and the difficult, even impossible, task of distinguishing between military and civil purposes in research and industrial production.

The position of the Truman Administration on arms control of the Federal Republic was modified and clarified in Acheson´s proposal to the UK and France at the tripartite foreign ministers meeting in Paris in November 1951. The US did not want to include certain heavy military equipment, such as tanks and artillery, as had been proposed by an expert group, but the prohibitions on the most important weapons, ABC weapons and carriers of strategic significance, were upheld. There should be no superior

Allied boards or agencies controlling the observation of the restrictions. A convention on control should be negotiated with the Germans. In addition, intelligence and the presence of Allied forces in Germany could be relied upon. Acheson's attitude to the problem was that restrictions alone were not reliable and that a certain production of arms in Germany was desirable. NATO, the EDC and the 'lack of resources'[2] would provide adequate protection, only 'certain broad categories' of prohibited weapons should be retained.[3] He wrote to Truman that a legal contract would give illusionary protection for an interim period yet become unworkable when needed. Security against Germany in the future lay more along the lines of tying Germany in every possible way to the West through mechanisms such as the ECSC, EDC and, eventually, NATO.[4]

European integrationists worked in a similar spirit. Jean Monnet believed that the only possible solution for arms control would be to abandon contractual arrangements and to rely on the common budget and procurement framework of the EDC to inhibit some forms of military production in Germany.[5]

The French were reluctant. They struggled to evade the equality principle as far as possible.[6] They were adamant in their opposition to German membership of NATO and wanted additional means of control. They were anxious to keep prohibition list for Germany as extensive as possible. The *Quai d'Orsay* [the French Foreign Ministry] complained that the Anglo-Americans focus on control of atomic weapons was not sufficient:

> In this there is a problem which affects France in particular. The British and Americans are convinced that, given the cost of modern armies and their equipment, it will be many years before the Federal Republic will be capable of establishing a military force sufficient to cause them disquiet; furthermore, the international situation and the presence in Germany of major contingents of their own forces gives them the impression that they have nothing to fear from a renascence of German military power. There is basically only one domain in which they would not wish to see Germany regain total independence, namely that of atomic weapons.[7]

The principle of equality was eventually modified by a formula which, without being openly discriminatory, applied to Germany but not to France. The agreed solution was that significant weapons manufacture should be forbidden in any area subject to seizure or destruction in the event of attack, a 'strategically exposed area'. A provision of this kind was included in the EDC Treaty.

The supranational arms procurement system with a common budget was a cornerstone of the EDC, in addition to the integration of armed forces. The existing (Germany had none) and future arms industries would become integrated and subject to common decision-making in a way similar to that of coal and steel in the already existing Community. The supranational executive organ of the EDC, the Commissariat, was responsible for the preparation and execution of common armament programs. There was a rule against an unequal distribution of the economic benefits between the member countries. It was foreseen that contracts received by a country's arms industry should not be less than 85 per cent, or more than 115 per cent, of the country's contributions to the budget.[8]

France and the Federal Republic would in this way control the arms production of each other, not through restrictions, but through cooperation and common decision-making. This part of the EDC also had economic functions. A national arms industry that was not competitive might be saved in a European context. After the collapse of the EDC, a similar system appeared as the French proposal for an 'Arms Pool'.[9]

Article 107 of the Treaty stipulated that production, import and export of war materials, and technical research, and so on, related to them, was forbidden, except if the Commissariat had granted a license. Two lists were annexed to the article, 'Annex I' and 'Annex II'. The first listed more or less all arms and war materials, from atomic weapons down to guns. The most important weapons (ABC-weapons and other weapons of strategic significance[10]) were listed in Annex II. The Commissariat was not empowered to grant licences for Annex II weapons in strategically exposed areas except by unanimous decision in the Council of Ministers. In this way France had a veto on German activities related to nuclear weapons and their carriers.

The term 'atomic weapon' was defined in a narrow way making it encompass parts of activities necessary or desirable for production of civil nuclear power, or being a necessary consequence of such activities.[11] Most importantly, a very small yearly production of nuclear fuel (500 grams) was allowed.[12] Such a quantity of plutonium is rapidly produced when operating any reactor other than a small research reactor.

Guidelines for delivering general licences were laid down. A country would be allowed to have war materials for overseas needs, but the Commissariat would control that these needs were not exceeded. It was envisaged that products related to weapons that were intended for civil uses would be granted a general licence; a control system would verify compliance. In the nuclear area, the various provisions meant that it would in principle be possible for other countries than the Federal Republic to exceed the 500 gram limit for civil purposes, and France would be free to produce nuclear weapons in its overseas territories up to the limit. France would, however, be subject to inspection of its nuclear energy program, still officially civil only. This was unpalatable to many, and there were French apprehensions that it might give the Germans access to plutonium technology.[13]

The provisions about atomic energy in the EDC Treaty were supplemented by declarations within the contractual framework by Chancellor Adenauer. He gave guarantees and accepted certain further restrictions, among them small upper limits for production, import and storage of uranium. German law would prohibit not only development and manufacture but also possession of atomic weapons. A comprehensive control over the nuclear sector would be maintained; the details would be agreed between the four countries.[14]

Another component of the total complex was a system of reciprocal guarantees between member states of the EDC, the UK and the member states of NATO. A declaration by the three Allies dealt with the question that was regarded by many, particularly in France, as the only ultimately effective protection against a resurgence of German militarism, the stationing of Allied troops in Germany. This guarantee was formulated in a way that was not binding ('station such forces...as they deem necessary and appropriate').[15] This was not satisfactory to the French. It was a main goal of French foreign policy to obtain firm commitments from the US and the UK for their continued military presence in the Federal Republic. The loose formula was however consistent with the long-run American goal of keeping the economy in balance by measures such as military withdrawal from the European continent.

After Adenauer's declaration had issued, but before the signature of the treaty complex on 26-7 May, the Germans tried to obtain a somewhat greater freedom of action in the nuclear field. Adenauer asked the Allies to agree to a research reactor size that would produce a little more nuclear fuel than the 500 grams, and to some other small adjustments, but the High Commissioners remained firm. They referred to the fact that concessions in this sensitive matter would raise a public storm in the Western countries. The British Commissioner expressed the reason for the factual discrimination: 'the fact that nuclear science in Germany lags behind that of other states is a consequence of losing the war'.[16] There had however been, and continued to be, internal differences between the US, on the one side, and the British and French on the other on this point. The US was prepared to permit a reactor program and production of nuclear fuel several times as large as Britain and France, but the point was not pressed.[17]

Negotiations on the details of the German atomic energy legislation went on for years after the signature of the EDC treaty within a quadripartite group of Allied and German officials. Also in connection with the work of this group it was clear that the American attitude to permitting the Germans to start working on a small scale reactor program before ratification of the EDC complex was more liberal than that of the British and French. Dulles however instructed that it was not worthwhile to press the matter in the face of British and French reluctance.[18]

The Additional Protocols of 1953

In the period after the signature of the EDC Treaty the dynamism of German economic development caused growing fears in France that Germany might eventually attain the ascendancy. France was handicapped by the drain of resources caused by the war in Indochina and the struggle to retain the African territories. France looked for discriminatory provisions in the collective arrangements, supplemented by US and UK guarantees, to curb German power. 'What she really cannot bring herself to accept is German equality, and Germany will accept nothing else...What she actually wants is to freeze Germany into a set of West European arrangements favourable to France and to her position as *primus inter pares*' it was observed in a State Department analysis with the somewhat resigned title 'France as a Problem for United States Foreign Policy'.[19]

In 1953 France presented various conditions declared to be necessary if ratification were to be attained. French prime ministers in successive governments told the Americans that at least three conditions were indispensable, (1) additional protocols to the EDC treaty, (2) a close association with Britain and an undertaking to maintain Anglo-American forces on the continent, (3) a settlement of the Saar issue.[20] The US opposed any French disposition to make EDC ratification dependent on a Saar solution, because of its potential for delaying the EDC, but worked actively to promote some adjustments on the two other points. The Americans were in principle prepared to accept most solutions for the Saar which the French and Germans could agree on, but wanted to avoid making the Saar 'a new Luxemburg'.[21] Much revolved around the question of the additional protocols.

When the René Mayer Government came to power in January 1953 it was a condition for the necessary Gaullist support that the Government would negotiate new protocols on the EDC to preserve the integrity and unity of the French armed forces. A first draft was put to the military chiefs for discussion. Their spokesman, Marshal Juin, answered the Government that the texts were unsatisfactory. He wanted changes, among them to Article 107, seeking national freedom '... to produce, import and export war materials necessary to the Armed Forces of certain Member States'. This of course also covered nuclear weapons. The Government adopted as the French negotiation bid most of the military standpoints, including this one.[22]

The French proposed six additional protocols to the EDC treaty and asked for clarification on a couple of other points.[23] The common underlying theme was the demand to retain a national sector that was not subject to supranational decision-making, the size of which would be decided by France, and at the same time to preserve the rights of decision on the common sector and thus on Germany.

France demanded that the US should be obliged to address its military aid to the EDC as such, not to single EDC states, after which it would be distributed by the EDC.[24] The demand was prompted by apprehensions that the US might choose to strengthen the military potential of Germany relative to that of France. The most important possibility concerned the nuclear transfer option. The US might equip German units within the European army with nuclear weapons without ensuring French superiority. The legal situation was intricate. The evidence indicates that both the US and the EDC had a veto on the allocation of US aid to nations and units within the EDC. According to US internal documents which analyzed the issue in connection with the later WEU affair the situation appears to have been this: In the EDC Treaty, arms from third countries would in principle be distributed by the EDC Council, but there was also a provision that individual states could receive arms, and that the transaction would merely be administered by the Commissariat.[25] Consequently, the US could deal with an individual nation. Similarly, the US could determine that a particular item of equipment should be shipped to a particular unit of the European Army - thus also to a German unit. Dulles retrospectively explained that ´...we would have retained under EDC right to determine on basis effective utilization allocation of equipment to individual EDC units in same way as we retain this right with respect to individual units of nations with which we deal...This retention of control by US with respect to designation of units to receive equipment was made clear to EDC countries and is part of negotiating record of military assistance agreement with EDC´.[26]

An important protocol from our point of view concerned Article 107. According to the French proposal, the general licences for production, import and export of war materials for overseas needs should be delivered by the Commissariat upon the entry into effect of the treaty and without limit as to duration. They should be irrevocable and contain no quantitative or qualitative indications. The control function of the Commissariat would be satisfied by receiving annual information from the beneficiary state. Thus no inspection.

The basis for differential treatment of France and Germany was of course the references to overseas needs. France had overseas possessions, Germany had none. The German *Amt Blank*, the precursor of the Ministry of Defence, considered the protocol to Article 107 to be, in particular, a material modification of the Treaty and a ´reason for serious concern´.[27] In the French historian Pierre Guillen´s view, the change was, in addition to serving the purpose of autonomously steering military capacity to the overseas possessions and maintaining the integrity of the French army, intended to keep the French national nuclear option open.[28]

Dulles responded cautiously when receiving the news that France would seek protocols in order to make ratification possible. He told his diplomats that the US believed in a flexible attitude toward minor modifications of the EDC Treaty provided that certain conditions were fulfilled, mainly that this could be attained without actual amendment to the treaty and without violating essential integration features.[29] The French invited the US to participate as observer in the negotiations in the executive organ of the EDC in the pre-ratification period, the Interim Committee.[30] After having read the French texts Dulles wrote that it seemed that most countries except Germany felt that they could be negotiated into acceptable positions. He commented that the ´protocols represent first French negotiating position, and that the French can be brought around to more reasonable position that will result in eliminating features of protocols which (a) give French a special position not required by realities of her overseas responsibilities or (b) discriminate against other parties to the Community, in particular Germany´. He opposed outright some features. With respect to the French proposal about Article 107, he wrote that the basic problem was one of balance. It was necessary to reconcile the fear of other EDC countries that France would use this protocol to build up its own armament industry for national forces, and the French fear that it would be hamstrung by the EDC in producing armaments for its forces in Indo-China. Dulles considered - apparently thinking of an arrangement compatible with US goals in Indo-China - that it would be possible devise a protocol such as to reconcile these views. EDC licensing would have to be handled with flexibility. Dulles opposed, however, the French demand for licences that were irrevocable, without quantitative limitation and without duration. In his view, this completely negated the content of Article 107, which gave the Commissariat the right to insure that licences were not used beyond certain specified needs.[31]

In the Interim Committee some minor adjustments were accepted by the other countries but dissent on essential points related to EDC´s supranationality remained.[32] The proposed protocol to Article 107 - that is, the demand for licences for producing weapons for overseas needs that were irrevocable, without a time limit, and without the right of inspection - was particularly unacceptable to the others. It was generally rejected by the partners as cancelling Article 107 completely.[33]

When the six foreign ministers met in Rome on 24-5 February 1953 they agreed on a formula regarding the thorny protocol issue, which could have caused the complete breakdown of the EDC. A breakdown was evaded, at least temporarily, by a sufficiently diffuse compromise. The French protocols were to be considered as what the Communiqué described as ´interpretative texts´, thus not affecting the treaty per se. The drafts were returned to the Interim Committee for further work.[34] After redrafting, the protocols were approved there in March and accepted by the governments in the six member states. There was no real clarity, however, because the protocols were not formally signed.[35]

However, the French military was dissatisfied with the version of the protocols which had been approved in the Interim Committee. A vivid polemics between politicians and the military took place. Marshal Juin and the General Staff asked for modifications designed to guard French autonomy but nothing that was satisfactory to the military was decided. After this, it became clear that the military turned against the EDC in a more definite way; it wanted to send the whole project 'to the Greek Kalends'[36]

The protocol question developed into a complicated political game in which the prospective EDC members were using legal arguments. The diffuse compromise in Rome was never really clarified. The central point was the legal status and force of the protocols. Had they the same validity as the treaty text, or had they, being interpretative, a lower validity, implying for example that the treaty text would prevail in case of conflict?

Internally in France the legal question seemed to be regarded as solved. The French nuclear programme would not be subjected to supranational regulation, and this was an important aspect of the protocols.[37]

The Germans had quite a different understanding of the validity of the protocols. The *Auswärtiges Amt* stressed that the compromise in Rome did not mean a change in the treaty but an interpretation only. The Court of the EDC would have the role of deciding in favour of the treaty text in case of conflict: 'In this way it should be ensured that the additional protocols, in the event of a conflict about interpretation being submitted to the EDC Court, would be subordinated to the Treaty text'. The German Government made a declaration to the *Bundestag* that the additional protocols were interpretive. Similar declarations were also made in Benelux and Italy.[38]

US diplomacy tried to promote agreement when the six states were negotiating about the final protocol texts in February–March 1953. Some accommodation to French wishes in order to help the French government to handle the domestic opposition to the EDC was regarded as inevitable. Dulles told the Frech - when looking back later - that 'he had counselled other European countries subscribing to the EDC not to agree to the French protocols until the French Government committed itself to act [to obtain ratification]. Finally, on the basis of assurances of the French Government, the other EDC countries with the U.S. urging had agreed to the protocols'.[39] The US Paris Ambassador, Douglas Dillon, reported that 'with US intervention', other European nations had reluctantly agreed to the protocols.[40] His assessment was premature, however. During the autumn of 1953, Dulles was troubled that the signatures of the governments were long in coming. Repeatedly, he stated that the protocol question had to be closed to prevent further delay of the ratification process: 'Until protocols have been signed by Foreign Ministers there will always be temptation for French to propose modifications or introduce further protocols'.[41] He wrote that Adenauer had indicated his willingness to sign.[42] The Germans, and the other EDC partners did not sign, however.

In the spring of 1954 France pressed for signature of the protocols and for reinforcement of their legal power. The French attempted to press their case by making the approval by the Allied High Commission of an issue in German constitutional reform dependent on signature of the protocols. Dulles reacted by writing to the French Foreign Secretary, Georges Bidault, and warned against such linkage. He stated that this would create a most dangerous situation and promised that he would urge Adenauer to sign.[43] The French retreated on the constitutional point. The French also negotiated directly with the Germans and asked that the protocols should be ratified by the Head of State, or given a similar legal form, thus confirming that they would have the same force as the Treaty. In June the French High Commissioner was still negotiating with Adenauer on this subject.[44]

In sum, agreement on the additional protocols had been reached because there remained obscurity in the formulations and as regards their validity in relation to the Treaty. The Germans refused to accept the French view that they had the same validity as the Treaty, and signatures were not forthcoming. The Americans urged the other Five to sign but did not want amendments to the Treaty. It seems, then, that the American position on the legal issue was close to the German one.

American and British Planning

The main obstacle to entry into force of the EDC-Contractuals package was the situation in the French Parliament. French ratification was regarded as uncertain from the outset, and doubts about the outcome of a vote were increasing as time went by.

Quite soon after the signature of the treaty complex in May 1952 agencies within the US foreign policy establishment had begun working on alternatives in case the EDC were not ratified. Papers on the subject were written during the last months of the Truman Administration. Various options were outlined, including German membership of, or association with, NATO, German rearmament independent of NATO, some form of German non-military contribution to Western defence, or US retreat to peripheral defence in Europe.[45]

A discussion of principle took place in January 1953 when the new Administration was coming in. Differing perspectives of the foreign policy leadership and the military were advanced. The Chairman of the Joint Chiefs of Staff argued that the EDC would be an acceptable solution, although not as good as German full membership of NATO. The problem was that the US was faced with more and more demands for restrictions on German production, which the French were pressing for in connection with the EDC. The Chiefs had been hoping that the Germans could produce many of the necessary items themselves. Peripheral defence was not a good solution from a military point view. Paul Nitze, of the State Department, also dismissed peripheral defence and stated that even the best alternatives from among the studies undertaken in the previous autumn did not look very good. Full German NATO membership was impossible; it would be vetoed by the French. Dulles outlined the pro-integration philosophy which he would profess on numerous occasions. He was surprised that the military considered full membership of NATO to be better than the EDC:

> From the political standpoint, EDC is much to be preferred. It would serve to combine Germany and France in a manner more trustworthy than a treaty relationship. The problem in Europe has been the recurrent conflicts between France and Germany leading to recurrent wars. Unless these conflicts are buried, difficulties between them are apt to reappear. We may find that treaty relationships, like the German-USSR alliance, will be torn up.[46]

However, from the negotiations standpoint it was useful to have alternatives, Dulles continued. If the French and Germans believed that peripheral defence was tolerable to the US that would create pressure on them. 'An alternative is necessary if we are to get it [the EDC]'.[47]

These themes were elaborated further in internal discussions in 1953. The cleavage between military and State Department points of view remained. The common conclusion was that none of the feasible alternatives was as satisfactory as the EDC.[48] President Eisenhower reflected that 'there were no suitable alternatives in any case, since Chancellor Adenauer himself was opposed to an independent German army and German general staff'. The President prohibited any public talk by officials on alternatives to EDC; if 'the French heard of such discussions they would become hysterical'.[49]

On 14 December Dulles issued his famous threat to France before the NATO Council in Paris: 'If ...the E.D.C. should not become effective...That would compel an agonizing reappraisal of basic United States policy'.[50] 'Agonizing reappraisal' was generally interpreted to mean that the US might withdraw its troops, retreating to isolationism or peripheral defence. The thinly veiled threat was not the first of its kind and came as no surprise in the EDC capitals. The President explained to Congress leaders that he had gone over the speech with Dulles; he 'believed the U.S. had to be firm, though not truculent, on the facts of life'.[51]

Was a hard line toward France credible? Part of the answer may be found in the perceptions of US policymakers of the importance of France in global strategy, and of French reactions in case the US activated the policy of 'agonizing reappraisal'. The dangers of France 'going commie' and its repercussions, for example in Indo-China and North Africa[52], were present in American minds. Dulles stated in the National Security Council that many people thought that the US should rearm Germany by unilateral action. However, he felt 'that any attempt to do this would probably result in a Communist France, with all that this implied for our forces in Germany'.

It was 'necessary to keep France on our side, and if we failed in the attempt to do so, a unilaterally armed Germany would prove useless to us'.[53] The spectre of France making an alliance with the Soviet Union was also there. It would, according to the military, 'be pretty tough having commies on one's line of communication' and if France was allied with the Russians 'we would be in a completely untenable position in Germany'.[54] Right-wing developments were not excluded either. Dulles told the National Security Council that, although 'he could not predict a coup d'état, there was some talk of it in France in connection with General Juin'; he stated his belief that 'General de Gaulle would not take the initiative in planning any coup d'état, but might move in on one if its success looked promising'.[55]

French politicians were well aware of the US dilemmas and were sometimes explicit when talking to Americans about possible consequences if the US attempted to implement the 'agonizing reappraisal' policy. For example, Maurice Faure, later French chief negotiator in the Common Market/Euratom negotiations, told State Department officials that 'if EDC fails, we must work out other solutions for if the US were to withdraw its troops from the continent, France would be forced to turn to Moscow'.[56]

In the spring of 1954 impatience mounted in the US. It was felt that the situation was approaching a crossroad; after waiting for two years since the signature of the treaty complex German rearmament had to be attained with or without the consent of France. Coordination with Britain was sought.

An Anglo-American meeting between Heads of Government and Foreign Ministers, the Churchill-Eisenhower talks, took place in Washington on 25-9 June. In the US view, the overriding consideration guiding a common EDC policy was the need to respond to the German insistence on ending the occupation regime. If sovereignty were postponed, frustration would be so great that Adenauer could not remain in power. The consequence would be neutralization as advocated by the Social-Democrats, and ultimately absorption of a unified Germany into the Soviet orbit. Eisenhower summarized his priorities in the words that 'we could not afford to lose Germany even though we were to lose France'. It was decided to separate the questions of Contractuals, that is, German sovereignty, from the condition about ratification of the EDC. The objective was to become 'legally lined up', that is, to prepare all the necessary parliamentary procedures required to implement the Contractuals in the absence of French ratification. Any public discussion of alternatives or open threats should be avoided. A German undertaking not to rearm unilaterally while the process was going on was required.[57]

When reporting to the National Security Council about the Churchill-Eisenhower talks Dulles indicated that the problem lying ahead was that Germany would refuse to accept limitations which applied to Germany alone. Accordingly, it would not be practical from the US point of view to try to induce Germany to accept an inferior position in NATO, as Eden and other likeminded statesmen wished. Eisenhower and Dulles agreed that Adenauer did not desire a separate national army for Germany, while he was at the same time opposing a special and inferior military status for Germany.[58]

An Anglo-American study group in London was charged with exploring the alternatives further. It submitted a report in July which anticipated various possible French reactions to a bilateral decision to restore German sovereignty and start rearmament by separating the Contractuals from the EDC Treaty. The American members of the group were however not yet authorized to support an alternative to the EDC. The separation raised a number of complicated legal problems for which texts and protocols were elaborated. The idea was to create a *fait accompli*, which would as little as possible militate against French ratification of the EDC later. The arms control issue was provided for. Under the proposed arrangement almost all weapons, and the manufacture of prototypes of and technical research concerning such materials should remain prohibited for the Federal Republic; exemptions could be granted by a commission, in which the US, the UK, France and the Federal Republic were represented on the basis of equality.[59]

The British, who had long been in favour of a 'NATO with safeguards' model, argued that, next to the EDC, this model was the best solution. An attached British paper argued that the essential prohibitions for Germany should be transplanted from the EDC Treaty to NATO. For example, 'certain types of arms production and research, including atomic and thermo-nuclear weapons, submarines and military aircraft' would only be permitted by the NATO Council. This would be supplemented with as many other guarantees as possible. The British also proposed an Arms Pool to be created primarily by the EDC countries - no doubt because it was hoped that Britain, having the most advanced arms industry in Europe, would have an export market on the continent.[60]

After having received the report of the study group, Dulles instructed his diplomats to inform the French government about the general lines of thinking of the group and the two governments. No details should be given. The French government should be told that other EDC partners had been informed in the same way.[61] Dulles then himself met the French Premier and put forward his arguments: the Russians were trying to neutralize and were winning Germany over, Congress would not appropriate a dollar for military aid unless Germany were rearmed, if the EDC were turned down there would be strong pressure for the US to engage in 'peripheral defense'. German sovereignty could not be partially restored, it must be fully restored, he said. He 'had been present during the work of the Versailles Treaty and felt that the results of that Treaty clearly demonstrated that it was folly to believe that permanent restrictions could be imposed on a great power'. Mendès France, in turn, stressed the argument that he used on all occasions in the EDC negotiations: he did not believe that there was a majority for the EDC in the French National Assembly. He would have to find some face-saving formula, perhaps in the shape of minor revisions, with the particular objective of securing the approval of Socialist deputies.[62]

A State Department memorandum in late July stated that if EDC or the interim model of the study group proved impossible the alternatives were (1) German NATO membership based on equality, and (2) armament of the Federal Republic by the US and Britain (this possibility which was described as less desirable was not discussed in detail). The NATO solution should not be pressed through against the will of France, it was argued. It could be made acceptable by constructing a separate US-UK-French-German security pact. Such a pact would have the double purpose ´of expressing the safeguards against resurgent militarism which the Federal Republic agreed to weave into the EDC "package", and at the same time bind the Occupying Powers by treaty to the observance of these assurances´. Among the restrictions that would be demanded by the Federal Republic were those contained in Article 107 of the EDC Treaty. The memorandum stated that the arms control problem would be the main knot in coming negotiations with the Allies. A three- or four-power mechanism for controlling German arms production would be unacceptable to the Germans. A NATO control system was problematic, and it was doubtful whether the US could participate in it. The British proposal for an arms pool would require a long negotiation period; the US should not permit it to be made a condition for German NATO membership. Integration of armaments programs within NATO to prevent independent national arming was imaginable but complicated: ´Admittedly, it will be difficult to persuade the British and then the French to agree to German rearmament without production controls extending beyond the prohibitions in Article 107. However, using NATO to limit production would be a complete distortion of its concept, and result in practical discrimination against Germany. Unless we can reach agreement on this, our efforts to achieve German membership in NATO may well be fruitless´.[63]

This was not far from the US standpoints in the coming WEU negotiations, although with the important difference that the WEU was organized without US membership.

German and French Planning

In Germany, the request for equality remained the fundamental principle upon which every policy should be built. The precursor to the Ministry of Defence, the *Amt Blank*, drafted an internal memorandum in July about demands concerning the German defence contribution in case the EDC were not ratified. Full NATO membership was anticipated. The memorandum enumerated a number of conditions, the common denominator of which was equal treatment, implying a degree of independence that was not very different from the other members. For example there would be a German military command under the Ministry of Defence. No unilateral qualitative or quantitative restrictions on the German troops should be allowed. There should also be freedom to the produce and import arms, and to conduct research and development. If the latter principle was accepted, an important concession was however imaginable. The *Amt Blank* considered that a voluntary restriction concerning A, B and C-weapons was possible.[64] The general argument was, then, that Germany should have very much greater freedom in the armaments field than in the EDC, and that this freedom would include missiles, warships, aircraft, and so on. The only exception would be ABC-weapons. The possibility of 'voluntary' denial on this point was a first sign and portent of Adenauer's *Kernwaffenverzicht* [renunciation of manufacture of nuclear weapons on the territory of the Federal Republic] in the WEU negotiations - a fundamental key to agreement there.[65]

French planning for an alternative to the EDC which might control German rearmament followed two tracks: a 'restriction track' based on including Germany in the alliance system without much supranationality but with restrictions, controls and British and US guarantees, and an 'integration track' based on unequal Franco-German integration and cooperation on production of armaments. Other French precautions were to orient the domestic nuclear programme, still officially civil only[66], increasingly toward future manufacture of nuclear weapons, and to fight restrictions on the French national option. The French believed, partly on the basis of the same arguments as the Americans, that NATO was unsuited for arms control purposes. The organization had no tools for it, and its objective was to enhance the defence effect, not to limit it. It had no means of steering the distribution of military aid, of limiting Germany's independence, of imposing standardization and of promoting joint production, and it had no means to enforce controls.[67] Moreover, NATO was an organization dominated by the US, and the French feared that the US might relax controls on Germany in the future.

The Army General Staff pronounced itself at the end of June, following the 'restriction track', to be in favour of a European defence organization by transformation and extension of the Brussels Treaty.[68]

The 'integration track' was based on the 'arms pool' part of the EDC. A French Socialist anti-EDC politician, Pierre-Olivier Lapie, had long argued that the arms procurement system in the EDC treaty was a self-contained whole, which might become a substitute for the EDC.[69] Franco-German integration in production of aircraft was also on the agenda; there were French plans to include this in the arms procurement system of the EDC. The French feared that American and British products would wipe out their unprofitable aircraft industry. It was concluded that only European arms programmes could save it. In the summer of 1954 joint Franco-German planning for aircraft production in North Africa was going on; it was reported that the US would be asked if it would be interested in a 1/3 stake, thus holding the 'balance of power' in the project.[70]

The *Quai d'Orsay* started favouring the arms pool concept. Common production of arms could give more secure controls, but the economic advantages were equally important. The price and cost relations between the products of French industry, working behind high tariff barriers, and those of Germany and other European countries, were unfavourable in many sectors. The arms sector, in which Germany had been prohibited to have industries, was seen as a field in which the possibilities for French competitiveness were good.[71]

A leading anti-EDC official at the *Quai*, Olivier Wormser, wrote a memorandum in which Franco-German cooperation on atomic energy was - perhaps for the first time - included as a suitable area for cooperation between France and Germany:

> Atomic weapons, military aircraft, guided missiles: these prohibitions were from the outset conceived by us as intended to facilitate Franco-German co-operation outside the territory of Germany. There was in fact no reason why Western Europe alone should not profit from the technical and intellectual contribution from Germany when it was German scientists who enabled different countries to make major advances in these very same sectors. It was also evident that if co-operation of this kind could not be established, the prohibitions would very soon be called in question by Germany, which would argue the necessity not to sterilise the intellectual and technical capital which West Germany represents for Western defence... To prevent any development of that kind a program of Franco-German co-operation in a European framework is indispensable.[72]

A working group chaired by the anti-EDC Secretary–General of the *Quai*, Alexandre Parodi, formulated a project for replacing the EDC with two agreements, representing a combination of the two tracks, one for a seven-power intergovernmental defence organization ('little NATO'), and one for supranational production of arms within a European arms pool. The defence organization would secure the participation of Britain[73] and incorporate some of the essential restrictions on Germany in the EDC. The arms pool would be built on the provisions for arms procurement in the EDC treaty.[74]

At the beginning of August *Quai* thinking crystallized around two alternatives for action. The first was the Parodi concept, 'little NATO' plus an arms pool. The second was modifications of the EDC Treaty through a new protocol along lines elaborated by another official (De Seynes), making it less supranational. The modifications should be presented to the other nations as exclusively touching on application and interpretation of the treaty.[75]

Bruce and Dillon reported that tension was mounting in Paris on both sides of the EDC question as Mendès continued successfully to conceal his views and intentions.[76] Mendès told Dillon that it was necessary for him, because of the effect on French Parliament and opinion, to make a conciliatory response to a Soviet note about a meeting on the German question, although he had certainly no intention to meet the Russians before the vote of the National Assembly. It was most important that the Russians should be made solely responsible for any lack of progress.[77] Mendès was probably quite sincere but the effect was to make the alternative of a deal with the Russians more visible. Dulles was upset, and his suspicions of Mendès France increased. He instructed Dillon to tell Mendès that this would be considered as further proof of French unreliability in the US, that it would undermine the very basis of Franco-American relations and that it would probably destroy Adenauer.[78]

The New French Protocol Proposal

Out of the alternatives discussed at the *Quai d'Orsay*, the protocol model was chosen. According to information received by Bruce and Dillon about discussions in the French Government ('no notes could be taken'), Mendès France flatly rejected the 'Little NATO' proposal of the Parodi group. The document prepared by De Seynes was taken as the basis for the negotiations. Intensive discussions went on in the Cabinet for two days.[79] Mendès France secured a majority, he judged, only by promising to respond to two years of Soviet notes by envisaging a Four-Power Conference after the vote in Parliament. Nevertheless, three Gaullist ministers resigned.[80] Mendès tried to explain to a distrustful Dulles the pressures to which he was subjected.[81]

The *Protocole français d'application* of the EDC treaty was submitted to the other states. The title signalled that it should be regarded as an interpretative supplement for application of the Treaty and the additional protocols of 1953, whatever the legal status of the latter, and thus requiring no further ratification. The document was described by Dillon as 'unacceptable beyond our worst expectations'. He informed Dulles that, once the 'Little NATO' proposal had been rejected by Mendès, the Parodi group had concentrated its energies on making the French suggestions to the coming Brussels Conference as anti-EDC as possible.[82]

The general tendency of the protocol was to reduce supranationality and increase Franco-German inequality. The most important changes were: (1) supranationality was almost eliminated through a number of proposals[83], (2) integration of troops was foreseen only within the 'strategically exposed areas' (that is, for German forces and Allied forces stationed in Germany), (3) far-reaching changes were proposed for the common arms procurement system. Further, the unsolved legal core point that had for long been disputed with Adenauer and others came back in new clothes; it was proposed that the protocol would be an integral part of the Treaty.[84] With respect to the atomic energy problem, which is our primary interest, the following points touching on the arms procurement system, should be mentioned:

The protocol proposed, first, that in the definition of atomic weapons resulting from the annexes to Article 107 the limitation to 500 grams of nuclear fuel yearly would not apply outside the 'strategically exposed areas'.[85] This meant that not even a general licence for production of nuclear fuel exceeding that quantity would be needed for France. There would be no legal restrictions whatsoever for France to go on with production under a civil label of fissionable material for later use in bombs or submarines, while the restrictions on the Federal Republic remained.

A second point concerned the distribution of commands for the most important arms between the EDC members. For example, it was proposed that there would be exceptions for Article 107/Annex II weapons from certain provisions in the Treaty aiming at a balanced distribution between countries (the 85/115 per cent rule).[86]

A third point proposed that a part of the common budget would be used by the Commissariat for establishing common means of production, including scientific research, while permitting the construction of installations outside the 'strategically exposed areas'.[87] The provision was apparently designed to favour joint projects safely located on French territory, and joint financing, for example the Franco-German aircraft project or the cooperation on atomic energy and missiles that had been conjectured by Wormser. A *Quai* official explained to an American diplomat that the proposal was intended to permit Germany, for example, which could not produce certain types of war material, to participate in the production of such material in other areas, for example plants for the construction of military aircraft in North Africa under joint Franco-German leadership.[88] The proposal was perhaps also a first sign of the ambition to obtain European financing for a plant for enrichment of uranium, an issue that would become crucial in the later negotiations about Euratom.[89]

Dillon delivered detailed criticism of various parts of the French proposal to Dulles. He pointed out, for example, that the demand that the protocol should be an integral part of the Treaty would require a new round of ratifications. The changes to the arms procurement system were discriminatory and would modify the Treaty; 'Agreement to apply provision of article 107 on atomic weapons only to Germany is clear case of discrimination against Germany and change in Treaty'. The proposal for certain exemptions from the rules for a balance in arms orders between countries he characterized as an effort to obtain economic advantage for France. This also applied to the proposal for separate budgeting for ABC weapons and the missile-warship-aircraft category: 'Under EDC Treaty as presently drafted French believe they will have advantage of obtaining large share of production of heavy military items. Having obtained this advantage, French would now like to get large share of some military items by manipulation of financial provisions...Proposal is definite change in Treaty'.[90]

The attitude of the State Department to the French protocol proposal was totally negative. Later, after the downfall of the EDC project, it was concluded that the provisions seemed designed to be unacceptable; the evidence suggested that Mendès France had not wanted an agreement.[91]

The French made vain attempts to persuade Washington to support the protocol in the capitals of the EDC partners. The Washington Ambassador, Henri Bonnet, visited the Acting Secretary, Bedell Smith, and later Dulles also. The State Department had already made a public declaration which affirmed that it was hostile to the abandonment of the supranational character of the Treaty, and to new discriminatory features. Bonnet reported that the Americans were worried by the declared intention of Mendès to answer recent Soviet notes, which proposed a Four-Power conference on Germany, by asking for clarifications. Bedell Smith had said that the Soviets were capable of taking very big risks in order to block the EDC, no price being too high for obtaining this result. But the *conditio sine qua non* was always the neutralization of Germany. Bedell Smith had warned that 'neutralisation would, sooner or later, mean the unilateral and uncontrolled rearmament of Germany and the possibility of German-Soviet collusion, two eventualities which America for its part wanted at all costs to avoid'. The fear of Soviet manoeuvres had given a more vivid tone to the American protests, and hardened resistance to French demands. Dulles had talked with emotion about the German problem, he had become 'animated when he recalled the consequences which defeat for Chancellor Adenauer would have in Germany, the threat of a return to militarism in power and to collusion with the USSR'.[92]

Hurried messages reflecting irritation and distrust were exchanged between Mendès France and Dulles. Mendès denied Dillon's interpretation that he was thinking of a Four-Power conference before the end of the ratification process.[93] The French suspected that the Americans were behind the opposition that was encountered everywhere. Dulles was informed by an emissary of Mendès that Mendès had the impression that it was the United States which was instigating opposition to his plan on the part of the Low Countries and Germany. Dulles denied this.[94] However, it may safely be presumed that the US was instigating opposition by the other EDC states. An American memorandum just before the conference proposed, for example, that the US should 'discreetly urge the other prospective members of EDC to resist any French efforts to further modify the existing draft of the EDC treaty'.[95]

The reactions of the EDC partners to the French protocol proposal were uniformly critical, with or without American inspiration.

The German Government was determined to oppose the protocol.

Adenauer told the French High Commissioner that the day he received the French text was the 'most painful day' of his chancellorship.[96] His confidant, Hallstein, informed Conant that four principles were guiding the Chancellor: '1. No changes can be accepted which would require further *Bundestag* ratification. 2. Proposals seriously damaging supranational character of EDC must equally be rejected. 3. No new discriminations against Germany can be agreed to. 4. Efficiency of defense machinery under EDC must be maintained'.[97] Adenauer and Hallstein discussed the situation with Spaak the night before the opening of the Brussels Conference. Adenauer was very suspicious of the intentions of Mendès France; he told Spaak that he had reliable information that Mendès' confidant, Boris, had said, scornfully laughing, that Mendès had not the slightest intention of letting the EDC be ratified. Adenauer and Spaak agreed that the French protocols transcended the limit of what they could accept. They also discussed the American attitude. Their common opinion was that the US emissary, Bruce, had signalled that it was better to close the matter now, rather than prolonging the uncertain situation. Bruce had had enough and was no longer striving for a compromise. Spaak stressed that it must also be kept in mind that not only was it impossible for the Europeans to go back to their Parliaments, but the US could not accept such a procedure either. Hallstein called attention to the fact that NATO's Commmander, General Gruenther, had argued that 'modern special weapons' were only of real value to the US if the Federal Republic were incorporated in the Western defence system.[98]

Regarding the Article 107 provisions, memoranda from the *Auswärtiges Amt* stated that the removal of the 500 gram limit for others than Germany was a clear modification of the Treaty, which required new ratification. By excluding nuclear fuels from the list of materials regarded as atomic weapons the manufacture of these fuels outside 'strategically exposed areas' was freed from all restrictions. Even if developments in the nuclear field made it reasonable to have more freedom in the production of fuels for civil purposes, there was no reason for making a one-sided concession to France. It was conjectured that this French proposal stemmed from the ambition to get more technical information from the US and Britain; as long as the EDC Commissariat had a right of control, nothing could be kept secret. The Germans also considered that the proposals concerning the distribution of armaments orders violated the equality principle, changed the Treaty and were economically disadvantageous for the Federal Republic. Some looser formulation than in the Treaty might be considered, however. On the other side, the French proposal that production of weapons that for strategic reasons was not possible on German soil could take place elsewhere was positive for the Federal Republic and demonstrated European spirit.[99]

The rest of the member states of the EDC were similarly negative, without exception. The Italians told the French that Italy opposed discrimination of Germany and any modification requiring new ratification; the interest of Germany's neighbours was to aid Adenauer to avoid a resurrection of Nazism. In addition, development toward supranationality was part of Italy's political programme.[100] The Dutch Foreign Secretary, Beyen, informed the French Ambassador 'in a rather solemn tone' that the propositions were unacceptable. They altered the supranational character of the Community. The increased discrimination of the Federal Republic was a grave political error. Furthermore, the economic provisions went against the interests of the small countries; they seemed intended to '"give a bonus to France" and to enable her to remain in the background, to her own advantage'.[101] The conclusion of the Belgian Foreign Secretary, it was reported to the Americans, was that the proposals were unacceptable; 'Spaak finds proposals contradictory, confused and in some cases insolent towards Germans'.[102]

The French looked for support from Britain. The French London Ambassador, René Massigli, tried to obtain a pledge for British support in Germany for the French propositions. He reported that the Foreign Office Under Secretary had declared that it was impossible to exercise very strong pressure if the Chancellor estimated that his weakened position prevented him from accepting new discriminations. The Under Secretary had appeared to exclude British support for discriminatory measures toward Germany when speaking with another French diplomat, and had given a few examples, among them 'the atomic question' and the non-integration of troops outside the forward zone.[103] The official British response to the Brussels Conference was a masterpiece of vague formulations and diplomatic balancing. The British Government was of the view that 'all parties concerned should go as far as they could in meeting the French Government's proposals half-way, and above all that these proposals should not be rejected right away'. The UK was preoccupied about manifest discrimination of Germany, which that country could not accept. There appeared to be a few points which might be considered discriminatory, among them the clauses concerning atomic energy:

> The clauses concerning atomic energy, which seem obscure in the protocol, have been explained by the French authorities in a manner satisfactory to Her Majesty's Government. The British Government's understanding is that the purpose of these clauses is to avoid what would in fact appear to be discrimination against France, where an atomic programme has already been put in hand, whereas in Germany it has not yet been started.[104]

In this manner, the British cautiously supported an EDC without any supranational restrictions on the French atomic energy programme, which the Americans never did. The most probable explanation is that although the British regarded a French bomb as undesirable they wanted to keep the possibility to cooperate with France without being referred to a European bloc. This applied both to civil atomic energy where the British were advanced and hoped to lead developments in Western Europe, and to a British-French military option. The British wish for bilateral nuclear deals appeared clearly in the negotiations about Euratom later.[105]

The Brussels Conference (19-22 August 1954)

The Brussels Conference between the Six opened with Spaak in the chair. Mendès France stressed his basic argument. He said that seven parliamentary commissions had rejected the EDC. It was necessary for about a hundred of the deputies hostile to supranationality to be won over to German rearmament, or to further political integration. He had to obtain some new element to give these parliamentarians the opportunity to justify their change of position; it was impossible for him to return to Paris empty-handed. The other five delegations opposed the French protocol proposal on point after point on the basis of two Belgian counterproposals which preserved most of the supranationality of the Treaty and did not increase discrimination in the Franco-German relationship substantially. The most important concession to French viewpoints was an offer to preserve the requirement for unanimity during an interim period, although much shorter than that proposed by the French.[106]

Dulles sent a conditional declaration of support to Mendès France; copies were sent to the other Five and to Britain. The message started by pointing out that all points that could be agreed on unanimously and spontaneously ought to be accepted. However, in bringing about this unity certain considerations should be kept in mind: no new ratifications, preservation of supranationality, non-discrimination. The message finished by indicating what would happen in case of non-agreement:

> If the Brussels conference breaks up without having reached agreement we shall face a grave crisis. Our intention would then be, in the first instance, to enter into immediate consultation with the United Kingdom and with those EDC member states that have ratified the treaty, with a view to determining as rapidly as possible what measures should be taken to associate Germany with the West on the basis of absolute equality, and to proceed to rearmament. [107]

It may be remarked that the reference to ´absolute equality´ carried overtones about various possibilities unpalatable to France, also concerning nuclear weapons. An absolute equality had always been regarded by the French as a threat, the question was how big the difference would be.

According to Spaak´s biographer Michel Dumoulin, Dulles´ message, which ´was to give rise to the legend according to which David Bruce was manipulating events in the back-ground, certainly did not create the happiest effect´.[108]

The French Prime Minister's irritation rose considerably on the last conference day when he was informed that Spaak had received another urgent message at 0.30 in the morning containing a similar threat about an immediate meeting between the Five, the US and the UK.[109]

The nuclear issue was not addressed directly at the conference, it was subsumed under the general problems of supranationality and the arms procurement system. The Belgian counterproposals with respect to Article 107 contained non-binding formulations about the distribution of arms orders between countries and they did not mention the nuclear issue directly. At the plenary session, Article 107 was hardly discussed; it was referred to a group of experts. Nothing satisfactory to the French delegation came out of this.[110]

In their judgement of the French protocol Dillon and the Bruce Mission concluded that the demand for exemption from the 500 gram limit for nuclear fuels was a clear case of discrimination against Germany and a change in the Treaty. A memorandum about the issue was written in the State Department. An official who had been involved in the matter in previous years tried to give an account of the background of the limitations about nuclear fuels on France. He wrote that his recollection was that the limitations had always been intended as safeguards against Germany. It had not been the objective of the limitation to control the production of nuclear fuel in France or the other countries. The French had announced in 1946 that they would not manufacture nuclear weapons and had never retracted or changed this statement of intent. The French had however accepted controls since this was the only way of achieving controls over Germany without undue appearance of discrimination. The official concluded that the exemption of France for civilian use was logical and would be unobjectionable if the Treaty had not already been ratified by several countries and if it could be accomplished without the appearance of discrimination. As this was not the case, however, 'it would seem that the French should be content with the understanding ...that any necessary license would be forthcoming more or less automatically'.[111]

It should be remarked that an official at this level may have had good reasons to believe that the safeguards had only been directed against Germany. It is improbable that intentions of restricting France as well were communicated outside a very limited circle at the top level. If it became known that the equality principle had this function the chances of French ratification would be very small indeed.

The Brussels Conference closed in a bitter and frustrated mood. Spaak concluded that the other governments had been shocked by several proposals for reducing supranationality and could not accept them. Mendès France said that he had got very little to bring home, and that there was no chance of ratification by the French Parliament. Adenauer stated in an ominous vein that the issue at stake was 'the life and death of Europe'.

Answering the question whether he was going to fight for the EDC, Mendès reserved the position of the French Government.

The final standpoints of the other Five were expressed in a common declaration after it had become clear that the conference had failed. On the issue of Article 107, and the arms procurement system generally, there were conciliatory formulations, but no substantial concessions. Instead, the French demands had been reduced to the prospect of eliminating some inconveniences of the control system if France wished to cooperate in the nuclear field with the US or Britain:

> They should undertake to give the necessary directives to the Commissariat to ensure that the controls referred to in Article 107 are not of a kind to affect international cooperation relating to research or to the production of nuclear fuels for civil use.

The French requests for modifications of the provisions in Article 107 which regulated the orders for armaments and the pooling of arms production were not accepted. The declaration of the Five in this respect contained non-binding formulations such as 'taking into consideration the particular situations of the Member States' and 'to observe a fair balance between the various industries of each of the signatory countries'.[112]

Last-Minute Attempts to Save the EDC

Mendès France met with Churchill and Eden at Chartwell the day after the Brussels Conference closed. Churchill had assured Dulles before the meeting that he was prepared to give Mendès France 'the works' and go all out in support of the EDC.[113] Mendès France complained to Churchill that he regretted that everything in Brussels had happened 'as if the negative attitude of the five European partners had been concerted, not only among themselves but also with the United States and even with certain pro-EDC elements in France'. Both Churchill and Eden stuck loyally to the exigencies of the 'special relationship'. They dismissed all other possibilities than the EDC. Mendès finished by cautiously evoking the 'little NATO' concept, outlining the possibility of a coalition between the Six which the United Kingdom would join. He explained that particular measures to bind Germany could be developed.

Thus, the 'Little NATO' concept of the Parodi group seemed, when the protocol approach had failed, to be the preference of Mendès. The British - at this moment when the vote on the EDC had not yet taken place - did not admit any interest in the suggestion.[114]

When Mendès spoke to Dillon the following day he said that the two possibilities, in the event of EDC failure, were direct German entry into NATO, unlikely to be accepted in France, and a 'little NATO' solution.

Dillon reported that Mendès had said practically nothing about his conversation with Churchill, but that it appeared to him that Churchill and Eden must have stood firmly behind the EDC.[115] Churchill and Eden sent messages about the talk with Mendès to Dulles assuring him that they had really stood firm.[116]

This was soothing to the State Department which was anxious to keep the US-British front firmly united. It wished to avoid the impression, which it believed Mendès France wanted to create, 'that UK will support Little NATO with discriminatory provisions toward Germany', but feared that the impression remained.[117] The exclusive US-British partnership and planning was seen as part of the pressure on France and necessary for upholding the thesis that there were no other possibilities than the EDC. When the British presented a request in Washington that the protocols from the Anglo-US talks in the summer be given to Mendès France, obviously in order to dispel French distrust of British intentions, the answer was negative. The State Department believed 'that the risk was too great that Mendes-France directly or indirectly utilize the possession of this document to mislead the Assembly into believing that he was working intimately with the UK and US on steps to be taken tripartitely immediately after the Assembly rejected the EDC'.[118]

Another part of the pressure was the interpretation of the so-called 'Richards Amendment' to the Military Security Act, which regulated US military aid to Europe. The original version of the Amendment from 1953 stated the principle that 50 per cent of the military aid to Europe would go to the future EDC or its member countries. A new version which had been underway in Congress for some time was adopted on 26 August, just days before the French vote on the EDC. In the new Amendment the equipment and materials planned for 1954 and 1955 should only be delivered to nations which had ratified the EDC and which participated in the common defence programmes in a manner that was judged satisfactory by the President. The amendment was interpreted extensively to include also the 'off-shore'- procurements, that is, American orders for weapons from European industries.[119]

During the last days before the vote in the French National Assembly hurried messages were exchanged between the capitals. Distrust was deep. Bruce reported pessimistically that pro-EDC political leaders in France were 'unanimous in view that Mendès-France is doing and will do his utmost to defeat the EDC Treaty'. He proposed that the British should be approached about the possibility of another mediating conference, with the participation also of the US and Britain, in order to put the French under stronger pressure.[120] Although the State Department showed interest, Churchill and Eden rejected the idea as futile.[121] Bruce then asked for authorization to say that the US accepted a conference, if the French proposed one, arguing that 'interesting developments are in course', and characterized the British position as regards the French as 'like the beaver kill after torrential rains' and added that 'fishing in troubled waters is not easy'.[122] Dillon however had to register during the last day of the debate on the EDC in the National Assembly that Mendès did not say anything about the possibility of resuming talks with other nations, thus closing this possibility.[123]

On 30 August the EDC was refuted by the French National Assembly.

Conclusion

We may draw some tentative conclusions about the effects that the EDC would have had on the three nuclear options that were outlined above - the national options in Germany or France, the transfer option and the European option. Some reservations should be made, however. The rules were complicated and open to interpretation, many questions were left for decision later and we do not know how the complex would have been implemented.

The goal of restricting and controlling Germany in the nuclear field was solved in a way that was satisfactory to the US and the EDC partners. The Federal Republic had a very limited freedom of action. The common arms procurement system contained a number of restrictions on the nuclear fuel cycle. To exceed these limits required approval by the EDC. The partners would have the right to inspect all installations in the nuclear and carrier sector, and it would be more difficult to hide anything than in the inter-war period because the production of arms in the Federal Republic would be subsumed under a supranational arms procurement system. Dulles was persuaded that restrictions without supranationalism were insufficient for arms control of Germany; his experience from Versailles had taught him, he said, that it was 'folly' to believe that permanent restrictions could be imposed on a Great Power.

But there were also supplementary safeguards. The EDC was part of a larger web of arrangements and conditions. The NATO integrated command structure was important. *All* German troops would belong to the EDC and be under the command of NATO's commander in Europe, who was always an American general. The presence of Allied troops in the Federal Republic was another check on the resurgence of German militarism, although the goal of the Eisenhower administration was to create a system that would permit withdrawal of American troops in the foreseeable future. In the nuclear field, the US and Britain - and France in its own sphere - controlled the actual production of uranium and other nuclear raw materials in the Western world, and the US controlled the entire supply of enriched uranium. Thus, the material base for an independent German nuclear programme was lacking for the time being.

The problem of the French national nuclear option was related to the German one but it was also a problem in its own right. The US and the prospective EDC partners - plus Britain, watching the process from the sideline - wanted supranational restrictions on the French option also. The problem was that there were limits to the pressure that could be applied on France. The alternatives to cooperation with France had been explored in the US, and by the US and Britain jointly; they all appeared unattractive. Dulles concluded that it was ´necessary to keep France on our side, and if we failed in the attempt to do so, a unilaterally armed Germany would prove useless to us´. Caution and balancing in US policy toward the EDC negotiations and the nuclear question was required.

The Treaty implied supranational bindings on both the military and civil side of atomic energy in France also. The basic rule was that the EDC Commissariat would decide about exceptions from the common arm programmes and about the right to exceed the small upper limit for nuclear fuel. A general licence for countries other than Germany to have a civil nuclear activity was envisaged. A civil programme for France would thus normally be allowed, and consequently also a programme that was officially civil up to the point of making the weapons decision on the basis of the civil programme. The final decision was however subject to EDC authority.

The EDC member countries would take part in a control system that was to be worked out. Thus, watching German eyes on French nuclear technology could be foreseen.

The Treaty gave France substantial but not complete freedom of action with respect to its overseas territories. In one of the additional protocols proposed by France in 1953 the substance of this supranational authority and the measures for effective control were however removed. The protocol would make it possible for France to manufacture nuclear weapons in the overseas territories without interference from the EDC. The question of the validity of the protocols was not completely clear, however. The French sought guarantees that they would have the same validity as the Treaty but the Germans never formally accepted this. Dulles balanced between the German and French positions, but he opposed the French demand that licences should be irrevocable, without quantitative limitation and without duration. If this had been accepted it would have removed the element of supranationalism which he regarded as crucial. Perhaps he believed, like the Germans, that, in case of future conflict between the Treaty text and the additional protocol, the EDC Court would decide in favour of the Treaty text.

The option of transfer of US nuclear weapons to the EDC or one of its members was subject to the provisions of a legalistic jungle. The Treaty seemed to indicate a kind of mutual US-EDC veto on allocation of US aid. This was not the American interpretation, however. Dulles later explained that the ´essential point´ was that under the EDC the US would have had the same ultimate right to determine the units which received equipment as in the American relationships with an individual nation.

The door to a common nuclear force of the EDC - the European option - was not closed if there was sufficient support for it in the EDC Commissariat and in the Council. This would take place according to the rules of the common arms procurement system. The EDC design however regulated the allocation of all kinds of EDC forces within the NATO context. This provided some protection against a development which was questionable from the US point of view, a development in the direction of an independent 'Third Force'.

The demands put forward by France at the Brussels Conference weakened the supranational features of the Treaty to the point of disappearance, and it increased Franco-German inequality. The nuclear issue was affected by this, like other issues. The specific demands bearing on nuclear activities indicated that all remaining possible restrictions on French nuclear activities would be removed. France requested a completely unfettered national military and civil nuclear programme and, it seems, the possibility of having the programme and weapon-carriers largely financed by the other member states. The EDC partners, supported and led by the US, refused to accept most of the French demands.

The nuclear dimension of the EDC and its effects on France do not seem to have been much discussed directly in the US at the time. There was an awareness that the French nuclear option was a very sensitive subject. Any traceable effort to prevent the French from getting nuclear weapons was predictably counterproductive. The best strategy was to talk about the matter as little as possible, also internally. The US opposition to the French option was tacitly included in the general criticism of lack of supranationalism and increased discrimination of the Federal Republic. It is a significant fact that the US did not at any time endorse a scheme that would have given France a permanent freedom to manufacture and possess nuclear weapons.

Were the supranational restrictions on French national nuclear ambitions in the EDC complex a main cause of the failure of the project? It was certainly a factor in the rejection, even if its weight cannot be ascertained precisely. The nuclear dimension occupied no prominent place in the heated French public debate at the time, and was limited to informed circles. Its impact was increasing, however. Even if the French nuclear programme had been designed from the outset to keep the national option open, the awareness that nuclear weapons were revolutionizing military strategy was growing rapidly. The 'New Look' influenced thinking in France as elsewhere. The conclusion of the military leadership and many politicians was that the new strategy had to be accepted, and that France should have its own nuclear weapons as soon as possible. The nuclear lobby in the *Commissariat à l'énergie atomique* criticized the fact that it had not been consulted sufficiently by the French EDC negotiators and rang the alarm bells; in its view the EDC restrictions on the nuclear freedom of action of France were unacceptable. The line of the military and the CEA was represented in the governments by the Gaullists and other forces of the Right and the Centre, and the Gaullists were included in governments during 1954 until the exit of their ministers before the Brussels Conference. For them, French national nuclear weapons were fundamental to the restoration of French *grandeur* and securing equality with Britain.[124]

Michel Debré, a leading EDC adversary at the time and later De Gaulle's Prime Minister, retrospectively emphasized the importance of ´la grande *affaire atomique*´ in his campaign to defeat the Treaty.[125] A historian, Jacques Bariéty, focuses on the nuclear question in explaining the French rejection of the EDC. Many factors contributed, he argues, but, ´for me the essential reason is absolutely clear: the possibility for France to manufacture the atomic bomb and the choice created by French political power to manufacture it, which became an essential factor in the balance between Germany and France in the Alliance, permitting the rearmament of the Federal Republic without too much anxiety and the hope that France would remain a Great Power´. He thinks that the partners did not realize the French ambition to make the bomb and that the EDC treaty was incompatible with it.[126] Some other authors are similarly definite about the cruciality of the nuclear factor. For instance, Gustav Schmidt judges that ´it is evident that France "killed" its own brainchild, the EDC, with a view to preserving its nuclear option and thus maintaining equality of status with Britain in a US-led transatlantic security partnership´.[127] My own opinion is that it impossible to say anything with certainty on this point. The nuclear issue was very important but it was one of several factors behind the vote in the National Assembly. We do not know what would have happened if the other countries had accepted in Brussels that part of the protocol proposal which would have given France complete nuclear freedom but rejected other parts. It is true that the importance of the nuclear issue was growing in 1954. It would also - as we will see in the next chapter - very soon be openly at the centre of attention in the negotiations about the Western European Union. But it is also true that we may tend to overemphasize the importance of this factor in retrospect, after decades of debate about the seriousness of the problem of proliferation of nuclear weapons.

3
The Nuclear Dimension of the Western European Union

The defeat of the EDC in the French National Assembly - 'the crime of 30 August' as it was called by the losing side - was the starting-point for a process toward negotiating a new treaty. 'Little NATO' with safeguards had, we saw, been the French alternative to the protocol approach during the summer, and 'NATO with safeguards' had for long been the British preference in spite of the official support for the EDC. Washington saw no better alternative but to accommodate to these developments.

German Signals about Self-Limitation

The British High Commissioner, Sir Frederick Hoyer Millar, was already the day after the defeat of the EDC charged with approaching Adenauer. The British approach was carefully coordinated with the US. Eden had suggested that the first soundings would be made without the participation of his American colleague, Conant. Conant was fully informed through a copy of the instructions to Hoyer Millar that was sent from the State Department. Hoyer Millar was instructed to tell Adenauer that the UK considered two major alternative policies, first, 'German entry into NATO with safeguards upon German rearmament', second, 'a looser non-supranational European Defence Community with United Kingdom participation' - that is, 'Little NATO'. Although the Government was working for the first of these solutions, it would be prepared to consider sympathetically a workable plan for the second one. It was essential to know whether the first alternative would be acceptable to Adenauer. There was reason to believe, however, that he would not be enthusiastic and would look critically upon safeguards regarded as discriminatory. Therefore, Adenauer should not at this stage be irritated by seeking his agreement to specific safeguards.[1]

At the meeting with Hoyer Millar, Adenauer declared that there were two solutions to the military problem, the NATO solution and a revised EDC which included Britain. He commented on the idea of self-limitation which, we saw, had had been prepared within the *Amt Blank* in July. The problem for a rearming Germany, Adenauer said, was how to offer restriction on arms without being subjected to discrimination. He was thinking of two possibilities, either voluntary self-limitation, or adaptation to the guidelines issued by the NATO Commander. He was prepared to accept voluntary limitations, the content of which should be agreed upon. Formerly, such limitations had not been necessary because integration, which submitted all to the same treatment, had been in the place of self-limitation.[2]

Churchill appears to have reacted favourably to Adenauer's hint. He sent a message to Adenauer in which he suggested self-limitation as a way out of the critical situation. He proposed that 'by a voluntary act of self-abnegation she [the Federal Republic] could make it clear that in any new arrangement as a substitute for EDC she would not ask for a level of military strength beyond that proposed in the EDC plan'. He informed Eisenhower of his message and added that he believed that it had had 'a fairly good reception'. Eisenhower answered that he thought Churchills's message was 'perfect' and that he hoped that Adenauer would respond favourably.[3] In his reply to Churchill, Adenauer avoided any direct commitment but confirmed that 'a voluntary act of self-abnegation' could be considered.[4] Hallstein informed Spaak about the German idea of self-limitation.[5]

When Eden met Adenauer during an exploratory tour of European capitals the British emphasized that German self-limitations were crucial for the chances of reaching agreement at a conference. The basic British idea about safeguards was to organize them within the NATO framework, but other possibilities might be considered. The arms pool part of the EDC could hardly be used any longer. The idea of limitation of arms in 'strategically exposed areas' must be maintained, particularly in the field of atomic weapons. However, the list of forbidden weapons in the EDC Treaty might be revised and abbreviated. Adenauer agreed that the necessary limitations and controls should be located in the NATO machinery. For psychological reasons a declaration about German intentions could also be made.[6]

The Germans indicated willingness to accept self-limitations as part of a new arrangement to the Americans also. Adenauer informed Conant that he had in mind a personal declaration, possibly confirmed by a vote of confidence in the *Bundestag*. He feared, he said, that German public opinion would feel that limitations were imposed on him by a conference rather than freely declared by himself.[7] He was 'prepared to accept a liberalized version of EDC restrictions on armament production'.[8] Bruce registered that 'Adenauer would agree to certain self-imposed limitations, but not, he thinks, enough to satisfy the French'.[9] Dulles was clearly in favour of the self-limitation concept. He told Eden that sovereignty had to be given Germany promptly, and that he agreed with Adenauer that the time was past when the position could be held by putting the Contractuals into effect (as had been envisaged in the Anglo-US study group in the summer), and added: 'From this it would follow that any secret limitations or conditions on German rearmament which were imposed or gave the appearance of being imposed on Germany would be a dangerous error. A voluntary and public declaration of self-imposed limitations would of course be another matter'.[10]

The French as well received news about the German attitude to self-limitation.[11]

Internally in Germany, the idea of self-limitation was made more specific in a memorandum about the guarantees that could be given, in the event that the Federal Republic was offered membership of NATO. The suggested limitations were more or less those which Adenauer accepted later at the London Conference, with only marginal differences. The list was a liberalized version of the EDC list. The Federal Republic would abstain from production of its own of ABC weapons and missiles-warships-strategic bombers. It would also agree to control of the German arms industry 'if a common arms programme is established for some or all European partners in NATO and if such controls also exist for these partners'.[12] That is, in some kind of arms pool and provided that others - meaning France - were controlled also.

It is not clear if the details of self-limitation were agreed between Adenauer and Dulles. I have not found any trace of this in my material.

Agreement on Negotiations about 'Little NATO'

In the post-EDC situation, the French Army General Staff seemed to come down in favour of a two-track (both restrictive and integrative) model, which included the possibility of nuclear integration. The Staff argued that the European defence group could only be imagined within the NATO framework and with British participation. This was a continuation of the ideas in June about transformation and extension of the Brussels Treaty. The Staff stated that the control of Germany in the field of conventional weapons might be taken care of through prohibitions and other measures. It was however necessary that the European defence group possessed atomic weapons in order to avoid complete dependence on the United States. Regarding atomic armament

...it is inconceivable to grant it to Germany, and it is indispensable that France should become an atomic power, but France alone cannot carry the burden of such arms while remaining on equal footing with Germany as regards conventional armaments. Nor would Germany be able to accept such discrimination.

The solution would be

...the creation, within the framework of an Atlantic Arms Pool, of an integrated European atomic force (with the participation if possible of the UK). The nations of Europe should contribute raw materials, technicians and money to establish collectively such a common force in areas that are reasonably secure. [13]

Although the formulations are somewhat ambiguous, the passage cited seems to open the door to German participation, primarily as a technical and financial contributor, in some kind of European nuclear weapons pool with common control over the joint stock, and it apparently also implied freedom of action to have a separate French national nuclear force which, aided by the production facilities of the pool, would become economically possible. With respect to the case that UK participation could not be obtained, the Staff was presumably thinking of a Franco-German arrangement as the core of the pool. The proposed programme would contribute to a stronger French and European role within NATO. [14]

This proposal from a most powerful institution in French society, which seems to imply German integration in the military nuclear field, was something new compared to the EDC model with its emphasis on prohibitions of German nuclear activities above the research level. It was close to the ideas behind the French proposals for Euratom six months later, and it explains much of them.

The two-track policy was adopted by the French Government. 'Little NATO' plus an arms pool were seen as the essential components of a solution for replacement of the EDC.

An illuminating account of the thinking behind the French position is contained in a note to Mendès France from his Under Secretary, Roland de Moustier, just before the opening of the London Conference. De Moustier outlined the dilemma confronting France in terms reminiscent of the perspective of 'two-level' negotiation theory. [15] The partners in London, he wrote, might criticize the French proposals as either discriminatory toward Germany or as too European, while the parliamentarians who must be persuaded were mainly those who might judge the project as too little European, or as offering insufficient guarantees toward Germany. It could be expected in London that some partners - Dulles, Eden - would try to locate the controls on Germany within a NATO framework. If they prevailed, the idea of an arms pool with real powers would be at risk, and there would also be a risk that some might propose that controls should be extended to zones other than Germany in order not to discriminate against Germany. For two reasons, the French argument should be, de Moustier argued, that control could only be exercised within a European framework. A technical reason was one of efficiency. A control agency with real powers, not just over prohibitions but also over production of arms, could not exist within NATO, at least not at its present state of development. The second reason was political:

> The second is political in nature and relates to the French conception of its role as a Great Power. In effect if, in the European framework, France

could impose on itself certain sacrifices and accept certain limitations, out of its desire to promote European unity thanks to the Franco-German reconciliation on the basis of the equality of rights, in the Atlantic framework, where each state is sovereign, France cannot accept a lesser position in relation to Great Britain and the United States, with which countries it shares the direction of world affairs, as is demonstrated by its membership of the permanent Group of Four. In consequence, if the controls which must apply to Germany were issued by the Atlantic organisation, France, to prevent the Federal Republic (which, sooner or later would find them discriminatory) from being tempted to renounce them, and to bind it in lasting fashion, would then be obliged to submit to them equally. Our country would thus find itself in a position of inferiority in relation to its British and American allies. - That is to say, in the Atlantic framework there can only be equality of rights as regards restrictions. In consequence they must not contain discriminations against either France or Germany. In that case Germany can no longer be controlled on a lasting basis. - That is why, given the real dangers inherent in German rearmament, it should be carried out in a European framework. - That, it seems, is the essential argument justifying in London what distinguishes the French project from the pure and simple accession of Germany to NATO. [16]

The gist of the argument was that control of Germany within the NATO framework alone would eventually result in Franco-German equality. The implication from the nuclear perspective which is in focus here, is that in order to keep the nuclear weapons option open to France, and deny it to Germany, a control system located solely within NATO was unacceptable. A European construct was necessary to obtain the required degree of inequality.

Eden and Mendès France met in Paris 15-16 September after Eden had made his tour of the other EDC capitals to make probes about a possible solution based on extension of the Brussels Pact of 1948. At the meeting, the British delegation informed about a number of guarantees which the Germans seemed prepared to give. It was further reported that Eden had obtained acceptance from the Germans that certain types of weapons would not be produced in 'strategically exposed areas'; the list of such weapons would however be much more limited than in the EDC. Mendès France said that he had been thinking about using the Brussels Pact, and he mentioned - without getting any reaction - the French arms pool concept, 'for the most important and largest projects one could envisage common, for example Franco-German, manufacturing plants situated in non-exposed areas'. Eden replied that he had certainly thought about extension of the Brussels Pact as an instrument of arms control within NATO. He insisted that Germany must become a member of NATO simultaneously as it was admitted to the

Brussels Pact, not after. Mendès was reluctant, explaining how difficult it would be for public opinion in France to accept this. After all, the EDC had been promoted with the argument that the only alternative, a worse alternative, was German membership of NATO. It was finally agreed that Eden's condition would be the point of departure for the coming conference.

The abandonment of the French four-year old fierce opposition to German NATO membership in any form was the essential concession, making negotiations worthwhile. The French views were elaborated in a memorandum that was sent to the other governments. The NATO commitment was not, however, expressed explicitly and the French position in this way remained uncertain, and was a cause for anxiety, until the London Conference had begun.[17]

When Eden met Dulles - as the last and most prominent of the leaders to be consulted - on 17 September and gave an account of his tour of the European capitals Dulles gave the green light to Eden's plan. According to Eden's report, Dulles saw no better alternative, he even called Eden's initiative 'brilliant and statesmanlike'. He had two reservations. First, the organization must not be an obstacle to the idea of 'real integration'. Dulles hoped that some means could be devised which would enable the others to go ahead without the United Kingdom in certain fields. Second, the Brussels organization might be used as a forum for fixing ceilings for forces, thus leaving NATO free to obtain maximum contributions, but a French veto on ceilings should be avoided.[18]

Dulles sent a circular telegram to missions, asking them to transmit his preliminary reactions to the French memorandum to the French. He complained that the memorandum was unclear on essential points. The US view was that Germany must be admitted to full NATO membership promptly. Anything else was out of question in the light of political realities in Germany. The US did not oppose making use of the Brussels Treaty for working out certain of the safeguards required by France. They must, nevertheless, meet certain criteria: they should be non-discriminatory and capable of prompt adoption, and should not duplicate existing NATO machinery. Dulles preferred 'positive measures', such as strengthening of the functions of NATO commanders, rather than 'negative measures' such as inspection of forces and armament production. He added that it was by no means sure that the US assurances to the EDC would be reaffirmed, nor that US military aid would be channelled through the Brussels organization.[19]

Revision of US European Policy

After the collapse of the EDC Eisenhower asked for thinking as regards the development of a substitute for the EDC - 'I take it that all of us agree we cannot sit down in black despair and admit defeat'. It seemed to Eisenhower that there were 'two possible approaches – or maybe even three':

Through the revision of the EDC idea by the nations concerned.

Through a meeting of the entire NATO group, with a view to including Germany as an equal partner therein.

Through unilateral agreements with Germany - to which agreements we would, of course, have to get the concurrences of a sizeable number of Western and Atlantic nations.

He asked that the planners should not send him 'a long dissertation'; he just wanted to know 'the direction of attack' which appeared to them to be the most hopeful.[20]

The State Department and the National Security Council started the process of considering what had gone wrong and evaluating the policy options. A series of memoranda were written within the Policy Planning Staff (PPS) in September. The themes in these reappeared in the NSC material and were developed further.

In three early memoranda PPS Staff member Leon W. Fuller suggested that a number of errors had been made in US policy, for example gearing European policy too much to a dubious estimate of Soviet military intentions in Western Europe, overstressing the supranational, federal concept while underestimating nationalist resistance ('We must admit that we went far in seeking to persuade and even coerce Europeans into making a surrender of sovereignty which we would not have made ourselves'), having intervened excessively, and having accepted too readily the British position regarding the relation to the continent. The basic question was now whether the US objectives should be changed in a radical way or not. Fuller enumerated alternatives, which he considered more or less unpalatable, for example isolationism, peripheral strategy, agreement with the Soviets on Germany, or bilateral US-German agreement. The purpose of the EDC had been to reconcile France and Germany, to provide for German rearmament with acceptable safeguards and restored sovereignty, and to promote the political integration in the heart area of continental Europe. A reconsideration of priorities might be desirable now. How urgent was for example the need for German armed forces if there was a revised estimate of Soviet intentions, and considering the existence of the New Look strategy and the development of nuclear capabilities on both sides? Had military integration been too much stressed compared to political and economic integration? An immediate necessary task was to satisfy the German demand for sovereignty. With regard to France, Fuller concluded that no viable European policy could dispense with France. The US 'must frame its future European policy with a view to according France a European role comporting with her capacity and willingness to cooperate fully as an ally, yet without permitting the achievement of our vital objectives to be hampered by French veto or obstruction'. The British role should be reconsidered. It seemed desirable that 'the UK should play a more intimate role in further projects of European unification, to a degree that will quiet French fears of political domination of a union by Germany. The US, however, should avoid pressure upon the UK to effect this while making clear its preference in the matter. This may mean a European evolution less along supra-national lines...'[21]

Later, further memoranda from the Policy Planning Staff developed these themes and added new aspects.[22] They discussed primarily (1) the viability of alternatives, (2) arms control - the level of 'reasonable' or 'acceptable' safeguards, and (3) the tactics to be used to ensure French acceptance of German rearmament and NATO membership:

The alternatives without France continued to be regarded as unsatisfactory. The alternatives 'should be attempted only as a last resort, and even then mainly as a device for putting political pressure on the French'.

With respect to arms control, the 'NATO with safeguards' concept could be implemented through a list of measures and additional NATO arrangements: renunciation of ABC-weapons and the missile-warship-aircraft category as itemized in the EDC Treaty (with possible revision), inclusion of all German forces under NATO command, reinforcement of the integrated command, and so on. It was necessary to prune the control and inspection features of the Mendès France plan down to something the Germans could accept. The French proposal for an Arms Pool, steered by the Brussels group, that would direct the manufacture of arms and guard against the manufacture of prohibited weapons in Germany as a strategically exposed area should be studied by the US, 'it might have possibilities of developing supranational institutions within the Brussels group within limits acceptable to the British'; the British war industries would 'obviously have to be excluded from the common pool'. It was however questionable whether the desirable goal of prohibition of ABC weapons and the missile-warship-aircraft category 'had better be undertaken by the Brussels group, or by NATO with respect to the whole continental area under NATO command'. The system proposed by the French suggested a bureaucratic and unworkable arrangement.

Regarding tactical considerations, it was stressed that the impression of excessive US intervention must be avoided. The US should 'resist the temptation to set forth a US plan'. The Europeans should have the initiative, and the US should only set limits to the concessions that could be safely made in areas vital to American paramount interests. The US position should be mediating, seeking to harmonize the divergent proposals. Certain commitments might be considered in order to promote better understanding, for example 'exchange of nuclear information and weapons'.

In the National Security Council memorandum on the subject, NSC 5433, the approach in the memoranda of the Policy Planning Staff was developed further. According to NSC 5433 the US was faced with a choice between continuing the present objectives, or determining what new objectives should be pursued. No radical change should be made at the moment, but radical alternatives should be explored. It was recommended that the US for the immediate future should make further vigorous efforts to achieve the present objectives in its European policy: containment of the USSR, defence of Western Europe, promotion of strength in Western Europe through integration, and attachment of the Federal Republic to the West through all feasible means. A programme of action was outlined. The essential points of the programme were: German sovereignty, German NATO membership, German rearmament with acceptable safeguards, fostering of political and economic aspects of integration, strengthening of NATO, and preparedness to make certain US commitments as a *quid pro quo* for European commitments. A condition for obtaining the policy objectives was French cooperation. France should be induced to cooperate by various means. If French reactions defeated one or more of the US objectives, policy should be governed by the result of the evaluation of the radical options.

In the matter of German NATO membership there was no objection to the concept of 'Little NATO', organized as a revised Brussels Pact. German membership of NATO was envisaged 'without precluding German participation also in the Brussels Pact or other European defense arrangements'.

The point about 'acceptable safeguards' on German rearmament focused on integration in NATO, and the need for modifying NATO for this purpose, but the door to a European Arms Pool was also kept open. The EDC prohibitions for Germany on certain kinds types of weapons were referred to, and it was proposed that certain restrictions should be maintained. Other measures were 'voluntary ' acceptance by Germany of limits on its initial military build-up, inclusion of *all* German forces except internal security forces in NATO, further integration of the NATO command structure and logistics system, and strengthening the authority of NATO's Commander in Europe.[23]

What kinds of instruments should be used to influence France? US aid could for example be slowed down, and France could be made aware of alternative strategic groupings 'far less attractive' to France. As a tactical matter, France should be given the opportunity later to cooperate to induce ultimate French acceptance of the programme.[24]

The point about possible transfer of nuclear weapons was opposed by the Joint Chiefs of Staff. They wrote that until 'reliability and support of the European Allies had been better demonstrated, it would be injudicious to enter into a commitment with such far-reaching implications'. Certainly, they argued, it should not be used as an inducement for acceptance of a US short-term programme.[25]

The Joint Chiefs discussed alternatives for the defence of Europe in various scenarios for French action. A German defence contribution was absolutely essential, and it should be sought preferably with the concurrence of the French and the British, but if this could not be obtained, the US should go as far as making a bilateral agreement with the Germans. The most negative scenario was a French withdrawal from NATO, cancellation of all bilateral military facilities and active obstruction of German rearmament: 'Under such circumstances, the rearming of West Germany should proceed without restrictions on the size and composition of forces and on her munitions production, such as contemplated in the Contractual-EDC arrangements'.[26]

At the meeting of the National Security Council when the NSC 5433 was discussed Dulles objected to this kind of thinking. France and Britain, at any rate, had now reached the point of no longer wishing to seem tied to the US coat-tails. America should not feel too bad about this; after all one of the great US objectives had been to get the Western European states to stand on their own feet. The important thing at the forthcoming meetings in Europe was to save NATO and German alignment with the West:

> The heart of the matter was whether or not we should be able to preserve NATO. The Soviets successfully used Mendes-France to kill, or at least to maim EDC. Will they now try to use him to destroy NATO? If they do that successfully the whole situation falls apart. There is no use talking about the U.S. proceeding unilaterally to rearm Germany. In such a situation Germany might well choose not to rearm. There would certainly be heavy pressure in these circumstances for Germany to accommodate to the Soviet Union. The latter could dangle the possibility of unification of Germany, rectification of the Polish frontier, and economic advantages. In short, there is no good alternative if the French torpedo the NATO solution, and we must not assume that we can go ahead independently to rearm Germany if the French won't agree.

It was discussed whether various kinds of economic support to France should be cut off at once unless France agreed to cooperate. Dulles explained to the more militant Secretary of Defense that he and Adenauer had talked about the possibility of cutting off everything, but the opinion of the latter had been 'no, not everything, but to slow down to the point where Mendes-France realizes that the flow is slowing down and whose hand controls the spigot'.[27]

The policy approved by the President differed somewhat from that proposed in NSC 5433. The specific *quid pro quo* points, for example about exchange of nuclear information and transfer of nuclear weapons, were, in accordance with the military view-points, replaced by a loose formulation that if a programme of action acceptable to the US was developed, the US would be prepared to give assurances generally similar to those given in support of EDC. It was also decided that limited forms of sanction should be introduced. The military aid to France should be slowed down until the situation had further clarified, and no new financial commitments should be made. Some more far-reaching measures that were contemplated in NSC 5433 were dropped.[28]

The conclusion of this top level review of US European policy was, then, that a radical 'agonizing reappraisal' of policy should not, or could not, be put into effect for the time being. French participation in an arrangement could not easily be sacrificed. It was seen as unwise to execute the threat as long as there were other advantageous options. The possibility of compromising should be explored first. Only moderate sanctions should be imposed as a reminder of more serious options. Binding nuclear commitments in order to facilitate compromise should not be made.

The basic question remained: What concessions could be made in order to induce the French Parliament to ratify a solution that was not so discriminatory that Germany would obstruct it?

Preludes to the London Conference

The main features of the revised Brussels Treaty were worked out at the Nine-Power (the Six, plus the US, Britain and Canada) Conference of Foreign Ministers in London under the chairmanship of Eden. The final adjustments were agreed at the ensuing conference in Paris three weeks later. Certain questions, above all those related to the end of occupation and German sovereignty, were regulated at intertwined Four-Power (US, Britain, France and the Federal Republic) meetings. There were also meetings with more restricted participation and meetings in committees for particular questions. The term 'the Paris Accords' covers a complex of treaty texts, agreements, declarations, and so on, regulating the termination of the occupation regime and restoration of German sovereignty, the accession of the Federal Republic to NATO and the approval of the revised Brussels Treaty, which was baptized the Western European Union (WEU), with Germany and Italy as new members.[29]

Three kinds of French conditions préalables for agreement were specified in the French memorandum: (1) satisfactory control of German rearmament, (2) guarantees for Anglo-American military presence on the continent, and (3) settlement of the Saar question. The proposals for control of German rearmament followed the 'two-track' pattern. They were based partly on prohibitions and restrictions, partly on integration of the arms industry. The armaments levels considered by NATO as minima would be maxima for the members of the Brussels organization. Manufacture of the most important weapons, as defined in the EDC Treaty - ABC weapons and the missile-warship-aircraft category - would be forbidden in strategically exposed areas and there would be a control system verifying this. There would be a common procurement system, that is, what was soon called the 'Arms Pool'. It was to be applied to the continental countries (thereby exempting Britain). The Council of the Brussels organization would procure and distribute arms on the continent, except those produced for export and for national forces not committed to NATO [that is, giving France, but not Germany, substantial freedom of action]. The Council would also have the competence to receive and distribute arms received from abroad [that is, mainly the US]. A system of zones would extend from East to West; joint new arms factories might be established in unexposed zones. The control system would verify that arms were not produced in areas in which they were prohibited, and that the ceilings were not exceeded in other areas. It would apply not only to stocks of armaments but to production as well. The Federal Republic would pledge itself not to raise any other forces than those placed at the disposal of the NATO Commander in Europe.[30]

Eden planned to make a striking move which - he explained to the British Cabinet - might become 'the key to the success of the Conference'. That was to make a commitment to maintain the existing British forces on the Continent and not to withdraw them against the wishes of the majority of the enlarged Brussels Treaty powers. Such a commitment was 'unprecedented', but it was required in order to reconcile (1) the German desire for sovereignty and NATO membership, (2) French reluctance to admit either, until elaborate safeguards had been agreed, 'notably a complicated and probably unworkable system for the control of armament manufacture on the Continent', (3) American reluctance or inability to repeat the undertakings that had been given in connexion with the EDC about maintaining American military strength in Europe. The Cabinet gave its approval. In the discussion, it was pointed out that if the French still refused to adopt a reasonable attitude, it would subsequently be easier to adopt the solution of the 'empty chair'. Churchill should cable to Eisenhower and ask for an equivalent American undertaking, but it was agreed that there was no advantage in making a British offer conditional on the American decision since if the US withdrew from Europe the whole NATO defence system would in any case collapse.[31]

Dulles met Mendès France the day before the opening of the London Conference. The themes were general, standpoints on arms control were not discussed. Mendès assured Dulles that, since his talks with Eden, he was no longer opposed to German membership of NATO. An expanded Brusssels Treaty would in his view make it possible to meet the two objections which explained the French Assembly's rejection of the EDC - its supranational character and the absence of the British. Dulles stressed the virtues of supranationalism and European integration. Even if there was indeed no good alternative to the EDC, a solution had to be found. It must meet three criteria. It should provide for German sovereignty, German rearmament, and make clear that the idea of unity was not dead. The supranational aspect of EDC was 'far, far, more important' than twelve German divisons. If the movement toward unity stopped, 'there was a very real chance that the American people would be disillusioned and would withdraw to their own continent feeling another world war would ultimately start in Europe and that we had no wish to be involved in it´.[32]

At a meeting of high-ranking US officials the French proposal for an integrated arms procurement system and its relationship to the ´NATO with safeguards´ concept was discussed. Dulles pointed out that one French purpose with an Arms Pool seemed to be to delimit zones in which certain types of production would be prevented or limited, for example atomic weapons. The other purpose was to obtain economic benefits by rationalizing arms production, and to make it impossible for any one country to provide a balanced arms programme independently of its neighbour. Probably France had also ulterior motives with a view to steering arms orders for the benefit of French industry. The US analysis of French motives, Dulles said, indicated that the French were concerned about two main points, to involve the UK on the continent and to prevent an independent German military potential. Some form of Arms Pool could help meet the second preoccupation, although it was clear that the British attitude was such that it would do little to meet the first. He felt that it was important to develop counter-proposals, possibly by agreement with the Benelux countries, so that the French could not say that there was only destructive criticism of their proposal. General Gruenther was also in favour of not opposing France directly on the issue. He reported that he had pointed out to Mendès France that an Arms Pool was not the most satisfactory method of meeting the French desire to control German military strength. NATO had ´a going concern´ for this, for example the logistics system and the command structure, and these measures could be deepened further. Mendès had replied that such a programme would be difficult to sell politically in France, and that he wanted SHAPE to accept responsibility for inspection of German factories. However, Gruenther explained to the American officials, this would be impracticable since SHAPE had no personnel for it, and it would be politically impossible for them to get into this field. The French Arms Pool plan in his view provided the germ of a programme which would be acceptable and could be developed. The meeting agreed that the principles of an effective scheme should be developed and used in discussions with other delegations in London.[33]

The American and British positions at the conference were coordinated at a dinner with Dulles and Eden, and officials. Eden informed Dulles that Britain was going to make the crucial offer of assigning specific forces to the continent and subject them to the majority vote of the Brussels countries. He had spoken about it only to the US, he said, and it was important that it was held close for use when it might do the most good.

The French Arms Pool project was another subject at the discussion. All believed that the plan that had been presented by Mendès France could hardly be accepted by Adenauer or by the other countries. Eden said that a ´genuine´ system of common procurement might have advantages both political and economic. It was agreed that it would be unwise merely to take a negative attitude to Mendès France's proposals. That would enable him to return to France and say that his efforts to obtain satisfactory safeguards by this means had been arbitrarily rejected by the others. To prevent this, it was desirable that a project for 'a bona fide Arms Pool' be developed. Dulles agreed to broach the subject with the Benelux countries and see whether they were interested in putting forward a proposal that would be more acceptable both to the Germans and themselves.[34]

The London Conference (28 September-3 October 1954)

One of the French *conditions préalables* was dealt with early in the negotiations, on 29 September. Dulles made a conditional and imprecise offer. He said that the pledge to the EDC about US commitment of troops to Europe could not be repeated now, but if the hopes of unity that were tied into the EDC could reasonably be transferred to new arrangements, he would be disposed to recommend to the President that the President should renew a comparable pledge. Eden made the move which he had planned as the key to the success of the conference. The United Kingdom undertook not to withdraw the existing level of British forces on the continent assigned to NATO, including Germany, against the wishes of the majority of the Brussels treaty powers, except in certain defined exceptional circumstances.[35] The British offer was greeted with emotion by Mendès France - 'After the meeting Mendès-France went up to Eden, with tears in his eyes, and thanked him for having bound the UK so closely with the fate of the states of Europe, particularly with that of France'.[36] Mendès had already accepted before the conference that the third French condition, agreement on the Saar, would be referred to treatment through bilateral Franco-German negotiations after the conference.[37]

There remained for discussion the problem of arms control of Germany. It was the critical issue and the pivot of the negotiations in London. All agreed that the functions of NATO for arms control should be strengthened in various ways, the most important of which was that *all* German forces would be assigned to the NATO command. NATO was not enough for the French, however. The discussions touched on three partly interconnected subjects: (1) the Arms Pool, (2) the influence of the Brussels organization over US military aid, and (3) prohibitions, restrictions and control within the Brussels organization.

The French tried to make their final approval of the negotiation package conditional on acceptance of the project for an Arms Pool.

The State Department was considering the implications of the proposal. Livingston Merchant wrote to Dulles that he was convinced that the Arms Pool would become the crux of the conference. Mendès must obtain something, but the practical difficulties were enormous. To negotiate a pool '*ab initio* would require more time than is allowed us if we are to maintain Adenauer's position in Germany'. There was also the fact that if the US supported an Arms Pool it would be over the deep-seated objections of the Benelux countries and against the deep suspicions of Germany and Italy. The British position was 'hostile but silent'. If the French plan was approved, the US would in fact be siding with Mendès France against his five EDC partners on a scheme in which the US were not a member. Merchant recommended a sympathetic attitude to the general idea of common procurement of arms. A plan should be prepared that would be lifted direct out of the EDC Treaty with only the necessary formal changes to conform to the new context and to provide for majority vote in the Brussels Council. He enclosed a memorandum with the principles of such a plan, containing many of the features of the EDC arms procurement system, for example the 85-115 per cent rule. Integration with NATO on various points was outlined. In such a type of plan, Merchant wrote, it seemed possible that the US could also accept distribution of the US military supplies by the Brussels organization, provided that the decisions of the Brussels Council were taken with the advice and consent of NATO's Supreme Commander.[38]

The Benelux states were completely negative to the French project, but did not submit principles for an alternative, as had been envisaged at the Anglo-American meeting. Adenauer did not openly dismiss the idea but insisted as always upon non-discrimination. Only the Italian Foreign Minister gave the pool qualified support. Dulles, in accordance with agreed tactics, did not reject the French project outright, but showed scepticism. When meeting Mendès France separately, he told him that suspicions regarding Mendès' purposes in this area were prevalent (adding diplomatically that he did not share them personally); there were 'doubts as to whether he might not have as his intention the prevention of any armament production in Germany and the concentration in France of the armaments industry of the entire community'.[39]

The French pursued the point that American military aid to Europe should be distributed by the Brussels organization. The argument was that the US had approved this for the EDC[40] and should do so under the new arrangement also. The background to this demand was apprehension that the US might send arms to Germany without French influence on the process, and give preferential treatment to Germany in the field of arms production. In particular, it was feared that the Americans might equip the Federal Republic with nuclear weapons. The issue was related to the Arms Pool project, as such a pool according to the French concept would distribute arms transferred from third countries. At the conference, Dulles emphatically declined any Brussels decision rights in the matter. The US wanted the arms distributed according to the recommendations of the NATO Commander in Europe, and off-shore orders were to a certain extent a reflection of American policy, he said.[41]

The problem of prohibitions, restrictions and controls was the object of lengthy discussions. It was however agreed early at the conference that an Armaments Agency would be organized and charged with control, and - if and when an Arms Pool were organized - supervising arms production under the authority of the Brussels Council.

The negotiations departed from a Belgian memorandum proposing prohibitions on ABC weapons and perhaps other weapons within strategically exposed areas as delineated in the EDC. The memorandum pointed out that civil needs should be considered, thereby, among other things, indicating the difficulty of drawing the line between the military and the civil side in the nuclear field. Spaak, in answering a question by Dulles, said that the delicate question about civil needs had not been fully investigated in the EDC, and that the experts should make precise delimitations.[42]

The arms control question was sent to a study group under the chairmanship of Viscount Hood. No agreement could be reached. A one-page report reflecting disunity was issued. Two models were sketched. The first was a recommendation that the manufacture of ABC weapons and, if possible, weapons in the missile-warship-aircraft category, should be prohibited in strategically exposed areas. The prohibition would apply only to the continent. However, unity on the delimitation of the term ´strategically exposed area´ could not be reached, the report stated. The German delegation did not accept a definition which applied to German territory only. An entirely different manner of approaching the problem had been proposed:

> In the course of the discussion, which had brought out the difficulties to be surmounted before a definition acceptable to all parties could be reached, there had been a proposal to tackle the problem in an entirely different way. It was that the Six continental powers of the Brussels treaty should conclude an agreement forbidding the production of arms in categories A B and C. The French delegation did not consider itself to be in a position to pursue this proposal.[43]

The second model would indeed mean an even more far-reaching commitment than in the EDC Treaty. While in the EDC Treaty the question was to be decided by the supranational mechanism, both Germany and France would under the new proposal bind themselves to renounce from all production of nuclear weapons. As no territorial limitation was mentioned, it applied in principle not only to the European continent, but to all French territories. The proposal was a bid to the French to accept Franco-German equality and the principle of non-proliferation. It was immediately declined by the French delegation.[44]

The Hood Report was discussed on the afternoon of 1 October and in the morning of the following day in a mood of irritation. Mendès France dismissed it out of hand as a very disappointing paper. The other countries had not taken into consideration the French points of view either about control or production, he said.

Dulles, who was generally keeping a low profile at the conference, made a lengthy statement at this moment. He touched on the Arms Pool concept, declaring that it was useful and necessary to create an Armaments Agency that would both organize production and be in charge of controls. This would require several months of work, however. The problem was now, he said, to organize a system for the transition period until the Agency functioned. He proposed that Germany would make a unilateral *temporary* [my emphasis] renunciation. Germany would engage itself during an interim period of for example two years not to *manufacture, import* or *export* [my emphasis] ABC weapons and the missile-warship-aircraft category approximately as defined in the EDC Treaty. During this period Germany would produce only other arms, defined by NATO and not covered by US deliveries. Meanwhile, the Agency would be organized and decided by a two-thirds majority. Decision-making by unanimity was unimaginable because in such case a country might prolong the interim system or cause it to collapse. After the interim period Germany would enter the permanent system. The Agency would be in charge of controlling and limiting, on a non-discriminatory basis, the production *on the continent* [my emphasis] of armaments by the member states. If the system were not in use within two years there would no longer be any control. All countries ought to be prepared to accept that some risks were involved.[45]

This meant supranational decision-making, which included decisions about nuclear weapons, in the permanent system, but it was not as radical as proposing Franco-German equality; the possibility of French manufacture on its territory outside the continent was not excluded in Dulles´ proposal. Germany would in the interim period - this seems to have been the bait for France - be prohibited not only to manufacture, but also to import or export strategic weapons, and would consequently not be allowed to receive nuclear weapons from the US. As a consequence of the reference to the EDC definitions, Germany would also seem to be barred from building up a capacity that could produce more than 500 grams of fissionable material during this time. If France did not accept, Germany would not be controlled by the Brussels states at all, only by NATO.

Dulles´ proposal was not supported in the discussion. Spaak believed that it postponed until later the solution of a very important problem that should be solved at the conference.

Mendès France declared that it was impossible for him to accept an unconditional prohibition to produce ABC weapons. He hinted at the French, or the Franco-German, nuclear option as a future opportunity for the others; the discussion on the matter was, he said, about ´activities and work which might in future even be of interest to the Community and which there is no reason to halt or prohibit´.[46]

On the last day of the conference, 2 October, the Belgian delegation submitted a new memorandum. In this paper, the continent was considered a strategically exposed area in which manufacture of ABC weapons should be prohibited. There were concessions to France such as a proposal that existing enterprises fabricating prohibited weapons in the strategically exposed area should not disappear [thereby permitting France for example to continue with the plutonium-producing reactors in Marcoule without supranational interference]. Extensions of plants would however require mixed WEU and NATO authorization, or WEU authorization only. For the arms for forces allocated to NATO, NATO decision-making would apply. And 'for the armed forces remaining at national disposition, the total quantity of weapons retained must be in accordance with their size and mission. This quantity must be notified to the Agency and *approved* [my emphasis] by it'.[48]

In the discussion, Spaak underlined the obvious fact that part of the French territory was not considered a strategically exposed area; on French territories outside the European continental territory France kept its freedom of action completely. He admonished the conference that it was necessary to have the courage to admit that there was no military definition of a strategically exposed area, it was a purely political one. Were there countries who wished authorization to manufacture ABC weapons? If so, they should say so and inform the experts accordingly. The politicians should accept their responsibility and not ask the experts to decide the difficult issues. Prohibition of ABC-weapons in the European zone was in any case the clearest concept. Spaak finished by making the declaration that Belgium would renounce from manufacturing ABC weapons, 'but on condition that everybody renounces them' - obviously not an impressive argument as the Benelux had no intention of making them anyway.[49]

Mendès France greeted the new Belgian proposal in conciliatory terms, but he repeated that he could not accept that the European continent should be considered a strategically exposed area. Spaak insisted on the concept as the only clear-cut one. An intense discussion took place about the definitions of the concepts 'strategically exposed area' and 'the continent'. If Germany was a strategically exposed area, what parts of, or the entire territory of, France and Benelux should also be considered as such? Other countries than France argued that if there were to be prohibitions and controls for them, France should also be subject to limitations.

It may be mentioned that Dulles, in one of his rare interventions, when the meaning of the word 'continent' was discussed, tended toward a broad interpretation. He said that 'It would perhaps be good to apply this arrangement [the proposals in the Belgian memorandum] to certain countries not covered by the Brussels treaty'. Dulles seemed in this way to indicate his propensity to use the occasion to promote the non-proliferation objective beyond the Six-state area in Europe.[50]

The conference seemed to end in deadlock on the issue of restrictions, prohibitions and control of strategic weapons. Adenauer at this point estimated that the time was ripe for making the ´voluntary´ renunciation, which he had for so long hinted might be possible. He made his historic *Kernwaffenverzicht*. He declared that the Federal Republic renounced voluntarily from manufacturing ABC weapons. When asked by Mendès France to extend this engagement to the missile-warship-aircraft category also, he said that he was ready to make a similar declaration about them, although he asked for modifications for economic reasons to produce somewhat larger warships and other aircraft than strategic bombers. In its final form the renunciation included that the Federal Republic would not *manufacture* [my emphasis] ABC weapons and the missile-warship-aircraft category (with some modifications compared to the EDC Treaty asked for by Adenauer) weapons *on its territory* [my emphasis]. The treaty texts defined ´atomic weapon´ essentially in the same way as the EDC Treaty although with a very important difference: the 500 gramme limit for production of nuclear fuel had disappeared.[51]

The *Kernwaffenverzicht* did not contain limitations that might have been expected. It was not limited in time, and there were no conditions tied to it. It contained carefully designed qualifications. First, even if it excluded a nuclear weapons option that was national from the first to the last stage of production, it did not exclude acquisition through cooperation with others, and manufacture outside the territory. This opened the door to two main possibilities. One was import of nuclear weapons from the US or acquisition of some degree of authority over US weapons deployed in Germany - that is, the transfer option. The other was nuclear cooperation with France of the kind which was already under consideration by the French Chiefs of Staff and at the *Quai d´Orsay*, and also cooperation in a related area, that of aircraft production. In this way, the cooperation might develop into a European option. Second, the declaration did not exclude production of fissionable material, labelled as civil, on German territory as long as it did not reach the final stage, that is, the assembly of reprocessed plutonium or highly enriched uranium into bombs. It was possible to argue that plutonium or enriched uranium which Germany might manufacture were intended for civil use. If this took place, the step to production of nuclear weapons would be extremely short. Third, the declaration did not exclude construction of propulsion reactors for civil vessels that were also useable in for example nuclear submarines. Fourth, the engagement was not directed to the Soviet Union or to the international community, but to Germany´s allies, who could in principle admit a change.

In his memoirs, Adenauer tried to reduce the scope of the declaration further. According to his account, Dulles had come over to him and said in a loud voice so that all could hear that he interpreted this to mean that the declaration, like all declarations and obligations under international law, was valid only *rebus sic stantibus*.[52] Adenauer answered, also in a loud voice: 'You have interpreted my declaration correctly'.[53]

There is no indication of any such intervention by Dulles in the record[54] of the conference. The question has been discussed in German historical research. Henning Köhler criticized the inadequate criticism of sources in the research about Adenauer on this point.[55] A very solid treatment of the *Kernwaffenverzicht* was published by Hanns Jürgen Küsters. Küsters gives an account of the background to the formulation in Adenauer's memoirs. The retired Chancellor was preparing them at a time when he was vehemently opposing German adhesion to the Non-Proliferation Treaty. He had often talked to his collaborators about the *rebus sic stantibus* limitation and wanted documentary support for his recollection. Archivists tried without success to find some corroborating document, but only Adenauer's own manuscript note, 'rebus sic stantibus', on the back of the press communiqué from the London Conference could be found. Adenauer's closest collaborators Blankenhorn and Hallstein were interrogated about their memories of the event. Blankenhorn could not remember anything 'from his own knowledge', but Hallstein 'from his certain recollection' confirmed the main lines of Adenauer's version. Adenauer saw this as sufficient to justify the inclusion of the passage in the memoirs. Küsters' conclusion is that it may be presumed that Dulles had in fact, not literally but in accordance with it, talked about the 'rebus sic stantibus' clause.[56]

It should be added that the main perspective of Küsters' article is the connection between the *Kernwaffenverzicht* and the question of German sovereignty that was treated simultaneously at the Four-Power Conference. That conference was dealing with legal matters about the formulation of German sovereignty and remaining Allied rights related mainly to all-German questions and Berlin. No common ground could be found between German demands for 'absolute' sovereignty and French insistence on 'relative' sovereignty, and the definition of these concepts and their application to specific disputed issues. Küsters' interpretation is that the *Kernwaffenverzicht* was the key to successful clearance of the total negotiation hurdle. Only this move made it possible to open the road to a compromise on the sovereignty issue: 'All parties concerned were clear that a successful outcome to the Conference could be attained only if the Federal Republic recognised the nuclear superiority of the three Western Powers and if the latter took the trouble to ensure that this discrimination was not too crassly apparent'.[57] It may be added, however, that the US and British negotiators no doubt hoped that the nuclear superiority' would apply only to the US and Britain, not to France.

It should be remarked that Adenauer himself two years later regretfully expressed his conviction that if the *Kernwaffenverzicht* had not been made, sovereignty would not have been obtained.[58] Franz-Josef Strauss, the later Minister for Atomic Energy and Minister of Defence, on the other side opined in his memoirs that 'if Adenauer had been firm, it would not have been possible to exact this renunciation from us '.[59]

After Adenauer's declaration, the representatives of Belgium, the Netherlands and Italy said they too were prepared to renounce from manufacture of ABC weapons. Mendès France said he was sorry that he could not make a similar declaration. What he was striving for was a solution that could be ratified in France.[60]

Adenauer's declaration made unnecessary the acrobatic exercises in constructing formulas that were both watertight in controlling Germany and apparently non-discriminatory which had characterized both the EDC and the discussions in London. There was no longer a need for the term 'strategically exposed areas'. In his memoirs Adenauer described the declaration as the only really 'lonely decision' during his period as Chancellor; for time reasons it had been impossible for him to consult the Government and the Party.[61] This is obviously not true. We saw above[62] that something of the kind had long been in preparation in Adenauer's close circle, even it did not reach the Cabinet. German industrial interests do not seem to have been involved, however. Some interests, for example the chemical industry, later complained about the economic consequences of the control system and criticized the fact that they had not been consulted.[63]

After Adenauer had made his declaration Mendès France raised the issue of the control system. It was insufficient, he argued, only to control that there were no stocks of prohibited weapons. It was necessary also to include the source, that is, production and import. Historical experience showed that if stocks only were controlled, the controls could easily be bypassed in various ways. For example, during the Vichy period the French Authorities had succeeded in hiding important stocks of arms from Nazi control. Vichy had however hardly been able to manufacture any weapons at all. It was very difficult to hide from serious control import and manufacturing equipment of the kind that was utilized exclusively or especially for manufacturing arms. If the other countries did not agree to an Arms Pool now, the control system must at least be effective, he said. A discussion followed about this problem, and about whether the arms industry in for example the Benelux countries, which, like Germany, had declared that they would renounce from making ABC weapons, should be subjected to control of this engagement. Beyen argued that there was no need for control of the Benelux countries. Adenauer and Spaak criticized the idea of control of production. Adenauer asked whether equipment especially utilized for production of arms really existed? He also declared that if the engagement of the Benelux countries was not to be controlled, he would prefer that they did not make any engagement at all, considering the impression on the German public if Germany were to be the only country to be controlled.[64]

An important step forward to ensure the success of the conference was taken when the French modified their standpoints in two respects. The first was that the control problem was referred to the expert study group for a proposal to the coming conference in Paris. The study group would define which weapons would be controlled, and propose a control system focusing on stocks. Thus, the French demand for control of production, which was tied to the Arms Pool question, was not pursued for the time being. Second, the whole question of the Arms Pool was turned over for negotiation later. This cornerstone of the French programme for arms control and economic checks on Germany was in this way not made a condition for agreement. A decoupling of the arms control question and the Arms Pool had become possible after the *Kernwaffenverzicht*.[65]

Adenauer raised the question whether his renunciation of strategic weapons would be permanent. Would it not be good to envisage a revision of the German engagement after two or three years? It was necessary to have the possibility to ask, for example, for new upper limits for sizes of ships. He described this as a real economic problem and was supported by Eden and others. Mendès France argued that if a change was decided later, the decision should be taken unanimously. The French demand was that ABC weapons and the missile-warship-aircraft category should be considered 'a homogenous whole'. This raised the temperature of the negotiations again. Eden refused flatly. A united Europe must be built on decisions by the majority, he said; he would never accept this kind of veto in the future. Italy's Martino asked if a two-thirds majority would be enough for France. Adenauer was perturbed. A compromise was reached. Adenauer accepted that the renunciation concerning ABC weapons would not be subject to revision without unanimous approval. Changes for the (modified) missile-warship-aircraft category could, on the other hand, be made by a two-thirds majority in the WEU after a request by the NATO Authorities.[66]

The heart of the compromise was that the possibility - in itself remote - that Germany might be given the right by the WEU majority and NATO [and thereby the US] to manufacture nuclear weapons without French approval was discarded. France had obtained not only a partial German nuclear renunciation - this goal was shared by all - but also a veto on change. The fact that Adenauer accepted the French veto supports the view that his later claim about a *rebus sic stantibus* provision is unfounded.

The discussions about ABC weapons in London ended on the last day of the conference with a dispute about whether France should also accept some restrictions of its freedom of action in the nuclear field. The Study Group delivered a second report in which it was proposed that ABC weapons would be included in the categories of weapons that would be regulated supranationally to some extent. This regulation consisted in rights for NATO as regards NATO arms, and for the Brussels Organization as regards non-NATO arms, to evaluate whether the production of ABC weapons was in excess of needs. Spaak argued that from the moment that certain countries had engaged themselves not to produce ABC weapons those who had not done so ought to accept some regulation. An intensive exchange between Mendès France and Spaak took place. Mendès indignantly declared that this was different from what had been agreed earlier, and that limitations in the nuclear area were non-ratifiable in France, particularly as France had not got the Arms Pool. Not even in the EDC had the French freedom of action been limited in his way. He insisted that the problem of control criteria should be the subject of further study. After recess in the conference, a formula was agreed which provided some appearance of equality without changing fundamentals. It was stipulated that 'when the development of atomic, biological and chemical weapons in the territory on the mainland of Europe' in countries 'who have not given up the right to produce them has passed the experimental stage and effective production of them has started there, the level of stocks' that the states concerned 'will be allowed to hold on the mainland of Europe shall be decided by a majority vote of the Council'.[67] In this way, the French freedom of action was restricted only marginally, and, as was to become clear later, only in theory. France did not accept implementation of the provision after having become a nuclear power in the sixties.

After returning home, Mendès France reported to the Parliamentary Commission of Foreign Affairs about the conference. On the subject of the nuclear freedom of action of France the discussions, he said, had been 'extremely painful and difficult'. An incident had occurred, 'the origin of which I have not properly understood' - apparently intimating that the origin was American. The incident had in fact been intended to prohibit France from producing atomic weapons: 'The Belgians, the Dutch and the Germans who had promised not to do so, agreed to consider that no reason could be seen why we should be authorised [to manufacture atomic weapons], at least without controls, and they envisaged that we could not be authorised to do so except to the extent that the military authorities of NATO recognized the need for it'. That had given rise to a rather sharp debate, Mendès France continued, in which he had defended French freedom of action, although he himself did not think that France should manufacture atomic bombs now. The French line had prevailed, and the outcome was completely satisfactory to French interests. The limitation on stocks on the continent that he had accepted was not a serious drawback. It was evident that a build-up and storage of nuclear arms could take place in overseas territories, and the arms could be brought to the continent, if needed.[68]

The Paris Conference (20-3 October 1954)

The task of the Paris Conference was to arrange the details and finalize the texts.

The *condition préalable* about the Saar was dealt with bilaterally at the meeting at Celle St. Cloud between Mendès France and Adenauer the day before the opening of the conference. A plan for europeanization of the Saar, to be approved in a referendum, was agreed; measures for Franco-German economic and cultural cooperation also. The Arms Pool question was introduced by the French, but the German reaction was cool. The meeting marked a turning point in the relations between France and the Federal Republic. After Celle St. Cloud more emphasis was put on the cooperative and integrative track in French German policy, less on prohibitions and restrictions.[69]

The main US preoccupation with respect to the Saar problem was to get a solution that was acceptable in both France and Germany, in order to clear the way for approval of the total package. Before the Franco-German meeting Dulles estimated in the National Security Council that there was a fair chance of agreement on the Saar. He recognized that a settlement was essential to Mendès France if he was to get parliamentary approval for the London arrangements. He doubted that Mendès would use the Saar issue as an excuse for abandoning the London arrangements, and predicted that he would try for a genuine settlement. Dulles was bothered, however, that Adenauer seemed to have a tendency to make more concessions to the French than were wise from the point of view of the Chancellor's own domestic political position.[70]

The negotiations about the field of application of the control system, which had been inconclusive in London, continued at the Paris Conference. The intricacies about control of stocks vs. control of import and production, and the border-line between civil and military production were topical again but no agreement was reached. Mendès France finally agreed to renounce the French demands for the moment, as the whole problem was tied to that of the Arms Pool.[71] In the final texts the matter was referred to further negotiations about defining the field of activity of the Armaments Agency. In a rather elastic formulation, the tasks of the Agency would be to satisfy itself about undertakings - including of course the *Kernwaffenverzicht* - and to control the level of stocks of arms on the mainland of Europe; this control should 'extend to production and imports to the extent required to make the control of stocks effective'.[72]

With respect to the nuclear field, the principle that civil production processes should not be controlled contained insoluble contradictions. On the one side, it was important to the French to verify that German nuclear activities - by definition civil - were not diverted to military uses. On the other side, it was a French goal that controls and inspections of the French programme - labelled as civil only at this time - should be avoided. Regardless of military intentions, inspections also had an undesirable industrial espionage aspect. The French nuclear programme had been underway for a decade, while the Germans had been restricted and had only been allowed to pursue limited nuclear activities of a scientific character. The Germans had more to gain from industrial espionage in this field.

A retrospective account about the application of the control system to the atomic energy sector throws further light on the matter. A British official told the Americans that the British perception of the proceedings on this point had been this:

> The British were aware, during the discussions, of the so-called loop-hole represented by civilian nuclear facilities in the general context of the control of atomic weapons. They proposed during the discussions that WEU recognize this by bringing certain civilian nuclear facilities under the cognizance of the Control Agency. The French...rejected this idea because they realized it would apply not only to German civilian nuclear facilities but also to French. When the British took the view that it was impossible to agree on an arrangement which applied in Germany but not in France, the French proposed that the Agreements not deal with atomic weapons. The British held that this was out of the question in an arrangement intended to control armaments. It was at this point...that Chancellor Adenauer's undertaking prohibiting the manufacture of atomic weapons in Germany was obtained.[73]

The final texts stipulated that ABC weapons and 'the factories solely earmarked for their production' would be controlled, but not activities for civil or scientific purposes. The term atomic weapon was defined in a new way.[74] The EDC method of defining nuclear fuel in excess of 500 grammes as an atomic weapon was abandoned. The term nuclear fuel was now based on two alternative criteria. The first was whether a weapon containing nuclear fuel, through explosions or radioactivity, was capable of mass destruction, mass injury or mass poisoning. Second, 'any part, device, assembly or material especially designed for, or primarily useful in' such a weapon would also be considered as an atomic weapon. Thus, the second criterion was based on intentions or primary use. This left a large grey-zone. Several activities in the nuclear field may result in products for either civil or military use; the purpose may be dual, the real purpose may be concealed, or it may change in the course of time. Nor is it always clear what is the primary use of an item in this field. In addition, the definition did not include nuclear submarines.[75]

The French efforts to obtain WEU authority over US military aid continued in Paris. Mendès France argued that an American concession on this point would increase the chances of ratification considerably. Dulles declared that he was not prepared for the moment to go any further than he had done in London.[76]

The French returned to the charge on the Arms Pool question. Mendès France worked hard to obtain a commitment that a conference on the Arms Pool would be arranged no later than 1 December. That was before the expected vote of the National Assembly on the Paris Accords. The Arms Pool was the most important of all French suggestions, he said, and the French Parliament had been very critical of the absence of results in London. The other delegations were on the whole negative. They were well aware that treatment of the Arms Pool question before ratification would re-inforce the French negotiating position on the issue and complicate things generally. It was finally agreed that a separate conference on the subject would take place after the Paris Accords had been dealt with in the French National Assembly.[77]

After the Paris Conference, the Germans started preparations for building up a nuclear programme. Heisenberg went to Washington to negotiate with representatives of the Allies. Adenauer made a declaration about limitation of production of nuclear fuel and reactor capacity during the next two years. These limitations had only formal importance as the Federal Republic was starting its build-up from a low level. It would hardly have been possible to produce more anyhow, even with an all-out effort. There was also some activity in progress to avoid the Anglo-American and French control of the raw material supply in the West. The planning committee for atomic energy had proposed that a search for uranium should be made in the entire territory of the Federal Republic in order to localize other domestic sources than those that had already been discovered in the Black Forest and Fichtelgebirge; otherwise, it could not be guaranteed that the fuel for a planned reactor driven by natural uranium would be available within two years.[78]

French Efforts to Obtain Further Concessions

There was a protracted period of uncertainty and further negotiations until the Paris Accords were finally ratified by France. The first and most important part of the ratification procedure took place during the last ten days of 1954 when the package was debated in the National Assembly, and approved by a vote of 287 to 256 on 29 December. The second part was the treatment in the Council of the Republic. The Council could not refuse ratification, but it had the competence, by making amendments, to refer the issue back for reconsideration in the Assembly. Thus, it had the power of delay, and of creating uncertainty about whether ratification was final. This could, however, in this matter be interpreted as tantamount to the power of denial. A favourable vote was finally taken in the Council also, on 27 March 1955, whereupon the complex entered into force. It should be kept in mind, then, that the French bargaining chip in negotiations with the other powers - 'accept this demand, or there will be a great risk of non-ratification' - was effective in both stages of the parliamentary process, although weaker in the second one.

The point of departure for US diplomacy during the months after the Paris Conference and the vote in the National Assembly was to assist Mendès France as far as possible in his dealings with domestic opinion and Parliament; French ratification was seen as probable but uncertain, at times very uncertain. There were definite limits to the possible, however. There was a determination in the US, and elsewhere, that the German question should be decided once and for all after years of bargaining, fiasco, and bargaining again. No further delay was considered tolerable. Beyond the acceptable limits were measures that might circumscribe the US freedom of action in the future. The tolerance threshold in German opinion and Parliament was another restriction. The German Social-Democrats opposed Adenauer's European policy; it was believed in the US that Adenauer's position must not be put in peril by too much accomodation to French demands. Eisenhower wrote to Gruenther that 'the answer to the European problem will probably be written in German' - thus expressing that the alliance with Germany was more important to him than that with France.[79]

A balancing act taking into consideration both popular and parliamentary opinion in Germany and France, and in the US Congress, was required. This made cooperation with the United Kingdom desirable; the US and UK positions, although not identical, were coordinated. Eisenhower told Churchill that he had instructed Dulles to confer with Eden in the ratification matter. His patience with French demands was not endless.[80]

The State Department saw the WEU as a rescue operation and a provisional solution to the problems created by the failure of the EDC. It was never regarded as satisfactory in the long run. It was however considered risky to admit this. The position paper for Dulles which was prepared for the visit of Mendès France to Washington in November provides an illustration. The paper stressed that it was 'doubtful that an organization embracing the UK can ever achieve the degree of economic and political integration for which the US has hoped, especially when the initial functions of this organization consist primarily of such negative matters as military controls'. Moreover, the consequences for NATO of further growth in the operational functions of the WEU had not yet been fully explored. Therefore, the US should be cautious in expressing views about the future status of the WEU. It was desirable, for tactical reasons, to avoid any discussion with French representatives about long-range prospects for European organizations at this time and of giving any appearance of exerting pressure for further integration later. The US should indicate an essentially 'open mind' and should avoid any commitment as to future US policy. The Mendès France Government had indicated 'a marked lack of enthusiasm' for European economic integration and there had been some evidence that it aimed at weakening the Coal and Steel Community whose successful operation was of vital importance if the economic integration movement were ever to regain the momentum that had been lost by the rejection of the EDC. Because of the importance of concentrating immediate attention on the the Paris Accords and the known UK reluctance about supranationalism 'it would appear counter-productive to suggest that the US will not be satisfied with the arrangements created by the Paris agreements but will thereafter push for major additional steps toward unity'.[81]

It was discussed whether the sanctions relating to US military aid should be used to influence the outcome in Paris. Was it, for example, an appropriate measure to continue the prevailing restrictions on off-shore procurements from French arms industry? Ambassador Dillon recommended prompt reconsideration of the restrictions. He believed that the freeze, 'now fully known to the French', as applied, seemed to be far more painful to US forces than to the French. Its effects on the French dollar position were long term and would not be felt in time to have any influence on the parliamentary debate. The policy was, in his view, totally ineffective.[82] When Dulles talked with Harold Stassen, responsible for foreign aid, Dulles 'thought it well to go slowly on these [the off-shore contracts] until after the French Chamber of Deputies had acted on the German treaties, but we should be ready to move promptly after that'. Some steps, he said, were already taken, with his approval, to mitigate certain harsh and unreasonable aspects of the cut off.[83] Consequently, when Mendès France visited Washington he obtained certain concessions on the military aid issue. Stassen told Mendès that France would receive the aid due for 1954 and that the off-shore procurements would start again in February 1955.[84]

In sum, the State Department line was that pressure tactics in favour of integration in Europe should only be used with great caution. It was thought preferable to keep a low profile, to be passive, to try to influence events by general conditions visible to all, or to act through intermediaries, such as the Benelux states. The methods that had been used in the EDC affair were subjected to heavy criticism from Congress and the media after the failure. The Department however resisted Congressional pressures for establishing a linkage between American aid and European integration, and to make American aid depend on progress in integration. Linkage of this kind was seen as counterproductive and as giving grounds for accusations of American imperialism. State Department officials argued that European integration, if it were to take root and was to last, had to be based on European initiatives. All America could offer was 'friendly aid' or counsel.[85]

The Mendès France Government endeavoured in talks with the Americans and the British to stretch the limits that had been drawn up in London and Paris, and to obtain interpretations that were acceptable to France. The argument was constantly that concessions to French wishes were necessary for, or improved prospects of, ratification. The main subject was arms control; the aim was to obtain further restrictions on German armament without accepting corresponding restrictions on France. Other issues, some of which had been presented in London as *conditions préalables*, were also discussed. For example, the French renewed their efforts to persuade the Americans to give binding guarantees about troop presence on the European continent, similar to those given to the EDC, and paralleling the key guarantee about British presence given by Eden at the London Conference. The Americans refused to move from the position announced in London. They stuck to the line 'first ratification, then possibly some kind of American guarantee'. Internally, the French efforts on this point were described by the President and Dulles as undue pressuring; it would be humiliating if for a second time the French were given all the assurances they wanted and then rejected the project.[86]

On the Saar question, Mendès France asked for a joint guarantee by the US and the UK of the Franco-German agreement in Celle St. Cloud up to the conclusion of a peace treaty with Germany. Dulles' answer was that the scales were so delicately balanced between France and Germany that he was not disposed to take any action which might be disturbing. He did not want to go further than declaring that it was probable that the US would support the French position at the peace conference. Mendès' reaction was that 'that won't help a lot' and that 'all France got from the war was the Saar'.[87]

Further, the French tried to persuade the British - and also the Germans - that a promise to hold a Four-Power conference on the German problem after ratification was necessary for countering possible Soviet moves before ratification and thus for improving the chances of a successful outcome in Parliament.[88]

With respect to the dominant problem of arms control of Germany, much of the French efforts concentrated on the issue of WEU authority over US military aid. The ominous possibility of transferring control of US nuclear weapons to the Federal Republic, as part of the New Look strategy, was the core of the problem, and a cause of grave concern in Paris.

If it proved impossible to accept WEU authority over the distribution of US military aid, the French argued, the WEU should at least be consulted. They also asked whether Washington could make a declaration of intent, stating that the US Government wished to harmonize its decisions on aid programmes with the programmes for arms production, thus tying the question to the Arms Pool project.[89] The modification of the US position that was eventually made was modest and did not change fundamentals. When the French ratification debate was approaching, the pledge to inform the WEU that had been made in London was finally supplemented with a cautiously circumscribed pledge to consult also.[90] Some of the leading

French newspapers reported that the declaration indicated US support for the French Arms Pool proposal. This was immediately denied by Dulles who cabled to US missions that such stories were inaccurate and misleading.[91] The Dutch expressed hope that the US would make it 'abundantly clear' to all WEU members that the US did not endorse the Arms Pool.[92]

Mendès France made a last-minute unsuccessful attempt to get Dulles change his mind. When the debate in the National Assembly was in progress, Mendès France phoned Dillon late in the night and said that the situation had been difficult during the day. He wondered if in view of his parliamentary difficulties it would not be possible to go further and give the US aid to the Agency of the WEU for distribution. Dulles' declaration had not been sensational, he said, 'what was needed now in the present temper of the Assembly was some new sensational fact that could change the tone of the Assembly'.[93] The plea was followed by silence.

Different interpretations concerning this point were made of the Paris Accords and of the regulation within NATO.

The point was raised in the ratification debate in the House of Commons on 18 November. Aneurin Bevan of the Labour Left asked whether the Paris agreements meant that the possession of nuclear weapons by the German armed forces was not excluded by the agreements. Could a German army with Nazi officers come in possession of the A-bomb? Defence Minister Harold Macmillan replied evasively that it was not a suitable matter for the agreements; it was a matter to be taken up between governments.[94] Eden gave a different answer. In response to a question in the House a few days later he said that it would be impossible for Germany to hold atomic or thermo-nuclear weapons without the approval of NATO, and such a decision required unanimity.[95] The issue remained controversial and unclear.

The French contended that France had a veto by reason of the NATO procedures which would establish stock levels, and that the Federal Republic could neither manufacture nor possess ABC weapons except by unanimous decision of the WEU Council. Thus, the French attempted to expand the veto on manufacture that was contained in the *Kernwaffenverzicht* to include possession also. Early in December the French diplomat Jean-Marc Boegner presented to the US Embassy in Paris a legal argument about the interpretation of two articles in conjunction in the Paris Accords. In his view, they showed that France had a veto. The Embassy was instructed to 'tell Boegner that we find difficulty in finding veto provision and would far prefer to see the matter handled by a statement that the question was academic as U.S. law forbade the transfer of nuclear weapons'.[96]

This was not soothing to the French. Another request was made on 19 December, the day before the opening of the debate in the National Assembly. A representative of the Embassy had emphasized to Mendès' collaborator Soutou, it was reported that the US could not accept the concept of a veto in NATO applying to U.S. forces. He also pointed out that we did not see any absolute prohibition in the Paris agreements, that a statement to that effect would adversely affect ratification[97], and that the French might take the line that a general system of controls had been established and that the specific manner in which it would function was being worked out. Soutou indicated he understood and said that Mendes would say as little as possible about the matter and endeavor to rely on WEU controls in what he did say.[98]

Although it was not 'either expressly or by implication' stated to the French that the US did *not* agree that London or Paris agreements provided a veto over German possession of atomic weapons, 'that was certainly our position', it was reported.[99] The American attitude was 'that the documents themselves are far from clear on this point and we have made an effort to play down a discussion of the problem until the agreements had been ratified'.[100]

The question of the transfer of nuclear weapons by the US to Germany was not much referred to specifically in the debate in the Assembly; it was part of the general theme of control of German rearmament and of US military aid.[101]

After the debate the French approached the Americans again. Boegner repeated his legal arguments about a French veto. He signalled that the French did not intend to be controlled in the nuclear field.[102]

The French tried to establish a common front with the British. Mendès France explained to the British Ambassador that if the Americans would agree to use the WEU machinery for the purpose of distributing their aid to Europe 'this would have much the greatest effect' on ratification.[103] The British were however unwilling to go far in this direction, even if a veto might have been regarded as desirable. The exigencies of the 'special relationship' worked against an Anglo-French standpoint that was incompatible with US policy in a matter as important as this one. The Americans were worried, however. Acting Secretary Murphy wrote to the London Embassy that the State Department was 'seriously concerned' lest responses to Soviet notes alleging that the London and Paris agreements contemplated giving ABC weapons to the Germans were not coordinated between the Allies. The Embassy was requested urgently to ask about the rationale of Eden's statement in Parliament and 'what if any plans UK has re coordination WEU replies'.[104]

Ambassador Aldrich answered that the French had not repeated their suggestion that the UK and French views on controlling supply of atomic weapons to the Federal Republic be concerted. The Foreign Office had no wish to discuss the question with the French, unless strongly pressed. The UK would not accept the principle that the Federal Republic must never have atomic weapons, even if, in the short run, any proposal to provide them would cause a political storm. The Foreign Office was 'inclined to think that the best course now was to leave the issue cloudy, with at least two different explanations on record'.[105]

Dulles concurred. He thought that the best course was to 'leave issue cloudy' and to avoid precipitating discussion of the problem as long as feasible.[106] Nothing indicates that a French veto over the transfer option was ever seriously considered in the State Department.

The French response to the civil-military control dilemma in the nuclear sector was to ask for special controls on Germany outside the WEU system. During the visit of Mendès France to the US in November his US interlocutors resisted French pressure to work out some special arrangements to check on the German undertakings, relying on the provisions for control under the WEU. The Americans estimated that too much inequality would be resented in Germany, and the US diagnosis was that the French standpoints were motivated not only by concern for security but also for the economy.[107] When Dulles met Mendès France in connection with the NATO meeting in Paris in December they touched on the problem of atomic energy controls on Germany. Dulles was reported to have made two points. First, was the French interest limited to information on German weapons production only, or did the interest extend over the entire field of atomic energy in Germany? Second, would the French proposal require some kind of spying in Germany?[108]

The French organized a minor diplomatic campaign at the beginning of 1955. A French official raised the problem with the State Department. He referred to an earlier French proposal about quadripartite (France, US, UK and Canada) discussions on the control of all atomic facilities in Germany. The State Department reported that Dulles' reply to the suggestion had been non-committal and that this position had been repeated in the talk with the Frenchman.[109] French officials continued to present arguments to the American and British Embassies in Paris. As was mentioned above[110], the British reported to the Americans that the French had talked at the London conference about the 'loophole', the fact that civil nuclear activities were not subjected to the control system of the WEU. The British were convinced that the French had been well aware of the loophole during the drafting of the Paris Accords and had been unwilling to take the steps necessary to plug it. Against this background, the British did 'not warm up' to the concern now expressed by the French. The British, for their part, were inclined to rely on three points in order to maintain some check on German production of nuclear weapons. First, that Adenauer in his declaration after the Paris Conference had offered to consult on German plans and intentions in the atomic energy field, second, that substantial production facilities and know-how related to the non-fissile aspects of the weapon production would be required and could be detected, third, that a test would be needed and could be detected.[111]

American and British Reactions during the Debate in the French National Assembly

US and UK policy-makers, although believing that ratification was probable, were nervous that something might upset the delicate balance at the last minute. An unfavourable vote on a key section of the Brussels Treaty late in the evening in the last debating day before Christmas, 23 December, caused uproar in Washington and London. Eisenhower exclaimed: 'Those damn French! What do they think they're trying to do? This would really upset the apple cart in Europe'. Hurried telegrams were exchanged. Dillon proposed, in agreement with the British Ambassador, that a joint Anglo-American statement should be issued that German rearmament would be undertaken with or without France. However, after having met Mendès France who hoped that the US and British Governments would limit any statements on the subject to the minimum, he withdrew the recommendation. Both Eisenhower and Dulles thought that it would be the wrong tactic and refused, even when Churchill insisted. Mendès strongly urged the Americans not to go into a formal statement with Churchill; this would do more harm than good. A more innocuous statement was issued.[112] When the situation looked brighter after another partial vote on 27 December, Dillon stressed that restraint was still necessary, 'We must talk and act during coming two months in a way that will make it as easy as possible for Council of Republic to take favourable action'.[113]

Preparations for alternative action were accelerated after the first negative partial vote. When Conant met Adenauer the latter was upset; he expressed the view that failure now would end the possibility of good French-German relations for some time to come and would kill any idea of European integration. If this happened, he believed that action must be taken immediately along the line of the empty chair theory. Otherwise public opinion in Germany would move rapidly into a completely neutralist attitude and perhaps shortly to one desiring negotiations with Russia on a neutralist basis. In further US-German discussions in Bonn the idea developed that a meeting between the US, the UK and the Federal Republic should be held within twelve hours after bad news from Paris. Conant supported this view. It would be a sign of the Chancellor's equal status; his domestic position would be strengthened.[114] Conant had grave doubts about the empty chair philosophy, however.[115] In an exchange of telegrams Eden and Dulles agreed that another conference, which Eden thought should include the Benelux, Italy and Canada, would be urgent in case of failure. Dulles was not too pessimistic. He thought that it looked as if the treaties would 'squeak through'.[116]

Mendès was frustrated after the negative partial vote in the Assembly. In a talk with Dillon he philosophized on the course of the bargaining process during the autumn. The crucial moment, he said, was the failure of either the US or the UK to support his Arms Pool proposal in London. He felt that if the Arms Pool had been accepted, it would have meant at least fifty additional votes. Furthermore, neither the US nor the UK had given him vitally needed help on the Saar the previous week, or on distribution of US military aid.[117]

An emergency meeting between Dulles and the British Washington Ambassador, Sir Roger Makins, and their aides took place on the last day of the debate and the day of the final vote. Although both Dulles and Makins believed that the package would pass, it was thought prudent to agree on immediate action in case of an adverse vote. Dulles said that the President had approved in the first instance the plans for Dulles to go to London to confer with Adenauer and Eden. It should be decided then what the next move would be, whether a conference with the Benelux countries or a NATO meeting. He referred to the Anglo-American planning that had taken place last summer, and said that he had given some thought as to whether a possible solution might be a Brussels Pact with six instead of seven members [that is, the 'empty chair']. He reflected, somewhat hesitantly, about the legal basis for leaving France out of a settlement on Germany; the objections to this alternative that had been raised in the summer seemed to remain:

> ...he had asked the Legal Adviser to give him a legal opinion as to whether the fact that France was in Germany due to the US and UK having invited her in, so to speak, might not constitute a legal basis for the US and the UK restoring sovereignty to Germany without French consent. In other words, we were guardians of German sovereignty as a result of our conquest (unconditional surrender) and occupation of Germany. We, so to speak, gave a share of this to France. Could we not give back to Germany the whole which had originally been ours, irrespective of French views?

Makins did not seem convinced that this was the best way; he suggested that in case of non-ratification 'it might be better to tackle the problem *de novo* without France'.[118] He remarked that the defection of France was likely to make the British Government less willing to take a new initiative for a Brussels Treaty without France without knowing precisely where the US Government stood.[119]

French Counterbalance: Reinforcement of the National Military Nuclear Option

There is a connection in time between the *Kernwaffenverzicht*, the finalization of the Paris Accords and French decision-making in the matter of national nuclear weapons. Immediately after the Paris Conference Mendès France made the first of a number of decisions intended to reinforce the national option. On 26 October, he signed a decree creating a committee for military nuclear applications; this committee never convened. On 4 November, another decree created the *Comité des explosifs nucléaires*, headed by a general, which started to function at once. Various agencies and officials cooperated in working out a secret nuclear armament programme. The programme was dated 20 December, the day when the ratification debate about the Paris Accords started in the National Assembly. It formed the basis of a meeting on 26 December, in the midst of the debate in the Assembly. The meeting took place in the office of Mendès France; Cabinet members, officials and military officers, about 40 in all, were present. A 'green light' to continue along the lines outlined in the programme was given by Mendès France. The literature on the history of French nuclear weapons generally considers this meeting as a crucial link, or as the most crucial link, in the chain of decisions leading to the bomb - or even as *the* French decision to make the bomb.[120] Not much attention is paid, however, to the direct connection between the meeting and the first and most important stage of the French ratification of the Paris Accords. A green light to go on with an intensified programme for making the bomb may be interpreted as the *sine qua non* for getting enough support for acceptance of a German rearmament programme partially bridled by the Western European Union.

The programme that was presented at the meeting contained a rough outline of the projects to be carried through, projects which were largely[121] realized during the next fourteen years up to the first H-bomb test in 1968. Two prototypes for nuclear submarines, the first fuelled by natural uranium, the second by enriched uranium, would be constructed by 1958 and 1961, respectively. Measures would be taken to conduct bomb tests in 1960-61, then to manufacture 4-5 A-bombs annually, and ultimately to pass to the H-bomb level. It was pointed out that the construction of propulsion reactors for submarines was important for the development of civil atomic energy. A budget was included. The allocations would not be distributed explicitly either to the Ministry of Defence or to the *Commissariat à l'énergie atomique*; the ministers concerned would later submit a proposal about how to obtain the credits from Parliament in a camouflaged way.

The programme enumerated the motives for acquiring nuclear weapons 'as regards our allies, as regards our possible enemies, as regards Germany, as regards the French Union'.

The first motive was contained in the traditional Gaullist argument about possession of nuclear weapons as a necessary condition for independence:

> Within a relatively short space of time no country will thus be able to claim real political independence unless it possesses atomic weapons, indeed even thermonuclear weapons, together with the means of delivery.

The thinking of the New Look about the military necessity of possessing nuclear weapons, and the later French doctrine of 'deterrence of the strong by the weak' was expressed:

> Those armed forces which do not possess them will become completely ineffective when faced by an adversary which has the possibility of using them. Conversely, the threat of destruction which such missiles exert must suffice to discourage an aggressor, even one much more powerful.[122]

There is no doubt that the dominant concern in the minds of those present at the meeting was Germany. The vote that would probably be decisive for regulating German rearmament after years of struggle lay only days ahead. It is possible - although I have no material corroborating it - that the 'green light' had been demanded by undecided Gaullists, Rightists and Centrists as a condition for support of the Paris Accords. Alternatively, Mendès France may have judged that the action was necessary for obtaining the marginal votes required. The negative partial vote of 23 December was a warning that the final outcome might be negative. Ratification was decisive for Mendès political future, and he was prepared to go far to adapt to parliamentary realities. The more so as the decision could be interpreted as not being final but as preservation of the freedom of action for a 'yes' or 'no' later.

The large number of persons present at the meeting, and the excited mood of the political elite at that time, seemed to guarantee that the decision would become known to relevant MP's.[123] If so, it would also become known to Adenauer and to the Americans. It can hardly be doubted that the 'green light' decision had an impact on US European policy once the Paris Accords had been disposed of.

The problem of obtaining nuclear military information from the US or the UK became more urgent. Much of the information continued to be closely guarded also under the new US Atomic Energy Act, although liberalization had taken place. French decision-makers asked themselves whether France would try to get the urgently needed technical information through espionage on its allies. A memorandum from the office of Mendès France stated that the latest session of the *Conseil Supérieur du Renseignement* had made clear that it was extremely difficult to obtain clandestinely nuclear information from the East. The information assembled in this way was fragmentary and uncertain. Until then, the intelligence agency, the S.D.E.C.E., had not been working in the US and the UK. Consequently, the memorandum continued, the French were in a position that was inferior to that of the East, which did not need to hesitate on this point:

> The question thus arises whether it is appropriate to put an end to this state of affairs and to admit that the S.D.E.C.E. can, at the request of the CEA or of the National Defence, try to obtain intelligence about some of the atomic know-how of our Allies. - It goes without saying that any such action should be shrouded in total secrecy and that the intelligence thus obtained should be jealously guarded by France.[124]

Negotiations about the French Arms Pool Project

The project for an Arms Pool had been referred to a special conference in Paris. It was scheduled to start on 17 January 1955. The work of the conference took place at the level of officials of the seven WEU countries, assembled in a 'Working Group'. Responsible for looking after American interests from the sideline were the US Permanent NATO Representative in Paris, John C. Hughes, and Ambassador Dillon.[125] The Americans of course remained at the centre of diplomatic activity. The European governments anxiously inquired about the American position and kept Washington constantly informed.

The French memorandum on the Arms Pool differed in some respects from that which had been presented in London three months earlier. The main difference was that the UK was now also included, and that a development in two stages was envisaged. There would be an interim period with non-supranational cooperation lasting to the end of 1956, and after that automatic transition to a permanent supranational regime with the same main characteristics as in the earlier proposal. Under the permanent regime there would be a common procurement and supply system covering at least - the language was unclear - the NATO sector. A licence for expansion of national production capacities would be required. Such a licence would, however, be required only for the mainland of Europe, thus excepting part of the French and the entire British arms industry.[126]

The main consideration behind the French proposal was to prevent an expansion of the German arms industry. As all German forces would be allocated to NATO the entire German arms production would be subjected to authorization. Consequently, Germany would be more closely restricted in the nuclear field also, while the French freedom of action would not be further circumscribed.

Before the opening of the conference the possibility of bilateral cooperation in the military nuclear field seems to have been discussed between French and German officials.

Some preparations for joint Franco-German production of arms had taken place in France in the autumn. Ideas for such cooperation had been discussed in the ministries, and the *Quai d'Orsay* had made a proposal for building up a continental industry for aircraft production, starting with the French, German and Italian industries. The Ministry of Defence had envisaged nuclear cooperation in a way similar to that which had been proposed by the Army General Staff in September. It had proposed to use the WEU Agency to pool European financial and technical resources and foster the accession of France to nuclear status 'alone or in a Community'. Suggestions for cooperation in the nuclear field had not been taken up by Mendès France, though.[127]

This subject was however taken up - according to the memoirs of a French participant - when collaborators of Mendès France and Adenauer met in Bonn a couple of days after the presentations of the French memorandum on the Arms Pool. The Germans showed interest in the production of 'new weapons' in a supranational context, and Mendès' confidant, Soutou, brandished the possibility of common nuclear installations in a French territory outside Europe:

> In speaking about the Arms Pool, our interlocutors declared their anxiety to come back to the subject in the Europe of the Six. They even proposed attaching this pool to the Coal and Steel Community, of making it a copy of that, and of extending it into the domain of new weapons. They are vaguely interested by plans for common establishments in North Africa. Soutou spoke to them about atomic installations in Guinea. As regards common production in the aeronautical field, they were much more reticent.[128]

The nuclear possibility was obviously intended as a strategic argument when trying to obtain German support for the Arms Pool. The facts are somewhat uncertain, however. The German record of the meeting does not mention it, but refers to the discussion as dealing with the importance of the pool - together with the issue of distribution of American military aid - for obtaining ratification in the Council of the Republic. The memorandum only mentions 'Common manufacturing plants and enterprises overseas' as one of the subjects that Soutou listed for the coming Adenauer/Mendès France meeting in Baden-Baden.[129]

Theodor Blank and his staff at the FRG central organization for military planning, *Amt Blank*, met US officials in Bonn a week later and informed them about the negative German reaction to the French memorandum. Blank saw a number of problems. The proposal was so far-reaching that it seemed to require a new ratification procedure. It was problematic, for example, that there was no limitation of orders that could be placed outside a country, like the 15-85% rule in the EDC. On the other side, there were some desirable features, such as the ambition to standardize. The Germans were not willing to renounce their rights to produce armaments as contained in the Paris Accords, but would consider entering into arrangements to produce certain types of armaments in one or two WEU countries, provided that this was done on a reciprocal basis. The Federal Republic strongly opposed channelling US military aid through WEU.[130]

Mendès France visited Italy and Germany to try to obtain support for the French proposal. On his way back to Paris from Rome he met Adenauer in Baden-Baden on 14 January.[131] Mendès France seemed prepared to compromise, indicating that the French memorandum was not the final word. He said that he had been informed that the Italians would readily join if agreement could be reached.[132] The situation in the Council of the Republic was discussed. Mendès was rather optimistic, the majority in the Council would be larger than in the Assembly, he opined.[133] This may be interpreted as a sign that Mendès did not want to press the issue as a *sine qua non*. Adenauer´s attitude was cautiously non-committal. The nuclear possibility of the Soutou/Blankenhorn meeting does not seem to have been discussed. The Germans were surprised at the conciliatory French attitude. They received the impression that the result in the Arms Pool issue was not the main thing for Mendès, but rather that he wanted to be able to counter his critics by referring to ongoing negotiations.[134]

There was relief in Washington after the positive vote in the National Assembly. The most important part of the battle had been won. Dulles had, we saw, envisaged that the US should go slow on the military aid to France until the Assembly had acted, but be ready to move promptly after that. Accordingly, it was decided to end the temporary freeze policy. The President approved that the construction and procurement limitations on US aid to France which had been imposed in September should be rescinded.[135]

Dillon cabled to the State Department that the idea of an Arms Pool deserved support. His study of the National Assembly debate on the Paris Accords had made him feel that the most striking element was the practically unanimous support from all non-Communist parties. One reason was that Europeanists saw it as a further step to European integration in a field where even the Gaullists did not object to the principle of supranationality. The second reason was that an Arms Pool was considered by all to provide for a surer method of controlling German arms production than other provisions in the Paris Accords. While Mendès France might earlier have been partly motivated by the desire to obtain a favoured position for the French armaments industry this was no longer an element of importance in French policy. In Dillon´s view, the US had no direct interest in the problem, and support would be in accord with the general US policy of favouring anything that would lead to closer integration in Europe. He felt that it would be appropriate and helpful to indicate to the Benelux countries, and in particular to the Netherlands, the importance which the US attached to the idea. The problem should be seen in the light of its bearing on eventual French ratification prospects. It was Dillon's 'considered opinion' that if there was no agreement on an Arms Pool and the Paris Accords were sent back by the Council of the Republic to the Assembly the chances were 'more than even' that they would be rejected.[136]

When the matter was discussed in Washington at a joint State/FOA/CIA meeting on 8 January the channelling of US aid was tied to the character of the Arms Pool. The uncertain factor was whether an Arms Pool would be 'genuine' and sufficiently supranational, or very biased in favour of French interests. Stassen argued that it would be in line with overall US objectives if a pool resulted in the most efficient use of available arms, for example standardization, and in increased economic cooperation. Bowie also believed that if a pool with supranational powers were capable of taking real decisions and furthering European integration, then the US should support it. He summarized the dilemma confronting Mendès France: 'If Mendes activated agreement on a genuine solution to the arms pool, he might lose votes in the Assembly, whereas an arms pool program which would secure French predominance would not command itself to the other WEU countries'. Dulles said that he was prepared to use the issue of control of US aid as an incentive to move the French toward an arms pool concept that was more palatable to the US and others. He requested Bowie 'to work up an elaboration of his earlier message to Mendes-France which would state that if the Brussels Powers evolve an efficient Arms Pool organization, we do not exclude working with it in a manner comparable to the EDC. Our objective in this would be to build up and strengthen an organization which would encourage further integration'. It should be made clear that any duplication with the NATO machinery should be avoided.[137]

The WEU countries communicated their largely negative reactions to the French plan to the Americans. The British stated that NATO should be the basis for any effort to standardize arms and that any body that might be established should avoid duplication with NATO. A British project would be elaborated, but timing was a critical factor. The British project 'should be proposed after it becomes clear to arms pool working group members (including, it is hoped, French) that French proposals are unworkable, but before negotiations have dragged on so long that French public believes they have actually failed'.[138] The Dutch dismissed the French plan completely. Spaak considered it impracticable and unworkable but argued that none of the governments concerned should give the impression of having a closed mind. It was necessary to carry the negotiations past the vote in the Council of the Republic. The only country that showed signs of hesitant support was Italy. The Americans were informed, however, that the Italian delegation had been instructed to keep in close touch with the US NATO delegation in Paris.[139]

The main question in the capitals was: Is the Arms Pool an absolute condition for the finalization of ratification of the Paris Accords in France? The general tendency was to give a negative answer to this question. The situation in the Council of the Republic was not as doubtful as Mendès for tactical reasons might wish to paint it. The Dutch had, it was reported, gone over the records of statements by Mendès France at the Brussels, London and Paris conferences and found repeated instances where he had emphasized that adoption of the Arms Pool plan was not a prerequisite for French parliamentary action, and they were 'ready to remind French of these statements'. Furthermore, new signs that seemed to indicate French de-emphasis had been registered. The Italians told the Americans that their Foreign Ministry had been much concerned lest the Arms Pool would be a condition, but the French had indicated to them during the last few days that it would not.[140]

After having weighed *pros* and *cons*, the US position was detailed in a telegram from Acting Secretary Robert Murphy before the first meeting with the Working Group. It would serve as guidance for the US personnel in Paris. Murphy stated that progress on arms standardization and rationalized arms production for NATO and for European integration was desirable in principle. The French proposal had, however, many serious shortcomings. There were obvious areas of duplication with NATO as well as some possible areas of serious potential conflict. The proposal contained a mixture of supranational features and national responsibilities which might prove very difficult in practice. It was unlikely to be accepted by other countries. In particular, the proposal for stage II was problematic. It was unrealistic to expect UK fully to participate in that stage. The shortcomings made it clear that the Working Group would not be able to reach agreement on the French proposal.

However, Murphy continued, everything must be measured in the light of the effect on ratification of the Paris Accords. The essential problem was to find an approach which would enable the Working Group to 'avoid breakdown of negotiations and produce at least enough positive results to prevent further ratification difficulties'. There appeared to be two possible means for accomplishing this. One was to modify Stage I and confine Stage II to a statement of general principles. The second was to build on something along the lines which the British were considering, standardization and coordination within a NATO framework. In the light of all these considerations the US would not take sides but underline the importance of ratification. Appropriate and discreet encouragement should be given to compromise efforts. The US should not give any encouragement to French proposals for placing orders for arms only after agreement with the Agency. It was highly desirable that the question of channelling US aid through WEU be kept entirely separate from the Arms Pool question. Murphy ended by instructing Conant that he should suggest to Blank that the German delegation should keep in close touch with the US NATO delegation in Paris as it would be in 'best position inform Germans of US thinking'.[141]

French diplomats who tried to probe the attitude of the State Department were told that it was not appropriate for the US to become involved in the substantive discussion at this time. Washington made clear that the guarantees in Dulles' earlier letter regarding a consultation procedure with the WEU about US military aid could not in any way be interpreted as a commitment towards an Arms Pool.[142]

The discussions in the Working Group went on for a couple of months without results.[143] The positions of the delegations did not deviate substantially from what the Americans had been told beforehand. The leader of the German delegation, Ludwig Erhard, led an offensive against the French plan. He reported about the initial period of discussions to the Cabinet in Bonn that the German delegation had declined the two main pillars of the plan, the creation of a supranational authority for procurement of arms and a procedure for approval of changes in national production capacities. The German refusal to accept the French project had been more or less supported by the other delegations.[144]

The news from the negotiations in the Working Group was soothing from the point of view of the Americans. Hughes reported that all the participants had accepted, at least tacitly, the necessity of avoiding any breakdown on specific issues prior to the Council of the Republic debate. Most importantly, the French representative, Parodi, appeared to be lending himself to this approach. There was a little uneasiness among other representatives who had participated in the Brussels Conference the previous August that at the last minute before the parliamentary debate the French would present the Working Group with some sort of ultimatum, but on the basis of what had happened so far they had, in Hughes' opinion, no reason to anticipate this. Meanwhile, the delegations engaged in strange ritual movements:

> No one has, of course, openly formulated at conference tactic of dragging out discussions and avoiding major disagreement. Hence there is certain air of unreality. In atmosphere of mutual exchange of bouquets, real objectives remain unstated. Tempo so far has been that of stately pavane, with each delegation going through set motions. Only Dutch and Germans have gotten slightly out of step, but this did not (repeat not) seriously interfere with basic rhythm...Such queasiness as exists arises largely from fact that no (repeat no) one can be quite sure just who is fooling whom, or whether anybody is being fooled at all. Hope of members of conference apparently is that at least those members of Council of Republic will be fooled to whom an Arms Pool with teeth is important, either as symbol of supra-nationality or as instrument of further control of Germans.[145]

Further instructions in the matter of WEU authority over US military aid were issued by the State Department. Dulles confirmed that existing principles were unchanged. He asked Conant to inform the Germans - who, we saw, also opposed any rights of the WEU in this respect - about US thinking. The basic reason, Dulles explained, was that the WEU was less supranational. Unlike EDC, it had no effective control over forces nor responsibility for raising and supporting them. Dulles mentioned that Mendès had pressed the US on the issue with the argument that the US should be willing to do under the WEU what it had been willing to do under the EDC. Certainly, he continued, the US had agreed to turn over title to equipment to EDC as an organization just as equipment normally was turned over to an individual country. But this had been a reflection of US support for the EDC and for its supranational structure. The US had in fact never abandoned its ultimate rights in the EDC either - and the Allies were aware of this fact.[146]

Renewed Discussion in the US about Alternatives in Case of Further Delay

There was an interregnum in France after the fall of the Mendès France Government. A delay in the ratification procedure could be expected during the period until a new government had been installed. There was some discussion among US diplomats on the site about the alternatives in case of further and unacceptable delay. Hughes communicated to Merchant that he was still generally optimistic about the French ratification. He believed, however, that the time was ripe to let it be known informally to the French that alternatives were under consideration. The very fact that the US had a plan ´would go a long way toward making it unnecessary to put it into effect´. He did not imagine explicit threats, but the plan could be made known through NATO colleagues.[147]

Merchant outlined two alternatives to Dulles. The first was simply to be patient and maintain an attitude of confidence for another few weeks. The second, ´predicated on action (or inaction) by the French signifying outright rejection or raising the prospect of "infinite delay"´ was the empty chair policy. After, possibly, a preliminary Dulles/Eden/Adenauer meeting, the nine ministers who had attended the London Conference would be promptly reassembled ´(a) to restore *de facto* sovereignty to the Federal Republic to the extent practicable by joint US/UK action and (b) to determine on measures for obtaining a German defense contribution on the basis of the arrangements provided by the Paris agreements to the extent this could be done ex-France, but leaving a "vacant chair" for the French´. Dulles believed that the first course of action was satisfactory. He was not prepared to ´crystallize a decision´ on the empty chair policy for the moment.[148]

Some reflections by PPS Staff member Leon Fuller about alternatives for US action may throw further light on the thinking in the State Department in the final phase of the WEU process. Fuller commented on opinions expressed by Conant on the empty chair policy, and added his own views. Conant had warned against precipitating rearmament if the Paris Accords were turned down, because Adenauer would meet greatly increased opposition to rearmament under any arrangement, which fell short of what was assured by the Paris Accords, and there were extreme legal complications if France was left out of the picture. Fuller commented that the US people in Germany, being accustomed to the conditions of the occupation period, had a degree of confidence in the future behaviour of the new ally that was not entirely justified by the facts. Perhaps due allowance was not made for a very different pattern of behaviour when Germany were on her own. Even if the Paris Accords went into effect, Germany would prove a most difficult problem for US diplomacy. A number of factors might pull the Federal Republic away from the alliance, and to adopt a policy of 'free wheeling': the pressure for reunification, the full realization of the implications of the NATO strategy for Germany, the impact of nuclear weapons, and the possibility of advantageous deals with Russia.[149]

Final French Attempts to Obtain Control of US Military Aid and the Transfer Option

When the new French Government had been formed the Foreign Minister, Antoine Pinay, made an attempt to modify the US position and open the door to a linkage between supranational integration in the Arms Pool and European control of US military aid. He asked that the language in Dulles' December declaration about a consultation procedure for US military aid should explicitly mention an Arms Production Agency, or be generalized to include both such agency and the Arms Control Agency. Pinay's argument was that an amendment about linkage had been unanimously adopted by a committee in the Council of the Republic.[150] This last-minute demand caused a final stir of diplomatic activity. The US Paris Embassy suggested to the French that the former declaration might be repeated. It also made clear that the US had reserved the same ultimate rights under the EDC.[151]

In the State Department, the analysis was that nothing short of a French limited veto over US assistance would satisfy the French; in any case 'we cannot give them what they want, so we might as well be honest about it'.[152] Merchant recommended against any substantive change in the earlier declarations. Dulles had no objections and instructed that he did not wish negotiations with Pinay on the subject. The request could not be met in substance, and 'should we nevertheless agree to ambiguous language which might imply a willingness to change our position, result would only be to raise false hopes among French supporters of WEU Arms Pool'.[153] A statement replacing the December declaration was issued a few days later. Nothing was changed in substance.[154]

Pinay had to take *ad notam* that this was the last word. He made an innocuous declaration on behalf of the Government in the debate in the Council of Republic.[155] The Paris Accords were finally comfortably approved without amendments on 27 March. The majority was proportionately larger than in the Assembly. An important factor was that the Gaullist spokesman, Michel Debré, recommended ratification without amendments. The Gaullists had a more pivotal role in the Council of the Republic than in the National Assembly.[156]

In his memoirs Debré throws an interesting light on views about the finalizing of ratification within the Gaullist camp. De Gaulle had publicly recognized that the Paris Accords were ´much preferable´ to the EDC, provided that certain conditions were fulfilled, the first one being that France would, before acceptance, take the lead in probing the chances for a *détente* with the Soviet Union. Debré writes that de Gaulle summoned Debré to persuade him to vote against the Paris Accords. Many Gaullists had voted against them in the Assembly, and de Gaulle had been told that if the Council rejected them, a ministerial crisis as a result of this new French refusal would be inevitable and a very difficult situation would arise. De Gaulle would have to be called back to lead the country. Debré objected that the result would not be a call for de Gaulle but the starting-point for an offensive by the integrationists that would this time be irreversible. Aided by American blackmail, one government or another would make France disappear in a European conglomerate, ´in order, they will say, "to avoid the worst" - that is to say, the recovery of France brought about by General de Gaulle!´ The Paris Accords were in fact a victory for Gaullism, Debré argued. The substitute for the EDC gave France a free hand in the field of military policy and armaments, and that would not be the case for Germany. According to Debré, his arguments made de Gaulle abstain from insisting.[157]

The demand for a French veto on US transfer of nuclear weapons came up a final time in the last minute of the long process of approval of the Paris Accords. The Accords would become legally valid when the instruments of ratification had been deposited, and the Edgar Faure Government had assured the US and British Governments that this would be done on 5 May. In the weeks before this date, the Gaullist minister Gaston Palewski requested that an agreement over German possession of atomic weapons be made a condition to the deposit of ratification. He referred to the fact that the US was fully free to furnish atomic arms to Germany regardless of French or WEU wishes. When Faure refused to postpone deposit, Palewski threatened to resign.[158] Dillon reported that Palewski was ´unfortunately unlikely to resign´ and recommended that the US should make no commitments.[159]

Soutou had talks with the American diplomat Achilles about the matter. Soutou explained that it was understood that US law currently forbade transfer. The French feared, however, an eventual change of the law.

They would like assurances in two respects: first, that no tactical or other atomic weapons would be transferred without unanimous agreement in the NATO Council, second, that cooperative measures be devised to assure that German atomic activities for peaceful purposes could not be diverted to military ends.[160] In another meeting Soutou asked that the US agree to an interpretation of the London protocols that ABC weapons could not be furnished to Germany except by unanimous agreement of the WEU Council. He now stated that the French did not and had never insisted that NATO had a veto on this subject. He also intimated that Dulles had agreed at the London Conference that the intent of the protocols was that the *Kernwaffenverzicht* would include possession also. While US experts who had been present in London might not be fully conversant with the intent of the protocols, he was sure that Dulles would be, as a result of the conversations between the ministers on the night when the London Conference had been deadlocked. He asked for official assurances covering three points: (1) that the US law prohibited transfer of atomic weapons to anyone and that there was no present intention of changing that prohibition, (2) that the US had noted the interpretation of the London protocols in an *aide-mémoire* that was to be delivered, and would comment on it, and (3) that the US considered control over possession by WEU members of atomic weapons as primarily a matter for WEU decision and that the US did not plan to take an initiative on the subject.[161]

The *aide-mémoire* that followed detailed the argument about interpretation. Even if it was not expressly indicated in the Paris Accords, the paper argued, it could not be doubted that the meaning was that the Federal Republic could neither manufacture nor possess ABC weapons except by unanimous decision in the WEU Council. This followed from the interplay between three articles. If this interpretation was not accepted, the impossible consequence was that a country which had not renounced from manufacturing or possessing ABC weapons would be bound to accept WEU's decisions about the levels of stocks, while a country which had renounced from manufacture could possess unlimited stocks of ABC weapons. A distortion of the original meaning had occurred between the agreement on principles in London and the codification in Paris.[162]

Merchant commented in a memorandum to Dulles. Regarding the French interpretation of the agreements in London he reported that no record had been found 'but you may perhaps recall if there were any such understanding among the Ministers'. He pointed out that the US position in the past had been to refuse to commit itself to an interpretation, 'the Agreements are ambiguous on this point and Defense has strongly opposed any step which would tie our hands in future deliveries of atomic weapons'. Merchant recommended an uncommittal reply.[163] This was done. It was affirmed that the Atomic Energy Act of 1954 prohibited the transfer of nuclear weapons to any other country and 'the United States Government has no present intention of modifying this provision´. An interpretation of the Protocols was declared not to be appropriate but primarily a matter for the WEU countries.[164]

Conclusion

After initial disappointment and anger the reaction of the State Department to the French rejection of the EDC was cautiously expectant. The first reviews of the situation contained elements of self-criticism. Had the US pressed too hard and had military integration been too much stressed compared to political and economic integration? Was British participation in some form necessary to obtain French consent to German NATO membership and rearmament? Dulles then and later was strongly critical about the lack of British support for the EDC and he thought it was a main factor explaining the failure. It seemed that neither Britain nor France could be bypassed in the critical situation that had arisen. The State Department´s view of the role of France in US European policy was unchanged. No viable policy was possible without France, although investigation of other possibilities should continue. In Dulles´ view, there was no use talking about the US proceeding unilaterally to rearm Germany; ´In such a situation Germany might well choose not to rearm´. Thus, it was necessary to accommodate to French demands to some extent. Dulles acknowledged that Britain and France no longer wished to seem tied to the US ´coat-tails´; the important objective was to save NATO and German alignment with the West.

Consequently, the rescue operation initiated by Britain and France was regarded benevolently in Washington right from the start. It offered a definite possibility of realizing the most important objective of tying Germany to the West and to make progress at least provisionally with the arms control problem. The National Security Council discussed a model for German membership of NATO with acceptable safeguards, consisting of a web of measures for arms control, among them voluntary acceptance by Germany of limits to the initial build-up of forces, and restrictions on certain types of weapons, possibly through designation of ´exposed areas´, or a European arms pool. This was a way of tackling the German nuclear problem, and also the French one; the German demand for equality and non-discrimination was the basis for restrictions on France also.

How did the outcome of the WEU negotiations affect the nuclear options: the German and French national options, the transfer option and the European option?

The restrictions on the German option were defined by Adenauer´s *Kernwaffenverzicht* at the London Conference. A ´voluntary´ offer on this crucial point had been considered in Germany at least since the summer as a means of untying the knots should the EDC fail. It is possible that there was a prior US-German understanding about the exact content of Adenauer´s offer, although I have not found documentary evidence for it. If Adenauer´s version in his memoirs about Dulles´ immediate reaction at the conference table (´*rebus sic stantibus*´) is correct, it may be interpreted in different ways, but it shows in any case that Dulles wanted to circumscribe the offer and avoid making it too comprehensive. Adenauer himself two years later regretted that he had had to make the *Kernwaffenverzicht*, but he also judged it absolutely necessary for a successful outcome of the conference; without it German sovereignty would not have been attained. The *Kernwaffenverzicht* focused on the German option only, it did not cover the transfer option and the European option. It was not in the American interest to exclude any of the latter options, and it was not in the French interest to exclude the European option. However, it was a paramount French goal to obtain authority over the transfer of American nuclear weapons to Germany.

The WEU outcome represented only a partial control on Germany, even in the area that was covered by the *Kernwaffenverzicht*. The French had avoided accepting a control system concept for the WEU which included the civil atomic energy sector because in that case the French atomic energy programme would have been subject to control also. The problems of distinguishing between military and civil production, and control of stocks versus control of production, caused lengthy and inconclusive discussions at the conferences in London and Paris. Many of these discussions had their roots in the French wish for control of the nuclear activities in Germany without accepting control of the French ones, and the wish of the US, Germany and others that the French activities should be controlled also. In order to avoid the contradictions France proposed that Germany should be controlled not only by the WEU control system, but by a supplementary system.

Many of the efforts at the two conferences were in fact dedicated to persuading the French to accept restrictions on the French national nuclear option, or even to renounce it, but all such attempts were instantly opposed by Mendès France as non-ratifiable in France. Dulles made a compromise proposal in London which was apparently intended to make France accept certain restrictions in the nuclear field in exchange for an engagement by the US not to transfer nuclear weapons to the Federal Republic for a limited period. As the restrictions would only apply to the continent, they would not have been an obstacle to the French option in the short run. However, as the proposal referred to supranational control of arms production on the continent, and the principle of equality, it may be interpreted as expressing Dulles´ hope that a first step in the supranational direction would be taken, a step that might later be followed by others to cover all the territories of the Six.

The possibility of envisaging transfer of US nuclear weapons to either France or Germany as a *quid pro quo* for cooperation was opposed by the Joint Chiefs of Staff and was not approved by the President. The German possibility was of course remote in the short run. Nevertheless, the French were very anxious to obtain guarantees against a future US change of policy and it therefore functioned as an American means of pressure on France. French diplomats made repeated attempts to obtain WEU control of the transfer of American aid. Legalistic arguments were advanced and a common front with Britain was sought. The French argued that the US should be prepared to do for the WEU what it had been prepared to do for the EDC. The US standpoint was, however, that American freedom of action on this point had in fact existed in the EDC also. Substantive concessions were refused. The analysis in Washington was that clarifications on this point should be avoided.

The transfer option was tied to the question of a WEU Arms Pool and the European option. The US attitude was that a European Arms Pool might be desirable in principle, provided that a US veto on distribution of aid remained. However, it was believed that an organization that embraced the UK could never achieve the necessary degree of integration. Second, the French project was considered as too biased toward French interests. Third, the Arms Pool seemed to imply enormous practical difficulties. It was a complicating factor in the finalization of the Paris Accords. Time was short if Adenauer's position in Germany was to be maintained and a drift toward 'neutralism' avoided.

In sum, the Paris Accords solved the immediate problem of German sovereignty, rearmament, and NATO membership. They promised to be a part of the system of measures controlling the German nuclear option, but they were insufficient because the *entire* German nuclear sector would not be controlled. With respect to the French national option only minor and hardly significant restrictions had been achieved, in spite of repeated efforts by the US and the partners to make France accept substantive restrictions.

4

Euratom and the Linkage to the Common Market: First Phase

Origins

In the period when the Paris Accords were negotiated and ratified ideas about military and civil uses of atomic energy were in the air in Europe. The US New Look strategy and Atoms for Peace policy were determining factors in this process.

Jean Monnet's role as *inspirateur* was important. Monnet was dissatisfied with the WEU as an insufficiently supranational framework for German rearmament and critical about the fact that the Paris Accords contained no itinerary for continued economic and political unification. For a while he gave thought to the French concept of an Arms Pool as a possible new Community and a wedge for a new supranational initiative but concluded that it had few chances of being accepted. He announced that he was going to resign as Chairman of the Coal and Steel Community, hoping to influence further developments by this move. In December 1954 the Assembly of the Community requested that its competences be extended to other sectors - transport, gas, electricity, atomic energy; some voices suggested the itinerary towards general economic integration. At the same time, Louis Armand, who had often supported Monnet's European initiatives and was preparing a report for the OEEC on the future of civil atomic energy, had a certain role. It appears that an American, Max Isenbergh, came up with the idea of a separate community for atomic energy around the turn of the year 1954-55, and that Monnet was immediately convinced about the usefulness of the concept.[1]

Different authors judge the question of the origin of the Euratom idea differently and there is some obscurity regarding Isenbergh's role.[2] It may be asked whether Isenbergh was a US emissary charged with the mission of planting the idea. Duchêne's view that Isenbergh acted only in a private capacity may be contested. Although I have not found any direct reference that Isenbergh was sent out to promote the idea of nuclear integration, it seems possible, even probable, that he was on a mission. Certain material of the period is still classified, including much CIA material. There is some indirect evidence that the idea of an American origin is not far-fetched. For instance, there is material showing that the Operations Coordinating Board

(OCB) - a White House agency for cooordinating various aspects of national security policy - was thinking of studying the possibility of using peaceful nuclear energy for promoting European integration as early as August 1954. Among a number of possible US courses of action in support of European unity an OCB memorandum recommended that the OCB in coordination with a working group for implementation of the Atoms for Peace policy should study ´the possibility of exploiting the President´s proposals for the peaceful uses of atomic energy *on a European basis* [my emphasis]´.[3]

Monnet now promoted the policy of expanding the Coal and Steel Community to include transport and classic sources of energy, and of founding a new community for atomic energy which would include Britain. The chances for acceptance of a nuclear community would be good, he believed, because there were still no vested interests in the field, atomic power promised to become economically extremely important in the long run, and it would make Europe less dependent on the import of oil. It thus seemed a suitable area for continuing toward European unification along sectoral lines. However, the consideration which, although it was not openly spoken of, was no doubt fundamental for Monnet was the prospect that integration in this field could be the instrument for preventing nationally controlled nuclear weapons in the hands of the hereditary enemies Germany and France.

Monnet obtained the consent of Spaak, his friend and fellow Europeanist, to work for sectoral integration, with an Atomic Pool as the priority project. Any open initiative had to wait until the Paris Accords had been ratified, however. Spaak regarded general economic integration as desirable but as too ambitious a project to have any chance of acceptance in the short run. Another defeat for an integration project would halt the process for years. He contacted his colleagues in the Netherlands and Luxemburg and tried to organize a common front about the best way of promoting integration. Dutch foreign minister Beyen reacted by sending to his colleagues in Belgium and Luxemburg a memorandum opposing the sectoral method for integration and suggesting that the Benelux states propose a customs union as a step towards the ultimate goal, an economic union (the Beyen Plan of 4 April 1955). Monnet and Spaak decided to combine their concept with the Dutch view. The two lines of action converged in the ´Benelux memorandum´ of 18 May. This was the prelude to the Messina Conference.[4]

The Messina resolution was the point of departure for almost two years of negotiations under the chairmanship of Spaak. First, of a more exploratory kind in the Intergovernmental Committee, ending with the ´Spaak Report´ of 21 April 1956, and its approval as negotiation base at the Conference of Foreign Ministers in Venice on 29-30 May. Second, in the Intergovernmental Conference, ending with the signature of the Treaties of Rome on 25 March 1957, about the Common Market and Euratom. Ratifications in the key countries, Germany and France, took place a few months afterwards on 19 and 24 July, respectively. Britain did not take part in the Messina Conference but participated as observer in the Spaak Committee for a time until the withdrawal on 17 November 1955.

When Monnet and Spaak prepared their initiative, the new French Government led by Edgar Faure was also on the trail of integration. Nuclear cooperation was the priority. Some urgent problems in the nuclear field were in need of solution from the French vantage point.

The first problem was that the Paris Accords had not solved the problem of controlling German nuclear energy. The *Kernwaffenverzicht* had been a fundamental condition for agreement, perhaps *the* fundamental condition. It was however partial in several respects. The control system would be oriented toward military production, not civil production that was eventually turned to military ends and the details would be agreed upon in further negotiations. The economic aspect of the control problem also played a role. There was a definite possibility that the Federal Republic would start to cooperate bilaterally with the US about atomic power development and this, in combination with German economic dynamism, might nullify the French ten-year advance. Both the military and civil aspects of the control problem made ´control through integration´ necessary.

The second problem was that France possessed no enrichment plant. The ´plutonium road´ for nuclear development had been chosen in the early fifties for resource reasons. For those French groups who wanted to follow the British example and advance to the H-bomb level access to high- and medium-enriched uranium was indispensable. Access to low-enriched uranium would also give greater freedom to choose technology in the civil field.[5] The only producers in the West were the US and Britain; the technology was highly classified. To build a national French enrichment plant was an extremely costly and technically complicated task. Aid seemed indispensable.[6] At the end of 1954 the French had asked for British technology for constructing a plant. The British had wanted to make a deal; the *quid pro quo* would be the sale of reactors to France. In February 1955, the British had to tell the French, however, that agreement was not possible because the Americans had opposed it with reference to Anglo-American agreements.[7]

The third problem was that uranium supply was not entirely assured. France had located substantial deposits in metropolitan France and African territories during a decade of prospecting efforts. It seemed uncertain, however, whether France could be independent in the long run if both a civil and a military programme were to be launched. It presupposed that the French Union could be kept under control, but the prospects for this were uncertain - the Algerian war had started. Most of the US and British supply up to then had come from the Belgian Congo and had gone to the nuclear armament under secret agreements between them and Belgium.

Negotiations about a new US-Belgian agreement were underway since the autumn of 1954. Thus one of the Six, Belgium, was thought to hold the key to an increased supply of cheap uranium, provided that the US gave its consent to Belgian deliveries to other parties.

The French Government and military establishment continued to favour a degree of Europeanism in the field. The *Comité de défense nationale*, a group gathering the most important ministers and the top military echelon, made fundamental decisions about French nuclear policy and European cooperation at two meetings at the end of March. Some of the military participants were against an immediate decision to procure nuclear weapons because France could not afford to do so simultaneously with keeping control over the French overseas territories by means of conventional weapons. The material submitted to the first meeting proposed that it should be decided to manufacture a small annual number of A-bombs within five or six years, using the plutonium produced in the reactor programme, that thermonuclear weapons on the basis of the initial effort would possibly follow, and that the decision would be kept secret for at least two years. No agreement could be reached, however. Several objections were raised at the second meeting. It was argued that France could not realize this alone, there were not enough technicians, and there was great reluctance among the actual technical staff to work for this objective. The 'European option' was discussed. Prime Minister Faure suggested 'that the possibility should be studied of a European experiment in which Germany could not question our leadership'. The conclusion of the meeting was not precise. It was decided, however, to construct two prototypes of nuclear submarines (one fuelled with natural and one with enriched uranium), to develop the infrastructure at an accelerated pace and to postpone the A-bomb decision 'because of the necessity of having first established the requisite infrastructure and the difficulty of maintaining secrecy'. The Foreign Secretary, Antoine Pinay, was charged with establishing the necessary contacts 'with a view to creating a European organisation for atomic energy' and the Minister in charge of atomic matters, Gaston Palewski, with coordinating the technical aspect of the negotiations.[8]

Thus, the *Comité* brought the national option a step further toward realization, even though it was considered prudent not to announce this to the world yet. New funds were allocated to the CEA and the Ministry of Defence. It was decided that negotiations for a European organization for atomic energy would be started. Other European states, notably the Federal Republic, would be formally approached and asked to participate and make financial and technical-scientific contributions.

Different interpretations may be made of whether a movement towards some kind of European military option was seen as a possibility, but it was apparently considered by some in the *Comité*, including the Prime Minister.[9] It is evident that it was not primarily the civil potential of atomic energy that was in the minds of French decision-makers, although this motive was also present. The most basic motive was to use the nuclear ´integration track´ to maintain and even increase French military superiority relative to Germany. A year later, the French chief negotiator, Maurice Faure, expressed the fundamental reason for wanting Euratom in the shortest possible way in talks with the British:

> ...if there were no Euratom, the Americans would have to make a bilateral treaty with Germany. Germany had already been allowed to have an army. With a powerful atomic industry she would have the fundamental elements of nationalism.[10]

To the meeting between Adenauer and Pinay in Bonn on 29-30 April Pinay submitted a memorandum about French ideas for European cooperation. This ´Pinay plan´ outlined a kind of confederation with harmonization in certain areas and a permanent diplomatic conference as an implementing organ; other OEEC members would be allowed to join. Thus, the French Government indicated preference for cooperation without supranationality in a context larger than the Six, and the main focus was on cooperation at the political level.[11]

Adenauer outlined his views about measures for further integration. The ECSC might be given certain new competences. Two complexes seemed propitious for treatment, the issue of peaceful uses of atomic energy, and communications. Adenauer also raised the question of German-French cooperation in the aircraft industry and pointed out that Mendès France had proposed this. Pinay stressed cooperation in the nuclear field. He declared himself to be in favour of a new European institution in the areas of communications and atomic energy but this cooperation should not take place within the framework of the ECSC. A separation from the ECSC would have the advantage that it would be easier for states other than the Six, notably Britain, to participate.[12]

Negotiations were carried out in parallel at the level of officials. The French side proposed, among other things, cooperation on enrichment between France, the Federal Republic and Belgium. There was no German reaction.[13]

The communiqué from the meeting pointed to the sectoral way as preferable for giving a new impulse to European cooperation. The role of atomic energy was singled out as particularly important.[14] Thus, it was now a public fact that there was a Franco-German understanding about atomic energy as a priority area for further European efforts. A *Quai d´Orsay* memorandum sketched the kind of nuclear cooperation that the French Government was striving for. Cooperation would be intergovernmental and not limited to the Six, each country would be free to carry out purely national activities, the members would grant one another free mutual access to their raw material resources, and a special agreement might perhaps be concluded between France, Germany and Belgium for the creation of a common industry for enrichment.[15]

In the Federal Republic, forces working for different models of cooperation and integration were forming. One was a 'political' group led by the Chancellor and the new Foreign Minister, Heinrich von Brentano, and Under Secretary Walter Hallstein. This group supported Monnet's concept of Six state sectoral integration that would spread to other sectors of the economies and later give the impulse to more comprehensive European integration.

There were two 'economic' groups within the Ministry of Economics. One was led by the Minister, Ludwig Erhard. It was backed by the continentally and globally competitive sectors of industry, which was the larger part. The group opposed sectoral integration projects and projects that were limited to the Six. It favoured general economic cooperation on an intergovernmental basis, as little intervention in the market mechanism as possible, and gradual liberalization of the economy within the broad frameworks of the OEEC and the GATT. It wished to develop trade relations with Britain first of all. It opposed supranational institutions, arguing that they were tainted with French *dirigisme* and ideas from plan-economic thinking.[16] Another group was likewise critical of the sectoral integration method but favoured general economic integration among the Six in a customs union equipped with supranational institutions. A Common Market would come first and be the basis of further liberalization in a larger regional and global context. The spearhead for this group was Hans von der Groeben. This tendency was supported by a smaller part of industry consisting of smaller firms and sectors vulnerable to competion from Scandinavia or Britain. It also had some potential support from agriculture, which enjoyed high protection and price support on certain products, although the attitude was cautious and ambivalent.[17]

The policy of the Erhard group was forcefully supported by the dynamic CSU-leader Franz-Josef Strauss (appointed Minister of Atomic Affairs in the autumn) but for different reasons. Strauss' motives were basically political. He opposed a Six-state supranational construct that would restrict German freedom to have access to nuclear weapons in the future (although not in a national but in a European framework).[18]

The differences were provisionally thrashed out before the Messina Conference. The essence of the compromise was that the concept of a Common Market with a customs union as the core, as advocated by the von der Groeben group, was accepted or at least not directly opposed. The 'sectoralists' of the *Auswärtiges Amt* adopted this course. The Erhard group reluctantly acquiesced.[19]

The resulting German memorandum to the Messina Conference was diffuse on several points but clearly in favour of the principle of general, as opposed to sectoral, economic integration, even if some sectoral areas were mentioned, in not very forceful terms, as areas for further study. The commitment to integration in the atomic energy sector was however strong; the communiqué from the Adenauer/Pinay meeting was referred to.[20]

At the Messina Conference on 1-3 June 1955 the sectoral and general economic lines of thought were brought together and presented as two parallel roads to the future.

The Federal Republic, Italy and the Benelux countries were all in favour of the Common Market idea and they also supported the possibility of sectoral integration. The German delegation expressed reluctance to create new sectoral communities except in the field of atomic energy, on which the ideas in the Benelux memorandum were supported without reserve. Pinay talked about the urgency of cooperation on atomic energy and initially opposed general economic integration. After having been pressed in overnight negotiations he declared, however, that France agreed to study such a project provided that certain problems that were particularly important to France were examined, mainly the methods of attaining a common tariff level, the harmonization of social charges, the creation of an investment fund for compensating disadvantaged areas, and the coordination of monetary policy. France requested that the studies should not commit the governments; the objective was not to elaborate treaties.[21]

The resolution from the Messina Conference stated, first, that the communication and energy sectors would be studied. Civil atomic energy was described in exaggerated and propagandistic terms as particularly important. Second, it was recognized that a European market, achieved in stages, was the objective in the field of economic policy. A number of harmonization measures and compensatory mechanisms related to such a market were outlined.[22]

During the summer of 1955, the Intergovernmental Committee under the chairmanship of Spaak ('the Spaak Committee') was organized. The negotiations took place in Brussels, much of them in two subgroups, one for the Common Market and one for Euratom (as the envisaged 'pool' for atomic energy was baptized; the other sectoral possibilities disappeared at an early stage). Britain participated initially, represented only by a medium-rank official.

The French and German negotiating positions were defined in the course of the summer.

American reports indicated that the French strived for incorporating the uranium from Belgian Congo in an atomic pool, and that they wanted scientific-technical information from the US to be given to such a pool, not to individual countries. The argument about uranium was that everyone should contribute according to ability; France had made big investments in research, Belgium could contribute uranium.[23]

A new US-British-Belgian uranium agreement, replacing the war-time one, was concluded at this time. In the new agreement most of the uranium would still go to the US and Britain for the period up to 1960, but Belgium could retain minor proportions of the production for civil purposes.[24] Thus, the US and the UK preserved their legal control of the Belgian uranium. The US had - with British consent - the opportunity to release it or not to release it in order to use it as a card in the European integration game. The Belgians assured US officials that they were not interested in Euratom alone and that they wished to do nothing in the field which would not have American approval.[25] Spaak regarded the Belgian uranium as an important factor in the coming negotiations. It was reported that he adopted the possession of uranium as his 'trump card' in the negotiations about Euratom, and the Common Market as well. This card would enable Belgium to become the 'catalyst' of general European integration. Spaak told the Americans that he would take an extremely defensive position, 'offering nothing, making no suggestions', until such time as the French particularly made clear their intentions. In doing this he wanted US cooperation in allowing him to choose the time and the framework for a request to the US for technical advice, or for a possible renegotiation of the agreement with Belgium. He felt that only in this way could he play this trump card with maximum effect.[26]

The main principles in the French memorandum that was delivered to the nuclear subgroup in Brussels were (1) supranationalism, but only partially (2) a common fuel system (with equal conditions of price and access for all members), and (3) common installations (among them an enrichment plant). The military question was bypassed in silence, except for a reference to the proposal that technical-scientific information should be exchanged in certain areas, but not concerning military studies and programmes.[27]

The French initial position in Brussels may be summed up as a demand for supranational restrictions on Germany, financial and technical contributions from the other Five, Belgian contributions of uranium to reinforce security of supply, and freedom of action for France in the military field and largely in the civil field also. The dominant underlying theme was to improve the future French relative position with respect to Germany and Britain.[28] The British commented sceptically: '...if there is one thing more certain than another it is that the French have no chance of securing parity with the United Kingdom in any nuclear arrangement because we are so far ahead of them, and because we do not so much care if Germany develops nuclear energy without special controls'[29]...'M. Palewski is seeking to secure two irreconcilable ends - a measure of control over a sovereign Germany, and full liberty of action for France'.[30]

The Germans presented a memorandum to the nuclear subgroup at the same time. The paper was very non-committal. The memorandum did not make definite proposals but opened up for the possibility of supranational developments in certain areas. It was apparently a compromise between pro-Euratom and anti-Euratom forces in the Federal Republic.[31]

The Early US Attitude to the Plans for a *relance européenne*

The principles agreed to in the Randall Report in early 1954[32] were the framework for the US attitude to general economic integration in Europe. The compromises in that report implied acceptance of regionalism while waiting for multilateralism, provided that the regional arrangement was reasonably compatible with the GATT principles and that a movement toward multilateralism could be foreseen. It also implied some sacrificing of short-run American economic interests in order to promote political goals, such as keeping up the momentum toward integration in Europe. After a decade of unchallenged US economic superiority the possible disadvantages of a common tariff barrier and a common trade policy in continental Europe were seen as bearable.[33]

The latter problematic took concrete shape in the spring of 1955. The US steel industry was demanding limitation of the export of American scrap iron to Europe. The European steel industry had grown remarkably since the establishment of the European Coal and Steel Community. The supply of European scrap iron to the industry was insufficient, the steel producers under ECSC authority imported increasingly from the US. This caused a price rise on the American market and increased the production costs of the US steel producers. The criticism by American steel interests of the restrictive practices of the ECSC was mounting. It was the first real conflict of economic interest since the foundation of the ECSC. The Chairman of the Council on Foreign Economic Policy wrote a memorandum to the State Departement complaining about the cartel practices of the ECSC and questioning American support for the Community. The State Department explained that it was against a change of US policy toward the ECSC because of the importance of the Community for the European integration process. Even if some restrictive practices remained, the ECSC was developing in the right direction, the Department argued. Simultaneously, Monnet, still ECSC President, offered to freeze the European import of scrap iron at the existing level. The political arguments of the State Department eventually prevailed. The Council on Foreign Economic Policy recommended in April that the existing commercial policy toward the ECSC should be maintained. After several months of negotiations between the State Department and the Department of Commerce the latter accepted that no export controls for scrap iron would be introduced for the time being.[34]

In the months after the Paris Accords Dulles was not inclined to deviate from his traditional concentration on the goal of supranational integration among the Six. The alternative of giving priority to the British strategy of developing the WEU and intergovernmental cooperation in the OEEC did not seem attractive to him. He favoured both the sectoral and the general economic paths toward supranationalism in principle, although he believed that the latter was more difficult and unlikely to be accepted in the short run. It was not yet time to take an official position on the plans for the *relance europénne*, however. Monnet reported that the governments of the Six, including the French, appeared willing to take further steps towards creating a united Europe, but warned Washington against interfering for the time being. He feared that 'any U.S. involvement with the Foreign Offices might have unfavourable effects'.[35] Internally, Dulles declared after the Messina Conference that he still backed European strongly, and he 'thought that in general the Benelux approach was probably the soundest; that in the main I would be disposed to support their initiative'.[36] He sent a telegram to Monnet's successor as President of the ECSC, René Mayer, assuring him that President Eisenhower saw the ECSC 'as the most hopeful and constructive development so far towards the economic and political integration of Europe'.[37]

The European countries were awaiting an official expression of Washington's position. The first response was prepared there. When the US representative to the ECSC, Robert Eisenberg, evaluated the prospects for the coming negotiations. Eisenberg recommended the sectoral approach as the right one for the time being. He estimated that the interested officials in the six countries felt that real progress toward integration could be expected only in the field of atomic energy. Several of them considered the Common Market to be a 'pretty nebulous project'. So many problems about harmonization, and so on, were listed in the Messina resolution that the negotiations could be expected to take a considerable time. It was not believed that the United Kingdom would participate in any closer form than that of an association. Cooperation on atomic energy might be possible, even if there was some doubt as to whether the French were ready to agree to the creation of a European authority. The success of the plan to create a Community for atomic energy depended, in Eisenberg's view, to a large extent on the attitude of the United States, because of its leading role, and the existence of the US-Belgian agreement and of other bilateral agreements: 'It is believed that the United States could kill the new integration plan outright if we insist on making bilateral agreements with each of the six countries'. Eisenberg warned against taking a position that might be interpreted as rejection of the atomic pool idea; the US should make clear that 'we have an open mind'.[38]

In Washington, there was a split between the views of the 'generalists' of the State Department, on the one side, and the 'nuclear specialists' there and in the Atomic Energy Commission, on the other. The AEC was already on its way to making bilateral nuclear agreements with a number of countries in cooperation with the American nuclear industry under the 'Atoms for Peace' programme. A supranational construct in Europe was considered problematic and disturbing.

Merchant wrote a memorandum for Dulles favouring, in the same vein as Eisenberg, a preliminarily positive attitude to the Atomic Pool idea. In Merchant's view the US had three kinds of interests in the matter: to revive European integration and to support the ECSC, to forge a new link between Germany and the West, and to permit the Europeans to make the best use of their inadequate resources in the field. He recommended that 'we treat a European common atomic authority modelled on the Schuman Plan in the same way as we treat a national state'. He also asked for authorization to discuss with the AEC the possibility of transferring to a pool the arrangements in the US-Belgian bilateral, and delaying new bilateral arrangements pending further developments in the negotiations in Europe. The memorandum focused entirely on the Atomic Pool; the Common Market was not mentioned.[39] The official in charge of atomic energy affairs, Gerard C. Smith, reacted instantly. He wrote that he did not concur with Merchant's recommendations; neither did the AEC. The Belgian uranium was needed in the US. The US should not support the Atomic Pool idea, even in principle, until it was sure that such integration was practical and desired by the European countries, and that the US was in a position to cooperate with such an authority.[40]

Dulles decided essentially in favour of Merchant's views. His decision governed American policy until it was substituted by a more explicit policy of support, endorsed by the President, for Euratom and the Common Market at the end of the year. The principles that Dulles proclaimed were: expressing officially an encouraging but unspecific attitude to supranational integration, envisaging the treatment of an Atomic Pool (it was increasingly called 'the European Atomic Energy Community' – 'Euratom') as a state, and brandishing the possibility of release of the Belgian uranium from the Anglo-American bonds. With respect to the bilaterals, he outlined a policy of balancing between making deals with individual countries - thinking primarily of the Federal Republic and France, of course - and at the same time with the Six as a group, and of using the bilaterals as a means of promoting integration.[41]

It was acknowledged in the State Department that the US position would be decisive for the success or breakdown of the negotiations about Euratom. By making bilateral agreements within the Atoms for Peace framework with either Germany or France and granting special favours to any of them, particularly with respect to enriched uranium, the US could wreck nuclear integration and possibly the Common Market negotiations also. In particular, it was certain that a 'power bilateral'[42] with Germany would torpedo Euratom. Conversely, by declaring that the US would also - in various degrees or exclusively - cooperate with Euratom, the US possessed a powerful instrument for increasing the chances of agreement. Germany, having no access to raw materials or fissile materials, was dependent on US assistance for many years to come. The actual German nuclear status was modest because of earlier restrictions. The Department was well aware of possibilities and contradictions in the relationship between bilateralism and promotion of European integration. The point of departure was, as expressed in a PPS memorandum, that the 'US might be well advised to refrain from additional bilateral agreements with any of the Six - as with Germany - until European ideas on nuclear integration have begun to crystallize, and adapt future agreements to the requirements of European nuclear organization'. A problem was that the powerful AEC and the infant American nuclear industry favoured bilateral arrangements and looked with scepticism on Euratom. Another problem was that the Atomic Energy Act of 1954 had not been framed with an eye to the question of joint international development.[43]

The German choice of path after having regained sovereignty was a cause of concern in Washington. Dulles wanted to ascertain whether the Germans had become less interested in his concept of integration. He met Adenauer in May when the Federal Republic participated in a meeting of the NATO Council for the first time. Dulles told Adenauer that the Western European Union was not sufficient and could not be an end-point of the unification process. If there were a standstill only a movement backwards could be expected. Adenauer expressed no clear preference between the Seven- or Six-state model, but seemed inclined to favour the latter. He assured Dulles that the Federal Republic would do all in its power to promote efforts toward integration.[44] At their next meeting - when Adenauer visited Washington after Messina - Dulles said that there had recently been a 'slight feeling' in Washington that the Chancellor's feelings about integration might have altered. In Dulles's view 'such concepts as the Coal and Steel Community were good and should be held on to'. Adenauer expressed full agreement.[45] Between these encounters Dulles also saw Ludwig Erhard and talked about his fears of a decline of interest in Germany. Erhard, while admitting in general terms the importance of unification, made his critical attitude to sectoralism clear. He questioned the method that had been followed in the ECSC and argued that the ECSC had not been intended to stand alone but to be combined with the EDC and other combinations.[46]

The 'political' group around the Chancellor and the 'economic' groups argued their cases in contacts with the Americans during the summer and autumn. Some examples may be given:

Soon after Messina, officials within the *Auswärtiges Amt* were emphatic about the necessity of American assistance to a supranational community for atomic energy. They did not believe that its competence should be added to the ECSC but be organized separately from but closely connected with the ECSC. Bilateral US-German agreements should be avoided. There existed a nationalist sentiment in West Germany, they said, which favoured conclusion of a bilateral agreement with the US and the undertaking of national projects in the field. This would be 'disastrous' and would 'leave the way open to a Soviet offer of a similar agreement'.[47]

Before the arrival of the Foreign Minister, von Brentano, in Washington in September it was expected that he would ask for negotiations about a 'power bilateral'. Merchant suggested delay without saying no. [48] However, von Brentano did not ask for a bilateral but insisted 'that it would be particularly helpful if the United States made it unmistakeably clear that it was interested in pooling atomic energy in Europe. If it were made known that future support of the United States depended on continued progress toward integration, this would provide a most useful support'.[49] Back in Bonn, von Brentano reported to the Cabinet that Dulles had told him that the US attached great importance to the continuation of European integration, and that 'this also applied particularly to a European solution of the nuclear question'.[50]

The industrial interests and Erhard's Ministry of Economics were coordinating their opposition to Euratom in the Brussels negotiations.[51] The US was also approached. An industrial delegation met officials from the State Department and the AEC in Washington. Its spokesman, Alexander Menne, said that he also represented the views of the Minister for Atomic Energy, F.-J. Strauss. He stated that industry had come to the conclusion 'that it was in Germany's best interest to establish a program on a bilateral basis with the United States'. However, 'radiation'[52] activities should be on a European basis as well as general research activity. Germany wanted nuclear materials and information from the US, and wanted to develop power reactors in cooperation with the US. He alluded to the alternative of cooperating with Britain; the British had envisaged that a bilateral agreement could be ready for consideration 'within a matter of weeks'. The AEC representative gave some support to the German views by indicating that the AEC was prepared to discuss a 'power bilateral' any time, a 'research bilateral' was however viewed as the first step. [53]

The *Auswärtiges Amt* tried to undermine the offensive by industry and the Erhard/Strauss' group in favour of bilateralism, by requesting American help to counter it. Ophüls asked the US Brussels Ambassador to recommend that the US Government let it be known that German industrialists would gain no advantage through a bilateral agreement with the US, that could not be had through participation in a pool.[54]

Dulles decided that the Germans should be told that it was too early to undertake any specific commitments until more had been decided about the content of Euratom. However, the US did not wish to see the Germans use any alleged US preference for bilateralism as a reason to prevent atomic integration arrangements. The intention to cooperate with Euratom should be explained to them. [55] A memorandum was delivered to von Brentano. It stated that the prevailing uncertainty regarding the US attitude might have a discouraging effect on Euratom. Although it was not possible to decide about US support until the Europeans themselves had agreed about the construction of the organization, the Executive Branch was prepared to seek Congressional approval for cooperation with it provided that the US judged it as 'possessing sovereign responsibility and authority' and as a contribution to a 'stronger and prospering Europe through integration'.[56] The Germans were also informed that a power bilateral could 'not be negotiated quickly'.[57]

The message that had been transmitted to the negotiating countries in Brussels was, then: (1) the Executive Branch was prepared to cooperate directly with Euratom, not just bilaterally with other countries, provided that it were sufficiently supranational, and (2) bilateral deals were suspended for the time being but would be resumed later.

French officials were very pleased with the American declaration. Dillon judged that it was bound to have positive repercussions in France 'far beyond atomic energy alone' and would be very helpful in the negotiations.[58]

Dulles' clarification had been made, it was explained internally, because the German industrialists and their supporters in the ministries had been 'spreading the word around' that the US preferred bilateral agreements to making arrangements with Euratom. This was understandable because the AEC people had said so to people 'all over Europe' in the summer. The 'first and main purpose' of the clarification 'was to align AEC squarely with the Department in this policy'.[59]

American industrial interests had also given Germans good reason to believe in bilateralism. A principal cause of the German reluctance to proceed in Brussels, it was reported, was assurances given by U.S. industrial firms to German industry about their ability to provide the Germans with what was necessary to get ahead with peaceful exploitation. Certain American industrialists had been particularly active.[60]

In sum, a transnational alliance for and against priority for US-German bilateralism in the nuclear field was forming. The standpoints of German industry, Erhard and F.-J. Strauss were supported by sectors of American industry which hoped to use continental Western Europe as a testing-ground for development of civil nuclear power, to conquer the market there and outdistance Britain. Germany, which lagged ten years behind, was the obvious first target. American power reactors would be introduced in the Federal Republic with as little state intervention and supranational steering as possible. The AEC supported bilateralism because it identified with the Atoms for Peace programme of launching civil nuclear power globally, and because it had close ties to the industry. Adversaries of priority for US-German bilateralism included those for whom the movement toward integration, non-proliferation, or political motives generally, were important, the State Department and the *Auswärtiges Amt*. Neither the State Department nor German integrationists wanted supranationalism only, both sides wanted to keep the possibility of bilateral deals. The attitude was similar to the earlier position on the issue of WEU steering of US military aid; such steering had been stubbornly refused.

The alliance against US-German bilateralism of course included France. France was anxious to prevent it, but a complete channelling of cooperation through Euratom was not desirable from the point of view of the majority in France. The French did not want that much supranationalism - if so, France would also be tied.

Models for Euratom at the End of 1955

In the Brussels negotiations, the various subgroups - on the Common Market, on nuclear energy and a couple of other areas - presented their reports at the end of October and the beginning of November. They were not definite proposals but summarized possibilities and made certain suggestions. There was some degree of understanding about principles for a Common Market but open disunity about Euratom.[61]

The proposal of the nuclear subgroup under the chairmanship of Louis Armand has been called 'the Armand concept'.[62] The two key suggestions were a system for Euratom monopoly on procurement and supply of fissile materials, and a system for financing of big industrial installations, notably an enrichment plant. An enrichment plant was described as fundamental for guaranteeing the possibility of independence in every atomic programme. It was important to start with it immediately, perhaps with broader participation than by the Six, without waiting for final agreement on Euratom, because enriched uranium would probably have an essential role during a relatively limited period only. The report conjectured optimistically that the US and Britain would be prepared to aid in the construction of a plant.[63]

The perspective of the report was the role of nuclear power in solving Europe's energy problem and the dependence on imported oil. The question of military uses of atomic energy and the intertwined civil-military relationships was not mentioned directly, although this was the primary factor behind the proposal for a fuel monopoly. The silence on this question - which was present in the minds of all concerned – reflected a wish not to disturb public opinion in the prospective member states.

With respect to the military question the implication of the 'Armand concept' was that manufacture of nuclear weapons in a national sector outside the community would be possible for France, while the Federal Republic would be legally bound by Adenauer's *Kernwaffenverzicht* to the WEU and materially checked by WEU's control system, by the fuel monopoly of the Community and the actual lack of raw material production in the Federal Republic. The enrichment plant wanted by France would be financed mainly by other European states. There was no proposal that Euratom should have exclusively peaceful purposes. Thus, the 'Armand concept´ also implied that nothing would prevent Euratom from becoming the point of departure for a European nuclear force.

The fuel monopoly also had another function from the French point of view. It would ensure that the Federal Republic would not outdistance France in the civil nuclear field through bilateral deals with the United States whilst France concentrated its scarce resources on the development of nuclear weapons.[64]

During the negotiations the German delegation had taken strong exception to Armand´s proposal regarding the supranational powers of Euratom. In particular, the granting of powers to allocate fissile materials had been opposed. In the end, the German delegation reserved its position on the Armand report.

Spaak went to the *Auswärtiges Amt* to protest about the German position. The key of the Brussels plan was the Euratom monopoly on procurement and supply of fissile materials, he said. The control of fissile materials was absolutely necessary and he regarded it as very important that Europe itself organized this control in friendship with the US. It was impossible at the actual time to proceed without the US because the US disposed of the sources of raw material; if the Federal Republic rejected Euratom it would be necessary to make a bilateral agreement with the US for supplies. Control would in such case be requested. It was also impossible for a single European country to build an enrichment plant alone and unaided. Belgium had bilateral agreements with the US and Britain about its uranium but could produce enough uranium to supply the European needs. Spaak was very critical of the German attitude to Euratom. It had caused a weakening of the French willingness to integrate. It was particularly bad if it was Germany which hesitated to choose the European road in the atomic field - such hesitation could only foster distrust and suspicions:

> It led in particular to reactions in France. It must be remembered that in London and Paris the French had not made clear whether they wanted to renounce the military use of nuclear energy. They certainly did not want it as a matter of prestige. But it is clear that the USA will not be prepared to release more Uranium 235 if they have any suspicion that this material might in France be destined for the production of nuclear weapons. Therefore all reservations of that kind are particularly damaging. The German reluctance looks like a rejection of control.

Von Brentano and Hallstein assured Spaak that they agreed in principle. Some time was needed internally, however, to clear up these things with industry. Germany was willing to be controlled, the resistance had other causes. There were also the tactical problems about the linkage (the German word *´Junktim´* was increasingly used in the negotiations about the twin projects, and will also be used here) between Euratom and the Common

Market, and the risk that the OEEC was presented as an alternative that would function as a rallying point for the anti-Euratom forces.[65]

It should be noted that Spaak used his 'trump card', the Belgian uranium, in his efforts at persuasion in Bonn. He saw it as part of the control arsenal that could forestall the German national nuclear weapons option. F.-J. Strauss complained to the British Ambassador in Bonn that he did not appreciate this 'rather hectoring attitude'. Strauss had 'got the impression that Spaak's main concern was that unless Germany joined Euratom they could expect to get no uranium from Belgian sources really to ensure that Germany did not embark on a military atomic programme. If this was really so and Spaak did not trust the assurances to the contrary given by the Chancellor, then, said Strauss, the proper thing was to ask the WEU to take the necessary supervisory measures to control German atomic activities'.[66]

The 'trump card' had however at this time lost much of its value, and Spaak knew it. The demand that Belgium should contribute its uranium to Euratom was accorded considerably less emphasis in French statements as time went by. A month earlier, a Belgian negotiator in Brussels had told the Americans that the information that had been released at the big atomic energy conference in Geneva in August had changed the picture: 'The Belgians would still like to use their uranium resources as a lever to nuclear achieve integration in this field, but since the Geneva conference on atomic energy they realized that their special position as one of the few countries with large supplies of raw materials was weakened'.[67]

British Policy toward Euratom

The Common Market aspect of the British attitude toward the integration negotiations in Brussels has been investigated thoroughly.[68] The nuclear aspect has been less studied.[69] The main theme of British policy for nuclear cooperation in Europe was - as for the Common Market negotiations - to try to steer the process toward the broader intergovernmental framework of the OEEC. Britain sponsored the less far-reaching proposals of the OEEC working party on nuclear energy that was set up in June 1955, shortly after the Messina Conference. Internally, the possibilities of a coalition with either France or Germany, or both, for building peaceful nuclear energy in Western Europe under British leadership were discussed. Britain had important commercial interests in the field. It was hoped that the British reactor type, based on natural uranium, would become the dominant technology for production of nuclear power in the future. Western Europe was the big prospective export market. It was an inescapable problem, however, that the British technology which had been developed with the dual purpose of producing electric power and plutonium for weapons was by definition a technology which made proliferation easier. The civil-military contradictions in British nuclear foreign policy were many, and the choices in the area were restricted by both the general and the nuclear special relationship with the US. It was in the British interest that the German *Kernwaffenverzicht* was controlled, that the French did not develop national nuclear weapons, and that no Franco-German nuclear axis were formed. In the first two respects British goals coincided largely with those of the US. However, while the Americans believed that supranationalism was necessary in order to ensure a really effective control, the British expressed a more sanguine view and argued that sufficient control could be obtained by other means.

In the autumn, while the positions within Armand´s subgroup of the Spaak Committee were being clarified, alternative nuclear combinations were explored by Britain, France and the Federal Republic. The enrichment issue was at the centre of these discussions. The French *Commissariat à l énergie atomique* asked the British in October to meet the material requirements of enriched uranium and other things for the ambitious French expansion plans. For the British this proposal had attractive features. It was feared that the French would consider building a joint Franco-German plant if Britain refused to build a plant in France. It was further felt that the US would step in to fill the void left by British inability (Britain had only a small plant) or unwillingness to supply France with enriched uranium. Therefore, Britain could lose potential atomic energy business with France and Europe. The possibility of preventing an emerging Franco-German nuclear relationship by approaching Germany was also under consideration. UKAEA felt that there were ´strong political (and indirectly commercial) reasons for desiring a close United Kingdom/German association in atomic energy development. We are unlikely to get this if the French and Germans have ganged up beforehand´.[70] The tactic was obviously to ally with Erhard, Strauss and German industry to prevent the emergence of Euratom.

The British Paris Ambassador, Sir Gladwyn Jebb, advised an initiative in the enrichment matter to support the OEEC in order to prevent the Six from slipping into neutralization or the ´Third Force´ trap. In Jebb´s view, Britain could induce the Six to agree to an OEEC solution if Britain was willing to make a major material contribution to an OEEC material organization.[71] The Foreign Office believed that all doors should be kept open and no engagements made while waiting for the American standpoint and hopefully the breakdown of the entire Messina venture.[72]

The Foreign Office instructed the Embassy in Washington to raise the issue of British assistance with the State Department and added that Britain itself would probably not make use of a European enrichment plant, ´we would prefer a joint venture with a Commonwealth country but please do not mention this to the Americans´.[73] The Ambassador, Sir Roger Makins, stressed that the matter was ´extremely delicate´; not the slightest hint of this possibility should be given to the OEEC until the British and the Americans were in complete agreement in advance.[74]

The British top advisory body for nuclear issues, the Official Committee on Atomic Energy, discussed the Brussels negotiations in order to make a recommendation to the Cabinet about participation or non-participation in Euratom. Euratom was judged to be in the focus of interest in Brussels, and also as having prospects of success because of the importance attached to keeping some sort of military control over Germany. The Committee however did not see it as a British interest to participate in Euratom. The priorities were: first, collaboration with selected countries on the basis of bilateral agreements, second, collaboration with the whole of OEEC, third, collaboration with the Six only. The Foreign Office representative, Sir Harold Caccia, made the optimistic but unrealistic forecast that a British decision not to join Euratom might well kill the project:

> It was very likely that a clear statement at this juncture that we could not join it would discourage the other countries concerned from pressing ahead with it. If, at the same time, we were able to offer some form of collaboration in O.E.E.C., this might provide the final *coup de grace*. There was a division of opinion between political and industrial interests, particularly in Germany on the desirability of setting up a supra-national organisation such as Euratom, and it was by no means certain that such an organisation would emerge, even without discouragement from us. The French would certainly sabotage it if they felt confident of sufficient co-operation from ourselves.[75]

The Cabinet followed the line of the Committee. The main considerations regarding Euratom were that Britain could not join because the organization was too supranational, and because of the mixed military-civil nature of the British nuclear programme. Such a vital part of the military sector could not be put under international control. The UK should not join Euratom, but the impression should not be given that the UK would obstruct the emergence of the organization; if it came into existence some form of collaboration should be considered. Regarding an enrichment plant, further study was required. The US should be informed without delay.[76]

A few days after his journey to Bonn Spaak came to London to try to convince the British leadership about the necessity of Euratom. Spaak made it abundantly clear that his main preoccupation in the negotiations about Euratom was the German question and the control problem. From a control point of view the OEEC was not at all sufficient. Within the OEEC, countries limited their collaboration only to those bits of the field from which they were likely to derive direct benefit. Spaak doubted that the nuclear problem could be handled effectively if it were compartmentalized in the way envisaged by the OEEC. It was not easy to see how a satisfactory form of control could be evolved without some degree of supranationality and monopoly powers about nuclear fuels. Lately, he said, the Germans had become very reticent in the Brussels negotiations and had reserved their Government's position. This, he believed, reflected the growth of nationalism in Germany. The British interlocutors admitted that some method of regulating the use of fissile material was extremely important, 'and if M. Spaak's proposals for a European structure introduced a greater possibility of security, we should be benevolent in our attitude to the organization.'[77]

The British explained to the negotiating countries the British withdrawal from the Spaak Committee. In a memorandum of 17 November the considerations behind the withdrawal from the negotiations about Euratom were given. The main reason referred to was the intermingling of civil and military purposes in the British programme. The French answer was more or less an official confirmation of military intentions and the will to be placed at the same level as Britain. It was added that nothing indicated that the organization that was considered in Brussels would exclude bilateral cooperation between member countries and third countries[78] - obviously a reference to the possibility of a Franco-British axis, whether Euratom came into being or not.

As instructed, Makins contacted the State Departement to obtain the US views. He emphasized to Merhant the need for Britain and the US 'to keep in step', particularly regarding demands for construction of a European enrichment plant. [79] A month later, he met Merchant again. The British felt, he said, that the French interest in the Common Market was 'phoney'. The UK saw Euratom in a 'somewhat different light'. The UK was quite willing to engage in nuclear cooperation with individual countries, but if they should see fit to band together in a supranational community, he assumed that his Government would cooperate with it.[80]

An American answer to the questions about possible British assistance for European enrichment was not forthcoming. The US policy with respect to a European enrichment plant had not been decided yet; it was a subject of discussions in Washington in December 1955 and January 1956. The British questions were simply ignored.

The outcome of British deliberations about enrichment was that Britain should do nothing for the time being. The UKAEA recommended against meeting most of the French requests for aid. Representatives of the French CEA arrived in London on 2 December to make another attempt to obtain cooperation about enrichment. The Frenchmen were informed that Britain could not help, since enrichment technology was classified.[81]

American Policy Decisions and Implementation Analyses in the State Department

When the Federal Republic had reserved its position on the 'Armand concept', and Britain had decided to withdraw from the negotiations in Brussels, the moment for further clarification of American policy towards the European projects had come.

At the meeting of the National Security Council of 22 November Dulles expounded his current views on European integration. His reflections demonstrated more than ever that his integration philosophy had its tap roots in the 'German problem'. In the less threatening world situation after the Geneva Foreign Ministers conference, he said, the big problem was Germany. The US must be prepared to do everything that it could effectively do to develop integration; 'if there was to be no reunification of Germany in the foreseeable future, it was incumbent on the United States to provide the Federal Republic and its people with the strongest possible sense of their future close relationship with Western Europe'. Several roads could be followed. The most important one was NATO. It was the instrument which was most effective in holding Western Europe together. He said that he believed that the most important thing the US could do was 'to give the Federal Republic some sort of vested interest in NATO through the development of a West German military establishment which was integrated with the West'. The US 'must make use of this military magnet to attract and retain the Federal Republic in integration with the Free World. Accordingly it was perhaps of very great importance that the United States provide more information to the NATO powers on our new weapons'. However, the US must also seek to develop alternatives to NATO in case the fear of aggression and general war continued to decline, with the effect of lowering solidarity. Without mentioning Euratom and the Common Market directly, Dulles expressed support for unification by all suitable methods: 'Perhaps the Coal-Steel Community was an alternative which offered significant possibilities; but almost any instrumentality was desirable if its use could develop the European principle rather than the national principle'.[82]

The President endorsed these views in even stronger terms. He made a dedicated argument for European unification and referred to his own long-standing support for the cause. Actually, he said, Dulles rather underestimated the case he had made: 'The unity of Western Europe today...would solve the peace of the world. A solid power mass in Western Europe would ultimately attract to it all the Soviet satellites, and the threat to peace would disappear' Everybody present should in their public appearances stress the great advantages of a more closely united Europe - cultural, economic, moral and otherwise. He saw 'the desirability of developing in Western Europe a third great power bloc, after which development the United States would be permitted to sit back and relax somewhat'.[83]

In this way, Eisenhower painted a picture in which the emergence of Europe as a powerful force in world politics should not be viewed with concern by the US, but as a main objective of American policy. In his vision, the aim of the New Look strategy to combine military strength with economic stability would ultimately be fulfilled. It is uncertain, of course, how far Eisenhower thought that independence should go. It may be presumed that he did not imagine a fully independent bloc capable of policies directed against fundamental US interests, but a benign Atlantic Europe in continuing alliance with the US. He probably believed that the common value basis would prevent undesired antagonistic developments, and that the US had the capacity to maintain sufficient military and economic superiority to keep the reins firmly in its hands.

After the NSC meeting Dulles ordered the initiation within the State Department of a ´clear-cut program for policy guidance´ of the problem of atomic energy and European integration.[84] Several memoranda were written by officials.

J. Robert Schaetzel at Gerard Smith´s office made what he called ´a first attempt at isolating the factors relevant to a decision on Euratom´. The paper listed the main issues that later became topical in US policy toward Euratom, and made proposals for policy. It may be described as a ´maximalist´ State view, a view which by no means coincided with that of the Atomic Energy Commission. The memorandum concentrated on the political and military dimensions. US economic interests in the development of peaceful nuclear energy were not discussed, neither was the question of the linkage to the Common Market. The subjects treated were (1) the German question and the German nuclear military option, (2) the French option and the general non-proliferation problem, (3) the relationship between OEEC and Euratom (4) the relationship between IAEA and Euratom, (5) bilateralism vs. US deals with Euratom only, (6) enrichment and reprocessing, (7) the Belgian uranium, and (8) the control of scientific-technical information:

The German question was in focus in the memorandum. Among US objectives in supporting Euratom Schaetzel listed the binding of Germany to the West as the first one. The major immediate problem was the German attitude. US support for Euratom should be sufficiently strong and tangible to overcome the approach preferred by German industrialists. The attack on the Brussels approach led by Ludwig Erhard could not be dismissed as mere nationalism, it was rooted in *laissez faire* philosophy and the hopes of developing a tremendous export market as well as meeting the foreseeable urgent energy requirements. The German industrialists, and large segments in other countries, ´seem either unaware of or are uninterested in the dangerous weapons potentiality of nuclear energy´. However, a national German programme might become a threat in due time. Schaetzel pointed to the existence of uranium in East Germany. He sketched the possibility of cooperation between the Federal Republic and East Germany, and the risks in the event of reunification:

> The long-range implications for US and Western security of an independent, national German atomic energy program should be carefully considered. It is evident that such a program would be increasingly dominated by German industry with only nominal Government control.

The lack of domestic uranium or thorium resources will drive Germany to seek assured outside sources of supply. East Germany has low-grade but extensive uranium resources...This suggests the prospect of ad hoc interdependent relationships between West Germany and East Germany, with the West German industry becoming increasingly dependent on the raw material supply. On the hypothetical assumption of a united but possibly uncommitted Germany, 20 years or more hence, and given the predictable advances in nuclear technology, there is created a formidable military threat.

In addition to the German case there was the case of France and the general concern for proliferation. Schaetzel proposed that US support for Euratom should be sufficiently strong also to 'break down French resistance to further integration as well as their reluctance to renounce the right to undertake an independent weapons program'. The French support for supranationality was 'equivocal...varied and obscure', France had been unwilling to commit its entire programme to the Community approach, and had specifically reserved the right to produce weapons. This could be explained by the French nuclear superiority on the continent and by nationalism.

One of the means to forestall the German or French national options was deployment of US tactical weapons: 'The US should supply through NATO channels, and permit physical custody if necessary, tactical atomic weapons to the participating nations, thereby removing a major incentive to the development of independent nuclear weapons programs'.

A rationale of the existing American policy of 'lying low' with regard to support for Euratom vs. OEEC appears, in this paper, to be the desirability of having a fall-back position in case Euratom did not become sufficiently supranational: 'Should the participating nations of Euratom be unwilling to endow that organization with supranational authority and provide means for effective control and inspection, Euratom might be less deserving of support than the emerging OEEC program covering the same limited substantive ground, but including a larger number of countries'.

Schaetzel went on to comment on the relationship between Euratom and the planned International Atomic Energy Agency. He sketched Euratom as a regional control system within a larger future IAEA framework. It is worth observing that the perspective that would lead to the Non-Proliferation Treaty fifteen years later was already present:

On January 23 there will be held in Washington the first meeting of the 12-nation IAEA preparatory committee. In developing with AEC the US position regarding the agency the Department staff has adopted a major premise, subject to NSC approval, that the proposed Agency should be invested with substantial control responsibility. If this is to be done major US decisions will be required covering the following key issues, relevant not only to the Agency but to the US position regarding Euratom: accountability, control and inspection as major functions of the agency; the Agency to have either brokerage or operating responsibilities for the international movement of fissionable material for peaceful uses; bilateral agreements should be subordinate to the Agency; membership in the Agency should include a renunciation of intention to develop nuclear weapons by the nations not now having such capacity. - Euratom having the responsibilities and powers outlined above, assisted and supported by the US, would not only be consistent with the notion of a strong Agency, but each organization should draw strength from the other. Without loss of its independence or strength, Euratom can be pictured as a regional operating arm of the Agency in the restricted but vitally important field of accountability and inspection. A Euratom undertaking to renounce the intention to produce nuclear weapons should make more feasible a similar renunciation by the Agency members.

Schaetzel recommended an end to bilateralism; in his view no further bilateral agreements should be concluded with any of the participating nations. Further assistance should be given to Euratom, and the countries should be told that assistance received by Euratom would be greater than that which would have been received individually. The US faced the imminent prospect of a request from Germany for a research bilateral, and from France for a power bilateral, he wrote. While being intrinsically a routine first step, such a bilateral with Germany could be construed as an indication of the US preference for the bilateral approach, or as evidence that Germany would make the most rapid strides in the field by the bilateral route. As for the French demand for a power bilateral, the French had bowed to the US argument that security arrangements were not yet sufficiently tight and had requested a research bilateral instead, but with the provision that the US would supply an amount of enriched uranium that was 6-7 times larger[85] than the customary amount in other such agreements.

The strategic role of enrichment was emphasized. Schaetzel recommended that 'full use is made of the present dominant US position in nuclear technology and, most importantly, as supplier of enriched nuclear fuel (U-235), bearing in mind that this is a wasting asset'. Schaetzel did not suggest support for a joint European enrichment plant, but proposed that enriched material should be supplied to Euratom. The dual objective would be to discourage the development of Euratom enrichment plants and to give the support most apt to be decisive for the success of the Community. With respect to reprocessing plants, on the other side, the US should join with Euratom in the construction of such facilities.

A continued supply to the US of the necessary amounts of Belgian uranium was described as a basic security interest. If this condition was satisfied, however, quantities of uranium sufficient to meet Euratom´s requirements should be released, at the initiative of and with the consent of Belgium, and with the consent of the UK.

Release of large amounts of scientific-technical information was proposed. All power reactor technology should be declassified immediately upon establishment of Euratom so that full US-Euratom technological cooperation would be possible: 'The substantial and broad security advantages to the US in both the political and atomic energy fields of Euratom should fully compensate for whatever, if any, concessions would be involved in the declassification program'.

Schaetzel concluded that US support for Euratom should be conditional upon the strengthening of the concept that had been proposed by the nuclear subgroup in Brussels [the 'Armand concept'] in certain respects: (a) a sufficiently supranational Council of Commissioners (b) unequivocal ownership and/or control for Euratom of nuclear ores and fuels no less comprehensive than in the US system, (c) renunciation by the nations in the treaty of 'the right and intention to develop nuclear weapons, as proposed by Monnet', (d) treaty provisions for accountability and inspection, 'including a commitment that these functions will be performed by the IAEA if and when the Agency is established'.[86]

Other State Department papers focused on the strategic role of enrichment in US policy toward Euratom. Two were produced within Gerard Smith's office by Philip Farley and by Smith himself, and one by Robert Barnett of the Office of European Regional Affairs.

Farley departed from a premise which had been formulated by the National Security Council in the spring: 'U.S production capacities and efficiency in producing U-235 [enriched uranium] and, less importantly in producing heavy water and processing spent fuel elements, give the U.S. the ability to maintain a commanding international position in the atomic power field'.[87] He observed that there was a rising pressure in Europe for an enrichment plant for political rather than economic reasons. The motive was to achieve independence of outside sources. Farley outlined three possible courses of action for US policy. The first was to refuse cooperation. The second was to make a commitment to supply enriched uranium to sweeten a refusal to cooperate. Unless some such compensating move were made, a refusal would be likely to stimulate joint European action 'by confirming their suspicions that we intend to keep them dependent'. Cheap enriched uranium might be offered either directly or through the IAEA. The third possibility was to concur in and cooperate with a European project. If the Europeans went ahead regardless of the US attitude, this course might be necessary. A regional plant would then probably be less of a threat of diversion of the product for military purposes than a plant built by a single nation. Farley recommended the second course as being most in the US interests, with the third course as 'the best fall-back position in view of the probable impossibility of preventing the Europeans from going ahead if they can agree to do so'.[88]

Barnett's paper was an argument for the third possibility. It stated that as a consequence of the very rapid advances in declassification of information that had taken place in particular since the Geneva conference on peaceful atomic energy the US no longer occupied a monopolistic position in the field. Of the various forms for cooperation that were available to the US it was improbable that any except cooperation on the erection of enrichment plants could at that time constitute a US initiative which would fundamentally influence the form and purpose of European development in the atomic energy field. Barnett referred to the role which Britain's commitment to place troops on the continent had played for French acceptance of the WEU. This action - 'as no amount of moral encouragement or philosophical explanation could have done' - had made possible a change in Franco-German relations. The memorandum ended with the recommendation that the US should make available the know-how for, and financially assist, the establishment of enrichment facilities, for example in the Saar. The common institution of the Six, with sovereign authority, would administer the plant. The 'authority would enter into treaty relations with the United States which would give both parties assurance, through development of an effective system for control and inspection, that the product of these facilities' would be used for peaceful purposes only'.[89]

Gerard Smith protested immediately against the adoption of such a policy. He argued further along the lines of his collaborators Schaetzel and Farley, using both economic and military arguments:

> The suggested contribution of a uranium enrichment plant might well have the most political appeal of any offer we could make. At the same time, it is not entirely clear to me that it would be the most economic move for the Europeans, even assuming substantial U.S. financing. Enriched uranium from the very large U.S. plants whose costs are being amortized over the life of weapons programs should be much cheaper – unless [Barnett's] proposal contemplates large U.S. subsidy of Europe's power bill. Enrichment plants are terrific *consumers* of electric power which is in short supply in Europe and the imminent shortage of which is the basic reason for European interest in atomic energy. Moreover, such a plant would take years to build - with some chance that at the end of that period, enriched uranium will be less essential than now appears likely... Such a proposal would probably be the most difficult to sell within the U.S. Government because of sensitivity of the technology, which is directly associated with weapons production know-how, and the specter of possible Communist take-over of the plant. We would be making the Europeans independent of us and giving up our monopoly on marketable enriched uranium.

Smith went on to consider other, not mutually exclusive, possibilities. One was that the US and Britain might release a part of the Belgian uranium, and that the US would provide enrichment services for it. Another was that the US might help in construction of fuel fabrication or reprocessing plants; 'if these became the sole European facilities of their kind, they would be very useful control mechanisms (against illegal weapons activities) and would make the individual nations dependent on group facilities, thus tying the Europeans together in a practical way'. A third possibility was that the US agreed to the British request for UK construction of an enrichment plant in Europe.

Smith also referred to the IAEA. It was a complicating factor for US policy on Euratom that a policy review for the IAEA negotiations was going on. Any offer to Euratom should be consistent with ultimate US policy on the IAEA: 'Our present view is that Euratom should be a useful adjunct to the Agency and could carry out Agency control functions'.

Finally, Smith argued that the guidelines of the NSC November meeting were too vague to be useful as a leverage on the AEC, which he obviously regarded as the main obstacle to any State Department policy steered by long-range political considerations. A more specific presidential decision was required, he argued. The basic question was whether the US should be prepared to incur a large cost to obtain the political and security advantages of Euratom.[90]

Dulles' Personal Diplomacy in Europe

Dulles now started to demonstrate determined support for Six-state supranational integration, particularly with respect to atomic energy. While in Paris for the meeting of the NATO Council in mid-December Dulles communicated US views to European leaders and leading integrationists. He met, in turn, Macmillan, Monnet, Spaak and von Brentano.

His meeting with Macmillan was preceded by a letter responding to the British explanations of the withdrawal from Brussels. Dulles reiterated the 'double containment' motive behind American support for supranational integration. The Soviet threat was now political and economic rather than military. Germany strived for reunification, this might cause neutralism or even orientation to the East after Adenauer. The task was to tie Germany now so firmly to the West through a complex of institutions that this became unthinkable. Dulles declared that the Six-state approach gave the greatest hopes for creating strength and cohesion. He downgraded the risks of protectionism and 'Third Force' developments. The main argument of the letter was that the two trends for increased unity in Western Europe, the Six-state approach and the OEEC approach, were not conflicting. Dulles asked for British support for the American policy.[91]

At the meeting with Macmillan he continued along these lines. He stressed that President Eisenhower ´felt strongly about European integration in general and in the atomic field in particular´. The whole question ought to be discussed during Eden´s forthcoming visit to Washington. He declared that he understood the British policy of ´balance´. Macmillan´s response was conciliatory. He did not promise support but indicated that the UK would not actively oppose the Six-state plans for the time being, provided that no high-tariff area were constructed. In the case of the EDC Britain had possibly waited too long to make clear its attitude and now wished to avoid any possible future opprobrium by announcing its intentions with respect to the Common Market and Euratom. Dulles and Macmillan were in agreement that the integration of the Six ought not to be allowed to develop into a high tariff ´Zollverein´.[92]

In Dulles´ talk with Monnet the latter pointed to the obstacles in Germany and the problem of British policy. In Germany, the Chancellor needed a firmer US attitude of support for integration, instead of bilateralism, as a basis for overruling the objections of the industrialists with respect to Euratom. The British were actively engaged in trying to discourage further progress toward integration; their main target was the Common Market. The market project, according to Monnet, would take years, perhaps ten years to achieve. The Action Committee for the United States of Europe which Monnet had created concentrated on sectoral integration in the nuclear field in the belief that if it was added to the ECSC that would revive the integration movement. Then progress could be made toward the Common Market. Monnet hoped that Dulles would speak to the British at the time of Eden´s planned visit to Washington. Dulles said that the British had not spoken to him about the atomic Community but had done so about the Common Market. He would do what he could with the Germans and the British. The US would try to assist in the creation of Euratom.[93]

The German question was in focus during Dulles´ talk with Spaak. Both men were of the view that the current situation was a transient historical opportunity for taking effective steps toward *Einbindung* of Germany, although the French and the British unfortunately did not fully understand this. The reunification matter was not finished, Dulles argued. Even if the French might prefer a divided Germany, this attitude was unrealistic. It would be most dangerous if the Germans had nothing to occupy their minds while waiting for reunification. It was necessary to ´inject creative element´ into the situation; progress toward European unity could be that element. Spaak fully agreed and stated that Adenauer would need all support possible. Spaak was seriously concerned about the recent British ´strong offensive´ against the Common Market concept. It had been launched precisely because the British believed that the Brussels negotiations had a real chance to succeed. Dulles was also concerned about British policy. President Eisenhower´s opinion was, he said, that if Britain had given strong support to the EDC at an earlier time, the EDC would have been a success. British support had come too late: 'We don't want to see British mistake over EDC repeated'.

With respect to atomic energy, Spaak hoped that the US would indicate to the Germans that they would get greater benefits on a multilateral basis than on a bilateral. He told Dulles that Adenauer had assured him, when Spaak visited Bonn, that he would give strong instructions 'along the right lines' to Franz-Josef Strauss on this matter.[94]

At the last in the sequence of meetings Dulles talked with von Brentano. The Common Market was not discussed directly, only Euratom. Dulles gave assurances of preferential treatment, that is, of greater support for the Community approach than in bilateral dealings. He was frank about the non-proliferation motive in the American policy for Euratom. He said that he felt that 'community approach would help solve problem of controls of materials of weapons quality produced in process of producing energy'. Von Brentano criticized Britain, which had given opponents in Germany additional arguments, and declared that he was convinced that the OEEC could not provide the necessary basis for action in the nuclear field. Some other institution, 'not necessarily supranational in character', was needed. Brentano finally asked whether the US could demonstrate a clear preference for the Six-state approach. Dulles answered cautiously that 'he doubted whether US could go that far', possibly thinking of French allergy to American pressure. While the US 'could not exert pressure, it could use its influence'.[95]

Dulles reinforced his message to the Germans by sending a letter to Adenauer. He wrote that he was extremely pleased by Adenauer's assurance that he would participate in measures for integration, 'whether it was a matter of the future creation of a Common Market or of the Atomic Community'. He would talk to Eden next month, and he hoped that Adenauer trusted that the US was ready to adopt a benevolent attitude towards proposals for closer integration.[96]

Dulles reported to Eisenhower that his talks with von Brentano, Spaak and Monnet had all showed that the British were 'working hard to block the development of the European idea in terms of atomic energy and a common market'. This was somewhat in the same pattern as the early British opposition to the EDC. Dulles felt that the matter had to be discussed 'seriously' with Eden and Macmillan when they came to Washington.[97]

Dulles finalized his efforts by informing US missions of the views which he had communicated to the Europeans, dwelling mainly on the importance of the German question and the non-proliferation aspect of Euratom. He informed the missions that the question whether the US planned something similar to the Richards Amendment[98] when cooperating with Europe in the development of peaceful atomic energy might be put to them. Without taking any initiative to discuss the question, the missions might then answer that the Administration had no intention of seeking similar legislation.[99]

American Diplomacy and German Developments

The balancing of the State Department between its own line, and German and French demands for immediate bilateral nuclear assistance and the AEC support for bilateralism, went on around the turn of the year 1955-56. State Department officials recommended continued suspension of bilateral agreements. For example, in a message to AEC Chairman Lewis Strauss it was explained that in the State Department's judgement active negotiations for a German research bilateral should be postponed. It was of overriding importance that no US action were taken which might make more difficult Spaak's further negotiations regarding Euratom. The tactics that was suggested was that Spaak should be informed in confidence that the US would be prepared to adopt a 'temporary standstill policy' on any new bilateral arrangement with the six nations.[100] In a draft letter to the President, it was suggested that the US should make an urgent study of a US contribution to a Six-state programme. Agreement should be sought with the Six 'to suspend all negotiations on bilateral arrangements for assistance in the field of power reactors until we can assess the success of their effort to create a genuine federation'.[101]

The outcome of internal German skirmishes was that an attempt should be made to obtain a 'research bilateral' with the US. The Ambassador in Washington, Heinz Krekeler, was instructed to raise the matter with the State Department. Krekeler requested that negotiations should be opened for a standard research bilateral at the beginning of January. He indicated that the German side would ask for more than the standard 6 kilograms of fissionable material in the 24 other US research bilaterals with various countries that were in effect or under consideration. The next day, he told Merchant that through an oversight he had failed to raise the matter of a power bilateral. Merchant reaffirmed US policy; the US was not prepared 'at the present time to enter into such negotiation'. Krekeler said that he was satisfied with this, 'the one answer he did not want to receive was that the U.S. would not under any circumstances negotiate bilaterally but would insist on any agreement being with a capital community or European authority'. He argued that developments in Europe in the nuclear field could not be expected to wait in suspense for the protracted period required for negotiations and ratification. He was opposed to an 'authority which would allocate materials or issue licenses for the raising of capital'. He hoped that the American position would remain uncrystallized at least until the forthcoming visit to the US of the Minister for Atomic Energy, Franz-Josef Strauss. The Minister was already directly in touch with the AEC Chairman, Lewis Strauss, he said.[102]

Several considerations relevant to the US balancing problem were listed in a State memorandum. The main argument for accepting a bilateral agreement was that Germany had been told several times in the past that the US was willing to negotiate such an agreement and that a modest start was urgent after the German ten year absence from the field. An argument against was that Euratom opponents in the Federal Republic would represent this as a further 'proof' that the US preferred the bilateral road. There were also the British and French factors. The British were prepared to act: 'The fact that the British have been talking of a bilateral engagement with the Germans, and also alleged to oppose EURATOM, will presumably be related to US-German negotiations'. The French had asked for an enhanced research bilateral calling for 40 kgs. of fissionable material and were unhappy about US unresponsiveness to their overtures. If the Germans got something in the absence of an affirmative response to the French this would result in a further deterioriation of the French attitude.[103]

Soon after, it was decided that negotiations about a standard research bilateral with the Federal Republic should be initiated.[104] This move was apparently also intended to put some lubricating oil in the negotiation machinery in Brussels. It was clear that the main problem in the Spaak Committee concerned Euratom and the German resistance to it.[105]

There is a direct line between the intensification of American diplomacy in December and January and the decision by Adenauer to impose his will on those members of his Government who were opposing six state integration in general and Euratom in particular. In a message to his ministers Adenauer evoked his constitutional right to make guidelines, *Richtlinien*, for the policy of the Government. Adenauer stressed that the leading statesmen of the West - Pinay, Spaak, the Americans - saw integration as the focal point of developments in Europe. As first priority for Germany integration between the Six, horizontal as well as sectoral, should be promoted by all possible methods. The negotiations about a Common Market should emphatically be brought to accomplishment. Sectoral integration should be accepted in certain fields, notably in the nuclear field. It was a compelling political necessity to disperse any doubts about the implementation of the commitments that had been made in Messina. Adenauer stressed the importance which the Americans attached to the nuclear issue: 'As they have officially declared, in a European Atomic Community which, in contrast to the OEEC, has its own rights and responsibilities the Americans see a determining moment of political development. They are ready to give very strong support to an Atomic Community of that kind'. The peaceful use of atomic energy could not, in the view of world public opinion, be separated in practical life from the manufacture of atomic bombs, he stated. A purely national German effort in the field would be seen with great distrust by other countries. Although discrimination should be avoided as far as possible, Germany could not decline europeanization of certain materials, if it was necessary for security reasons. Adenauer did not, however, mention the other main part of the 'Armand concept': common installations, notably an enrichment plant.[106]

The Monnet Concept

The Action Committee for the United States of Europe was formed by Monnet in the autumn of 1955. Monnet´s rationale for organizing the Committee was that the EDC failure had showed that support for integration at the governmental level was not sufficient, a broad backing in parliaments was also necessary. He believed that it had been a mistake to have governmental agreements which subsequently failed to be ratified. The Action Committee was a broadly based international pressure group. The Committee may be seen as a parallel arena to the negotiations in Brussels. It was composed of a number of influential personalities from non-Communist parties and trade unions in the six countries. The Social-Democrats had a particularly important role. The division among the French Socialists had been decisive for the EDC failure. The French and German party leaders, Guy Mollet and Erich Ollenhauer, were pivotal members of the Committee. Mollet´s membership signalled that he intended to unify his party around a pro-European policy. He also became Prime Minister in the Government that was formed on 31 January after the fall of the Edgar Faure Government and the elections in early January. Ollenhauer´s participation signified that the German Social-Democrats were now orienting themselves toward integration, instead of giving priority to reunification.

The Committee convened for its first session in Paris for a couple of days in mid-January and its ´Declaration´ and ´Resolution´ brought what may be called the ´Monnet concept´ to the Brussels negotiations and the public scene.[107] The ´Declaration´ was short, it dealt only with atomic energy and the (unfulfilled) intention was that the national parliaments concerned would vote on it in the spring. The important issues covered by the Declaration/ Resolution were (1) supranationalism, (2) exclusively peaceful purpose, (3) the common fuel system, and (4) the linkage (´*Junktim*´) between Euratom and the Common Market:

The Committee agreed unanimously that a supranational Atomic Community should be built up, although there were differences on the modalities. The model for this, supported by a majority consisting of Socialists/Social-Democrats, was reminiscent of the American ´Baruch Plan´ of 1946.[108] A supranational authority would manage the common fuel system, and it would authorize in advance the construction and use of nuclear installations. It would also manage relations with countries outside the Community. The German CDU-representative, Hans Furler, argued in the debate that a measure of bilateralism should be maintained, but this was not accepted.[109] The Declaration proposed a Community monopoly on relations with third countries, particularly with respect to the supply of nuclear materials. Thus, the proposed scope of supranationalism in Euratom was very wide. There was no question of large national sectors working in parallel, as in the ´Armand concept´.

The most important point of the debates at the meeting in Paris was the issue of ´peaceful purpose´ for the Community. Should Euratom have an exclusively peaceful purpose? The issue at stake was future German, French or European nuclear weapons. According to Furler´s account the efforts to reach unity almost split on the issue. The exact implications of the positions are not always clear in the account, however. Did they mean renunciation of nuclear weapons for Euratom as such, of the European option generally, of the national options, or of a combination? Perhaps the obscurity reflected the need for ´constructive ambiguity´ in order to make agreement possible. Jean Monnet´s first draft suggested that the six states would limit themselves to developing atomic energy exclusively for peaceful purposes. Guy Mollet declared on behalf of the French Socialists that renunciation of the manufacture of nuclear weapons was a basic condition for the acceptance of Euratom. His main argument was that without this restriction the Federal Republic would have the opportunity to manufacture nuclear weapons within the Community. All Socialists and the Benelux delegates were in favour of renunciation, while the Italian liberal Malagodi argued that a renunciation of the manufacture of atomic weapons - presumably the European option - might be seen as neutralization of Europe. Furler declared on behalf of the CDU that the CDU favoured clear restrictions in the field of peaceful uses of atomic energy and that Germany had no intention of escaping from the *Kernwaffenverzicht* by means of Euratom. Mollet thanked the Germans for unequivocally supporting the position that Euratom should be limited to peaceful development of atomic power. Jean Monnet, for his part, made a striking appeal for comprehensive renunciation and for supranational authority over *all* nuclear resources of the member countries. His argument was that not only individual states but even the Community lacked the financial resources for developing the civil and military side of atomic energy simultaneously.[110] Monnet´s aim was Atlanticist. He was a dedicated adversary of all three military options, the German, the French and the European.[111]

The formulation that was finally approved was:

> The European Community must develop nuclear energy for exclusively peaceful purposes. This option demands a control without cracks. It opens the way to a general control on a world scale. It in no way affects the fulfilment of all international engagements currently in force.

The latter provision, Monnet told an American diplomat, was intended to reassure the US in particular ´that EURATOM will not become rallying ground for neutralist sentiment, i.e. expression EURATOM´s part peaceful intent in no way can be construed as being against NATO or other western European defense agreements´.[112] In this way - it should be noted - the Declaration was not an obstacle to the transfer option, that is, the possibility of transferring control of US nuclear weapons to a country or group of countries. Nor was it to be an obstacle to the actual plans for deployment - without transfer of control - of US nuclear weapons in Western Europe.

It should be added that Guy Mollet shortly afterwards, in his investiture speech to the French Parliament when elected Prime Minister, continued to oppose the use of Euratom for making bombs but was less clear about the national option:

> Is it necessary to create a European nuclear industry to permit the manufacture of atomic bombs, which in practice could not be carried out at the national level? My answer is quite clear: No. [113]

With respect to the common fuel system, the Action Committee decided after substantial debate that the system should be constructed in such a way that the Commission of the Community retained *exclusive ownership* [my emphasis] of nuclear fuels throughout processing'. There was a cleavage between the Socialist and trade union members of the Committee on the one side, and the Christian-Democratic and Liberal parties on the other, the former preferring that the supranational agency should have authority over fuels, and over nuclear installations also, while the latter wanted a greater degree of private ownership.[114] There was also a cleavage within the Socialist/Social-Democratic camp. The German leader, Ollenhauer, argued that everything that was related to production and use of atomic power should be publicly controlled and public property. This more far-reaching *socialization* proposal was not accepted by a number of other Committee members of the Left. The majority however agreed that Euratom ownership of fuels was necessary for effective control.[115]

Furler reported that the delegations from Benelux and Italy, as well as himself, had been strongly in favour of a *Junktim* between Euratom and the Common Market. However, the entire Monnet Action had as its point of departure that the atomic Community should be realized first and the Common Market later. At the meeting, Monnet had wanted to prevent a linkage between the two projects. Only a loose formulation about the *Junktim* was included in the Resolution.[116]

In sum, the *Monnet concept*, by combining supranational competence over the important parts of the nuclear field of the member countries (the fuel cycle in particular) and exclusively peaceful purpose seemed to exclude both the possibility of nationally controlled nuclear weapons and a European nuclear force in the Euratom organization as such. It possibly even excluded a common nuclear force among the Six, or some of them, outside Euratom. The concept was based on equality between France and Germany. In Monnet's thinking, but not in that of several others backing the Action Committee, NATO and the US nuclear umbrella were sufficient.

The Declaration/Resolution of the Action Committee brought the military issue, which had hitherto been hidden behind technicalities in the Brussels negotiations, to the forefront. Both the Brussels group and another group, which was exploring the possibilities of nuclear cooperation within the OEEC, had remained silent on the question of the implications of national energy programmes for weapons production.[117] Open discussion of the crucial proliferation issue had been avoided.

What was the American attitude to the 'Monnet concept'? It would show more clearly later, as policy developed in the spring of 1956, that US policy coincided with it on vital points, diverged on others. The Americans did not act in favour of as comprehensive a supranationalism for Euratom as in the 'Monnet concept', but promoted a large measure of bilateralism while also dealing with a supranational entity. Like the Action Committee, the Americans requested Community ownership of nuclear fuels. Like Monnet himself, but unlike the Committee majority, they were against the *Junktim*.[118]

What about the question of 'exclusively peaceful purpose'? It is clear that Dulles, as in the 'Monnet concept', would have preferred to limit Euratom's field of action to peaceful purposes only. This is illustrated by Dulles' reaction to a report from Paris about French reactions to Monnet's plans. It was reported from Paris that Goldschmidt had informed the Americans that the forthcoming Monnet resolution would pledge peaceful uses only for Euratom, and that this was taken to mean that marine nuclear propulsion would be excluded for countries joining Euratom. Goldschmidt had argued that this complicated things for the French and might jeopardize the whole endeavour.[119] Dulles instructed clarifyingly that the State Department's tactics with respect to Euratom during the actual formulative period was to see that the participating nations had a free range to develop a programme which they believed would best serve their interests. While Dulles did 'heartily agree with Monnet's objective of restricting EURATOM to peaceful uses only', it did not seem to him 'that peaceful propulsion should be excluded from nuclear activities of adhering nations', thus indicating that propulsion of civil ships and other vessels should be within the scope of Euratom, while for example propulsion of submarines should not.[120] Dulles' reply seemed to indicate that he did not want to define 'peaceful purpose' so narrowly that the Brussels negotiations were jeopardized, nor that potential civil markets for US propulsion reactors would be excluded. At this time, it may be added, many experts believed that nuclear propulsion for merchant ships had a bright future.

Even if Dulles preferred that the European option should also be excluded - not only the national options - he does not seem to have considered this feasible if the Euratom project were to obtain sufficient support. According to an account by Monnet's collaborator Jacques van Helmont, the Americans in no way suggested that Euratom should undertake to renounce nuclear weapons. Once advanced by the Committee, the Americans did not support or approve of the idea of renunciation. Robert Bowie of the State Department advised Monnet against taking this line.[121]

The appearance of the 'Monnet concept' triggered lively debate and controversy, particularly in France. Very soon after the issue of the document the nationalists mobilized. French generals started to write to the Government and to publish articles about the danger of the 'Monnet concept' with respect to the French national nuclear option. Michel Debré came out strongly in favour of atomic energy cooperation within the OEEC framework. He attacked the Euratom project, characterizing it as the work of those who wanted supranationality in revenge for the defeat of EDC. He also suggested that Euratom was a German-American plot to enable the Germans to escape from the *Kernwaffenverzicht* in the WEU.[122]

German officials informed the American Embassy in Bonn about German reactions. Von der Groeben said that many felt that there was a recent exaggerated emphasis on Euratom at the expense of the idea of the Common Market - 'Monnet was too successful in Paris'. A decision about Euratom without agreement on the Common Market would lead to the establishment of another High Authority busy solving the problems of another industry, but this would not lead to a United States of Europe. The Germans would be willing to accept controls if these were accompanied by an acceptance of Common Market proposals.[123] Karl Carstens of the *Auswärtiges Amt* confirmed that the *Junktim* was seen in Germany as an absolute condition for agreement. Any measure of control over importation, distribution and use of nuclear fuel would be acceptable. Community ownership of fuel was however contrary to German socio-economic principles. Nevertheless, the guarantee of exclusive peaceful purposes was a favourable feature of the Action Committee's proposal. It would provide a basis of answer to those Germans who argued that a Community which permitted Germany's partners to make nuclear weapons could involve unacceptable discrimination of the Federal Republic. The OEEC appproach and the Euratom approach could be developed simultaneously, and there would be no difficulty on agreement regarding a common enrichment plant.[124]

US Domestic Bargaining: State-AEC Coordination

When the first studies in the State Department had been done Dulles wrote to the President, referring to the general guidelines decided by the National Security Council in November. He stressed the German question, the non-proliferation problem and the need for effective control. Control would be simplified and a precedent would be set for similar regional arrangements elsewhere. He proposed a common State-AEC study on an urgent basis. The US should 'make a maximum contribution' in order to consolidate and enlarge integration among the Six. Dulles did not suggest, however, that bilateralism should be abandoned. He suggested that any resulting agreement from the ongoing early phases of bilateral negotiations should reflect in some way the possibility of assignment of the bilateral agreements to Euratom.[125] Thus, he diverged from, for example, the ideas of Schaetzel, who had argued that the US should deal *only* with the new Community.[126] He also diverged in this respect from the ´Monnet concept´ that was soon to appear in public. Perhaps he anticipated that the AEC, which was preparing its offensive for exporting American nuclear technology to Europe, would never agree to give up the bilateral approach at this time. He may himself have believed in the importance of a rapid beginning to trade in nuclear technology. Perhaps he also believed in bilateralism as a useful instrument in order to win acceptance of Euratom.

Eisenhower agreed to Dulles´ proposals and directed that a joint AEC-State study be made.[127] Subsequently he also agreed to AEC Chairman Lewis Strauss´ proposal that enriched uranium, 20,000 kgs. of U-235, should be allocated to American industry for atomic power purposes for a period extending through and beyond the next ten years. This was a huge amount and a large part of the output from the mammoth American enrichment plants. Dulles then raised the question ´whether it would not be desirable to make and announce an allocation of a substantial amount, additional to previous allocations, for peaceful uses including power production by our allies´. After discussion there was consensus that there would be great value in an early announcement of an allocation in the order of 1,000 kgs. for stimulating peaceful uses of atomic energy abroad.[128]

Before approaching the AEC about the joint study some preparations were made in the State Department. Resistance was expected. A memorandum by Barnett was included in a briefing package that was sent to Dulles.[129]

Barnett stressed that the vital element in the US attachment to integration was the Franco-German tie. For the foreseeable future the tie would not be created by pressures only from within France and Germany, or even from within the Community of the Six. For them to be created the US must be - Barnett was using a phrase that was sometimes used in American documents - ´the catalytic agent´. The time for action was limited because with the passage of time the value and potential impact of the American resources would decline:

The consequences of independent atomic energy developments in Europe can be so critical for the United States, the West, and the entire balance of world power that we should identify precisely and concretely what elements are essential for genuine ´integration´, if it is in atomic energy integration that we see safety and strength for the West. These elements, viewed in the framework of the Europe now existing, are no less than:

Common Franco-German responsibility and authority for internal security in all matters relating directly or indirectly to controls over materials, information, and personnel involved in atomic energy programs;

Common Franco-German responsibility and authority for all government expenditures which might lead directly or indirectly to production or utilization of nuclear energy;

Common Franco-German responsibility and authority for all plans and operations relating directly or indirectly to production and employment of atomic weapons.

Considering, then, that ´our real problem is France and Germany´, the two parts of the problem that, in Barnett´s opinion, should be studied by the State Department and the AEC were:

What is the maximum contribution in U.S. resources - material, personnel, financial, or technological - which the U.S. would be prepared to make in order to induce France and Germany, in an appropriate multi- and supranational framework, to abandon separate and national atomic energy programs in favor of one program carried forward in common?

In the three sectors mentioned above, what could constitute a genuine fusing of Franco-German responsibility and authority?[130]

In another memorandum by Barnett he reflected that the State Department should be governed by certain premises in its own handling of the bargaining assets that the US possessed, and which would become clear in the work with the AEC. Barnett sketched a priority order for desirable outcomes, going from close integration, as in the ´Monnet concept´, to building bilateral networks, and, in the last resort, to US-UK coordination close to the British model for European cooperation:

1) The Monnet Resolution expresses most satisfactorily a relationship between the Western European countries which would necessitate the Franco-German association which we call the core of ´integration´. To the extent that the work of the Messina Group, or the actions of national parliaments, give promise of implementation of that program, we should give it our full support.

2) If the Monnet approach fails, we should not abandon our interest in the Franco-German atomic tie, but rather explore urgently possibilities of according them preferential, but open-ended treatment provided arrangements worked out with them would be harmonized with multilateral arrangements encompassing the Six, or even the OEEC group of countries.

3) We should also explore the possibility of arrangements between the U.S. and France and Germany that could be coordinated and harmonized with U.K. interests and commitments in Europe in such a way as to represent a commitment of U.S. and U.K. influence and responsibility in what Europeans could construe as the core of an Atlantic Community in atomic energy programs.[131]

The State-AEC meeting took place on 21 January. Dulles gave an account of Eisenhower's and his own persuasion about the importance of European integration, and expressed hope that the AEC 'would not think in terms of existing laws, regulations and inhibitions, but rather define in maximum terms what lay within the realm of possibility'. Laws could be changed. Dulles pointed out that 'the Congress supported European integration perhaps more vigorously than the Executive Branch itself'. Time was short. There were three general approaches to advancing US interests in the nuclear field. All three could be pursued at the same time. One was the IAEA, but this Agency would come into being very slowly. The second was the bilateral approach. Dulles emphasized that the bilaterals would continue, and that he had specifically opposed a suggestion that bilateral negotiations be suspended. The third was US support for an integrated institution in Europe. Merchant added a few remarks. He mentioned the possibility that the British might take a part of the nuclear market in Western Europe unless Six-state nuclear integration succeeded. He also warned against concluding a bilateral with Germany in advance of conclusion of a bilateral with France since this would generate French suspicions and undesirable tensions.

Lewis Strauss responded to the arguments in conciliatory terms. He stated that the State Department and the AEC were in agreement that the United States should expand the peaceful atom and back developments leading to integration in Europe. He made clear, however, that 'the Commission objected to any foot-dragging in the handling of bilateral negotiations', and he expressed concern about transmitting nuclear information to France. France was a security problem, and 'the French problem in a sense defined the general problem of security presented by dealing with a group of countries since the lowest common denominator of the group might well be controlling'.

Much of the discussion dealt with US enrichment policy. The possibility that had been proposed in Barnett's December memorandum[132] - that the US should assist in the establishment of European enrichment facilities - was not advanced by the State representatives. Merchant stated in general terms that it was the view of the State Department that the Europeans were determined to achieve atomic energy independence with or without the help of the US. What the US could offer was a wasting asset. Bowie said that Monnet had told him that the erection of European enrichment facilities made little sense from an economic standpoint, but Monnet had reiterated the very strong sense of compulsion on the part of the Europeans to achieve atomic independence.

The AEC commissioners and officials were negative to the idea of assisting Europe in building enrichment facilities, although export of the product, enriched uranium, was imaginable. Several objections were made:

> Mr. Libby observed that the French appeared to want to produce atomic weapons. Mr. Murray said that he believed that weapons manufacturing capacity would be developing in a number of countries. To forestall this would require keeping the French out of the gaseous diffusion process. Mr. Hall observed, however, that if the purpose of European integration is to achieve atomic independence, they should have a gaseous diffusion plant but perhaps such a development was precisely what was clearly contrary to United States interests. Mr. Libby added that the Europeans could well do this without our help, but that it would be extremely expensive and, in any case, we could not help them with it on account of inhibitions of United States law...Mr. Libby stated flatly that the United States could not tell the Europeans how to make a gaseous diffusion plant. Mr. Merchant wondered if this might not be a premature judgment at this stage. Mr. Libby quickly replied that the British gaseous diffusion plant does not work, that he doubted the efficiency of the Russian process, and that we do effectively possess a monopoly in this sector of the whole field. - Admiral Strauss added that a gaseous diffusion plant to be efficient would produce quantities of material far beyond the foreseeable power requirements of Europe. Further, for it to be operated, it would consume enormous quantities of power. We may however, be in a position to supply the Europeans with materials which, from a price standpoint, would be advantageous for them to obtain from us rather than to produce themselves.[133]

Conant - having received the minutes from the State-AEC meeting - reacted with a long letter to Merchant in which he wrote about the connection between integration and non-proliferation, the attitude to nuclear weapons in the Federal Republic, and his conclusions with respect to US policy towards Euratom. Conant expressed strong suspicions toward Germany's most famous physicist, Heisenberg, leader of the German nuclear programme during and after the war, 'who always had and still has strong nationalistic feelings'. The dismal technical performance of the atomic bomb project during the Nazi period was irritating to Heisenberg, Conant wrote. Conant felt sure that Heisenberg 'will be on the side of those who urge the Germans to be "independent" and develop their own atomic energy schemes as far as possible in secrecy and with the minimum of national interference let alone supranational interference'. Such ambitions coincided with those of other forces, like German industrialists and certain promoters in the US. These forces hoped that the atomic energy law in the US would soon be amended to put ownership of fissionable materials in the hands of private industries, with concomitant relaxation of controls, and they mistakenly believed that a power bilateral with the US would be an easy matter to arrange. In any case, the reprocessing of fuel elements would produce plutonium and this was a long step towards manufacture of atomic weapons:

> Although all the Germans preface their remarks about atomic energy by disclaiming any desire to manufacture atomic weapons, I begin to detect signs of uncertainty on this point. Unless I am mistaken people are saying quietly that it is out of the question for Germany to be kept in a position of inferiority by not having the ability to make atomic weapons now that it is generally proclaimed atomic bombs for tactical purposes are a necessary adjunct to any ground defense of Europe. This feeling, needless to say, would be enormously increased it there were any discussion of France being in a position to produce atomic weapons.

Another factor, Conant continued, working against German participation in a supranational nuclear scheme was that the shadow of socialism hung over all these discussions. The fact that socialists in other countries and to some extent in Germany supported Monnet's concept fed the fears of industrialists and those supporters of the Government who were 'religiously committed to the doctrine of private initiative and free competition'. Conant believed that the demands for a *Junktim* between the Common Market and Euratom were 'in part put forward by those who realize how difficult it will be to reach a common market and who think that by inserting this provision they can be certain that the EURATOM scheme will fail'. What was needed now was 'a very large carrot in the form of what United States is offering would have to be put in front of the mouths of six donkeys'. Conant supported the AEC line of offering enriched uranium to the Six. His main suggestion was that the US should offer a large amount of enriched uranium together with an offer of helping in construction of a reprocessing plant [for separating plutonium and burnt-out uranium] within a supranational framework. France was already developing a reprocessing plant and would be in a position to produce plutonium before too long whether an enrichment plant was built or not, he argued. Conant asked himself whether it was not in the interest of the US and the stability of the world that such a reprocessing plant be operated by a Six-state supranational authority: 'Would not this plutonium eventually make them sufficiently independent of United States controls to satisfy their vanity (national and supranational)'?[134]

The Eisenhower-Eden Talks and the Evolution of the British Position

Around the turn of the year 1955-6 it was clear that the British were going to concentrate their efforts on launching the OEEC as an alternative to the Six state projects in the general economic sphere as well as for nuclear cooperation. An intergovernmental model strongly supported by Britain was attractive to many in Europe, not least in the nuclear field, in which Britain was by far the most advanced European country.

The French propensity to support Euratom was underestimated in British judgements. The Foreign Office made optimistic forecasts about what the French attitude would be when the full implications were thought out in France. Caccia wrote that the French Government would be no more disposed than the British to adhere to any form of cooperation on the civil uses of atomic energy which would limit their freedom of action in the military field. If any organization of this kind came into being he was doubtful whether the French could be parties to it on the civil side and yet remain ´fancy free´ in the military field. He also judged that if the French believed that ´third countries´ - that is, the US or Britain - would be ready to conclude bilateral agreements with individual members of a closely integrated Euratom, they were unrealistic. Other countries would hesitate before giving assistance to a member of the Six which would automatically be circulated to the other five.[135]

The meeting between Eisenhower and Eden in Washington about various world problems was scheduled to take place 28 January - 1 February. One of the issues on the agenda was the general situation in Europe and European integration. The split between the Americans and the British about the best way of tying Germany to the West and the means of organizing effective control, came out clearly in papers by British officials in the weeks before the talks in Washington. The view of the Foreign Office was that it was highly doubtful whether supranationalism was necessary for effective control. Control could be based on the joint enterprises that were most important from a proliferation point of view [that is, enrichment plants and reprocessing plants]. The difficulties in devising a security control over such enterprises should be no greater in an OEEC scheme than those entailed in devising one for operation through Euratom.[136]

An evaluation of the difference between American and British approaches to the control problem was provided by the Deputy to the Ambassador in Bonn, Roger Allen, when the Embassy was asked to judge the prospects for tying Germany to the West through a Common Market and Euratom:

The American belief was, Allen wrote, that existing restrictions on German civil use of atomic energy were insufficient. When Adenauer disappeared, German industry and its allies on the right wing were likely to become more powerful. They would have a financial interest in developing civil atomic power and giving Germany a commercial advantage over her neighbours as a result. The step from civil atomic development to military atomic development was short:

> It is therefore essential, the Americans would say, that Germany's atomic potential should be linked as closely as possible to that of her neighbours who have the greatest interest in seeing that neither her industrial nor her military potential is misused. The best way of doing this is to set up some supra-national authority to which Germany will be bound by treaty and which, if it can be built in to some fuller scheme of political integration, will mean that Germany cannot break free in the atomic field without breaking the whole Western connection at the same time. She must in fact be brought to make a surrender of sovereignty for this purpose. At the very least, in the American view, supra-national control should be established over atomic fuels which should not be left in individual national ownership or in the hands of private industry.

Allen contrasted the American view with his own (which was close to mainstream Foreign Office thinking). Supranationalism was not the only way of obtaining effective control:

> Whatever sort of institution may be set up, its efficacy will, in the last resort, depend on the goodwill of its members, and their readiness to make it work. If Germany was really determined to break away from her Western connections, she could break out of a supranational organisation with little more difficulty than she could break out of an O.E.E.C.-type set-up...It is doubtful whether even a supra-national organisation can establish controls so pervasive that they could not be evaded by individual enterprises which were determined to do so. If, however, it is possible to devise security controls over the supply of fuel and over other atomic activities, this can be done on the general lines of the plan put forward by the O.E.E.C. working group, aided by the already existing W.E.U. controls.[138]

British diplomats reported about discussions with American officials at the OEEC about the integration problem. They saw indications that the State Department did not believe that the Common Market would be realized, at least not as a low-tariff project. The British had been told that Dulles was 'completely sold' on Euratom as a step toward integration in Europe and seemed 'impervious to argument'. The Americans had argued that the British ought to concentrate on the compatibility of the two schemes, not to regard them as alternatives. Euratom could exist in close relationship with the O.E.E.C. scheme. If reconciliation were not achieved, the Americans 'were terrified that they would have to come down in favour of EURATOM' in the OEEC Council.[139] The compatibility theme was communicated to the Foreign Office in other ways also, for example by an official at the US London Embassy who transmitted 'policy guidance on (as he put it) the U.S. attitude to the U.K. attitude on European integration'.[140]

Before Eden went to Washington, the American Ambassador in London, Aldrich, forecast that proposals about supranationality including the UK would fall on deaf ears: 'Hence, UK decision not to join Euratom will almost certainly remain firm and participation at this time in Common Market is unthinkable. Best that can now be hoped for is cooperative arrangement with EURATOM and neutrality vis-à-vis Common Market'. Aldrich added that priority attention was devoted in Britain to peaceful nuclear energy at the moment. There was a shortage in coal production, causing import and dollar drain, and the crucial dependence on Middle East oil had been acknowledged.[141]

Dulles expected to include a discussion about atomic energy at the meeting with Eden but his estimate of the chance of agreement was pessimistic. 'The British tradition, almost instinctive, is to favor European divisions rather than emergence on the Continent of greater unity and strength', he sighed.[142] Incoming reports stressed the importance of British positions for the outcome. Luxemburg's Foreign Minister, Josef Bech, judged for example that 'final success of Euratom might be determined by UK position'.[143]

The talks in Washington about world problems took place in a cordial atmosphere, although Eisenhower initially thought that the British 'were prepared to be a little sticky on one or two points'. He had 'had to ask them to decide which is more valuable, friendship in this country or somebody else'.[144] After the meeting Eisenhower wrote warmly in his diary that he had never attended any international talks where the spirit of friendship had been more noticeable than in this one. European problems had been talked about 'a great deal', although they had been one of the 'minor subjects'. In the European field 'there was no acute matter to be taken up and we merely reviewed our general policies on which we largely agreed'.[145]

The British position on integration was presented by the new Foreign Secretary, Selwyn Lloyd. He predictably referred to the OEEC as the valuable instrument. He admitted, however, that the two projects were compatible. The UK had no prejudice against Euratom, but the UK itself could not participate because in its programmes for military and peaceful uses of atomic energy were 'completely intermingled'. With respect to the Common Market, the British 'felt strongly' that France would accept it only on the basis of a high protective tariff. The whole exercise would probably lead to a repetition of the EDC experience. Lloyd concluded that the British position was 'hostile' to the Common Market. In the area of arms control, he felt that the most promising means of promoting friendship between Germany and France lay in the system provided for in the Western European Union.[146]

Thus, the differing British attitude to Euratom and the Common Market, respectively, which had been expressed in various contexts had been confirmed at the top level and cleared with Washington: Britain preferred the OEEC/WEU approach to nuclear matters but would not fight to launch the OEEC as an alternative that excluded Euratom. Britain was willing to cooperate with Euratom or its members within the OEEC framework, if Euratom in spite of all came into being. A Foreign Office memorandum described the background to the British position:

> If, as reports from Paris and Bonn suggest is not unlikely, the Six run into difficulties over Euratom we should have incurred ill-will amongst the 'Europeans' and some Americans, quite unnecessarily. From the start, we have taken the line that we ought not to show hostility to Euratom, or try to 'hustle' the Six. Rather, we should concentrate on making the OEEC alternative possible, as far as our powers and interests permit, leaving the rest to the Six. If they can really see their way to going ahead with Euratom they are unlikely to be deterred by any demonstration by us in favour of OEEC. But by supporting an OEEC scheme at the [OEEC] Council meeting we might still hope to get them to fit their closer grouping into the wider framework.[147]

The Common Market was another matter; Britain was resolutely opposed to it. The adjustment toward a more positive approach to the project however started at this time. In February, Macmillan, as Chancellor of the Exchequer, ordered a review of means for a new policy towards Europe. This would in due time become the 'Plan G' for a Free Trade Area compatible with the Common Market. [148]

American officials informed the French and Germans about the British attitude at the Eden talks. Assurances were given that the US would continue to give 'every possible support' to the Six-state model. To the French it was emphasized that the main reason why Washington supported supranational integration was the German problem. The American Government very keenly desired a rapid solution for Euratom because of the psychological effect of integration in this new area, and because it wanted the control of peaceful nuclear activities regulated within a European framework. The Common Market was not so urgent.[149] The message to the Germans was that the US was as anxious as ever to obtain Six-state supranational nuclear integration. Conant told von Brentano that the mention of the OEEC in the common declaration from the Eden talks did not mean that the US and British standpoints had come closer to each other. The US position had not changed, nuclear cooperation should be organized supranationally within the Six state framework, although cooperation with others was of course not excluded. The American Government wished this opinion to be communicated to the six countries before the opening of the Conference of Foreign Ministers in Brussels few days later.[150] The American standpoint was emphasized by Under Secretary Hoover, then visiting Bonn. Dulles, and especially the President, he said, had taken a strong position with the British in stating that, while NATO and the OEEC were helpful, they did not believe these organizations would in any way take the place of closer integration in such projects as Euratom.[151]

The *Auswärtiges Amt*, when communicating with the British, supported the standpoint that restrictions on German atomic energy must be effectively controlled. The OEEC model was not effective enough because it would only provide for control of nuclear material supplied through the OEEC; if any country obtained nuclear fuel from other sources it could use it without restraint. The *Amt* even expressed surprise that the British view of control fell short of the German level of acceptance.[152] The leading figure in the German anti-Euratom coalition, F.-J. Strauss, worked in the opposite direction, trying to forge an alliance with the British. When talking to the British Ambassador, Hoyer Millar, he sketched a programme for nuclear cooperation with Britain. Strauss objected to Euratom for several reasons. It would place in the hands of a supranational authority the control of raw materials, the programmes of the participating nations, and patents, and it would have the ability to conduct ´atomic foreign policy´. Most importantly, it would exclude the United Kingdom. He would much rather see something on the lines of the WEU. Alternatively, could not Euratom be built into the OEEC?[153]

The British hope was, then, that it would be possible to fit Euratom into the wider OEEC framework. To achieve this, it was believed that a substantive offer had to be made. The Foreign Office was convinced that United Kingdom participation in a European enrichment plant would be the crucial factor. ´We know´, it was argued in a Foreign Office memorandum, ´that a declaration of U.K. willingness to participate, or at least to help in the construction of, a European diffusion plant, in the OEEC context, would persuade Europe that our support for OEEC is not mere lip-service´. The hurdle was that enrichment technology was classified and American consent was required.[154] In joint Foreign Office/Atomic Energy Authority deliberations it was pointed out that ´the European diffusion [enrichment] plant had become the emotional centre of the European movement´. Another possibility for Britain was to cooperate with Canada and aid in construction of a plant there. It was judged impossible, however, to participate fully in a plant in Canada and Europe at the same time. It was agreed that the views of the US should be obtained and that the question of a Canadian plant should be studied. After that, participation in the European project should be considered. At the coming OEEC meeting no commitments should be made.[155]

Makins was instructed to obtain the American views. He reminded the State Department that no response to the November enquiry had been received. [156] At a meeting with Merchant Makins inquired what the US attitude would be at the OEEC meeting, particularly with respect to the enrichment question. Merchant replied that there was no prospect of obtaining an answer before the meeting of the OEEC. He anticipated, however, that the answer would be 'strongly negative'. The construction of an enrichment plant in Europe was 'the last thing' the AEC envisaged. The US delegation would resist discussion in the OEEC as premature and the American representative would remain completely silent on the subject at the meeting. It was possible that the US would decide to transfer enriched material to the European countries. Merchant admitted that there would be economic advantages in this.

The British asked if it would make a difference whether the European countries concerned reserved their rights individually or collectively to embark on a military programme. The answer was that the US arguments against an enrichment plant for Western Europe over-rode any such considerations.

The possibility of the OEEC undertaking a joint reprocessing plant - the other main kind of installation that was vital from a proliferation point of view - was mentioned. The British stated that the UK would not want to participate in such a plant.[157] This policy was to change later, however.[158]

Makins' report to the Foreign Office about the meeting was very critical of the idea of using enrichment as a bargaining chip to promote the OEEC concept against the Euratom concept. In Makins' view, it would be impossible for Macmillan to go further in the OEEC than the position that had already been conveyed to the OEEC Working Party in November.[159] The political advantages seemed to him 'marginal' and the economic and commercial advantages 'doubtful and hypothetical'. There were strong counterarguments. Britain was in dire need of American nuclear assistance:

> On the other hand, quite apart from our obligations to them [the Americans] in regard to declassification, there are strong, immediate and practical reasons for staying in line with the Americans. In the next few weeks or months we expect the Administration to secure Congressional approval for the transmission to us of information on marine propulsion and package reactors, and the ratification of the deal for the supply of uranium 235 as well as to give their cooperation in the conclusion of contracts for the supply of Canadian uranium which we must have. We are also in the process of developing cooperation with the Americans under the two bilateral agreements. These are matters of vital importance to us and their realization would be prejudiced if we were to try to take a different line from the Americans on the European diffusion plant...For the same reason I would think it most impolitic to suggest either to the

Americans or in the O.E.E.C. that the only reason why we are not prepared to cooperate with European countries in a diffusion plant operation is an American objection. I can say with confidence that the Americans would very much resent such an attitude on our part.[160]

The day after this Anglo-American meeting President Eisenhower made the announcement that a very large quantity of American enriched uranium would be allocated for distribution abroad.[161]

In the circumstances, no British attempt was made at the meeting of the OEEC Ministerial Council to reinforce the OEEC alternative, as compared to the Six-state projects, by playing the enrichment card.

Atoms for Peace, IAEA and the European Scene

Some complications in the relationship between US disarmament proposals to the Soviet Union, European integration, the non-proliferation problem, and export of American technology for civil nuclear power abroad were discussed in Washington in February. These were all aspects of the two year old Atoms for Peace policy. Certain implementation decisions were required. One crucial question was whether it was possible to make renunciation of nuclear weapons a condition for receiving US civil nuclear assistance through the three channels: IAEA, the bilateral system and Euratom.

An interagency meeting which included Dulles, Lewis Strauss and disarmament negotiator Harold Stassen was called in order to consider the plans for the coming twelve-nation meeting on the IAEA Statute. The basic question was whether the Agency should operate with limited controls designed merely to ensure that nuclear assistance was not diverted to military uses, or whether the Agency should be used to attempt to keep fourth countries from producing nuclear weapons. The State Department had proposed that a comprehensive control should be exercised by the IAEA. The obvious problem was that partial control was not effective for the objective of non-proliferation, ´assistance from the Agency, even though limited to peaceful purposes, would simply free the other resources of a nation to support a parallel weapons program´. AEC Chairman Strauss recognized that this was so, but nevertheless urged a policy of partial control. It appeared to him extremely difficult to get agreement on a broader control. A ´no weapons´ pledge would not be feasible, and France in particular would not accept such a pledge. Demands for reciprocal inspection in the US would come. IAEA inspection of the US power reactor progamme appeared difficult to accept; the US would not accept sufficiently strict inspection and control of its programmes to satisfy prudent requirements for safeguards abroad. US refusal would serve as an excuse for other countries to limit inspection to what the US would accept. The military representative supported Strauss.

Dulles admitted that 'it would be difficult for nations to forego permanently their right to make nuclear weapons while the U.S., USSR and UK continued to make them'. Countries would not come into the IAEA if this was required. A *moratorium* [my emphasis] might however be realistic. In Dulles' view,

> ...it might be possible to get agreement by other countries to forego weapons production as an interim measure, looking toward the institution of international control of atomic energy which would apply to all countries including the present military atomic powers...what we must ask is that they agree, for a specified period of time, as a self-denying move, not to complicate the problem of nuclear disarmament by engaging in atomic weapons production, while the great powers try to bring the world situation, and their own stocks of these weapons under control.

Stassen supported Dulles.[162]

At a meeting with the National Security Council few days later the proliferation problem was embedded in a general discussion of disarmament policy. Eisenhower's perspective was, in essence, the same as the one which had once motivated his Atoms for Peace proposal. He tried to combine disarmament and economic perspectives. A method for stopping the drift toward war had to be found, he said. Otherwise the world was headed for an armaments race that would be ended in only one way, 'namely, a clash of forces which could not result in victory for anybody, or at least, stupendous expenditures for an indefinite period...if we could somehow eliminate the H-weapon, the world would be better off...some of our thinking overlooked a transcendent consideration - namely that nobody can win a thermonuclear war'. He hoped that his advisers would bring forth new ideas as to how the production of nuclear material could be channelled for peaceful purposes. If the US could only do this, 'we could be safe in that our plants which produce this material could keep running for a long time, even without an effective disarmament agreement'. Eisenhower referred in positive terms to a proposal for distributing fissionable material abroad which he had received from the AEC Chairman.[163] The proposal was that, in connection with the ear-marking of 20,000 kgs. of fissionable materials for domestic distribution, there would be a corresponding offer to ear-mark 20,000 kgs. for peaceful uses elsewhere in the world. The IAEA would receive 1,000 kgs. as an out-and-out gift, Euratom 5,000 kgs. (but not as a gift), the remaining 14,000 kgs. would be made available to other nations of the world. This would be a five-year programme, and it would be combined with an offer to match contributions from all other nations [that is, the USSR] in the world, even if they exceeded the 20,000 kgs. Obviously, the amount of 20,000 was a very radical change compared to the 1,000 kgs. for stimulating the peaceful atom abroad that had been envisaged only three weeks earlier.[164]

Dulles' entourage at this stage felt that coordination of the many intertwined threads of American nuclear policy toward Europe was urgent. Merchant and Gerard Smith sent a top secret memorandum to the Secretary demanding a comprehensive political analysis of the nuclear problems the US was facing in the European arena, including examination of the means by which and the extent to which it was politically feasible to achieve US objectives. An effort to obtain interdepartmental agreement between State, Defense, the AEC, and Stassen's disarmament agency should be made. The memorandum, although still, it seems, only partly available[165], gives an insight into the the balancing between different policy goals at the top level in the State Department.

The realization of the largely interrelated US objectives, the memorandum stated, raised a host of problems. Five objectives were mentioned: non-proliferation, implementing the New Look strategy in Europe, promoting civil nuclear power, encouraging European integration, and winning the propaganda war with the Soviet Union:

> 1. Our disarmament objective is to prevent, retard or minimize the development of nuclear weapons programs by nations other than the three who have already achieved a competency in this field.
> 2. In the European area, it is still our objective to build and maintain an effective deterrent based on an atomic strategy. This is accepted NATO doctrine to which we have given our concurrence.
> 3. On the peaceful use side, it is our objective, within security limitations, to assist friendly governments in the development of non-military programs. As yet unresolved is the issue of whether we will extend such assistance to countries which seek to develop a nuclear weapons capability.
> 4. It is our objective to encourage European integration by the Community of 6 and we believe the proposed EURATOM project gives the greatest hope for progress in this direction.
> 5. Nuclear questions will increasingly engage the interest of the public and be exploited as far as possible by the Soviet Union for propaganda purposes. It is our objective to persuade world public opinion that the U.S. and the West in general is 1) willing and able to help other peoples to advance in the peaceful uses of atomic energy and reap the benefits they provide, and 2) sincerely desirous of cooperating in steps to remove the threat of nuclear warfare, within the limitations imposed by reasonable free world security requirements.

On the military side, the paper reviewed the dilemmas in the relationship between NATO strategy, the transfer option, and the national nuclear options, of which the French one was of immediate concern:

> On the one hand, we are encouraging our NATO allies to cooperate in the building of an effective deterrent based on the use of nuclear weapons. On the other hand, we wish to discourage the inauguration of nuclear weapons programs by 4th countries and, at the same time, are not presently willing or able to furnish our allies with such weapons from our own resources...For reasons of national prestige and legitimate defense concern, there is strong pressure in certain European countries for the development of a national nuclear weapons program. [deletion] For us to pursue a policy of discouraging the development of French nuclear capability and, at the same time, to withhold furnishing such weapons from our own resources is likely to create a host of problems affecting the whole range of our relationships with France. The problem, while less acute in other countries, is likely to be a developing one. Further problems arise, in this connection, from the WEU Agreements prohibiting the development of a nuclear weapons industry in Germany [deletion]...If we wish to obtain the military storage and use rights which we require in foreign countries, we must be prepared to pay some price for them. In some cases at least, our allies will probably desire that the price takes the form of an increased sharing of nuclear know-how, assured availability of weapons for their own defense, and participation in decisions with respect to use.

On the peaceful side, there were additional problems with far-reaching political implications:

> 1. What should be the nature of our support for EURATOM if, as appears probable, Monnet's efforts are not successful to bring about a permanent foreswearing by national Governments of the right to produce nuclear weapons?
> 2. Is it politically feasible for us to make our peaceful uses through IAEA or in bilateral arrangements dependent on a renunciation of or moratorium on weapons development by 4th countries?[166]

In sum, the memorandum formulated clearly the two interrelated priority goals for American European policy: Six-state integration and non-proliferation. Euratom was described as the most promising road to integration. The non-proliferation goal was to *'prevent, retard or minimize'* [my emphasis] the development of nuclear weapons by other nations than the three who already had them. Decisions about certain problems seemed particularly urgent: Was it politically feasible to make renunciation of the French and other national options, or a moratorium, a condition for giving US civil nuclear assistance (enriched uranium essentially)? What concessions were necessary to obtain French cooperation with respect to military storage and use rights (for example, transfer of some degree of control of US nuclear weapons, transfer of nuclear know-how)? What would be the nature of US support for Euratom if the French did not accept renunciation or a moratorium?

American Diplomacy around the Brussels Conference (11-12 February 1956) up to the Spaak Report

The Conference of Foreign Ministers of the Six in Brussels was arranged in order to discuss the results of the negotiations in the Spaak Committee and its subgroups. An important motive for arranging the conference was the wish to find out whether the new French Government, led by Mollet, with Christian Pineau as Foreign Minister, would continue the policy of the previous Government.

The State Department received a series of warnings from Dillon before the conference that a decisive issue for the fate of Euratom was the question of French nuclear weapons. Dillon underlined that he felt he should raise a ´serious warning flag´ against demanding permanent renunciation of the French right to manufacture nuclear weapons. The concept which had been worked out by Monnet during the last two months, and which had ´apparently been wholeheartedly adopted by Guy Mollet´ would create great difficulties for final ratification. Renunciation might well mean the end of Euratom as far as France was concerned. The capability for manufacturing nuclear weapons was the only respect in which the French position was more favourable than the German position. Secondly, it was very important to avoid the danger that the French should come to believe that US favoured their renouncing the right to manufacture atomic weapons. The chance of French permanent renunciation was extremely slight, and it would certainly be ruined if it could be labelled as an American project to deprive France of military power. Dillon added an admonition against demands from the other negotiating countries for a *Junktim*. The chances of Euratom were not good if the Belgians and the Germans intended to insist on any very definite progress on the Common Market as the price of their support for Euratom.[167]

In further telegrams Dillon reported about exchanges with Pineau, and with Jean Monnet. Pineau had told Dillon that he saw great difficulties ahead if a renunciation of the right to manufacture nuclear weapons were requested in the Euratom negotiations. Pineau had drawn a line between strategic and tactical nuclear weapons [thus referring to the divison of labour between America and Europe in the New Look strategy][168]. He had marked a distance from his Party leader on the issue. He had opined that Mollet had gone too far in his investiture speech and should have limited himself to renouncing the right to build strategic nuclear bombs. He had doubted the wisdom of France giving up forever the right to manufacture of tactical weapons and he had pointed to complications with respect to nuclear propulsion of submarines.[169]

Dillon's account of his talks with Monnet made clear that Monnet's and his own judgement differed on the wisdom of making permanent renunciation of nuclear weapons a condition in the negotiations, but they had the same opinion about the necessity of the US treading 'very warily' in the field. Monnet was emphatic on the ideological importance of the principle that all members of Euratom should forever forswear right to manufacture nuclear weapons. Dillon did not believe this was possible. Monnet was more optimistic than himself regarding the chances of a renunciation being accepted by France provided that the US kept out of the fight. Monnet had also set out his views of what the US could do to help, Dillon reported. First, and most urgent, 'use every possible argument to persuade the British to cease obstructing EURATOM's efforts'. Second, 'the USA could release immediately nuclear material to EURATOM when it had jelled'.[170]

Monnet tried to counteract the possible influence with the Americans of René Mayer, his successor as President of the Coal and Steel Community who was currently visiting the US. Monnet explained that Mayer now numbered among those French who did not wish France to renounce weapons potential, and he intimated that Mayer's interest in Euratom stemmed from his ambition to return to French politics. It was important that the US did not publicly show interest in Euratom until some request for help had been received.[171]

Mayer in fact raised the subject of French renunciation of nuclear weapons when meeting Dulles in Washington. Mayer made clear his strong belief that France would never give up atomic weapons and that, if this was a condition for Euratom, it would never be accepted by the French Parliament. Dulles then mentioned the idea of a moratorium which, we saw, he had few days before discussed with L. Strauss and Stassen. He suggested that 'in connection with the UN Atomic Energy Agency there might be an agreement that "fourth countries" would not make atomic weapons for a period of time - say five years - during which an effort would be made to eliminate these weapons by agreement between the United States, the Soviet Union and the United Kingdom'. He optimistically observed that 'Mayer seemed to think that this would be acceptable'.[172]

An American input to the Brussels Conference of Foreign Ministers was, we saw, assurances to the Six that the US continued to support firmly a supranational Six-state model for nuclear integration. The intergovernmental concept sponsored by the British, tied to the OEEC, should be seen not as an alternative but as a supplement.

Another cornerstone of American diplomacy in the negotiations about Euratom seems to have been introduced at this time. It was communicated to the Germans just before the start of the conference that the US wished Euratom *ownership* of fissile materials. This was, we saw, an essential part of the 'Monnet concept'. Ambassador Krekeler in Washington reported that the newly appointed US Representative to the Coal and Steel Community, Walton Butterworth, had told him that 'the "special nuclear fuel", which was produced in plants in the Euratom area must remain the property of the supranational authority'. Krekeler added that he was certain that Butterworth's statement reflected the official position of the US Government.[173]

At the Brussels Conference, von Brentano reaffirmed support for the Common Market, and also declared that nuclear collaboration was indispensable for political and economic reasons and because a really efficient control must be organized. He talked about the desirability of a *Junktim* between the projects in the sense that definite steps forward on the more time-consuming Common Market project should have been taken when a treaty on Euratom was ratified. He did not insist on simultaneous ratification, however.[174] The Conference gave the green light to go on with both projects in principle.

Spaak raised the question of nuclear weapons. He opposed a national military option. Would it be possible to organize the Community if a country reserved a certain quantity of nuclear fuel for military purposes? A common renunciation would however in his view be politically unwise, even if he himself had been a long-time partisan of the idea. He referred to the problem of obtaining parliamentary approval of such a renunciation.[175] The six countries should not definitely give up common military uses and might examine in common, at a later stage, whether other than exclusively peaceful use would be possible. In this way, Spaak dissociated himself from the renunciation of the European option in the 'Monnet concept'. Spaak was supported by the representatives of Italy, the Netherlands and Luxemburg. Von Brentano did not express a position, and Pineau, tying the problem to the development of disarmament, made no commitments on either the national or the European option.[176]

A public statement largely along the lines in the AEC proposal that had been discussed at the meeting of the National Security Council two weeks earlier was made on 22 February. The President offered for domestic producers 20,000 kgs. of U-235 and for peaceful purposes abroad an allocation of another 20,000. The IAEA and Euratom were mentioned in positive terms, but the pattern of distribution between the three channels - bilaterals, IAEA, and Euratom - was not specified. Details about prices and distribution between countries were not given. It was declared that they would be announced in the near future. It was stated that 'it is not intended that nations which are presently producing uranium 235, or the Soviet Union and its satellites, shall share in this distribution´. The earlier idea to match the contributions of ´all other nations´ - the USSR - was not included in the statement. The value of the 40.000 kgs. total was estimated to be one billion dollars - an enormous sum at the time.[177] The quantity was enormous also - ´with 20 tonnes of enriched uranium one could blow up the planet´.[178]

Dulles informed relevant US missions of the background to the President´s statement. Consideration had been given to including a specific and substantial suballocation for Euratom; this was however considered premature ´in view uncertainty as to what specific proposals six countries will agree to and US desire maintain initiative in European hands´. The formulation that U-235 would not be available to countries ´presently producing´ this material had been interpreted by some Europeans as an effort by the US to prevent Europe from constructing enrichment facilities, Dulles stated. The US was aware that one of the major drives behind the Brussels work was the European desire to ´stand on their own feet´ in the atomic field and that the construction of an enrichment plant in Europe might have become a symbol of this desire. However, several factors related to non-proliferation and the economy made a European enrichment plant problematic. Further State-AEC study was required and a decision had not yet been made. Dulles added a hint about an American means of pressure: ´It might be noted that should the Europeans decide to proceed with construction of separation facilities, they would in the interim period be in great need of US assistance as a source of U-235´.[179]

The President thus had decided to offer export of the product, enriched uranium, instead of enrichment technology. In American internal discussions the option of helping the Europeans to build an enrichment plant now had little backing. Lewis Strauss told the British that anyone who was thinking seriously about encouraging such a plant in Europe ´ought to have his head examined´.[180] The President described the offer of enriched uranium as unique; he placed it in the perspective of infusing life and vigour into the Atoms for Peace programme. He wrote an irritated letter to Lewis Strauss and recapitulated the development of the programme since his initial speech in 1953. Between intermittent bursts of activity there had, Eisenhower wrote, been ´silence´ or ´complete silence´. He ordered Strauss to work out a plan based on the offer of enriched uranium which included ´speeding up whatever negotiations and decisions are involved´. Regarding the offer, he wrote that the phrase ´unprecedented in history´ was a very convenient phrase that was used all too often:

> However, in the case of the American offer of fissionable material to the world this is an absolutely unprecedented offer, so tremendous in all its aspects that it cannot be grasped, cannot be appreciated and in a real sense cannot be implemented unless these repeated periods of silence

are filled, at least partially, by some public recognition of activity on our part.[181]

It was clear to all concerned in Europe that a European plant could never produce as cheaply as the American production complex. The economic rationale for a European plant had vanished. It was equally clear that the American offer meant dependence on American willingness to honour supply agreements for many years, and that dependence could in any case not be avoided for a period of perhaps 5-7 years while a European plant was being constructed. The American move was received with mixed feelings in Britain. The Foreign Office - aware of Makins´ warnings against doing anything in the enrichment matter without American consent - informed the Washington Embassy that in the light of the American offer everyone would need to reexamine very carefully ´whether it would not be more desirable to postpone consideration of a European plant until the economic and other implications of that offer could be examined´.[182] In France, the American offer was seen by many, not least in nationalist circles, as a means of sabotaging French and European efforts to achieve independence.

The Atomic Energy Commission delivered in April the study that the President had ordered in January. It was remarkably positive towards Euratom and European integration as compared to the Commission´s earlier priority for bilateralism, presumably as a result of the President´s pronouncements in favour of integration.

The study contained a number of recommendations for providing materials and information in order to promote European nuclear integration. A general principle was expressed. The ´United States must be prepared to extend assistance and privileges to the Community equal to or greater than that now, or in the future, to be extended to any one member of the Community under a bilateral arrangement, with the possible exception of Belgium...´ This contained the possibility of *preferential treatment* and was a change compared to the weaker signal that had been sent since the autumn of 1955. The earlier message had been that the Executive Branch was prepared to cooperate directly with Euratom, not just bilaterally with other countries, provided that it were sufficiently supranational.

The study suggested that up to half of the quantity of enriched uranium that had been announced might go to Euratom. The offer meant that ´the technical need for early construction of a gaseous diffusion plant may be deferred´. Nevertheless, Euratom might decide to construct a plant for political reasons. If so, it ´may be that the opportunity to be a part owner in a gaseous diffusion plant plant will be a greater incentive to the integration of the atomic energy effort than any other single factor´. The study proposed that the US should do nothing which would prevent the Community from constructing a plant if desired.[184]

The Spaak Report and the Spaak Compromise

The Spaak Report, with proposals for the Common Market and Euratom, was issued on 21 April.[185]

The Common Market part of the Report - which was the foundation for what was to become a truly revolutionary change in economic and political relations in Europe - will merely be mentioned here. Suffice it to say that the Report outlined the principles for a Common Market for industrial goods, services, capital and labour and harmonization of different kinds of associated national policies - a gigantic project that would not approach full realization until half a century later. The immediate and most precise proposals concerned the liberalization of trade in industrial goods. It was also proposed that a common agricultural policy for regulation of agricultural markets, with no barriers within the area and a common external wall, should be built up. Free trade in industrial goods within the Six state area and a common external tariff - in principle a mean of existing tariffs - would be effectuated in three stages over a period of 12-15 years. The transition between the stages would be automatic and decided in advance. The process would be irreversible, and there would be no right of exit from the system.[186]

The other part of the Report concerned Euratom.

It was initially stated that the resources required to develop atomic power exceeded the capacity of any European country in isolation. The future European energy situation was precarious, and atomic power was needed much more in Europe than in the US. The US Government had spent in total about 15,000 million dollars in the nuclear field and the British Government about 1,500 million. In comparison, France had spent about 200 million dollars. A number of proposals for developing atomic energy in continental Europe were made. The most important issues[187] were:

1. The question of *military use*
2. A *common fuel system*, or, more precisely, a supranational fuel and control system, with
   a) Euratom purchase priority and monopoly of distribution to users (I will use the term ´supply monopoly´ for both aspects)
   b) Euratom legal authority over fuels (´*sui generis*´ instead of ´ownership´)
   c) A system for control to ensure that nuclear fuels were not used for other purposes than intended
3. *Sharing of information*
4. *Common installations*, most importantly a European enrichment plant within or outside the framework of Euratom

1. It proved impossible to include anything about the military question in the Spaak Report. A moratorium was discussed, and the Draft Report of 8 April recommended a moratorium of five years in the manufacture of atomic

weapons, defined as ´uncontrolled explosive devices´ [thus not including submarine reactors]. The French Cabinet was however unable to agree to the moratorium, and the French delegation to the Spaak Committee was consequently unwilling to discuss it.[188] In the Report the military question had been taken out; it was referred to a higher political level.[189]

2. The common fuel system was vital for obtaining effective control of the entire atomic energy sectors of the member countries, but nothing was said explicitly about this non-proliferation function. France had requested a common fuel system in the negotiations also for other reasons than the wish to control Germany militarily. France wanted protection against the possibility that Germany, by operating on its own in the fuel area and making bilateral agreements with the US and/or Britain, would catch up with and outdistance France in the civil nuclear field.[190] Further, the system would provide protection against the possibility that the Anglo-American bloc steered the stream of raw materials and enriched uranium to Europe in a way that created difficulties for France, particularly in the event that France decided to procure nuclear weapons.

The Report proposed that the purchase priority would apply to fuels ´not committed´, and that ´fissile materials produced in non-Community installations should be reserved for the enterprises which produced them or to those for which they are intended under the programme that binds these enterprises together, including in those cases where they are shared out´. This was the concept of ´tied programmes´. It was a complicated and discreet way of saying that existing arrangements, essentially French and Belgian ones as Germany and the others had only small activities yet, would not be affected by the supply monopoly.[191] Maurice Faure, when negotiating with the British a couple of months later, explained the importance of these clauses for guarding the military option for France:

> Membership of EURATOM would not involve any change in her programme at Marcoule[192] whether as regards power production or the production of plutonium. France would also retain the right to build more such installations, if required. - As to EURATOM´s right of purchase, M. Faure said that this would be the general rule, but there would be a very important exception, namely, for ´tied programmes´. Where production was tied to a certain consumer there would be an ´escape´ from EURATOM´s monopoly of purchase. The consumer might be a power station, or it could be a Ministry of Defence.[193]

The Report proposed a number of rules for supply of fuels, and for the control system. The general principle was supply monopoly for Euratom, equal access to fuels for users, and Euratom physical custody of fissile materials that were not actually in use. Rules were proposed for fixing of prices and for situations of scarcity. An exception to the supply monopoly was proposed: if Euratom was unable to deliver fuels to a user, the user who received an offer from elsewhere could take advantage of it, 'in conditions to be defined'. This proposal covered for example the possibility that Germany might be allowed to make bilateral deals in case of scarcity. It was designed to create an exception to the supply monopoly in response to German fears of discrimination, as the Federal Republic had no uranium production of its own.

The rules about price setting and supply in situations of scarcity were disputed both before and after the appearance of the Report. The Germans criticized them, arguing that they were designed to bolster high-cost production in French uranium mines and to make German users pay prices above world market prices.

The word 'ownership' was not mentioned in the Report. This sensitive issue, which was included in the 'Monnet concept' and soon forcefully supported by the Americans, was hidden behind a diffuse compromise. It was argued that the consequence of the rules for supply and control was that the contracts about fuels were of a particular kind, 'sui generis'. It was envisaged that the fuels would be rented by users in certain specified cases, for example for particularly dangerous materials.[194]

The principles for the control system were sketched loosely and without going into controversial questions like the extent of inspection, and so on. The aim of the security control was not formulated in the usual way as control of clandestine diversion from civil to military uses, but as guaranteeing 'that nuclear materials will not be diverted to uses other than those for which they are intended'. This formula was no restriction for French national nuclear weapons, but for German ones, taking the *Kernwaffenverzicht* into account. The sanction in case of violation was refusal or prohibition to supply nuclear fuels.[195]

3. There were a number of proposals concerning sharing of information: common research projects in parallel to the national research efforts, exchange of scientific-technical information, participation in patent rights, and so on. The general principle was voluntariness, and the maintenance of the provisions about information that existed in agreements with third countries - that is, in bilaterals with the US and the UK.

4. It was proposed that installations for production of 'concentrated fissile materials', should be managed by Euratom. The Report contained a conciliatory but not binding formula, apparently designed to appease France and sufficiently loose not to bind the others to participate in a European enrichment plant. The question would be studied without delay by a Study Group which was being organized. The French delegation had without success insisted on a definite proposal for construction of the enrichment

plant. The other kind of project that was important from a proliferation point of view, a reprocessing plant, was referred to a more distant future.[196] Spaak´s private attitude to a European enrichment plant was less than enthusiastic. He indicated to the US Ambassador in Brussels that ´if the United States could assure sufficient enriched uranium for EURATOM purposes for the next ten to fifteen years, he would wish to take the lead in opposing the construction of a diffusion (isotopic separation) plant by EURATOM´.[197]

As the question of military use had been taken out of the Report, Spaak decided to propose in a personal capacity a moratorium. His confidential letter to the Foreign Ministers contained essentially the passage that had been taken out of the Draft Report. It became known as the ´Spaak Compromise´. In the opening sentence of the letter, Spaak wrote:

With the prospect of efforts to achieve world disarmament, the member states would agree for a fixed period to renounce production of strategic nuclear weapons (for mass destruction) and tactical nuclear weapons (shells).[198]

In changed circumstances, the Council would decide unanimously about a change of policy. The renunciation would not apply to transfers from other countries. After the fixed period a member state would regain the right of manufacturing weapons only after agreement by at least two other states. Euratom would be in charge of the fuel and control system. The rules would be the same for military and civil uses, and special provisions would apply for allocation in situations of scarcity. No mention was made of propulsion reactors.

This made the compromise more palatable for the French who were busily engaged in the programme for constructing submarine reactors. This feature also appeared to be attractive to the Germans. An *Auswärtiges Amt* memorandum concluded that the Spaak Compromise was a ´useful basis´ for the discussion because it did not include propulsion reactors, and because the rules for control and supply of nuclear fuels were the same for civil and military uses.[199]

In sum, the moratorium proposed in the ´Spaak compromise´ was a supranational moratorium. It covered all kinds of nuclear explosives, tactical as well as strategic , the A-level as well as the H-level. It would not allow France to go on independently with any kind of nuclear weapons after the period of renunciation.

Franz-Josef Strauss´ Exploratory Visit to the US

The front figure of the German anti-Euratom coalition, the Minister for Atomic Energy F.-J. Strauss visited the United States on 14-17 May to probe the American attitude. The briefing material for Dulles anticipated that Strauss would ask for US-German bilateralism, and that he would argue the case for a strict *Junktim* between Euratom and the Common Market. Dulles was advised not to discuss the possibility of a power bilateral at the current delicate stage of the negotiations in Europe, but to envisage ´preferential treatment´ for Euratom as compared to a bilateral agreement.[201]

Strauss first met Dulles´ collaborators, then Dulles also. He declared that he had heard of two US views, one favouring Euratom, the other the OEEC. The German Government would like to have Euratom as part of the OEEC approach. The Germans would not like to have the British left out, ´without them EURATOM would consist of five blinds and one half-blind (which he identified as France)´. Strauss declared that the ´Monnet concept´ was absolutely unacceptable to the German Government and Parliament. Strauss proposed a moderate version of the *Junktim*. He realized that the Common Market could not be fully achieved at once. To insist on simultaneous realization would be to sabotage Euratom. But there must be some sort of ´real step, or ´first step´, as the German Government expected that it would take twelve to fifteen years to achieve a Common Market. If there were no such step in connection with Euratom, the Common Market would never be accomplished. At the luncheon with the State Department officials he began to ´talk more freely´. He said that ´…if any attempt were made in Germany to proceed with EURATOM separately from the common market he would immediately leave the Cabinet. He also said that the majority of Adenauer´s Ministers would follow suit, and that this would bring about the collapse of the present Government´. Needless to say, this scenario was repugnant to the Americans, who placed their faith in Adenauer and saw his Government as a bulwark against dangerous tendencies towards neutralism.

Strauss addressed the military question squarely, indicating that he was in favour of keeping a European option and against a French national one. There were also problems in drawing the dividing line between military and civil uses:

Military use: He would not wish to see all Europe abandon military use. This has nothing to do with Germany. In any case, weapons should not be produced by one Western European nation alone. However, it would encourage Moscow and might eventually become a means of neutralization. Mr. Strauss said he did not want raw materials divided into civilian and military use and did not want research and technical secrets treated differently, e.g. withheld from the partners in EURATOM on the grounds of military use.

Dulles talked about the necessity of integration, and the American right to try to bring it about, considering that the US had been drawn into two world wars that had started in Europe. He gave his assessment of the two integration projects, seeing the Common Market in the perspective of the economic struggle with the USSR. The US was ´all in favor of the common market idea´, he said. ´With the common market Europe would be a third force along with the US and the Soviet Union. If Europe does not have a common market, it will remain weak.´ He opposed the *Junktim*, though: ´...if a common market is made an absolute condition for unity in atomic power development, Europe may end up with nothing.´ [202] He exposed in a very direct way the non-proliferation motive behind the US effort to get approval of Euratom, and the appalling prospects unless the spread of nuclear weapons could be halted:

> The problem is to have controls to insure that atomic energy is being used for peaceful purposes. Because of the by-product of plutonium, the efficacy of controls will be most important. It is our thought that the larger and more responsible the safeguard organization the more control will be facilitated. This would be better than multiple controls of many individual countries involving complicated policing. It is appalling to contemplate a multiplicity of uncontrolled national atomic developments leading to multiplying atomic weapons programs. If you set up a pattern allowing the thing to spread on national lines there will be the danger of irresponsible action. While certain nations are capable of the responsibility there are other places in the world without the necessary sense.

Strauss stated, however, that the German Government was against ownership of fissile materials and purchase monopoly in Euratom´s common fuel system, and also against compulsory exchange of information. The Government would feel differently if the supranational authority, like the AEC in the US, were an instrument of a European government.[203]

Comments in the State Department on the Strauss visit were critical. Strauss had wanted to satify the American requirements by controls only over materials from the US. The only utility he had seen in Euratom was its function in bargaining for French acceptance of the Common Market. [204] His attitude had not been reassuring with respect to critical sections in the Spaak Report, for example the ´loophole´ of members contracting for nuclear material when Euratom could not meet the demands of member states.[205] The Embassy in Bonn was instructed to see Adenauer or von Brentano and tell them about Strauss´ ambiguous attitude. Although Strauss had professed support for Euratom, the proposals he had made raised doubts as to his sincerity. Strauss´ public statements in America about bilateralism would have ´most unfortunate impact on Brussel´s Group´s efforts´.[206]

In Paris, Monnet reassured Maurice Faure that the Americans had stood firm with respect to Strauss' proposals. They had talked about preferential treatment for Euratom and they had rejected bilateralism so long as there remained a hope that a European Community would be created.[207]

The US Message to the Europeans before the Venice Conference

Those European integrationists who were in regular contact with the Americans and were well-informed about the situation in France incessantly urged them to exert influence but to do it discreetly in order not to hurt French feelings. Dillon's reports from Paris followed a similar pattern.

The efforts intensified in the period between the appearance of the Spaak Report and the Conference of Foreign Ministers in Venice which would decide about the fate of the Report. Monnet exhorted Lewis Strauss to 'tread wearily' in the matter of allocating enriched material to Euratom. It would be difficult for public opinion to understand why the US should allocate materials to Euratom before it had been formed. The public might conclude that pressure was being brought on Europe in order to bring about the creation of Euratom. Monnet advised that 'any announcement should follow the raising of the question by the European powers rather than precede it'.[208] Louis Armand, when meeting a group of US diplomats and a representative of the AEC in Paris, talked about the importance of Euratom for the development of a huge atomic energy industry in Europe, for research, and so on. OEEC had also a role to play, but the Six should join this kind of cooperation via the common organization. Armand stressed that the atomic weapons provision in Euratom should be left aside. The French themselves would renounce the construction of bombs within two or three years. He warned the Americans against giving any of the Six, except Belgium, a power bilateral pending the completion of the negotiations on Euratom. The US should use its 'full influence' to promote Euratom, although this had to be done with discretion and tact, 'one can say it without saying it'.[209]

Dulles decided however not to be silent but to communicate American positions directly and officially. He was possibly influenced by the fact that the President in a talk with him had seemed to disagree with the position that the US should do nothing about integration, unless asked by the French.[210] Dulles summarized the US standpoints which had been evolving for about a year and more or less clearly communicated through diplomatic channels, in a memorandum to the relevant US missions in Europe. The missions were asked to try to clear up any misunderstandings about US positions in the minds of the participants in Venice. This was a direct intervention at a strategic moment and represented an exception to the general rule of not officially exercising pressure on the negotiations in Europe.[211]

The memorandum started by enumerating the reasons for US support of Euratom: the need for tying Germany organically to the West, to submerge Franco-German rivalry, to get an integrated organization with the necessary control powers and safeguards, and to get rapid development of nuclear industry in continental Western Europe. These objectives could only be met through a Six-country supranational organization. The principle of preferential treatment was proclaimed: The US ´could make available substantially greater resources and adopt attitude of substantially greater liberality towards real integrated community´ than for countries separately.

The question that was most emphatically stressed was the need for a common fuel system. Dulles would be ´greatly concerned´ if there were to be compromise on the points of (a) ownership of fuel, and (b) the possibility for member states to go outside Euratom to obtain nuclear materials. The US view was that Euratom ´must have authority fuel, which if not ownership, is as complete as if Euratom owned fuel´. Separate arrangements for procuring materials outside Euratom seemed to ´strike at heart of Euratom concept´. The Six should be informed that failure to meet these points would ´raise problems with respect future ability US cooperate substantially with Euratom´.

Dulles gave confidential [´for your information´, FYI] instructions about two other major issues that were likely to arise in Venice. First, the question of military uses. The US was against proliferation and supported the Spaak Compromise, but the official posture was neutrality:

Military uses. FYI. We consider desirable discourage atomic weapons production in countries not now producers. Atomic weapons moratorium would also postpone day when Germans raise discrimination issue and seek end WEU ban on production in Germany of nuclear weapons. Therefore US views favourably moratorium proposed Spaak letter ... However, in view delicacy French internal problem this subject, with Cabinet split and Pineau consequently likely to go to Venice uninstructed, we are concerned that expression at this time of US view would do more harm than good. End FYI. Therefore, official posture US officials at this time should be to leave the matter for Europeans themselves to decide.

The second issue was the *Junktim*. Even if the US was preliminarily sympathetic to the Common Market, it was not in favour of a linkage between the two projects:

Common Market Tie. The Germans, in particular, and Dutch and Belgians to lesser degree, assert Euratom by itself is insufficient step toward integration. Strauss, German Minister for Atomic Energy Affairs, would even condition German ratification of Euratom on simultaneous ratification of the Common Market by Germany's partners. US sympathetic desire Six countries establish Common Market though we have not completed study Common Market report. However, we would certainly hope that approval of Treaty for Euratom, which of such immediate importance, would not be held up until complex and doubtless lengthy Common Market negotiations concluded. FYI. Additional reason for US opposition to link is indication that chances for French ratification of Common Market are presently far more uncertain than for ratification of Euratom. End FYI.

Dulles finished by complaining about the use of the OEEC by the British 'to undermine Euratom effort'. He criticized a British suggestion for a common reprocessing plant[212] within the OEEC framework. Such a plant would 'tend to reduce apparent technical advantages of Six-power approach and can be used by opponents of European integration to argue Euratom not urgent'. Recent inferences that the US preferred the OEEC over Euratom were incorrect, Dulles stated, although the OEEC also had a role to play as a framework for broad cooperation.

The enrichment question was not mentioned.

Spaak was pleased with the exposition of American policy. He thoroughly agreed, it was reported. The American message would be most helpful and strengthen his position in Venice.[213]

Dulles also opened up for release of Belgian uranium to Euratom. The move should be seen in conjunction with the memorandum and as a part of the general policy to promote the Six-state projects - a policy which also included Eisenhower's enrichment offer. Replying to a letter from Spaak, in which Spaak had proposed to study possible changes in the US-Belgian bilateral in order to facilitate agreement on Euratom, Dulles wrote that he left it for Spaak's determination if such studies should be undertaken.[214] Spaak was gratified, it was reported. He said that if the Euratom principle was approved in Venice he would now be in a position to inform the other foreign ministers that he expected to enter negotiations with the US and UK about tranfer of uranium rights to Euratom.[215]

The US missions in the capitals of the Six sent estimates of the integrative propensity in their host countries with respect to both Euratom and the Common Market, transmitted the US message, and reported about reactions. Dillon sent a pessimistic report about the prospects for approval of Euratom in France. The key question, 'the Gordian knot of whole problem', seemed to him to be the question of manufacture of atomic weapons. The Foreign Affairs Committee of the National Assembly was not prone to take a vote on the Monnet Resolution - 'name which even its active supporters try to avoid for psychological reasons' - before summer. If it did, it was improbable that a majority could be obtained. Even a number of those members of the Committee who were in favour of integration would probably oppose the

Resolution on the ground that France should not renounce the right to manufacture atomic weapons. Time worked against approval of Euratom. The interest in European integration was, in Dillon´s view, a subject of much less passionate interest than at the time of the EDC. The North African problems were the principal preoccupations of French politicians. Various supporters of Euratom had told the Embassy that action was needed during the ongoing session in the Assembly. The parliamentary calendar made this difficult, however, and it was far from certain that there existed majority for Euratom: 'There was not a majority for the EDC when it finally came to a vote and this lesson should be remembered'. Furthermore, the issue was unresolved within the Government. Dillon estimated that unless something unforeseen occurred, the French representatives in Venice would not have a position on the issue of weapons manufacture.[216]

The day before the opening of the Venice Conference, Dillon met Pineau´s Under Secretary and spokesman in Brussels, Maurice Faure. The situation was discussed in detail. The talk showed that the American and French positions appeared to coincide on two key points, Euratom ownership of fuels and the *Junktim*. Faure´s view of the crucial ownership issue was something new - the French had not, it seems, sent similar signals before this meeting:

Dillon reported that Faure was pleased with the memorandum generally and with the reiteration of the US 'hands off position on military uses'. Faure stated that the French position was now in favour of ownership of fuel by Euratom and if that did not prove to be possible the French shared the US view that Euratom must have authority over fuel as complete as if it owned the fuel. Faure added that the only difficulty in this regard would come from Germany. Faure further interpreted the prospect about preferential treatment of Euratom as dealing with the control which would be required by the US. He went on to the *Junktim*. He was, Dillon reported, particularly pleased by the US position on this point. When questioned, Faure answered that he felt that it should be possible to negotiate a Euratom treaty within approximately two months, whereas it would take six months to a year to negotiate a treaty on the Common Market. Faure informed Dillon that it was 80 per cent sure that the French would propose in Venice that overseas territories of the member countries would be included in the Common Market. It was difficult to proceed rapidly with the Common Market at a time when France was severely strained financially by military costs in Algeria. Finally, Faure declared that the only problem with Euratom lay in Germany, in particular with German industrialists. He exposed the French views about America´s task in calling them to order and asked for even stronger American resistance against US-German bilateralism. He said that he understood that F. -J. Strauss had returned to Germany disappointed in the prospects for purely bilateral assistance from the US. If this attitude could be maintained and reinforced, in particular during Adenauer´s forthcoming visit to the US, the prospects for a really integrated Euratom were good, he argued.[217]

In Bonn, Conant made parallel efforts. He reported that the German Cabinet had decided to accept the Common Market and Euratom projects in the Spaak Report as a whole as basis for further negotiations, and to stand firm on the *Junktim*.[218] Together with the American representative to the Coal and Steel Community, Walton Butterworth, he met a number of ministers, officials and leading industrialists, and underlined the themes in the US memorandum. The industrialists were very loath, Conant reported, to accept Euratom if it was not a ´probable first step´ to the Common Market. They were worried lest Euratom by itself would be a means of curbing German technical ability, and a means of expansion of power by the French or by a series of Socialist governments in other European states. Furthermore the prestige of German industry was to some degree involved.[219]

The Venice Conference (29-30 May 1956)

The Conference of Foreign Ministers in Venice was a milestone in the negotiations, giving the green light for continuing with both projects. It became clear at once that the French Government was in favour of continuing to negotiate about the Common Market on the basis of the Spaak Report, provided that certain conditions were accepted. Pineau also introduced the new element, which Faure had signalled to Dillon. He demanded the inclusion of overseas territories in the Common Market, a question that had not been dealt with in the Spaak Report. He also proposed that the transition between stages in the Common Market would not be automatic. The leader of the German delegation, Hallstein, stressed that the transition between stages had to be defined as irrevocable in the treaty, and he added - obviously as an appetizer to the French and also reflecting the outcome of deliberations by the German farming organizations - that a solution for agriculture had to be included.

The nuclear component of the bargain played its role. Pineau supported the principles about Euratom in the Spaak Report and suggested, concerning the military question, that the Ministers might take the Spaak Compromise as basis for discussion. Hallstein reiterated the German standpoint that the Federal Republic supported Euratom albeit conditionally. He expressed reservations about the common fuel system and the control system; details would be presented later. The common fuel system should assure a sufficient and non-discriminatory supply, and security controls should not be excessive but permit economic development and sufficient freedom. Furthermore, the same rules and controls should apply to all military as well as civil applications.[220]

Spaak said that the military question was urgent, the Ministers could not wait too long for a solution. In his view, a treaty on Euratom could not be elaborated without it. He suggested a new ministerial meeting about the issue after the vacations. Italy's Gaetano Martino stressed that Euratom's common fuel system had to be comprehensive, there should be no possibility of procuring fuels outside it. On the military question he argued that production of nuclear weapons would require a long preparatory period. Meanwhile, the ties between the members could be reinforced. And, referring to the European option, 'it would be inopportune for continental Europe to renounce *a priori* the most modern means of defence'. According to an American report about the proceedings, Martino also referred to the US memorandum and raised the question of a joint approach to the US with respect to nuclear materials. However, Pineau 'brusquely shelved discussion this issue implying it indiscreet of Italians have brought US views into conference with danger of resulting publicity'.[221]

Although France agreed to continue the negotiations on the Common Market, the French stuck to the position that the time perspectives for the Common Market and for Euratom were different. This was partly for tactical reasons. All the other countries stood behind the *Junktim*.

The Conference decided that the work on drafting treaties for the two organizations would continue at an Intergovernmental Conference under the chairmanship of Spaak. The Ministers would reconvene periodically and pronounce themselves on two issues in particular, the military question and the inclusion of overseas territories. A door was kept open for Britain and others, but no concessions were made. A country could be invited after agreement by all Six, but every invitation would 'presuppose the acceptance by the third country concerned of the common basis for negotiation on which the Six have reached agreement'.[222]

Thus, with respect to Euratom, no decisions had been taken in Venice on the issues that were central in US policy: renunciation of military uses or a (supranational) moratorium, common ownership of fuels, and the supply monopoly. 'Neither French nor Germans were ready lay cards on table and no attempt made negotiate at Venice meeting'.[223]

The Germans, we saw, had requested that the same rules and controls should apply to all military as well as civil applications. I will call this condition *minimum equality*. The principle was tied to different points in the Spaak Report. If France was to have full military freedom of action and no supranational bonds whatsoever, this would require exceptions - with reference to military needs - from the common ownership of fuels, from the supply monopoly, and from the control system.[224] The negotiations about Euratom in the Intergovernmental Conference until the signature of the Treaty dealt largely with the problem of to what extent the 'minimum equality' principle would be upheld. The French and the Germans played the principal parts in the negotiation battle. The other Four, and, acting in the background, the Americans supported 'minimum equality'.

Conclusion

The Paris Accords had solved acute problems but the solution was deficient from the American point of view. The WEU model contributed very little to general supranational integration and to the proliferation problem only partly. A system without loop-holes for controlling Germany in the nuclear field had not been obtained, and France retained more or less full freedom of action.

Dulles had learnt from the EDC failure that direct and visible US intervention in European negotiations was an extremely sensitive matter, particularly in France, and too much pressure could result in a backlash. The tactic now was to avoid open threats and ultimata that were not sufficiently credible, and to use indirect means and intermediaries as far as possible.

The American interest focused from the start on the nuclear part of the *relance* plan that was developed by Monnet, Spaak and the Dutch. It is even possible that the US had a role in the origins, although I have found no direct evidence of this, only circumstantial indications. The Common Market part of the plan also fitted well with the general perspective of the importance of regional supranational integration for double containment and the principles for support of regional economic integration that had been outlined in the Randall Report a year earlier. The State Department declared support for the Common Market idea in general terms. A Common Market was however seen as a much more difficult and uncertain project. It was believed that it would require a protracted negotiation period even if the resistance from important economic groups in France could eventually be overcome.

It was obvious to the Six that the dominant American position in the nuclear area, and the immense resources and know-how that were concentrated in the US, provided a basis for deciding about the fate of the European nuclear project. The US could 'kill the new integration plan outright' if it insisted on dealing only with individual countries and not with the Six as a group.

Very early it was decided in the State Department that a solution should be sought in which deals with a supranational entity and individual countries could go on in parallel. The State Department did not take the line that nuclear cooperation could take place only if the Six integrated sufficiently in the field. There was a strong domestic and transnational combination of forces opposing such an idea. The AEC and domestic industrial interests were on the offensive to sell American civil nuclear technology to Europe, notably to Germany. The nuclear lobby had substantial backing in Congress. German industry and other European groups which opposed Euratom allied with these American interests.

Britain was also an unobtrusive member of the anti-Euratom alliance. For the continental powers, cooperation with Britain was an alternative to cooperation with the US. Both German and French interests explored the possibilities and the British gave them encouragement. The British launched the OEEC as a non-supranational framework for development of civil nuclear energy, and they argued that sufficient safeguards against clandestine military uses could be developed. The American response was to accept officially that Euratom and the OEEC were two parallel and non-conflicting roads to the future. The priority for the Six state model and for Euratom was however expressed first diffusely and later clearly. The British were told that even if they did not want to participate themselves they should not try to sabotage the Six-state projects, at least not Euratom. The positions were agreed during the Eden talks in Washington in February. The Americans refused to accept any kind of subordination of Euratom under the OEEC, and the British - while 'hostile' to the Common Market - agreed not to oppose Euratom and not to advance the OEEC as an alternative, only as a compatible project.

In American planning the possibility of an agreement on disarmament and non-proliferation with the Soviet Union was always present. Dulles explained internally that he saw three general approaches to advancing US interests in the nuclear field, and that all could be pursued at the same time: the IAEA, the bilateral approach, and US support for an integrated institution in Europe.

Departing from these considerations the US standpoints with respect to the negotiations about Euratom were elaborated in the months between the appearance of the French-inspired 'Armand concept' and the Venice Conference. They concerned (1) the balance between bilateralism and deals with Euratom as a group (2) enrichment policy, (3) renunciation or moratorium on manufacture of nuclear weapons, (4) Euratom's fuel and control system, (5) the linkage between Euratom and the Common Market, and (6) release of the Belgian uranium. In parallel, pronouncements of general support for the Common Market were made from time to time, normally with the reservation that further study was required and that it was understood that the average tariff level against third countries would not be raised.

The formula that was developed for channelling US aid to Euratom or in bilateral deals was 'preferential treatment'. That is, it was indicated that substantially greater resources and scientific-technical information would be allocated to a sufficiently supranational Euratom than in agreements with individual members of the Six. The Germans and the French wanted to retain the opportunity of making bilaterals between themselves and the US, but they also wanted to block US bilateral preferential treatment of the other party. From the horizon of the State Department the problem of bilateralism became a problem of balancing and temporizing.

The enrichment monopoly and the secrecy surrounding enrichment was a key factor in the American bargaining position; the importance of this factor can hardly be overestimated. The US possessed a huge productive capacity that was no longer needed for producing bombs. The construction of a European plant would take 5-7 years and in this period the US and - to a very small extent - Britain would be the only possible suppliers. For France, European aid in the difficult task of constructing and financing an enrichment plant was a main factor behind the French priority for Euratom. Access to enriched uranium without conditions for civil use only was necessary for H-bomb aspirations and crucial for the nuclear submarine programme. It was evident that there was no economic rationale for building a European plant, only the wish to avoid dependence on the US and Britain during a limited period. It was considered internally in the US whether the US should offer participation in the construction of a European plant as a means of promoting integration, but the possibility was discarded. The AEC Chairman admonished that anyone who was thinking seriously about encouraging such a plant in Europe 'ought to have his head examined'. British plans for offering enrichment technology as a means of promoting the British concepts of European cooperation were halted by the Americans. President Eisenhower offered American export of enriched uranium in unprecedented quantities before the appearance of the Spaak Report. Prices were not specified, but it was envisaged that the material would be much cheaper than that which might be produced in a European plant.

It was discussed in interagency talks whether renunciation of nuclear weapons and a comprehensive control over the entire nuclear sector in a recipient country could be made a condition for receiving US aid. The question affected all three channels for distribution of nuclear resources and information, the IAEA, the bilateral channel and regional organizations like Euratom. It was concluded that if this were to be requested, many nations, France in particular, would not adhere to the IAEA, and Euratom would most certainly fail. Dillon in Paris sent repeated warnings against accepting the 'Monnet concept' in this respect. Dulles admitted that it was difficult or impossible to make other countries forego the nuclear weapons options as long as the existing nuclear powers continued to produce them. It was decided that the realistic way seemed to be to try to 'prevent, retard, or minimize' the emergence of nuclear weapons by other means. Dulles said internally that it might be possible to get agreement about a moratorium, and he mentioned the possibility in talks with Europeans. The American support for a moratorium explains much of its role in the European negotiations in the following months. In the 'Spaak Compromise'- the concept of a supranational moratorium was introduced, and Dulles supported it discreetly in the American message to the Europeans before the Venice Conference.

The theme that was most emphatically underlined in that message was the need for a common fuel system in Euratom. Dulles stressed the necessity of supranational authority over the nuclear fuel cycle in the member states. This meant that the ambitions had been reduced compared to the Baruch Plan a decade earlier. In that plan the supranational authority would be global and it would comprise both the important installations, like reactors, and the fuel cycle. It was made completely clear in the message that the issues of *ownership* and *supply monopoly* were crucial for US support of Euratom. Euratom must have authority over fuel, 'which if not ownership, is as complete as if Euratom owned fuel'. Separate arrangements for procuring materials outside Euratom were not acceptable. Unless these points were met the US could probably not cooperate substantially with Euratom.

Dulles communicated repeatedly to the Europeans that he thought that the linkage between Euratom and the Common Market was a bad idea. However, both the pro- and anti-Euratom factions in Germany were united in the demand for the *Junktim*, as were other negotiating countries than France, notably the Dutch. The demand was not given up. The Germans argued that Euratom without guarantees for the Common Market could not be ratified in Germany. The unspoken argument was: 'If Germany accepts supranational control without loop-holes of the nuclear weapons option, France should accept "minimum equality", and also accept the Common Market.'

Finally, Dulles communicated to Spaak that the Belgian uranium and the preferential treatment that had been accorded to Belgium in previous US-Belgian agreements might be transferred to Euratom if Euratom was accepted in principle in Venice. There was however an increasing awareness that the epoch of scarcity of uranium was coming to an end. Uranium was no longer, as Spaak had believed at the beginning of the negotiations, a 'trump card' for promoting agreement on integration.

In sum, the central American goal was to subject the *entire* nuclear fuel cycle in Germany to supranational authority. This was the most important among the various means for arms control of that country. Euratom ownership of fuels and the supply monopoly would put restrictions on France also. These might perhaps prevent, but at least retard and minimize, development of French nuclear weapons. The German demand for 'minimum equality' could only reinforce this strategy.

5

Euratom and the Linkage to the Common Market: Second Phase

US Signals to Germany and France after the Venice Conference

Dulles met first Adenauer, then Pineau, after the results of the Venice Conference had been digested in Washington. Dulles' message - essentially elaborations of the positions in the US memorandum - constituted an additional American input to the Intergovernmental Conference.

In briefing papers for Adenauer before the meeting it was stressed that it was necessary to obtain American understanding for the necessity of the *Junktim*. A specific argument might impress the Americans. That was that sectoral integration without simultaneous general integration would entail social and economic disturbances to which Germany, having an exposed political situation, could not be subjected. The questions of ownership and the supply monopoly in Euratom were characterized as questions of 'technical expediency', not of 'principle'. The German views should conform with American negative conceptions of a protective *dirigisme* that took decisions on research and the economy. It was important to find out whether the Americans would make their preferred solutions in these respects an absolute condition for cooperation with Euratom:

> It can safely be assumed that what interests the Americans more than anything is an absolutely reliable control of nuclear fuel, which could however also be guaranteed by acceptance of the German proposal. For that reason it would be useful to establish whether the American Government will really make acceptance of its wishes a *sine qua non* for cooperation with EURATOM.[1]

At the meeting with Adenauer, Dulles did not mention the non-proliferation aspect directly. He talked about how vital both integration projects were for the salvation of Western Europe. He emphasized the economic threat from the Soviets. The USSR was 'transforming itself rapidly, with the benefit of forced labour, into a modern and efficient industrial state in which atomic energy would be important'. The rate of industrial growth was more rapid than that of Western Europe. He 'did not think Western Europe could survive economically with what in many countries are obsolete plants, with cartels, with small markets, all resulting in high costs. He thought that at the present time the economic danger from the Soviet Union was perhaps greater than the military danger'. Dulles also talked about the danger of interruption of the flow of Middle East oil: 'The industry of Western Europe would be paralyzed and the operation of NATO would be greatly impaired if the USSR or its friends or agents were able to cut off this oil'. Adenauer reaffirmed his long-standing support for integration, but did not seem impressed by the picture of economic danger painted by Dulles. He seemed sceptical about the economic importance of atomic energy in East-West competition. He remarked that he had learnt from his recent visit to the Soviet Union that there were many economic problems there, for example in agriculture. He had also got different views of the future of atomic energy when speaking to Soviet leaders: 'Khrushchev had given him a glowing account of Soviet development of atomic energy. However, Malenkov had told him that this was far from true and that he did not agree as to the possibilities of nuclear energy. Malenkov had said he thought the British atomic energy program was too optimistic'. Adenauer's opinion was that 'one should take a calm view of developments in the Soviet Union'.

Adenauer also referred to the Saar problem. He mentioned his successful negotiations with Mollet the previous week about the Saar. The Saar would be united with Germany on 1 January, 1957: 'A price would have to be paid for this, but this would do no harm'. [2]

At dinner the same night there was some further discussion about Euratom. Dulles said that the US did not consider the *Junktim* wise. Adenauer said that he favoured the Euratom idea in principle but he was afraid that it was being set up in such a way as to promote socialism. Hallstein explained that the Federal Republic had been compelled to make a reservation about the common fuel system in Venice...'the agency should not retain ownership, but should exercise all the controls that could be exercised if there were ownership'. [3]

Few days later, on 18-19 June, Dulles met Pineau. In connection with discussion of NATO problems Pineau argued that more could be attempted in the field of economic cooperation - apparently wanting to probe whether the US might be interested in widening the negotiation context for the ongoing negotiations in Europe and support the French standpoints directly in NATO. Pineau suggested that certain economic problems might be taken up in NATO. It would be useful to discuss political aspects of purely economic organizations there, he said, for example the possibility of establishing the Common Market by graduated steps, which would require a modification of GATT. He also suggested that there would be certain large joint undertakings which would be of strategic benefit to the whole NATO area. [4] Dulles rejected such ideas. He 'saw a danger in attempting to take steps which might turn NATO into a substitute for agreements between countries.

Any development of NATO should not be such as to suggest that it could be a substitute for close agreements between members, such as Euratom and the Common Market. NATO should remain essentially as a forum in which political consultation can take place'.[5]

Pineau reviewed the results of the Venice Conference. The French Government felt that Euratom should be ratified first, the Common Market later. Thus, no *Junktim*. Euratom should exercise control over fissionable material. While Adenauer personally might agree to this, there was opposition in Germany.[6] The French Parliament was reluctant to commit France never to make an atomic bomb, but was in favour of a moratorium. If this situation was not taken into account, there would be a risk that Euratom would fail.[7] Some French groups were hostile to the restriction that Euratom would be exclusively dedicated to the peaceful uses of atomic energy, he said.[8] With regard to the Common Market he pointed to the French demands for social harmonization, flexibility of stages, and the inclusion of overseas territories. Pineau finished by asking whether Dulles could tell him what Adenauer was thinking in these matters.

Dulles stressed as usual the necessity of European integration and Eisenhower's and his own early commitment to the idea. As when talking to Adenauer, he dwelled on the theme that the recent Soviet economic offensive made integration even more important. About his talks with Adenauer, he said that he could say that he had told Adenauer that he was against the *Junktim*. It seemed to him, however, that the Germans were for it. The fundamental problem with regard to Euratom was the establishment and maintenance of adequate controls. The US position was that both Euratom ownership of fissile materials and strict controls were required.[9] If Euratom did not, however, retain actual title, then the control to be exercised should be as complete in all respects as if title were retained. He told Pineau that when Adenauer had said that control by Euratom might lead to socialization of the atomic energy industry Dulles had retorted that the system for ownership of fissionable material that he favoured existed in the US and did not mean socialization. Further, he had advanced the 'preferential treatment' argument. He had emphasized that 'the US would undoubtedly have a closer relationship with Euratom than with individual countries'.[10] Dulles did not - this was fully in conformity with general American strategy when dealing with the French - take up directly with Pineau the key question of French nuclear weapons.

Thus, after the talks with Adenauer and Pineau, the message that had been transmitted by Dulles was this: (1) he had told both the Germans and the French that the US continued to support both Euratom and the Common Market in principle, and he had referred particularly to the Soviet economic danger; (2) he had told both the Germans and the French that the US did not consider the *Junktim* a good idea, but he had not appeared to be decidedly against it in all circumstances; (3) to the French he had said that the control question was central, and that both common ownership of fissile materials, or at least something equivalent, and strict controls were necessary, without going into the question whether this would apply in the same way to France, that is, to a possible military sector there, as to Germany; (4) the nuclear weapons question had not been mentioned directly either to the German or to the French; (5) US 'preferential treatment' of Euratom combined with continuation of bilateralism had been reaffirmed, without going into specifics.

Franco-British Negotiations

Maurice Faure visited London in mid-June for talks with the British foreign policy leadership, Selwyn Lloyd and Anthony Nutting. The talks were arranged to explore the chances of Franco-British rapprochement, about Euratom primarily, at a time when the British were trying to accommodate to the unforeseen vital force of the Six-state projects. A French motive was that the Government wanted to refer to the fact that everything possible had been done to try to persuade the British to join. This was important for obtaining sufficient parliamentary support.

Before the meeting some principles for British standpoints crystallized among officials of the Foreign Office and the Atomic Energy Authority. The negative attitude to UK membership of Euratom was unchanged. The officials agreed that there for the UK was no commercial or scientific advantage in joining. The proposed supply monopoly in Euratom would not be compatible with existing contractual arrangements for the purchase of uranium nor with the British military programme. Moreover, it was generally preferable not to be committed to cooperation with only a limited group of countries. Neither could the UK assist the European countries in the construction of an enrichment plant because of American hostility to the project. A joint reprocessing plant for chemical separation of plutonium and irradiated uranium was an alternative, however. It could be a key venture for promoting British policy for nuclear cooperation and it could provide the basis for a programme under OEEC auspices. If all fuels were treated in a common plant, sufficient guarantees against proliferation of nuclear weapons could be obtained. The possibility of British assistance for a joint reprocessing plant had been set forth in the OEEC committee on nuclear energy during the spring. It was not clear, however, from the behaviour of the French representatives whether France was seeking to make a reality of this new venture. The officials hoped that the UK might count on French support for this objective during the next month before the meeting of the OEEC Ministerial Council in July. In the talks with Faure it was, however, advisable to be cautious:

The U.K. security proposals in O.E.E.C., to use only joint separation plants for the purification of irradiated fuels, appear to us to offer the best hope of obtaining real security in this field; they should effectively guard against the development of any surreptitious military programme. This should provide a satisfactory framework within which Euratom can operate. (In fact, the O.E.E.C. scheme goes further than anything Euratom has so far provided. On this point the Euratom scheme is still obscure, primarily because of the French difficulty; she wishes Germany to be controlled without herself accepting a similar control. Unless M. Faure himself leads the discussion on to this point, it would be best to avoid it. There is no point, at this stage, in making clear that the present O.E.E.C. scheme might in this connection be even more difficult for France to accept than Euratom.) [11]

The last remark probably indicates that one of the motives for the British wish for a reprocessing plant under OEEC was that it might subject French plutonium to international control - and thus prevent not only German but also French nuclear armament. Another motive was that reprocessing would make the British reactor concept (based on natural uranium and possible recycling of burnt-out uranium and plutonium) more competitive in Europe. There were great expectations in the middle fifties that British nuclear power technology would become the basis for an important future industry.

At the meeting with Nutting and the British delegation[12] Faure initially made clear the French point of departure for the talks. The French hoped that a fruitful cooperation with the OEEC could be established, ´but first EURATOM must come into being´. Before that, it would be impossible to define the relationship between the two. Faure answered negatively to Nutting´s question whether the British might be represented in the Brussels negotiations in order to make sure that EURATOM would be complementary to the O.E.E.C. scheme. The Six had decided in Venice, Faure replied, to negotiate on the basis of the Spaak Report. If other countries were to attend for the purpose of trying to bring them back to the O.E.E.C., all the expert work they had done would be wasted. Faure then detailed the situation with respect to the disputed issues in the Euratom negotiations. The question of ownership of fissile materials ´was still open, with a tendency to give this to Euratom...ownership would make it easier for the United States to transfer control over United States fissile materials to EURATOM´ (he did not mention that he had recently told Dillon that France was in favour of Euratom ownership of fuel, or authority over fuel as complete as ownership). He explained the French version of a moratorium on nuclear weapons (a moratorium that was not subjected to supranational bonds) [13] and hinted that the situation might be different if Britain decided to join: ´If the United Kingdom joined, the proposed temporary renunciation of military use might even be given up'.[14] He explained intricacies in the Spaak Report that would allow France to keep part of the uranium and the fissile material to preserve the material basis for a military programme[15], and said that 'the question of control over national military use remained open'. Nutting asked whether Faure thought that 'Germany would be prepared to join an organisation where she alone would be debarred from producing nuclear weapons', and Faure replied '"In 1956, Yes". But the future was not certain...It would be safer for Germany not to be autonomous as regards atomic supplies'.

The British expressed the hope that the French would proceed with both schemes - Euratom and the OEEC scheme - as fast as possible, and the British with the one. The key offer which was planned in Britain, the joint reprocessing plant, was mentioned, but only indirectly and without going into specifics. The security control aspect of the OEEC scheme, the British said, was based on following up the product of joint enterprises; 'This was eminently a field where EURATOM would be going further. But we thought that there must be optional facilities, in the O.E.E.C. scheme, for joint enterprises...the object was to prevent the diversion of products from a joint project'.

At this Franco-British meeting the Common Market negotiations were referred to only briefly and in general terms. Faure placed them in the context of the desirability of European cooperation to support French African territories as a step to developing a strong economic area, *Eurafrique*. The dominant subject of discussion was Euratom. Faure described it as really the last chance to relaunch Europe. If this failed there would be no Europe at all. The project for a Common Market would take far too long too realize. The British did not wish any detailed talks about the Common Market at this moment either - their preparations for launching the Free Trade Area had not been completed.[16]

The British Paris Ambassador, Jebb, reported that Faure, back in Paris, had expressed gloomy views to him when talking about the results of his London visit. It had become clear to Faure that there was a complete, and indeed unbridgeable gulf between any project for Euratom, which contained a very limited measure of supranationality, and any proposals for atomic cooperation within the framework of the OEEC. It appeared to him that the UK could never agree to such a system however limited the supranational field outlined in the treaty might be. Unfortunately, Faure did not think that without the new impulse which would be given to the whole thing if the UK were prepared to join some kind of Euratom the Six would succeed in overcoming the national resistances which were now beginning to emerge both in France and Germany. If, moreover, the UK were not prepared to join in any subsequent Common Market, both Germany and France would gravitate more and more towards the East.[17]

The 'unbridgeable gulf' to British acceptance of any measure of supranationality remained. The British continued to try to develop the OEEC as the British alternative for nuclear energy cooperation under which Euratom might be subsumed, in the same way as it was hoped that the Common Market would be subsumed under the larger Free Trade Area. The principle of compatibility between the two European nuclear schemes was established at the meeting of the OEEC Ministerial Council on 17-19 July. It was decided to set up a permanent body to deal with nuclear energy; it would comprise all the members of the OEEC, including the prospective members of Euratom together with the US and Canada. Macmillan talked at a press conference of the British readiness to help in the construction of a joint reprocessing plant, although Britain did not need the capacity itself. He did not mention, however, the plant´s most basic function of getting the plutonium produced on the continent under control, but referred to economic reasons.[18]

French Conditions about Euratom

The French acceptance in Venice of the Spaak Compromise as the basis for discussion was not maintained. Strong domestic forces, spearheaded by the military and nuclear lobby, insisted that French freedom of action must not be restricted by any supranational bonds or internationally binding commitments. A simple moratorium on weapons tests might be accepted - it would take 3-4 years before a test would be possible anyway. A decisive meeting between Maurice Faure and representatives of the French military establishment concluded that an agreement could be made on the basis of three principles: (1) moratorium on the *manufacture*[19] of nuclear arms for three or four years, (2) resumption of unilateral freedom of action in the military field after that period, and (3) no diplomatic or technical obstacle for France to use that freedom.[20]

The matter had thus been more or less settled when Spaak met Faure the day after and set forth his arguments face to face with the French chief negotiator. Spaak asked if France was capable of simultaneously manufacturing atomic bombs and developing civil nuclear energy, and assuming the economic sacrifices necessary for Algeria, Morocco, Tunisia and Black Africa? Why risk the entire negotiation in Brussels by demanding freedom of action when France perhaps had not decided to make bombs? Spaak also referred to French wishes for independence. Although he was a friend of the US, he said, he also judged that Europe needed a real autonomy in the field and could not place itself in total dependence on the Western hemisphere. It was possible to ´escape American tutelage in this field only through joint efforts which would require indispensable sacrifices by all´. Spaak was ´extremely firm´ on the question of the *Junktim*. As in past discussions in the Spaak Committee, he refused to accept the argument that signature of the Euratom treaty was the only way of getting the French Parliament to ratify the Common Market, although he conceded that there might be a small time difference, provided it was kept to the minimum.[21]

The 'French moratorium' was something quite different from that proposed in the Spaak Compromise. It was a moratorium without supranationality or other bonds. Mollet and Pineau now took the decisive step of accepting that it would be a condition for French approval of Euratom that nothing going beyond this rather innocuous moratorium would be approved. They decided to submit Euratom to the National Assembly for a decision of principle based on this premise. The purpose was to keep the governing coalition together, and to ask for a standpoint that would bind the Assembly to ratification later. The EDC experience had not been forgotten.

In the Assembly debate, the spokesmen for the Government - Mollet, Pineau and M. Faure - gave assurances that complete freedom of action for France remained in the military field. It was stated that the Spaak Report contained a 'fundamental exception' to the supply monopoly in the common fuel system, an exception for existing arrangements and contracts.[22] This would give France the material possibility of deciding alone about the use of the fissile material produced in the national programme. Euratom could even increase the French possibilities of obtaining fissile materials, by means of common installations, for instance the construction of a plant for highly enriched uranium: 'Whatever the circumstances, Euratom would thus in no way diminish the possibility to supply any future military programme. It could only improve it by the complement which could be furnished by the communal enterprises it would have created'. Mollet stated that Euratom ownership of fuels was also a French interest. In order to construct a control 'without cracks' France requested that Euratom should retain 'exclusive ownership of all nuclear materials and, in particular, of enriched materials'. Mollet gave solemn formal assurances that Euratom would not be an obstacle to possible French manufacture for military purposes - while at the same time stating that such a decision had not been made and that he personally was against it. France undertook not to explode the prototype of an A-bomb before 1961. Meanwhile, nothing would prevent France from going on with research on military applications and there would be no delay. After the expiry of the moratorium there were no material or legal bonds whatsoever on French freedom of action, he said. Pineau added that there would be no ban on construction of propulsion reactors.[23] Further, it was stated that France retained the right to be represented in the IAEA, instead of agreeing to an arrangement whereby the Six would be represented in the IAEA by Euratom. Pineau also talked about the British reticence about cooperation in nuclear matters. Britain had a privileged relationship with the US and next year the first thermonuclear weapon would be tested. If anything could bring Britain, 'this country where things evolve only slowly', to consider a new approach to the problem, it was 'the success of a powerful and efficient European atomic organisation'. On the issue of the *Junktim,* Pineau rejected the opinion that the Common Market was the price that France had to pay to get Euratom. The other countries had the same interest in Euratom as France, and France also had an interest in the Common Market as such - the agricultural organizations were convinced that it was good for French agriculture - although a number of particular issues had to be solved. Therefore, it was not possible to link the Euratom and the Common Market in time.

The vote in the Assembly, which approved negotiations on the basis of the Government's statements, gave a surprisingly comfortable majority of 342 votes against 183. The majority in the Council of the Republic was even larger.[24]

Would the Germans accept Euratom when the French Parliament had made clear that Euratom must not be an obstacle to French nuclear weapons, while it was also clear that one of its main tasks would be to serve as a barrier against German ones? The fact that Germany went on negotiating in Brussels was in itself sufficient to demonstrate that acceptance was not excluded. The subsequent negotiations about Euratom touched largely on the different aspects of 'minimum equality' that Germany had demanded in Venice.[25]

A New Approach to Euratom?

What would be the American reaction to the French Parliament's condition? A memorandum from the *Quai* estimated pessimistically that nothing indicated that the Americans would maintain indefinitely their support of Euratom. It was explained that the Americans had two motives for their support, first, they saw the organization as a stage in building Europe, second, they saw it as a means of preventing the spread of nuclear weapons. Even if the first motive was still valid, the second had lost much of its force after the parliamentary vote in France. The US might consider that concluding atomic bilaterals with the European powers would be more efficient in preventing the manufacture of atomic bombs on the continent. There was no doubt whatsoever that if the US offered Germany a bilateral that was really attractive, a bilateral which included a large amount of enriched uranium, Euratom would be killed instantly.[26]

There were indeed worried voices in the State Departement after the French vote. It was argued that the Euratom project was in peril and the entire negotiation process was stagnating. The recommended course was not, however, withdrawal of US support for Euratom and concentration on bilateralism. Instead variants of 'a new approach' in US policy toward the European integration process were proposed.

G. Smith and Elbrick wrote that there was now a distinct possibility that Euratom might turn out to be a limited cooperative arrangement, whose principal function would be the intrinsically negative safeguard and control responsibility. If the French position on weapons prevailed, the safeguard and control function would become appendant, because the six nations would be authorized to do the very things that safeguards were supposed to prevent. The US tactical position was exceedingly difficult, they argued. The opponents of Euratom and European integration generally were alleging that Euratom was conceived and sponsored by the US, the supporters staunchly replied that the US had nothing whatsoever to do with it. Rather than trying to influence the Europeans by pleading privately and being officially neutral it was now time to use the 'carrot' by offering a large programme of partnership in developing nuclear power. In this way it would be possible to develop a new atomic energy complex in Europe which could have an equal status with the US and the USSR.[27]

Barnett argued that it might be worth the risk of seriously damaging the possibility of Soviet acceptance of the IAEA if a genuine Euratom were probable. It might not be worth taking if an OEEC-type grouping of the Six was the most likely outcome. It was unwise to step in and tell the Europeans what they should do. A better alternative was to become associated in the European efforts on a footing of reciprocal partnership. Barnett proposed - in the same vein as he had done without success the previous December - that the Six should be allowed to acquire a significant equity in the American enrichment plants. This would have an 'electrical impact' upon the Six. Such a move could be combined with a promise of possession under NATO supervision of a few weapons from the US stocks. In return, the US should get a commitment from the Six of no weapons production, no access to the US weapons programme, and so on, for five years. If this was done, Barnett believed, 'all we would have to do would be to hand the plan to Spaak'. [28]

Toward the end of the month Smith and Elbrick produced a more detailed version of their proposal for a 'new approach'. They recommended that Dulles should suggest to the AEC Chairman a joint memorandum to the President for a new US initiative to the Six. This would however require 'a substantial adjustment in AEC operating habits, acquired in ten years of domestically-oriented programs and largely free from the need to work in harness with other agencies'. A draft letter from the President to Spaak contained an outline for a partnership arrangement for a broad and accelerated development programme in the civil uses of atomic energy.[29]

The 'new approach' showed up in the strategy of Monnet's Action Committee. There were good lines of communication between the State Department and Monnet and other members of the Committee. Influences went both ways.

After the French vote in July the Action Committee faced a grave crisis. The German Social-Democrats, in particular, were frustrated.[30] The executive body of the Action Committee met at the end of July to consider the situation. The representative of the German trade unions declared that the trade union movement would only support Euratom if it was exclusively peaceful. Mollet explained what had happened in the National Assembly and the formal character of the approved French moratorium. The necessity of a second line of defence against national options was discussed. Mollet was questioned whether he supported Euratom ownership of fissile materials and control of the French military sector:

> On the other hand, if one country can use the atom for military purposes, Euratom will not for all that renounce either the ownership of fissile materials or its possibilities for control. - Guy Mollet declared himself in agreement on this point during the meeting which he granted the Committee. - It is in all events excluded that any one country should be able to produce fissile materials and not be subject to control.[31]

Thus, Mollet declared his intention to stand firm on the remaining restrictions on French freedom of action, although it would show later that he was forced to retreat on these points also in the last stage of the Brussels negotiations.

The Action Committee convened in plenary session on 19-20 September. A resolution drafted by Monnet was approved. An introductory statement reflected disillusion but referred hopefully to the ownership and control issues:

> The Committee hopes that it will still be possible, under these circumstances, to ensure complete control over the use of all fissional substances, in accordance with its resolution of 18 January. It noted that, in the French view, Euratom´s control over and ownership of fissional substances should also cover substances ultimately intended for military use.

The Resolution exhorted the Governments dutifully to expedite the signature of the treaty on the Common Market and to make a rapid study of the UK proposal for incorporation of the Common Market in a Free Trade Area. It concentrated, however, on the most ´serious and urgent problem´, the energy problem. The energy situation in Europe was described as precarious; the Suez crisis was a serious warning. Atomic energy would make it possible to keep the oil and coal imports of the European countries within reasonable limits. If Europe obtained a large enough share of the enriched uranium which the US President had allocated for foreign distribution, it would be possible to accelerate the joint effort. The Committee asked the Governments to take the necessary steps for ratification of the Euratom Treaty before the end of the year. A concrete programme for atomic power had to be worked out in parallel with the negotiations in Brussels without waiting for Euratom to come into operation. The Resolution proposed that three distinguished personalities, 'Three Wise Men', should be appointed to submit a report within two months.[32]

Thus, the core of the 'Monnet concept' remained and was adapted to new circumstances: Euratom first - no *Junktim* - and a supranational fuel and control system based on ownership and supply monopoly. It was now combined with the prospect of a US-European effort for developing atomic power. This was the starting-point for the 'Three Wise Men' action, which in early 1957 worked out a plan for a huge joint US-Euratom programme for the development of nuclear power in Europe.[33]

The State Department stayed cautiously in the background. A careful balancing was required in several respects, among them in establishing the attitude to the OEEC and the Grand Design, that is, to Britain and the British role in the European negotiations. The US continued to follow the principle of priority for Six-state integration, that is, establishment of supranational six-state integration first, promotion of intergovernmental efforts within the OEEC possibly later. When Dulles met the Secretary General of the OEEC, René Sergent, in September he expressed general but diffuse sympathy with the British 'Grand Design' concept.[34] Dulles assured Sergent that the US regarded the projected study between the proposed Common Market and the Free Trade Area with deep interest. Britain, formerly hostile to the Common Market, seemed, he said, to be approaching the question 'in a much more objective way, and... there had been a considerable shift in Britain's thinking on the matter' since Eden's visit to Washington six months earlier. Sergent said that it been realized since July that there was compatibility between the nuclear projects of the Six and within the OEEC.[35]

With respect to the nuclear dimension, the analysis of the State Department continued to be that Euratom because of its critical importance from a US foreign policy standpoint had priority for the time being over the launching of OEEC's nuclear energy programme; 'the US will temporarily withhold any form of support to OEEC which might have an adverse effect on the current EURATOM negotiations'. However, 'careful handling will be required to avoid the impression that the U.S. is reluctant to support important OEEC programs'.[36] British officials were approaching the US London Embassy looking for hopeful signs, arguing that the OEEC and EURATOM concepts for atomic energy cooperation were tending to converge. They got no encouragement. The American attitude was one of polite neutrality. The British were told that it was 'obviously up to the Europeans to decide whether they preferred the EURATOM or the OEEC approach'.[37]

Franco-British and Franco-German Talks

In September, Mollet visited London to make a probe about the British attitude to cooperation with France and Europe. He may have had several motives. An alliance with Britain was important in order to balance a powerful Germany, and he was already allied with Eden about Suez. He was trying to cope with the Algerian uprising and was in need of support from the other major European power with a colonial heritage.

When Mollet met Eden he went as far as suggesting that Eden reconsider Churchill's proposal of 1940 for Anglo-French union.[38] Leading Foreign Office officials suggested that Mollet be told that this was a limited and antiquated concept and that the United Kingdom should move instead toward wider European unity. This was endorsed by the Cabinet.[39]

At another encounter with Eden - in Paris two days before Mollet's meeting with Adenauer - Mollet said that the French Government favoured a slow approach to the Common Market; several problems were still unsolved. He emphasized the immense hope there was in France that the UK would take its place in Europe and lead the movement towards closer European unity. Neither the WEU nor the OEEC were moving very fast in the direction Mollet desired, he said. The opportunity must be seized to push ahead, 'and to make progress with arms standardisation and atomic co-operation'. The UK and France had to draw closer together. Eden was non-committal, talking about the need for cooperation on a broader basis and about probable new proposals to the European allies after coming discussions with Commonwealth representatives, and, with respect to cooperation on arms, remarked vaguely that Britain was 'anxious to push on W.E.U.'s work in the armaments field'.[40]

The deliberations about Mollet's suggestions went on for some time in Whitehall. The reaction was mostly negative, although Eden was personally in favour. The arguments turned around the question whether the limiting factor for a new kind of Commonwealth was supranationalism or the prospect of it becoming a 'Third Force' and thereby alienating the US. The discussions never crystallized into clear-cut policy. The question disappeared in the stream of urgent matters in the midst of the Suez crisis.[41]

From the summer of 1956 the German leadership focused much more than earlier on European self-reliance and on the role of nuclear weapons in German rearmament. The impact on Adenauer's thinking of British signals about troop reductions in Germany and increased reliance on thermonuclear deterrence in defence policy, and, not least, of the American so-called Radford Plan, is stressed in research about German foreign policy. Adenauer's concern about the Radford Plan had its origin in an article in the New York Times in July which contained the information that the Chairman of the US Joint Chiefs of Staff, General Radford, recommended a major reduction of American forces in Europe and concentration on nuclear weapons in plans for its defence. This revived Adenauer's fears of American withdrawal from Europe and dramatized the dangers of relying exclusively on the New Look strategy. Adenauer felt that Dulles had left him in the dark about the American plans.[42] At a Cabinet meeting on 20 July, Adenauer argued that if Western strategy continued to switch over to nuclear weapons the Federal Republic would have to reconsider the *Kernwaffenverzicht.* Strauss added that a nation that did not produce nuclear weapons itself was ´downgraded´.[43]

These perspectives were gradually introduced into the public sphere. A first sign came in early August when a spokesman in Bonn told journalists that his Government was interested in more cooperation with some non-nuclear European powers and that the Federal Republic fully recognized the leading role of France in this context.[44]

The concept of increased European self-reliance within the Atlantic framework was exposed programmatically in a speech by Adenauer in Brussels on 25 September. He talked about a ´European Confederation´ that would not destroy NATO but take care of specific European interests. He stressed in particular the importance of the United Kingdom in this context and directed a special appeal to Britain. In Conant´s report about the speech he characterized it as the culmination of a series of events designed to increase cooperation and to bring pressure on the British to give greater weight to European interests. Accompanying the ´extreme sensitiveness´ in the Federal Republic to reports about possible US and British withdrawal was a growing demand that the Germans ´as equal partners must be equipped with most modern weapons (including, we presume, atomic weapons)´.[45]

Two Franco-German top-level meetings took place in September. Maurice Faure made a preparatory visit to Bonn at the middle of the month and Mollet went there to meet Adenauer two weeks later.

Shortly before Faure´s arrival, Adenauer, when talking to Jean Monnet, seemed prepared to forego the German demand for *Junktim* in order to pave the way for Franco-German agreement. The French position was still, we saw, that the time perspectives for the two projects should be different. Monnet explained to Adenauer that the French Parliament´s condition about preserving the nuclear option was a setback for the integration movement, but at the same time - he stated optimistically - the first success of the European cause since the defeat of the EDC. For a short moment Monnet apparently succeded in persuading Adenauer to drop the demand for *Junktim*. Washington was informed by Matthews in the Hague that Monnet had told Adenauer that the German attitude about the *Junktim* represented ´mortal danger´ to Euratom, and that Adenauer had understood the warning and agreed to take action to bring about a change in the German position. However, Matthews reflected, Adenauer might be unable, ´politically or technically´ to bear down on the specifics of the problem.[46] This proved to be so. Adenauer´s collaborators acted immediately, and successfully, to make him revert on the decision.[47]

Faure's mission was to probe the German attitude to components of a total package: Euratom, the Common Market and the *Junktim*, cooperation on arms, and remaining details about the Saar. It was seen as appropriate that France and Germany tried to reach agreement first. The results that might be obtained about Euratom and the Common Market would then be submitted to the other four states for approval - 'the Franco-German *tête-à-tête* has to be discreet but on this question it is fundamental'. An agreement would be so constructed that Britain would have the opportunity to join.[48]

Neither the French nor the German positions on the Common Market changed during the Faure talks. The main disputed issues were: social harmonization, a special regime for preservation of certain French import taxes and export subsidies, and protective clauses for situations of balance of payments difficulties.[49]

On the subject of Euratom, Faure made far-reaching promises about future Franco-German equality with respect to control and information. He further envisaged that if the political situation so required Germany too must be armed with nuclear weapons; it would be impossible for the Six to renounce military uses for all time. He assured von Brentano and Hallstein that 'France has no intention to evade controls on nuclear weapons' and reminded them that 'it is the manufacture of tactical nuclear weapons and not formally the possession of them that is forbidden to Germany by the Paris agreements' - obviously referring to the possibility that France might provide them.

> M. Faure gave an assurance that, since the question of military use had been raised, France had never asked to withdraw from all control of nuclear material. Nor had it any particular rule for the division between Member States, and in this connection had not sought any distinction between military and peaceful uses. Thirdly, it supported an exchange of information about procedures and patents, including those relating to production for military purposes. These would be three formal assurances.

Hallstein's reaction was that this was new to him; Faure promised to send a memorandum.[50]

The memorandum dealt with cooperation on arms. It was in fact a follow-up to a similar one that had been delivered to the Federal Republic five months earlier and had been received negatively then.[51] It was in principle the old French Arms Pool proposal in new clothes. The new memorandum acknowledged the very positive recent response from the Federal Republic to the French ideas. It argued that the discussions on arms cooperation within the WEU were secondary for the time being, even if they should be revived later, and that Mollet and Adenauer at their forthcoming meeting should decide to develop a bilateral programme of action for close cooperation on production of arms. The nuclear issue was not mentioned.[52]

Adenauer and Mollet met on 29 September in a broad setting of ministers and officials. Much of the outlook on European problems was coloured by the views of the risk of American abandonment and of nuclear devastation of Western Europe, and the feeling that independence should be increased. Adenauer delivered a diatribe against US nuclear strategy and its devastating consequences for Europe at a time when the American homeland had become vulnerable. He saw a development towards isolationism in the US. Therefore, the Common Market and Euratom should be finalized as soon as possible and the WEU must be activated. Mollet said that he shared Adenauer's concerns. In his view, there was a development in American policy not toward isolationism but toward 'peripheral defence'. The dormant project about an Arms Pool from the WEU negotiations had to be revived. The door to European cooperation should be kept open for Britain. It was urgent to make progress in the negotiations about Euratom and the Common Market. In addition, the two Governments should support the idea of appointing 'Three Wise Men' to make a proposal for a programme for civil atomic energy - that is, the idea that had recently been advanced by Monnet's Action Committee. Mollet argued that France had made a positive contribution to the Common Market lately; it was now up to the Germans to be accommodating on the issues of ownership of fuels and the supply monopoly in Euratom. Pineau added that the French reservations on the Common Market were of a purely tactical nature - the French Government wanted to submit Euratom to Parliament first and the Common Market later - while the German reservations about the Euratom plan were fundamental.

The arguments by the German side touched mainly on Euratom and the *Junktim*. No concessions were made on the issues of fuel ownership and supply monopoly.[53] F.-J. Strauss stated, about equality of control and information (the prospects for which, we saw, Faure had painted in bright colours earlier), that if the control also applied to the military materials 'the problem would already be half solved', and if exchange of information would also be possible, 'the problem would be completely solved'. Faure declared that it was understood in principle that military nuclear information should be exchanged, although there had to be a necessary minimum of military secrecy. Military information which had any significance for civil purposes should however be communicated.

There was a clarification about the actual status of the *Junktim* in an exchange between Hallstein and Mollet. Hallstein declared that it would be impossible to get approval for the Euratom plan in Germany if there was no certainty that the Common Market would also be ratified by the French Parliament. Mollet answered that there should be no doubts that the majority of the French people saw the Common Market as an unconditional necessity although there were reservations on certain points because of the difficult situation in France. The elaboration of a treaty would necessarily require more time because of the thorny problems involved, such as the questions of overseas areas and agriculture. Mollet then proposed - this was something new - 'to sign the Euratom treaty as soon as possible and to ratify it immediately in France, while Germany could delay ratification until French support on the Common Market was assured'. Hallstein responded that he considered this to be fair, but the *Bundestag* and the *Bundesrat* would have the last word.

The French memorandum about cooperation on arms does not seem to have been discussed.[54]

It was reported to the State Department before the meeting that Government circles in France did not hide their hopes that Mollet would be able to get the Chancellor to change the German positions on ownership and supply of nuclear materials.[55] Spaak, however, made a pessimistic forecast of the German propensity to make concessions on Euratom. His recent conversations with Adenauer had given him little reason to think that much would come out of the Adenauer/Mollet meeting as far as the German Euratom stand was concerned.[56]

State Department officials and Conant had recommended Dulles and Murphy that a personal message be sent to Adenauer. The argument was that the meeting and the coming Paris Conference would be decisive for the fate of Euratom. A discreet US intervention with the Chancellor might be effective, it was argued. Adenauer was not committed on the ownership question, and he had not been involved until recently. There was 'some doubt that even he can overrule Strauss and his supporters, and thus avert a serious split among the Six, without a good deal of support'. A message would be a means of strengthening his hand against the German opponents of Euratom.[57] Dulles followed the advice, although the message was delivered to Conant only after the Adenauer/Mollet meeting. Conant was instructed to approach the Chancellor and stress the importance which the US attached to the ownership and supply issues. Dulles formulated more explicitly the threat that had been expressed more diffusely already in the memorandum to the Venice Conference: It would be possible for the US to cooperate very closely with Euratom if it had common authority and responsibility. If not, Euratom could not hope to get fissionable materials from the US. The US 'in view of our own domestic U.S. legislation could not transfer fissionable material to EURATOM unless latter were in position maintain ownership of material'.[58] Conant transmitted the message in a letter to Adenauer on 3 October. Adenauer's reply was non-committal. He indicated readiness to meet with Conant to discuss the subject.[59]

Obviously, Dulles' threat was ominous. Without access to enriched uranium during the period of 5-7 years before the material could be produced in Europe the Federal Republic could participate only marginally in the development of what was depicted as the key technology of the future.

German Decisions before the Paris Conference

The German Government was now ready to decide about the strategy at the impending Foreign Ministers Conference in Paris about the Common Market and Euratom. This was done at Cabinet meetings on 3 and 5 October.

Adenauer set forth to his Cabinet the foreign policy themes which he returned to many times in the autumn of 1956, although in other contexts in a less straightforward way. He argued that the Federal Republic should follow two parallel roads in its European policy, one with a somewhat more distant perspective based on cooperation with Britain in a revised WEU, and one for more immediate action in the Six state context. He saw it as necessary to construct Europe as a 'Third Force'. He estimated that the US was not opposed to 'Third Force' ambitions and referred to recent public statements by Dulles. The fate of single European nations could not be dependent on the power of Russia and the US only: 'There is a threat of a *pax atomica* between the two Super Powers on which all other states would be dependent'.[60]

Erhard and Strauss expressed a wish to participate personally at the Brussels Conference side by side with von Brentano; permission to do so was granted. One part of the discussion delineated possible German concessions on the Common Market. The general tendency was a preparedness to make necessary adaptations to get acceptance of the project. However, French demands about social harmonization and escape clauses that would permit France in certain circumstances to withdraw unilaterally, or refuse to proceed to the next stage, should be opposed. Well-defined temporary measures intended to help overcome acute French economic problems might be accepted.

The discussion on Euratom and the *Junktim* throws light on various motives within the German Government concerning the nuclear question at a moment when the decision about the fate of the integration projects was perceived to be near. The opposing views of the Chancellor and Strauss dominated the exchange:

Strauss admitted that Mollet had made a concession about the *Junktim* at the meeting with the Chancellor but advised against accepting the proposal. Even if the German ratification instruments of Euratom would not be deposited until France had ratified the Common Market, Germany would be subjected to pressure from the Americans, and to moral pressure as perhaps the only country that had not completed ratification. Euratom was rather a sacrifice than an advantage, and it was less a construct for support of German development than for control of it. Adenauer turned against Strauss and summarized why he was in favour of Euratom:

> The Federal Chancellor opposes this view. *Through Euratom he would like as soon as possible to obtain the possibility to manufacture nuclear weapons himself* [my emphasis]. He also thinks that we would not be able to catch up the French lead in that sector of research very quickly. Furthermore, German industry is not so generous as the Federal Minister for Atomic Affairs assumes. Industry would certainly like to join in so long as nothing occurs against it, but would be little disposed to pay. The Euratom Treaty would for that reason definitely be beneficial to Germany too.

Thus, Adenauer told the Cabinet clearly enough about his intention of using Euratom for getting out of the *Kernwaffenverzicht*, and used as a side-argument the benefits that could be drawn from access to ten years of unrestricted French nuclear research.[61]

In further discussion about the *Junktim*, Hallstein recommended sticking to the principle, but for tactical reasons - 'the *Junktim* is our strongest means of pressure on the French'. Adenauer believed that Mollet's suggestion at the recent meeting was fair. He would, however, reconsider his opinion, if the French showed a reticent attitude in the negotiations about the Common Market.

On the question of supply monopoly both Strauss and Adenauer stated that there had to be exceptions for situations of scarcity or unfair prices. With respect to ownership of fuels, Strauss argued that Euratom should own materials produced by the organization and those furnished by the Americans under restrictions required by them, but should not own other materials. He used the usual arguments about risks of socialization, industry's resistance, and so on, but he also advanced a very explicit military argument. It referred to the fact that weapon-carriers were required for use of atomic bombs, and that these were national and could not be provided by Euratom. This led to further discussion which, in a diffuse way, dealt with the significance of Euratom ownership of fuels as obstacle to French and German national military options, and its relationship to the issue of weapon-carriers:

> On military use the Federal Minister for Atomic Affairs [Strauss] explained that Euratom should retain ownership if the Community itself produced plutonium or obtained the raw material from the United States. In any case these materials should finally be handed over to a national state, since the Community had no aircraft from which to drop bombs. For the rest individual Member States of the Community could also manufacture nuclear weapons. The Federal Minister for Bundesrat Affairs proposed that raw material that would be used for military purposes should lose its status as national property. Under Secretary Prof. Dr. Hallstein wanted, however, to know for sure that the raw material from which

bombs would be manufactured would remain the property of Euratom. The Federal Minister for Atomic Affairs argued that it was necessary for Euratom to obtain sufficient raw material from its own plants or from America. Under Secretary Prof. Dr. Hallstein requested that the question should be left open. The Cabinet agreed. [62]

Thus, the questions of ownership and supply were left open in spite of Dulles' efforts at persuasion. However, feelers about possible compromise solutions were transmitted to the Americans. Conant reported about an approach by a prominent official at the *Auswärtiges Amt*, Wilhelm Hartlieb. Hartlieb had outlined a model which contained the unsolved points of French production of nuclear weapons, Euratom ownership of fuels, the supply monopoly and the *Junktim*. Conant judged that it was possible but not certain that Hartlieb's remarks represented policy at the highest levels of the German Government. At the receiving end in the State Department, Cleveland's reaction was that the deal rang true as a possible German proposal, and he added his evaluation of the different points. Regarding French weapons, Hartlieb had suggested:

> Question of French production of atomic weapons can be settled in following manner: French could be given 'formal right' to manufacture atomic weapons, with there being at same time informal understanding that they would not in fact do so. On other hand, there would be agreement (perhaps in secret protocol) that EURATOM itself could produce atomic weapons for use of France and other member countries (including Federal Republic) which might in future need them. Plants producing such weapons would of course not be located in Federal Republic.

Cleveland's judgment was that the first half of this was 'fine'. The second half - about a European option - was, Cleveland stated, obviously what a number of people, including Spaak and possibly even Monnet, had had in mind for a long time. Cleveland doubted, however, that a secret protocol was feasible, word of it would certainly leak out. It was also unclear to him what would be the German SPD's reaction to that kind of proposal. Some thinking about the US reaction was required.

On the ownership point, Hartlieb had envisaged that the German atomic energy law could be modified to provide for state instead of private ownership of fissionable material. Cleveland judged this to be a step in the right direction.

On the supply monopoly, Hartlieb had suggested that Euratom would purchase practically all the fuels while a member state might, if necessary, purchase a small and definitely limited additional amount. This was in Cleveland's view 'possibly intended to save Strauss' face'. He added that it was very much like the proposal on this point in the Spaak Report - that is, *sui generis* - to which the US had ´objected vigorously´ in the memorandum before the Venice Conference.

Hartlieb had finally said that the French seemed to be prepared to acknowledge the *Junktim* in a manner satisfactory to the Germans. Internal German opposition to Euratom might be diminished by limiting the life of the agreement to a period of five or ten years. Cleveland reflected that he was not sure that he liked the idea, but if the organization worked within that period the chances for a longer life were considerable.[63]

The package deal that had been outlined by Hartlieb was seen as a serious threat by others in the State Department. A memorandum for Dulles, endorsed by some key officials, and a telegram with instructions for Butterworth in Luxemburg was drafted. The memorandum observed that a compromise on the nuclear weapons question whereby France would be given the formal right to manufacture nuclear weapons was now in the making, and the essence of the citation above from the Hartlieb conversation was given. It was suggested that the Brussels negotiating group should have some idea of the US views on the sensitive subject, but they should be put forward ´without seeming to inject the U.S. into the negotiations´. The tactic proposed was that Butterworth should pass the Department´s informal comments to Franz Etzel, and to Etzel only, using him as the channel into the Brussels group. This approach would take advantage of Etzel´s close relations with Monnet and the trust in which he was held by Adenauer.

There are no indications that the draft telegram was approved by Dulles and sent for action. It deserves some attention, however, because it throws light on the priorities with respect to the different nuclear weapons options - the German, the French and the European - that were harboured within the State Department. The draft listed some implications regarding US ability to cooperate with Euratom ´if community is to be actual or potential weapons producer´, among them that Euratom would not have fissionable material for weapons for many years, and that an escape clause for French weapons development would give the Soviet Union ammunition to renew their earlier charges that Euratom was a transparent cloak for a European military programme. Further, if a ´compromise gave exception to nascent French weapons program, then it would be only matter of time before Germany insisted on release from her WEU commitments and embarked on nuclear weapon production herself´. The draft went on to explain that if the other Five were obliged to accept the French national option, the European option was a less bad alternative from the US point of view:

> Aware of force and importance of motivation Brussels group for independent atomic energy program, US has carefully refrained from intrusion into negotiations. Injection US into treaty discussions at

this juncture with advice on weapons questions likely to backfire. Also recognize that Brussels group may in final analysis find itself obliged accept some weapons compromise as sine qua non French participation EURATOM. While difficult, US could assist and cooperate with EURATOM, even should it have some weapons activities, if latter program were segmented thus permitting US cooperation along general lines UK-US bilateral relations. *While US reluctant to see development nuclear weapons production capability in countries not now having that capacity, if forced make choice, it would be more in US interest to have common EURATOM weapons development program than to have independent competitive nuclear weapons programs among six nations* [my emphasis].[64]

Possibly as a consequence of Hartlieb's feelers, Conant requested clarifications from the Department about the exact US standpoints on certain points regarding ownership and the supply monopoly. He asked if ownership would apply to all fissionable materials, or only to quantities given to Euratom from the US, and if Euratom would possess *exclusive* rights over acquisition and distribution of fissionable materials. The questions thus touched on the central problem of whether the entire stock of fissionable materials in Germany and France would be subjected to supranational authority, or whether there would to some extent be loopholes for the national weapons options. Dulles' answer left no doubts about his position at the time of the supposedly decisive conference of the Six. He instructed that the Department 'had in mind ownership all materials, not simply those made available by the US'; this would 'contribute materially to effective control and safeguarding'. He added that the Department 'has not taken position on whether such ownership should be over both special nuclear materials (i.e. fissionable materials) and source materials (i.e. natural uranium, thorium)'. With respect to the supply monopoly he explained that the Department felt that the various objectives desired by the US were much more likely to be fulfilled 'if EURATOM possesses exclusive rights over acquisition and distribution fissionable materials as well'.[65]

The Paris Conference (20-1 October 1956) and its Impact in Bonn and Paris

As a whole, the Conference of Foreign Ministers of the Six in Paris was not a success. No agreement on the principles for a Euratom/Common Market package solution was achieved. The start of the conference was not ideal; the appearance of Erhard and Strauss at the opening meeting caused considerable surprise and was not helpful psychologically with the French. A professorial lecture on a liberal economy which was delivered by Müller-Armack, apparently at Erhard's insistence, contributed further to the unfortunate atmosphere which developed.[66]

Most of the discussions concerned the Common Market, Euratom was treated more briefly.

Many of the Common Market exchanges dealt with the French demands for social harmonization and Germans objections to it; other delegations were also reluctant to accept social harmonization. In the German delegation there were internal splits. Attempts to elaborate a compromise formula were determinedly opposed by Erhard. The French demand for a special regime for keeping French import taxes and export subsidies was accepted by the Germans, provided that it was for a limited period and with ceilings. Pineau made a major concession on the issue of the transition between stages - this was a French ´escape clause´ that had for long been firmly opposed by the others. After a long discussion, adjournment and consultation with Mollet, he accepted that the issue would be decided by qualified majority after a certain period. A compromise of roughly this kind was accepted by all the others. However, after further dispute about social harmonization which gave no concrete German promises, Pineau declared that, in these circumstances, he was obliged to witdraw the concession about stages that he had just made. The issue of overseas areas that had been a major theme in Venice was not treated at this conference.

When Euratom was on the agenda the Germans made concessions on the issue of the supply system. The supply monopoly in the Spaak Report was accepted in principle. Von Brentano proposed two exceptions. The users would be free to procure fuels outside Euratom if the organization was unable to deliver sufficient quantities (this had been proposed in the Spaak Report), or offered at prices not related in a normal way to the world market price level. He envisaged that this was a temporary model. The system might be valid for three years, a revised system might be decided by a majority after that, and a final decision about a permanent system would require unanimity. The German offer was conditional, von Brentano stated. It presupposed equality of control and information. The reactions of the other delegations were inconclusive.

The issue of legal authority over fuels - the alternatives were ownership or *sui generis* [67] - seemed to come close to agreement. Von Brentano referred to the *sui generis* principle, and Pineau also supported it, but only partly. He envisaged that, when fixing how far this right would extend, a distinction might be made between, on the one side, ´the ores and fertile materials which do not cross the frontiers of the producer countries´ and, on the other side, ´the fissile materials which must be followed more rigorously´. The positions were reflected in two memoranda. The first, supported by all delegations except the French, proposed that the *sui generis* would apply to all fuels. A French memorandum proposed *sui generis* for minerals and fertile materials, and exclusive Euratom ownership for fissile materials.

Von Brentano reiterated the ´minimum equality´ demands that had been requested by the Germans since Venice: equal access to information, and equal control in both civil and military areas. A single country could not be allowed itself to define what was military and what was not. Pineau answered that the French Government did not intend to renounce definitely from nuclear explosives but the concept of military secret should be 'very tightly drawn', it would not apply to research, only to 'the military device'. He seemed to open up for possible supranational decision about drawing the border line between military secrets and other nuclear information, wondering 'whether the definition of what should remain a military secret could not be entrusted to the Community itself'. The exchange of military secrets between the six countries could be regulated outside the treaty. This was rejected by von Brentano as impracticable. He 'would not wish a military Euratom to be created' and argued that if the task of defining what is secret were entrusted to the Community, 'the result would be even more secrets and that, in consequence, this solution cannot in the end be adopted'.

With respect to the ownership issue Benelux and Italy - as was indicated above - had made a concession to the Germans and were not insisting on full ownership by Euratom of fissionable material, but had agreed upon a *sui generis*-interpretation which would subject all fissionable material to complete control by the Community. This, then, was a compromise that would have subjected the French national weapons option to a certain restriction while the efficiency of the control of the German *Kernwaffenverzicht* would have been reduced.

The ultimate stumbling block at the conference was the issue of harmonization of wages. The outcome was however regarded by many as only a temporary setback that would be corrected at the meeting between Adenauer and Mollet in Paris two weeks later.[69]

When the German Cabinet evaluated the negative result of the Paris Conference it was decided that an effort should be made to put the negotiations on the right track again at the meeting with Mollet. Adenauer argued that it was fundamentally important to reach agreement in the actual world situation. He talked about Suez, Hungary, American isolationism, and so on. The alternative in case of failure was to relate to the British proposal about a Free Trade Area; he would talk about it with Macmillan. Brentano, Erhard and Strauss were exhorted to agree on the German standpoints before his meeting with Mollet. Brentano warned against the risk of bankruptcy of European policy, and estimated that the French Parliament would hardly be prepared to give a positive vote on the complicated Common Market proposal. He judged that Britain's preparedness to agree to a Free Trade Area presupposed the existence of the Common Market. The attitude of the rallying figure for resistance to Euratom, Strauss, was more complacent than earlier. He did not object to a German offensive to save the Six-state projects, possibly because of Adenauer's explanations about the role of Euratom in solving the German nuclear weapons question at the earlier meeting. His attitude was registered as being: 'France and Germany need Europe-Success. Back to simple forms'.[70]

A few days later von Brentano warned Adenauer that Erhard believed that the decisions in Messina and Venice could no longer be realized. A proposal for a looser project that was close to the OEEC concept was under preparation in the Ministry of Economics. This led to a private talk with Adenauer in which Erhard was forced to give up the fight. He agreed to a compromise on the basis of the results that had been reached in the negotiations. At a meeting with Adenauer and the ministers involved limits for possible adjustments, mainly on the issue of social harmonization, were defined.[71]

The French Government communicated to the German side that it was anxious to untie the remaining knots. Mollet sent a personal message to Adenauer specifying the unsolved issues that would have to be treated at their forthcoming meeting: the common supply system and ownership of fissile materials in Euratom, harmonization of certain social charges and a special temporary regime for France in the Common Market. Mollet wrote that the unsuccessful outcome in Paris proved that 'although they look no more than technical, the problems posed in Brussels have major political importance'.[72]

Before the meeting with Adenauer briefing papers for Mollet were drafted in Paris. They set out the difficulties on the subject of military use, which concerned three points: exchange of information, fuel supply and control. It was noted that 'the French position remains to be precisely defined, by trade-offs between the French authorities concerned'. Thus, the French attitude to the German request for 'minimum equality' in Euratom had not been decided internally. The signals about full or almost full equality of control and information which Faure and Pineau had emitted during the autumn had obviously been intended to facilitate agreement in Brussels. It would soon prove that there was no domestic basis for these promises.[73]

The issue of European foreign policy coordination and cooperation on arms was also dealt with in the briefing material. Several European combinations for regular meetings of foreign ministers were described as possible - 'Seven', 'Six', 'Two (Franco-German)', 'Three (Franco-Anglo-German)'. A revitalization of the WEU and closer collaboration with Britain 'would deserve careful attention'. A new French memorandum that would be communicated to the Germans was attached. The paper did not differ in principle from the earlier ones, except that it contained a proposal for forming a Franco-German Military and Technical Committee. The information was given that the Minister of Defence intended to elaborate a list of about fifty kinds of equipment and research subjects, which the French would be prepared to start in common with the Germans. The

Arms Committee of the WEU would be informed about the progress. It was pointed out that discretion about the subject was required. If it came up at the meeting with Adenauer it might be preferable to do so in a restricted group; it should not be mentioned in the Final Communiqué.[74] Couve de Murville handed over the memorandum to Adenauer and reported that the reaction of the Chancellor had been 'very favourable'. His only preoccupation had seemed to be Italian reactions to an exclusively Franco-German agreement: 'What are we going to do for Italy?'[75]

American Reactions

After the Paris Conference, there was a stir of American activity. Hurried telegrams were exchanged between the State Department and the missions. There was a feeling that this was the decisive stage and the 'moment for action'.[76] American representatives were informed of the details of what had happened by officials in the participating countries. The diagnoses varied, responsibility for the stalemate in Paris was placed differently. The general tendency was that Germany was mainly to blame. Proposals for US intervention were advanced from the missions.

The French outlook was, according to Dillon's synthesis of views by a number of French officials, that some concessions had been made by both sides. However, the outcome was regarded on the working level in France as a small crisis that could be overcome at top level meetings.[77] When Dillon met Faure and Marjolin, Faure said that remarkable progress had been made on the Common Market, even if the negotiations had broken down over a social harmonization issue. Over Euratom the progress had been much less. The Germans had refused Euratom ownership of fuels, even if only for fissile materials. The German concession on the supply monopoly issue had been made dependent on conditions which deprived the concession of all substance. While the exceptions about situations of scarcity or abusive prices might seem reasonable, the effect would be seriously to undermine Euratom: 'Germany because of her industrial power could in bilateral deals with countries producing uranium offer considerably more than would be possible for EURATOM organization'. The proposal that the supply monopoly would last only for a limited period was totally unacceptable. The net of the divergences was that the Germans had not budged from their original reservations about the Euratom concept. Faure asked for US intervention; 'any help which the United States could give in influencing the German Government regarding EURATOM problems prior to Mollet/ Adenauer meeting would be most helpful and welcome'. Dillon fully supported this proposal. Adenauer would definitely have to overrule Erhard and Strauss on Euratom. Dillon recommended all-out action to press the Germans at this decisive moment: 'It appears to me that Mollet/Adenauer meeting will indeed be crucial and that now is the time for United States to use any or all influence it may have with Adenauer to get him to understand the necessity for ownership and monopoly supply of nuclear materials by Euratom'.[78]

German views were communicated to the Americans by Carstens and Hartlieb of the *Auswärtiges Amt*. Carstens informed about the various concessions that had been made - and withdrawn - in Paris. He stated that the Germans did not consider themselves bound by the German offer on the fuel supply issue in Euratom, in view of the failure to agree on Common Market issues. He also said that the French had agreed that Euratom could maintain control over material, and that each state would be bound to supply full information to Euratom. He considered this to be a significant advance in the French position.[79] Carstens' views were - it should be remarked - incorrect or overoptimistic, considering what had actually happened at the conference and later French unwillingness to move in the direction of 'minimum equality'. In the meeting with Hartlieb, an American official was told that issues with respect to the Common Market, not Euratom, now stood in the way of agreement. A way of helping France must be found. Hartlieb said, 'in strictest confidence', that the Auswärtiges Amt was recommending the Chancellor that he offer Mollet in the forthcoming meeting a long-term loan of 5 billion DM.[80]

The Belgian message was that the chief blame for the failure of the conference lay with the Germans and not with the French. Although the meeting had ended on a sour note, agreement had been near and, contrary to press reports, there were not grounds for pessimism.[81]

The integrationists also expressed their views. Monnet was reported to be bitter about the failure of von Brentano to counterbalance Strauss and Erhard. He expressed the belief that the Germans wanted neither Euratom nor the Common Market. In discussing Euratom, he raised the ownership problem. He threw out the suggestion that the problem of Euratom ownership of fissionable materials could perhaps be solved by having such ownership lodged with Euratom for only five years, at the end of which the six countries would take another look at the problem.[82] His assistant, van Helmont, opined that the only progress that had been achieved 'lies in fact that Germans learned to hear term "supply monopoly" without raising hands in horror'. The French concession on the issue of transition between stages in the Common Market was however also important. Van Helmont intimated that Monnet was unhappy over Spaak's 'fuzzy' position on ownership of fissionable materials.[83]

Butterworth and Conant, like Dillon, reached the conclusion that this was the moment to discuss personally with Adenauer and to explain further the American positions. They discussed the situation with Etzel, Monnet and Bech. Butterworth and Conant reported to Dulles and recommended action. Bech had been pessimistic, Monnet and Etzel had been optimistic, but all held the view 'that it was make or break within near future and another ministerial meeting terminating in failure would be the end'. The US should try to strengthen Adenauer's hand. To this end Butterworth and Conant proposed that Conant should remind Adenauer that the US would give Euratom preferential treatment with respect to access to fissionable materials, and so on.

Butterworth provided further arguments in another telegram. The US assurances about preferential treatment to Euratom had had 'good effect before the Venice meeting in May', he estimated. The problem was that negotiations about bilaterals since then had deprived these assurances of 'effective purposeful meaning'. Butterworth believed that some of the German resistance to Euratom could be explained by the fact that Adenauer did not completely understand the political implications of the technical issues involved. He trusted that Conant could put things right, '...of course Conant is uniquely qualified[84] to make the Chancellor understand the whys and wherefores of ownership, supply, control problems, et cetera, and there is no doubt that he has been exposed to much misinformation and illusory misconceptions so widely held in German industrial and official circles supporting Strauss'.[85]

Butterworth's views about Adenauer's incomplete understanding were no doubt off the mark considering what we now know about the Chancellor's efforts to keep the military option open and his statements in the German Cabinet about this.

The conclusion drawn in the State Department from incoming reports was that the main reason for the failure in Paris was the intransigence of the German delegation. Elbrick and Farley wrote a memorandum for Dulles explaining that the Germans had broken up the meeting on the issue of harmonization of wage policies to which the other five had agreed. No agreement had been reached despite a substantial French concession - that of dropping the veto on transition of stages in the Common Market. Elbrick and Farley concluded that the real cause of the failure had not been disagreement about the Common Market, but about Euratom: 'Although the breaking point came on a common market issue, it seems clear from the reports that Erhard and particularly Strauss were motivated by a desire to prevent a compromise agreement on Euratom control of fissionable materials'. The success of Euratom and the Common Market now depended on a Franco-German package covering the whole range of issues on both treaties. There were prospects of agreement at the coming meeting between Adenauer and Mollet. Whether it would be possible therefore depended 'on whether the Chancellor can carry the Cabinet with him over the opposition of Strauss and probably of Erhard'. The memorandum supported Butterworth's and Conant's proposal for a US move to help strengthen Adenauer's hand.[86]

Dulles agreed. He instructed Conant to express to Adenauer his serious concern about the way the situation was developing.[87] Elbrick detailed to

Conant that he might 'review with the Chancellor previous statements of United States position in order to counter rumors apparently being circulated to the effect that this position has changed'. Elbrick proposed to Dulles that the issue should be brought to Eisenhower. The President, who was going to meet the German Ambassador the following day, should drop a few words reflecting his continued strong support of integration and his concern that the Federal Republic might be turning away from this policy.[88]

On 29 October the President made a contribution to the intensified effort by making a statement in Miami - 'which came on the President's own initiative without prompting from the State Department' - in support of the Common Market and European integration generally.[89]

After having met Adenauer, Conant was optimistic. He had emphasized to the Chancellor, he wrote, the importance the US attached to government ownership of fissile materials. Adenauer had appeared already convinced by Conant's letter of 3 October[90] and had 'agreed it was rather absurd that some Germans were taking attitude against government ownership when United States with its deep commitment private enterprise system has as late as 1954 reaffirmed principle government ownership fissionable material'. He had assured Conant that 'we need have no worry on this point, that he was quite prepared to yield on this issue and as he remarked in passing Strauss was now occupied with other matters'. Conant had reiterated the US standpoint about preferential treatment of Euratom, but this was 'clearly forcing an open door'. When Adenauer had complained about some French demands in regard to the Common Market, Conant had not responded because he felt that this was beyond his competence.[91]

Dulles expressed satisfaction with Adenauer's 'apparent confidence in his ability deal with Strauss on question ownership and supply fissionable materials'. With respect to the Common Market, he was 'impressed' by the fact that the French had made a major concession in Paris [majority decision about transition between Common Market stages, presumably] and that all except Germany had been prepared to go along with French proposals on social harmonization. He added a comment which illustrates the continuing American focus on Euratom as compared to the Common Market. Common Market issues were 'details':

> In any case, we would certainly hope that matters of such major importance as agreement on Euratom should not be held up because of inability agree on relatively less important details of common market arrangements.

Dulles wanted a final move to complete the American effort. He instructed Conant to seek an opportunity to go over with the Foreign Minister the same ground as he had covered with the Chancellor to make sure Brentano was aware not only of US policy but also of the Chancellor's reaction.[92] Von

Brentano received an American official in the afternoon of 5 November, just hours before the German delegation took the night train for Paris. Conant reported that the Foreign Minister had said that he entirely agreed with the views of the Chancellor and 'concurred United States position re government ownership of fissionable material'.[93]

Conant sent a last-minute warning that the US should consider that it was impossible for Germany to go further on the issue of social harmonization (working week and overtime pay). Germany had made 'numerous concessions' in the Common Market negotiations and this was the 'last straw'. Practically all in Germany were against it and even Adenauer could not force acceptance. Conant implied that it was preferable to press France on this point instead: 'Given substantial concessions likely to be made by Germans on EURATOM issue believe corresponding concessions by French on common market issue would pave way for successful conclusions along line desired by Department'.[94]

During the short period of the 'moment for action' the State Department was also trying to cope with a disturbing tendency toward bilateralism. Pressure for bilateral deals with the US in the nuclear field was coming from several directions. There were French, Italian and German requests for bilateral assistance, and the AEC was impatient to make deals with European countries, Germany above all, as quickly as possibly.

The French, urged by the *Commissariat à l'énergie atomique*, had recently asked for negotiations on a power bilateral and they had for long been anxious to obtain enriched uranium for the submarine programme. The scientific leader of the CEA, Frances Perrin, had proposed to Lewis Strauss that an arrangement be made whereby the US would provide France with enriched uranium for submarine reactors in exchange for weapons grade plutonium which France would shortly produce.[95] An Italian diplomat asked State Department officials about the possibilities of starting negotiations for providing Italy with a large amount of enriched material. He said that conversations with the AEC had indicated that an unclassified bilateral agreement could be negotiated very quickly. He informed the Americans that some Italian technicians argued that 'what was needed to bring about German agreement to EURATOM was a slight jolt such as the realization that other people were going ahead and that a bilateral with Italy would provide the needed impetus'. The answer was that a bilateral with Italy would have 'just the opposite effect'.[96] A German electric power company sent a delegation to the State Department asking for a specific small agreement for an atomic power project, the first German one, intimating that the German Government would be prepared to back the request. Butterworth reported that von Brentano had expressed his worries to Monnet about 'information from an official American source to a private German person', according to which the US could eventually negotiate a bilateral agreement which did not contain provisions for US control or public ownership.[97]

The reports caused Dulles to act. A request was made to Maurice Faure that the French should postpone demands for bilateral assistance. Faure agreed that this was wise. Dulles informed US missions that Faure had made a commitment to refrain from negotiations until early 1957 and that the commitment should remove French bilateral negotiations as a disruptive factor. No mention should be made to the Germans of the discussions with the French. The Italian Government should be made aware of possible ramifications of further Italian bilateral discussions with the US at the particular moment.[98] The missions were instructed to refute any report that might reach the German Government that the US was prepared to enter into a full-scale nuclear power agreement without regard to Euratom.[99]

The Adenauer/Mollet Compromise

Adenauer and Mollet met in Paris on 6 November in dramatic circumstances - the Hungary and Suez crises were culminating. Back in Bonn again, Adenauer reported to the Cabinet that 'all in all it had been a day of extraordinary tension and major events, which those involved will probably never forget'. The danger of a third world war had passed, he said.[100]

At their meeting, the two leaders initially delegated to their aides to make an intense effort to reach agreement as far as possible on open issues in the Brussels negotiations. Adenauer and Mollet then talked about the critical international situation and Europe's role in the world. They did not discuss specifics in the Brussels negotiations but simply signed the compromise package on the Common Market and Euratom that had been worked out by the officials at the end of the day. Discussions took place between Brentano and Faure and their experts in the afternoon, and Adenauer and Mollet joined this meeting towards its end. The French proposals about European foreign policy coordination and on cooperation on arms was one of the subjects treated by Brentano and Faure. The 'Adenauer/Mollet compromise' consisted, then, of agreed standpoints on (1) the Common Market (2) Euratom, (3) foreign policy coordination and cooperation on arms, and (4) a few other minor issues, which will be disregarded here. It may be added that the last details about the Saar had been solved a week earlier. The treaty about returning the Saar to Germany from 1 January 1957 had been signed, and this finalization of the protracted Saar problem was a factor contributing to agreement.[101]

Adenauer talked about themes that had long occupied his mind: the risk of a deal beween the superpowers at Europe's expense and of American abandonment of Europe in the event of a Russian attack. Adenauer mentioned circumstances that had increased his suspicions about US intentions. He knew, he said, that for two and a half years now there had been a direct line of communication between the White House and the Kremlin which by-passed the State Department. He had told Dulles so, and Dulles had not denied it. Bulganin's letter to Eisenhower in connection with the Suez crisis, proposing a close cooperation between the two superpowers, 'that is to say to share out the world between them', was a confirmation of the situation. The US had not responded to the offer of cooperation but had not rejected it one hundred per cent. The US general perspective was that world peace could be maintained thanks to nuclear weapons, if America could keep its advance. The US did not understand the European situation:

The United States is so ill-informed about the situation in Europe and about European politics that one could weep. In their defence, it has to be said that they have abandoned hope of a united Europe. Mr Dulles has several times said to Mr Adenauer that there is no hope of opposing the Soviet bloc unless Europe is united. - If not, the United States will have to come to an agreement with the Russians, and they will do so under the *Pax atomica*.

Europe had to unite against America, in whatever form, he said. After the presidential elections one should ask the Americans what they wanted. Naturally, Britain should take part in the uniting of Europe. The Americans denied that the Radford Plan existed but Adenauer knew that it existed. He did not believe that the Russians could implement their threats about Suez, since the Americans would not allow it; their troops in Europe would be in danger. They had to withdraw their troops first, and that was precisely what was envisaged in the Radford Plan.

Mollet agreed, although with some objections and in less dramatic terms, that there was indeed a risk of a 'world carve-up', and that European unification was more necessary than ever. His feeling of abandonment by the US in Suez was obviously a factor that contributed to agreement at this moment. Furthermore, in the course of the meeting it became clear that his ally in Suez, Eden, had ceded to American pressure without consulting him. He received a telephone call from Eden with the message that Eden had ordered a cease-fire in Suez.[102]

The Franco-German compromise can be interpreted as having two corner-stones, one dealing with the Euratom/Common Market package, and one with foreign policy coordination and common production of arms.

In the agreement about the Common Market and Euratom the concessions that had been explicitly offered at the Paris Conference - and partly withdrawn - were finalized. The main significance of the Common Market part was that the French Government crossed the Rubicon and accepted the Common Market without assured escape clauses and a guarantee of a large degree of social harmonization (although the important issues of overseas territories and agriculture were left aside for treatment later). At the Paris

Conference, the Germans had, we saw, accepted a special regime for keeping French import taxes and export subsidies, provided that it was for a limited period and with ceilings. The French now agreed to these conditions. A special regime for France would be possible, but it could ultimately be ended by a supranational mechanism if certain conditions mainly related to the balance of payments situation were fulfilled. Second, the major French concession that had been made and withdrawn in Paris, the renunciation of the French right to decide about transition between stages, was confirmed. It was accepted that general social harmonization would no longer be a condition for the concession.[103] The counterpart to this was that Adenauer accepted, in a declaration of intent, the principle of harmonization of social costs, and certain possibilities for France to have a special regime and an escape clause if certain goals were not achieved. But there was little specific, practical detail, and in consequence the complicated web of concessions and conditions in the field of social harmonization would prove of little importance later.

For Euratom, Germany confirmed the concession which had been made at the Paris Conference about the supply monopoly, with exceptions if Euratom could not satisfy the demand or set excessive conditions and prices. The French approved the exceptions, but the situations in which they were applicable should be defined through institutional and supranational procedures. The system would be revised periodically. It would be established for a period at the end of which it could be confirmed by a supranational procedure.[104]

The compromise did not contain a clarification of the crucial point of supranational ownership of fissile materials, to which the Americans attached so much importance. The ownership issue was postponed, as was the German demand for 'minimum equality'.

> The French Delegation put down a reserve on the question of the ownership of fissile material. The German Delegation pointed out that the question of reciprocal information and control of the use of fissile material must be looked at again in detail.[105]

It was thus clear that the optimism in Conant's report from his meeting with Adenauer was unfounded.[106]

A week after the meeting Mollet sent an insistent personal message to Adenauer about what he called 'this last obstacle' in the Brussels negotiations, 'on which depends the political scope of Euratom'. He reiterated Pineau's demand at the Paris Conference that Euratom should have exclusive ownership rights of fissile materials. The *sui generis* solution that had been envisaged in Paris was not sufficient with respect to these materials. However, Euratom ownership could be limited to a certain period, the length of which could be discussed, and ownership by users could be admitted for other materials, for minerals and non-enriched materials. Mollet put forward the ´American argument´. The reason for his suggestion, he stated, was the need to develop atomic power in cooperation with the US to prevent future dependence on Middle East oil. Further, it was of the highest political importance that only Euratom itself exercised control of imported or produced nuclear materials. If the Six were to obtain acceptance from the US for the principle of self-control instead of external [US or IAEA] control it was absolutely necessary to establish the system for ownership that was already applied in the US and the UK. Maurice Faure was ready to go to Bonn to discuss the issue in more detail with the Chancellor if the latter so wished.[107] This message went unanswered for two months.

Another core issue in the Euratom negotiations seems not to have been discussed at the Adenauer/Mollet meeting and was in any case left out of the documents on the compromise. The compromise did not contain anything about the common enrichment plant, vital for French work on the H-bomb option. It may be presumed that Mollet and Pineau were not interested in pushing this pet project of French nationalists.

It was however agreed that the ´Three Wise Men´ group would be formed. Armand, Etzel and an Italian would be the members, and Spaak[108] would be asked by the two Heads of Government to be Chairman. In this way, Mollet and Adenauer opted for exploring the possibilities that might be contained in the ´new approach´ idea that had taken shape in the State Department and among the European integrationists: a joint US-European programme for development of civil nuclear power. The alternative of joining forces with Britain in the nuclear power field does not seem to have been considered.[109]

The *Junktim* had been informally acknowledged, we have seen, at least since the earlier meeting between Adenauer and Mollet in September, but it had not been formally accepted, because withholding recognition functioned as a French bargaining chip, and because Mollet believed that the model ´Euratom first-Common Market later´ would facilitate approval of the Common Market in the French Parliament. The *Junktim* was not mentioned in the compromise.[110]

The second cornerstone of the Adenauer/Mollet compromise concerned foreign policy coordination and cooperation on arms. The agreement on these points reflected a wish to keep the door open for Britain. The intentions for foreign policy coordination were formulated loosely. The summoning of periodical meetings of ministers in the European countries in order to promote political coordination was envisaged. With respect to arms cooperation a possible solution was to activate the Armaments Agency of the WEU. The other states would be asked to participate in the planning for a new European Arms Pool.[111] The proposal in the French memorandum to form a Franco-German *Comité militaire et technique* to start planning of concrete projects was not accepted by the Germans at this time, the possibility of British participation should be explored first.

It should be noted, however, that on the day of the Adenauer-Mollet meeting in Paris parallel Franco-German discussions about arms cooperation took place in Bonn. The French General Valluy came to Bonn for talks with F.-J. Strauss who had recently been appointed Minister of Defence. The material from these talks does not seem to have been declassified. It is not far-fetched, however, to assume that possibilities of Franco-German military nuclear cooperation were mentioned. The French Ambassador reported that Strauss was at this time constantly making public declarations about the priority of quality over quantity in solving the difficulties in building up the *Bundeswehr* and about the necessity of having ´the most modern weapons´. In private conversations he adopted the same position as the Chancellor with respect to cooperation on arms with France and Italy. He also expressed the wish to visit the French installations in Colomb-Béchar in Algeria.[112]

In sum, after the Adenauer/Mollet meeting, a number of issues were still more or less in the pot and seen as components of a comprehensive deal between the leading actors, France and the Federal Republic. The principal ones were:

1. For Euratom:
   - Euratom ownership of fissile materials for military as well as civil uses
   - equality of control
   - equality of information
   - exception to the supply monopoly for military uses
   - a European enrichment plant
2. For the Common Market:
   - agricultural policy
   - the size of contributions to French overseas areas
   - the height of the tariff wall against other countries
3. Formal French acceptance of the *Junktim*
4. The specification of the agreement in principle to cooperate about arms

Was a central part of the Adenauer/Mollet compromise an acceptance by Adenauer that Euratom would not constitute an obstacle to French national nuclear weapons? The material bearing on this question is unclear. Incoming reports to the State Department from talks with French officials indicated that the issue of military uses of atomic energy had not been discussed at all and remained to be resolved.[113] The most thorough studies[114] of the Six state negotiations and accounts by participants[115] do not say anything about it. The French historian G.-H. Soutou has however argued that the main outcome of the meeting was that Adenauer decided to unblock the Euratom negotiation on this point of capital importance. The negotiation partners had hitherto wanted to impose the interdiction. At the meeting, Adenauer conceded that the future organization would not prevent a nuclear military effort in a member state.[116] The basis of the argument is a reference to the observation by historian Pierre Guillen that Adenauer was prepared after the meeting to make concessions to prevent the downfall of Euratom; this led to the German concession in January that control of the use of fissile materials would not apply to military installations in a member state.[117]

My view is that the thesis that Adenauer unconditionally gave the ´green light´ to French nuclear weapons in the Adenauer/Mollet compromise is a simplification. The process continued for another two months. The German position during this period was to stick to the demand for ´minimum equality´ and its abandonment was tied to the specification of a Franco-German nuclear option in the arms cooperation project. Mollet and the French Socialists continued for long, but not to the end, to support Euratom ownership and to avoid exception for military uses in the supply system. This was the last chance to put some, albeit weak, European restriction on French nationalists and a completely national French nuclear weapons programme. It was also essential in order to retain the support of the German Social-Democrats and thereby to obtain ratification of Euratom in the Federal Republic. This endeavour coincided with that of US diplomacy.

After the Adenauer-Mollet meeting French interlocutors told American officials that the entire package was now probably ratifiable in France, even if many difficulties, such as agriculture and overseas areas, remained to be met. A member of Pineau´s staff assured that, although the ownership issue had scarcely been discussed, Mollet had not given up the idea; Spaak´s *sui generis* compromise was ´sweeping matter of ownership under rug´ and it had little appeal. Marjolin said about the *Junktim* that the official French position was still that enactment would be easier if the two treaties were presented separately. The Euratom treaty would be ready for presentation to parliaments in January, the Common Market Treaty few months later.[118]

The Germans made an effort to dispel any impression in the State Department that they were becoming interested in Third Force ideas. Mollet and Adenauer had agreed, the Americans were assured, that the events in Hungary demonstrated the need for more effective European unity. Mollet had suggested regular foreign ministers meetings in ´a restricted European circle´, which the Germans took to mean the UK, France and the Federal Republic. Adenauer had made it clear that he did not want any arrangements which would tend to exclude the US or the other European countries. As regards Suez, the Germans had avoided any commitment on solidarity with the French.[119]

Butterworth´s judgment was that the successful Adenauer/Mollet talks represented a decisive step, ´Germany has now made the required concessions´. He was however concerned that the Euratom negotiations could not be closed without waiting for the Common Market because of the gradual French acceptance, in practice if not formally, of the *Junktim*. The American attitude in the matter was in his view up to revision. Butterworth delivered an epitaph of the *Junktim,* which the US had for so long tried to prevent:

> My hunch is that in days to come France will re-emerge as center of difficulties when, for example, the detailed provisions regarding agricultural and overseas territories have to be negotiated and when it has to be faced that through the general process of negotiation a definite link has grown joining EURATOM and common market. To this link French themselves importantly contributed for example: By not fostering basic decisions re EURATOM at Venice conference; by helpful attitude of Faure and Marjolin in Brussels in respect to both questions; by permitting St Cloud [Paris] conference to break up on common market issue without consolidating agreements reached on EURATOM questions et cetera. Furthermore, Adenauer-Mollet communique and subsequent statement of Faure that 'all questions concerning common market and EURATOM which had not been solved at last meeting of Foreign Ministers have been settled' recognizes the link. Thus to predilections of German and Belgian governments to unite these two questions the French have in practice fallen in accord.[120]

The views of integrationists - Monnet and Armand - were communicated to Schaetzel in the State Department:

Monnet said that he felt that a Euratom treaty could now be drafted. Control was his major preoccupation. The WEU control function had not worked, basically because the British were not prepared to accept the same control required of the Germans and the French. Hence, the French had never taken action to implement their part of the arrangements. He explained that he considered that in the case of Euratom the US should no longer stick to the normal principle that US inspectors controlled the whereabouts of material received from the US but should allow self-policing in Euratom. Otherwise there would be two control systems:

> Euratom will own and control not only material received from the U.S., but indigenously produced material as well. If the U.S. should insist on the same type of control vis-a-vis Euratom [as] called for under the bilaterals, or control to be administered by the Agency [IAEA], then the Europeans would be compelled to limit outside control to only that nuclear material coming from the U.S. This would create a division in Euratom's control system making it less than complete and thus vitiate a basic objective of Euratom.

Monnet stressed the relationship between ownership and the supply monopoly. If the treaty provided for ownership combined with the supply monopoly, even for a limited period of time, 'then the irrepressible German efficiency would make it work so that at at the end of the period there would be no incentive to eliminating this function'. The importance of common ownership was in the authority it gave to Euratom. Without it, the whole programme would collapse. Schaetzel warned Monnet that the US next year might be amending its legislation to allow for private ownership of fissile materials, and Monnet cautioned against passing this information around.[121] Monnet seemed to be sure, Schaetzel observed, 'that the control system will include any weapons project, for the weapons material will come from the common stock (pointing up again the importance of common ownership'. Monnet also pleaded - he continued to do so in the following months - that it was time for the US to bring to life to the transfer option to help avoid the threatening national options: '...it is in the interest of the U.S. to make available, in good time, finished weapons to the Europeans'.[122]

At the meeting with Armand, Schaetzel pointed out that there was pressure in the US for bilateral programmes with various countries. As a year had passed without Euratom coming to fruition these pressures were developing. Some people in America seemed to feel that not much would come out of Euratom, or conversely that it might assist in the development of a neutralist Europe. Armand confessed that he had initially seen Euratom from the angle of an economist and industrialist as a means of solving Europe's energy problem. Now he had come to the conclusion that it was perhaps politically more important than economically. Therefore he thought it ten times as important as the OEEC effort in the nuclear energy field. Euratom was a means of overcoming Franco-German rivalry. The idea of manufacturing atomic weapons had become the pet theme of the ardent French nationalists. There was no risk of Third Force developments; Armand 'pooh-poohed the idea of a neutralist Europe emerging from a closely integrated group of six'. He stressed the control and ownership issues, warning 'that we all had to watch out for French and German nationalists if we wanted the project to succeed and a strong community to emerge with wide powers of security control as well as fissionable materials ownership'.[123]

Franco-German Arms Cooperation with Nuclear Components

The first trace in my sources about a nuclear dimension in the agreed programme for Franco-German arms cooperation is a French letter of 21 December reporting about the excellent relationship that had emerged when F.-J. Strauss had met the French Minister of Defence, Maurice Bourgès-Maunory. The latter, describing Strauss enthusiastically as 'a statesman', had offered to accompany Strauss personally to show the installations for missile tests at Colomb-Béchar in Algeria. The author of the letter wrote that he was convinced, now more than ever, about the necessity of close military cooperation, and that studies about cooperation should be made, among other things, about 'the atomic problem'.[124]

In Colomb-Béchar an agreement was signed on 17 January 1957 by Strauss and Bourgès-Maunoury. This agreement was the formal starting point for Franco-German arms cooperation with a nuclear component which eventually, from late in 1957, became the so-called F-I-G [France-Italy-Germany] project. The basic principle, which developed fully in the autumn of 1957 and went on until De Gaulle's coming into power in 1958, was production of nuclear weapons, including means of delivery, on French territory and German and Italian participation in research, production and financing.[125] It seems that the text of the Colomb-Béchar agreement is still not available.[126] There is no doubt, however, that Strauss was authorized by Adenauer to sign the agreement. The historian Colette Barbier concludes - on the basis of secondary sources and an anonymous interview - that the elaboration of a comprehensive plan was probably envisaged, a plan which included several elements including the production of fissile material. She also refers to a French secondary source indicating that the construction of an enrichment plant was discussed at the Strauss/Bourgès-Maunoury meeting.[127] It is unclear whether agreement on this point was reached, however.

F.-J. Strauss wrote in his memoirs that the agreement in Algeria was 'without nuclear components'.[128] Substantive evidence of the presence of nuclear components is however found in a diary entry by Adenauer's close collaborator Herbert Blankenhorn. It is noteworthy that Blankenhorn judged the emerging Franco-German entente about arms cooperation to be *more* important than the Common Market and Euratom, which were now approaching completion:

> Meanwhile Franco-German relations have entered a further stage of close cooperation. The negotiations on the Common Market and Euratom have made very good progress, so that one can now count on new Community organisations. *Still more significant* [my emphasis], however, seems to me the fact that the Minister of Defence, Strauss, has succeeded, in personal discussion with the French Minister of Defence, Bourgès-Maunoury, in establishing close cooperation with regard to necessary arms production. This cooperation extends in essence to the production of tanks and aircraft, but also to the manufacture of *missiles and atomic armament* [my emphasis], in which German experts are to work together with their French colleagues in the Sahara training-grounds in the future. Such agreements contribute more than any others to reinforcing France's sense of security and to eliminating posssible distrust towards us which understandably may still persist.[129]

The US and other NATO allies were informed very early about the talks about Franco-German arms cooperation. According to the historian Gustav

Schmidt, the German general Heusinger, who accompanied Strauss to the talks in Algeria, informed NATO staffs about the meetings. Schmidt adds that the US was not only informed about the trilaterateral impetus but offered moral and material support.[130] It is to be doubted, however, that the US offered support, at least not for any nuclear component. It is uncertain whether the atomic weapons part of the agreement, which Blankenhorn mentioned in his diary, was reported to NATO. It can be presumed that it was kept secret. An American official in Bonn reported the fact that Heusinger had told the NATO staff about the agreement right after the event, but, the author added, 'There is no evidence that this agreement relates to the development of atomic warheads'.[131]

Controversies about Enrichment and Bilateralism

After the Adenauer/Mollet compromise American foreign policy makers decided that time was ripe for the implementation of US enrichment policy, the principles of which had been announced in February, that is, the allocation of 20,000 kgs. U-235 for distribution abroad. The long-awaited announcement of precise conditions and prices for uranium with various degrees of enrichment, and other materials, was made by the President and the Atomic Energy Commission on 18 November. The conditions were even more financially advantageous than expected. For example, prices were about 33 per cent lower than the prices that had been envisaged at the Geneva Conference about peaceful uses of nuclear energy in 1955, advance commitments for supply for more than 10 years were made, and assurances were given that plutonium and other materials produced from the US fuels would be bought back at advantageous prices [a purpose of this was to 'mop up' plutonium that would otherwise eventually find its way into weapons] and used only for peaceful purposes. The promise of 'preferential treatment' for Euratom as compared to bilateral relations was reiterated.[132]

The American offer meant that there was no economic rationale for a European enrichment plant. It was recognized in France that the US prices decisively reduced the chances of agreement on a European plant. There was disappointment in the CEA. Goldschmidt told the British that it would be almost impossible to secure agreement to the construction of a plant for civil purposes. It was likely that the only diffusion plant which might be constructed on the continent would be to provide material for military purposes. The French would have to go ahead on this project on their own. Guillaumat said to the Americans that it was not clear to him what the US could do for Euratom in excess of what it was apparently prepared to do in bilateral arrangements.[133] The *Quai d'Orsay* similarly judged that agreement about a plant had become improbable. One of the principal attractions for France of Euratom had disappeared. The pricing-structure showed 'little concern to give the Europeans a taste for acquiring independence' in this field. Interpreted less favourably, 'the objective of this decision is to obtain an advantage for the export of American reactors'.[134]

Reports from France's partners confirmed that the construction of a European plant had become commercial nonsense. A Dutch source stated that the American announcement virtually amputated one leg of the three on which the Euratom concept stood - monopoly ownership, the common budget and the enrichment plant. The effect of the loss of this leg should not be underestimated. Another Dutch diplomat interpreted the French strategy to be to bring about a low-enrichment plant, the output of which would be fed through the Marcoule reactor complex, producing plutonium that would be assigned to the weapons programme. France would demand in Brussels that when the Governments signed the Treaty, they would also decide to start building an enrichment plant in 1957. Euratom was, in effect, to be an accessory to the French bomb plan.[135]

Butterworth issued warnings about the effect of the US announcement on the negotiations in Brussels. The fact that the announcement had come in the atmosphere engendered by differences with the US over Suez had given rise to distrust concerning the US motivation among participants in the Brussels negotiations. Some asked themselves whether the US did not prefer Europe to remain dependent for fissile material for reasons of political and commercial advantage. An idea was circulating that the US, after securing European dependence through the bait of low uranium prices, might subsequently raise the prices in order to exploit the dominant supply position. The question of dependence was again at the forefront. It was argued that Europe needed to develop full mastery of atomic technology to regain its ability to play the role of a major world power.[136]

At the negotiations in Brussels the French standpoint was that a decision of principle should be taken to construct an enrichment plant before the signature of the Euratom Treaty. The German position was non-committal.[137] At the meeting of the Heads of Delegation on 4-5 January 1957 - after which the general opinion was that there were no unsolved questions serious enough to wreck the negotiations - the positions did not change. It was noted that the work of the Study Group about enrichment had made no headway; the French criticized the fact that the group had been unable to obtain data from Germany about methods for enrichment that had been studied there. A factor that contributed to the reluctance to make commitments before signature of the treaties was that Israel had asked for membership of the Study Group; the request obviously accentuated the military and political complications of the enterprise.[138]

When M. Faure discussed the unsolved questions with the German leaders in Bonn a week later enrichment was one of them. Faure talked about the US attempt to discourage the European plant through 'veritable dumping'. Hallstein and Carstens made no commitments. They referred to the high cost and the risk that a plant would be antiquated within a few years.[139]

However, when the question came up for decision in the German Cabinet on 15 January 1957 - few days after Faure's visit and the arms cooperation agreement in Colomb-Béchar - Adenauer made statements, which made clear that he was now prepared to agree to this project which the French had solicited from the beginning. It is evident that his motive was the importance of the enrichment plant for the Franco-German nuclear weapons option:

> The *Federal Minister for Atomic Affairs* [Balke] now dealt with the question of constructing an isotope-separation [enrichment] plant. The plant would be very expensive and already outdated technically, and would cost from half a billion to a billion DM. One should therefore wait, in order to avoid a wrong investment. The French were of course pressing hard, but their principal interest in the plant was of a military nature. The *Chancellor* was of the view that it would be more advantageous for us to participate in the plant and that France should not build it alone. *Only in that way would we have the possibility to take part in discussion about military development* [my emphasis]. The *Federal Minister for Foreign Affairs* supported this opinion. The Federal Republic had an interest in taking part in the construction of a possible isotope-separation plant. However, to avoid a wrong investment one should if possible not give any binding commitment. But one should aim to include in the treaty on the basic agreement to build an isotope-separation plant a reserve on the financial question and a more thorough study of the technical problems. The Cabinet so agreed.[140]

Elbrick and Farley discussed the acute danger of bilateralism in a memorandum for Dulles in the period when the final decisions about Euratom were to be made. They referred to a recent request from the German Embassy in Washington for immediate negotiation and early conclusion of a power bilateral, to a similar approach from the Italians and to the French decision in October to withdraw their request for a power bilateral.[141] The line of the State Department for the past year had been 'to insure that any negotiations from the Six were made by the Governments concerned after weighing fully the possible impact on Euratom; we have not ourselves taken any action to suspend such negotiations'. When the problem of the impact on Euratom had been brought to the attention of the French they had withdrawn their demand, but 'other governments have been more willing to close their eyes to this impact under pressure from their own immediate domestic interests'. Ambassadors Conant, Dillon and Butterworth had all warned that bilateral negotiations at this point, especially with Germany, could disrupt the Euratom negotiations. The memorandum suggested that the primary responsibility for deciding whether to ask for bilateral negotiations should be turned back to the Six.

Accordingly, Dulles sent a circular telegram and instructed the missions to explain to the Six, particularly Adenauer and Italian Prime Minister Segni, that it would be inappropriate for the US to assume responsibility for decisions as to the possible effects of bilateral negotiations on Euratom.[142]

Faure, who was about to go to Bonn to discuss with the German leaders, was 'very pleased' and felt his position was 'greatly reinforced' by the US action. It would also make his position easier with the CEA which had gone over the *Quai d'Orsay*'s head straight to Mollet in its push for bilateralism. The situation had become so acute that Mollet had called for a special restricted Cabinet meeting about the matter. Now, Faure 'would have no trouble holding the line with French Government provided he was successful in persuading Germans to adopt same policy'.[143]

Monnet was also active in the fight against bilateralism. He warned Dulles that if the US agreed to give 'bilateral aid of a substantial character to Germany before EURATOM was signed up, it would almost surely mean the end of EURATOM'. Dulles replied that he thought 'we could hold the line for a week or so at least'.[144] A week later Monnet reported to Dulles that he had had a five-hour talk with AEC Chairman Strauss to explain the importance of the Euratom project for the creation of Europe. Monnet felt that Strauss now understood Euratom better and, although he had not committed himself, he had said that 'he thought he would not press for the bilaterals as long as there was an early prospect of the Euratom treaty being signed'.[145]

Erosion of 'Minimum Equality'

In December, it was obvious to American policy-makers that the French would not be satisfied with anything less than complete legal and technical freedom for the national option. The French would not allow Euratom to be constructed in a way that might interfere with the condition that had been set up by Parliament in July. The realization of this state of affairs resulted in a search in the State Department for possible instruments for discouraging and delaying French nuclear weapons in the short run and for bringing about a reversal of policy in the long run. Schaetzel drafted a memorandum on the subject. Although the formal status of the paper is uncertain, it throws light on lines of thought that were topical in the Department. Several of the actions proposed fitted well with policies that were applied later.[146]

The alarming side effect of Suez, the paper stated, was that there had been renewed pressure within the French Government for the acceleration of the weapons programme as compared to the four-year period that had obtained tacit consent in July. In subsequent elaboration M. Faure had stated that France did not wish to withdraw from consultation with the partners nor from the control of the Community, even if this would be a 'special control'. The memorandum enumerated the disadvantageous consequences for the US of the accelerated French programme: the implications of the fourth country example for complicating disarmament and increasing the risk of a general nuclear war, the weakening of European unity, the risk of a revocation of the German pledge to WEU and the loss of Socialist support for Euratom. It was essential that steps be taken ´to discourage or at least delay such a French program, or to keep it at a token level´. However - this was an axiom in the State Department by then - any overt US attempt to block France would be resisted, and indeed might have the effect of accelerating the French weapons-development activities.

A number of arguments that could be used in an effort of ´Persuasion, as a Means of Discouraging French Weapons Development´ were listed: A limited nuclear weapons production capacity would not help France in resisting nuclear blackmail from the USSR, as shown by the British experience from Suez. A programme would be an economic drain. If the French decided on nuclear weapons development it was inevitable that the Germans would seek escape from their WEU commitment. The recent support from German Social-Democrats for the Common Market and Euratom would be undercut. Finally, France and the other partners would lose the benefits of an integrated European programme including preferential US assistance.

The memorandum went on to list ´Promises the U.S. Might Make´ and ´Actions which the U.S Might Take´. The US might promise, for example, training in handling of nuclear weapons, and to ´...transfer weapons to French custody, retaining U.S ownership of the nuclear components´.[147] Among the actions proposed were several that became the object of US-French bargaining in the following years: The US could for example encourage French utilization of plutonium as a reactor fuel, and as a means of diverting plutonium from weapons use, and offer exchange of French plutonium for enriched uranium. The greatest French interest in U-235 was for a submarine reactor. The French had recently proposed such an exchange themselves. Provision of U-235 for a French submarine could be part of a strong US effort to focus the French work on the military aspects of atomic energy on non-explosive manufacture.[148] The paper also discussed the potential of what was called above the ´new approach´ to Euratom (an approach that was concretized in the visit to the US of the ´Three Wise Men´ in February 1957). The ongoing effort to set very ambitious atomic power targets for Euratom would have the effect of committing available French physical and scientific atomic energy resources to non-military projects, ´...the central concept of an integrated atomic energy effort will make it increasingly difficult for the French to separate out and compartmentalize a national weapons development program´.

Barnett delivered comments on the memorandum which provide further illustration of American thinking. The US could not, he wrote, cooperate with institutions which were contrived to contribute materially to French bomb capabilities. In the situation that had developed the US could do one of several things. It could object and oppose, ´and the results of doing so night well be nil, or possibly the demise of "Euratom"´. It could promise something along the lines of the ´new approach´. Or, it could ´meet the weapons issue head-on, and urge that it be dealt with explicitly in either the WEU or NATO context´. The choice was related to the basic strategy for Euratom. There had been two broad concepts in Washington planning, Barnett wrote. The first was that the treaty should describe something truly supranational and the US should be dissatisfied with anything that fell very far short of this. The second was that the treaty was merely a first step. It did not matter too much how defective it was as long as a start was made; improvements could be made later.[149]

During the period from the Adenauer/Mollet compromise up to the turn of the year there were cleavages in France between the integrationists and the nationalists about whether a measure of ´minimum equality´ should remain, or whether France should demand complete military freedom of action while maintaining restrictions on Germany. The differences related to the issues of ownership, control of the French military sector, exceptions in the supply monopoly for feeding materials to that sector, and obligations to give away information about it. The possible consequences of the decisions in these respects for the US attitude to cooperation with France vs. Germany were constantly in mind.

Marjolin attempted to sound US views at a meeting with Schaetzel and Tuthill shortly after the Adenauer/Mollet compromise. He told the American officials that although the ownership issue had not been settled at the Adenauer/Mollet meeting, Adenauer would probably agree to the position of the five countries who were supporting Euratom ownership of fissionable materials, ´at least partly because of American intervention´. Marjolin asked for confirmation of the importance that the US attached to ownership and for an explanation of the reasons. The reasons given by Schaetzel were that it facilitated effective control, had juridical value and strengthened Euratom against influences tending towards bilateralism. When asked whether the American position was that Euratom would own and control the fissionable material received from the US, or all fissionable materials from any source, Schaetzel confirmed that the US objective was ownership and control of all fissionable materials from any source. The US was very worried about the French reservations on military use, Schaetzel said. It was difficult to know if effective controls could be possible in the event that there were ´closed rooms´, and if members had the right to retain and operate independently with fissionable material from outside sources.[150]

Still in mid-December Marjolin confirmed that France intended to accept a measure of control of the French military sector. He told Dillon that, ´following a meeting with Mollet...it had been decided that France would accept EURATOM inspection and control in military field through the process of manufacture of atomic weapons. Their disposition thereafter for storage or use would be beyond jurisdiction of EURATOM but presumably might fall within competence of WEU'.[151]

The French had, we know, for long accepted, indeed requested, Euratom ownership of fissionable materials. Common ownership was part of the 'minimum equality' formula, and it was an adaptation to US signals that common ownership would probably be necessary for US cooperation with Euratom. There were complications in the French attitude to ownership, however. They emerge clearly in a *Quai d'Orsay* paper. Common ownership could be a step towards the European option - but it could undermine the French national option:

> ...the wish to assign to Euratom all possibilities for cooperation with America led the Prime Minister to ask Chancellor Adenauer to accept Euratom ownership of all fissile materials. It is manifest that this idea is totally alien to the German mentality. But above all it will be said that, if material which forms the explosive or fuel for submarines belongs to the Community, it will establish German participation in the ownership of atomic weapons. Some will see in this a step towards the creation of a European nuclear armament, others a threat to our freedom to manufacture and use these weapons.

> On the political plane, the preoccupation with making a treaty that America will approve will disturb those who fear pressure by the United States on France to abandon her freedom on the question of arms. A treaty which from the United States' point of view was 'perfect' in all its clauses would always be at fault on this point. We might then fear pressure from America and our partners to abandon the only arrangement which would prevent collaboration.[152]

Internal French differences seem to have been thrashed out at a meeting at which M. Faure was one of the participants. The other participants are not indicated, but there is good reason to believe that the meeting had a similar character to the one of 25 June when limits for concessions on the military question were agreed in a small circle.[153] It may be presumed that key military representatives and representatives of the CEA were present. Several problems that had been raised by the CEA were discussed and agreement was reached on a number of points. Most of them aimed at removing any imaginable remaining obstacle for the national military option. The impression given by the minutes is that if these limits were crossed, the nationalists would blow the trumpet for a battle against Euratom in the National Assembly. The most important point in the agreement is a reversal of French policy on the ownership issue. The decisions related to the military question were:

1. Abandonment of Euratom ownership of fissile materials
2. A Belgian proposal in the Brussels negotiations that 'tied programmes' [programmes tied to existing arrangements] bearing on fissile materials would be subject to supranational approval should not be accepted
3. With respect to the supply system, France would demand priority for a certain quantity of uranium for construction of an enrichment plant, either national or European
4. Maintenance of the control system that had been established.[154]

What was at stake behind these technical issues was whether the US and the negotiating partners in Brussels would accept removal of remaining obstacles to French nuclear weapons. The French line was accepted - in a mood of resignation - during the first weeks of January. The ownership issue was still, however, the object of a number of bargaining moves that were dictated by tactics and ulterior motives that are not always transparent. The major stages in the process were these:

Faure tried to explain the reversal of French policy on ownership to the Americans on 9 January. A report - probably written by Dillon - accounted for the talk with Faure:

Faure suddenly asked me 'does United States really insist on ownership of fissile material by Euratom?'...Faure said that as we knew France has always strongly favored ownership by EURATOM of all fissile material but now found herself in uncomfortable and equivocal position. French decision to go ahead with national military program is now firm and without such decision there would be no chance for ratification of EURATOM. If all fissile material should be owned by EURATOM weird situation would evolve whereby French atomic weapons were owned and controlled by French but fissile material within such weapons remain property of EURATOM...Thus French find themselves in equivocal position of being leading proponent of EURATOM ownership of fissile material and at same time only country to request exception to such ownership for their own national needs. Faure said that German reaction to such approach was obvious and would be 'why bother with EURATOM ownership. Whole problem can be simplified by allowing national ownership with strict system of control by EURATOM'.

The American's comment to the State Department was that it appeared that the French were preparing to give up the fight for common ownership in return for German concessions in other areas, unless the US could provide a more convincing argumentation than before regarding the necessity of Euratom ownership.[155]

The following morning, Faure met Hallstein in Bonn. Hallstein reaffirmed the standpoint that Bonn could not see why Euratom should be the sole owner. In this conversation, Faure did not discuss the French intentions for exception for French military uses, nor did he offer the Germans any relaxation of the demand for common ownership, as the American diplomat had conjectured. He just briefly referred to the well-known US views about ownership.[156] Faure probably met Adenauer and Brentano later in the day (he had told the American diplomat that he would do so). I have no material from that meeting. There is good reason to believe, however, that the French demand for full freedom of action and the required exceptions for France was a central subject at such encounter.

A few days after Faure´s visit Adenauer sent a very belated reply to Mollet´s request for Euratom ownership of fissile materials which had been sent after the Adenauer/Mollet meeting two months earlier.[157] The reply contained no concessions. Adenauer wrote that he had the impression that the delegations at the Paris Conference had found a satisfactory solution to the problem.[158] He admitted that it was important to receive materials from the US in coming years and that a system based on common ownership might be preferred by the Americans. He invited Mollet to join him in trying to persuade the Americans that it was quite unimportant whether Euratom retained ownership or not.[159]

It must be presumed that Adenauer, when this letter was sent, had made up his mind that the Federal Republic, if necessary, would yield on this last but crucial point in the Euratom negotiations. Two days later, the ownership issue was treated at the Cabinet meeting which dealt with German standpoints at the final Conference of Foreign Ministers. Erhard and Balke, following up earlier warnings, expressed scepticism about giving way on this point, but did not outright oppose doing so. Von Brentano referred to the US system of Government ownership, which had not fostered tendencies to socialism. Adenauer advanced several arguments which indicate that he considered that the time had come for giving up the long-standing German resistance to supranational ownership of fuels/fissile materials. The only important thing, he said, was that the enterprises received the material they needed, ´the ownership concept is not decisive´. Besides, if the Federal Republic did not adhere to the treaty, a sales embargo would be applied to it, because the country would be considered a ´trouble-maker´. The only decisive question was whether the treaty was harmful to German economic interests. It was certain that without the treaty the Federal Republic could not do anything important in the nuclear field, if only for financial reasons. The treaty opened the possibility to take part in the lead of the others. Hallstein added that it was politically noteworthy that the US and France had a very great interest in ownership monopoly for fuels in Euratom. It was however advisable to continue negotiating on the basis of the previous German line and offer resistance as far as possible. The Brussels negotiations should not be allowed to break down on the issue, he said. So was decided.[160]

Adenauer's remarks about an embargo in case of non-compliance were not off the mark. Dulles sent another input to the ongoing deliberations about the ownership issue, addressed primarily to Germany. Spaak should be informed that 'U.S. under existing policy prepared to transfer special nuclear material in nuclear power quantities only when governments prepared to accept ownership such material and retain title to it. On assumption EURATOM would meet test permitting bilateral agreement to be concluded with it, same policy on transfer special [fissile] nuclear material would apply'. This should also be made clear to the German Government.[161]

It should be observed that Dulles' message was weaker than earlier when only Euratom ownership, not just governmental ownership had been acceptable to the US. Thus the dilemma for American policy at this point was that Euratom ownership could no longer be requested and made a condition for US cooperation. Then the French would not ratify. On the other hand, Germany had to be subjected to satisfactory safeguards. German governmental ownership combined with Euratom self-control of the entire German nuclear sector seemed to be acceptable to Dulles at this moment.

However, on the same day as this message was sent Butterworth warned Dulles against 'national ownership' and proposed a model that was ultimately adopted in the Euratom Treaty. Butterworth argued that the alternative of 'national ownership' as had been referred to by Faure would ultimately end up with the Germans reverting to F.-J. Strauss' ideas of private ownership. Butterworth proposed that 'in effort forestall such major retreat…proposal be made to French that they continue sponsor EURATOM ownership but seek agreement that ownership rights to materials in nuclear weapons would pass to French Government at same point that EURATOM control ceases to apply to such weapons. (At latter point WEU military control might apply)'.[162]

Mollet - without knowing that the German decision to accept Euratom ownership had already been made - was momentarily prepared to accept Adenauer's demand to join him in asking the Americans if they would accept cooperation and Euratom self-control even if there were no Euratom ownership. He envisaged that Faure should discuss this possibility with Hallstein.[163] Apparently, he was prepared to accept something less than Euratom ownership of German fissionable materials if the Americans did.

It is uncertain whether a common Franco-German *démarche* was made. Five days later he sent a letter to Adenauer proposing that, 'because of the extreme political importance of this problem', it should be solved at the coming meeting of Heads of Government in Paris, together with the other essential remaining question, the association of overseas territories to the Common Market.[164]

The other reservations related to 'minimum equality' (equality of control and information) had already been abandoned by Germany in December.

The French representatives in Brussels had proposed Community control, without discrimination, on both military and civil manufactures, although up to a point only, that of making an ´operational device´. The Germans had for long refused to consider any kind of exception in the control system for the French military sector.[165] Now this position was abandoned. It was agreed that control would in no case extend to the operational device.[166]

Similarly, the German delegation lifted its general reservation on the chapter in the draft treaty about the circulation of information. The French delegation made a small concession while not giving up the essence, the French right to define the borderline between civil nuclear technical information and military secrets.[167]

According to a later account by Monnet´s collaborator, Jacques van Helmont, the final formula concerning the French exceptions to control and obligation to pass information about French military applications was preliminarily agreed between Mollet and the leaders of the German Social-Democratic party, Ollenhauer and Wehner, as members of the Action Committee.[168]

Van Helmont´s thesis seems to imply that the German Social-Democratic Party had the final say about the fate of Euratom, in the sense that if the Party had decided to fight Euratom the treaty would not have been ratified in Germany. The Party´s original goal was that Euratom would restrict both Germany and France from having nuclear weapons. Now, the leadership apparently judged it necessary to agree to a model that would bind Germany only, because it was obvious that Euratom would not be ratified in France if France were bound. The alternative to agreeing to Mollet´s demand was that neither country would be restricted.

The main components of the legal formula that eliminated ´minimum equality´ and was eventually adopted in the Euratom Treaty were: (1) the control should aim at ensuring that materials were not used for other purposes than those that had been declared, (2) the control should not include materials destined for defence purposes, and there should be no discrimination because of the purpose, (3) Euratom should have ownership of the fissile materials that were subjected to control, and (4) a member state could demand secrecy by referring to defence purposes. This formula gave France more or less[169] full legal freedom of action for the national military option, while subjecting the entire nuclear sector in the Federal Republic to control because of the *Kernwaffenverzicht* to the WEU.[170]

Spaak delivered a frank evaluation of the entire Euratom affair by the time that he met the British leadership at No. 10 Downing Street on 15 January. He uttered some bitter words about the outcome compared to his initial hopes. He interpreted Adenauer´s motives for accepting the French unrestricted national option accurately enough, considering what the

German documents now indicate about these motives. He also seemed to put some blame on the Americans for not having prevented this development:

> Originally it [Euratom] had specifically excluded any military programme, but the German Government had now agreed that the French Government would be entitled to a military atomic programme within the framework of the Treaty. He thought that Chancellor Adenauer had been led to make this concession to the French by his fear lest the United States withdraw their troops from Europe and by the idea that if the French were permitted to have a programme it might also be possible for the Germans to have a programme in say five or ten years time. He himself considered that for the French to start a military atomic programme was plain foolishness. It would dislocate entirely the already shaky French economy and would have unfavourable consequences for the whole problem of disarmament etc. But M. Mollet had been under extremely heavy pressure...[Spaak] had warned the American Government of what was on foot but he did not know whether the French Government had themselves said anything to the Americans. He was really becoming very hesitant about accepting his new appointment with NATO[171] in the light of these developments...M. Spaak suggested that what was really necessary was to persuade the United States Government to advance a little from their present offer of atomic weapons to NATO. We should try to make them go beyond the present formula, which might be summed up as 'We will make bombs for you and put them in the European cupboard but General Norstad must keep the key'. Perhaps it might be possible to find some solution by working forward from the NATO decision about the use of nuclear weapons which was reached at the end of 1954.[172]

The US Position on the Common Market and the British Free Trade Area Proposal

The American preference for regionalism rather than multilateralism in Europe remained unchanged during the entire period studied here, 1953-57. After the Venice Conference in May 1956 it had become clear that there was a good chance that the Common Market would be realized, and the British were preparing their 'Plan G' for a Free Trade Area compatible with it (it was announced publicly on 3 October). It became necessary for Washington to take a closer look at the political and economic consequences for the US of the European market plans. The American attitude since the beginning of the Brussels negotiations had, we know, been that the US was preliminarily sympathetic to the Common Market, although further study was required and no decisions could be taken until the project had advanced further.

Some preoccupations had been expressed now and then about the risk of restrictive business practices and the effects on US agricultural export in particular. A *Junktim* between Euratom and the Common Market had been discouraged with the argument that the negotiations on the latter project would be complex and lengthy.

In mid-August the newly created Council on Foreign Economic Policy (CFEP) established a subcommittee to study the effects of regional economic integration on US trade and other economic interests. The committee limited its focus to Western Europe, it did not study other regions of the world. The Council's chairman, Clarence C. Randall, wrote an enthusiastic letter to Dulles in early October in which he praised the Common Market as 'the most significant economic event in my generation'. In his Miami speech on 29 October President Eisenhower supported both the Common Market and the Free Trade Area in principle but he gave clear priority to the Common Market. In various US agencies, uncertainty remained about whether the ultimate British objective in launching the FTA plan was to torpedo the Common Market or to build a bridge to it.[174]

In November, the CFEP subcommittee delivered a report with detailed arguments and a policy statement. The report was a compromise between agency interests in the subcommittee. It was close to the State Department's positive line, as against the much more reserved attitude of the Treasury and the Federal Reserve. It passed the CFEP without change, and the NSC Secretariat concluded that it did not deviate from previous NSC statements on US policy toward European integration. The policy statement and explanatory notes were handed over and discussed with representatives of various European countries.[175]

The report discussed the net effect of the proposed Common Market and Free Trade Area on US political and economic interests. With respect to the political aspect it was summarily stated that the Common Market would reduce the danger of another European war and the FTA would lessen both the fears and chances of German domination of Europe. There was a 'slight political risk' of Third Force-developments and neutralism, but a stronger Europe would probably, in its own self-interest, strengthen the Atlantic Community. Moreover, 'if the US were to adopt an unsympathetic policy, there would be the risk that such an attitude toward proposals initiated by our principal Allies in their self-interest might drive Europe into the very neutralism that we seek to avoid'. The political considerations, it was concluded, pointed toward a position of general support, while the economic risks should be minimized.

Economic risks and advantages were weighed. There were short-term risks of protectionism resulting in displacement of some US exports to Europe and more competition from European products. The US should ensure that, in accordance with GATT principles, the resultant single tariff would be no more protective on the average and with respect to commodities important to the US than the tariffs of the member states separately. There was no *a priori* basis for inferring that US export would be either helped or hindered by the contemplated external tariff arrangements. Further, many of the short-term disadvantages might be off-set by long-term economic benefits. For example, insofar as the Common Market and the FTA fostered more rapid economic growth and more efficient production in Europe, Western European demands for US goods and the ability to pay for them would increase. US private investment in Europe would be stimulated. The economies in question were so large and the intra-trade barriers so significant that the world economy would probably benefit from the elimination of these barriers. Only through improvement in the relative competitive position of Europe could the persistent balance-of-payments difficulties be resolved.

Agriculture was a special problem. The possible effects on US agricultural exports were especially hard to judge, the report estimated. The proposals for the Common Market to deal with the special agricultural problems by Community organization of production, markets, pricing and subsidization could hit agriculture hard in the US and in other countries. However, this would be true only to the extent that it would make the situation worse than it might otherwise have been. For example, in the case of wheat, the French had already concluded a long-term marketing arrangement with Germany, which suggested future disadvantages for the US, Common Market or not. The importance of the agricultural sector in the French economy had to be taken into account in the total negotiation context, ´indeed, the opportunities for expanding production and stabilizing farm incomes that this marketing organization may offer France are probably a *sine qua non* for sufficient votes in the National Assembly for French ratification´. With respect to the FTA-Common Market relationship agriculture was a complicating factor. An exclusion of foodstuffs from the FTA would avoid difficult problems. But the Common Market countries were understandably reluctant to grant free entry of virtually all British exports to the Common Market while Britain offered to grant free entry to only part (67 per cent) of the Common Market exports to the UK.

The American views on economic integration were announced publicly by the State Department on 15 January 1957. It was declared that the two market plans were welcome and compatible with the traditional policies of the US: to support European cooperation and to promote non-discriminatory multilateral trade and currency convertibility. A Common Market based on expansion of internal and external trade would have the support of the US; it was however presupposed that its construction would be consistent with the regulations of the GATT and the IMF. Certain reservations with respect to agriculture were expressed. The European market for agricultural exports from the US was important, and the possible impact of common market arrangements on it would be studied carefully. The Free Trade Area was commented on in positive terms. The formulations made clear, however, that US policy remained: Common Market first, Free Trade Area later.[176]

The French wanted to be certain that possible American hesitations about the Common Market and its provisions for agriculture in particular, would not complicate the Brussels negotiations at the last minute. The Americans were told that M. Faure stressed the importance of decisive action while the Mollet Government was still there and could get the treaties through. Technical points or the desire to dispose of agricultural surpluses, especially wheat, must not lead to 'active US prodding' to change treaty provisions. If so, the negotiations might be interminably delayed. Overall political considerations should be put in the balance and outweigh technical, economic and commercial policy considerations in determining the US attitude.[177]

The Germans, for their part, solicited the US views on the other big open question in the Common Market negotiations, besides agriculture, the question of Europe's relationship to overseas territories, that is, the French vision of *'Eurafrique'*. Dulles was informed that Adenauer wanted to know the US attitude on this point; the Germans did not want to see Germany labelled as a colonial power. Dulles responded positively. He supported enthusiastically the working out of an association between Europe and Africa as part of a peaceful process of Africa gaining political independence from colonialism. If one looked at the map, he said, it was apparent that Africa was 'the big hinterland of Europe'; 'a whole new force in the world' could come out of an association. Germany could further this development.[178]

Revitalization of the Anglo-American Nuclear Special Relationship

The German and French inclination to keep the door open for Britain in a bloc aiming at increasing European autonomy had its counterpart in the 'Grand Design' ideas that were presented by the British Foreign Secretary, Selwyn Lloyd, in December 1956 and January 1957.[179] A main motive was to obtain French consent to the British Free Trade Area plan. It is also very probable that Lloyd was influenced by the emerging Franco-German entente in the armaments field. It could no doubt be observed from London, although it is uncertain whether the British knew the details of the process that led to Colomb-Béchar. In any case, Eden's Cabinet Committee on the Long-Term Defence Programme had discussed the possibility of nuclear cooperation with Germany and France on 18 December and had noted that 'Germany and France were known to be averse to relying entirely on the United States for the provision of atomic weapons and warheads and there might be advantage in our co-operating with such European allies in the nuclear field'.[180]

At the meeting of the NATO Council on 12 December, Lloyd told the

Council that he

> ...saw a grand design now emerging for [the] Atlantic Community made up of three elements; (1) high military and political directorate as represented by WEU and NATO; (2) economic co-operation under and associated with OEEC, including [the] Coal and Steel Community, European Payments Union, [the] projected Common Market and EURATOM; (3) single assembly in Parliamentary lines.[181]

This triggered a debate within the British Foreign Office on the future of British policy towards Europe and NATO. Whilst the debate was going on, Lloyd presented a startling additional element to the 'Grand Design' to the Cabinet on 5 January 1957. Lloyd proposed that Britain should join with the rest of the WEU in developing A- and H-bomb capacity. The proposal meant that Britain would make a radical change of traditional foreign policy by endeavouring to become the leader in developing the European option:

> ...if we are to be a first-class Power with full thermo-nuclear capacity, it can only be done in association with other countries. Britain and Six other Western European Union...Powers have a combined population of over 210 million, together with a very considerable industrial capacity, resources, and skill. If these were pooled, the resultant association could afford to possess full thermo-nuclear capacity.[182] [He suggested] a joint R & D programme for atomic and thermo-nuclear weapons including all the means of delivery.[183]

Lloyd appears to have believed that since Britain would be the leader of the European group it could prevent any drift into neutralism, or the withdrawal of the US from Europe. His idea was not to create a Third Force, the perspective was completely Atlanticist. The bloc would develop as a powerful group within NATO 'almost as powerful as America and perhaps in friendly rivalry with her'.[184] Lloyd's intention was to reduce British and European dependence on the US but to keep NATO as the central feature of British foreign and security policy. A WEU bomb was an 'insurance policy' in case the US would not honour its commitments, not an alternative to NATO. Other factors that influenced him were that the project would make the British deterrent cheaper and dampen criticism in Germany of planned British troop reductions.

Lloyd's plan met strong resistance in Whitehall. Some were concerned that the US should approve the policy. This was - considering Eisenhower's many pronouncements about European self-reliance and his vision of American withdrawal in the long run - not excluded. Others forecast that the US would not approve it. For example, the Minister of Defence quite correctly anticipated that the US was unlikely to proceed with it; the US would not sanction Britain´s giving the other WEU members US nuclear data. Makins argued that any hope of restoring the nuclear special relationship with the US would be extinguished. He also pointed out that Britain was dependent on the US for the uranium supplies for its civil nuclear programme.

The nuclear version of the ´Grand Design´ was short-lived. After Macmillan had become Prime Minister in early January, the British reaffirmed traditional policy of attempting to persuade the US to restore the Anglo-American nuclear special relationship of the war years. The Foreign Office pressed ahead with other aspects of the plan. General cooperation on arms was still considered, and a closer association with Europe in other than nuclear respects was a priority goal for Macmillan.

The Americans were informed that the French Defence Minister Bourgès-Maunoury had told the British that he had held ´intimate and useful talks´ with Franz-Josef Strauss on research problems - the reference was obviously to Colomb-Béchar. Fears that Britain would be left aside increased. The British wanted to raise the subject in US-UK defence talks. They were ´anxious to obtain a US reaction to the possibility of developing some coordinated research among British, French and German scientists as a nucleus around which a new WEU Armaments Committee program could grow´, it was reported to Washington.[185]

The British and American positions on these and other matters were coordinated at the Conference in Bermuda on 21-3 March 1957. Different aspects of British European policy and policy on nuclear cooperation were agreed between Eisenhower and Macmillan. In essence, there was agreement to reconstruct and fortify the ´special relationship´ after the damage caused by Suez.

Before the Bermuda Conference Dulles sent a circular telegram to missions, containing preliminary views on Lloyd´s ´Grand Design´, from which all nuclear perspectives had now been eliminated. He developed his views on the role of the WEU in the European structure in terms which indicate that a Third Force development outside NATO was not in the US interest. He explained that the US Government questioned the desirability of conceiving the WEU as an ´inner circle´ in NATO. NATO´s primacy in the political and military field must be clearly recognized. However, there was no lessening of US interest in WEU´s activities ´in fields clearly assigned to it, in particular arms control´. This interest was particularly relevant ´in view role WEU expected to play in connection control any atomic weapons production by EURATOM members´. A major weakness in the British Grand Design was, Dulles continued, that there was a tendency to blur the vital distinction between merely cooperative arrangements and ´genuine´ integration. He was concerned over the implication that Six-country developments should in some way be subordinated to the OEEC. Another problem was timing. During the next six months attention must be concentrated on bringing to fruition the Six-state projects that were already in process. The US feared discussion in the official, parliamentary and public arena of new proposals, regardless of their merits.[186]

In the briefing material for Eisenhower for the Bermuda Conference these themes were repeated and others were added. It was stated that the US welcomed bilateral and trilateral new weapons research and development coordination in Western Europe generally of the type that was being instituted among the UK, France and Germany. However, the US should ´not make a general statement which could be interpreted by the British as giving them general approval for making available to WEU information about research and development projects covered by ABC arrangements or which contain U.S. information´. All such matters had to be examined on a case-by-case basis. With respect to the Franco-German arms cooperation project it could be expected that the British delegation might ´urge the desirability of tying Germany into a wider European effort from the point of view of allaying Soviet concern that bilateral Franco-Geman collaboration in new weapons might some day result in a nuclear-equipped Germany on its old borders´.

> The British may express concern over the close bilateral coordination which the French and Germans are apparently in the process of establishing in the new weapons field. In this event it is believed that the U.S. representatives should state that we perceive important political, military and economic advantages in this collaboration; that we have been informed by the French that they wish to bring the U.K. and other WEU states, if they desire, into the arrangement; but that we agree with the British that this situation should be closely watched, preferably through the U.K. becoming a partner in the enterprise. We have no information that the French have assisted or would contemplate assisting the Germans to produce ABC weapons, which Germany is presently prohibited, under the Brussels Treaty, from producing.

A part of the briefing material dealt with ´Atomic energy problems´; these should however only by raised at British initiative. The information was given that the US had been informed before the conference, on 14 March, that the UK had been approached in January by the French Defence Minister with a request for assistance for the French nuclear weapons development programme. It was recommended that the UK reaction should be fully explored. If it appeared that the UK were negative, the US should concur. If the UK showed interest in the French proposal the US should ´plead surprise´ and point out that this would require thorough US-UK staff discussions. For example ´consideration must be given...to possible negative implications for U.S.-U.K. military atomic energy cooperation as well as such effects on WEU and NATO. The U.K. might inquire of Mollet as to whether the French Minister of Defense inquiry represents a Government decision´.

The briefing paper mentioned some details about British dependence on uranium. The US controlled the production in the US and Canada, and the production from South Africa, the Congo, Australia and Portugal was covered by contracts with the US and UK. However, 'The U.K.'s joint interest in these contracts is not considered sufficient to provide the UKAEA with an adequate supply of uranium for its presently projected atomic energy program'.

It was further anticipated that the British would propose a frank discussion about the 'fourth country' problem. They might suggest that the US might make nuclear components available to NATO nations 'on condition that they not undertake military atomic programs of their own'. It was recommended that the British should be told that Washington did not favour such a policy. Although the US did not wish to see additional countries capable of manufacturing nuclear weapons, a direct approach, including such a bargain, 'has not appeared feasible or likely to be productive'.[187]

At Bermuda, the British relationship to the WEU and the American views of the limits to 'Third Force' developments were discussed. Dulles stated that the US had realized already in 1954 that a question could arise whether the center of gravity would be in NATO or in WEU. He would not object to seeing Europe and the UK becoming a force just as long as it was not neutralist. The US wished a strong Europe but not as an intermediary playing the USSR and US off against each other. He foresaw, however, no development in Europe in the next generation which was likely to relieve it of dependence upon the deterrent power of the US. Lloyd assured that even if there were some even in the UK who advocated an independent development the British Government was going to prevent the driving of a wedge between Europe and America. A closer association of the UK to the WEU was however rather important politically, particularly to help cushion the shock of British troop reductions in Germany. Britain wanted to cooperate with the WEU about development of arms but UK-Canadian-US relations would remain a limiting factor. When Eisenhower pointed out that it was important to maintain the 'special relationship' Lloyd replied that the contemplated cooperation 'of course' did not include any nuclear matter.[188] Macmillan confirmed this in a memorandum to Eisenhower: 'We would still exclude all atomic matters, but we would like to exchange information about new weapon projects, such as guided missiles, and discuss future cooperation in their development and production'.[189]

The 'fourth-country problem' was approached on the last day of the conference. Dulles and Lloyd discussed separately what the US and the UK should do about the French and Franco-German nuclear ambitions. It was agreed that three courses of action were possible: first, to join together in opposing the development of a nuclear military programme in France or in any other 'fourth' country; second, to associate themselves either jointly or separately with any French or Franco-German programme in order to be able to influence it; or, third, to adopt a neutral attitude of neither actively assisting nor actively hindering any such French or joint Franco-German plan. Dulles and Lloyd were not in favour of the first two possibilities. The first course might arouse nationalist feelings and create political difficulties. The second was difficult, both for reasons of policy and security. It was agreed to keep a low profile for the time being.[190]

The understanding that had been established at Bermuda developed further in 1957-58. The Macmillan Government 'tied its privilege of nuclear collaboration with the United States to the aim of reaching a joint US-UK position against French nuclear aspirations'.[191]

The Final Stage of the Negotiations on Euratom and the Common Market

The remaining disputed issues about the twin projects were solved at the Conference of Foreign Ministers in Brussels 26-8 January, and at the Conference of Foreign Ministers and of Heads of Government in Paris 18 and 19-20 February, respectively. The Brussels Conference was essentially devoted to the settlement of a French *sine qua non* issue, the principles for a common agricultural policy. Before the Paris Conferences the 'Three Wise Men' committee for US-Euratom cooperation visited the US, and Spaak also went to Washington to obtain clarification about the American view of the draft Euratom treaty.

The 'Three Wise Men' were received warmly in Washington by Dulles and the President. The 'new approach' received official blessing. Eisenhower talked in more positive terms than ever about 'Europe as a third great force in the world' and about Euratom as a 'great hope for the whole free world'. The committee painted a gloomy picture of the energy situation in Europe in the next decade. Coal was running out, oil had to be imported and energy prices were double those in the US. Europe might solve the problem by cooperating with the US in a bold programme for development of nuclear power. The Communiqué from the meeting outlined a 15,000 megawatt US-Euratom reactor programme in Europe based on the American offer of enriched uranium. In this way, the objective of stabilizing European fuel imports early in the 1960's could be achieved, it was declared. An integrated Community could help European industry to mobilize the necessary resources to base new power plant construction after 1962 on nuclear energy rather than coal and oil. In addition, Euratom 'would provide a political entity competent to afford adequate safeguards' - an indication that self-control of resources obtained from the US would be allowed.[192]

Spaak met Dulles and Lewis Strauss; the 'Wise Men' were also present. Spaak explained that his intention was to ask whether the Euratom draft treaty provided an adequate basis for future cooperation with the US, and whether Belgium might make available Congo uranium to the Euratom partners. He now appeared less frustrated about Euratom than when talking to the British leadership three weeks earlier.[193] The treaty was good, he said, but not entirely what he had first intended because the negotiators had had to take account of the French political problem on the question of military use. The 'maintenance of at least a theoretical possibility to engage in the weapons program was the price which had to be paid to the moderate Right in France for their support of EURATOM *and also of the Common Market* [my emphasis]'.

The crucial unfinished issue, ownership of fissile materials, was discussed. Elbrick's brief for Dulles at the meeting had explained that the weakening of the supply provisions of the Euratom Treaty over the past months made common ownership through Euratom even more important: 'Spaak's position on this subject may be of key importance, as we understand the German Government is prepared to accept EURATOM ownership if Spaak joins the French in insisting thereon'. At the meeting, Spaak explained that he had not supported the French demand for complete Euratom ownership of all fissionable materials because of the dilemmas created by the French insistence on the right to engage in military uses. [Spaak was apparently referring to his support for *'sui generis'* instead of ownership and his hope that refusal to accept Euratom ownership for German fissionable materials might force the French to make some concession about French military materials]. The Americans suggested the solution that was eventually adopted in the Euratom Treaty, 'Euratom... ownership up to the point where control of fissionable material passed from its hands into those of the WEU'. They did *not* signal that cooperation would be problematic unless France accepted Euratom ownership of all French fissionable materials. The resigned formula was: 'While we did not take a firm position that we could not cooperate with EURATOM unless the Treaty provided for common ownership, we would certainly be happier if it did so'.

The answer to Spaak's question about the Belgian uranium was that the US would probably have no objections to releasing it to Euratom. The question of whether a European enrichment plant would play some role in obtaining agreement in Paris was not discussed. In Elbrick's brief it had been forecast that the question was likely to be raised by Spaak, although 'Spaak, himself opposed to a European isotopic separation plant, believes it best to let studies continue on the grounds the plant itself will never be built'.[194]

At the final conferences in Paris the two essential missing pieces in the Common Market/Euratom puzzle - association of overseas territories to the Common Market and ownership of fissionable materials in Euratom - were put in place. With respect to the overseas territories decisions were made about market access for certain products, the size of a development programme and contributions from different countries. A five-year investment programme, one-third of which was financed by Germany, was agreed. On the ownership issue, Adenauer made the concession which had long been decided but withheld 'for tactical reasons' - among other things, perhaps, in order to keep down the German contribution to the overseas programme.[195]

When the outcome in Paris was discussed in the German Cabinet the Minister for Atomic Affairs, Balke, expressed preoccupation about the decision that all fissionable material would be owned by Euratom, since the FRG had renounced from military use. Adenauer's reply was that 'the German renunciation of military use could be withdrawn any time'.[196] It is hardly likely, however, that he himself believed that this could be done without drastic and unforeseeable reactions from the surrounding world - after all, Germany had lost the war.

The enrichment question was not brought to decision before the signature of the Rome Treaties. The inflamed issue was buried for the time being. The Study Group for enrichment delivered an interim report on 22 January and the French asked for commitments on the construction of a plant before signature of the treaties. No commitments were forthcoming, however. The Foreign Ministers declared merely that the construction of a plant was 'highly desirable' and asked for further studies.[197] This fitted well with Spaak's hopes that a European enrichment plant would never come about. The French declared that they would go on with the project with or without aid from others.

A mood of disillusion about the outcome of the Euratom negotiations reigned in the State Department. Bowie talked about the 'wretchedness' of the final draft of the Euratom Treaty. The main *raison d'être* of Euratom - European integration - would be effectively smothered by 'wholesale and contagious exercise of the "national" reservations'. A deficient safeguards system in Euratom would inevitably diminish the acceptance of IAEA standards elsewhere.[198] Schaetzel wrote that the French reservation about weapons production was 'a hard fact of life' and the problem now was how to move on to seek effective means of dealing with it. It was a 'bid for time - time to meet the need for a nuclear weapons capability through NATO and also to continue our efforts to make some headway, no matter how limited, on world-wide control'. The US interests - and the interests of Europe - were not served by forcing the French nuclear weapons activities out of the Euratom system and into a strictly national effort. The basic strategy must be not to hit the French directly but rather to 'envelop' them. Regional arrangements still offered the most promising approach to control. A secure control system within Euratom might depend as much on the large US-Euratom cooperation programme and in particular on common ownership of fissionable material as on the relationship between Euratom and the IAEA. The control issue should, in Schatzel's view, not be overplayed. The cause of safeguards would not be furthered in the longer run if the US were tagged as primarily interested in developing international control mechanisms, 'which of course do not apply to us'.[199]

After the final conferences all substantive questions in the negotiations about Euratom and the Common Market had been solved. The rest was detail. A few significant points related to the further development of the nuclear dimension should be mentioned briefly.

During the spring the French made unsuccessful efforts to obtain German consent to participation in the enrichment enterprise. Adenauer's inclination in January to participate in order to have the possibility to take part in the discussion about military development did not materialize in definite agreement. It is not far-fetched to assume that the American opposition was an insuperable obstacle. The report of the 'Three Wise Men' in May contributed to undermining the project. The report pleaded strongly for acceptance of the American enrichment offer: the product from a European plant would probably cost two to three times as much, several years would elapse before it could operate, and the future requirements for enriched uranium were very uncertain since the plutonium that would be produced in the power reactors might be useable for enrichment and breeder reactors would become available later. The conclusion was that no decision about a European plant had to be taken before a programme for the production of nuclear electricity had been launched.[200] The French resigned. It was decided in France to build a small national military plant based on French resources only.

The Treaties on the Common Market and Euratom were signed in Rome 25 March 1957 and submitted relatively rapidly for ratification. The Treaties were ratified in Germany and France in July with large majorities. There were no serious preoccupations in the State Department that ratification was uncertain, as in the cases of the EDC and the WEU. Dulles occasionally relapsed, however, into 'agonizing reappraisal' thinking. For example, he informed the Germans that 'he had repeatedly emphasized to the French his opinion that failure on their part to ratify the Common Market and EURATOM agreements, following on the defeat of EDC, would have a catastrophic effect on United States attitudes toward Europe'.[201]

The Franco-German intentions for cooperation on arms, as codified in Colomb-Béchar, became a full-fledged programme for developing the European nuclear option by France, Italy and Germany in the autumn of 1957 and the spring of 1958. The project had no chances under de Gaulle, however. Only nineteen days after his return to power he ordered: 'We should not continue cooperation in the atomic field, a field which we reserve entirely to ourselves'. Gaullist diplomacy undermined the American objectives that Euratom should become a vehicle for US-European cooperation on development of civil nuclear power and for putting a curb on French nuclear military ambitions. The organization did not develop as the State Department and the European integrationists had hoped.[202] It retained the basic function of controlling *all* German fissionable materials, however. It had already served the purpose of unlocking the door to final agreement on the Common Market.

Conclusion

After the Venice Conference and the debate about Euratom in the French National Assembly the situation had clarified. The *sine qua non* for French ratification of Euratom was freedom of action for procuring nuclear weapons. The outcome of the aggregation of interests of the economic forces in France, agriculture in particular, was a green light to proceed with the Common Market in principle, and to aim at obtaining contributions from the other five for development of French overseas territories and guarantees for protection of the French economy in the event that something went wrong. From now on there was a basis both in France and Germany for going on with parallel elaboration of treaties for the two Communities, although the French standpoint was still that Euratom should be finalized first and the Common Market later. This was, however, advanced with less conviction and partly for tactical reasons.

The alternative of Franco-British cooperation as the core of a future European construct was investigated in a final round of visits to London by French leaders in the summer and early autumn. Adenauer was also interested in a revival of the WEU, backed by Britain, as a means of obtaining greater European independence within NATO in a somewhat longer perspective. It became apparent, however, that British policy remained ambiguous and torn between undecided priorities about relationships to the US, the Commonwealth and Europe. The British developed the concept of the Free Trade Area in an attempt to obtain equal access to industrial markets on the continent and to resume leadership in Europe on British terms without supranationalism. The same model was applied to cooperation in the nuclear field. Many in Washington suspected that the primary British goal was to torpedo the Common Market and Euratom. The US reacted by declaring general but unspecific support for the Free Trade Area and the OEEC approach. It was underlined that the Six-state projects had priority and that British plans must not interfere with them.

The French Assembly's condition might have caused American abandonment of Euratom. The moratorium that had been approved by the Assembly was no real obstacle to the French weapons option, and was different from the supranational moratorium that had been envisaged by Dulles and Spaak. The US nevertheless continued to support Euratom. A ´new approach´ to the project was developed in the State Department and in Monnet´s Action Committee. The main idea was that it was time to use the ´carrot´ by offering a large joint US-European programme of partnership in developing civil nuclear power. The national programmes would become embedded in a common programme, and Euratom would retain much of its significance for preventing the spread of nuclear weapons. There were also strong economic arguments for this approach. Western Europe was seen as the propitious area for developing nuclear power to the point where it could compete with conventional sources of energy. It was, beside the US, the only advanced industrial area of the West, the conventional energy resources were scarce, dependence on imported oil was increasing rapidly, and energy prices were about double those in the US.

The Franco-German project for cooperation about arms became one of the pillars of the Adenauer/Mollet compromise which untied the knots in Brussels. Washington made no attempt to halt the plan, partly because it was seen as functional in finalizing the negotiations about Euratom and the Common Market. It is not clear whether the details of the agreement in Colomb-Béchar - which was judged by Adenauer's confidant Blankenhorn to be more significant than the Common Market and Euratom - were known in the State Department. In any case, there was good reason to believe that the agreement included nuclear components. The Franco-German project caused worries in Britain. Foreign Secretary Lloyd outlined the alternative of a nuclear 'Grand Design' for a British-Franco-German deterrent within the NATO framework. The plan was short-lived, however. There was little domestic backing for it and Dulles questioned the desirability of conceiving the WEU as an inner circle in NATO. Instead, the US-British nuclear special relationship was revived to some extent few months later at Bermuda. This was part of the work to repair Anglo-American relations after the damaging impact of Suez. When the French and German ambitions were discussed Dulles and Lloyd agreed that, for the time being, the most appropriate way of handling the problem was to neither assist nor actively hinder any French or joint Franco-German nuclear plan.

The increased likelihood that the Common Market could be realized in the near future caused closer examination of its economic effects in Washington. The risks were considered in the Council on Foreign Economic Policy in the autumn. Its analysis was that the long-term benefits to the US outweighed the possible short-term disadvantages, provided that the resultant single tariff would be no more protective on the average and with respect to the commodities important to the US than the tariffs of the member states separately. Agriculture was a problem, but protective measures against US agricultural exports existed already in Europe and an agricultural solution acceptable to France appeared to be a *sine qua non* for French ratification of the entire package.

When the Brussels negotiations approached finalization the Common Market received official American blessing. The State Department underlined that it had to be consistent with the regulations of the GATT and the IMF. Dulles had no objections to the draft treaty. He told the Germans that he sympathized with the French ideas about 'Eurafrique', thus promoting agreement on the last unsolved major issue, the association of overseas areas.

The opposition to the *Junktim* disappeared gradually in the autumn of

1956 when the chances of French acceptance of the Common Market were increasing and when it became apparent that a treaty could be finalized without delaying Euratom.

The US standpoints with respect to nuclear cooperation which had been outlined in general terms before the Venice Conference were adjusted and specified as the negotiations in Europe made progress. The main issues were: (1) enrichment policy, (2) Euratom's fuel and control system, (3) implementation of the 'new approach', (4) postponing bilateral agreements, and (5) initiation of discussions about transfer of military nuclear resources and information.

When the conditions for deliveries of enriched uranium were issued in November after the Adenauer/Mollet compromise it was more evident than ever that there was no economic rationale for a European enrichment plant - it could be justified only as a means of independence of the US. Adenauer however said to his Cabinet in January that he was now prepared to agree to the project - only in this way could the Federal Republic have a say about future military nuclear developments. The implication was that he wanted to take a decisive step towards a Franco-German thermonuclear option. Later, however, the Federal Republic abstained from participating in the French enrichment plant.

The American demand for a sufficiently supranational fuel system as the probable condition for cooperation had been the central point in the message to the Venice Conference. The demand was the main instrument for trying to close the German and French national nuclear options. In the autumn repeated efforts were made to impress on Adenauer and von Brentano that Euratom ownership of fissionable materials as a minimum was absolutely necessary. Before the Paris Conference Dulles communicated to Adenauer that the US could not transfer fissionable materials [enriched uranium essentially] to Euratom unless Euratom retained ownership. He also made clear that he had in mind *all* materials, not only those supplied by the US. The *sui generis* solution in the Spaak Report as a replacement for Euratom ownership was accepted at the Paris Conference by all except France, which, like the US, requested Euratom ownership of fisionable materials at least. At the Adenauer/Mollet meeting the ownership issue was postponed, and apparently referred to Franco-German and intra-German bargaining the details of which are difficult to retrace fully. The outcome was German renunciation of 'minimum equality'. In January, the German Government decided to accept Euratom ownership of all fissionable materials in Germany, although the concession was to be withheld for a while for tactical reasons. Other components of minimum equality - equality of control, information and supply - were also given up. The French military sector would not be controlled, France would not be obliged to give away information from it, would itself determine the dividing-line between military and civil information, and the supply of materials to that sector would not be bound by Euratom's fuel system. In return Adenauer obtained the hope of a Franco-German nuclear option, the starting-point of which was the agreement in Colomb-Béchar. Adenauer's preparedness, as communicated to his Cabinet, to agree to the French enrichment plan may also have been a part of a comprehensive Franco-German deal.

The Americans were informed by Maurice Faure that France had made an about-turn in its policy on ownership and control. The cardinal question for US policy at this moment was: Should the French receive the same message as the Germans, that is, that the US could not transfer enriched uranium and other fissionable materials to Euratom, or cooperate in other ways, unless the principle of Euratom ownership of all fissionable materials and all-embracing control were approved? No such ultimatum was issued. Spaak was disappointed. Various reasons for a soft attitude were listed internally in the US. A basic reason was that it was impossible to induce France to refrain from the national option at this time without endangering the negotiations about Euratom and also the Common Market. A new EDC failure could not be risked. France had sufficient resources to proceed alone, and the coalition against the French option was not as strong as that against the German one. The conclusion of the State Department was that other ways had to be tried in order to embed French national ambitions in a European-Atlantic context.

The implementation of the 'new approach' started with the visit of the 'Three Wise Men' to the US in February 1957. The importance which Washington attached to their mission was underlined in various ways. The message to the Europeans was that the Administration was prepared to seek Congressional approval for a huge programme for development of nuclear power in cooperation with Euratom, a programme based on deliveries of American enriched uranium. This was confirmed in the report of the 'Three Wise Men' after the signature of the Rome Treaties. The report pleaded for acceptance of the American enrichment offer and argued that enriched uranium would be needed for a limited period only; the resulting dependence would be temporary.

The need for balancing carefully in the final stage of the Brussels negotiations was expressed in the attitude to bilateralism at that moment. Pressures for finalizing negotiations about bilateral agreements were coming from domestic interests and from the French and the Germans. The State Department tried to postpone all deals until after completion of the treaties by exhorting the Europeans to agree among themselves about postponement.

The State Department could also use as an incentive that the US would assist the nuclear military posture of European countries in various ways. The leading integrationists, Spaak and Monnet, proposed that the US should envisage transfer of tactical nuclear weapons as a means of persuading the Europeans that there was no need to develop them themselves. The State Department accepted the French demands for starting discussions about transfer of enriched fuel and technology for submarine reactors.

It was unquestionably within the power of the US to decide the fate of Euratom. The US had an overwhelmingly strong position in the nuclear field and controlled the necessary resources, enriched uranium in particular. The Euratom project was simply not viable if the US decided to oppose it or not to cooperate. A central question is, then, whether the Common Market project would have survived if the US had opposed the model for Euratom that developed in the course of the negotiations?

It seems very probable that it would not, particularly during the first negotiation phase up to the Venice Conference. In that phase, the French priority was agreement on Euratom. The domestic base for the Common Market as an isolated project was uncertain. In the second phase, when the powerful agricultural sector gave conditional backing to the Common Market and the partners seemed prepared to take their shares of the costs of developing French overseas territories, the chances of French acceptance improved considerably. It can certainly be argued that the Common Market would have been ratifiable in France even if the kind of Euratom that finally developed had been rejected by Germany. There was, and is, much uncertainty on this point. My view is, however, that a solution to the German security problem that was acceptable to France remained an absolute condition for agreement in the economic field. The main components that were outlined in the Adenauer/Mollet compromise and agreed during the following months - the unsolved issues in the Common Market and Euratom, and arms cooperation with a nuclear perspective - were all necessary prerequsities for the Treaties of Rome. Economic factors and security factors were completely intertwined.[203] The US, which accorded priority to security, was a dominant actor in the game. The role of security considerations in this case is admitted - to some extent - by Moravcsik, although he stresses the preponderance of the economic considerations. When discussing the relative weight of security and economics in the explanation of the *relance* he concludes that ´Geopolitical ideas and security externalities were not entirely unimportant. Had economic interest been the sole motivation, European governments would probably have converged toward something like an FTA, not a customs union with quasi-constitutional institutions.´[204]

But this is a decisive difference. If the nuclear issue had not been solved in a way that was acceptable to France the result might have been international cooperation but not *integration*.

A second counterfactual question is whether the Common Market project would have survived if it had been opposed by the US. What would have happened if the main line in American policy had been to request European economic development along multilateral lines instead of supporting the regional approach? It should be remembered that regionalism was chosen primarily for security reasons. I think the simple answer is that in that case the Common Market project could not have been successfully negotiated and ratified.

Conclusion: Integration and Non-Proliferation

There were two main goals in American European policy in the period studied here: integration and non-proliferation. They were derived from the most general foreign policy goals such as containing the Soviet Union and Germany, tying Germany to the West, and preventing the spread of nuclear weapons globally. Thus, the motives for US interventions in the negotiations about cooperation and integration in Europe were related to considerations of security and world power above all. Washington wanted to build a security complex in Europe that would prevent Soviet dominance in the Eurasian hemisphere and eliminate Europe's, particularly Germany's, potential for causing another world war. Sovietization of Europe, Germany in the first place, would, it was feared, tip the balance of world power. Economic conditions were seen, much more so than later, as a means of strengthening security in Europe. The US was often, at least up to the late fifties, prepared to sacrifice some short-term American economic interests in the interest of security and power. Thus, economic regionalism was seen as a necessary but temporary stage on the road towards the goal of world multilateralism in trade and payments - the traditional goal of the leading economic power since the epoch of British economic dominance in the nineteenth century. Washington's priority for security and power explains why the normal imperial rule of conduct, *divide et impera* [divide and rule], was temporarily suspended in favour of the watchword: 'Europe, unite!'.

The present study indicates that the non-proliferation goal in US policy was stronger in these years than is generally appreciated in the literature. The objective of non-proliferation in American foreign policy did not have its origins in the sixties (when the American President called it 'the most important task on earth'[1]).

The interaction between the integration and non-proliferation goals as implemented in Europe is the red thread running through my study. The policy in favour of non-proliferation pursued by the US and others was a strong undercurrent in the European negotiations in the fifties. It focused on the two leading countries on the continent, Germany and France. US non-proliferation policy was however more complex and included more contradictions in the fifties than later, because of the New Look strategy which propagated the normalcy of nuclear weapons. US policy did not signify that national decision-making about nuclear weapons should be excluded in all circumstances, only that the process should be approved by Washington and take place within the Atlantic structure and be limited to the tactical A-bomb level. The distinction between this level and the strategic H-bomb level was almost as important as that between conventional and nuclear weapons later. There were several means for keeping the nuclear ambitions of the European countries in control. European integration was one of them, and the most essential. Other important means were to embed the rearmed Federal Republic completely in NATO's military structure, to embed France also in NATO as far as feasible, and to try to uphold control of nuclear resources and information as long as possible. The enrichment monopoly was crucial in this connection. There was an awareness, however, that US dominance in the nuclear field was a diminishing asset.

A principal aim of the 'Atoms for Peace' policy was to explore the possibilities of cooperating with the USSR about submitting the fissile material in the non-nuclear countries to international control by the projected International Atomic Energy Agency. The American leadership believed very early, and quite realistically, that sooner or later some material would find its way into weapons in several countries if it was not internationally controlled. In the 'Atoms for Peace' perspective there were three different ways of controlling the fissile material: the bilateral way, the regional way - as in European integration - and the IAEA way. The crucial aim when trying to obtain an effective barrier against proliferation was to submit *all* the fissile material in a country to effective control, and this could in Washington's view only be obtained in the regional way or in the IAEA way. Obviously, effective control could never be achieved if only the part that was affected by assistance and export from the US were controlled. It was not however considered feasible to request control of the entire nuclear sector in a country through pressure, for example by setting it up as a condition for US aid in the bilateral system. The key countries would not agree to subject an important part of their energy sector to control by a single country.

Thus, European integration was, among other things, and along with the more distant IAEA alternative, a means for obtaining control of *all* fissile material in Germany and France. The duality with respect to the roles of the European organizations and the IAEA in US policy was perceived clearly in Europe. When Adenauer and Mollet in late 1956 talked about the role of nuclear weapons in world politics they saw a risk of a deal between the superpowers at Europe's expense. Adenauer was apprehensive about the 'two-track approach' in American policy, and Mollet saw a risk of a 'partition of the world'.

The European projects treated in the book affected the three nuclear weapons options: the national option, the transfer option and the European option. The unfinished EDC project, the WEU and Euratom all restricted the national options, and they left the transfer option and the European option intact.

The EDC would have restricted the national options in both Germany and

France. France tried for long to obtain exceptions that would have permitted full national freedom of action, but neither the US nor the five partners in the EDC accepted the demands. This was one of the reasons for the French refusal to ratify its own 'brainchild'. The WEU partially closed the German option through Adenauer's *Kernwaffenverzicht*. The bindings on Germany were weak in several respects. The main deficiency was that the WEU was not sufficiently supranational and that it was doubtful whether the control system that would be elaborated would subject all the fissile materials in the country to a control without cracks. If the WEU had been constructed to ensure this, the German demand for equality would have meant that all French fissile materials would have been controlled also. This was not ratifiable in France. In Euratom the loop-holes with respect to control of Germany were finally closed, but the French managed to resist the pressures from the US, Germany and others. The French option remained unbound after years of negotiations about the different projects. Adenauer gave up the demand for equality. In return, he obtained the prospect of becoming a junior partner in developing the Franco-German nuclear option and virtual certainty that France would ratify the Common Market. For Adenauer, the Franco-German arms cooperation project was also useful as a means of pressing the US to approve transfer of nuclear weapons. This was a crucial step in the development of the 'uncertain alliance'[2] that was based on French political and German economic leadership.

Washington was not at any time prepared to accept any European project constructed in a such a way as to limit the freedom to transfer nuclear weapons to any of the participating countries, or to a European organization. In the WEU negotiations the French made strong efforts to persuade the Americans to let the Europeans decide about transfer of American military aid, but the Americans refused to make any real concession. The possibility of transfer was a vital part of the New Look strategy, and it also served to persuade the European countries that they did not need to develop nuclear arms themselves. Further, it was a reminder to the French that these weapons might be transferred to Germany if the French decided to manufacture them. The implicit threat was not sufficiently credible, however.

The European option was not excluded in any of the three projects, even if Jean Monnet and parts of the Action Committee lobbied for excluding it in Euratom in order to prevent developments in the direction of a 'Third Force' outside NATO. In the US, it was considered impossible to make the Europeans accept renunciation of the European option, for example by making it a condition for US cooperation. It was difficult to say at the same time that the Europeans must unite and defend themselves, but not possess the weapons that were propagated in the New Look strategy as necessary for defence. Many in Europe were unwilling to close the European option. A main reason was that it was evident that the US would become increasingly hesitant to risk attack on the homeland for Europe's sake when the balance of deterrence in the arms race was approaching.

There was a tendency within the Eisenhower Administration, visible above all in pronouncements by Eisenhower himself, to regard European nuclear autonomy within a supranational framework as essentially a positive development. If it was realized, the US could send troops back home, cut down the military budget and 'sit back and relax somewhat'. The backing for this idea, at least if it meant risks of a Third Force that was not safely embedded in the Atlantic context, was however weak in other parts of the Administration and in Congress. Dulles, for example, warned against measures that could endanger NATO and US leadership in the long run. The policy that was established was essentially that the European option was not desirable but not as bad as the national ones. As expressed in a State Department memorandum, 'if forced make choice' a common weapons development programme was more in the US interest than competitive national programmes.

The reconstruction of a nuclear special relationship with Britain that was agreed at the Anglo-American summit in Bermuda should be seen as one of the ways of avoiding a strong European option. It was highly undesirable from the American point of view that Britain after Suez would be tempted to join and reinforce a Franco-German nuclear armaments bloc that was in the making. The British short-lived nuclear 'Grand Design' plan had been a signal that a radical change of traditional British foreign policy was not excluded.

What was the outcome of the European integration process in these years as compared to the US goals for the nuclear dimension?

The main goal was to prevent manufacture of nuclear weapons in Germany and France. The outcome was that Germany was restricted and France was not. In this sense American policy was obviously not successful. However, the two steps in restricting the German nuclear option, in the WEU and in Euratom, were steps toward a more comprehensive non-proliferation policy. The combined effect of the arrangements was that the German option could be expected to be rather effectively controlled within a regional supranational framework, as part of a larger web of precautions. It was the first time that the entire nuclear sector in a country was submitted to international control. Germany and Italy were those primarily affected as they had both accepted restrictions in the military nuclear field. Thus, the nuclear side of the 'German problem' was temporarily solved soon after German sovereignty had been granted. A vital part of the double containment goal had been attained. The combined WEU-Euratom regime was to last until it was supplemented and superseded by the Non-Proliferation Treaty and IAEA's control system in the late sixties.[3]

It is true that other expectations about Euratom were not fulfilled. Euratom never became a vehicle for US-European cooperation about joint development of civil nuclear power, and Europe did not become the place for market-driven introduction of the American reactor type in the energy systems. The 'new approach' in American policy and in the policy of Monnet's Action Committee that started in the autumn of 1956 was realized only to a modest extent. Nevertheless, Euratom was much more important than judged by some authors.[4] The most essential American goal - a goal that was extremely important also to others - had been achieved. Euratom was the strategic missing piece for arms control of Germany.

Notes

Introduction

1   I will normally use the term 'Germany', also when referring to 'West Germany'
2   Moravcsik's *The Choice for Europe* is an indispensable point of reference for studies of the history of European integration. It makes its theoretical points of departure explicit and uses its conceptual scheme in organizing a very large body of material to investigate the main thesis about the primacy of economic factors as compared to geopolitical factors in explaining integration. The thesis is an elaboration of, and additive contribution to, views that have been put forward by economic historian Alan S. Milward in several reputed works. Moravcsik 1993 and 1998; Milward 1984 and 1992; Milward et al. 1993.
3   Gowing 1974, 63-130, 241-321
4   The concept of a 'penetrated political system', developed by James N. Rosenau, has been used by some scholars to describe the German situation after the war. In a penetrated political system non-members of a national society participate directly in the decision-making process. Penetration may also take place without direct participation if decision-making is strongly affected by external events and trends. Cf. Grabbe 1990.
5   Cf. also John Gillingham's objections to 'the Milward approach'. Gillingham argues that it excludes, for example, the possibility that different influences were critical in successive phaces of the integration movement. Gillingham 1996,3.
6   Certain documents from the major countries have also been obtained from the Historical Archives of the European Communities in Florence, in which there are copies of some series
7   For example: Fursdon 1980 and Maier 1990 (EDC); Thoss 1993 (WEU); Küsters 1982 and Gerbet 1987 (Common Market); Weilemann 1983 (Euratom); Duchêne 1994 and Wilkens 1999 (Common Market and Euratom)
8   Among studies from the last 10-15 years, for example: Hewlett-Holl 1989, Helmreich 1991, Winand 1993, Romero 1993 and 1996, Mai 1993, Duchêne 1994, Bossuat 1994, Schröder 1994, Schwabe 1995 and 1998, Conze 1995, Lundestad 1998, Dumoulin 1999, Pitman 2000, Un Général..., Neuss 2000
9   For Germany, for example: Christian Deubner, Michael Eckert, Peter Fischer, Catherine McArdle Kelleher, Hanns-Jürgen Küsters, Hans-Peter Schwarz. For France, for example: Jacques Bariéty, Gérard Bossuat, Elena Calandri, Bertrand Goldschmidt, Pierre Guillen, Frances Lynch, Gustav Schmidt, Georges-Henri Soutou, Maurice Vaïsse. For the United Kingdom, for example: Miriam Camps, Anne Deighton, Saki Dockrill, James Ellison, Margaret Gowing, Richard T. Griffiths, Wolfram Kaiser, Elizabeth Kane, Jan Melissen, Alan S. Milward, Mervyn O'Driscoll, Andrew J. Pierre, John W. Young

1   The European Policy of the Eisenhower Administration

1   Leffler 1994
2   Lundestad 1998, 'Empire'..., 4, 22-8; Mai 1993; Costigliola 1997, 177
3   Trachtenberg 1999, vii

4   Report by the Policy Planning Staff, 'Review of Current Trends, U.S. Foreign Policy', 24 February 1948, FRUS 1948, Vol. I, 515
5   Schwabe, 1995, 122-5 (7 July 1949)
6   Citations in ibid., 125-6 (24 October 1949); Maier 1994, 162-7
7   Milward 1984, 126-87, 362-420; Rappaport 1981
8   Leffler 1992, 383-7
9   Ibid., 386-7
10 Ibid., 408-16
11 The United Nations and Disarmament 1945-1965, 12-13; Blackett 1948, 103-15; Myrdal 1976, 103-9
12 Cf.: 'In effect, the Americans were working for years on a "crash programme" basis, with ore feedstocks below the theoretical emergency level. Though the programme did not break down during the crucial years, the raw material staff of the US Atomic Energy Commission lived in a state of continuing crisis, and were frenetically determined to secure more and more uranium ores, at any cost'. Gowing 1974, 364. - In 1953, there was no acute shortage. The Chairman of the Atomic Energy Commission reported to the National Security Council that raw material supplies were being assured, with the annual procurement goal apparently well within achievement by 1960. Lewis L. Strauss at 162nd NSC meeting, 17 September 1953, DDEL/AWF/NSC, box 4
13 Gowing 1974; Hewlett-Duncan 1969; Helmreich 1986; Skogmar 1993
14 To give an idea of the size, it can be mentioned that the enrichment plants consumed 12 per cent of the production of electricity in the US in 1956. (Chemical and Engineering News, 17 December 1956). The plants in Oak Ridge consumed as much as the entire production of electricity in France (Jean Crouzier, Assemblée Nationale, 5 July 1956, Journal Officiel, AN, 3285). During the war, the Americans had explored three possible methods for enrichment. The gas diffusion process was chosen, then and later.
15 For example, highly enriched uranium is used for A-bombs and for the A-bomb detonator in H-bombs, and medium-enriched uranium for naval reactors. Low-enriched uranium cannot be used directly in H- or A-bombs, but it is necessary for the kind of civil power reactors that became dominant later (light-water reactors based on the naval reactor technology that had been developed in the US).
16 Førland 1991, 41
17 Wheeler-Bennet and Nichols 1972; Myrdal 1976, 42
18 Riecke 1996, 192-4
19 Biological and chemical (BC) weapons are of course also strategically significant weapons, but less crucial. Use is hazardous and risky for the user.
20 Trachtenberg 1991, History..., 126-9; Trachtenberg 1999, 156
21 134th NSC meeting, 25 February 1953, FRUS 1952-1954, Vol. II, 1111
22 Wenger 1997, 52, 91-3 (citation from David Alan Rosenberg). Sections of the 'Chance for Peace' speech, FRUS 1952-1954, Vol. II, 1204-6
23 165th NSC meeting, 7 October 1953, ibid., 528
24 NSC 162/2, 'Basic National Security Policy', ibid., 577-97; 'Atoms for Peace' speech, Public Papers of the President of the United States: Dwight D. Eisenhower, 1953, 813-22
25 NSC special meeting, 31 March 1953, DDEL/AWF/NSC, box 4. For a comprehensive account of the 'New Look' strategy of the Eisenhower Administration, see Dockrill 1996. Cf. also Freedman 2003, 72-113, 288-314.

26   NSC 162/2, FRUS 1952-1954, Vol. II, 580; Tamnes 1991, 92; Heuser 1997, 5
27   Trachtenberg 1996, 121
28   Cited in Trachtenberg 1999, 159 (emphasis in original source)
29   Trachtenberg 1999, 147-79 (the citations: viii, 159, 162, emphasis in original sources). - Eisenhower wanted to supplement the extreme reliance on nuclear weapons with keeping the possibility of nuclear disarmament open. His inclination not to forget the olive-branch shows up, for example, in Dulles' notes from a discussion with the President, prompted by a letter from Churchill. 'This led to a general discussion of the use of atomic weapons, and the President reiterated his conviction that if in fact we could get an effective elimination of atomic weapons, we should do this, irrespective of a military ban on conventional weapons. He felt that as long as the United States was not in peril of immediate destruction, our industrial power would turn the balance and would operate as a deterrent to use by the Russians of their superior ground forces.' Meeting Eisenhower/Dulles, 17 January 1955, ML/JFD/WH, box 3
30   About perceived Soviet bomber capacity, see Quester 1970, 126-39
31   'Armaments and American Policy', January 1953, FRUS 1952-1954, Vol. II, 1056-91 (citations, 1065-6, 1072). The committee was chaired by the 'father of the atomic bomb', Robert E. Oppenheimer, and counted among its members Allen W. Dulles, head of the CIA and brother of the Secretary of State.
32   132d NSC meeting, 18 February 1953, FRUS 1952-1954, Vol. II, 1107
33   134th NSC meeting, 25 February 1953, FRUS 1952-1954, Vol. II, 1112. – The surplus capacity had arisen because new scientific-technical discoveries showed that most of the enrichment capacity would no longer be needed for the H-bombs. The AEC Chairman's forecast about the impossibility of using the enrichment plants for peaceful purposes soon proved to be inaccurate, as the use of low-enriched uranium for power reactors became the centrepiece of the Atoms for Peace policy and the basis for the American light-water reactor technology that became internationally dominant later.
34   NSC special meeting, 31 March 1953, DDEL/AWF/NSC, box 4
35   Bowie 1985, 18-20
36   Ibid., 21
37   Atomic Power and Public Enterprise, US Congress, Joint Committee on Atomic Energy, December 1952
38   'Statement by the Under Secretary of State Concerning Legislation Designed to Foster the Development of Atomic power'(delivered to the Congressional Joint Committee on Atomic Energy), 25 June 1953, FRUS 1952-1954, Vol. II, 1180-4. In a previous draft of the statement, dated 4 June 1953, it was stated that a disadvantage of a policy of the proposed kind was that the negotiations for procurement of uranium ore from other nations would become far more difficult. All countries were concerned about the conservation of a natural resource which was regarded as patrimony for the future. Hitherto it had been possible to counter these arguments by recalling that the day of atomic power was not yet in sight, but the enactment of legislation designed to promote the development of atomic power would be taken as an overt sign that it was already at hand. However, it was stated, the Department did not believe that these considerations should stand in the way of the development of atomic energy for peaceful purposes. NA/RG 84/FSPF-F, box 67

39 When the two officials who were responsible for coordinating policy, C.D. Jackson and Lewis Strauss, later tried to reconstruct the history of the Atoms for Peace policy they agreed that Eisenhower was the originator of the pool concept. Jackson: 'Conversation between yourself and the President, I believe in Denver, where he, sort of thinking out loud, expressed the very vague and general term of the "pool" idea'. Strauss: 'This is a very important paragraph. The basic idea of the pool must remain unquestionably the President's.' Jackson to Strauss, 25 September 1954; Strauss to Jackson, 27 September 1954, DDEL/AWF/Adm., box 5

40 Memo by Cutler for Strauss and Jackson, FRUS 1952-1954, Vol. II, 1213

41 Dulles to Eisenhower, 23 October, 1953, FRUS 1952-1954, Vol. II, 1234-5;

42 Bohlen to DOS, 21 December 1953, FRUS 1952-1954, Vol. II, 1303-5

43 And also on the military side, as part of the nuclearization of Europe, to permit giving information to allies, primarily about the effects of nuclear weapons.

44 United States, United Kingdom, Canada, France, Belgium, South Africa, Australia and Portugal

45 15 November 1954, cited in Bechhoefer 1959, 48

46 Skogmar 1979, 104, 140

47 Statute of the International Atomic Energy Agency, article III, in Participation Act for the International Atomic Energy Agency, Hearings, US Congress, July 1957

48 Dulles in 1957, cited in Bechhoefer-Stein 1957, 1383

49 Dulles, n.d., cited in Knorr 1957, 108. On Atoms for Peace and non-proliferation cf. also Holl 1985; Hewlett-Holl 1989, 305-25; Tal 2001.

50 Winand 1990, 71-4 (citations from US documents)

51 Bossuat 1994, 309-10

52 'Certain European Issues Affecting the United States', Office of the United States Special Representative in Europe, 14 April 1953, III-7-9, DDEL/WHCF-Confid./ Subj., box 99. The committee was presided by the Special Representative, William H. Draper.

53 Romero 1993 and 1996; Lynch 1993, 61

54 Draper Report, ch. V (the citation, V-18)

55 Romero 1993, 160-5

56 The citations, from US documents, in Trachtenberg 1999, 155

57 Heuser 1997, 130. This was called the double-key system.

58 267th NSC meeting, 21 November 1955, FRUS 1955-1957, Vol. XIX, 150-1.

59 Trachtenberg 1999, 149.

60 Bossuat 1994, 344

61 Conze 1995, 311

2 The Nuclear Dimension of the European Defence Community

1 McCloy to Acting SecState, 26 November 1951, FRUS 1951, Vol. III, 1719-21

2 In the nuclear field, the essential resource lacking in the Federal Republic was uranium

3 US/British/French Foreign Ministers meeting, November 23, 1951, FRUS 1951, Vol. III, 1715-19; de la Tournelle to French Embassy, London and other missions, 26 November 1951, BDF, Bd. 1, Nr. 19; Maier 1989, 77-8

4 Acheson to Truman, 30 November 1951, FRUS 1951, Vol. III, 1730-2

5   As reported in Acheson to AmEmbassy, Paris, 13 December 1951, FRUS 1951, Vol. III, 1736-7

6   The French interpretation of the equality principle was later reported to be: 'In the course of the negotiations the French Government has defined the rights specified in the treaty as follows; "Equality of rights consists in treating identical situations identically, and different situations differently" '. Answer to question by Coste-Floret to the Foreign Minister in Commission des affaires étrangères, March 25 1954, AN/363AP (René Mayer), box 29

7   Memo by de Guiringaud, March 4, 1953, BDF, Bd. 1, Nr. 21

8   Fursdon 1980, 163-4

9   Below, 75-6, 86-7, 93-4, 98, 101-7, 114

10 The latter will be referred to here as 'the missile-warship-aircraft category'. For definitions of this category, see Fursdon 1980, 165; Bundesgesetzblatt 1954, Teil II, Nr. 3, 371-5

11 The origin of the definition appears to be a US proposal to Britain and France when preparing the Allied standpoints in the negotiations with the Federal Republic. The EDC definition followed it in all essentials. Webb (Acting Secretary) to Amembassy, London, 5 October 1951, FRUS 1951, Vol. III, 1703-4

12 The term nuclear fuel was defined, among other things, as plutonium and uranium enriched to more than 2.1 per cent

13 Goldschmidt 1980, 143-4

14 Briefe des Bundeskanzlers, 7 May 1952, Bundesgesetzblatt 1954, Teil II, Nr. 3, 416-8. Possession meant national possession. It was not excluded that German EDC contingents should be equipped with atomic weapons. Hirsch to Staats, 6 July 1954, NSA/NNP/164

15 Three-Power Declaration, 27 May 1952, Bundesgesetzblatt 1954, Teil II, Nr. 3, 419-20

16 Besprechung Bundeskanzler-Hohe Kommissare, 12 Brief über Atomenergie, 15-16 May 1952, AA-PA/B2, Bd. 186

17 Wendel to Steers, 21 September 1953, NA/RG 59/LF 57D688, box 409

18 Reber to Robinson, 15 and 30 January 1953, NA/RG 84/FSPF-F, box 3; Matthews to Robinson, January 25, 1953, ibid.; Dulles to Robinson, 17 February 1953, ibid.; Minutes from quadripartite meetings, 27 February and 14 December 1953, ibid.

19 Memo by L. W. Fuller, 'France as a Problem for United States Foreign Policy', 13 May 1954, NA/RG 59/LF 65D101, box 87

20 Bruce to DOS, 12 March 1953, FRUS 1952-1954, Vol. V, 766-9; Fessenden to Wolf, ibid., 21 July 1953, 798-800; Meeting Dulles/Bidault et al., 17 February 1954, ibid., 875-7

21 Dulles to Amembassy, Paris, 26 March 1953, ibid., 781-784; Memo by W.J. Williams on White House visit by five Bundestag leaders, 1 April 1953, DDEL/AWF/Int., box 14; Blankenhorn diary (the citation), 24 March 1954, BA/N 1351/30b

22 Cf. also Guillen 1983, 21-31

23 Wettig 1967, 534-40

24 Dunn to DOS, 12 February 1953, FRUS 1952-1954, Vol. V, 719-725; Wettig 1967, 536-8.

25 Cf. below, 107, 110-11

26 Dulles to HICOG and Amembassies in the Hague and Paris, 26 January 1955, NA/RG 59/DF 740.5, box 3114. See also E. Martin to Palmer 28 January 1955, ibid.

27 Maier 1989, 141-3

28 Guillen 1983, 20-1; Maier 1989, 143
29 Dulles to Amembassy, Paris, 24 January 1953, FRUS 1952-1954, Vol. V, 706-8
30 Dunn to DOS, 12 February 1953, ibid., 719, n. 1. The American observer was David Bruce. See also Bruce to DOS, 27 February 1953, ibid., 741-3
31 Dulles to Amembassy, Paris, 18 February 1953, ibid., 734-9
32 Sitzung des Lenkungsausschusses des Interimsausschusses der Konferenz zur Schaffung der Europäischen Verteidigungsgemeinschaft vom 20.2.1953, Bericht CD/CR/12, 25.2.1953, BDF, Bd. 1, Nr. 125
33 Ibid. (meeting 21 February 1953), BDF, Bd. 1, Nr. 126
34 Fursdon 1980, 207-9
35 Heuseler to Nebel, 8 June 1954, BDF, Bd. 1, Nr. 129; Editorial note, FRUS 1952-1954, Vol. V, 775.
36 Guillen 1983, 23-4
37 Memo 'Origine et historique des protocoles', n.s., 4 May 1954, AN/363 AP (René Mayer), box 29. Cf. also Dockrill 1991, 114-32.
38 Heuseler to Noebel, 8 June 1954, BDF, Bd. 1, Nr. 129
39 Meeting Dulles/MacArthur/Mendès France, 13 July 1954, FRUS 1952-1954, Vol. V, 1019-21
40 Dillon to DOS, 20 September 1953, ibid., 811
41 Dulles to Amembassy, Paris, 9 November 1953, ibid., 839
42 Dulles to Amembassy, Paris, 5 October 1953, ibid. 818; Dulles to Amembassy, Paris, 9 November 1953, ibid., 839
43 Dulles to Bidault, 24 March 1954, ibid., 917-8
44 Heuseler to Noebel, 8 June 1954, BDF, Bd. 1, Nr. 129
45 Editorial note, FRUS 1952-1954, Vol. V, 693-4
46 Meeting DOS/MSA/JCS, 28 January 1953, FRUS 1952-1954, Vol. V, 712. The editors add: 'Reference is presumably to the Nazi-Soviet Pact of August 1939'.
47 Ibid., 711-17
48 Editorial note, FRUS 1952-1954, Vol. V, 859-60; Wesley Jones to Bonbright, 7 December 1953, ibid., 860-3; Fuller to Bowie, 10 December 1953, ibid., 863-5. Cf. also Duchin 1992.
49 174th NSC-meeting, 11 December 1953, DDEL/AWF/NSC, box 5
50 Editorial note, FRUS 1952-1954, Vol. V, 868; Creswell 2000, 225-8
51 Memo 'Legislative Leadership Meeting', 18 December 1953, DDEL/AWF/Diary, box 4
52 Meeting DOS/MSA/JCS, 28 January 1953, FRUS 1952-1954, Vol. V, 711-7 (espec. Dulles, 715)
53 159th NSC meeting, 13 August 1953, FRUS 1952-1954, Vol. VII, 502
54 Meeting DOS/MSA/JCS, 28 January 1953, FRUS 1952-1954, Vol. V, 715 (Bradley and Hull)
55 177th NSC meeting, 24 December 1953, DDEL/AWF/NSC, box 5
56 Meeting M. Faure/Merchant, et al., 30 November 1953, FRUS 1952-1954, Vol. V, 858
57 Ibid., 985-90 (Eisenhower and Eden citations, 986); FRUS 1952-1954, Vol. VI, 1076-7, 1080-1, 1126-7, 1135-6.
58 205th NSC meeting, 2 July 1954, DDEL/AWF/NSC, box 5
59 5-12 July 1954, FRUS 1952-1954, Vol. V, 997-1016

60 N.d., ibid., 1013-16
61 Ibid., 1016-18
62 Meeting Dulles/MacArthur/Mendès France, 13 July 1954, ibid., 1018-23; 206th NSC meeting, 16 July 1954, DDEL/AWF/NSC, box 5. Dulles reported to the NSC that 'he was very well impressed with the sincerity, frankness and simplicity of the French Premier'.
63 Maier 1989, 204-6 (citations from: Murphy to Dulles, 27 July 1954); cf. also FRUS 1952-1954, Vol. V, 995, n. 3. The memorandum was written as a basis for final discussions with the Joint Chiefs and the British about an agreed position.
64 Maier 1989, 202-3
65 Below, 83-5
66 The official basis of French nuclear policy was the so-called 'Parodi declaration', which had been submitted to the United Nations in 1946 by the French delegate Alexandre Parodi: '...one essential trait marks these studies, these projects and these realizations [about atomic energy]: it is that they are entirely oriented toward the works of peace, toward activities whose essential goal is the welfare of humanity. - I am authorized to say that the goals the French Government has assigned to the research of its scientists and technicians are purely peaceful.'(cited in Scheinman 1965, 20)
67 Calandri 1995, 39 (referring to memo by Olivier Wormser, 26 June 1954)
68 Guillen 1983, 32 (30 June 1954). This was one of a series of alternatives to the EDC that had been suggested within the French military establishment since 1952. - The thought of using the Brussels Treaty as an alternative to the EDC appeared in Britain also. A considerable amount of planning for this possibility had already been going on both in the UK and France when Eden, according to his own account, had the idea after the fall of the EDC. Eden 1965,151; Soutou 1987, 461; Deighton 1997, 17
69 The Americans observed that the origin of French thoughts about common pro-duction of arms was 'the so-called Lapie Plan, developed in 1951 to deal with the need for greater integration in aircraft procurement'. Meeting Dulles/Gruenther et al ., 27 September 1954, FRUS 1952-1954, Vol. V, 1283.
70 Gibson to DOS, 27 July 1954, NA/RG 59/DF 762A.5622, box 3905; Joyce to DOS, 18 August 1954, ibid. A French motive, it was observed, for locating such production in North Africa was 'that if German aircraft is manufactured in Germany it would be too close to the Germans to "shake hands" with the Russians in an alliance of some sort'.
71 Cf. answer by the Foreign Secretary to Robert Schuman and Alfred Coste-Floret in the parliamentary Foreign Affairs Commitee, 25 March 1954, AN/363AP (René Mayer), box 29
72 Cited in Calandri 1995, 40-1 (10 July 1954) - The remark 'from the outset', appears to refer to the German atomic and rocket scientists who had been recruited to laboratories on the French side of the Franco-German border since the war. The question of what would happen to them if the EDC came into effect was discussed in Parliament in March. Answer by the Foreign Minister to General Billotte in the parliamentary Foreign Affairs Committee, 25 March 1954, AN/363AP (René Mayer), box 29
73 According to a memorandum, one of the most objectionable features of the EDC was that it established a profound inequality between the position of Britain, 'a sovereign and independent power, and that of France, militarily enslaved in a

system of Six'. MAE memo, 'Grande-Bretagne et C.E.D.', n.s., 20 July 1954, BDF, Bd. 1, Nr. 131

74 de Beaumont to Mendès France, 6 August 1954, DDF 1954, no. 44; Calandri 1995, 39

75 de Beaumont to Mendès France, 6 August 1954, DDF 1954, no. 44

76 Bruce and Dillon to DOS, 5 August 1954, FRUS 1952-1954, Vol. V, 1025

77 Dillon to DOS, 12 August 1954, ibid., 1027-8

78 Dulles to Dillon, 12 August 1954, ibid., 1029-31

79 Dillon and Bruce to DOS, 13 August 1954, FRUS 1952-1954, Vol. V, 1033-6

80 Mendès France to Bonnet, 13 August 1954, DDF 1954, no. 63

81 Mendès France to Dulles, 17 August 1954, DDF 1954, Annexes, Ch. III

82 Dillon to DOS, 15 August 1954, ibid., 1039. Spaak had warned Mendès France in late June that US-British planning about alternatives to the EDC was going on; they had agreed that a conference between the Six would be arranged before the French ratification debate. Meeting Mendès France/Spaak, 30 June 1954, IPMF/CED 2

83 For example, countries would have a veto over actions of the Commissariat for an initial interim period of 8 years and the interim period should not be terminated except by unanimous vote, the reference to the EDC as a first step towards European unification was struck out, withdrawal from the Community was allowed if NATO ceased to exist or if the US and Britain withdrew their troops from Europe, the Court should be deprived of its authority to review the decisions of the Commissariat.

84 DDF 1954, Annexes, Conférence de Bruxelles, annexe 1, 105-12; Dillon to SecState, 15 August 1954, NA/RG 59/LF 64D181, box 56

85 DDF 1954, Annexes, Conférence de Bruxelles, annexe 1, titre VI, point 1

86 DDF 1954, Annexes, Conférence de Bruxelles, annexe 1, titre VI, points 2, 3

87 DDF 1954, Annexes, Conférence de Bruxelles, annexe 1, titre VI, point 3

88 Joyce to DOS (about talk with Sauvargnes), 18 August 1954, NA/RG 59/D 762.A.5622, box 3905

89 Below, 135-40, 149-54

90 Dillon to SecState, 15 August 1954, NA/RG 59/LF 62D181, box 56

91 'The last days of the EDC', Oral presentation by Robert Bowie at Planning Board Meeting, 30 August 1954, DDEL/NSC-S/SSF, box 3

92 Bonnet to Mendès France, 16 August 1954, DDF 1954, no. 70; Bonnet to Mendès France, 19 August 1954, ibid., no. 78. Until the end of the EDC it was suspected in the State Department that Mendès was preparing a deal with the Russians. He 'seemed to envision the possibility of an agreement by which the USSR would exchange neutralization of Germany for the giving up of EDC...It has been suggested that the defeat of the EDC was the Soviet price for a settlement in Indochina. There is no evidence, however to support this speculation.' Oral presentation by Robert Bowie at Planning Board Meeting, 30 August 1954, DDEL/NSC-S/SSF, box 3

93 Mendès France to Dulles, 17 August 1954, DDF 1954, Annexes, 35-6; Bonnet to MAE, 19 August 1954, ibid., 37; Dulles to Amembassy in Brussels and other missions, 20 August 1954, NA/RG 59/LF 62D181, box 56

94 Dulles to Amembassy, Brussels, and other missions (memo of conversation with André Meyer 18 August 1954 was enclosed), 20 August 1964, NA/RG 59/LF 64D199; Sprouse to SecState, 21 August 1954, NA/RG 59/LF 62D181, box 56

95 Memo for the Operations Coordinating Board, 'Progress Report on OCB checklist of Courses of Action to Enhance Progress toward National Objectives for Western Europe', 24, 18 August 1954, DDEL/NSC-S/OCB, box 82

96 François-Poncet to Mendès France, 17 August 1954, DDF 1954, no. 76

97 Bruce to DOS, 15 August 1954, FRUS 1952-1954, Vol. V, 1042, n. 4

98 Meeting Adenauer/Hallstein/Spaak, 18 August 1954, AA-PA/B 10-Abt. 2, Bd. 1252. Hallstein's contribution to the meeting was to provide the information that NATO's Supreme Commander, General Gruenther, had concluded that 'modern special weapons' [apparently referring to the tactical nuclear weapons required by the New Look strategy] were only of real value to the US if the Federal Republic was built into the Western defence system.

99 Stellungnahme MR Vialon zu Title VI', n.d.; 'Vorläufige Beurteilung der neuen französischen Protokollverschläge', 15 August 1954; Memo, 20 August, 1954, AA-PA/B 10, Bd. 1952-3

100 Sébilleau to MAE, 18 August 1954, DDF 1954, no. 77

101 Garnier to Mendès France, 16 August 1954, DDF 1954, no. 71

102 Amembassy, Brussels, to DOS, 17 August 1954, FRUS 1952-1954, Vol. V, 1042, n. 4; Sprouse to DOS, 16 August 1954, ibid., 1041-2

103 Massigli to Mendès France, 17 August 1954, DDF 1954, no. 73

104 DDF 1954, Annexes, Conférence de Bruxelles, annexe 10, 128-30; Massigli to MAE, 17 August 1954, DDF 1954, no. 75.

105 Below, 130-3

106 DDF 1954, Annexes, Conférence de Bruxelles, 45-95, and annexes 2 and 4; Dumoulin 199, 480-86

107 Ibid., annexe 3, 20 August 1954.

108 Dumoulin 1999 483

109 Spaak explained in his memoirs that he had not communicated the message to Mendès in order not to provoke his anger, and because Spaak did not agree with the proposed policy. He did in fact, however, talk about it with Mendès. Dumoulin 1999, 485-6 (Dumoulin had access to Spaak's personal archives).– The incident was referred to in an American report: 'Spaak did not (repeat not) read his message from the Secretary to open meeting. He had long meeting with Mendes afterwards. He showed Mendes message from the Secretary. Spaak told Mendes that he thought it preferable to show him message rather than face him with it in open meeting. Mendes thanked Spaak saying that no (repeat no) representative of France had suffered humiliation such as he had suffered today and that reading this message tonight would have been too much'. Sprouse to SecState, 22 August 1954, NA/RG 59/LF 62D181, box 56

110 DDF 1954, Annexes, Conférence de Bruxelles, 80, 91, and annexes 2, 4, 7

111 Miller to Reinstein, 'Limitation on Production of Nuclear Fuel', 19 August 1954, NA/RG 59/LF 57D688, box 409

112 DDF 1954, Annexes, Conférence de Bruxelles, annexe 8

113 The last days of the EDC', Oral presentation by Robert Bowie at Planning Board Meeting, 30 August 1954, DDEL/NSC-S/SSF, box 3

114 Meeting Mendès France/Churchill/Eden, 23 August 1954, DDF 1954, Annexes, 131-40;

115 Dillon to DOS, 24 August 1954, FRUS 1952-1954, Vol. V, 1071-77. Bowie reported later that Churchill had apparently been firm: 'This is the strongest statement we have had from the British in support of EDC. There was no discussion

between Mendes-France and Churchill of alternatives although Mendes-France gave out a story that there had been. This was one of a series of French-inspired news stories...The U.S. got the British to issue a statement denying that there had been any discussion of alternatives between Churchill and Mendes-France and making it clear that the British felt that EDC was the best solution to the problem of German rearmament. This story did not appear in a single French paper'. 'The last days of the EDC', Oral presentation by Robert Bowie at Planning Board Meeting, 30 August 1954, DDEL/NSC-S/SSF, box 3

116　Churchill to Dulles and Eden to Dulles, 24 August 1954, FRUS 1952-1954, Vol. V, 1077-9

117　W.B. Smith to Amembassy, Paris, 27 August 1954, FRUS 1952-1954, Vol. V, 1082-3

118　Meeting W.B. Smith/Scott et al., 26 August 1954, NA/RG59/LF 64D199, box 2

119　MAE memo, Direction générale des affaires économiques et financiers, 5 November 1954, DDF 1954, no. 318

120　Bruce to DOS, 26 August 1954, FRUS 1952-1954, Vol. V, 1079

121　W.B. Smith (Acting Secretary) to Amembassy, Paris, 26 August 1954, ibid., 1081-2

122　Bruce to DOS, 27 August 1954, ibid., 1087

123　Dillon to DOS, 30 August 1954, ibid., 1091-2

124　Goldschmidt 1980, 142-4; Soutou 1989, Die Nuklearpolitik..., 606-7

125　Debré 1988, 161-225, espec. 181, 220, 225

126　Bariéty 1993 (the citation, 383). The latter point is to be doubted. There is no reason to believe that the partners did not understand, nor that US policy-makers did not understand, but it was probably considered counterproductive to talk about the matter.

127　Schmidt 1995, 148

3　The Nuclear Dimension of the Western European Union

1　DOS to Conant, 1 September 1954, NA/RG 59/LF 62D181, box 56

2　Meeting Hoyer-Millar/Adenauer/Hallstein/Blankenhorn, 2 September 1954, BA/1351 (Blankenhorn), Bd. 33b; Küsters 1994, 500-1

3　Churchill cited his message in Churchill to Eisenhower, 3 September 1954, FRUS 1952-1954, V, 1144-5. Eisenhower's answer, ibid., 1145, n. 3. Whether Churchill reacted or had the idea of self-limitation first is not quite certain, as his message to Adenauer is not dated in FRUS.

4　Fischer 1992, West German Rearmament ..., 388

5　Memo 'Gespräch mit Spaak', n.s., 5 September 1954, BA/N1351 (Blankenhorn), Bd. 33b

6　Meeting Adenauer/Eden et al., 13 September 1954, BA/N1351 (Blankenhorn), Bd. 33a. On the British role in organizing the WEU, see Dockrill 1991, 133-50; Deighton 1997; Ruane 2000, 102-72.

7　Conant to DOS, 7 September 1954 (two telegrams), FRUS 1952-1954, Vol. V, 1152-4

8　Conant to DOS (about meeting Adenauer/Murphy/Conant), 13 September 1954, ibid., 1181-4 (the citation, 1182)

9   Meeting Hallstein/Bruce, 9 September 1954, HAEC/JMAS 167 (copy of David Bruce Diary)
10 Dulles to Eden, 14 September 1954, FRUS 1952-1954, Vol. V, 1192-4 (the citation, 1192). On US views of the German situation, cf. Hershberg 1992, 545-9
11 François-Poncet to Mendès France, 17 September 1954, DDF 1954, no. 188
12 Memo by Kielmannsegg, 'Zur Frage möglicher Garantien (anzubieten durch die Bundesrepublik für den Fall einer Aufnahme in NATO)', 7 September 1954, AA-PA/B10, Bd. 1252
13 11 September 1954, cited in Guillen 1983, 33. The paper was received by Mendès France. Similar ideas about the necessity of the 'integration track' appeared in other French agencies at this time. See Calandri 1995, 41.
14 Cf. Coutrot 1985, 312; Pitman 2000, Un Général..., 50. The thoughts of the French military were tied to the goal of France participating in the decisions taken by the two nuclear powers within NATO. G.H. Soutou observes: 'Thus it was, that the first version of the French plan of September 1954 comprised the creation of a Tripartite Strategic Directorate. Thus it was, that the meeting of the Defence Council held on 10 September, without taking a formal decision, moved in the direction of acquiring nuclear weapons. Thus it was, that at the London Conference Mendès-France fought to ensure that the controls and restrictions in the future WEU would not render impossible a French nuclear armament programme'. (Soutou 1987, 468)
15 The theory aims at tying together international bargaining and domestic influences on foreign policy decision-making. Cf. Putnam 1988; Evans-Jacobson-Putnam, eds., 1993
16 De Moustier to Mendès France, 25 September 1954, IPMF/Accords de Paris
17 Meeting Eden/Mendès France, 15-16 September 1954, DDF 1954, Annexes; Conférence de Londres, annexe 1 (18 September 1954). The Americans were informed that Mendès France had told Eden that he had slept little that night, had summoned his staff, and was now of the opinion that it was desirable to consider admission of Germany to NATO. Dillon to Conant, 16 September 1954, FRUS 1952-1954, Vol. V, 1200. See also Dillon to DOS, 24 September 1954, ibid., 1256-9
18 FO to Britembassy, Washington, 18 September 1954, PRO/PREM 11, 843.
19 Dulles to certain US missions, 23 September 1954, FRUS 1952-1954, Vol. V, 1245-6
20 Eisenhower to W.B. Smith, 3 September 1954, DDEL/AWF/Diary, box 8
21 Memo by Fuller, 'Post-EDC Reappraisal', 2 September 1954, NA/RG 59/LF 65D101, box 84; Memo by Fuller, 'Post-Mortem on EDC', 3 September 1954, ibid.; Memo by Fuller, 'US Policy toward Europe -Post-EDC', 10 September 1954, FRUS 1952-1954, Vol. V, 1170-7. Cf. also memo by Moore, 'US Position on Alternative to EDC', 10 September 1954, ibid. 1164-7.
22 Memo by Fuller and Bowie, 'U.S. Policy Toward Europe - Post-EDC', 13 September 1954, NA/RG 59/LF 65D101, box 84; Memo by Fuller, 'A US Position Respecting the Association of the German Federal Republic with the West (with specific reference to the forthcoming Nine-Power and NATO Conferences)', 21 September 1954, ibid.; Memo by Fuller, 'Primary Considerations in Determining a US Negotiating Position at London', 22 September 1954, ibid.
23 NSC 5433, 'Immediate US Policy Toward Europe', 16 September 1954, FRUS 1952-1954, Vol. V, 1205-9
24 On this point a less militant formulation was proposed by State, a more militant one by Defense

25 Radford to C. Wilson, 22 September 1954, FRUS 1952-1954, Vol. V, 1247-8
26 Memo for the Secretary of Defense (s. Radford), 'Strategic Issues Confronting the U.S. in Europe', 22 September 1954, DDEL/SANSA/Brief., box 19. When answering questions related to NSC 5433 on 22 October - the time of the Paris Conference - the JCS stated that these views were unchanged. Ibid.
27 NSC meeting, 24 September 1954, FRUS 1952-1954, Vol. V, 1263-8. Adenauer sometimes argued, when speaking to Americans, that the US was too patient, giving out too much money without asking for something in return. See for example meeting Adenauer/Murphy, 14 September, 1954, BA/N1351 (Blankenhorn), Bd. 33a. - When accompanying Dulles to the airport after his visit in Bonn, Adenauer told Dulles that he felt that the way to influence Mendès France was through financial pressures and that in this way he could be 'steered'. He thought that Mendès France's heart was in the economic and financial recovery of France and that everything else was marginal. Memo by Dulles, 17 September 1954, NA/RG 59/LF 62D181, box 56. - Voices within the US Administration also proposed economic reprisals. For example the Director of the Foreign Operations Administration, Harold Stassen, suggested that France should be notified that, in view of the fact that the contemplated programme was not carried out in either Indo-China or EDC, US aid should be suspended until Congress decided otherwise. Stassen to Dulles, 14 September 1954, NA/RG59/LF 64D199, box 2
28 NSC 5433/1, 'Immediate US Policy Toward Europe', 25 September 1954, FRUS 1952-1954, Vol. V, 1268-71
29 The various components of the treaty complex are listed in DDF 1954, Annexes, Conférence de Londres et Réunions de Paris, Introduction, 5-7. The essential approved texts related to arms control are printed in Young, ed., 1966, Appendix A
30 DDF 1954 Annexes, Conférence de Londres, 25-33; Annexe 1, 18 September 1954; W.B. Smith to certain US missions, 20 September 1954, FRUS 1952-1954, Vol. V, 1231-4
31 Draft Cabinet paper, 'London conference', 26 September 1954, PRO/PREM 11, 843; Meeting at 10, Downing Street, 28 September 1954, ibid.
32 Meeting Dulles/Merchant/Mendès France, 27 September 1954, FRUS 1952-1954, Vol. V, 1283-8 (the citation, 1286)
33 Meeting Dulles/Gruenther/Merchant/Bowie et al., 27 September 1954, FRUS 1952-1954, Vol. V, 1281-3 (the citation, 1282)
34 Meeting Dulles/Eden et al., 27 September 1954, ibid., 1275-8
35 Ibid., 1312-13, 1357-63. In Dulles' report to the President he called the British pledge a 'historical decision tying England to the continent in a way which has never been done before'. Dulles to Eisenhower, 29 September 1954, HAEC/JMDS 89
36 Blankenhorn 1980, 199
37 Dillon to DOS, 24 September 1954, FRUS 1952-1954, Vol. V, 1258
38 Merchant to Dulles, 29 September 1954, NA/RG59/DF 740.5, box 3490; Memo by E. Martin, 'Principles for Establishment of Armaments Pool', 28 September 1954, NA/RG59/LF 62D181, box 57. - Dulles reported to Eisenhower that 'the most difficult point remains the so-called arms pool, which many feel is desired by France in order to exclude Ruhr industrialists from participation in army industry and to concentrate that industry in France'. Dulles to Eisenhower, 29 September 1954, HAEC/JMDS 89

39   Meeting Dulles/Merchant/Mendès France, 29 September 1954, FRUS 1952-1954, Vol. V, 1308-11 (the citation, 1309). After having returned home Dulles complained to the National Security Council about the 'very tricky definitions' devised by the French in order to exclude Germany and concentrate arms production in France. 216th NSC meeting, 6 October 1954, ibid., 1380.

40   Internally in the US, the French parallel to the EDC was described as factually incorrect: 'Prior to the Paris meetings, the French had proposed that the Brussels Treaty Organization be given authority to allocate US end-item aid among the Brussels Treaty countries. Mendès-France argued that the U.S. had agreed to give the EDC Commissariat such authority and a similar arrangement should be agreed for WEU. (This was based on a partial misunderstanding of the EDC arrangements. In the negotiations with the EDC Interim Committee we had agreed to turn title to US equipment over to the EDC Commissariat, but had carefully retained for the U.S. the same rights regarding the determination of the ultimate destination of U.S. equipment as we have with respect to individual countries.)'. Position paper, 'Mendès-France Talks', n.s., November 1954, NA/RG 59/ LF 62D181

41   DDF 1954, Annexes, Conférence de Londres, 103-4

42   Ibid.

43   Ibid., annexe 11

44   Such a proposal for unconditional renunciation does not appear in the verbatim record of the discussions in the DDF. Spaak proposed, during discussion of the Hood Report, that all the continental members of the WEU would engage themselves not to produce ABC weapons on the continent, 'a kind of disarmament agreement'. This obviously did not mean renunciation for France, but permission to produce nuclear weapons except in Metropolitan France. DDF 1954, Annexes, Conférence de Londres, 184.

45   Ibid., 180-3. The corresponding summary in FRUS 1952-1954, Vol. V, 1323, is much less clear.

46   DDF 1954, Annexes, Conférence de Londres, 186-8

48   Mendès France opposed the word 'approved'. DDF 1954, Annexes, Conférence de Londres, 218-19 and annexe 13.

49   DDF 1954, Annexes, Conférence de Londres, 197-205 (the citations, 203-4)

50   Ibid., 201

51   Ibid., 205-11 (Adenauer's declaration was made on 2 October; WEU, Protocol III, Annex II, in Young, ed., 1966. The new definition made it possible to clear the path for German civil nuclear activities. As long as such an extremely restrictive limit remained, it was not possible to start building a civil nuclear industry. It was thus accepted that Germany should not, or could not, be prevented from building such an industry. The WEU was concerned with the regulation and control of armaments, not civil production. The dilemma was that there is no clear border line between the two in the field of nuclear energy.

52   An elastic term of international law meaning that it was applicable in present circumstances only

53   Adenauer 1966, 347.

54   The record was made by the Belgian delegation and published without changes in the French DDF Collection

55   Köhler 1994, 841-5

56   Küsters 1994, 527-35. Further details are given in Schwarz 1991, Adenauer und die Kernwaffen, 577-8.

57 Küsters 1994, espec. 512-33, 535-6 (the citation, 535)
58 Schwarz 1991, Adenauer: Der Staatsmann..., 299
59 Strauss 1989, 310
60 DDF 1954, Annexes, Conférence de Londres,. 209-21, espec. 209.- The Italian declaration had no factual, only symbolic, significance because the Italian Peace Treaty already barred Italy from owning, manufacturing or testing nuclear weapons.
61 Adenauer 1966, 347
62 65-7
63 Thoss 1990, 481; Fischer 1994, 141-2; Eckert 1990, 316-17. According to Eckert (1990, 317, n. 15), referring to FRUS 1952-1954, Vol. V, 1144 f. and particularly 1164-5, the *Kernwaffenverzicht* had been prepared carefully with Britain and the US. The first source referred to is Churchill's message to Eisenhower about his proposal to Adenauer (above, 66), the second a memorandum by the Director of the Office of European Regional Affairs, Ben T. Moore. Moore outlined a 'NATO with safeguards' programme for German membership in NATO on which efforts should be made to reach agreement first with the British and Germans and then with the other EDC countries and Canada. One of the elements of the programme was that Germany would undertake to produce certain kinds of arms, 'She would state, however, that she would not produce atomic and thermo-nuclear weapons, military aircraft, etc. (other items in Annex II of Article 107 of the EDC Treaty) because of her exposed strategic position except as agreed by NATO'. Cf. also Eckert 1989, 124, n. 24. - The available sources leave no doubt about the fact that Britain and the US supported the idea of the *Kernwaffenverzicht*, and it was shown above that Adenauer emitted unspecific signals that something of the kind might be possible. Although I have not found confirmation that it had been carefully prepared in the sense that the details had been agreed upon beforehand with the US and Britain it appears probable that they had.
64 DDF 1954, Annexes, Conférence de Londres, 214-29
65 FRUS 1952-1954, Vol. V, 2 October 1954, 1324-8; Thoss 1993, 44-5
66 DDF 1954, Annexes, Conférence de Londres, 2 October 1954, 229-35; WEU, Protocol III, in Young, ed., 1966
67 DDF 1954, Annexes, Conférence de Londres, 271-8 and annexe 15; WEU, Protocol III and IV, in Young, ed., 1966. Mendès France made some comments about the necessity of a different kind of control for three kinds of arms, ABC weapons, the missile-warship-aircraft category, and other arms. This was questioned by Spaak and Dulles. The meaning of this exchange is far from clear. Was it part of the French effort to keep the 'loop-hole' for French freedom of action in the nuclear field? The discussion on this point seems to be the basis of Soutou's interpretation: 'But then there arose the problem of the control of manufacture of nuclear weapons for countries which might embark on it - in reality for France. Mendès France would have liked to institute a special control, the modalities of which would have been defined later by a special commission. His partners, and in particular Spaak, insisted that this control should not differ from the general control established on arms in their entirety, which would be one of the essential functions of the WEU. In reality, what was at stake was fundamentally, the freedom of action of France in the nuclear field'. Soutou 1989, La politique nucléaire..., 323.
68 Commission des affaires étrangères, Audition Mendès France, 6 October 1954, AN/AP/505(II)/6 (Edgar Faure)

69 Calandri 1995, 48; Altnöder 1998, 182-96; Seydoux 1975, 192-3
70 217th NSC meeting, 14 October 1954, DDEL/AWF/NSC, box 6
71 DDF 1954, Annexes, Réunions de Paris, 408-15
72 WEU, Protocol IV, Article 7, in Young, ed., 1966
73 Meeting Hamilton/Roper, 11 February 1955, NA/RG59/LF57D688, box 403. - On the basis of earlier discussions on the subject between the British Washington Embassy and the State Department, Roper had undertaken to check on the subject further with his Government, and then gave the information cited.
74 WEU, Protocol III, Annex II, ibid.
75 DDF 1954, Annexes, Réunions de Paris, 408-15, 422; WEU, Protocol III, Annex II, in Young, ed. 1966. The control should, in any case, only be exercised on the mainland of Europe.
76 DDF 1954, Annexes, Réunions de Paris, 424-9; Dillon to DOS, 13 October 1954, FRUS 1952-1954, Vol. V, 1387-9; Thoss 1990, 481
77 DDF 1954, Annexes, Réunions de Paris, 430-41; Guillen 1990, La France et l'intégration..., 88
78 Eckert 1989, 124-26
79 Eisenhower to Gruenther, 2 November 1954, DDEL/AWF/Diary, box 8
80 Eisenhower to Churchill, 14 December 1954, FRUS 1952-1954, Vol. V, 1498-501
81 'Mendès-France Talks, Position Paper', n.s., November 1954, NA/RG 59/LF 62D181, box 57
82 Dillon to SecState, 16 October 1954, NA/RG 84/FSPF-O 1953-57, box 67-8
83 Meeting Dulles/Stassen, 23 October 1954, NA /RG 59/LF 64D199, box 2
84 'Voyage aux Etats-Unis', n.s., n.d., IPMF/Relations internationales
85 Cf. Schwabe 1995, 118-19; Mélandri 1975, 54-6. Schwabe's view is that the 'soft line' was counterproductive: 'In the final analysis one could argue that the State Department's reluctance to put more than rhetorical pressure on the Europeans may even have contributed to the setbacks that the process of European integration suffered in the mid-1950's'.
86 Bonnet to Mendès France, 10, 11 and 14 December 1954, DDF 1954, nos. 431,438 and 449; Mendès France to Bonnet, 14 December 1954, ibid., no. 445; Bonnet to Mendès France, 14 December 1954, ibid., no. 449; Dulles to Mendès France, 16 December 1954, FRUS 1952-1954, Vol. V, 1504-5; Dulles to Eisenhower, n.d., ibid., 1497; Dulles to Dillon, 14 December 1954, ibid., 1497-8
87 Meeting Eisenhower/Dulles/Mendès France et al., 18 November 1954, FRUS 1952-1954, Vol. V, 1481-4; 'Voyage aux Etats-Unis', n.s., n.d., IPMF/Relations internationales; Meeting Dulles/Mendès France et al., 19 November 1954, FRUS 1952-1954, Vol. V, 1484-5; Meeting Dulles/Eden/Mendès France et al., 16 December 1954, ibid., 1505-7 (the citation, 1506)
88 Jebb to FO; 3 January 1955, PRO/PREM 11, 843; Meeting Adenauer/Mendès France, 14 January 1955, BA/N1351/39 (Blankenhorn)
89 'Voyage aux Etats-Unis', n.s., n.d., IPMF/Relations internationales; Mendès France to Bonnet, 1 December 1954, DDF 1954, no. 406; Meeting Dulles/Bonnet, 2 December 1954, NA/RG 59/LF 64D199, box 2; DOS-HICOG, 9 December 1954, NA/RG 59/DF 740.5
90 Dulles to Amembassy, Paris, 7 December 1954, NA/RG 59/DF 740.5, box 3490
91 Dulles to Amembassy, Paris, and certain other missions, 11 December 1954, ibid.
92 Matthews to SecState, 15 December 1954, NA/RG59/DF 740.5, box 3490
93 Dillon to DOS, 23 December 1954, FRUS 1952-1954, Vol. V, 1515-7
94 DOS instruction (containing citations from the debate), NA/RG59/DF 762A.5611,

box 3905; Aldrich to DOS, 19 November 1954, FRUS 1952-1954, Vol. V, 1485-6

95 Amembassy, London to DOS (containing citations from the debate), 15 January 1955, NA/RG 59/DF 740.5, box 3114

96 State Department official Joseph J. Wolf discussed some legal intricacies of the French and German positions: 'Article 14, particularly as related to Article 18 of Protocol IV which he [Boegner] said were expressly designed by the French to give France that protection (Boegner was the draftsman of these two Articles and obtained last-minute technical changes in them at Ministerial level)'. Wolf observed that the German interpretation seemed to be similar: 'The German submission of the pacts to their Parliament was accompanied by a precis of the agreements. In essence the Germans indicate that control over import of nuclear weapons was in general contemplated, and indicate that Article 14 provides that NATO will establish the requirements for ABC weapons for Germany. In other words, they appear to agree with Boegner's line of thinking'. Wolf to Merchant, 'Control of ABC Weapons by Germany Under London and Paris Pacts', 14 January 1955, NA/RG 59/LF 57D688, box 403

97 Elsewhere than in France, presumably

98 Wolf to Merchant, 14 January 1955, NA/RG 84/LF 57D688, box 403; Dulles to Amembassies in Paris and London, and HICOG, Bonn, 29 December 1954, NA/RG 59/DF 762A.5611, box 3905

99 Dillon to SecState, 26 April 1955, ibid., box 3569

100 Hamilton to G. Smith, 29 March 1955, NA/RG84/LF 57D688, box 403

101 Amembasssy, Paris, to DOS, 6 January 1955, NA/RG59/DF 740.5, box 3113; Journal Officiel, 21 December 1954, 6710 (Duclos), 6874-5 (de Moro, Giafferi)

102 Wolf to Merchant, 14 January 1955, NA/RG 84/LF 57D688, box 403

103 Jebb to FO, 3 January 1955, PRO/PREM 11, 843

104 Murphy to Amembassy, London, 14 January 1955, NA/RG 59/DF 740.5, box 3114

105 Aldrich to SecState, 21 January 21 1955, ibid.

106 Dulles to Amembassy, Paris, 25 January 1955, ibid.

107 Hamilton to G. Smith, 29 March 1955, NA/RG59/LF 57D688, box 403

108 'Memorandum for the files', n.s., 19 January 1955, ibid.

109 Meeting de Juniac/Merchant/Tyler, 21 January 1955, ibid.

110 P. 89

111 Meeting Hamilton/Roper, 11 February 1955, NA/RG 59/LF 57D688, box 403

112 Dillon to DOS, 24 December 1954, FRUS 1952-1954, Vol. V, 1519-20; Diary entry by Hagerty (the citations), December 24, 1954, ibid., 1520-3; Churchill to Eisenhower, 24 December 1954, ibid., 1524-5

113 Dillon to DOS, 28 December 1954, ibid., 1528-9

114 Conant to DOS, 24 December 1954, ibid., 1523

115 Conant to Merchant, 27 December 1954, ibid., 1526-8

116 Eden to Dulles and Dulles to Eden, 27 December 1954, ibid., 1525-6

117 Dillon to DOS, 24 December 1954, ibid., 1524

118 Meeting Dulles/Makins et al., 29 December 1954, FRUS 1952-1954, Vol. V, 1531-5

119 Makins to FO, 29 December 1954, PRO/PREM 11, 843

120 Cf. particularly Scheinman 1965, 111-6; Goldschmidt 1980, 146-7; Coutrot 1985, 312-3; Soutou 1989, La politique nucléaire..., 324-30

121 The important exception is the submarine prototype fuelled with natural uranium. The project proved to be technically impracticable and was abandoned later.

122   Soutou 1989, La politique nucléaire..., 323-9 (the citations, 326)
123   An indication that this might *not* have been the case may be mentioned. Michel Debré, strategic MP in the Council of the Republic, wrote in his memoirs that he did not know about the decision until 1958: 'And Mendès France (as I would not learn until 1958) can decree research into the atomic bomb'. Debré 1988, 227
124   Memo, Présidence du Conseil, n.s., 17 January 1955, IPMF/Energie atomique
125   The German delegation was however headed by the Minister of Economics, Ludwig Erhard. Hughes advised against US participation of any kind in the Working Group. Hughes to SecState, 11 January 1955, NA/RG 59/DF 740.5, box 3113; Murphy (Acting Secretary) to Amembassy Paris, 14 January 1955, ibid.
126   DDF 1955, Annexes, t. 1, Entretiens des Ministres des Affaires Etrangères concernant les problèmes européens et échanges de messages, Annexe 1, 'Mémorandum français sur la standardisation et la production des armements', 3 January 1955; Hughes to SecState, 8 January 1955, NA/RG 59/DF 740.5, box 3113; Garnier to E.Faure, 2 February 1955, DDF 1955, t. I, no. 62, n. 1; Thoss 1993, 98
127   Calandri 1995, 47-53 (the citation, 49)
128   Bérard 1977, 605-6. The meeting took place on 5 January, the participants were Soutou and Bérard, Blankenhorn and von Maltzan.
129   Meeting Soutou/Blankenhorn, 5 January 1955, BA/N1351/38a (Blankenhorn)
130   Conant to SecState, 12 January 1955, ibid. German industry was critical of French Arms Pool plans. When visiting the US in December, its spokesman, Fritz Berg, when questioned by Dulles, had stated that the idea of a pool was perhaps too restrictive and would hinder the maximum utilization of European arms production. What was needed was some kind of clearing system which would enable each country to devote its production facilities to those items that it could make most efficiently. Meeting Dulles/Berg et al., 7 December 1954, NA/RG 59/LF 64D199, box 2
131   Dulles had sent a personal message to Adenauer before the meeting pointing out that a positive vote in the Council of the Republic was probable and that the US was prepared to help both Adenauer and Mendès France to overcome the difficulties. He did not mention the Arms Pool; thus Adenauer was not asked to make concessions to the French in the matter. 13 January 1955, BA/N1351/38a (Blankenhorn)
132   This was perhaps part of an endeavour to invite Franco-German-Italian cooperation as an initial step. An article in Combat, interpreted in NATO circles as officially inspired, had indicated that Mendès' journey to Rome and Bonn, was intended to lay the foundation for a future trilateral Franco-German-Italian arms pool which might make it possible to overcome the resistance of the UK and the Benelux. Thoss 1993, 100.
133   Meeting Adenauer/Mendès France, 14 January 1955, BA/N1351/39 (Blankenhorn) and DDF 1955, Annexes, t. I, Ch. XI
134   Thoss 1993, 100-1
135   230th NSC meeting, 6 January 1955, DDEL/AWF/NSC, box 6
136   Dillon to SecState, 4 January, 1955, NA/RG59/DF 740.5, box 3113
137   Meeting Dulles/Bruce/Bowie/Stassen et al., 8 January 1955, NA/RG59/LF 64D199, box 3
138   Butterworth to SecState, 17 January 1955, NA/RG 59/DF 740.5, box 3114
139   Durbrow to SecState, 18 January 1955,ibid.; Meeting Plaja/Stabner, 11 January 1955, ibid; Durbrow to SecState, 16 January 1955, ibid.; Meeting Luciolli/

Merchant/Freund, 17 January 1955, ibid; Matthews to SecState, 8 and 10 January 1955, ibid., box 3113; Hughes to SecState, 11 January 1955, ibid.; Alger to SecState, 7 January 1955, ibid.; Alger to SecState, 13 January 1955 (2 telegrams), ibid., box 3114

140 Matthews to SecState, 10 January 1955, ibid., box 3113; Hughes to SecState, 11 January, ibid; Matthews to SecState, 12 (the citation) and 18 January 1955, ibid., box 3114

141 Murphy (Acting Secretary) to Amembassy, Paris, 15 January 1955, ibid.

142 de Juniac to Mendès France, 11 January 1955, DDF 1955, t. I, no. 22; Murphy (Acting Secretary) to Amembassy, Paris; Meeting de la Grandville/Palmer, 13 January 1955, NA/RG 59/DF 740.5, box 3114; Hughes to SecState, 20 January 1955, NA/RG 59/DF 740.5, box 3114

143 See Calandri 1995, 57-63

144 Kabinettssitzung 26 January 1955, KAB 1955, 106-8. Erhard's memorandum, of 14 January, is printed in DDF 1955, Annexes, t.1, Annexe 2

145 Hughes to SecState, 26 January 1955, NA/RG 59/DF 740.5, box 3114

146 Dulles to HICOG and Amembassies in the Hague and Paris, 26 January 1955, ibid

147 Hughes to Merchant, 16 February 1955, ibid., box 3115. Hughes wrote that Achilles was in general agreement.

148 Meeting Dulles/Merchant/Conant et al., 17 February 1955, NA/RG 59/LF 64D199, box 3

149 Fuller to Bowie, 21 February 1955, NA/RG59/LF 66D70

150 Dillon to Dulles, 8 March 1955, ML/JFD/Tel.conv., box 3; Achilles to SecState, 9 March 1955, NA/RG 59/DF 740.5, box 3116; Meeting Merchant/de Juniac, 9 March 1955, ibid.; Meeting Palmer/van Baarda, 11 March 1955, ibid.

151 Achilles to Sauvagnargues, 10 March 1955, ibid.

152 Palmer to Cleveland, 10 March 1955, ibid.

153 Dulles to Amembassy, Paris, 16 March 1955, ibid.; Merchant to Dulles, 11 and 15 March 1955, ibid.

154 Dulles to Amembassy, Paris, 19 March 1955, ibid.

155 Achilles to SecState, 26 March 1955, ibid.

156 Gibson to DOS, 28 March 1955, ibid.; Debré 1988, 225-33

157 Debré 1988, 230-1

158 Dillon to SecState, 26 April 1955, NA/RG 59/DF 762A.5611, box 3569; Dillon to SecState, 27 April 1955, NA/RG59/DF 740.5, box 3118

159 Dillon to SecState, 27 April 1955, NA/RG 59/DF 762A.5611, box 3569

160 Dillon to SecState, 22 April 1955, ibid.

161 Dillon to SecState, 26 April 1955, NA/RG 59/DF 762A.5611, box 3569. Bérard and Robinson were also present.

162 Dillon to SecState, 26 April 1955 (translation of French aide-mémoire), ibid.

163 Merchant to Dulles, 28 April 1955, ibid.

164 Dulles to Amembassy, Paris, 30 April 1955, ibid.

4   Euratom and the Linkage to the Common Market: First Phase

1   Monnet 1976, 466; Küsters 1982, 68-73; Weilemann 1983, 25-6; Gerbet 1989, 68-9; Fischer 1994, 202-8; Duchêne 1994, 262-6; Schröder 1994, 387-90; Varsori 1999, 345-7; Wilkens 1999, 174-80. Armand was in charge of the French railways and also a member of the Board of the *Commissariat à l' énergie atomique*. He supported the concept of an atomic pool in common with Britain and West Germany, and later baptized it ´Euratom´. - Isenbergh was a deputy legal counsel of the US Atomic Energy Commission who was on leave in Europe in order to study the control of civil nuclear power in order to prevent military proliferation.

2   Weilemann (1983, 25), referring to an interview with Uri by Erling Bjøl, attributes the Euratom idea to Isenbergh; Bjøl's account does not mention Isenbergh, however (Bjøl 1966, 380-5). Fischer 1994 (203, n. 55) refutes Weilemann on this point and argues that Armand was the inspirator, referring to his interviews with Monnet's collaborators Max Kohnstamm and Pierre Uri. Uri writes in his memoirs that Monnet elaborated the project in close collaboration with Armand and Isenbergh (Uri 1991, 112). According to Guillen, official France was not the originator of the Euratom idea, even if some Frenchmen played a role behind the scenes (Guillen 1994, 111-13). Duchêne's view is that Isenbergh ´seems not to have been on a mission in any way, rather to be enjoying Europe in self-imposed exile and playing the clarinet´ (Duchêne 1994, 264).

3   Memo for the Operations Coordinating Board, ´Progress Report on OCB checklist of Courses of Action to Enhance Progress toward National Objectives for Western Europe´, 18 August 1954, 32, DDEL/NSC-S/OCB, box 82. - The OCB had been established in September 1953 in order to provide for the integrated implementation of national security policies by the several agencies of the Federal Government. It included representatives of, among others, State and Defense, at the Under Secretary/Deputy Secretary level, and the Director of the CIA (the latter was Allen Dulles, the brother of the Secretary of State). FRUS 1952-1954, Vol. II, 455, 1736-7, 1855-7, 1875. A working group on nuclear energy was formed. A memo noted that the ´OCB, assisted by a new working group, has been given the responsibility to advise with Agencies in the Government concerning the foreign impact of US nuclear energy programs´. Several types of action were planned, the memo reported, among them ´some early planning on peaceful applications of nuclear energy which may affect Western Europe´. OCB, Meeting of Working Group on Western Europe, 6 May 1954, DDEL/NSC-S/OCB

4   Küsters 1982, 73-4, 95-9, 100-3; Weilemann 1983, 26-8; Dumoulin 1999, 504-6

5   Daviet 1995. - High-enriched uranium was necessary for the A-bomb detonator of the H-bombs of the time; plutonium would not do. Medium-enriched uranium is necessary (even if the French were not yet aware of this in the spring of 1955) for propulsion reactors for nuclear submarines. Low-enriched uranium is necessary or useful for several types of power reactors.

6   The Gaullist Minister of Defence, Gaston Palewski, described the enormous difference of magnitudes of the US, British and French nuclear efforts (´US spends 700 billion francs yearly, UK 100 billion, France 6 billion 1952, 9 billion 1953, 10 billion 1954´). Dillon to SecState, 11 April 1955, NA/DF 851.1901, box 4579

7   Goldschmidt 1967, 225-7. The Anglo-American agreements were war-time agreements (with later amendments). Above, 5, n. 3

8   L´aventure de la bombe 1985, espec. 61, 82-3 (testimonies by General Jean Crépin and Pierre Guillaumat; Crépin had been secretary of the *Comité* and based his account on the minutes). Cf. also Guillen 1985, 397.

9   Guillaumat however stated that the *Comité* had 'discarded the idea of a European weapon'
10   Meeting Nutting/Hope/Caccia/M. Faure/Marjolin et al., 15 June 1956, PRO/FO 371/1122028
11   Adenauer 1967, 23-7; Küsters 1992, 104-5; von der Groeben 1995, 272. Consultations between the Six about the plan took place later but the interest was weak.
12   Meeting Adenauer/Pinay, 29-30 April 1955, BA/N1351/45a,b (Blankenhorn). The US Ambassador was informed by the *Auswärtiges Amt* of the content of the talks. Conant to SecState, 4 May 1955, NA/RG 59/DF 740.5, box 3118
13   French minutes from meeting Wormser/von Maltzan et al., 30 April 1955, BDF Bd. 1, Nr. 130. - According to Fischer's account of the Adenauer/Pinay meeting, Pinay proposed the construction of an enrichment plant on a bilateral basis, but Adenauer's reaction was evasive. Fischer 1994, 209-12
14   'Communiqué', 30 April 1955, DDF 1955, Annexes, t. I. Fischer observes that Adenauer had agreed to nuclear cooperation without consulting the nuclear scientists and industry; there were some protests from them after the event. He interprets this to be a consequence of Adenauer's conviction that the nuclear field was central in Franco-German relations and in European cooperation. Adenauer wanted no interference in his judgment of what was politically desirable in the long run. He was well aware that France had already started concrete preparations for a military nuclear programme. Fischer 1994, 209-12. - Possibly Adenauer was already at this early stage thinking of European integration as the natural way for Germany to acquire nuclear weapons, as he did a year and a half later (below, 204). But this is in the realm of speculation. - For British worries about the signs of impending Franco-German cooperation in the nuclear field, cf. O'Driscoll 1998, Missing..., 138
15   MAE memo, May 1955, BDF, Bd. 2, Nr. 214
16   Küsters 1982, 79-88; Lee 1995, 43-8
17   Lee 1995, 46-8; Moravcsik 1998, 96-9
18   Heuser 1998
19   Küsters 1982, 116-18; von der Groeben 1995, 272-4. According to Sabine Lee, Adenauer was not interested in economics and had no preference as to the methodology of integration. Later, when he saw the Common Market negotiations to be promising, he started supporting this course. Lee 1995, 48
20   'Memorandum über die Fortführung der Integration', 1 June 1955, BDF, Bd. 2, Nr. 215 (the citation, 750); Küsters 1982, 118-19; von der Groeben 1995, 274-5.
21   Extract of German minutes from the Messina Conference, 1-2 June 1955, BDF, Bd. 2, Nr. 216; Pinay to certain French missions, 10 June 1955, DDF 1955, t. I, no. 332; Küsters 1982, 119-27; Resolution of the Messina Conference, 2 June 1955, Documents on International Affairs 1955
22   Resolution of the Messina Conference, 2 June 1955, Documents of International Affairs 1955
23   Meeting Rotschild/Sprouse, 8 June 1955, NA/RG 59/LF 57D688, box 362; Sprouse to G. Smith, 9 June 1955, ibid.; Dillon to DOS (about talk with Sauvargnes), 10 June 1955, FRUS 1955-1957, Vol. IV, 293-5; Dillon to SecState (about meeting with E.Faure/Pinay/Gaillard), 14 July 1955, NA/RG 59/DF 840.1901, box 4403; Meeting Hall/Palmer/G. Smith et al., 15 July 1955, FRUS 1955-1957, Vol. IV, 315
24   L. Strauss to Eisenhower, 15 June 1955, DDEL/WHCF-Confid./Subj., box 7
25   Alger to SecState, 11 July 1955, NA/RG 59/DF 840.1901, box 4403

278   *Notes to pp. 114-85*

26   Schaetzel to Palmer, 8 August 1955, NA/RG59/LF 57D688, box 362
27   'Note de la délégation française', 18 July 1955, MAE/DE-CE, 599; Weilemann 1983, 37-8.
28   Memo 'Préparation des instructions pour la délégation française à la Conférence de Bruxelles, Comité interministeriel du 5 juillet 1955', MAE/DE-CE, 612; Memo 'Instructions pour la délégation', July 1955, BDF, Bd. 1, Nr. 179. Palewski, whose main objective was to protect the French national military option, admonished Pinay that the common financial effort in the proposed areas, which he regarded as desirable, should not in any circumstances be allowed to infringe on the national nuclear budget. If so, French independence would be compromised. Palewski to Pinay, 7 July 1955, MAE/SD
29   de Peyer to Edden, 27 July 1955, HAEC/JMDS 97
30   de Peyer to Edden, 3 August 1955, ibid.
31   'Note de la Délégation allemande', MAE/DE-CE, 599. According to Weilemann - who also studied the preparatory work in Germany - the memorandum was oriented toward supranationalism and the ECSC model, expressing the line of the *Auswärtiges Amt*. Weilemann 1983, 36-7
32   Above, 33
33   The attitude changed in 1958, after the entry into force of the Rome Treaties. Cf. Romero 1996.
34   Schröder 1994, 391-3; Neuss 2000, 286-9
35   Merchant to Dulles, 12 April 1955, FRUS 1955-1957, Vol. IV, 279; Schröder 1994, 394-5
36   Hanes to Merchant and Hollister (about meeting Dulles/Stassen), 9 June 1955, NA/RG59/LF 64D199, box 3
37   Dulles to R. Mayer, 8 June 1955, FRUS 1955-1957, Vol. IV, 292-3
38   Eisenberg to Palmer, 30 June 1955, FRUS 1955-1957, Vol. IV, 301-3
39   Merchant to Dulles, 1 July 1955, ibid., 304-5
40   G. Smith to Dulles, 1 July 1955, ibid., 306-7
41   Memo by Dulles, 5 July 1956, ibid., 309
42   The more ambitious type of agreement on cooperation about civil uses of atomic energy. The less ambitious type was 'research bilateral'.
43   Fuller to Bowie, 'Current Status of European Movement: Problem of US Policy', 18 August 1955, NA/RG 59/LF 66D70, box 96
44   Adenauer to Dulles, 7 and 11 May 1955, BA/N1351/416 (Blankenhorn)
45   14 June 1955. Editorial note (extracts from memo by Lyon), FRUS 1955-1957, Vol. IV, 297
46   Meeting Dulles/Erhard et al., 7 June 1955, FRUS 1955-1957, Vol. IV, 291-2
47   O'Shaughnessy to DOS (about talks with Ophüls and Harkort), 15 June 1955, NA/RG 59/DF 840.00, box 4386
48   Merchant to Dulles, 29 September 1955, NA/RG 59, LF 57D688, box 363
49   Meeting Dulles/von Brentano, 30 September 1955, FRUS 1955-1957, Vol. IV, 330 (Editorial Note); Memo by Boochever, 'Atomic Energy, von Brentano Discussions', 30 September 1955, NA/RG 59, LF 57D688, box 363
50   Sondersitzung 11 October 1955, KAB 1955, 564
51   Conant to SecState, 13 October 1955, NA/RG 59/DF 840.00, box 4386
52   Presumably a hint that parts of the fuel cycle relevant for nuclear weapons might be subjected to some European arrangement
53   Meeting Menne/Hall/Margolies et al., 12 October 1955, NA/RG 59/LF 57D688, box 409

54 Alger to DOS, 21 October 1955, FRUS1955-1957, IV, 332-4
55 Hoover to Amembassy, Bonn, 24 October 1955 (two telegrams), ibid., 335-7
56 Annexed to O'Shaughnessy to DOS, 8 November 1955, NA/RG 59/DF 840.1901, box 4403. The memorandum was distributed to the other five also. According to Conant, it created 'favourable stir' in the Spaak Committee although most representatives felt that it did not 'go far enough'. Conant to SecState, 17 November 1955, ibid.
57 Hoover (Acting Secretary)-Amembassy, Bonn, 9 November 1955, NA/RG 59/DF 840.1901, box 4403
58 Dillon to SecState, 11 November 1955 (3 telegrams), NA/RG 59/DF 840.1901, box 4403, and DF 611.5197, box 2509
59 Barnett to E. Martin, 26 October 1955, NA/RG 59/LF 57D688, box 363
60 E. Martin to Timmons, 10 November 1955, FRUS 1955-1957, Vol. IV, 346-8
61 Küsters 1982, 161-205
62 Weilemann 1983, 42
63 Rapport de la Commission de l'énergie nucléaire, 5 November, 1955, MAE/DE-CE, 599; Commission de l'énergie nucléaire, Sommaire des conclusions no. 4, 4 November 1955, ibid.; Note du Service de coopération économique, 14 November 1955, ibid., 612; Weilemann 1983, 42-7
64 Memo, n.s., Secrétariat Général, Coordination des questions atomiques, 21 December 1956, DDF 1956, t. III, no. 316
65 Meeting Spaak/von Brentano/Hallstein et al., 14 November 1955, AA-PA/B2, Bd. 106
66 Hoyer Millar to Macmillan, 21 November 1955, HAEC/JMDS 97
67 Meeting Hupperts/Vance/Chapin, 13 October 1955, NA/RG 59/DF 840.00, box 4386
68 See for example Camps 1963, 20-53; Kaiser 1996, 28-60; Ellison 2000, 13-36
69 A valuable exception is an article by Mervyn O'Driscoll (O'Driscoll 1998, Missing...)
70 O'Driscoll 1998, Missing..., 144-5, 150
71 Ibid. op.cit., 143-7, 149 (citation from PRO document)
72 FO to Jebb, 11 November 1955, HAEC/JMDS 98
73 FO to Britembassy, Washington, 15 November 1955, PRO/PREM 11, 2848
74 Makins to FO, 18 November 1955, PRO/PREM 11, 2848
75 'Extract from A.E. (O)(55)20th Meeting', 15 November 1955, PRO/AB 6/1654
76 The Vice Chairman of the Official Committee on Atomic Energy to Hancock with enclosed annex, 14 November 1955, HAEC/JMDS 97
77 Meeting Salisbury/Plowden/Spaak, et al. (memo by Strath), 18 November 1955, PRO/AB 6, 1654; Meeting Cockroft/Jebb, 22 November 1955 (memo by Strath), ibid. At a WEU ministerial meeting a month later, Spaak was very critical of British policy.
78 'Aide-mémoire', 22 December 1955, PRO/FO 371, 116057; O'Driscoll 1998, Missing..., 148
79 Meeting Makins/Merchant et al., 22 November 1955, FRUS 1955-1957, Vol. IV, 350-1
80 Meeting Makins/Merchant/Elbrick (memo by Elbrick), 22 December 1955, NA/RG 59/LF 57D688, box 363
81 O'Driscoll 1998, Missing..., 146, 148-9 (citations from PRO documents)
82 About the roots of Dulles' integration philosophy, see Görtemaker 1993
83 267th NSC meeting, 22 November 1955, DDEL/AWF/NSC, box 7 (Eisenhower's views are printed in FRUS 1955-1957, Vol. IV, 348-9, Editorial Note)

84   Dulles to Hoover, 22 November 1955, ibid., 349-50; 'Decision by the Secretary' (for Merchant), 25 November 1955, NA/RG 59/LF 57D688, box 363
85   40 instead of 6 kilogrammes
86   Memo by Schaetzel, 'Europe and Atomic Energy', 2 December 1955, NA/RG 59/LF 57D688, box 363
87   NSC 5507/2, 'Statement of Policy on Peaceful Uses of Atomic Energy', 12 March 1955, FRUS 1955-1957, Vol. XX, 46-55 (the citation, 51)
88   Memo by Farley 'Notes on Proposal for European Isotope Separation Plant' [enrichment plant], 28 November 1955 , NA/RG 59/LF 57D688, box 363
89   Memo by Barnett, 'Peaceful Uses of Atomic Energy and European Integration', 6 December 1955, FRUS 1955-1957, Vol. IV, 355-60
90   G. Smith to Merchant, 8 December 1955, ibid., 360-2
91   Dulles to Macmillan, 10 December 1955, FRUS 1955-1957, Vol. IV, 362-4. According to Acting Secretary Herbert Hoover Jr., the intention of Dulles' letter was to express the hope that, if the British could not associate themselves in the US efforts, they would agree at least 'not to impede' them. Hoover-L.Strauss, 12 December 1955, HAEC/JMDS 98
92   Dulles to DOS, 16 December 1955 (about meeting Dulles/Macmillan, 15 December), FRUS 1955-1957, Vol. IV, 370, n. 4; Minutes from meeting Dulles/Macmillan, PRO/FO 371/116057
93   Meeting Dulles/Bowie/Monnet, 17 December 1955, FRUS 1955-1957, Vol. IV, 367-8
94   Dulles to DOS (about meeting Dulles/Spaak et al.), 17 December 1955, FRUS 1955-1957, Vol. IV, 370-1
95   Dulles to DOS (about meeting Dulles/von Brentano), 17 December 1955, ibid., 372
96   Adenauer 1967, 99-103
97   Dulles to Eisenhower, 17 December 1955, FRUS 1955-1957, Vol IV, 369
98   Above, 60
99   Dulles to Amembassies in the Six, and London, 27 December 1955, NA/RG 59/ DF 840.00, box 4386
100   Dulles to L. Strauss (draft letter by Schaetzel), 5 December 1955, NA/RG 59/LF 57D688, box 363
101   Dulles to Eisenhower (draft letter by Barnett), 13 December 1955, ibid.
102   Meeting Merchant/Krekeler (memo by Merchant), 21 December 1955, ibid., box 409
103   Draft memo for Dulles (by Schaetzel), 21 December 1955, ibid.
104   Merchant to Dulles (draft letter), 29 December 1955, ibid.; Decision by the Secretary, 4 January 1956, ibid.
105   This was for example confirmed by the German Common Market negotiator, von der Groeben, who informed the Americans that agreements had been reached in the Spaak Committee on all points except Euratom and some aspects of agricultural integration. Amembassy, Bonn, to SecState, 30 December 1955, NA/RG 59/DF 840.00, box 4386
106   Adenauer to the members of the Government, 19 January 1956, BDF, Bd. 1, Nr. 180
107   Résolution et Déclaration commune du Comité d'Action pour les Etats-Unis d'Europe, 17-18 January 1956, La Documentation Française no. 0309, 21 January 1956; Gerbet 1983, 205-7
108   Above, 14-15

109 Wilkens, ed., 1999, Dokument 2

110 Ibid; 'Exposé de M. Jean Monnet à la première réunion du Comité d'action pour les Etats-Unis d'Europe', HAEC/JMDS 117, 16 January 1956 (Max Kohnstamm archives)

111 Above, 3

112 Achilles to SecState, 17 January 1956, NA/RG 59/DF 840.1901, box 4403

113 Cited in L'année politique 1956, 257. Mollet thus explicitly excluded common weapons but not French ones, he only depicted the latter as unrealizable in practice. As a member of the Action Committee, he seemed, we saw, to support the stronger 'Monnet concept'. - A French memorandum concludes that the national option was not excluded in Mollet's investiture speech: 'In this respect the Ministerial statement is less categoric [than that of the Action Committee]: it certainly proposes that the Community should be forbidden to undertake any military production, but it does not explicitly say that all its members should renounce it'. 'Note', JT/LV, 9 February 1956, IPMF/Energie atomique

114 Joyce to DOS, 'Meeting of Monnet Committee for United States of Europe and Reactions Thereto in France', 25 January 1956, NA/RG 59/DF 840.1901, box 4403

115 Monnet later informed Maurice Faure that the German Social-Democrats insisted on Euratom ownership of fuels, but, on the other hand, 'would be conciliatory as regards military applications of nuclear energy'. Telephone conversation Monnet/M. Faure, 26 May 1956, MAE/SD. - Monnet possibly meant that the German Social-Democrats would be conciliatory about the European option, not the national ones, because they saw it as a means of greater independence of the US.

116 Spaak's collaborator Rotschild however told the Americans that the Belgians considered that the loose formulation was a considerable improvement compared to Monnet's original proposal, which did not mention the Common Market. Sprouse to SecState, 20 January 1956, NA/RG 59/DF 840.1901, box 4403

117 Barnett at meeting Dulles/L. Strauss et al., 25 January 1956, FRUS 1955-1957, Vol. IV, 397

118 Cf. Van Helmont 1986, 61

119 Achilles to SecState, 13 January 1956, NA/RG 59/DF 840.1901, box 4403

120 Dulles to Amembassy, Paris, 17 January 1956, ibid.

121 Van Helmont 1986, 61

122 Joyce to DOS, 'Meeting of Monnet Committee for United States of Europe and Reactions Thereto in France', 25 January 1956, NA/RG 59/DF 840.1901, box 4403

123 Dowling to SecState, 24 January 1956, NA/RG 59/DF 840.1901, box 4403

124 Dowling to SecState, 25 January 1956, NA/RG 84/FSPO-O, box 67.

125 Dulles to Eisenhower, 9 January 1956, FRUS 1955-1957, Vol. IV, 388-9

126 Above, 137

127 11 January 1956, FRUS 1955-1957, Vol. IV, 389, n. 2.

128 Conference Eisenhower/L. Strauss/Dulles et al., 13 January 1956, DDEL/AWF/Diary, box 12

129 Merchant and G. Smith to Dulles, 24 January 1956, NA/RG 59/LF 57D688, box 363

130 Barnett to Merchant, 'State-AEC Study of Atomic Energy and European Integration', 16 January 1956, ibid.

131 Barnett to Merchant, 'Tactical Considerations: Atomic Energy and European Integration', 16 January 1956, ibid.
132 Above, 139
133 Meeting Dulles/L. Strauss et al., 25 January 1956, FRUS 1955-1957, Vol. IV, 390-9
134 Conant to Merchant, 10 February 1956, NA/RG 59/LF 57D688, box 363
135 Caccia to Jebb, 29 December 1955, PRO/FO 371, 116057
136 Draft policy brief for Eden talks, 'European Integration', January 1956, PRO/FO 371, 122022; Caccia to Hoyer Millar, 12 January 1956, PRO/FO 371, 116057
138 Allen to Caccia, 24 January 1956, PRO/FO 371, 122022.
139 Meeting Sergent/Ellis Rees/Vultee/Shearer, 19 January 1956, PRO/FO 371, 121949
140 Memo by Rodgers (about discussion with Dale), 'U.S. Policy Guidance on European Integration', 1 February 1956, PRO/FO 371, 122022
141 Aldrich to DOS, 24 January 1956, FRUS 1955-1957, Vol. XXVII, 615-6
142 Dulles at meeting Dulles/L. Strauss et al., 25 January 1956, FRUS 1955-1957, Vol. IV, 395
143 Buchanan to SecState, 22 January 1956, NA/RG 59/DF 840.00, box 4386
144 Eisenhower/Dulles, Telephone calls, February 1, 1956, DDEL/AWF/Diary, box 12
145 Eisenhower Diary, 8 February 1956, FRUS 1955-1957, Vol. XXVII, 653-4
146 Meeting Dulles/Eden/Hoover/Lloyd et al., 30 January 1956, ibid., 620
147 Memo by Edden, 'O.E.E.C. and Euratom', 8 February 1956, PRO/FO 371, 121950
148 Kane 1997, 88-90
149 Couve de Murville to Pineau (about talks with Merchant and Cleveland), 4 February 1956, DDF 1956, t. I, no. 74
150 Meeting Conant/von Brentano, 9 February 1956, AA-PA/B 1, Bd. 155
151 Hoover to DOS (about meeting Hoover/Conant/von Brentano), 14 February 1956, NA/RG 59, LF 57D688, box 363
152 Barnes to R. Wilson, 22 February 1956, PRO/FO 371, 121951
153 Meeting Hoyer Millar/F.-J. Strauss, 8 February 1956, PRO/FO 371, 121950
154 Memo by Edden, 'O.E.E.C. and Euratom', 8 February 1956, PRO/FO 371, 121950
155 Extract from A.E. (O)(56)1st meeting, 15 February 1956, PRO/AB 6, 1654
156 Above, 133. Memo by Makins, 'Record of Conversation' (with Merchant), 6 February 1956, PRO/FO 371, 121950
157 Meeting Makins/Merchant et al., 21 February 1956, PRO/FO 371, 121951 (the citations); Meeting Makins/Merchant et al., 'Atomic Energy and European Cooperation: OEEC Ministers Meeting', 21 February 1956, NA/RG 59/ DF 840.1901, box 4403
158 Below,189-92
159 The (non-committal) position had been that if the military/security problems could be surmounted, Britain might participate by contributing know-how on a commercial basis, and would not rule out the possibility of participating in a joint venture and taking some of the product. FO to Britembassy, Washington, 25 February 1956, PRO/FO 371, 121951
160 Makins to FO, 22 February 1956, ibid.
161 Below, 167-8

162 Meeting Dulles/L.Strauss/Loper/Stassen et al., 3 February 1956, FRUS 1955-1957, Vol. XX, 307-11. Cf. also Hewlett-Holl 1989, 321-5.

163 The matter had been discussed with the President the day before. Eisenhower said he would be willing to have the fissionable material held outside the US 'under international control'. Strauss said 'that it could be so diluted that to remove it would be a major operation'. Dulles stated that 'the cessation of the production of fissionable material, except for peaceful purposes, could be made into something worthwhile' and 'fully approved' the project of sending 20,000 kgs. abroad. Meeting Eisenhower/Dulles/L. Strauss, 6 February 1956, ML/JFD/WH, box 4

164 275ᵗʰ NSC meeting, 7 February 1956, FRUS 1955-1957, Vol. XX, 319-28

165 The document appears not to be entirely declassified, at least not in the National Archives. In my copy large parts are deleted.

166 Memo by Merchant and G. Smith (drafted by Palmer) for Dulles, 'European Atomic Problems', 21 February 1956, NA/RG 59/DF 840.1901, box 4403

167 Dillon to DOS, 3 February 1956, FRUS 1955-1957, Vol. IV, 401-2

168 The distinction resurged later in Spaak's proposal in the matter, the 'Spaak Compromise'. Below 173-4.

169 Dillon to SecState, 4 February 1956, NA/RG 59/DF 840.1901, box 4403

170 Luce to DOS (Luce met Monnet at Dillon's home), 4 February 1956, FRUS 1955-1957, Vol. IV, 402-3; Dillon to DOS, 6 February 1956, NA/RG 59/DF 840.1901, box 4403 (partly printed in FRUS 1955-1957, Vol. IV, 403, n. 3)

171 Dillon to SecState, 6 February 1956, NA/RG 59/DF 840.1901, box 4403

172 Memo by Dulles (about meeting Dulles/L.Strauss/R. Mayer/Couve de Murville), 6 February 1956, FRUS 1955-1957, Vol. IV, 406-7. - Duchêne's interpretation is: 'Given the very low risk of disarmament, Dulles in effect told the French that the United States would not make a fuss about the Bomb. For anyone inclined to go ahead, this was virtually a green light' (Duchêne 1994, 296). - This could be so, but other interpretations are certainly possible. Dulles may have hoped for another outcome than French national nuclear weapons, if the decision could be postponed. This is indicated for instance by the NSC discussion the day after the Mayer meeting. Discussions about sharing US weapons with Allies in a NATO context were going on. Further, the moratorium which Dulles had in mind was no doubt of a supranational kind, like that proposed later in the 'Spaak Compromise' (below, 173-4). Such a moratorium was not the same thing as a green light. - Weilemann writes that Spaak had already brought the moratorium idea into the debate at the Brussels Conference in February (Weilemann 1983, 105).

173 Krekeler to AA, 10 February 1956, AA-PA/B1, Bd. 48

174 Before going to Brussels Pineau had told the Board of his Party that he would defend the line 'Euratom first-Common Market later' in Brussels because there was otherwise a risk that everything would be rejected by the French Parliament. He had also said that the powers of Euratom must be limited to control and not extend to production, and that nuclear energy must be restricted to peaceful uses. He had added, however, the crucial reservation that if the French example were not followed 'we reserve our rights as regards other uses'. OURS/CD, 6 February 1956.

175 Mollet's Chef de Cabinet, Emile Noël, judged retrospectively: 'It had been Jean Monnet's wish that France (and the other five countries) should go further

and collectively renounce all military use of atomic energy. Guy Mollet had taken up this idea in his statement on appointment [as Prime Minister] and his Foreign Minister, Christian Pineau, had raised the question at the first meeting of the Six Ministers of Foreign Affairs in which he took part (February 1956). He reported immediately thereafter to Guy Mollet and the other Socialist Ministers at their weekly meeting on Tuesday evening. None of the other Five Ministers had supported such a formulation, the general view being that it was not wise to make a unilateral concession of that kind; it smacked of a gratuitous gesture from which the Soviet Union would derive advantage in the negotiations on general disarmament, without having made any concession in return. The continuation of defence research in the *Commissariat àl'énergie atomique* (which Guy Mollet was to confirm publicly during the debate in the National Assembly at the beginning of July 1956) was the outcome of the negative conclusion of this discussion among the Six'. Noël 1989, 375

176   Projet de procès-verbal de la Conférence des Ministres des Affaires Etrangères des Etats members de la C.E.C.A, Brussels, 11-12 February 1956, MAE/DE-CE 610; Rivière to Pineau, 6 February 1956, DDF 1956, t. I, no. 80.; Küsters 1982, 232-6; Weilemann 1983, 68, 76-80

177   Statement issued by the President, 22 February 1956; Statement issued by the Chairman of the U.S. Atomic Energy Commission, 22 February 1956, American Foreign Policy: Basic Documents, 1956, Docs. 362-3. Before publication Strauss assured the President that the allocation would not interfere with the plans for military uses up to 1965. L. Strauss to Eisenhower, 20 February 1956, DDEL/ AWF/Adm., box 4

178   Monnet's collaborator, Max Kohnstamm, at meeting with the Executive Committee of the Action Committee, 25 July 1956, HAEC/JMDS 118

179   Dulles to Amembassy, Paris (and other missions), 29 February 1956, NA/RG 59/DF 840.1901, box 4403

180   Britembassy, Washington, to Plowden, 23 February 1956, PRO/FO 371, 121951

181   Eisenhower to L. Strauss, n.d., DDEL/Jackson, box 69

182   FO to Britembassy, Washington, 25 February 1956, PRO/FO 371, 121951

184   L. Strauss to Dulles, 13 April 1956, with annex 'Action in the Field of Atomic Energy to Encourage Integration of the Community of the Six', FRUS 1955-1957, Vol. IV, 423-9

185   Rapport des chefs de délégation aux ministres des affaires étrangères, 21 April 1956, MAE/DE-CE, 600. The version in German language is published in Schwarz, ed., 1980, Nr. 33. There were also some proposals concerning other sectors than atomic energy, for example the air communication sector; these are disregarded here.

186   For a detailed account of the Common Market provisions, cf. Küsters 1982, 239-51

187   They all had something to do with the nuclear weapons options. Mendès France's adviser, George Boris, wrote that the only really important thing about Euratom was the military question: '...the more one re-reads the papers on Euratom, the more one comes back to the conclusion that the only question of major importance is that of the renunciation of military uses. The rest always puts you in mind of the mountain and the mouse'. He added that the supply monopoly in Euratom's fuel system had no longer any meaning except to control military manufacture, because henceforth the risk of scarcity of uranium had disappeared completely. Boris to Mendès France, 21 April 1956, IPMF/Energie atomique

188 Sprouse to DOS, 18 May 1956, NA/RG 59/DF 840.00, box 43, 86
189 Spaak Report, Part 2, Ch. 6
190 Cf. a *Quai d'Orsay* analysis: 'Through its monopoly of supply Euratom also offers certain guarantees against the danger that Germany might exploit its industrial power to develop its nuclear power outside the circle of its European neighbours, that is to say in direct association with the USA. It should provide an assurance that the development of nuclear energy would not become a simple reflection or auxiliary of the American programmes. In that case France, which declines to renounce the production of nuclear weapons would be left to its own devices. Our programme could be carried out but it might one day be overtaken both qualitatively and quantitatively by that of our neighbours. And the European idea would lose one of the pillars on which it might be based, to the advantage of American influence in the affairs of our continent'. 'Note pour le Secrétaire Général', Secrétariat général, Coordination des questions atomiques, 21 December 1956, MAE/SD
191 According to an interpretation - correct or not - of the expression 'the resources not committed' by Mendès France's collaborator Boris, the expression referred exclusively to the Congolese uranium which Belgium would deliver to the US and the UK. Boris to Mendès France, 21 April 1956, IPMF/Energie atomique.
192 The reactor complex under construction in the Rhône valley
193 Meeting M. Faure/Nutting et al., 15 June 1956, PRO/FO 371/122028 (above, 189-92). Similar assurances - although less frankly expressed - were given by Mollet and Pineau in the debate on Euratom in the National Assembly in July (below, 193-4)
194 The definition of one of the cases is apparently a supranational restriction on manufacture of nuclear weapons: '[The organisation] would employ a leasing contract...for products such as fuels that are highly enriched or particularly dangerous for any other reason, by decision of the Commission; such a decision, adopted for reasons of security, with the agreement of the Council and subject to the Court, should apply in regard to all users, without discrimination.' Spaak Report, Part 2, Ch. 4.
195 Spaak Report, Part 2, Introduction and Ch. 2
196 Ibid., Part 2, Ch. 3
197 G. Smith to Dulles, 27 April 1956 (not sent), NA/RG 59/LF 57D688, box 363 (the citation); G. Smith to Bowie, 1 May 1956, ibid.
198 Spaak to von Brentano, 26 April 1956, AA-PA/B 22, Bd. 22. The sentence cited is from an English translation in Butterworth to SecState, 6 May 1956, NA/RG 59/DF 840.1901, box 4404
199 Memo by Hädrich, 'Aufzeichnung', 28 April 1956, AA-PA/B 22, Bd. 19
201 G. Smith and Elbrick to Dulles, 11 May 1956, NA/RG 59/LF 57D688, box 409; Schaetzel to G. Smith, 11 May 1956, ibid.
202 Hoover later wrote that the Americans had stressed the political disadvantages from a German viewpoint of being tagged with the responsibility for the failure of Euratom by insisting on a formal link with the Common Market, or by attaching other conditions. Hoover to Amembassy, Bonn, 28 May 1956, NA/RG 84/FSPO-O, box 67
203 Meeting Elbrick/F.-J. Strauss et al., 14 May 1956, FRUS 1955-1957, Vol. IV, 435-8; Meeting Dulles/F.-J. Strauss et al., 14 May 1956, ibid., 438-41
204 Hoover to Amembassy, Bonn, 28 May 1956, NA/RG 84/FSPO-O, box 67
205 G. Smith to Robinson, 15 May 1956, NA/RG 59/LF 57D688, box 363

206   DOS to Amembassy, Bonn, 18 May 1956, ibid.
207   Telephone conversation Monnet/M. Faure, 26 May 1956, MAE/SD
208   Meeting Monnet/L.Strauss/Robinson, 28 April 1956, FRUS 1955-1957, Vol. IV, 432-3
209   Meeting Armand/Schaetzel/Boochever/Hall et al., 7 May 1956, NA/RG 59/LF 57D688, box 363
210   Dulles wrote that Eisenhower had turned to a telegram 'purporting to recount a conversation which I had with Mollet and in which I was reported as saying that we should not be saying anything about the integration of Europe unless Mollet asked for it. I said this was not correct and that there must have been some misunderstanding. I had said to Mollet, as reported, that he should feel free to let the President or me know if any particular action on our part would be helpful. I had not said the reverse, namely, that we would not say anything unless it were helpful'. Memo by Dulles, 7 May 1956, ML/JFD/WH , box 4
211   Dulles to US missions in the Six and at the ECSC, 24 May 1956, FRUS 1955-1957, Vol. IV, 442-4. The parts that were not marked as FYI ['for your information'] appear to have been handed over to at least some of the governments. Cf. a French version, 'Principaux extraits du mémorandum américain du 25 Mai 1956 sur la position du Gouvernement des E.U. vis-à-vis de l'Euratom', MAE/SD. In French literature the document has sometimes been referred to as the 'US memorandum' (for example in Goldschmidt 1980, 150-1, 308-10).
212   Below, 189-92
213   Sprouse to Dulles, 25 May 1956, NA/RG 84/FSPF-O, box 67
214   Dulles to Spaak, 24 May 1956, FRUS 1955-1957, Vol. IV, 445
215   Amembassy, Brussels, to DOS, 25 May 1956, ibid., 445-6, n. 4 (the citation); Dillon to Dulles, 25 May 1956, NA/RG 84/FSPO-O, box 67. In July, the US-Belgian agreement was amended to allow a transfer of the rights and obligations of Belgium to an integrated group, if Belgium so requested, and the integrated group, in the judgement of the US, could 'effectively and securely carry out the undertakings'. Helmreich 1990, 65, and 1991, 403.
216   Dillon to SecState, 22 May 1956, NA/RG 59/DF 840.1901, box 4404
217   Dillon to SecState, 28 May 1956, ibid.
218   Conant to SecState (about talk with Müller-Roschach), 24 May 1956, ibid.
219   Conant to SecState, 26 May 1956, ibid. Industry's spokesman, Berg, had empasized the importance of the *Junktim* to Adenauer after the appearance of the Spaak report: 'As hitherto, German industry holds unconditionally to a *Junktim* between Euratom and the Common Market'. Berg to Adenauer, 9 May 1955, AA-PA/B 22, Bd. 22
220   See also German preparations before the conference, memo by Müller-Roschach 'Aufzeichnung, Betr.: Ressortbesprechung auf der Ebene der Abteilungsleiter und Staatssekretäre am 18. Mai, 1956', BA/N1337 (Carstens), Bd. 642
221   Gerrity to SecState, 31 May 1956, NA/RG 84/FSPO-O, box 67
222   Projet de procès-verbal de la Conférence des Ministres des Affaires Etrangères des Etats members de la C.E.C.A, Venice, 29-30 May 1956, and Communiqué de presse, MAE/DE-CE, 610; Wilkens 1999, 192
223   Gerrity to SecState, 31 May 1956, NA/RG 84/FSPO-O, box 67
224   From the German point of view sharing of information with military implications was also essential

5 Euratom and the Linkage to the Common Market: Second Phase

1 Memo by Müller-Roschach, 'Aufzeichnung, Betr.: Besuch des Herrn Bundeskanzlers in den USA; Gesprächsthema: Deutsche Haltung bei der Fortführung der Europäischen Integration', 31 May 1956, AA-PA/B 32, Bd. 22 (the citation); Memo by Ophüls, 'Betr.: Euratom und Gemeinsamer Markt in den Gesprächen des Herrn Bundeskanzlers in Amerika', 2 June 1956, ibid.

2 Meeting Dulles/Adenauer et al., 12 June 1956, FRUS 1955-1957, Vol. XXVI, 107-20 (the citations 118-19, 108); Position paper 'European Integration and Euratom (To be raised by the Secretary)' n.s., n.d., NA/RG 59/LF 62D181, box 107. - The Saar problem remained a factor that was always present as a piece in the European jig-saw puzzle, although it was not directly discussed at the Brussels negotiations. The referendum in the Saar in October 1955 had rejected the European statute that had been agreed between Adenauer and Mendès-France at Celle St. Cloud in the autumn of 1954. After the referendum it had been evident that the Saar would become German; the issue at stake was economic compensation for France. Loth 1991, 126. - Adenauer's remark about a price may of course have referred to many things, perhaps to the investments in French overseas areas that had been demanded in Venice.

3 Meeting Dulles/Adenauer et al. (among them L. Strauss and Hallstein), 12 June 1956, FRUS 1955-1957, Vol. XXVI, 121

4 On this point, Pineau gave the rather far-fetched example of a tunnel under the English Channel. Was he thinking of the enrichment plant?

5 Meeting Dulles/Pineau et al., 18-19 June 1955, FRUS 1955-1957, Vol. XXVII, 64-5; DDF 1956, t. I, no. 417

6 In the French minutes ownership was included. The formulation was 'at the same time ownership of fissile materials and the control of their use'.

7 This is only in the US minutes

8 This is only in the French minutes

9 In the French minutes: 'The reply given to Mr. Adenauer was that the question was not a problem of property law, but of control. Control was best exercised through ownership of fissile materials; it was only in its absence that recourse to the control of use would be necessary'.

10 Meeting Dulles/Pineau et al., 18-19 June 1955, FRUS 1955-1957, Vol. XXVII, 73-5; DDF 1956, t. I, no. 417

11 FO meeting (Caccia/Plowden/Edden et al.), 13 June 1956, PRO/FO 371/121959; Memo by Nutting, 15 June 1956, FO 371/121959 (the citation). - The FO meeting added a complication. The British had prematurely promised that British civil plutonium would also be included in the OEEC control system: 'We have undertaken in O.E.E.C. to accept control of our own purely civil atomic energy projects as part of a general O.E.E.C. control system. When this decision was made it was thought that highly irradiated plutonium could be used for civil purposes and that U.235 was better for our nuclear weapons. Our scientists now believe that the use of highly irradiated plutonium as a fuel element will be more difficult than they had thought. They think on the other hand that it might be in demand for weapons. If the new assessment was correct we might wish to withdraw our offer since it would disclose the amount of highly irradiated plutonium going from our civil power reactors into our defence programme'.

12 There was first a lunch meeting of a more general and informal character in which Selwyn Lloyd participated. It can be mentioned that Faure then asked for

Lloyd's view of the possibility of developing the WEU; Lloyd 'suggested that the most effective means of achieving this would be to press on with its activities in connection with arms control'. Lloyd to Jebb, 19 June 1956, FO 371/1220228

13   Below, 192-3

14   Faure had already broached the subject of the moratorium with Nutting on the way in from the airport and Nutting had answered that any kind of moratorium would be unacceptable to the United Kingdom.

15   'Tied programmes', and so on, in the Spaak Report. Above, 171

16   Meeting Nutting/Hope/Caccia/Faure/Marjolin, 15 June 1956, PRO/FO 371/1122028; Memo by Nutting, 15 June 1956, FO 371/121959; Memo by Nutting, 15 June 1956, FO 371/121959

17   Jebb to Nutting, 23 June 1956, FO371/122029

18   Memo 'United Kingdom Contribution to the O.E.E.C. Scheme', n.s., n.d.. PRO/FO 371/121963

19   The italics are in the source, thus emphasizing that all kinds of preparations, except actual manufacture, would be permitted during the moratorium

20   Meeting M. Faure/Marjolin/general Lavaud/colonel Buchalet et al., 25 June 1956, DDF 1956, t. I, no. 430

21   Meeting M. Faure/Spaak, 26 June 1956, DDF 1956, t. I, no. 432

22   That is, the concept of 'tied programmes', and so on.

23   That is, the planned submarine reactors

24   Journal Officiel, AN, 3313-17 (Pineau, 6 July 1956); 3382-85, 3388 (Mollet, 11 July 1956)

25   Above, 181-2

26   Memo 'Etat des négociations de Bruxelles', n.s., 24 July 1956, MAE/SD

27   G. Smith/Elbrick to Bowie, 5 September 1956, NA/RG 59/LF 57D688, box 364.

28   Barnett to Schaetzel, 10 September 1956, ibid. Cf. above 139

29   G. Smith/Elbrick to Dulles, 'A new U.S. Approach to Euratom' (with 2 annexes), 25 September 1956, ibid.

30   One of its leaders, Herbert Wehner, who was also a member of the Action Committee, stated retrospectively that the objectives of the Action Committee had been 'indisputably blocked' on an essential point by Mollet's decision [not to restrict the French option]. Monnet however succeeded in preventing the Committee from breaking up. Wilkens 1999, 194

31   Meeting of the Executive Committee of the Action Committee for the United States of Europe, 25 July 1956, HAEC/JMDS 118

32   'Action Committee for the United States of Europe, Third Session, Meetings of 19 and 20 September 1956, Paris, (translation from French)', HAEC/JMAS 83

33   Below, 244-7

34   On the 'Grand Design', see Kaiser 1996, 61-87; Ellison 2000, 37-98

35   Meeting Dulles/Timmons/Sergent, 26 September 1956, FRUS 1955-1957, Vol. IV, 464-6

36   For example Hogerton to Payne, 'Review of Problems of U.S. Representation in Nuclear Energy Activities of OEEC', 20 September 1956, NA/RG 59/DF 840.1901, box 4404

37   Meyers to DOS, 2 October 1956, ibid.

38   It seems that Mollet did not tell the Germans about this proposal when meeting von Brentano in Paris few days afterwards. Meeting von Brentano/von Maltzan/Mollet, 14 September 1956, AA-PA/B1, Bd. 155

39   Kane 1997, 90; GEN 511/2, 27 September 1956, PRO/PREM 11, 1352

40 Meeting Eden/Mollet, 'European Problems', 27 September 1956, PRO/PREM 11, 1352
41 Kane 1997, 90-4
42 Cf. for example Grabbe 1990; Wampler 1993; Schwarz 1991, 291-5; Adenauer 1967, 197-214
43 Pitman 2000, Un Général..., 52
44 Heuser 1998, 86, n. 52 (referring to an article in Stuttgarter Nachrichten of 4 August1956)
45 Schwarz 1991, 296-8; Conant to SecState, 26 and 27 September 1956, HAEC/ JMDS 98
46 Matthews to SecState (about talk with van der Beugel), 20 September 1956, NA/ RG 59/DF 840.00, box 4387
47 Wilkens 1999, 194-5. Adenauer´s thinking about Euratom as a means of acquiring nuclear weapons (below, 204) may wholly or partly explain his transitory propensity to accommodate to Monnet on this crucial point
48 de Margerie (on behalf of M. Faure) to Pineau, 17 September 1956, DDF 1956, t. II, no. 185
49 Meeting Erhard/M. Faure, 16 September 1956, BDF, Bd. 2, Nr. 227
50 Meeting M. Faure/von Brentano/Hallstein, 17 September 1956, DDF 1956, t. II, no. 188 and 'Aufzeichnung', AA-PA/B1, Bd. 155. Faure met Adenauer also. The themes were general. The risks of military abandonment of Europe by the US and Britain were discussed. Adenauer expressed his concerns about the Radford Plan and the necessity of increased military cooperation between the European states. Meeting Faure/Adenauer/Hallstein, 17 September 1956, DDF 1956, t. II, no. 188
51 The earlier memorandum, of 28 April, had proposed various kinds of military cooperation, particularly extensive industrial cooperation, in order to reduce costs. French diplomats had then brought the subject to discussion at an economic meeting in May. The Germans had been totally negative and had referred to NATO and the WEU. Soutou 1996, 47-8
52 Memo, 25 September 1956, BDF, Bd. 1, Nr. 214.
53 See next note
54 Meeting Adenauer/Mollet (and von Brentano/Erhard/Hallstein/F.-J. Strauss/ Pineau/M. Faure/Couve de Murville et al.), 29 September 1956, AA-PA/B1, Bd. 155 (extract also in BDF, Bd. 2, Nr. 231); 'Kurzprotokoll', 1 October 1956, BA/N1337/643 (Carstens); Pineau to French missions, DDF 1956, t. II, no. 235, Communiqué, Documents on International Affairs 1956, 699-700; Pitman 2000, Un Général..., 56-7. Pineau´s circular telegram observed that the discussions about the Saar and other matters had taken so much time that concrete European problems had been referred to the next meeting planned between Adenauer and Mollet.
55 McBride to DOS, 28 September 1956, NA/RG 59/DF840.00, box 4387
56 Alger to SecState, 29 September 1956, NA/RG 59/DF 840.1901, box 4404
57 Elbrick and Farley to Dulles, 26 September 1956, FRUS 1955-1957, Vol. IV, 466-7; Memo for Murphy, 'German Position on Euratom' (drafted by Cleveland), 28 September 1956, NA/RG 59/DF 840.1901, box 4404
58 Dulles to Conant, 30 September 1956, FRUS 1955-1957, Vol. IV, 467-8. Dulles´ message was reinforced in a personal talk between Murphy and Adenauer in Bonn. Adenauer made no commitments, but simply asked Murphy to discuss the question with F.-J. Strauss. Gufler (from Murphy) to DOS, 4 October 1956, FRUS 1955-1957, Vol. IV, 468, n. 3, 472-3.

59   Conant to SecState, 17 October 1956, NA/RG 59/DF 840.1901, box 4404. See also FRUS 1955-1957, Vol. IV, 468, n. 3.
60   Kabinettssitzung 3 October 1956, KAB 1956, 609-12
61   As has been pointed out by Trachtenberg, Hans-Peter Schwarz was the first to challenge the dominant view that Adenauer's position in favour of Euratom was due to his wish to establish the Common Market at any price. My view is that Schwarz is basically right. However, Schwarz states that it is evident that Adenauer at the Cabinet meeting was thinking of a German option, not of European nuclear weapons. (Schwarz 1991, 299). This is, I think, questionable, even if Adenauer used the expression 'himself' [selbst]. He may as well have been thinking of a European (Franco-German) option. Adenauer was generally in favour of *Einbindung* to guard against possible dangerous nationalistic developments in Germany. Another aspect in the interpretation of the confidences at this meeting is the tactical-domestic one. Adenauer's visions would obviously be welcomed by Strauss, in particular, and would perhaps be an argument for Erhard also, thus making it easier for Adenauer to get acceptance for the Euratom-Common Market package by his foremost opponents.
62   Kabinettssitzung 5 October 1956, KAB 1956, 620-9
63   Conant to SecState, 4 October 1956, NA/RG 59/DF 840.1901, box 4404; Cleveland to Timmons, 5 October 1956, ibid. The conversation with Hartlieb took place on 3 October, the day of the German Cabinet's session on integration.
64   Farley and Beam to Dulles (drafted by Schaetzel, concurrence of PPS), 16 October 1956, NA/RG 59/LF 57D688
65   Conant to SecState, 17 October 1956, NA/RG 59/DF 840.1901, box 4404; Dulles to Amembassy, Bonn, 23 October 1956, ibid.
66   Alger to SecState, 24 October 1956, NA/RG 59/DF 840.00, box 4387; Dillon to SecState, 24 October 1956, ibid.
67   'Sui generis' which had been proposed as a compromise formula in the Spaak Report was a legal notion applicable to certain juridical relations not forming part of a well defined category. It meant that both Euratom and the users would have ownership rights over the fuels.
69   Projet de procès-verbal de la Conférence des Ministres des Affaires Etrangères des Etats members de la C.E.C.A., Paris, 20-21 October 1956, MAE/DE-CE 610; Carstens to Hallstein, 22 October 1956, BDF, Bd. 1, Nr. 187
70   Kabinettssitzung 24 October 1956, KAB 1956, 656-65. Strauss' standpoint was formulated in private notes by Seebohm.
71   Enders 1997, 159-60
72   Pineau to Couve de Murville, 31 October 1956, DDF 1956, t. III, no. 75
73   Cf. below, 231-2
74   Memo 'Note pour le président du Conseil en vue des entretiens prévus au cours de la visite à Paris du chancelier Adenauer', n.s., 3 November 1956, DDF 1956, t. III, no. 123
75   de Murville to Pineau, 3 November 1956, ibid., no. 104
76   Butterworth to SecState, 28 October 1956, NA/RG 59/DF 840.00, box 4387
77   Dillon to SecState, 24 October 1956, ibid.
78   Dillon to SecState, 26 October 1956, ibid.
79   Trimble to SecState, 25 October 1956, ibid.
80   Conant to SecState, 27 October 1956, ibid.
81   Alger to SecState (about talk with Snoy), 24 October 1956, NA/RG 59/DF 840.00, box 4387
82   Dillon to SecState, 25 October 1956, ibid.

83 Dillon to SecState (from Goldenberg about talk with van Helmont), 24 October 1956, NA/RG 59/DF 840. 1901, box 4404
84 Conant was originally a scientist and he had worked on the war-time atomic bomb project
85 Butterworth to SecState, 26 October 1956, FRUS 1955-1957, Vol. IV, 478-9
86 Elbrick and Farley to Dulles, 26 October 1956, NA/RG 59/DF 840.1901, box 4404. *Ex post* - after the Adenauer/Mollet meeting - Butterworth pointed to another explanation. He reported that he had been informed that the German splitting of the conference on social harmonization was Erhard's tactic for dropping the Common Market altogether: '...following his disruptive tactics at St Cloud [Paris] conference Erhard advocated abandonment of common market project and submitted to Adenauer 40 (sic) page memorandum which my informant, (not Etzel) who saw it, described as designed to sabotage common market and substitute a loose, limited free trade area. The real motive behind this manoeuver was revealed to Chancellor at Cabinet sub-committee meeting presided over by him and attended among others by Erhard and Etzel. In course of heated discussion, Erhard stated that harmonization of 40-hour week was insignificant problem. Asked by Etzel why in that case German delegation permitted disruption of St Cloud conference on this issue, Erhard revealed that his real purpose was for Germany to have a free hand and to be able to go it alone and in this connection he referred to the developments within satellites vis-a-vis USSR. It therefore became clear to Chancellor that his basic European policy was in this wise being challenged, and he was accordingly prepared to act decisively'. Butterworth to SecState, 9 November 1956, ibid.
87 Dulles to Amembassy, Bonn, 27 October 1956, NA/RG 59/DF 840.00, box 4387
88 Elbrick to Dulles, 26 October 1956, NA/RG 59/DF 840.1901, box 4404
89 Cleveland to Sprouse, 23 November 1956, FRUS 1955-1957, Vol. IV, 486, n. 4
90 Above, 202
91 Conant to SecState, 30 October 1956, FRUS 1955-1957, Vol. IV, 480-1. It may be remarked that 'government ownership' is not the same thing as 'Euratom ownership'. The former is national, the latter supranational. Perhaps Adenauer was using 'constructive ambiguity'.
92 Dulles to Amembassy, Bonn, 2 November 1956, NA/RG 59/DF 840.1901, box 4404, partly printed in FRUS 1955-1957, Vol. IV, 480, n. 4
93 Conant to SecState, 5 November 1956, NA/RG 59//DF 840.1901, box 4404; Memo by Weber, 'Aufzeichnung', 5 November 1956, AA/-PA/B1, Bd. 156.
94 Conant to SecState, 3 November 1956, NA/RG 59/DF 840.1901, box 4404. Cf. also Conant to SecState (about talk with von der Groeben), 6 November 1956, ibid.
95 Meeting Farley/Schaetzel/J. Martin, 24 September 1956, NA/RG 59/LF 57D688, box 406; AEC meeting No. 1230, 28 September 1956, NA/RG 326/AEC, Vols. 17-18, box 9
96 Meeting Ortona/Wesly/Torbert, 23 October 1956, NA/RG 59/LF 57D688, box 364
97 Butterworth to SecState (about talk with Monnet), 28 October 1956, NA/RG 59/DF 840.00, box 4387
98 Dulles to Amembassy, Bonn, 23 October 1956, NA/RG 59/DF 840.1901, box 4404; Dulles to Amembassy, Paris, 23 October 1956, NA/RG 59/LF 57D688, box 364
99 Dulles to Amembassy, Bonn, 1 November 1956, NA/RG 59/DF 840.1901, box 4404

100   Kabinettssitzung 7 November 1956, KAB 1956, 693-4
101   Carstens 1976, 598-601; Carstens 1993, 204-9; Grewe 1979, 288; Pineau-Rimbaud 1991, 219-23
102   Meeting Adenauer/Mollet, 6 November 1956, DDF 1956, t. III, no. 138 (these minutes contain only the discussion on the international situation)
103   According to one source Spaak had told Chaban-Delmas that he had suggested to Mollet before the Adenauer/Mollet meeting that France might be given an escape clause, the right to withdraw from the Common Market after the first stage, but Mollet had refused to take this into consideration. Bousquet to MAE, 1 February 1957, MAE/SD
104   The Americans were informed that the period in question was four years although it had not been put in writing. Meeting Percival/Sachs, 11 November 1956, NA/RG 59/LF 57D688, box 364; Meeting Pauls/Lisle, 11 November 1956, ibid.
105   Memo by Illig, ´Aufzeichnung´, 9 November 1956, AA-PA/B1, Bd. 156;
106   Above, 214
107   Mollet to Adenauer, 13 November 1956, DDF 1956, t. III, no. 165. German Euratom sceptics were worried about the demand. Strauss´successor as Minister for Atomic Affairs, Balke, emphasized to Adenauer that he had not got information about Mollet´s demand until 29 November, and that the demand was incompatible with the draft for a German atomic energy law. Balke to Adenauer, 12 December 1956, BDF, Bd. 2, Nr. 240.
108   The Italian who was appointed later was Francesco Giordani. Spaak apparently declined the offer.
109   Memo by Illig, ´Aufzeichnung´, 9 November 1956, AA-PA/B 1, Bd. 156
110   Arbeitsgruppe deutscher und französischer Sachverständiger zu EURATOM und dem Gemeinsamen Markt, Aufzeichnung 6 November 1956, BDF, Bd. 1, no. 188; Pineau to certain French missions, 8 November 1956, DDF 1956, t. III, no. 146; Memo by Carstens, ´Aufzeichnung´, 8 November 1956; AA-PA/Abt. 2-B22, Bd. 23; Memo by Illig, ´Aufzeichnung´, 9 November 1956, AA-PA/B1, Bd. 156; Conférence de Bruxelles, Réunion des chefs de délégations du 16 novembre 1956, MAE/DE-CE 618. Cf. also Küsters 1982, 324-32; Weilemann 1983, 130-2; Carstens 1976, 599-600; 1993, 206-9; Grewe 1979, 281-91; Fischer 1992, Das Projekt...147
111   Memo by Carstens, ´Aufzeichnung´, 8 November 1956; AA-PA/B22, Bd. 23; Memo by Illig, ´Aufzeichnung´, 9 November 1956, AA-PA/B1, Bd. 156
112   Couve de Murville to Pineau, 9 November 1956, DDF 1956, t. III, no. 149. About the Franco-German agreement with nuclear components at Colomb-Béchar two months later, cf. below, 223-5
113   Dillon to SecState (about talk with Marjolin), 8 November 1956, NA/RG 59/DF 840.1901, box 4404; Meeting Percival/François-Poncet, 8 November 1956, NA/RG 59/LF 57D688, box 364
114   Weilemann 1983, 130-2; Küsters 1982, 324-33
115   Müller-Armack 1971, 123; Carstens 1976; 1993, 206-9; Grewe 1979, 281-91; Blankenhorn 1980, 257-9
116   Soutou 1989, Les problèmes..., 228; 1994, 129; 1996, 61-3
117   Guillen 1985, 403, 406. Guillen´s thesis is debatable though. Would France have abstained from the enormous gain of getting effective control through Euratom of the German *Kernwaffenverzicht* if Germany had insisted that the French military nuclear sector would be subjected to Euratom´s control system?

118 Meeting Tuthill/Bode/Valéry/Clappier, 7 November 1956, NA/RG 59/DF 840.1901, box 4404; Meeting Percival/François-Poncet, 8 November 1956, NA/RG 59/LF 57D688, box 364; Dillon to SecState (about talk with Marjolin), 8 November 1956, NA/RG 59/DF 840.1901, box 4404. Marjolin made available to Dillon the texts of the Franco-German agreements.

119 Meeting Brand/Cleveland, 14 November 1956, NA/RG 59/DF 840.1901, box 4404

120 Butterworth to SecState, 9 November 1956, ibid.

121 Dulles had often defended Euratom ownership to German critics, who denounced it as 'socialism', with the argument that federal ownership of fissile materials was required in the US and this was not 'socialism'

122 Meeting Schaetzel/Monnet/van Helmont, 12 November 1956, NA/RG 59/LF 57D688, box 364

123 Meeting Schaetzel/Percival/Armand, 14 November 1956, ibid.

124 BDF, Bd. 1, Nr. 216. The letter (in French) is from the Christian-Democratic archive, Nachlass Jansen. The names of the sender and addressee (a minister) could not be established.

125 Cf. McArdle Kelleher 1975, 65-88, 104-5, 123-55; Strauss 1989, 310-19; Barbier 1990; Nuti 1990; Conze 1990; Schwarz 1991; Fischer 1992, Das Projekt...; Heuser 1997, 148-51; Heuser 1998; O'Driscoll 1998, Les Anglo-Saxons...

126 The BDF refers to the later more defintive agreement about the F-I-G project, dated 25 November 1957, as 'textually largely in accord' with the Colomb-Béchar agreement. The November document refers, among other things, to cooperation about 'the different families of guided missiles' and 'the military applications of atomic energy'. BDF, Bd. 1, Nr. 217, n. 2, and Nr. 221.

127 Barbier 1990, 90-2

128 Strauss 1989, 311

129 Extract from Blankenhorn's diary of 17 January 1957, BDF, Bd. 1, Nr. 257

130 Schmidt 1995, 156, n. 100

131 Linebaugh to Schaetzel, 29 March 1957, NA/RG59/LF 57D688

132 Hoover (Acting Secretary) to Amembassy, Luxemburg, NA/RG 59/DF 840.1901, box 4404; Alphand to Pineau, 23 November 1956, MAE/Amérique, Etats-Unis 1952-1963, 466; Memos by Ophüls and Poensgen, 27 November 1956, AA-PA/B 22, Bd. 23

133 Memo by Michaels, 'Note of visit', 5 December 1956, PRO/FO 371, 121970; meeting Isenbergh/Guillaumat/Goldschmidt, 26 December 1956, NA/RG 59/LF 57D688, box 364. The French decided about the military enrichment plant in Pierrelatte in 1957. Goldschmidt has later in books and articles set out his views about the decisive impact of the American prices on the European project. Cf. for example Goldschmidt 1980, 313-16

134 Memo, n.s., Secrétariat Général, Coordination des questions atomiques, 21 December 1956, DDF 1956, t. III, no. 316

135 Matthews to DOS (about talk with van der Beugel), 30 November 1956 and Barnett to DOS (about talk with Eschauzier), 24 December 1956, NA/RG59/ 840.1901, box 4404

136 Butterworth to SecState, 11 December 1956, ibid., box 4404

137 Comité des chefs de delegation, Meeting 16 November 1956, MAE/DE-CE, 606

138 Comité des chefs de delegation, Meeting 4-5 January 1957, MAE/DE-CE, 607; Memo 'Conférence de Bruxelles', Brunet to MAE, 8 January 1957, MAE/SD; Sprouse to SecState, 7 January 1957, NA/RG 59/DF 840.1901, box 4405. - There

was know-how in Germany about a less established technology for enrichment based on ultra-centrifuges (particularly the so-called Becker process). Ultra-centrifuges had been studied there during and after World War II.

139   Meeting Faure/Hallstein/Carstens et al., 10 January 1957, MAE/SD; Kabinetts-sache, 10 January 1957, BA/N1337/644 (Carstens)

140   Kabinettssitzung 15 January 1957, KAB 1957, 87-99 (the citation, 91), ; Kabinettsvorlage, n.d., AA-PA/B 10, Bd. 916; Memo by Carstens 'Aufzeichnung, Kabinettsbeschlüsse zum Gemeinsamen Markt und Euratom', BA/N1337/644 (Carstens). Erhard, but not F.-J. Strauss, was present at the meeting. Balke had set out his objections beforehand; see: Balke to the Under Secretary of the Chancellery, 11 January 1957, ibid.

141   Above, 215-16

142   Dulles to Amembassies in the Six, 4 January 1957, FRUS 1955-1957, Vol. IV, 498-500; Conant to SecState, 10 January 1957, NA/RG 59/DF 840.1901, box 4405

143   Amembassy, Paris, to SecState, 10 January 1957, ibid.

144   Memo by Dulles (about talk with Monnet), 10 January 1957, FRUS 1955-1957, Vol. IV, 501

145   Memo by Dulles (about talk with Monnet), 18 January 1957, HAEC/JMDS 102;

146   G. Smith to Dulles, 'US Action to Discourage Accelerated French Nuclear Weapons Program', 19 December 1956, NA/RG 59/LF 57D688, box 407. The memorandum is a draft of a proposal to Dulles, mentioning concurrence by, among others, Bowie and Elbrick. It bears the hand-written note 'not sent'. There is also a preliminary draft (Schaetzel to G. Smith, 6 December 1956, ibid.)

147   This was the 'double key' system that was introduced in several countries later

148   The protracted negotiations about possible US assistance to French nuclear submarines has been accounted for in depth by Maurice Vaïsse (Vaïsse 1994)

149   Barnett to Schaetzel, 27 December 1956, NA/RG 59/LF 57D688, box 364

150   Meeting Marjolin/Schaetzel/Tuthill, 15 November 1956, ibid.

151   Dillon to SecState, 12 December 1956, NA/RG 59/840.1901, box 4404

152   Memo, n.s., Sécrétariat Général, Coordination des questions atomiques, 21 December 1956, DDF 1956, t. III, no. 316

153   Above, 192

154   Minutes, 'Réunion chez M. Maurice Faure le 20 decembre 1956', MAE/SD

155   Amembassy, Paris, to SecState, n.s., 10 January 1957, NA/RG 59/DF 840.1901, box 4405

156   Meeting Faure/Hallstein/Carstens et al., 10 January 1957, MAE/SD. At this meeting remaining questions about the Common Market, and the enrichment plant in Euratom, were also discussed.

157   Above, 218-19

158   That is, the *sui generis* formula

159   Adenauer to Mollet, 14 January 1957, BDF, Bd. 1, Nr. 192

160   Kabinettssitzung 15 January 1957, KAB 1957, 89-91

161   Dulles to Amembassy, Brussels, 16 January 1957, NA/RG 59/DF 840.1901, box 4405

162   Butterworth to SecState, 16 January, 1957, ibid.

163   Noël to François-Poncet 18 January 1957, MAE/SD

164   Mollet to Adenauer, 23 January 1957, AA-PA/B1, Bd. 48

165   Conférence intergouvernementale pour le Marché Commun et Euratom, Groupe de l'Euratom, 10-12 December 1956; Comité des chefs de délégation, 13-14 December 1956, MAE/DE-CE, 606, 609

166 Comité des chefs de delegation, 23-4 January 1957, ibid., 607
167 Ibid.
168 Van Helmont 1986, 64
169 There were, it should be remembered, certain restrictions in the WEU
170 Traité instituant la Communauté Européenne de l'Energie Atomique (EURATOM) et documents annexes, mainly articles 24-5, 77, 84, 86
171 Spaak became Secretary General of NATO in May 1957
172 Meeting Spaak/Macmillan/Lloyd et al., 'Euratom', 15 January 1957, PRO/PREM 11, 2848
174 FRUS 1955-1957, Vol. IV, 482-6; Winand 1993, 109-12
175 'Effect of Regional Economic Integration on U.S. Trade and Other Economic Interests', DDEL/NSC-S/CFEP 539/3, 15 November 1956, FRUS 1955-1957, Vol. IV, 482-6 (the policy statement); 'Regional Economic Integration', CFEP 539, 20 November 1956, DDEL/NSC-S/CFEP, box 7 (the full report); NSC-memo, 'CFEP 39', 19 November 1956, ibid; Alger to SecState, 6 December 1956, NA/RG 59/DF 840.00, box 4387; Tuthill to Wormser, 11 December 1956, ibid.
176 'Department of State Announcement of United States Views Concerning the European Common Market and Free Trade Area', 15 January 1957, Documents on American Foreign Relations 1957, 126-8
177 Yost to DOS, FRUS 1955-1957, Vol. IV, 518-9
178 Meeting Dulles/Krekeler, 11 February 1957, FRUS 1955-1957, Vol. IV, 523-4; Meeting Dulles/Krekeler/Ollenhauer et al., 18 February 1957, ibid., 525-6. Critical American voices were heard, but splits were avoided until ratification of the Common Market had been obtained. Winand 1993, 114.
179 The following account is based mainly on: Schmidt 1995, 156-9; Kaiser 1996, 98-100; Kane 1997, 92-7; O'Driscoll 1998, Les Anglo-Saxons..., 112-4, Ellison 2000, 95-103
180 Cited, from a British document, in Ellison 2000, 101
181 Cited, from a US document of 13 December 1956, in Kane 1997, 94. – This vision, it may be remarked, was in principle a new version of the so-called Eden Plan of 1952. The Eden Plan proposed that the Council of Europe would be a ministerial and parliamentary organ for the Coal and Steel Community, the EDC and other future specialized European agencies. The construct would be intergovernmental, not supranational.
182 Cited (from British document of 5 January 1957) in Kane 1997, 95
183 Cited (from ibid.) in O'Driscoll 1998, 'Les Anglo-Saxons'...,112
184 Cited in Ellison 2000, 97
185 Perkins to DOS, 4 February 1957, NA/RG 59/LF 57D688, box 386
186 Dulles to certain US missions, 6 March 1957, FRUS 1955-1957, Vol. IV, 534-6
187 Memo by Goodpaster, 'Bermuda Meeting March 21-23, 1957', DDEL/WHCF-Confid./Subj., box 9. (the document was not declassified until 1998); Memo 'Bermuda Meeting March 21-23, 1957' (partly identical, n.s.), NA/RG 59/LF 62D181
188 Meeting 22 March 1957, FRUS 1955-1957, Vol. XXVII, 727, 751-52
189 Macmillan to Eisenhower (with enclosed memo), 23 March 1957, ibid. 762-4
190 'Agreed note on military nuclear programmes of fourth countries', 23 March 1957, ibid., 766. The minutes of this talk appear still not to be declassified.
191 Melissen 1999, 109
192 Meeting Dulles/Armand/Etzel/Giordani et al., 4 February 1957, FRUS 1955-1957, Vol. IV, 512-15; Briefing memorandum for the President by Dulles, 6 February 1957, NA/RG 59/DF 840.1901, box 4405; Meeting Eisenhower/

Armand/Etzel/Giordani et al. 6 February 1957, FRUS 1955-1957, Vol. IV, 517-18; Communiqué, 8 February 1957, Documents on American Foreign Relations 1957, 128-29 (the citation)

193 Above, 235-6

194 Meeting Dulles/L. Strauss/Armand/Etzel/Giordani et al., 8 February 1957, FRUS 1955-1957, Vol . IV, 519-22; Elbrick to Dulles, 'Call of Belgian Foreign Minister Spaak', 8 February 1957, NA/RG 59/LF 57D688. It should be added that Butterworth had reported that the Germans had decided to accept Euratom ownership in the final round, although they withheld the decision for tactical reasons. Butterworth to SecState, 25 January 1957, NA/RG 59/DF 840.1901, box 4405. Cf. also Helmreich 1991, 406-8.

195 Carstens to German missions, 20 February 1957, BDF, Bd. 1, Nr. 196; 'Pressekonferenz über Gemeinsamen Markt und Euratom', 21 February 1957, ibid., Bd. 2, Nr. 246

196 Kabinettssitzung 21 February 1957, KAB 1957, 156

197 'Declaration of the Foreign Ministers of the CSC countries adopted February 4, 1957', NA/RG 59/LF 57D688, box 364

198 Amembassy, Paris, n.s., to Schaetzel (about talk with Bowie), 14 February 1957, ibid

199 Schaetzel to Isenbergh, 26 March 1957, ibid.

200 A Target for Euratom, 32-3. About developments 1957-58, Hewlett-Holl 1989, 430-48

201 Meeting Dulles/Adenauer/von Brentano et al., 26 May 1957, FRUS 1955-1957, Vol. IV, 557-8

202 Polach 1964, 115-36; Gorove 1967; Skogmar 1979, 130-42 and 1995, 209-12; Schwarz 1992, 304-11 (the citation, 304)

203 Cf. Charles Maier's discussion of the twin themes of productivity and containment in the foreign policy of the Truman Administration, and Paul Pitman's observations of the interplay of geopolitical and economic concerns in French and German policy-making in the fifties. Maier 1994, espec.160; Pitman 2000, Un Général...

204 Moravcsik 1998, 90

Conclusion: Integration and Non-Proliferation

1 Lyndon B. Johnson, cited in Skogmar 1979, 187

2 Soutou 1996

3 The Social-Democrats were in power in Germany then. Adenauer likened the NPT with the Morgenthau Plan [the proposal after the war that Germany should be deindustrialized and transformed into a purely agrarian country] and F.-J. Strauss talked about the danger of 'a new Versailles of cosmic dimensions'. Brandt 1989, 172.

4 Guillen judges that 'the mountain gave birth to a mouse' and Asbeek Brusse that 'it seems almost a farce to regard the Euratom Treaty as a milestone in the process of European integration'. Asbeek Brusse however mentions a crucial aspect when observing that 'the negotiations on Euratom had, at times, helped keep the momentum of the common market negotiations going when they might otherwise have stalled'. Guillen 1985, 411; Asbeek Brusse 1990, 222.

Bibliography

Unpublished sources

Auswärtiges Amt, Politisches Archiv, Berlin [AA-PA]
AA-PA/B 1	Ministerialbüro
AA-PA/B 2	Büro Staatssekretäre, B 2
AA-PA/B 22	Friedliche Verwendung der Kernenergie
AA-PA/ B 32	Amerika

Archives Nationales, Paris [AN]
Archives privées:
AN/363 AP	René Mayer
AN/505 AP	Edgar Faure

Bundesarchiv, Koblenz [BA]
Nachlässe:
BA/N 1239	Heinrich v. Brentano
BA/N 1254	Franz Etzel
BA/N 1337	Karl Carstens
BA/N 1351	Herbert Blankenhorn

Dwight D. Eisenhower Library, Abilene, Kansas [DDEL]
Eisenhower, Dwight D.: Papers as President of the United States 1952-1961 (Ann Whitman File) [AWF]
DDEL/AWF/Adm.	Administration Series
DDEL/AWF/Diary	DDE Diary Series
DDEL/AWF/Int.	International Series
DDEL/AWF/NSC	NSC Series

Dwight D. Eisenhower: Records as President (White House Central Files), 1953-61. Confidential File [WHCF-Confid.]
DDEL/ WHCF-Confid/Subj.	Subject Series

White House Office, Office of the Special Assistant for National Security Affairs: Records, 1952-61 (NSC-Series) [SANSA]
DDEL/SANSA/Brief.	Briefing Notes Subseries

White House Office, National Security Council Staff: Papers, 1948-61 [NSC-S]
DDEL/NSC-S/CFEP	CFEP (US Council on Foreign Economic Policy) Series
DDEL/NSC-S/OCB	Operations Coordinating Board (OCB) Central Files Series

DDEL/NSC-S /SSF   Special Staff File Series
DDEL/Jackson   C.D. Jackson: Papers

Historical Archives of the European Communities, Florence [HAEC]
HAEC/JMAS   Jean Monnet American Sources
HAEC/JMDS   Jean Monnet Duchêne Sources

Institut Pierre Mendès France, Paris [IPMF]
IPMF/CED 2
IPMF/Accords de Paris
IPMF/Énergie atomique
IPMF/Relations internationales

Ministère des Affaires Etrangères, Paris [MAE]
MAE/EU   Série Amérique, sous-série Etats-Unis 1952-1963
MAE/EUR   Série Europe 1944-1960, sous-série Généralités
                        1956- : Questions internationales européennes
MAE/ DE-CE   Direction des affaires économiques et financières,
                        Service de coopération économique 1945-1966
MAE/SD   Special delivery to the author, file not marked

National Archives and Records Administration, College Park, Maryland [NA]
Record Group 59, General Records of the Department of State [RG 59]

Central Decimal Files [DF]:
NA/RG 59/DF 611.5197   US-French bilateral agreements on atomic energy
NA/RG 59/DF 740.5   Europe, national defense affairs
NA/RG 59/DF 762.5611   Germany, atomic bombs
NA/RG 59/DF 762A.5622   Federal Republic of Germany, military aircraft
NA/RG 59/DF 840.00   European integration (1950-57)
NA/RG 59/DF 840.1901   Europe, atomic energy, peaceful purposes
NA/RG 59/DF 851.1901   France, atomic energy, peaceful purposes
NA/RG 59/DF 851.2546   France, uranium, other atomic material

Office or Lot Files [LF]:
NA/RG 59/LF 57D688   Records relating to atomic energy matters
NA/RG 59/LF 62D181   Conference files
NA/RG 59/LF 64D199   Secretary's Memoranda of Conversation
NA/RG 59/LF 65D101   Policy Planning Staff
NA/RG 59/LF 66D70   Policy Planning Staff

Record Group 84, Foreign Service Post Files of the Department of State [RG 84/FSPF]
NA/RG 84/FSPF-O   Office of African & European Operations Regional
                        Organizations Staff, Subject Files 1948-57
NA/RG 84/FSPF-F   Paris Embassy, 1936-55

Record Group 326, Records of the Atomic Energy Commission
NA/RG 326/AEC   Minutes of the meetings of the Commissioners

National Security Archive, Gelman Library, Georgetown University, Washington, D.C. [NSA]
NSA/NNP   Nuclear Non-Proliferation, 1945-1990

Office universitaire de recherche socialiste, Paris [OURS]
OURS/CD   Procès-verbaux du Comité directeur du Parti socialiste

Public Record Office, Kew, London [PRO]
PRO/AB 6   UK Atomic Energy Authority: Correspondence and Papers
PRO/FO 371   Foreign Office General Correspondence
PRO/CAB 130   Cabinet Miscellaneous Committees: Minutes and Papers (GEN series)
PRO/PREM 11   Prime Minister's Office

Seeley G. Mudd Manuscript Library, Princeton University Library, Princeton, New Jersey [ML]
ML/WH   White House Memoranda Series

Published sources

BDF   *Die Bundesrepublik Deutschland und Frankreich:* Hrsg. von der Historischen Kommission bei der Bayerischen Akademie der Wissenschaften und dem Institut für Zeitgeschichte; hrsg. von Horst Müller und Klaus Hildebrand, München: Saur 1997-99
    Bd. 1: Aussenpolitik und Diplomatie, 1997
    Bd. 2: Wirtschaft, 1997
    Bd. 4: Materialien, Register, Bibliographie, 1999
DDF   *Documents diplomatiques français,* Paris: Imprimerie nationale
    1954, Tome II
    1954, Annexes
    1955, Tomes I-II
    1955, Annexes
    1956, Tomes I-III
    1957, Tomes I-II

FRUS   *Foreign Relations of the United States,* Washington, DC: Government Printing Office
    1948, Vol. I, General; The United Nations (1975-6)

1951, Vol. III, European Security and the German Question (1981)
1952-1954, Vol. II, National Security Affairs (1984)
1952-1954, Vol. V, Western European Security (1983)
1952-1954, Vol. VI, Western Europe and Canada (1986)
1952-1954, Vol. VII, Germany and Austria (1986)
1955-1957, Vol. IV, Western European Security and Integration (1986)
1955-1957, Vol. XIX, National Security Policy (1990)
1955-1957, Vol. XX, Regulation of Armaments; Atomic Energy (1990)
1955-1957, Vol. XXVI, Central and Southeastern Europe (1992)
1955-1957, Vol. XXVII, Western Europe and Canada (1992)

KAB   *Die Kabinettsprotokolle der Bundesregierung*, hrsg. für das Bundesarchiv von Hans Brooms
1954, Bd. 7, Boppard am Rhein: Harald Boldt 1993
1955, Bd. 8, München: R. Oldenbourg 1997
1956, Bd. 9, München: R. Oldenbourg 1998
1957, Bd. 10, München: R. Oldenbourg 2000

American Foreign Policy 1950-1955: Basic Documents, Vols. 1-2, Washington, DC: Government Printing Office 1957
L'Année politique 1956, Paris: Fondation nationale des sciences politiques (1875-1963)
Atomic Power and Public Enterprise, US Congress, Joint Committee on Atomic Energy, Washington, D.C.: Government Printing Office December 1952
Bundesgesetzblatt, Bonn
Chemical and Engineering News, 1956
Documents on American Foreign Relations 1957, New York: Council of Foreign Relations (1939-73)
Documents on International Affairs 1955-57, London: Published for the Royal Institute of International Affairs. London: Oxford University Press (1929-1973)
Furler, Hans, 'Notizen über die Sitzungen des Aktionskommitees für die Vereinigten Staaten von Europa (Atomgemeinschaft – Monnet) am 17. und 18 Januar 1956 in Paris', in Wilkens, ed., 1999, Dokument 2
Journal Officiel, Paris
Participation Act for the International Atomic Energy Agency, Hearings, US Congress, Washington, D.C.: Government Printing Office July 1957
Schwarz, Jürgen, hrsg., *Der Aufbau Europas: Pläne und Dokumente 1945-1980*, Bonn: Osang 1980
A Target for Euratom, Report submitted by Mr. Louis Armand, Mr. Franz Etzel and Mr. Francesco Giordani at the request of the Governments of Belgium, France, German Federal Republic, Italy, Luxembourg and the Netherlands, May 1957

Traité instituant la Communauté Européenne de l'Énergie Atomique (EURATOM) et documents annexes, Bruxelles: Secrétariat du Comité intérimaire pour le Marché commun et l'Euratom 1957
The United Nations and Disarmament 1945-1965, New York: United Nations 1967

Memoirs and diaries

Adenauer, Konrad (1966-1967), Erinnerungen 1953-1955 (1966); 1955-1959 (1967), Stuttgart: Deutsche Verlags-Anstalt

Alphand, Hervé (1977), L'Étonnement d'être: Journal (1939-1973), Paris: Fayard 1977

Bérard, Armand (1977), Un ambassadeur se souvient: Washington et Bonn 1945-1955, Paris: Plon

Blankenhorn, Herbert (1980), Verständnis und Verständigung: Blätter eines politischen Tagebuchs 1949 bis 1979, Frankfurt-am-Main: Propyläen

Brandt, Willy (1989), Erinnerungen, Frankfurt-am-Main: Ullstein

Carstens, Karl (1976), 'Das Eingreifen Adenauers in die Europa-Verhandlungen im November 1956', in Blumenwitz et al., Bd. I, 591-602

Carstens, Karl (1993), Erinnerungen und Erfahrungen, Boppsard am Rhein: Harald Boldt

Debré, Michel (1988), Trois républiques pour une France: Mémoires 1946-1958, Paris: Albin Michel

Eden, Anthony [the Earl of Avon] (1965), The Eden Memoirs: Full Circle, London: Cassell

Eisenhower, Dwight D. (1963), Mandate for Change, 1953-1956, New York

Eisenhower, Dwight D. (1965), Waging the Peace, 1956-1961, New York

Grewe, Wilhelm G. (1979), Rückblenden 1976-1951, Propyläen

von der Groeben, Hans (1995), Deutschland und Europa in einem unruhigen Jahrhundert: Erlebnisse und Betrachtungen, Baden-Baden

van Helmont, Jacques (1986), Options européennes 1945-1985, Brussels: Com-mission des Communautés européennes

Marjolin, Robert (1986), Le travail d'une vie: Mémoires 1911-1986, Paris (English version: Architect of European Unity: Memoirs 1911-1986, London: Weidenfeld and Nicholson)

Massigli, René (1978), Une comédie des erreurs 1943-1956: Souvenirs et réflexions sur une étape de la construction européenne, Paris: Plon

Monnet, Jean (1976), Mémoires, Paris: Fayard

Müller-Armack, Alfred (1971), Auf dem Wege nach Europa: Erinnerungen und Ausblicke, Tübingen

Noël, Émile (1989), 'Jean Monnet et la négociation d'Euratom (1956/1957)', in Témoignages à la mémoire de Jean Monnet (1989), Lausanne: Fondation Jean Monnet pour l'Europe, Centre de recherches européennes

Pineau, Christian - Rimbaud, Christiane (1991), Le grand pari: l'aventure du traité de Rome, Paris: Fayard

Rotschild, Robert (1997), Un Phénix nommé Europe: Mémoires, 1945-1995, Bruxelles

Seydoux, François (1975), Mémoires d'outre Rhin, Paris: Grasset

Snoy et d'Oppuers, Jean-Charles (1989), Rebâtir l'Europe: Mémoires, Bruxelles-Lausanne

Spaak, Paul-Henri (1969), *Combats inachevés: De l'indépendance à l'Alliance*, Paris: Fayard
Strauss, Franz-Josef (1989), *Die Erinnerungen*, Berlin: Siedler
Uri, Pierre (1991), *Penser pour l'action: Un fondateur de l'Europe*, Paris: Odile Jacob

Books and articles

Abelshauser, Werner (1994), '"Integration à la Carte": The Primacy of Politics and the Economic Integration of Western Europe in the 1950s', in Martin, ed., 1-18
Aldrich, Richard J. (1995), 'European Integration: An American Intelligence Connection', in Deighton, ed., 109-28
Andreini, Ginevra (2000), 'EURATOM: An Instrument to Achieve a Nuclear Deterrent? French Nuclear Independence and European Integration during the Mollet Government (1956)', *Journal of European Integration History*, no. 1, 109-28
Anfänge westdeutscher Sicherheitspolitik 1945-1956; Bd. 2, *Die EVG-Phase* (1990); Bd. 3, *Die NATO-Option* (1993), Militärgeschichtlicher Forschungsamt, Frei-burg, München: R. Oldenbourg
Asbeek Brusse, Wendy (1990), 'EURATOM', in Griffiths, ed., 209-31
Asbeek Brusse, Wendy (1996), 'The Americans, GATT, and European Integration, 1947-1957', in Heller-Gillingham, eds., 221-49
Atoms for Power: United States Policy in Atomic Energy Development , The American Assembly, Columbia University 1957
L'aventure de la bombe: De Gaulle et la dissuasion nucléaire (1958-1969), Paris: Plon 1985
Barbier, Colette (1990), 'Les négociations franco-germano-italiennes en vue de l'établissement d'une coopération militaire nucléaire au cours des années 1956-1958', *Revue d'histoire diplomatique*, no. 1-2, 81-113
Bariéty, Jacques (1993), 'La décision de réarmer l'Allemagne, l'échec de la CED et les accords de Paris vus du côté français', *Revue belge de philologie et de l'histoire*, no. 71, 354-83
Bechhoefer, Bernard G. (1959), 'Negotiating the Statute of the International Ato-mic Energy Agency', *International Organization*, no. 1, 38-59
Bechhoefer, Bernard G. – Stein, Eric (1957), 'Atoms for Peace: The New Inter-national Atomic Energy Agency', *Michigan Law Review*, no. 1
Bédarida, F. – Rioux, J.-P. (1985), eds., *Pierre Mendès France et le mendèsisme, l'expérience gouvernementale (1954-1955) et sa postérité*, Paris: Fayard
Beloff, Max (1963), *The United States and the Unity of Europe*, London: Faber and Faber
van der Beugel, Ernst H. (1966), *From Marshall Aid to Atlantic Partnership: European Integration as a Concern of American Foreign Policy*, Amsterdam: Elsevier
Bjøl, Erling (1966), *La France devant l'Europe: La politique européenne de la IVe République*, København: Munksgaard
Blackett, P.M.S. (1948), *Military and Political Consequences of Atomic Energy*, Lon-don: Turnstile Press
Blumenwitz, D. et al., eds. (1976), *Konrad Adenauer und seine Zeit: Politik und Persönlichkeit des ersten Bundeskanzlers*, Bd. 1-3

Bluth, Christoph (1992), 'Nuclear Weapons and British-German Relations', in Heuser-O'Neill, eds., 139-56

Bossuat, Gérard (1992), *La France, l'aide américaine et la construction européenne 1944-1954*, 2 vols., Paris: Imprimerie Nationale

Bossuat, Gérard (1994), 'Jean Monnet, le Département d'État et l'intégration européenne (1952-1959)', in Girault-Bossuat, eds., 307-45

Bossuat, G. - Wilkens, A., eds. (1999), *Jean Monnet, l'Europe et les chemins de la Paix*, Actes du Colloque de Paris du 29 au 31 mai 1997 organisé par l'Institut Pierre Renouvin de l'Université Paris-I/Panthéon Sorbonne et l'Institut Historique Allemand de Paris, Série Internationale No. 57, Paris: Publications de la Sorbonne

Bowie, Robert R. (1985), 'Eisenhower, Atomic Weapons and Atoms for Peace', in Pilat et al., eds., 17-24

Bowie, Robert R. - Immerman, Richard H. (1998), *Waging Peace: How Eisenhower Shaped an Enduring Cold War Strategy*, Oxford: Oxford University Press

Bunn, George, (1992), *Arms Control by Committee: Managing Negotiations with the Russians*, Stanford, Ca.: Stanford University Press

Calandri, Elena (1995), 'The Western European Union Armaments Pool: France's Quest for Security and European Cooperation in Transition 1951-1955', *Journal of European Integration History*, no. 1, 37-63

Camps, Miriam (1956), 'The European Common Market and American Foreign Policy', Memorandum no. 11 for the Center for International Studies, Princeton University

Camps, Miriam (1964), *Britain and the European Community 1955-1963*, London: Oxford University Press

Cioc, Mark (1988), *Pax atomica: The Nuclear Defense Debate in West Germany during the Adenauer Era*, New York: Columbia University Press

Cohen-Boulakia, Sophie (1987-8), *Louis Armand et les origines de l'Euratom*, Paris: Mémoire de Maîtrise à l'Université de Paris I – Sorbonne

Conze, Eckart (1995), 'Hegemonie durch Integration? Die amerikanische Europa-politik und ihre Herausforderung durch de Gaulle', *Vierteljahrshefte für Zeitgeschichte*, no. 2, 296-340

Costigliola, Frank (1997), 'The Nuclear Family: Tropes of Gender and Pathology in the Western Alliance', *Diplomatic History*, no. 21, 163-83

Coutrot, Aline (1985), 'La politique atomique sous le gouvernement de Mendès France', in Bédarida-Rioux, eds., 310-16

Creswell, Michael (2000), 'Between the Bear and the Phoenix: The United States and the European Defence Community', in Dumoulin, ed., 215-34

Daviet, Jean-Pierre (1995), 'Pierre Guillaumat et l'enrichissement de l'uranium 1952-1962', in Soutou-Beltran, eds., 131-53

Deighton, Anne, ed. (1995), *Building Postwar Europe: National Decision-Makers and European Institutions, 1948-63*, London: Macmillan

Deighton, Anne, ed. (1997), *Western European Union 1954-1997: Defence, Security, Integration*, The European Interdependence Research Unit, St. Anthony's College, Oxford

Deighton, Anne (1997), 'Britain and the Creation of the Western European Union, 1954', in Deighton, ed., 11-27

Deubner, Christian (1977), *Die Atompolitik der westdeutschen Industrie und die Gründung von Euratom: Zur Rolle des westdeutschen Kapitals im westeuropäischen Integrationsprozess*, Frankfurt am Main

Deubner Christian (1979), 'The Expansion of West German Capital and the Foundation of Euratom ', *International Organization*, no. 2 , 203-28

Diefendorf, J. – Frohn A., Rupepier H.-J., eds. (1993), *American Policy and the Reconstruction of West Germany, 1945-1955*, German Historical Institute, Washington, D.C.: Cambridge University Press

Di Nolfo, E., ed. (1992), *Power in Europe? II. Great Britain, France, Germany and Italy and the Origins of the EEC, 1952-1957*, Berlin: Walter Gruyter

Dockrill, Saki (1991), *Britain's Policy for West German Rearmament, 1950-1955*, Cambridge: Cambridge University Press

Dockrill, Saki (1996), *Eisenhower's New Look National Security Policy, 1953-61*, Basingstoke: Macmillan

Dockrill, M. - Young, J.W., eds. (1989), *British Foreign Policy, 1945-56*, Basingstoke: Macmillan

Duchêne, François (1994), *Jean Monnet: The First Statesman of Interdependence*, New York: W.W. Norton

Duchin, Brian R. (1992), 'The Agonizing Reappraisal: Eisenhower, Dulles and the European Defense Community', *Diplomatic History*, no. 2, 201-21

Dumoulin, Michel (1989), 'Les travaux du comité Spaak (juillet 1955-avril 1956)', in Serra, ed., 195-210

Dumoulin, Michel (1999), *Spaak*, Bruxelles: Éditions Racine

Dumoulin, M., ed. (2000), *La Communauté Européenne de Défense, Leçons pour demain?/ The European Defence Community, Lessons for the Future?* Euroclio, Etudes et documents, Bruxelles: Peter Lang

Dumoulin, M. - Guillen, P.- Vaïsse, M., eds., (1994), *L'énergie nucléaire en Europe: Des origines à l'Euratom*, Euroclio, Etudes et Documents, Bern: Peter Lang

Duval, Marcel-Melandri, Pierre (1995), 'Les États-Unis et la prolifération nucléaire: Le cas français', *Revue d'histoire diplomatique*, 193-220

Eckert, Michael (1989), 'Die Anfänge der Atompolitik in der Bundesrepublik Deutschland', *Vierteljahrshefte für Zeitgeschichte*, no. 1, 115-43

Eckert, Michael (1990), 'Kernenergie und Westintegration: Die Zähmung des deutschen Nuklearnationalismus', in Herbst et al., 313-34

Ellison, James (2000), *Threatening Europe: Britain and the Creation of the European Community, 1955-58*, Palgrave Macmillan

Enders, Ulrich (1997), 'Integration oder Kooperation? Ludwig Erhard und Franz Etzel im Streit über die Politik der europäischen Zusammenarbeit 1954-1956', *Vietelsjahrshefte für Zeitgeschichte*, no. 1, 143-71

Evans, P.B.-Jacobson, H.K.-Putnam, R.D., eds. (1993), *Double-Edged Diplomacy: International Bargaining and Domestic Politics*, Berkeley: University of California Press

Fischer, Peter (1992), 'Das Projekt einer trilateralen Nuklearkooperation: Französisch-deutsch-italienische Geheimverhandlungen 1957/58', *Historisches Jahrbuch*, 1. Halbband, 143-56

Fischer, Peter (1992), 'West German Rearmament and the Nuclear Challenge', in Heller-Gillingham, eds., 381-401

Fischer, Peter (1994), *Atomenergie und staatliches Interesse: Die Anfänge der Atompolitik in der Bundesrepublik Deutschland 1949-1955*, Nuclear History Program, Baden-Baden: Nomos

Freedman, Lawrence, *The Evolution of Nuclear Strategy*, 3d ed., Basingstoke: Palgrave Macmillan 2003

Førland, T.G. (1991), *Cold Economic Warfare: The Creation and Prime of CoCom, 1948-1954*, diss., University of Oslo

Fursdon, Edward (1980), *The European Defence Community: A History*, London: Macmillan

Gerbet, Pierre (1983), *La construction de l'Europe*, Paris: Imprimerie nationale

Gerbet, Pierre (1987), *La naissance du Marché Commun*, Paris: Editions Complexe

Gerbet, Pierre (1989), 'La "relance" européenne jusqu' à la conférence de Messine', in Serra, ed., 61-91

Gillingham, John R. (1991), *Coal, Steel and the Rebirth of Europe, 1945-1955: The Germans and French from Ruhr Conflict to Economic Community*, Cambridge

Gillingham, John R. (1995), 'American Monnetism and the European Coal-Steel Community in the Fifties', *Journal of European Integration History*, no. 1, 21-36

Gillingham, John R. (1996), 'Introduction', in Heller-Gillingham, eds., 1-21

Girault, R.- Bossuat, G., eds. (1994), *Europe brisée, Europe retrouvée: Nouvelles réflèxions sur l'unité européenne au XXe siècle*, Paris: Publications de la Sorbonne

Goldschmidt, Bertrand (1967), *Les rivalités atomiques 1939-1966*, Paris : Fayard

Goldschmidt, Bertrand (1980), *Le complexe atomique: Histoire politique de l'énergie nucléaire*, Paris: Fayard

Gorove, Stephen, 'Inspection and Control in Euratom', *Bulletin of the Atomic Scientists*, March 1967, 41-6

Görtemaker, Manfred (1993), 'John Foster Dulles und die Westintegration der Bundesrepublik Deutschland: Zur konzeptionellen Entstehung der Dullesschen Europa- und Deutschlandpolitik', in Steininger et al., eds., 9-38

Gowing, Margaret (assisted by Lorna Arnold) (1974), *Independence and Deterrence: Britain and Atomic Energy, 1945-1952*, Vol. I, *Policy-Making*, Bristol: Macmillan

Grabbe, Hans-Jürgen (1990), 'Konrad Adenauer, John Foster Dulles and West German-American Relations', in Immerman, ed., 108-32

Griffiths, R., ed. (1990), *The Netherlands and the Integration of Europe 1945-1957*, Amsterdam: NEHA

Griffiths, Richard T., ed. (1993), *Socialist Parties and the Question of Europe in the 1950's*, Leiden: European University Institute

Griffiths, Richard T. - Asbeek Brusse, Wendy (1989), 'The Dutch Cabinet and the Rome Treaties', in Serra, ed., 461-93

Griffiths, R. T., ed. (1997), *Explorations in OEEC History*, Paris: OECD

Groom, A.J.R. (1974), *British Thinking about Nuclear Weapons*, London: Francis Pinter

Guillen, Pierre (1983), 'Les chefs militaires français, le réarmement d'Allemagne et la CED (1950-1954)', *Revue d'Histoire de la Deuxième Guerre mondiale et des Conflits Contemporains*, no. 129, 3-33

Guillen, Pierre (1985), 'La France et la négociation du traité d'Euratom', *Relations Internationales*, no. 44, 391-412

Guillen, Pierre (1992), 'Europe as a Cure for French Impotence? The Guy Mollet Government and the Negotiation of the Treaties of Rome', in Di Nolfo, ed., 505-16

Guillen, Pierre (1994), 'La France et la négociation du Traité d'Euratom', in Dumoulin et al., eds., 111-29

Hackett, Clifford (1995), *Monnet and the Americans: The Father of a United Europe and his U.S. Supporters*, Washington, DC: Jean Monnet Council

Haftendorn, Helga (1983), *Sicherheit und Entspannung: Zur Aussenpolitik der Bundesrepublik Deutschland 1955-1982*, Baden-Baden: Nomos

Haftendorn, Helga (1996), 'Die Allierten Vorbehaltsrechte und die Aussenpolitik der Bundesrepublik Deutschland: Eine Einführung', in Haftendorn-Riecke, eds., 9-26

Haftendorn, H. – Riecke, H., eds. (1996), '...die volle Macht eines souveränen Staates': Die allierten Vorbehaltsrechte als Rahmenbedingung westdeutscher Aussenpolitik 1949-1990, Baden-Baden: Nomos

Hanrieder, Wolfram F. (1989), *Germany, America, Europe: Forty Years of German Foreign Policy*, New Haven, Conn.: Yale University Press

Harryvan, Anjo G. - Kersten, Albert E. (1989), 'The Netherlands, Benelux and the Relance Européenne 1954-1955', in Serra, ed., 125-57

Heller, F. - Gillingham, J., eds. (1992), *NATO: The Founding of the Atlantic Alliance and the Integration of Europe*, London: Macmillan

Heller, F. - Gillingham, J., eds. (1996), *The United States and the Integration of Europe: Legacies of the Postwar Era*, New York: St. Martin's

Helmreich, Jonathan E. (1986), *Gathering Rare Ores. The Diplomacy of Uranium Acquisition*, Princeton: Princeton University Press

Helmreich, Jonathan E. (1990), 'Belgium, Britain, the United States and Uranium 1952-1959', *Studia Diplomatica*, no. 3, 27-81

Helmreich, Jonathan E. (1991), 'The United States and the Formation of EURATOM', *Diplomatic History*, no. 15, 387-410

Herbst, L. - Bührer, W. - Sowade, H., eds., (1990), *Vom Marshallplan zur EWG: Die Eingliederung der Bundesrepublik Deutschland in die westliche Welt*, München

Hershberg, James G. (1992), 'Explosion in the Offing: German Rearmament and American Diplomacy, 1953-1955', *Diplomatic History*, no. 4, 511-49

Heuser, Beatrice (1997), *NATO, Britain, France and the FRG: Nuclear Strategies and Forces for Europe, 1949-2000*, London: Macmillan

Heuser, Beatrice (1998), 'The European Dream of Franz-Josef Strauss', *Journal of European Integration History*, no. 2, 75-103

Heuser, Beatrice – O'Neill, Robert, eds., (1992), *Securing Peace in Europe, 1945-62: Thoughts for the post-Cold War Era*, Oxford: Macmillan

Hewlett, Richard G. (1985), 'From Proposal to Program', in Pilat et al., eds.

Hewlett, Richard G. – Duncan, Francis (1969), *Atomic Shield 1947/1952: A History* of the United States Atomic Energy Commission, Vol. II, The Pennsylvania State University Press

Hewlett, Richard G. - Holl, Jack M. (1989), Atoms for Peace and War 1953-1961: Eisenhower and the Atomic Energy Commission, Berkeley: University of California Press

Hitchcock, William I. (1998), France Restored: Cold War Diplomacy and the Quest for Leadership in Europe, 1944-1954, London: Chapel Hill

Hudemann, R. – Kaelble, H. – Schwabe, K., eds. (1995), 'Europa im Blick der Historiker: Europäische Integration im 20. Jahrhundert: Bewusstsein und Institutionen', Historische Zeitschrift, Beihefte, Neue Folge, Bd. 21, München: R. Oldenburg

Immerman, R. H., ed. (1990), John Foster Dulles and the Diplomacy of the Cold War, Princeton: Princeton University Press

Kaiser, Wolfram (1996), Using Europe, Abusing the Europeans: Britain and European Integration, 1945-63, London: Macmillan

Kane, Liz (1997), 'European and Atlantic Community? The Foreign Office and "Europe" 1955-1957', Journal of European Integration History, no. 2, 83-98

Kaufman, Burton I. (1982), Trade and Aid: Eisenhower's Foreign Economic Policy 1953-1961, Baltimore

Killich, John (1997), The United States and European Reconstruction, 1945-1960, Edinburgh: Keele University Press

Knorr, Klaus (1957), 'American Foreign Policy and the Peaceful Uses of Atomic Energy', in Atoms for Power

Kohl, Wilfrid L. (1971), French Nuclear Diplomacy, Princeton, N.J.: Princeton University Press

Köhler, Henning (1994), Adenauer: Eine politische Biographie, Frankfurt am Main: Propyläen

Kollert, Roland (1994), Die Politik der latenten Proliferation: Militäre Nutzung 'friedlicher' Kerntechnik in Westeuropa, Wiesbaden: Deutscher Universitäts Verlag

Kramish, Arnold (1963), The Peaceful Atom in Foreign Policy, Council of Foreign Relations, New York: Harper & Row

Küsters, Hanns Jürgen (1982), Die Gründung der Europäischen Wirtschaftsgemeinschaft, Baden-Baden: Nomos (rev. ed.: Fondements de la Communauté économique européenne, Bruxelles-Luxembourg 1990)

Küsters, Hanns Jürgen (1994), 'Souveränität und ABC-Waffen-Verzicht: Deutsche Diplomatie auf der Londoner Neunmächte-Konferenz 1954', Vierteljahrshefte für Zeitgeschichte, no. 4, 499-536

Küsters, Hanns Jürgen (1995), 'Die Europapolitike der Bundesrepublik Deutschland im Spannungsfeld von EWG- und EFTA-Grundung 1956-1958', in Hudemann et al., eds., 203-39

Küsters, Hanns Jürgen (1998), 'Walter Hallstein and the Negotiations on the Treaties of Rome 1955-57', in Loth et al., eds., 60-81

Larres, Klaus (1995), Politik der Illusionen: Churchill, Eisenhower und die deutsche Frage 1945-1955, Göttingen: Vandenhoeck & Ruprecht

Lee, Sabine (1995), 'German Decision-Making Elites and European Integration:

German "Europolitik" during the Years of the EEC and Free Trade Area Negotiations', in Deighton, ed., 38-54

Leffler, Melvyn P. (1992), *A Preponderance of Power: National Security, the Truman Administration, and the Cold War*, Stanford, Ca.: Stanford University Press

Leffler, Melvyn P. (1994), 'National Security and US Foreign Policy', in Leffler-Painter, eds., 15-51

Leffler, M. P. - Painter, D. S., eds. (1994), *The Origins of the Cold War: An International History*, London: Routledge

Loth, Wilfried (1991), *Der Weg nach Europa: Geschichte der europäischen Integration 1939-1957*, Göttingen: Vandenhoef & Ruprecht

Loth, W. - Wallace, W. - Wessels, W., eds. (1998), *Walter Hallstein, the forgotten European*, Basingstoke: Macmillan

Lundestad , Geir (1990), *The American 'Empire' and Other Studies of US Foreign Policy in Comparative Perspective*, London: Oxford University Press

Lundestad, Geir (1998), *'Empire' by Integration: The United States and European Integration, 1945-1997*, Oxford: Oxford University Press

Lundestad, G., ed. (1998), *No End to Alliance: The United States and Europe: Past, Present, Future*, Nobel Symposium 105, Basingstoke: Macmillan

Lynch, Frances M.B. (1993), 'Restoring France: The Road to Integration', in Milward et al., 59-87

Lynch, Frances M.B. (1997), *France and the International Economy: From Vichy to the Treaty of Rome*, London: Routledge

Mai, Günther (1988), 'Dominanz oder Kooperation in Bündnis? Die Sicherheitspolitik der USA und der Verteidigungsbeitrag Europas 1945-1956', *Historische Zeitschrift*, no. 246, 327-64

Mai, Günther (1993), 'American Policy toward Germany and the Integration of Europe', in Diefendorf et al., 85-109

Maier, Charles S. (1994), 'Hegemony and Autonomy within the Western Alliance', in Leffler-Painter, eds., 154-74

Maier, Klaus A. (1989), 'Die internationalen Auseinandersetzungen um die Westintegration der Bundesrepublik Deutschland und um ihre Bewaffnung im Rahmen der europäischen Verteidigungsgemeinschaft', in *Anfänge...Bd. 2*, 1-234

Maier, Klaus A. (1992), 'The Anglo-Saxon Triangle, the French and Western European Integration', in Heller-Gillingham, eds., 403-12

Martin, Stephen, ed. (1994), *The Construction of Europe: Essays in Honour of Emile Noël*, Dordrecht: Kluwer

McArdle Kelleher, Catherine (1975), *Germany and the Politics of Nuclear Weapons*, New York: Columbia University Press

Mélandri, Pierre (1975), *Les États-Unis et le 'défi' européen, 1955-1958,* Paris: Presses universitaires de France

Mélandri, Pierre (1995), 'The United States and the Process of European Integration', in Varsovi, ed., 102-16

Mélandri, Pierre (1998), 'The Troubled Friendship: France and the United States, 1945-1989', in Lundestad, ed., 112-33

Melissen, Jan (1993), *The Struggle for Nuclear Partnership: Britain, the United States and the Making of an Ambiguous Alliance 1952-1959*, Groningen: Styx

Mendl, Wolf (1970), *Deterrence and Persuasion: French Nuclear Armament in the Context of National Policy, 1945-1969*, London: Faber & Faber

Milward, Alan S. (1984), *The Reconstruction of Western Europe 1945-51*, London: Methuen & Co.

Milward, Alan S., with the assistance of George Brennan and Federico Romero (1992), *The European Rescue of the Nation-State*, London: Routledge

Milward, Alan S. (1992), 'NATO, OEEC and the Integration of Europe', in Heller-Gillingham, eds., 241-52

Milward, Alan S. - Lynch, Frances M.B. - Ranieri, Ruggero - Romero, Federico - Sørensen, Vibeke (1993), *The Frontier of National Sovereignty: History and Theory 1945-1992*, London: Routledge

Mongin, Dominique (1997), *La bombe atomique française 1945-1958*, Bruxelles: Bruylant

Moore, Ben T. (1958), *The American Interest in the European Atomic Energy Community*, The Twentieth Century Fund

Moravcsik, Andrew (1993), 'Preferences and Power in the European Community: A Liberal Intergovernmentalist Approach', *Journal of Common Market Studies*, no. 4, 473-524

Moravcsik, Andrew (1998), *The Choice for Europe: Social Purpose and State Power from Messina to Maastricht*, London: UCL Press

Myrdal, Alva (1976), *The Game of Disarmament*, New York: Pantheon

Neuss, Beate (2000), *Geburtshelfer Europas? Die Rolle der Vereinigten Staaten in europäischen Integrationsprozess 1945-1958*, Baden-Baden: Nomos

Nuti, Leopoldo (1990), 'Le rôle de l'Italie dans les négociations trilatérales', 1957-1985, *Revue d'histoire diplomatique*, no. 2, 77-158

O'Driscoll, Mervyn (1998), 'Missing the Nuclear Boat: British Policy and French nuclear ambitions during the EURATOM foundation negotiations, 1955-6', *Diplomacy & Statecraft*, no. 1, 135-62

O'Driscoll, Mervyn (1998), '"Les Anglo-Saxons", F-I-G and the Rival Conceptions of "Advanced" Armaments Research & Development Co-operation in Western Europe, 1956-58', *Journal of European Integration History*, no. 1, 105-30

Pierre, Andrew J. (1972), *Nuclear Politics: The British Experience with an Independent Strategic Force 1939-1970*, London: Oxford University Press

Pilat, Joseph F. -Pendley, Robert E. - Ebinger, Charles K., eds. (1985), *Atoms for Peace: An Analysis After Thirty Years*, Boulder: Westview Press

Pitman, Paul M. (2000), '"Un Général qui s'appelle Eisenhower": Atlantic Crisis and the Origins of the European Economic Community', *Journal of European Integration History*, no. 2, 37-59

Polach, Jaroslaw G. (1964), *EURATOM: Its Background, Issues and Economic Implications*, Dobbs Ferry, NY: Oceana

Pruessen, Ronald W. (1982), *John Foster Dulles: The Road to Power*, New York: Free Press

Putnam, Robert D. (1988) 'Diplomacy and Domestic Politics: the Logic of Two-Level Games', *International Organization*, no. 3, 427-60

Quester, George H. (1970), *Nuclear Diplomacy: The First Twenty-Five Years*, New York: Dunellen

Rappaport, Armin (1981), 'The United States and European Integration: The First Phase', *Diplomatic History*, no. 2, 121-49

Riecke, Henning (1996), 'Die Bundesrepublik Deutschland als Nichtkernwaffenstaat: Der Einfluss der Allierten Vorbehaltsrechte auf den Bonner Kernwaffenverzicht', in Haftendorn-Riecke, eds., 187-226

Riondel, Bruno (1994), 'Maurice Faure et la négociation des traités de Rome', in Girault-Bossuat, eds., 347-364

Romero, Federico (1993), 'Interdependence and Integration in American Eyes: from the Marshall Plan to Currency Convertibility', in Milward et al., 155-81

Romero, Federico (1996), 'U.S. Attitudes towards Integration and Interdependence: The 1950's', in Heller-Gillingham, eds., 103-21

Roussel, E. (1996), *Jean Monnet, 1888-1979*, Paris: Fayard

Ruane, Kevin (2000), *The Rise and Fall of the European Defence Community: Anglo-American Relations and the Crisis of European Defence, 1950-55*, Basingstoke: Macmillan

Rupepier, Hermann-Josef (1991), *Der besetzte Verbündete: Die amerikanische Deutschlandpolitik 1949-1955*, Opladen

Salewski, M., ed. (1991), *Nationale Identität und Europäische Integration*, Göttingen

Sayer, Ghislain (2000), 'Le Quai d'Orsay et la construction de la Petite Europe: l'avènement de la Communauté Economique Européenne (1955-1957)', *Relations Internationales*, no. 101, 89-105

Schaetzel, J. Robert (1964), *The Unhinged Alliance: America and the European Community*, New York

Scheinman, Lawrence (1965), *Atomic Energy Policy in France under the Fourth Republic*, Princeton, N.J.: Princeton University Press

Schmidt, Gustav (1991), 'Grossbritannien, die Gründung der Europäischen Wirtschaftsgemeinschaft und die "Sicherheit des Westens": "The American Connection"', in Salewski, ed., 169-231

Schmidt, Gustav (1995), '"Tying" (West) Germany into the West - But to What? NATO? WEU? The European Community?', in Wurm, ed., 137-54

Schröder, Holger (1994), *Jean Monnet und die amerikanische Unterstützung für die europäische Integration, 1950-1957*, diss., Marburg Universität, Europäische Hochschulschriften/31; 263, Frankfurt am Main: Peter Lang

Schwabe, Klaus (1993), 'Die Vereinigten Staaten und die europäische Integration: Alternativen der amerikanischen Aussenpolitik', in Trausch, ed., 41-54

Schwabe, Klaus (1995), 'The United States and European Integration: 1947-1957', in Wurm, ed., 115-36

Schwabe, Klaus (1998), 'Atlantic Partnership and European Integration: American-European Policies and the German Problem, 1947-1969', in Lundestad, ed., 37-80

Schwartz, Thomas (1993), 'Die USA und das Scheitern der EVG', in Steininger et al., eds., 75-98

Schwarz, Hans Peter (1991), *Adenauer, Der Staatsmann: 1952-1967*, Stuttgart: Deutsche Verlags-Anstalt

Schwarz, Hans-Peter (1991), 'Adenauer und die Kernwaffen', in Migliazza-Decleva, eds., 563-96

Schwarz, Hans-Peter (1992), 'Adenauer, le nucléaire et la France', *Revue d'Histoire diplomatique*, no. 4, 297-311

Schwarz, Insa (1992), 'The United States and the Creation of the European Atomic Energy Community 1955-1958', *Lettre d'information des Historiens de l'Europe/ Historians of Contemporary Europe Newsletter*, December 1992, 209-24

Serra, Enrico, ed. (1989), *Il rilancio dell'Europa e i trattati di Roma*, Actes du colloque de Rome 25-28 mars 1987, Baden-Baden: Nomos

Skogmar, Gunnar (1979), *Atompolitik: Sambandet mellan militärt och civilt utnyttjande av atomenergin i amerikansk utrikespolitik 1945-1973* (Atomic Politics: The Interdependence between the Military and Civil Uses of Atomic Energy in American Foreign Policy 1945-1973), Malmö: Frank Stenvall

Skogmar, Gunnar (1980), 'Nuclear Energy and Dominance: Some Interrelationships between Military and Civil Aspects of Nuclear Energy in U.S. Foreign Policy since 1945', *Cooperation and Conflict*, no. 1, 217-35

Skogmar, Gunnar (1993), *Nuclear Triangle: Relations between the United States, Great Britain and France in the Atomic Energy Field 1939-1950*, Copenhagen: Copenhagen Political Studies Press

Soutou, Georges-Henri (1987), 'La France, l'Allemagne et les Accords de Paris', *Relations Internationales*, no. 52, 451-70

Soutou, Georges-Henri (1989), 'Les problèmes de sécurité dans les rapports franco-allemands de 1956 à 1963', *Relations Internationales*, no. 58, 227-51

Soutou, Georges-Henri (1989), 'La politique nucléaire de Pierre Mendès France', *Relations Internationales*, no. 59, 317-30

Soutou, Georges-Henri (1989), 'Die Nuklearpolitik der vierten Republik', *Vierteljahrshefte für Zeitgeschichte*, no. 4

Soutou, Georges-Henri (1994), 'Les accords de 1957 et 1958: Vers une communauté stratégique et nucléaire entre la France, l'Allemagne et l'Italie', in Vaïsse, ed., 1994, 123-62

Soutou, Georges-Henri (1996), *L'alliance incertaine: Les rapports politico-stratégiques franco-allemands, 1954-1996*, Paris: Fayard

Steininger, Rolf (1990), 'John Foster Dulles, the European Defense Community, and the German Question', in Immerman, ed., 79-108

Steininger, R.- Weber, J. - Bischof, G. - Albrich, T. - Eister, K., eds. (1993), *Die doppelte Eindämmung: Europäische Sicherheit und deutsche Frage in den Fünfzigern*, Tutzinger Schriften zur Politik, Bd. 2, München: v. Hase & Koehler

Tal, David (2001), 'Eisenhower's Disarmament Dilemma: From Chance for Peace to Open Skies Proposal', *Diplomacy and Statecraft*, no. 2, 175-96

Tamnes, Rolf (1991), *The United States and the Cold War in the High North*, Oslo: Ad Notam

Thoss, Bruno (1990), 'Die Lösung der Saarfrage 1954/55', *Vierteljahrshefte für Zeitgeschichte*, no. 38, 225-88

Thoss, Bruno (1993), 'Der Beitritt der Bundesrepublik Deutschland zur WEU und NATO im Spannungsfeld von Blockbildung und Entspannung (1954-1956)', in *Anfänge...* Bd. 3, 1-234

Trachtenberg, Marc (1991), *History and Strategy*, Princeton, N.J.: Princeton University Press

Trachtenberg, Marc (1996), 'La formation du système de défense occidentale: Les États-Unis, la France et MC 48', in Vaïsse-Mélandri-Bozo, eds., 115-27

Trachtenberg, Marc (1999), *A Constructed Peace: The Making of the European Settlement 1945-1963*, Princeton, N.J.: Princeton University Press (with Internet Supplement: http://www.history.upenn.edu/trachtenberg)

Trausch, Gilbert, ed. (1993), *Die europäische Integration vom Schuman-plan bis zu den Verträgen von Rom: Pläne und Iniativen, Enttäuschungen und Misserfolge/The European Integration from the Schuman-Plan to the Treaties of Rome: Projects and Initiatives, Disappointments and Failures*, Publications of of the European Community Liaison Committee of Historians, vol. 4, Contributions to the Symposium in Luxemburg May 17-19, 1989, Baden-Baden: Nomos

Vaïsse, Maurice (1990), 'Autour des accords Chaban-Strauss 1956-1958', in Vaïsse, ed., 77-9

Vaïsse, Maurice (1994), 'La filière sans issue: L'histoire du premier sous-marin atomique français 1954-1959', in Vaïsse, ed., 101-21

Vaïsse, M., ed. (1994), *La France et l'atome: Etudes d'histoire nucléaire*, Bruxelles: Bruylant

Vaïsse, M. - Mélandri, P. - Bozo, F., eds. (1996), *La France et l'OTAN: 1949-1996*, Bruxelles: Complexe

Varsori, Antonio, ed. (1995), *Europe 1945-1990s: The End of an Era?* Basingstoke: Macmillan

Varsori, Antonio (1999), 'Euratom: une organisation qui échappe à Jean Monnet?', in Bossuat-Wilkens, eds., 1999, 343-56

Volkmann, Hans-Erich (1999), 'Adenauer, Frankreich und die Europäische Verteidigungsgemeinschaft', in Wilkens, ed., 161-86

Wall, Irwin M. (1991), *The United States and the Making of Postwar France, 1945-1954*, Cambridge

Wampler, Robert A. (1993), 'Die USA, Adenauer und die atomare Strategie der NATO', in Steininger et al., eds., 261-82

Warner, Geoffrey (1993), 'Eisenhower, Dulles and the Unity of Western Europe, 1955-1957', *International Affairs*, no. 2, 319-29

Weilemann, Peter (1983), *Die Anfänge der Europäischen Atomgemeinschaft: Zur Gründungsgeschichte von EURATOM 1955-1957*, Baden-Baden: Nomos

Weilemann, Peter (1989), 'Die deutsche Haltung während die Euratom-Verhandlungen', in Serra, ed., 531-45

Wenger, Andreas (1997), *Living with Peril: Eisenhower, Kennedy and Nuclear Weapons*, Lanhern, Md.: Rowman and Littlefield

Wettig, Gerhard (1967), *Entmilitarisierung und Wiederbewaffnung in Deutschland 1943-1955*, München: R. Oldenbourg

Wheeler-Bennet, John – Nicholls, Anthony (1972), *The Semblance of Peace: The Political Settlement after the Second World War*, London: Macmillan

Wilkens, Andreas (1999), 'Jean Monnet, Konrad Adenauer et la politique européenne de l'Allemagne fédérale – Convergence et discordances (1950-1957)', in Bossuat-Wilkens, eds., 147-201

Wilkens, A., ed. (1999), *Interessen verbinden: Jean Monnet und die europäische Integration der Bundesrepublik Deutschland*, Pariser Historische Studien, Bd. 50, herausgegeben vom Deutschen Historischen Institut, Paris, Bonn: Bouvier

Winand, Pascaline (1990), *Presidents, Advisers and the Uniting of Europe: American Policy toward European Integration*

Winand, Pascaline (1993), *Eisenhower, Kennedy, and the United States of Europe*, New York: St. Martin's Press

Wolfe, Bertram (1985), 'No Leadership without being a Leader', in Pilat et al., eds., 187-96

Wurm, Clemens (1995), 'Two Paths to Europe: Great Britain and France from a Comparative Perspective', in Wurm, ed., 175-200

Wurm, C., ed., (1995), *Western Europe and Germany: The Beginnings of European Integration 1945-1960*, Oxford: Berg Publishers

Young, Hugo (1998), *The Blessed Plot: Britain and Europe from Churchill to Blair*, Basingstoke: Macmillan

Young, John W. (2000), *Britain and European Unity, 1945-1999*, 2nd ed., Basingstoke: Macmillan

Young, John W. (1989), '"The Parting of Ways?" Britain, the Messina Conference and the Spaak Committee, June-December 1955', in Dockrill-Young, eds., 197-224

Young, W., ed. (1966), *Existing Mechanisms of Arms Control*, London: Penguin

List of Persons

ACHESON, Dean G., US Secretary of State, January 1949-January 1953, 12-14, 37-8, 261

ACHILLES, Theodore C., Chief of Mission of the US Embassy in Paris, September 1952-October 1954; Minister, October 1954-May 1956, 109, 275, 281

ADENAUER, Konrad, FRG Chancellor, 1949-63, and Foreign Minister, 1951-55; Chairman of the CDU, 1950-66, 5-6, 37, 39-40, 44-8, 50, 52,54-6,58, 65-7, 74, 77, 79, 83-6, 88-91, 96-8, 100, 102-3, 107-8, 111- 13,118, 120, 125, 128, 140-2, 144, 155, 174-5,179, 186-8, 198-204, 206, 209-222, 224-5,227-8, 230-1, 233-6, 239, 245-52, 254-5, 266-7, 269-72, 274, 277-8, 280, 286-7, 289-92, 294, 296

ALDRICH, Winthrop W., US Ambassador to the UK, February 1953-February 1957, 95, 157, 273, 282

ALGER, Frederick M., Jr., US Ambassador to Belgium until March 1957, 275, 277,279, 289-90, 295

ALLEN, Roger, Minister at the British Embassy in Bonn, 155-6, 260, 276, 282

ALPHAND, Hervé, French Ambassador to the US 1956-65, 293

ARMAND, Louis, Managing Director and Chairman of the French Railways, 1949-57; member of the 'Three Wise Men' committee 1956-57; President of Euratom 1958-59, 114, 128-9, 131, 133, 138, 144-5, 176, 183, 219, 222-3, 276, 286, 293, 295-6

Van BAARDA, C. Th.R., First Secretary, Dutch Embassy in Washington, 275

BALKE, Siegfried, FRG Minister for Atomic Energy, 1956-62, 227, 233, 246, 292, 294

BARNES, E.J.W., Counsellor at the British Embassy in Bonn, 282

BARNETT, Robert W., Officer in Charge of Economic Organization Affairs, Office of European Regional Affairs, Department of State, after November 1954, 138-9, 150-2, 195, 229-30, 279-82, 288, 293-4

BEAM, Jacob D., Deputy Assistant Secretary of State for European Affairs, Department of State, October 1955-June 1957, 290

BECH, Josef, President, Foreign Minister and Minister of Foreign Trade, Luxemburg, 157, 212

BÉRARD, Armand, French Deputy High-Commissioner in Germany 1949-55; Adviser to the Prime Minister 1955-56, 274-5

BERG, Fritz, President of the German Association of Industry, 1949-71, 274, 286

Van der BEUGEL, Ernst, Director General for Economic and Military Affairs, Dutch Foreign Ministry, Chairman of the Cabinet Committee on European Integration, 289, 293

BEVAN, Aneurin, British MP (Labour), 94

BEYEN, John Willem, Dutch Foreign Minister, 1952-56, 56, 85, 115

BIDAULT, Georges, French Foreign Minister, January 1953-June 1954, 45, 262-3.

BILLOTTE, French General, 264

BLANK, Theodor, FRG MP (CDU), 1949-72; Head of Amt Blank, 1950-55; Minister of Defence, 1955-56, 102,105

BLANKENHORN, Herbert A.H., Director of the Political Affairs Section of the FRG Foreign Ministry from March 1951, 84, 103, 224-5, 249, 262, 267, 269, 272, 274, 277-8, 292-3

MALENKOV, Georgij, Soviet Prime Minister, 1953-55; Deputy Prime Minister 1955-57, 187

Von MALTZAN, Vollrath, Head of the Division of Commercial Policy in the FRG Foreign Ministry, 1953-55; Ambassador to France, 1955-58, 274, 277, 288

De MARGERIE, Roland, Director General for Political and Economic Affairs at the French Foreign Ministry, 1955-56, 289

MARJOLIN, Robert, Secretary General of the OEEC, 1948-55; Technical Adviser of the French Foreign Minister, 1956-57; Deputy Leader of the French Delegation in the Brussels negotiations, 1956-57, 211, 221-2, 230, 277, 288, 292-4

MARGOLIES, Daniel F., Officer in Charge of Economic Affairs in the Office of German Affairs, Department of State, after November 1953, 278

MARTIN, Edwin M., US Deputy Representative on the North Atlantic Council, after June 1953, 262, 269, 279

MARTIN, Jacques, Official at the French Foreign Ministry, 291

MARTINO, Gaetano, Italian MP (liberal), Foreign Minister, 1954-57, 86, 181

MASSIGLI, René, French Ambassador to the United Kingdom, 1944-55; Under Secretary of the Foreign Ministry, 1955-56, 56, 266

MATTHEWS, H. Freeman, Deputy Under Secretary of State, Department of State, July 1950-September 1953, Ambassador to the Netherlands thereafter, 199, 262, 272, 275, 289, 293

MAYER, René, French Prime Minister, January-June 1953; President of the High Authority of the ECSC, 1955-57, 41, 123, 166, 262-4, 278, 283

McBRIDE, Robert H., First Secretary at the US Embassy in Paris, 289

McCLOY, John J., US High Commissioner for Germany, June 1949-July 1952, 261

MENDÈS FRANCE, Pierre, French Prime Minister and Foreign Minister, June 1954-February 1955, 48, 52, 54-5, 57-61, 68-70, 72, 76-83, 85-100, 102-5, 107, 112, 118, 263-6, 268-72, 274-5, 284-5, 287

MENNE, Alexander., Deputy Chairman of the German Association of Industry after 1949; Chairman of the Association's Committee for Atomic and European Questions, 126, 278

MERCHANT, Livingston T., US Assistant Secretary of State for European Affairs, March 1953-May 1956, 78-9, 107-8, 110, 124, 126, 133, 143, 152-3, 160, 163, 263, 269-70, 273, 275, 278-83

MEYERS, Howard, First Secretary at the US Embassy in London, 288

MILLER, William K., Office of German Economic Affairs, Department of State, 266

MOLLET, Guy, Leader of the French Socialist Party 1946-69; Prime Minister February 1956-June 1957; Member of the Action Committee for the United States of Europe, 145-7, 165, 187, 193, 196, 198-204, 208-13, 216-22, 225, 228, 230, 233-6, 239, 242, 249-50, 252, 254, 281, 283-6, 288-9, 291-2, 294

MONNET, Jean, President of the High Authority of the ECSC, 1952-55, President of the Action Committee for the United States of Europe, 1956-75, 5-6, 8, 12, 30, 38, 114-6, 119, 122-3, 138, 140-2, 145-52, 154, 164-7, 172, 174, 176, 178, 182, 184, 195-7, 199, 201, 205-6, 212, 215, 222-3, 228, 235, 248, 251, 255, 257, 276, 280-1, 283-4, 286, 288-9, 291, 293-4

MOORE, Ben T., Director of the Office of European Regional Affairs, Department of State, after September 1952, 268, 271

De MOUSTIER, Roland, Under Secretary in the French Foreign Ministry (Independent), 68, 268

MÜLLER-ROSCHACH, Herbert, Official at Political Division of the FRG Foreign Ministry, 1952-June 1956, 286-7

ROTSCHILD, Robert, Paul-Henri Spaak´s Head of Cabinet, 277, 281
SALISBURY, Lord (Robert A.J.G. Cecil), British Acting Foreign Minister, June-October 1953; later Lord President, 279
SAUVARGNES, Jean, Deputy Director at the Administration Central Europe of the French Foreign Ministry, 1949-54; Head of Division, 1954-55; Technical Adviser at the Cabinet of the Foreign Minister, 1955, 265, 277
SCHAETZEL, J. Robert, Office of the Special Assistant to the Secretary of State for Atomic Energy Affairs, Department of State, from August 1955, 135-9, 150, 222-3, 228, 230,246, 278, 280, 285- 6, 288, 290-1, 293- 4, 296
SCHUMAN, Robert, French (Republican Popular Movement), 1946-62; Foreign Minister, 1948-53, 13, 30, 124, 264
SCOTT, Walter K., Director of the Executive Secretariat, Department of State, from June 1953, 267
SEEBOHM, Hans C., FRG Minister for Traffic Services, 290
SÉBILLEAU, Pierre, Head of Bilateral Agreements at the French Foreign Ministry, 1955-56; Chargé d´affaires at the Embassy in Rome thereafter, 266
SEGNI, Antonio, Italian Prime Minister, 1955-57, 228
SERGENT, René, Secretary-General of the OEEC, 197, 282, 288
De SEYNES, Philippe, Official at the French Foreign Ministry, 51-2
SHEARER, Official at the US Delegation to the OEEC, 282
SMITH, Gerard C., Consultant to the US Secretary of State until January 1956; Special Assistant for Atomic Energy Affairs, January 1956-October 1957, 124, 135, 138-40, 163, 194-5, 273, 277- 8, 280- 1, 283, 285, 288, 294
SMITH, Walter Bedell, US Under Secretary of State until October 1954, 23-4, 54, 267-9
SNOY ET D´OPPUERS, Jean-Charles, Baron, Belgian Official, Adviser of Spaak, 290
SOUTOU, Jean-Marie, Deputy Director of the Cabinet of the French Foreign Minister, 1954-55, 94-5, 102-3, 109-10, 220, 258, 264, 267-8, 271, 273- 4, 289, 292
SPAAK, Paul-Henri, Belgian Foreign Minister, 1954-57, President of the Assembly of the ECSC, 1952-54; Secretary General of NATO, 1957-61, 5-6, 55-8, 66, 80-2, 85- 7, 104, 115-6, 120-1, 129-33, 140- 4, 165, 167, 170-1, 173, 175- 8, 180- 2,184-5, 190-3, 195, 202, 205- 6 208, 212, 219, 221, 234- 6, 244- 6, 248, 250- 1, 265-7, 270- 1, 279-81, 283, 285- 6, 288, 290, 292, 295-6
SPROUSE, Philip, Counselor at the US Embassy in Paris, November 1952-September 1953; thereafter Counselor at the Embassy in Brussels, 265-6, 277, 281, 285- 6, 291, 293
STAATS, Elmer B., Executive Officer, US Operations Coordinating Board, 262
STABNER, Wells, Second Secretary at the US Embassy in Rome, 274
STALIN, Josef, Soviet dictator until March 1953, 17- 8
STASSEN, Harold E., US Director for Mutual Security from January 1953; Director for Foreign Operations Administration from August 1953, 92, 104, 161-3, 166, 269, 272, 274, 278, 283
STEERS, Office of the US High Commissioner for Germany, 262
STRATH, Official at the United Kingdom Atomic Energy Authority, 279
STRAUSS, Lewis L., Admiral, Chairman of the US Atomic Energy Commission, 24, 143, 150, 152-3, 161, 166, 168, 176, 215, 228, 244, 259, 261, 277, 280-84, 285- 7, 296
STRAUSS, Franz-Josef, FRG Minister for Atomic Energy until October 1955; Minister of Defence thereafter, 84, 119, 126-7, 130-1, 142, 143, 159, 174-5, 177, 179, 199, 201- 5, 207, 209, 211-4, 220, 223-5, 234, 241, 271, 282, 289- 90,292- 4
TIMMONS, Benson E.L., Director of the US Operations Mission in France after December 1954, 279, 288, 290

De la TOURNELLE, Guy Le Roy, Head of Political and Economic Affairs at the Central Administration of the French Foreign Ministry, 1950-54, 261
TORBERT, Horace G., , Official at the Office of Western European Affairs, Department of State, 291
TRIMBLE, Official at the US Embassy in Bonn, 290
TRUMAN, Harry S., President of the United States, 1945-52, 10, 14, 17, 30, 37- 8, 45, 261
TUTHILL, John W., Minister for Economic Affairs, US Paris Embassy, 230, 293- 5
TYLER, William B., Deputy Director of the Office of Western European Affairs, Department of State, after May 1954, 273
URI, Pierre, Collaborator of Jean Monnet, Director in the High Authority of the ECSC, Co-author of the Spaak Report, 276
VALÉRY, François, Head of the Section for Economic Cooperation and Integration at the French Foreign Ministry after 1948; Head of the Economic Cooperation Division, 1955-61, 293
VANCE, Sheldon B., Second Secretary at the US Embassy in Brussels after July 1954, 279
VIALON, Friedrich-Karl, Official in the German Ministry of Finance, 1950-56, 266
VULTEE, Howard, Official at the US Delegation to the OEEC, 282
WEBB, James E., US Under Secretary of State, January 1949-February 1952, 262
WEBER, Hans-Otto, Official at the FRG Foreign Ministry, 291
WEHNER, Herbert, FRG MP (Social-Democrat), Member of the Party Board after 1952; Member of the Action Committee for the United States of Europe, 235, 288
WENDEL, Clarence A., Special Assistant to the Director of the Office of Political Affairs, Office of the US High Commissioner for Germany, 262
WESLEY JONES, John, Official at the Office of Western European Affairs, Department of State, 263
WILLIAMS, Walter, US Under Secretary of Commerce after January 1953, 262
WILSON, Charles E., US Secretary of Defense from January 1953, 269
WILSON, Hon. Richard John McMoran, Foreign Services Officer at the British Foreign Office, 282
WOLF, Joseph J., Officer in Charge of Political Military Affairs, Department of State, after July 1952; Special Adviser for NATO Affairs after July 1954, 262, 273
WORMSER, Olivier, Deputy Director-General for Economic and Financial Affairs at the French Foreign Ministry, 1950-1954; Director-General, 1954-66, 51, 53, 264, 277, 295

Index

Action Committee for the United States of Europe, 141, 145-9
  French and German attitudes, 149
  role in 'new approach', 195-7; *see also* new approach to Euratom
  US attitude, 148-9
Amt Blank [precursor to FRG Ministry of Defence], *see* Germany
Armand concept, *see* Euratom
Arms Pool, *see* cooperation on arms
Atomic Energy Commission (AEC), US, 4, 22-4, 160-3, 176, 184, 195, 225, 259, 276, 284
  attitude to bilateralism v. Euratom, 123-8, 135-7, 140, 143, 149-54, 167-9, 215, 228
  part of transnational alliance, 127-8, 182-3
Atomic Pool, *see* Euratom
Atoms for Peace policy
  bilateral agreements, *see* bilateral agreements for civil uses of atomic energy
  negotiations on IAEA, 27-9
  origins, 21-6, 261
  promotion of civil nuclear power, 26-7, 163
  relationship to integration, 24-5, 114-15
Auswärtiges Amt [FRG Foreign Ministry]; *see* Germany
Baruch Plan, 14-15, 24-6, 28, 145, 185
Belgium, 30, 56-8, 80, 82, 85, 87, 115, 165, 169, 171, 176, 177, 212, 222, 232, 261, 270, 281; *see also* Benelux countries
  uranium, 116-19, 120-1, 123-4, 129-30, 135, 137-8, 140, 178, 183, 185, 244, 285-6
Benelux countries, 5-6, 13, 44, 77-9, 82, 85, 97-8, 115, 120, 123, 146-7, 274

as intermediaries for US, 92, 103-4
Bermuda Conference, 241-4
bilateral agreements for civil uses of atomic energy
  'bilateralism' v. Euratom, 124-8, 137, 143-4, 149-52, 215-16, 227-8
  one of three approaches in US policy, 152
  origins, 26-9
  'preferential treatment', *see* Euratom
  pressure from AEC and industry, 127-8
Canada, 27, 75, 96-7, 159-60, 192, 243, 261, 271
Central Intelligence Agency (CIA), US, 114, 260
Colomb-Béchar agreement, *see* cooperation on arms
Commissariat à l'énergie atomique (CEA), *see* France
Common Market /European Economic Community (EEC)
  Brussels and Paris Conferences (26-8 January and 18-20 February 1957), 244-6
  different UK attitudes to CM and Euratom, 157-8
  French-German talks, September 1956, 199-202
  French domestic backing, 193-4, 201-2
  initiative, 115, 119-20
  main disputed issues, 120, 179-80, 200, 203, 207-21, 244-6, 287, 291-2; *see also* Junktim
  Messina Conference, 119-20
  Paris Conference (20-1 October 1956), 207-9
  part of Adenauer/Mollet compromise, 216-20
  relationship to UK Free Trade Area plan, 191, 196, 236-9

D1564261

The Cavaliers in Exile

The Cavaliers in Exile

1640–1660

Geoffrey Smith

© Geoffrey Smith 2003

All rights reserved. No reproduction, copy or transmission of this publication may be made without written permission.

No paragraph of this publication may be reproduced, copied or transmitted save with written permission or in accordance with the provisions of the Copyright, Designs and Patents Act 1988, or under the terms of any licence permitting limited copying issued by the Copyright Licensing Agency, 90 Tottenham Court Road, London W1T 4LP.

Any person who does any unauthorised act in relation to this publication may be liable to criminal prosecution and civil claims for damages.

The author has asserted his right to be identified as the author of this work in accordance with the Copyright, Designs and Patents Act 1988.

First published 2003 by
PALGRAVE MACMILLAN
Houndmills, Basingstoke, Hampshire RG21 6XS and 175 Fifth Avenue, New York, N.Y. 10010
Companies and representatives throughout the world

PALGRAVE MACMILLAN is the global academic imprint of the Palgrave Macmillan division of St. Martin's Press, LLC and of Palgrave Macmillan Ltd. Macmillan® is a registered trademark in the United States, United Kingdom and other countries. Palgrave is a registered trademark in the European Union and other countries.

ISBN 1–4039–1168–1

This book is printed on paper suitable for recycling and made from fully managed and sustained forest sources.

A catalogue record for this book is available from the British Library.

Library of Congress Cataloging-in-Publication Data

Smith, Geoffrey, 1938–
  The cavaliers in exile, 1640–1660 / Geoffrey Smith.
    p.   cm.
  Includes bibliographical references and index.
  ISBN 1–4039–1168–1
  1. Great Britain – History – Puritan Revolution, 1642–1660. 2. Royalists – Great Britain – History – 17th century. 3. British – Europe – History – 17th century. 4. Exiles – Europe – History – 17th century. I. Title.

DA406.S6   2003
941.06′3 – dc21

2003053577

10 9 8 7 6 5 4 3 2 1
12 11 10 09 08 07 06 05 04 03

Printed and bound in Great Britain by
Antony Rowe Ltd, Chippenham and Eastbourne

Contents

Preface

During the planning and writing of this book I have benefited from assistance and advice given generously by many persons and institutions, in Australia, the United Kingdom and the Netherlands. I am particularly grateful for the support and wise guidance over many years that I have received from Dr Don Kennedy. I appreciate also the encouragement and advice of several friends and colleagues, in particular Dr John Reeve at the Australian Defence Force Academy, Canberra, Professor Peter McPhee and Dr Barry Collett at the University of Melbourne, Dr John Adamson and Dr David Smith at Cambridge University and Professor Marika Keblusek at the University of Amsterdam. Over the years I have benefited greatly from the intellectual stimulus and friendship of many of those who are now former students and ex-colleagues in the History and English departments at Melbourne Grammar School.

The support and guidance, expressed in many emails between Basingstoke and Melbourne, of Ms Luciana O'Flaherty, editor at Palgrave Macmillan, has been much appreciated.

My wife has been a perceptive and critical reader of drafts. Both she and the rest of my family have tolerated patiently for many years my frequent absences into the seventeenth century. To Margaret, and to Madeleine, Jacqueline, Belinda, Jeremy, Nicholas, Annabel and Emily, for whose computer skills I have often had cause to feel especially grateful, I owe an enormous debt of gratitude, for their patience, support and encouragement. This book is dedicated to them.

List of Abbreviations

Add. MSS	British Library, Additional Manuscripts
Bod. L.	Bodleian Library, Oxford University
Carte, *Letters and Papers*	*A Collection of Original Letters and Papers, Concerning the Affairs of England . . . 1641, 1660, found among the Duke of Ormond's Papers*, ed. Thomas Carte, 2 vols., (London, 1739)
CCC	*Calendar of the Proceedings for the Committee for Compounding*, ed. M. A. E. Green, 5 vols., (London, 1889–92)
CClSP	*Calendar of the Clarendon State Papers*, ed. W. H. Bliss, W. D. Macray and F. J. Routledge, 5 vols., (Oxford, 1868–1970)
Clarendon, *Life*	Edward Hyde, Earl of Clarendon, *The Life of Edward, Earl of Clarendon . . . in which is Included a Continuation of his History of the Grand Rebellion, from the Restoration in 1660 to his Banishment in 1667*, 2 vols., (Oxford, 1857)
Clarendon, *Rebellion*	Edward Hyde, Earl of Clarendon, *The History of the Rebellion and Civil Wars in England*, ed. W. D. Macray, 6 vols., (Oxford, 1888)
ClSP	*State Papers Collected by Edward, Earl of Clarendon*, ed. R. Scrope and T. Monkhouse, 3 vols., (Oxford, 1767–86)
CSPD	*Calendar of State Papers, Domestic Series, 1640–1680*, ed. M. A. E. Green, (London, 1875–86)
CSP, *Ireland*	*Calendar of State Papers, Ireland, 1630–1675*, ed. C. W. Russell, J. P. Prendergast and R. P. Mahaffy, (London, 1870–1910)
CSP, *Venetian*	*Calendar of State Papers . . . relating to English Affairs . . . in the Archives and Collections of Venice*, ed. R. Brown, (London, 1864–)
DNB	*Dictionary of National Biography*, 22 vols., (Oxford, 1885–1901)
HMC	*Historical Manuscripts Commission*
NP	*The Nicholas Papers: Correspondence of Sir Edward*

	Nicholas, Secretary of State, ed. G. F. Warner, Camden Society, 4 vols., (London, 1886–1920)
PRO. SP	Public Record Office. State Papers
TSP	*A Collection of the State Papers of John Thurloe, Esq.*, ed. Thomas Birch, 7 vols., (London, 1742)

Cavaliers living in exile in Europe had to become familiar with a variety of different currencies and with two calendars, the Gregorian or New Style in use on the continent and the Old Style, which was ten days behind, still used in England. All dates given are Old Style except that the year has been taken as beginning on 1 January and not on 25 March. In this period one pound sterling had the approximate value of 4.8 thalers or rix dollars, or 10 guilders, or 12 livres tournois or 10 Dutch florins. Spellings in quotations have been modernised.

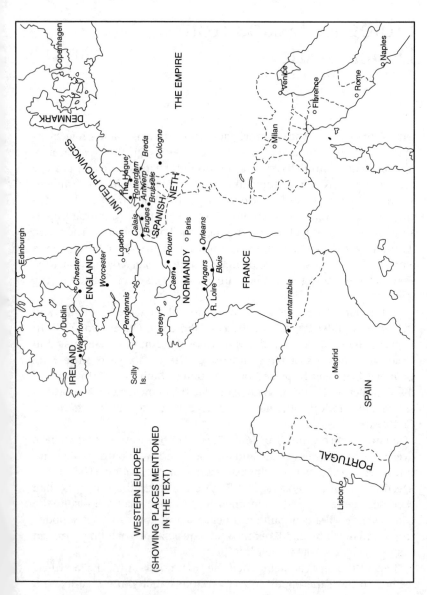

Western Europe in the 1650: places frequented by exiled Cavaliers

Prologue: Escape from Dover Castle

On 4 February 1655 the Channel packet boat, having made a safe crossing from Dunkirk, entered Dover harbour. Although the crossing may have been uneventful, its conclusion was not. There was no easy passage through customs and for some of the passengers their journey came to a sudden halt in the cells of Dover castle. For when the travellers disembarked they were met, according to one of them, by 'a restraint upon all passengers by order from his highness the Lord Protector'. They were all interrogated by the lieutenant governor of the castle, and several, whose reasons for their visits to England were considered unsatisfactory, were detained, being either held in the castle itself or billeted in the town.

In February 1655 the Commonwealth of England, Scotland and Ireland was under the rule of the Lord Protector, Oliver Cromwell. In England the political situation was tense, the atmosphere uneasy and laced with rumours of plots and risings. It was six years since King Charles I had been beheaded on the scaffold built against the wall of the Banqueting House in Whitehall, but the achievement of a lasting and stable political settlement continued to elude the victors in the Civil Wars.

At last, by the beginning of 1653, the Commonwealth seemed to have overcome all its enemies. Ireland and Scotland were both passive and exhausted, held down by English armies of occupation. The radical Levellers had been broken. The English royalists, the Cavaliers, had been defeated again and again; their leaders were dead or in exile, the young Charles II a debt-burdened pensioner of Louis XIV, his supporters ground down by punitive fines and sequestrations of estates, banned from playing any role in political life.

Then, at the very moment when the Commonwealth's civilian rulers seemed to have the opportunity to restore stability and security to a republican England, they were suddenly overthrown. In April 1653 the Purged Parliament – better known by its later acquired nickname of the Rump – was expelled by the victorious army's commander, Oliver Cromwell. The Protectorate, succeeding to the authority of the Commonwealth and sustained by the power of the army, seemed at first a

more stable and secure regime than its predecessors. But it had many enemies. It was hated by Scots and Irish, by Levellers and Common-wealthsmen (as republicans were usually called) and, perhaps most bitterly of all, by the Cavaliers. There were many committed Cavaliers still not prepared to accept the Cromwellian Protectorate as the final act in the tragic drama of the British Civil Wars. Instead, they looked for leadership to the young man they recognised as King Charles II and to the leaders of his little court in exile. It is against this background of continuing political instability and newly raised military power that we must consider the curious events at Dover in the first two weeks of February 1655.

Thanks to four letters in the Thurloe State Papers, preserved today in the Rawlinson MSS in the Bodleian Library at Oxford, we are able par-tially to reconstruct what happened at Dover in early February.[1] John Thurloe, Secretary of State to the Lord Protector, comes across in his correspondence as a fairly colourless but efficient bureaucrat. Among his responsibilities was the preservation of the security of the regime, a duty that involved him in counter-espionage against the regime's enemies, an activity assisted significantly by his additional office of Post-master General. The Thurloe State Papers include reports and despatches from agents, military officers and government officials, private corre-spondence, intercepted letters, copies of treaties and agreements, all together a wide variety of documents. Many of them deal with the activ-ities of Charles II and the Cavaliers in exile.

The four letters are insignificant items in the great mass of Thurloe's papers, but they enable us partially to reconstruct a mysterious and dra-matic incident that opens a window onto much wider events and issues that invite exploration. On the surface what happened is clear. The packet boat making the regular Channel crossing between Dunkirk and Dover reached port on 4 February. The passengers were questioned by Captain Thomas Wilson, Lieutenant Governor of Dover Castle, and several were detained, including one calling himself Nicholas Wright, who 'pretended his business to Newcastle to settle his family there; that he came from Rotterdam, being a merchant there'.[2]

Wilson immediately had his suspicions of Nicholas Wright, the alleged merchant from Rotterdam, informing Thurloe by letter on 11 February that 'of all the men that ever I secured, both formerly and now, at first I was not more unsatisfied in a man than him.' When Wilson told Wright that he was to be kept in custody in the castle, the gover-nor 'perceived a trouble of spirit upon him, therefore was the more careful of him'.[3]

Unfortunately for Wilson, his prisoner was not prepared to sit resignedly in his cell and allow events to take their course. On 4 February, the day he was detained, he wrote a letter to one Sir Robert Stone:

> Kind salutes. I had the convenience of a passage from Dunkirk to Dover in the same boat with your man Mauris, but here we found a restraint upon all the passengers by order from his highness the Lord Protector: by this means your servant is made prisoner in the town of Dover, and I in the Castle, till we send to our friends, that the officer that commands here may have an order from above to give us our freedom. I beseech you do me the favour to prevail with some of your friends near his highness the Lord Protector, to get me leave either to come to London or return back to Rotterdam. . . . I know you will not forget your friends in trouble, that makes me now give you this. Pray direct your letter to Mr Robert Day, Clerk of the Passage. I have desired Mauris to send this to you.[4]

Wright's letter somehow reached 'Mauris' – there are various spellings of his name – and from Dover it was conveyed immediately to London. Sir Robert Stone had it by 5 February for on that same day he passed it on to Thurloe with a covering note, supplemented shortly afterwards by a further brief letter, that gave the Secretary further information about the man calling himself 'Nicholas Wright'.

According to Stone, the writer of the letter he forwarded to Thurloe 'hath taken up the name of Wright'. But if he were examined 'our merchant Wright in Dover Castle I understand will prove Mr Armorer, one of the princess Royal's gents'. The Princess Royal was Mary Stuart, sister of Charles II and widow since 1650 of Prince William II of Orange; her little court in the Hague was a natural magnet to exiled Cavaliers. Furthermore, Stone claimed that Armorer alias Wright 'hath been here [in England] lately' and had links with certain notorious royalist conspirators, in particular 'Norwood and the Litteltons, now in hold [prison]'. Stone concluded his letter with conventional expressions of his willingness to be of service to Secretary Thurloe.[5]

Thurloe responded quickly, writing immediately to Captain Wilson but, luckily for Armorer, the letter arrived too late. By the time Thurloe's instructions reached Dover, 'Merchant Wright' was no longer occupying a cell in the castle. Wisely, he had not relied solely on the good offices of his old friend Sir Robert Stone to obtain his release. Instead, he had also turned to Robert Day, Clerk of the Passage, who obligingly had guaranteed 'Wright's' good behaviour and the genuineness of his

merchant status to the Dover Commissioners of the Passage, the civilian customs authorities at the port.

Confronted with these guarantees from the civilian port authorities of 'Merchant Wright's' respectability, Wilson had unwisely released his prisoner. Almost immediately he was compelled to justify this rash action. In a letter written on 11 February in reply to one from Thurloe received the same day Wilson explained how 'he was very much troubled at Wright's being released, especially considering that particular bloody design you mention'. Desperately, Wilson tried to push responsibility for the blunder onto the port commissioners and in particular Robert Day, 'whom in your last [letter] you mention'. As for 'Merchant Wright', who had immediately vanished, Wilson piously trusted that 'the Lord will graciously disappoint his horrid intentions'. In the absence of the real thing, Wilson provided Thurloe with a description of his ex-prisoner:

> The said Nicholas Wright is a pretty full and somewhat ruddy faced man, of a middle stature, of about thirty-five or thirty-six years of age, having a deep brown hair, short beard, his hair on his beard and face much of a colour.[6]

This curious little episode raises several questions. Who was Nicholas Wright/Armorer, what exactly was he up to and what happened to him? What role did Robert Day, the Clerk of the Passage, have in the affair? Who was Sir Robert Stone and why did he betray his friend? After all, if Thurloe had acted only slightly more quickly or if Wilson had ignored the recommendations of the Dover Commissioners of the Passage, Armorer would certainly have ended in the Tower and possibly on the scaffold. For Stone was correct. The prisoner at Dover was not a legitimate 'Merchant Wright' but Major Nicholas Armorer, a Cavalier veteran of the Civil Wars, at this time living in exile in Holland.

To answer these questions it is necessary to explore the world of Nicholas Armorer in the 1650s. This was a world in which exiled royalists were scattered throughout a dozen European countries, and where their struggle to survive led many of them to become conspirators, soldiers of fortune or hangers-on at one or other of the little courts that gathered around the exiled Stuarts. In this often desperately difficult existence the highest principles of courage and loyalty coexisted with treachery and bitter factionalism. It is the world inhabited by exiled Cavaliers like Nicholas Armorer that this book attempts to explore.

Part I
Flight

1
A Sad and Long Exile

> The history of an exile is almost by definition a melancholy one.
>
> (P. H. Hardacre)

On 1 December 1640, Sir Francis Windebank, Secretary of State to King Charles I, was denounced to the House of Commons of the Long Parliament as a protector of popish priests and recusants. With Charles I's most energetic and capable minister, the Earl of Strafford, already impeached and a prisoner of the Tower, and with the ferocity of Parliament's attacks on the King's so-called 'evil counsellors' rapidly intensifying, Windebank's never particularly strong nerve broke. Rather than answer before the House the charges against him, Windebank fled, making 'a passage . . . full of hazard' in an open boat across the Channel to France. He was never to return to England; after wandering from France to Italy and back again, he died in Paris in 1646. Sir Francis Windebank, and his nephew and secretary Robert Read who fled with him, were the first English royalists to go into exile.[1]

Almost nineteen years later, in the summer of 1659, an elaborate but poorly coordinated and organised rebellion to overthrow the republican Commonwealth regime and restore the exiled Charles II broke out. The scattered and ineffectual royalist risings were suppressed quickly. Sir George Booth, the rebel leader whose forces achieved a short-lived local success in Cheshire, was decisively defeated at Winnington Bridge in August. Unconvincingly disguised in female clothes – he did not have time to remove his riding boots and was in need of a shave – Booth fled south but not surprisingly was soon captured. The hunt was on for other royalists involved in organising the rising. John, Viscount Mordaunt, a daring and energetic, but also tactless and prickly conspirator who had

3

played a major part in organising the rising, went into hiding in London with a warrant out for his arrest. On 7 September he successfully escaped across the Channel to Calais. As Windebank was the first, so Mordaunt and the other conspirators escaping from the suppression of Booth's rising, were the last Cavalier exiles.[2]

Between Windebank's flight in December 1640 and Mordaunt's in September 1659, hundreds of English, Scottish and Irish royalists went into exile in Europe. The length of time between the totally different circumstances of Windebank's and Mordaunt's hurried passages across the Channel shows that the flight of royalists into exile was not one isolated and distinct event, prompted by a single cause such as the military defeat of Charles I's armies in the Civil War. Rather, the emigration of the Cavaliers can be seen as a series of overlapping waves, with major surges and fluctuating currents, lasting for almost twenty years, for practically the whole period between the first meeting of the Long Parliament in November 1640 and the restoration of the monarchy in May 1660.

The life of the exile is by its nature bitter and melancholy. Historians like Eva Scott and Paul Hardacre, who have studied the lives in exile of Charles II and his followers, have referred to 'the weary, sad-hearted men who maintained the cause of Charles I . . . and when that cause was lost . . . followed his son across the seas, into a life of suffering, material and intellectual poverty, frustration and paralysing unhappiness.'[3] According to David Underdown, the exiled Cavaliers' existence was marked by 'years of grinding penury, of delusory plots and frustrating failure, of the tedious triviality of court intrigue, of the repeated disappointment of ill-founded hopes'. A similar view is presented in John Miller's biography of James II, where he refers to 'the constant nagging disadvantages of exile: the poverty, the uncertainty and the endless, sterile faction-fighting'.[4] The men and women who endured this grim experience, and who survived to return to England at the Restoration, apparently returned as persons deplorably changed for the worse by their ordeal. To the historian of the Tory Party, Sir Keith Feiling, they were stamped with 'the brand of the emigré', their actions marked by a 'fierce un-English bitterness towards opponents', by 'personal feuds', by the 'depravity of public and private morals', and by 'enervating sloth'.[5] The vice of sloth has been identified by more than one historian as a significant debilitating side effect of exile. G. R. Balleine, the biographer of Sir George Carteret, the royalist commander in Jersey until the conquest of the island by Commonwealth forces in 1651 forced him to go into exile in Paris, praises Carteret

because, 'unlike most of his fellow exiles, he did not idle about doing nothing'.[6]

Is this picture of the royalist emigration as a totally negative and demoralising experience accurate? Before one can begin to answer this question it is necessary to define the scope of this book. The subjects of this study are those active and committed adherents of Charles I or Charles II who, as a consequence of their beliefs and activities, went into exile in Europe between 1640 and 1660. The exiled Cavaliers comprised not only Charles II and other members of the Stuart family, loyal magnates like the marquesses of Ormonde and Newcastle, royal counsellors like Sir Edward Hyde and Sir Edward Nicholas, military commanders like Lord Byron and Lord Gerard, and a few faithful courtiers. They included hundreds of 'ordinary' royalists, often accompanied by their families and servants. This book is concerned with the fortunes of these exiled Cavaliers and their families. It is not directly concerned with the Anglican clergy excluded from their livings by the victorious Parliamentarians, many of whom also went into exile, nor with other victims of this period of upheaval and civil war who found it desirable to leave England in a hurry, like the one-time parliamentary leader Denzil Holles, or the Leveller Edward Sexby.

A study of the Cavaliers in exile presents a number of challenges. First, there are the basic questions of how many and exactly which royalists chose to go into exile rather than conform to and live quietly under a regime they may have loathed but which was on the whole prepared to tolerate them if they behaved. After all, the majority of the exiled Cavaliers were never banished formally; their lives would not have been in danger if they had remained in England. There was no reign of terror directed against members of the 'King's Party' in England, although the situation was rather different in Ireland and Scotland; no seventeenth century equivalent of the guillotine, no English version of the Scottish 'Maiden', was set up in Charing Cross. Most of those royalists who fled into exile would certainly have been permitted to return to England and expiate their legal Delinquent status by paying composition fines, determined according to their degree of Delinquency, and taking oaths of loyalty to the government of the day. Many exiled Cavaliers sooner or later, in most cases sooner, did exactly that, but a significant number did not.

Having made the decision, in the words of the Worcestershire Cavalier Major Henry Norwood, to 'fly from their native country as from a place infected with the plague', the fugitive Cavaliers were confronted with the problem of where to live until their fortunes and those of the

King improved.[7] Biographies of Charles II and other leading royalists like Sir Edward Hyde, later Earl of Clarendon, have concentrated on the exiled court – its fortunes and its factions – but the exiled Cavaliers were dispersed through many countries, from Portugal to Russia. Like English debtors fleeing from their creditors, down to the days of Lady Hamilton and Beau Brummell, most took refuge in towns in the Netherlands and northern France, sometimes in Channel ports like Calais and Boulogne where, as Strafford's friend Sir George Radcliffe confided to his fellow exile Colonel Gervase Holmes in February 1652, 'there is cheapness and frequent means to hear from my friends, or send to them'.[8] But many Cavaliers were more enterprising or more restless, travelling widely in search of employment or adventure, turning up for example in the armies of the kings of France, Spain and Sweden, of the republic of Venice and of the grand duke of Tuscany, even of the tsar of Russia. The exiled royalists' choices of destinations, the reasons why they settled in one particular town, or decided to move from one place to another, or even in some cases refused to stay put anywhere, engaging instead in restless wandering, help to illuminate important aspects of the experience of exile.

The answer to the question of where to live in exile was largely determined by the much more important question of how to live. How did the exiled Cavaliers cope with the constant, critical shortage of money, of sometimes being, like the north country Cavalier Captain Thomas Carnaby in Paris 1657 'in danger to perish from want of bread and clothing'?[9] Exile meant poverty, separation from families, the exclusion from traditional social and political roles, bitterness and frustration as a consequence of the royalist defeats in the Civil Wars and in the various failed conspiracies and risings against Commonwealth and Protectorate regimes. Did these forces all combine to make exile an overwhelmingly miserable and melancholy ordeal? Or did the experience, for at least some Cavaliers, have certain positive features?

Unlike other notable groups of political emigrés, the Jacobites or the White Russians for example, most of the exiled Cavaliers survived to return to England at the Restoration, finally on the winning side. They returned expecting to be rewarded appropriately, even generously, for their loyalty and their sufferings. Were their expectations met and how had they been affected by the experience of exile? Along with their hopes and expectations, what other values and attitudes did the returning Cavaliers bring back with them from their years of deprivation and disappointment in military camps in the Netherlands and in impoverished Stuart courts in Paris and Cologne, the Hague and Brussels;

from lodgings in Calais and Caen, in Boulogne and Bruges; and from battlefields from Crete to Copenhagen?

This study of the Cavaliers in exile attempts to answer these questions. An examination of the wide variety of circumstances and situations encountered by the exiles shows that there are no convenient, all-embracing stereotypes of the exiled royalists, whether they are portrayed as idle, licentious companions of Charles II at his wandering and impoverished court or as unhappy wretches huddling in miserable lodgings hiding from their creditors. Rather, the exiled Cavaliers were a fascinating and varied 'crowd of fugitives', uprooted from their previous existences and scattered through a dozen countries for periods of time ranging from a few weeks to twenty years. In the alien soil in which they were transplanted it will be seen that some withered and succumbed, some hung on grimly and survived and some even flourished. All of them, noblemen and generals, country gentry and courtiers, soldiers and civilians, wives and mistresses, scholars and desperadoes, children and servants, spies and traitors, coped with the experience of exile and were shaped by that experience, but in many different ways.

2
Court Papists and Army Plotters

'If he had not made his escape from thence (the Tower of London) very dexterously in a lady's dress, he had been in danger of his life.'

(Edward Hyde, Earl of Clarendon on Daniel O'Neill)

The first wave of royalists fleeing into exile was set in motion by the meeting of the Long Parliament in November 1640. In an atmosphere of anger and mistrust directed at the court, which was held responsible for all the ills of the nation, the removal of Charles I's 'evil counsellors' ranked high in the programme of the House of Commons. With an empty treasury, and a Scottish army occupying Newcastle and the northern counties of Northumberland and Durham, the King was in no position to resist Parliament's onslaught on his closest adherents and advisers.

Especially odious to the angry members of the Long Parliament were those ministers who had been the instruments of royal authority during the eleven years of Charles I's personal rule, and those Catholic courtiers who made up the circle around Queen Henrietta Maria – the so-called 'Spanish party' – whose political influence was regarded as both undesirably far-reaching and unremittingly malevolent. The impeachment and arrest of the King's most capable but most hated minister, Thomas Wentworth, Earl of Strafford, and of William Laud, Archbishop of Canterbury, were accompanied by Parliament's investigation into the activities both of other ministers, particularly the Secretary of State Sir Francis Windebank, and the Lord Keeper Lord Finch, and of the 'court papists' who surrounded the Queen.

Parliament's investigations, carried on against a tumultuous background of anti-Catholic petitions and public demonstrations, uncov-

ered what the Commons leader John Pym called a conspiracy 'to alter the kingdom both in religion and government'.[1] The exposure of this alleged 'Catholic conspiracy against English liberties and religion' launched the first wave of exiles led by the unfortunate Secretary Windebank.[2] Windebank belonged to a family that had served the Crown for generations but, without social connections and wealth himself, he had always depended on patronage from great men at court, like Archbishop Laud and the Catholic diplomat Lord Cottington. Suddenly, he was on his own. Attacked on all sides, and accused before Parliament of protecting Catholics from the law by issuing licences of exemption from recusant fines and prohibiting the prosecution of Catholic priests, Windebank decided not to stand and defy his enemies while relying on the King's protection. Accompanied by his nephew and secretary Robert Read, another member of the 'Spanish party' around the Queen, Windebank fled, escaping from Deal across the Channel to Calais in an open boat, enduring difficult and foggy conditions, and suffering from seasickness.[3]

Windebank never recovered from his hasty flight into exile and never returned to England. Read, writing from Calais on 14 December to Windebank's son Thomas, reported that 'my uncle is very much dejected, still making account that he and his family are utterly ruined', longing for the King, vainly as it turned out, 'to avow Mr Secretary gallantly, as in honour and justice he is obliged'. Windebank's letters to Thomas from Paris, where he died in September 1646 after converting to Catholicism, show him as querulous and complaining, unreconciled to his fate, the first royalist casualty of exile.[4]

Windebank was the first but certainly not the last. On 21 December the Lord Keeper, Lord Finch, appeared under summons before the Commons to answer various charges concerning his judicial role during the years of Charles I's personal rule, the most serious being that he had prostituted his own conscience by upholding the legality of the Ship Money tax. Finch did not wait to follow Strafford and Laud into the Tower. The next day he was on his way across the Channel and was in the Hague by the end of December. There, in the Netherlands, Finch remained – John Evelyn encountered him in Amsterdam in August 1641 – while in 1644 Parliament sequestered his estate and in 1647 rejected his petition for permission to return to England.[5] But Finch was in all ways a stronger man than Windebank. He survived to see the Restoration and 'at the age of seventy-six he would totter triumphantly back to a seat in the House of Lords'.[6]

The flight of Windebank and Finch was followed quickly by the

disintegration of Henrietta Maria's circle of 'court papists'. Prominent in this group were the Queen's secretary Sir John Winter; the notorious convert to Catholicism, Wat Montagu, brother of the future Earl of Manchester and parliamentarian general; Sir Toby Mathew, another convert, son of the Archbishop of York; Sir Kenelm Digby, son of a Gunpowder Plotter; and the Queen's principal fund-raiser in the Catholic interest, Sir Basil Brooke.[7] Not quite so closely associated with the Queen's circle was Endymion Porter, Groom of the Bedchamber to Charles I, connoisseur of paintings and the King's close companion, a Catholic sympathiser rather than an open convert.[8]

Certain significant characteristics were common to most of the members of the Queen's circle. They were cosmopolitan, cultured, well-travelled; at home both in the company of scholars and artists and in the princely courts of Catholic Europe. Toby Mathew had travelled widely in France and the Spanish Netherlands where, in 1616, he had assisted Sir Dudley Carleton, the English ambassador to the Hague, in his negotiations to buy paintings by Rubens, and had lived for quite long periods in Tuscany and Spain. Wat Montagu had also travelled extensively in western Europe. In Paris in 1624, he had been involved in the negotiations for the marriage between Charles I and Henrietta Maria. He also travelled in Italy and France in the 1630s with another future Cavalier emigré, Tom Killigrew. Montagu's friend, Sir Kenelm Digby, who enjoyed the company of scientists and philosophers and was a correspondent of Thomas Hobbes, spent much of the 1630s in France and Italy. Endymion Porter, who had a Spanish grandmother, was more familiar with Spain. Some of his early years were spent in the household of Gaspar de Guzman, Count-Duke of Olivares, chief minister of Philip IV. As an authority on the customs and conventions of the Spanish court he accompanied Prince Charles and the Duke of Buckingham to Madrid in 1623 for the ill-fated Spanish Match negotiations; he was later sent to Rome on a diplomatic mission.[9]

During the years before the Civil War these 'court papists' had made themselves equally at home in Madrid or Brussels, Paris or Florence, as they were in Whitehall. Exile for them did not hold the terrors that it did for someone like Windebank. 'I live in Florence,' wrote Mathew in August 1608 to his friend Carleton in Venice, 'in an excellent cool terrain, eat good melons, drink wholesome wines, look upon excellent devout pictures, hear choice music'.[10] The campaign by the Long Parliament, spurred on by Pym, to root out the popish conspiracy that threatened the lives, liberties and religion of loyal Protestant Englishmen destroyed this cosmopolitan and cultivated way of life.

In the early months of 1641 the Queen's circle was scattered as Parliament conducted interrogations, demanded arrests and petitioned for the banishment of papists from court. The proselytising activities of George Con, the papal agent at the English court; the attempts to raise money from English Catholics, largely organised by Sir Basil Brooke and Sir John Winter, to finance the war effort against the Scots Covenanters; the rumours of imminent invasion by a savage Irish army acting in concert with a rising of English papists: all these factors combined to increase the popular fear of a widespread papist conspiracy. In this atmosphere the queen's circle evaporated. Toby Mathew went first, 'run away for fear of further questioning', retiring first to Raglan castle, the Welsh Marches stronghold of the Catholic Earl of Worcester, and then to the English college at Ghent where he spent the rest of his life, dying there in 1655. Although interrogated by the Commons during January and February, Montagu and Digby held out longer, before they too followed Mathew across the Channel. Digby returned to Rome as Henrietta Maria's agent, while Montagu withdrew to France, where eventually he became abbot of St Martin's at Pontoise near Paris. In the years to come the abbey at Pontoise would be a source of refuge for many exiled Cavaliers. Brooke withdrew to his estate on the Welsh border. For the time being Porter and Winter rode out the storm and remained at court; it was not until the final defeat of the armies of Charles I in 1646 that they too went into exile.[11]

The flight of the 'court papists' into exile in the winter of 1640/1641 was followed closely by that of a second group of very different royalists, although most were also courtiers, forced to leave England for a very different reason: their involvement in the so-called army plots of 1641. The two army plots of the spring and summer of 1641 were fuelled by the genuine discontent of the demoralised English army in the north, angered by their long arrears in pay and believing that Parliament was more sympathetic to the demands of the Scots than it was to their own grievances. The overlapping plots ranged from proposals for an army petition to much more extreme and far-reaching plans to march on London, intimidate Parliament, occupy the Tower and save Strafford.[12]

The plotters were all officers in the English army, most had court connections, particularly with the circle around the Queen, and several had sat in the Short or Long Parliaments. Unlike the 'court papists', they were almost all Protestants. Prominent among them were Henry Percy, a brother of the Earl of Northumberland; George Goring, a professional soldier and governor of Portsmouth; the Cavalier poets Sir John Suckling and William Davenant; Henry Jermyn, the Queen's Master of

the Horse; Sir John Berkeley, a diplomat as well as a soldier; and two veterans of the siege of Breda, Henry Wilmot and the Irishman Daniel O'Neill. Like the 'court papists', they had almost all travelled and lived in western Europe but, more soldiers than courtiers, they were more familiar with the siege lines of Breda than with the artistic glories of Florence.[13]

As the confused and conflicting details of the army plots were exposed in the early summer of 1641, the plotters identified and their plans revealed and denounced in the Commons, several of the principal actors, according to Sir Edward Hyde, Earl of Clarendon, 'resolved not to trust themselves with such judges (whose formality was first to imprison, and after, at their leisure to examine), and so fled into France'.[14] Berkeley and O'Neill, who were with the army in York, learning just in time that the serjeant-at-arms of the House of Commons was on his way north with warrants for their arrest, fled in June to Holland. Rashly, with Parliament in recess, the two Cavaliers returned to England in September, promptly to be arrested on the orders of Parliament's standing committee. Although Berkeley was later released, O'Neill, who was considered to be deeply implicated in the plot 'to bring up the army against the Parliament, and to interrupt the proceedings thereof', was impeached for high treason and imprisoned in the Tower.[15]

Daniel O'Neill was clearly a person of courage and resource; he was to become one of the most active and enterprising of the Cavaliers in exile. Born in about 1612, the eldest son of Con O'Neill, lord of Upper Clandeboy in Ulster, and Eilis, sister of the redoubtable Owen Roe O'Neill, Daniel was brought up in England as a ward of the crown, his father having died in 1619, having first contrived by various means to lose almost all his estate.[16] Raised as a Protestant, O'Neill was introduced early into the court of Charles I. According to Clarendon, 'he was very well known in the Court, having spent many years between that and the Low Countries, the winter season in the one and the summer always in the army in the other'. O'Neill's familiarity with the Netherlands was to prove very useful in the 1650s. Clarendon also observed in him other valuable qualities: 'a natural insinuation and address which made him acceptable in the best company. And he was a great observer and discerner of men's natures and humours . . . and he had a courage very notorious. And although his inclinations were naturally to ease and luxury, his industry was indefatigable when his honour required it, or his particular interest.'[17]

O'Neill's personal qualities and his career as a courtier/soldier almost made it inevitable that he would become involved in the army plots.

According to Sir Philip Warwick, O'Neill at court was a follower of the Earl of Holland, a prominent member of the Queen's circle, while at the siege of Breda in the summer of 1637, at which he was wounded, O'Neill served under Colonel George Goring, a prominent actor in the army plots.[18]

O'Neill returned from the Netherlands to take part in the campaign against the Scots Covenanters in 1640. After being one of the very few officers in the English army to distinguish himself in the disastrous battle of Newburn, where he was captured but shortly afterwards released, O'Neill was employed as a secret courier between the court and the army. It was this activity that led to his imprisonment in the Tower at the end of 1641, with a charge of high treason hanging over his head. O'Neill remained in the Tower for over five months as England stumbled towards civil war. Then, on 6 May, the proceedings of the House of Commons were interrupted by the arrival of the lieutenant of the Tower who announced that Daniel O'Neill 'is gotten out'. Having escaped from the Tower, 'very dexterously in a lady's dress' according to Clarendon, O'Neill got away to Brussels, despite a watch on the ports for a man 'of a sanguine complexion, a middle stature, light brown hair, about the age of thirty, and little or no beard, and of late hath been sickly'.[19]

With the exception of Suckling, who died in Paris in 1642 (the first Cavalier to die in exile), the men who fled abroad as a result of the exposure of the army plots all returned to England in 1642 or 1643 to support the royalist cause in the Civil War. For example, within three months of his escape from the Tower, O'Neill was back in England, at Charles I's court at York. When Prince Rupert landed at Tynemouth on 20 August O'Neill was among the party of Cavaliers waiting to meet him and escort him to Nottingham where, two days later, the royal standard was raised.[20] For these returning army plotters, a second much longer period in exile lay ahead. It is remarkable that Berkeley, Goring, Jermyn, Davenant, Percy, Wilmot and O'Neill all fought in various royalist armies during the Civil War, and all survived the war only to go into exile again. This second much longer period of exile they did not all survive.

3
To Go Beyond the Seas

The Princes Rupert and Maurice 'to go beyond the seas at any time within the said six months, with their said servants, horses, arms and goods'.

(From Prince Rupert's passport to go into exile)

The outbreak of the Civil War in August 1642 brought the exiled army plotters hurrying back to England to join the forces being raised to fight for Charles I. As they returned, other royalists were crossing the Channel in the opposite direction; a trickle would become a flood as the fortunes of war turned gradually against the Cavaliers. Royalists who left England in the early stages of the Civil War included Anglican clergy expelled from their livings and Cambridge fellows ejected from their colleges, like the poet Richard Crashaw who went into exile in Paris in 1643 after his ejection from Peterhouse by parliamentary authorities. Some royalist victims of hostile treatment in their localities also found it necessary to leave England for a time. For example, in 1642 the Catholic landowner William Leveson of Wolverhampton, a quarrelsome fire-brand, fled to France after his weapons were confiscated as part of the measures taken by the Staffordshire gentry to secure the county against a feared rising of papists. He returned to England early in 1643 when the fortunes of war seemed to be favouring the royalists and as governor of Dudley castle he generated, in about equal amounts, terror among the parliamentarians and anger among the royalists in the neighbourhood of his miliary activities. The trickle of the King's supporters across the Channel in the early stages of the Civil War also included those royalists of a cautious or nervous disposition who, although not technically going into exile, decided that this was a very suitable time for a leisurely contemplation of the sights of Florence and

Venice. John Evelyn, for example, obtained in October 1643 'a licence of His Majesty, dated at Oxford and signed by the King, to travel again'. Evelyn sailed from Dover to Calais in November and did not return to England for four years.[1]

When Evelyn left England, the prospects for an eventual royalist victory in the Civil War still seemed reasonable, but during 1644 the royal cause suffered a series of military disasters. Ralph, Lord Hopton's western army, weakened by the losses suffered in its brilliant campaign in the south-west and its heavy casualties at the storming of Bristol in the previous July, was defeated on 29 March at Cheriton, eight miles east of Winchester. In the north also the news for the King's adherents was increasingly ominous. In January, John, Lord Byron, the royalist commander in Cheshire, was defeated by Sir Thomas Fairfax's northern parliamentary army at Nantwich. Among Byron's troops scattered or destroyed at Nantwich were the infantry veterans shipped over from Ireland by Charles I's loyal Lord-Lieutenant, James Butler, Marquess of Ormonde. The defeat at Nantwich was followed closely by more bad news for Charles I: the crossing of the border by the Scots Covenanters' army in alliance with Parliament, a further victory by Fairfax over the Yorkshire royalists at Selby, and then the 'Great and Close Siege of York' by three parliamentary armies. Prince Rupert's dramatic march north to raise the siege of York ended on 2 July with the battle of Marston Moor, the largest and bloodiest battle of the English Civil War, and a catastrophic defeat for the Cavaliers. William Cavendish, Marquess of Newcastle, the royalist commander in the north, rejected Prince Rupert's plea to rally his men and to continue the struggle, with the response: 'I will not endure the laughter of the court'. Telling Rupert that he intended instead to 'go into Holland', he sailed from Scarborough, still held for the King by Sir Hugh Cholmley, with approximately seventy attendants and companions.[2]

The flight of Newcastle and other northern Cavaliers into exile was soon duplicated in southern England as, despite victories at Lostwithiel and Cropredy Bridge, the royalist forces were increasingly forced onto the defensive. The decisive defeat of the principal surviving royalist field army by the newly created New Model Army at Naseby on 14 June 1645 was followed by the advance of parliamentary forces into the royalist controlled west country and the Welsh marches. By the end of 1645 only Bridgnorth, Ludlow and Lord Newport's fortified house at High Ercall near Shrewsbury still held out in Shropshire for Charles I. The garrison at High Ercall, which had withstood two separate sieges during 1645, was commanded by Captain Nicholas Armorer, a younger son of

a minor Northumbrian gentry family. He had served in Ireland in the English forces sent to attempt to suppress the Irish rebellion in 1641 and was one of the veterans of the Irish wars shipped over to England by Ormonde to strengthen the royalist armies. At the end of March 1646, after enduring another sustained assault, High Ercall surrendered. Armorer did not go into exile yet; instead, he made his way to Worcester, still holding out under its defiant governor Colonel Henry Washington and packed with royalist refugees and diehard Cavaliers.[3]

The fall of these last strongholds in Wales and the marches, and the news of the Marquess of Montrose's crushing defeat at Philiphaugh on 13 September 1645, led to a scattered exodus of Cavaliers from the few coastal towns still remaining in royalist hands: Carlisle, Chester and some little ports in Wales. Some royalists withdrew to the Isle of Man, some to the continent and some to continue the struggle in Ireland, where Daniel O'Neill had been since August 1645, engaged in protracted and fruitless negotiations aimed at raising an Irish army to come to the assistance of an increasingly desperate Charles I.[4] The once elegant connoisseur of the arts, Endymion Porter, found a ship in south Wales to carry him to France, arriving in Paris with neither money nor suitable clothes in which to appear at court, 'having nothing but the poor riding suit I came out of England in'. After the destruction of the last remnant of Sir Marmaduke Langdale's Northern Horse on Carlisle Sands on 24 October, following their tragic final ride, Langdale and George, Lord Digby, Charles I's fatally charming and plausible Secretary of State, O'Neill's friend and Rupert's *bête noire*, escaped in a 'cock-boat' to the Isle of Man. Digby possessed the remarkable quality of remaining serene and undismayed through all the disasters that beset the Stuart cause, many of which he had contributed significantly to bring about. Having escaped the destruction of the Northern Horse, Digby 'stayed a month for a wind in the Isle of Man', until eventually, as he wrote to Sir Edward Hyde from Dublin on 5 January 1646, 'I and my companions were very securely conveyed here in a light frigate of his Lordship's [the Earl of Derby]'. Shortly after Digby left Man, Colonel John Robinson, a veteran of several sieges and campaigns in north Wales and Cheshire, arrived on the island. Having been in the garrison of Beaumaris castle, one of the last remaining royalist strongholds in Wales, he escaped to the Isle of Man 'in the disguise of a labourer' when the castle finally surrendered in June 1646.[5]

Not all Cavaliers fled from England in such haste and secrecy as Porter or Robinson or in such chaotic conditions as Digby and Langdale. Sir Hugh Cholmley, a year after farewelling from Scarborough the Marquess

of Newcastle and his entourage following the disaster of Marston Moor, surrendered the castle on terms, having endured a long siege. During the siege 'my wife, who would not forsake me, desired me to send into Holland my two girls, whom I parted with not without great trouble, for I was fond of them'. Cholmley made certain that his daughters would be well cared for in exile. 'With them I sent to wait on them a French gentlewoman, a chamber maid, a man-servant; and a grave minister, one Mr Pennington, and his wife, to be superintendents over all.' Cholmley's daughters and their attendants were certainly better off in Holland than they were sharing with the scurvy-ridden garrison the horrible conditions of the siege in the battered and bombarded castle. When the castle finally surrendered Cholmley had to decide whether to march south to join the King in Oxford or attempt to bring together in exile his scattered family: 'by the articles of surrender we had liberty to march to the King, or [receive] passes to go beyond seas'. Cholmley, who clearly saw Charles I's cause as lost, 'took ship for Holland', for the time being leaving his wife behind. It was not until March 1647 that the whole family was finally united in Rouen, being joined by the eldest son William 'upon his return out of Italy', and the youngest son Hugh, 'who had been left at Paul's School in London'.[6]

The flight of Charles I to the Scots army besieging Newark, which was soon followed by the surrender of Oxford to Sir Thomas Fairfax and the New Model Army in June 1646, caused more prominent royalists to leave England. For some it was a leisurely and drawn-out process. The passport issued by Fairfax for Prince Rupert and his younger brother Maurice 'to go beyond the seas . . . with their said servants, horses, arms and goods' listed approximately seventy persons authorised to go with them. The original pass permitted the princes 'to abide for the space of six months free from any molestation whatsoever' while they put their affairs in order, but this generous concession was suddenly over-ruled by Parliament who ordered the princes to leave England within ten days. Less than a month after the surrender of Oxford Rupert sailed from Dover to join Queen Henrietta Maria and Prince Charles in Paris. Another royalist in the Oxford garrison, Sir Edward Nicholas, one of Charles I's secretaries of state, way more successful than Rupert in achieving a leisurely passage into exile. On his way to the south coast from Oxford, Nicholas visited his estate in Wiltshire to settle its affairs, before continuing on to Weymouth 'with his six servants to take passage thence beyond the seas, by virtue of a pass by his Excellency Sir Thomas Fairfax . . . and for that the said Sir Edward Nicholas hath here freighted a barque called *The Nonesuch* of this port . . . to transport himself, his

lady, his son George and six servants with his necessaries'. The pass from Fairfax was issued on 24 June but Nicholas did not reach Weymouth until the second week of October.[7]

The last royalist strongholds fell and the last military forces crumbled and disintegrated in an atmosphere of bitterness and bloody-minded quarrelling among the defeated generals. Worcester, with no prospect of relief and hopelessly overcrowded with royalist refugees and officers who no longer had units to command, finally surrendered on 20 July. The list of those in the garrison when the town surrendered included three lords, sixteen knights, forty-four esquires, nine colonels, nine lieutenant-colonels, sixteen majors, sixty-eight captains, forty lieutenants, twenty-four cornets and forty ensigns. The non-combatants included 'one bishop, many Doctors [of Divinity], parsons, vicars, curates, ladies not a few'. Among the captains listed was one Nicholas Armorer.[8]

By this time, with the exception of Pendennis castle and the Scilly Islands, the west country had been subdued by Fairfax's forces. The young Prince of Wales and the members of his Council had watched helplessly as one royalist stronghold after another fell to the apparently irresistible New Model Army. In this atmosphere of defeat and disinte-gration the Prince's civilian councillors, notably Sir Edward Hyde, Lord Culpepper and the Secretary to the Council, Sir Richard Fanshawe, quar-relled constantly and bitterly with the generals, particularly with Lord Goring who, according to Clarendon, had a 'perfect hatred of all the persons of the council, after he found they would not comply with his desires, and to his particular ambition'. Goring was now General of the Horse, following the arrest on the King's orders of his one-time fellow army plotter Lord Wilmot at the head of his regiment on 8 August 1644, while Hopton had replaced Lord Percy as Master of the Ordnance. Wilmot and Percy had once more gone into exile, joining Queen Henrietta Maria at the Louvre, where their resentment at their dismissals simmered, to break out in a rash of quarrels and duels when they were joined in Paris two years later by some of those royalists, notably Digby, whom they held responsible for their disgrace. When the generals – Goring, Lord Wentworth, Sir John Berkeley, the ferocious Sir Richard Grenville – were not quarrelling with the Prince's civilian councillors they were in fierce dispute with each other.[9]

By the middle of 1646 the Scilly Islands and Pendennis remained the last royalist toeholds in Cornwall. When Prince Charles, his councillors, a few faithful members of his household and a ragtag following of atten-dants landed at St Mary's in the Scilly Islands on 4 March, Sir Richard Fanshawe's wife Ann was not impressed:

The next day, after having been pillaged and [being] extremely sick and big with child, I was set ashore almost dead in the land of Scilly. When we had got to our quarters near the castle where the Prince lay, I went immediately to bed, which was so vile that my footmen ever lay in a better . . . In one of these [rooms] they kept dry fish . . . and in this my husband's two clerks lay; one there was for my sister, and one for myself, and one amongst the rest of our servants. But when I awaked in the morning I was so cold I knew not what to do, but the daylight discovered that our bed was near swimming with the sea, which the owner told us afterwards, it never did so but at spring tides. With this we were destitute of clothes, and meat or fuel . . . and truly we begged our daily bread of God, for we thought every meal our last.[10]

The Scilly Islands obviously did not have the resources to sustain for long Prince Charles and the crowd of refugees accompanying him. Jersey, still held for the King by Sir George Carteret, was a more attractive prospect to the Prince's councillors. Anxious letters from Henrietta Maria to Hyde, in which she declared, 'I shall not sleep in quiet until I hear that the Prince of Wales shall be removed from thence', and the appearance of a parliamentary fleet near the islands, confirmed the necessity for further flight. After 'three weeks and odd days', according to Ann Fanshawe, 'we set sail for the Isle of Jersey, where we safely arrived, praised be to God, beyond the belief of all the beholders of that island; for the pilot, not knowing the way into the harbour, sailed over the rocks, but being spring tides and by chance high water, God be praised, His Highness and all of us came safe ashore through so great a danger'. Sailing with Prince Charles and his Council into exile on Jersey were approximately 300 persons: soldiers, courtiers, clerks, Cornish officials and servants, in some cases accompanied by their families.[11]

Now only Pendennis castle, defended by the indomitable John Arundell of Trerice, remained in royalist hands in the west. With the garrison starving, decimated by disease and desertions, Arundell finally negotiated the castle's surrender on 17 August. While some of the garrison chose to submit to Parliament and were permitted to return to their homes in Devon and Cornwall, others preferred to go into exile and took ship to St Malo or Jersey. In this latter group were two prominent figures in the royalist war effort in Cornwall, Joseph Jane, MP for Liskeard in the Long Parliament, and Sir Henry Killigrew, MP for West Looe, one of Hopton's most trusted officers and a man greatly admired by Hyde, who considered him a 'very gallant gentleman . . . of excellent

parts and great courage'. Killigrew's time in exile was extremely brief. He died of wounds at St Malo while on his way to join the forlorn community of exiled Cavaliers in Jersey.[12]

As the forces of Parliament stamped out the last flickers of resistance, all round the coasts of England and Wales, from Carlisle and Newcastle in the north, to Chester and Pendennis in the midlands and the west, Cavaliers passed into exile. Sometimes in haste, as fugitives on the run, and sometimes at their leisure and in some style, hundreds of royalists departed from England, either to continue the struggle from Ireland, or even the Isle of Man or Jersey, or to seek refuge on the continent. They did not necessarily go into exile unaccompanied. The inevitable tendency to focus on the chronicled movements of military commanders – Hopton, Newcastle, Goring, Langdale, Grenville, Wentworth, and the like – or courtiers and councillors like Hyde, Nicholas, Culpepper, Digby and Fanshawe, should not cause us to overlook the presence of their families, dependants and attendants, who often accompanied or followed them into exile. This emigration of the Cavaliers also embraced wives and children, chambermaids and chaplains, secretaries and servants.

Although the greatest wave of those Cavaliers who chose to go into exile flowed at the end of the first Civil War, this was by no means the end of the royalist emigration. The great majority of the supporters of Charles I remained in England, hopeful that a negotiated settlement between the King and the commissioners of Parliament and the Scots would be accomplished quickly. Only then could the wounds caused by the Civil War start to heal, and the royalists begin to recover, both from the personal and emotional consequences of military defeat and from the huge economic losses caused by four years of warfare and by the various financial exactions imposed by both sides. Those royalists who remained in England could not foresee that no general settlement would emerge from the negotiations at Newcastle; instead, a series of military campaigns, attempted invasions, risings and conspiracies lay ahead, all of which would prompt further waves of fugitives to flow across the Channel. Those royalists who fled into exile at the end of the first Civil War comprised certainly the largest of the various groups of distressed Cavaliers who would make sudden appearances in the maritime ports of western Europe until the eve of the Restoration, but they were not the last. A number of royalists and their families, who remained in England in 1646 believing that, for better or for worse, the war was over, would likewise find themselves making hasty flights across the Channel in the years to come.

Similarly, as we shall see, the correspondence of Cavaliers who went into exile after the first Civil War shows that they did not expect to have to remain away from England for very long. Defeat and exile were concepts that would take a considerable time for some royalists to assimilate. Instead, during the dark months after the surrender of Oxford, they looked hopefully to more optimistic prospects: the conclusion of a negotiated settlement between Charles I and Parliament or a dramatic recovery in the fortunes of the King's party. There were a number of possible developments which encouraged this first great wave of fugitives to hope that their exile would be shortlived: a successful royalist invasion from Ireland or Scotland, foreign military aid, or divisions among the victors – Independents against Presbyterians, generals against civilians, Scots against English – which the King and the royalists could exploit. Events were to prove that this optimism was unjustified.

4
The Road to Worcester

> Many who had made escapes arrived every day in France,
> Flanders and Holland.
>
> (Edward Hyde, Earl of Clarendon, *The History of the Rebellion*)

The Cavaliers who went into exile on the continent as a consequence
of the defeat of the armies of Charles I in the first Civil War did not
expect their enforced absence from England to last very long. Either
there would be a settlement between Charles I and the victorious, but
surely essentially moderate Parliament, or there would be a dramatic
reversal in the King's military fortunes, achieved by a combination of
resurgent royalism in England and an invasion either from Ireland or
from Scotland by an army that would rescue and restore Charles to his
rightful position. There was even the possibility of foreign aid, to be
generously provided by a range of possible potentates, from the King of
Denmark to the Duke of Lorraine. Secretary Nicholas was one of those
optimistic exiles who clung to the first possibility. On 5 July 1647 he
wrote to a fellow exile Dr Isaac Basire, who had been a chaplain to
Charles I in Oxford during the Civil War, expressing his 'hope it will not
be long before we hear that peace in England is in so good forwardness,
as that honest men may return with comfort to their homes'.[1] Sadly for
Nicholas and his family, it was to be nearly thirteen years before he
returned to his home in Wiltshire.

The failure of the prolonged and fruitless negotiations to reach a
settlement between Charles I and either the Scots, the commissioners
from Parliament or the senior officers, the 'grandees', of the New Model
Army, led to the outbreak of the second Civil War in the summer of
1648. The total defeat of the Duke of Hamilton's invading Scottish army
at Preston in August 1648, accompanied by the suppression of the

scattered royalist risings in England, was followed by the purging of Parliament of those members who favoured continued negotiations with the King. The trials and executions, not only of Charles I but also of Hamilton and several leaders of the risings, combined with these military disasters to demoralise the royalist party.

These catastrophic events caused the flight into exile at the end of 1648 of many royalists who were involved in the risings. For the second time in just over two years the Yorkshire Cavalier Sir Marmaduke Langdale narrowly evaded capture and once more fled to the Netherlands, where he had the company of many recently arrived distressed royalists. The exiled John Bramhall, Bishop of Derry, wrote to Ormonde on 1 October to report the arrival in Rotterdam of Sir Thomas Glemham, at different times governor of York, Carlisle and Oxford during the first Civil War, Sir John Marlay, late governor of Newcastle, and 'forty Gentlemen and Officers' who had sailed from Berwick. The last English troops still 'on foot for the king', after the defeat of the Scottish army at Preston, they had tried to withdraw into Scotland, but had been assured by Hamilton's brother the Earl of Lanark that 'it was not safe for them to do so, which caused their voyage hither'. The flight into exile of these northern royalist leaders was to some extent also duplicated in the south, where, with the government's attention focused on the trial and execution of Charles I, the resourceful General Edward Massey and Lord Loughborough successfully escaped respectively from St James's palace and Windsor castle. Loughborough's safe arrival in Rotterdam was reported on 16 March 1649, 'whither are come many persecuted Cavaliers'.[2]

In the winter of 1648–49 the choices facing the exiled Cavaliers suddenly became much bleaker. The more defiant and committed, those who were unwilling to admit that the royal cause had been finally defeated, looked to Ormonde in Ireland or to either Montrose or an alliance with the Presbyterian Covenanters in Scotland to restore the young prince they now recognised as Charles II. But those who had already had enough of life in exile welcomed the willingness of the Commonwealth regime to allow most royalist exiles to return to England and apply to compound, even though this meant a humiliating 'acknowledgment of delinquency' and the at least nominal abandonment of what Hyde, writing to Nicholas from Jersey in December 1646 to stiffen his resolve, called 'the obligation of natural allegiance'.[3]

The flow of what may be called the 'short-term' exiles began almost before the first Civil War had ended. As early as 24 October 1646 Hyde

wrote from Jersey to his friend Lady Dalkeith, in Paris with the young Princess Henrietta Anne whom she had just secretly brought from England, that he heard 'no news from England or France but that of a multitude of men of honour running to compound'. One of the first emigrés to return was the indecisive and muddled Earl of Peterborough, who had been changeable in his loyalties during the Civil War, and was older brother to that very different character, the energetic and daring royalist conspirator, John Mordaunt. On 25 April 1646 Peterborough petitioned the Committee for Compounding that, 'having withdrawn himself for the space of a year's past from Oxford, and removed into foreign parts and unwilling to continue long where he might give offence to the Parliament', he now desired to be received again 'into your favour'. Peterborough duly returned from exile, 'made his Composition with this noble Committee and paid part of his fine and secured the residue'. Most unwisely, he then had a rush of blood to the head, made another disastrous change of sides, and in 1648 became 'unfortunately engaged in the late action of the Earl of Holland in taking up arms against the Parliament'. Unlike Lord Holland he retained his head but, in exile once more, Peterborough made a new series of abject approaches to the Committee for Compounding, submitting obsequiously to the Committee's 'favourable censure' and applying once more to compound, 'being fully resolved never more to transgress in the like kind'. Although Hyde warned him of the dangers of 'putting yourself into the hands of those devils', in 1649 Peterborough returned to England from his second period of exile, paid his composition fines and embraced the quiet life.[4]

The drift back to England of exiled Cavaliers, in the aftermath of the military defeats in the second Civil War and the abolition of the monarchy, was not confined to muddled and easily discouraged supporters of the Stuart cause like Peterborough. The composition regulations, with the various deadlines for applications to compound, and a range of penalties for late applications, were an effective combination of threat and temptation that many emigrés found impossible to resist. Sir Hugh Cholmley, the heroic defender of Scarborough castle, had no qualms about returning to England when the opportunity offered. With 'money falling short' after two years living in Rouen, Cholmley's 'dear wife, with her two daughters, resolved for England', sailing from Dieppe in February 1649. Cholmley then moved from Normandy to Paris, 'where, having notice that the Parliament had admitted the King's party to a composition (but some few excepted persons), I thought fit to return to England'. Although he had originally himself been on a list of royalists

excepted from pardon, Cholmley returned to England in May to rejoin his family and was admitted to compound, being fined £850.[5]

Cholmley was not the only Cavalier to return to England in 1649 who ignored the fact that officially he had been excepted from pardon. It is a remarkable illustration of the indecisiveness and inconsistency of Commonwealth policies, wavering between a hardline determination to except notorious Delinquents from pardon and a recognition of the need to reconcile as many royalists as possible to the new regime, that so many notorious Cavaliers, including some of the 'court papists', were able to return to England from exile and sometimes even recover portions of their forfeited estates. Endymion Porter returned from Brussels in April 1649 to appear before the Committee for Compounding although the committee had previously recommended that he be sentenced to 'perpetual banishment and confiscation'. Another notorious 'court papist', Sir John Winter, once Henrietta Maria's secretary, and 'the plague of the forest [of Dean]' during the Civil War had joined the Queen in Paris when the war ended. Although excluded from pardon, and with his lands and estates declared forfeited to the Commonwealth for treason, he soon returned to England, only to be imprisoned in the Tower for four years.[6]

A minority of the exiled Cavaliers during the dark days of 1649 were not prepared to accept the humiliating requirements to sign Engagements of loyalty to the Commonwealth, Covenants and Negative Oaths, or to endure harassment from Parliamentary county committees, or to pay composition fines. Instead, they looked to the young Charles II and his councillors and generals to take decisive action to restore the shattered fortunes of the royalist party. Unfortunately for those Cavaliers who were determined to continue the struggle against the regicide republic, the exiled court was beset by divided counsels and mutually hostile factions, competing against each other for royal support for their different schemes and plans to set the King back on his throne again.

The arguments and disagreements had emerged three years earlier, on Jersey in April 1646, following the sudden arrival of Prince Charles, his Council and about three hundred of his followers, fleeing from the Scilly Islands which they believed were about to be assaulted by a parliamentary fleet. Although peaceful Jersey had many attractions and advantages for the refugee Cavaliers, it could only be a temporary resting place. The island provided the conditions in which Hyde could begin work on his magisterial *History of the Rebellion* while, according to Ann Fanshawe, the Lieutenant Governor Sir George Carteret 'endeavoured with all his power to entertain His highness and court with all

plenty and kindness possible'.[7] But while Charles enjoyed a carefree few weeks in Jersey the pressure was building for him to join Henrietta Maria, who divided her time between her apartment in the Louvre and the palace of St Germain just outside Paris. The 'great disputes about the disposal of the Prince' contributed to the division of the exiled court into hostile factions. Culpepper, Digby, who had turned up from Ireland to make his usual calamitous contribution to the Prince's counsels, and Jermyn, one of the leaders of the so-called 'Louvre' group, wanted Charles to join the Queen in Paris. Their policy, as Sir John Berkeley later expressed it to Hyde, was 'to give one hand to the Catholic Roman, and the other to the Presbyterian, and join with them both to the destruction of our common enemy'.[8] Charles could not withstand the summons from his mother to join her in Paris; escorted by Digby and Jermyn, he left Jersey for St Germain on 25 June. Those councillors who feared the influence of the Queen and her circle on the Prince, 'the Paragons now at Jersey' as Berkeley rather contemptuously labelled them, lingered for a while on the island; then, one by one, they moved on to other destinations. The Earl of Berkshire, a comparative nonentity among the forceful and variously talented members of the Prince's Council, and Hyde's friend Lord Capel returned via France to England, in Capel's case to death on the scaffold after the second Civil War. The Fanshawes also returned to England for a time, although they left the baby daughter born in June on the island 'with a nurse under the care of Lady Carteret'. When Hopton also left Jersey for Rouen, Hyde was left with the hospitable Carterets to work at his *History* in peace. This period of peaceful writing was broken when the news reached Jersey that Hamilton's army had crossed the border, the parliamentary fleet in the Channel had mutinied and royalists had risen in a number of places in England and Wales. In June 1648 Hyde was urgently summoned by both Jermyn and Digby to join Prince Charles in Holland.[9]

The arguments that began at Jersey in June 1646, were continued among the reconstituted Council in Paris and Holland between 1646 and 1649. Following first the defeat of the royalists and their Presbyterian allies in 1648 and then the execution of Charles I and the establishment of a republic, they were renewed at Breda in the spring of 1650. The court and the Council divided into hostile factions, not only over the rival merits of expeditions to Ireland or Scotland but also over the opposing claims to support of the Covenanters in power in Edinburgh or of Montrose, who intended to overthrow the leaders of the Kirk and replace them with a genuine royalist regime. Traditionally, three main factions have been identified: the 'Louvre party' who for purely prag-

matic reasons favoured a Presbyterian alliance; the 'Old Royalists' who remained faithful to Anglican and constitutional principles; and the 'Swordsmen', a loose group of military men who looked to Prince Rupert for leadership and despised everybody else.[10] These labels misleadingly oversimplify the factional divisions in the exiled court. There were personal relationships, ancient friendships or enmities, which could be complicated by patterns of clientage, the ties between patrons and clients. There were sometimes bitter quarrels over the responsibility for failed campaigns or lost battles, which made it impossible for certain Cavaliers, Wilmot and Digby for example, ever to cooperate with each other. Then there were the national and confessional differences. All these elements could be just as important in shaping the factions as disputes over principles or policies.

At first Ireland, where Ormonde held out optimistic hopes of achieving the impossible and uniting the various mutually hostile Irish Confederate, Ulster Irish, Ulster Presbyterian, Old English and recently arrived English royalist forces under his authority, seemed to hold out the best opportunity for a revival of royalist fortunes. The landing of Cromwell in Ireland on 15 August 1649, shortly after the defeat of Ormonde at Rathmines during a failed attempt to capture Dublin, soon shattered those hopes. Henry Seymour, a groom of the bedchamber to the King, and a trusted and reliable courier, was sent to Ireland in October to gain 'a true account of affairs', returning to Charles in December with a gloomy picture of Ormonde's condition.[11]

The collapse of resistance in Ireland before the relentless advance of the Commonwealth's armies drove into exile another group of distressed Cavaliers. Having survived a midwinter Atlantic gale off the coast of County Clare, Ormonde escaped to France in December 1650, settling at first in Caen, while Lady Ormonde returned to England to try and recover those of the family estates which had been her own inheritance. Ormonde was accompanied into exile by lords Inchiquin and Taaffe, and by two of his most loyal followers, his secretary George Lane and one of the most trusted and resourceful of his officers, John Stephens.[12] Daniel O'Neill had already left Ireland about six months earlier, to join Charles II in Holland. About this time Nicholas Armorer also turned up in Holland, having last been heard of in the garrison at Worcester when it surrendered at the end of the first Civil War. After the surrender of Worcester, Armorer may have returned to his home in Northumberland for a time, although, as he had served in the English army in Ireland in 1642, and was to demonstrate in later years a close relationship with both Ormonde and Stephens, it is probable that

Armorer spent at least some of the time between 1646 and 1651 fighting in the savage Irish wars.[13]

Despite the unrelieved sequence of disasters befalling the royalist cause, there were still plenty of exiles determined to continue the struggle. The second Duke of Hamilton, who had inherited the title on the execution of his older brother, writing to Langdale from the Hague on 8 May 1650, stressed the need to 'not faint under our afflictions, but unite all our spirits and powers in the pursuit of a just revenge'.[14] Hamilton had been drawn to Holland by the desire to take part in the negotiations between Charles and the Presbyterian commissioners, sent from Edinburgh by the hard-line Covenanter regime now in power in Scotland after the defeat and death of his brother. The authority of the new government was strengthened in 1650 by the capture and execution of Montrose, who had failed to repeat his spectacular military successes of six years earlier.

With Ormonde's forces disintegrating and Montrose dead, an alliance with the Scots Covenanters seemed to many of the young king's advisers the only choice he had left, especially as the possibility of significant aid from any European ruler seemed remote. A major diplomatic effort by Charles during 1649 and 1650, with missions despatched to a range of European countries from Portugal to Russia, had brought only modest results: some money, many expressions of goodwill but no military alliances.[15] Certainly, the times were not propitious for any European country to offer significant support to the exiled Stuarts. The end, at last, of the Thirty Years War in 1648 had left Germany ruined and devastated, no city more ruined than Heidelberg, the capital of the reduced, in all senses of the word, Palatinate of the Rhine, finally restored to Prince Rupert's older brother, Charles Louis. France and Spain remained at war, with intermittent campaigns in the Spanish Netherlands occasionally disrupting the movements of exiled Cavaliers. France also, with the boy King Louis XIV under the control of his mother Anne of Austria and his Machiavellian chief minister Cardinal Mazarin, was gradually slipping into the series of aristocratic revolts known as the Fronde. The sudden and premature death from smallpox in November 1650 of Prince William II of Orange, husband to Charles's sister Mary, had deprived the King at the worst possible time of his most energetic supporter among the princes of western Europe. Although in the short term the failure of Charles II to receive significant foreign support may be seen as disastrous for the exiled royalists, in the long term the opposite was the case. It meant that the Restoration, when it finally came in 1660, was a purely British affair. Charles II avoided the

humiliating situation of Louis XVIII in 1814, of entering his capital in the baggage train of a foreign army.

The negotiations between Charles and the Scots commissioners at Breda in March and April 1650 horrified many exiled Cavaliers, with their anger and disapproval cutting across traditional factional loyalties. Sir John Berkeley, an old friend of Hyde's but also a 'Louvrian', in a letter to Hyde on 22 March referred critically to a cabal of those who opposed the projected alliance: 'Herbert, Wyndham, Elliot, Progers, Loving or those that are in all appearance joined with them, Gerard, Nicholas, Hopton & c.'[16] This list includes both 'Old Royalists', friends of Hyde like Nicholas and Hopton, and 'Swordsmen', enemies of Hyde like Gerard and Wyndham.

Opposition to the negotiations with the Scots commissioners led to the withdrawal and even the exclusion from the royal counsels of several prominent exiles. At a meeting of the Privy Council on 6 April, Nicholas and Hopton were 'set aside' for their opposition to the terms demanded by the Scots commissioners. The influence of Jermyn and the young and volatile second Duke of Buckingham, a fairly recent arrival at the exiled court, who both favoured the Scottish alliance, was now in the ascendant. According to Nicholas, Jermyn had told Hopton that 'those who obstructed the King's counsels ought to be removed from his counsels'.[17] The royalists despatched on diplomatic missions to different European courts at this time also included a number who were opposed to the Scottish alliance, including Hyde who, with the elderly Catholic diplomat, Lord Cottington, set off reluctantly on an unwelcome and fruitless journey to Spain. Having arrived eventually in Madrid, Hyde once again encountered the Fanshawes and once again Ann Fanshawe was pregnant. 'That woman will undo him', Hyde predicted sourly to his wife, left behind in Antwerp, although whether he was referring to Ann Fanshawe's behaviour, her condition or simply to her presence, he did not make clear.[18]

Despite the opposition of Hyde, Hopton, Nicholas and many other prominent exiles, by the end of April Charles had reached an agreement, riddled with evasions and insincerities on both sides, with the Scots. In June he sailed for Scotland accompanied by a substantial following of Cavaliers, most of whom were regarded by the dour leaders of the Kirk as totally unacceptable companions for a devout Presbyterian King. Left largely in ignorance of events in Scotland, the royalists left behind on the continent swung between optimistic and unrealistic hopes that a decisive military victory was at hand and their triumphant return from exile imminent, and gloomy fears that another military disaster was

looming, leading to a reluctant recognition that perhaps the time to return to England and compound had finally arrived.

This pessimistic outlook was strengthened by the arrival back in Holland of household servants and other followers of the King, expelled by the Scots Parliament for being unacceptable companions for a godly ruler. Foremost among the King's attendants to be banished was Daniel O'Neill, who had reached the Hague after his escape from Ireland just in time to join Charles's expedition to Scotland. O'Neill was especially odious to the leaders of the Kirk, both 'for being an Irishman, and having been in arms on the late King's behalf in the late war'. He was arrested on landing and then released on condition that 'he will leave Scotland within eight days . . . nor return to Scotland without a pass from the Parliament, Committee of Estates, or Secret Council, upon pain of death'. By the end of August O'Neill was once again in the Hague.[19]

O'Neill was merely the first of the King's entourage to be ordered onto a ship back to Holland. The correspondence of the émigrés records the return into exile of other members of Charles's household. On 18 November Abraham Cowley, writing to Henry Bennet from Paris, reported that 'Mr Long, Mr Progers, Mr Seymour and Dr Fraser are again banished', and on 4 December Nicholas informed Lord Hatton that Dr Fraser and Edward Progers had arrived at the Hague, 'being both banished out of Scotland'.[20] Writing to Sir George Carteret on the same day, Nicholas deplored the fact that 'there are none of the King's servants now left to attend on his person in Scotland except the D[uke] of Buck[ingham], the Ld. Wilmot, Mr Harding, Mr Smith, Mr Rootes and Mr Pooley [sic]'. By early 1651 Richard Harding and John Poley, respectively a groom of the bedchamber and a gentleman of the privy chamber to Charles II, were also back in Holland.[21]

These depressing developments caused some of the exiled Cavaliers to come close to giving up the struggle. In the spring of 1651 two stalwarts of the out of favour 'Old Royalist' faction, Secretary Nicholas and Lord Hopton, discussed together whether the time had come to cut their losses and apply for permission to return to England. In the opinion of Nicholas, 'now the King's party are in a manner destroyed in England, I do not see how I can be any use or service to his Majesty, and shall therefore take the best course I can to preserve myself and my poor family from starving'.[22] This attitude was probably widespread at this time among the exiled Cavaliers.

Widespread perhaps, but it was not unanimous. Not all exiles felt so pessimistic about the prospects of Charles II in Scotland. Events in Scotland, in particular the invasion of the English army and Cromwell's

spectacular victory at Dunbar, gradually weakened the political influence of the leaders of the Kirk party. As Charles's own position strengthened, symbolised by his coronation on New Year's Day 1651, genuine royalists, like the Duke of Hamilton, emerged from their enforced seclusion to gather around the King. Among them was the irrepressible Daniel O'Neill. Showing the same contempt for the threats of the Scottish Parliament as he had for those of the Long Parliament nine years earlier, O'Neill returned to Scotland in May. He was just in time to join the King and his army at Stirling, from where he wrote optimistically to Ormonde on 20 June, informing his patron that 'His Majesty will in a very few days march with a much more numerous army than Cromwell's, and . . . all entirely at his command'.[23] As the Scottish army plunged southwards into England, other exiles were invited to join the desperate venture. Hamilton wrote to Ned Progers, a groom of the bedchamber and close companion of the King, who had been one of Charles's attendants banished from Scotland in November and was now in Paris, encouraging him 'to make all the haste you can' to join the army. Charles added his own hasty postscript to the letter: 'The army being on their march I could not write to you myself, pray make all the haste you can hither. Remember my service to xxx. [Lucy Walter?]. C.R.'[24] Luckily for Progers, he was not given the time to act on this pressing invitation.

News that the Scottish army had crossed the border and that it had been joined on its march by English royalists aroused the wildest hopes among some of the exiled Cavaliers. According to Clarendon, 'the king's friends in Flanders, France and Holland, who had not been permitted to attend upon his majesty in Scotland, were much exalted with the news of his being entered England with a powerful army, and being possessed of Worcester, which made all men prepare to make haste thither'. A minor skirmish at Warrington Bridge, when a small force under General Lambert withdrew out of the path of the Scottish army, was magnified in reports to the exiles as a major victory. On 30 August Lord Byron in Paris wrote exultantly to Ormonde, who was still in Caen, of the 'news brought hither by an express from Scotland which assured us that the King marched into England . . . with his whole army consisting of 15,000 foot and 6,000 horse with a good train of artillery'. Byron related how 'His majesty's army is much increased since his coming into England, and at Warrington Bridge he forced his passage with so great a slaughter of the army that opposed him under the command of Harrison and Lambert that . . . they were forced to run as far as Utoxeter [*sic*] in Staffordshire, leaving the King a fair and

uninterrupted march to London, from where in all probability he cannot now be far distant.'[25]

Four days after Byron wrote his letter Cromwell shattered the royalist army at Worcester. Of the several thousand prisoners taken, many were penned in the cathedral, where Hamilton died of his wounds a few days later. Other royalist leaders who had returned from exile were captured in the city or in flight outside it, including generals Massey and Middleton and Fanshawe. The escape of Charles II, frequently recounted in later years by the King himself and even more frequently recounted by historians and novelists, is one of the most well known events of the Civil Wars. As Wilmot was a companion of Charles for some of the time he was a fugitive, the details of his escape are also known. Buckingham and O'Neill also got away; unfortunately, we do not know how they managed their escapes. O'Neill did not reappear at the Hague until November, by which time Charles II was safely back in Paris.[26]

If the royalist army was shattered at Worcester, the exiles were equally shattered when, as Clarendon expressed it, the 'assurance of that fatal day' reached them. Once again there was a two-way traffic of Cavaliers across the Channel. In flight from England, fugitives from the Worcester campaign 'who had made escapes arrived every day in France, Flanders and Holland'. At the same time, disillusioned exiles, their hopes and resources exhausted, were returning to England. On 21 October Nicholas at the Hague wrote gloomily to Hyde about the 'abundance of royalists gone for England from these parts and many more are going, as having little hopes left them'. Hopton was one prominent exile who seriously considered returning to England on receiving 'the sad news of our fatal overthrow at Worcester', as 'where little hope is left of sudden employment', the main remaining imperative was 'to save something of my estate'. In the event, Hopton remained in exile, dying in Bruges a year later.[27]

Those Cavaliers who either decided to remain in exile, or who had no other choice but to do so, now faced the realisation that their period in exile stretched indefinitely ahead, with no immediate prospect of either a political transformation in England or a stunning military victory to bring it to a sudden end. They needed to come to terms with the kind of society on the continent in which they found themselves, to learn patience and to fall back on faith in providence to eventually create the conditions in which they could safely return home. Ormonde's serene letter to the anxious Nicholas, written in Caen on 19 October, illustrates the qualities he believed were needed if the experi-

ence of exile was to be successfully endured. 'All imaginable trials for the recovery of the royal interest have been made and failed; there remains to hope for . . . either a division among the Rebels or some such miracle as the Peace of Christendom and then their election of the English Rebels as a common enemy even before the Turk'. Ormonde recommended patience and calm resignation as the qualities now most needed. 'His not blessing all our endeavours in so just a cause I would fain understand to be a command to stand still and see the salvation He will work for us'.[28]

5
The Crowd of Fugitives

> The crowd of fugitives who hung upon them [the court] for bread.
>
> (J. Oldmixon, *The History of England during the Reigns of the Royal House of Stuart*, (London, 1730))

On 3 June 1656 a Protectorate agent in Brussels wrote to John Thurloe, that 'the English with Charles Stuart are colonel Sydenham, Price, Philips, Cairless, who set on the tree with Charles Stuart after Worcester fight, Sir Edward Walker, Mason, Lane and Harding, and of Scots, colonel Blackater, Borthwick and his brother, and major John Stone.[1] There are many similar lists in the intelligence reports sent to Cromwell's Secretary of State. The challenge is to rescue these men from obscurity, to transform the lists of names into real people, to distinguish them both as individuals and as elements in any group portrait of the exiled Cavaliers. Before we examine what the experience of exile was like, how the Cavaliers maintained themselves and their families, and how they related to their fellow exiles, we need to discover who the exiled royalists actually were, in other words, to construct their group portrait.

For there is a gap in our understanding of the lives of a large number of men and women who were involved on the royalist side in the English Civil Wars and as a consequence went into exile. This ignorance of the portion of their lives that some Cavaliers spent in exile is illustrated clearly in the *Dictionary of National Biography* entry on the Welsh Cavalier, Colonel John Robinson. The entry first details his exploits in the Civil War. 'Although only twenty-six years of age, [Robinson] . . . held the rank of lieutenant colonel, and was made governor of Holt Castle in Denbighshire in November 1643. He was present at Nantwich

34

in January 1644. In the following year he commanded a company at the battle of Rowton Heath in Cheshire; on 1 February 1646 ... he was one of the commissioners to negotiate the surrender of Chester ... [He] acted in a similar capacity when Colonel Richard Bulkeley surrendered Beaumaris, 14 June, 1646.' The entry then glosses quickly over the significant period of his life Robinson spent in exile. 'On the triumph of the parliamentary cause, Robinson, who was marked out for special vengeance, fled from Giversyllt in the disguise of a labourer, first to the Isle of Man, and then into France. His estates were confiscated. His name appears on the bill for the sale of delinquents' estates (26 September 1650).' The entry picks up the narrative again ten years later. 'At the Restoration in 1660 he recovered his estates and received other marks of royal favour ... Colonel of the militia for Denbighshire, Member of Parliament for Beaumaris in July 1661, Vice-Admiral for North Wales in 1666 ...' and so on.[2] Nor has Robinson been the only royalist victim of this Rip Van Winkle approach to writing history.

This group portrait is intended to rescue from obscurity the time spent in exile by men like Robinson and the companions of Charles II listed by Thurloe's spy in Brussels. Our concern is with those Cavaliers who, because of their royalist activities and beliefs, and who were sometimes accompanied by their families, went into exile in Europe between the meeting of the Long Parliament and the Restoration. Immediately, there is a problem: how to distinguish these 'genuine' exiled Cavaliers from the large number of other English, Irish and Scottish men and women living and travelling on the continent in the 1640s and 1650s. J. W. Stoye has described vividly the extent to which the English were travelling in Europe in the seventeenth century, 'scattering, to a degree not always appreciated, and it will never be easy to ... range in order the different groups into which they fall ... exile colleges of priests, nunneries and communities of Separatists; bands of neglected soldiery, ships and crews at sea, factors and their servants in foreign ports; the ambassadors' households, the gentry learning languages in Siena and Saumur, and even individual wanderers, scholars, musicians and jewellers.'[3]

The world of the royalist exiles overlapped with this larger world of the British expatriates in Europe. For many expatriates had royalist sympathies. This was obviously the case in the households of the Stuart princesses Mary of Orange and Elizabeth of Bohemia at the Hague, whose little courts were natural magnets to Cavaliers looking for some way in which to maintain themselves in exile. It was also the case with some of the English merchants, in particular the enormously resourceful and generous John Shaw of Rotterdam, who features so prominently

in Hyde's correspondence.[4] Other royalist sympathisers of this kind included the obliging creditor of the extravagant Marquess of Newcastle, Mrs Beynham of Rotterdam, remembered approvingly by Lady Newcastle as the 'widow to an English merchant, who had always been very loyal to his Majesty the King of England, and serviceable to his Majesty's faithful subjects in whatever lay in his power'. Religious houses on the continent also contained royalist sympathisers and, as in the cases of Toby Mathew and Wat Montagu, could become havens for royalist exiles. Mary Knatchbull, for example, a Benedictine abbess in Ghent, was also a regular correspondent of Hyde's and her abbey served as a kind of safe clearing-house for letters between royalists in England and in exile.[5]

It is normally a fairly straightforward matter to distinguish the genuine exiled Cavaliers from these respectable and prominent royalist sympathisers living in Europe: men like Lord Craven, Elizabeth of Bohemia's devoted admirer and benefactor, or John Shaw of Antwerp, or the faithful Sir Richard Browne, Charles I's resident ambassador in Paris since July 1641, who continued to try and protect the interests of Charles II throughout the 1650s. However, it is not always so easy to distinguish the emigrés from other English expatriates. It was common for young men with royalist sympathies making what was soon to be labelled the Grand Tour to move sometimes in exile circles, to attend – as John Evelyn did – Anglican services at the residence of Sir Richard Browne in Paris or to pay their respects to Charles II. To second generation royalists there was now a further reason to make the Grand Tour: to demonstrate one's loyalty to the Stuart monarchy while escaping, at least for a time, the humiliation of submission to the detested Commonwealth regime. To the young Yorkshireman Sir John Reresby, who 'left England in that unhappy time', remaining in England 'appeared worse than banishment; which caused most of our youth (especially such whose families had adhered to the late King) to travel; amongst others myself'. But Reresby and the other young men who shared his views had not taken part in the Civil War, although, as they tended to cluster around the exiled court of Charles II, it is sometimes difficult to distinguish them from the genuine exiled Cavaliers.[6]

The exiled Cavaliers also need to be distinguished from other English expatriates who cannot be so easily classified into neat groups as can the merchants, gentlemen on the Grand Tour, members of religious orders, or place-holders at the courts of Elizabeth of Bohemia or Mary of Orange. For the exiled Cavaliers moved among a colourful and dubious assortment of adventurers, mercenaries and soldiers of fortune.

Mysterious characters of ambiguous loyalties like Colonel Sir Thomas Rokeby and the treacherous Sir Robert Stone, who flit in and out of the correspondence of the exiles, can easily be mistaken for Cavaliers, until one investigates them more closely.

Sir Thomas Rokeby, although he moved in exile circles and was apparently quite highly regarded, at least at first, by Sir Edward Nicholas and Sir Marmaduke Langdale, was no Cavalier but a professional soldier who had fought in the Thirty Years War. Unlike so many of his comrades in arms, he did not hurry back to England when the Civil War broke out; instead, he remained in France and served under the Prince of Condé in the civil wars of the Fronde. His subsequent fortunes during the 1650s were, to put it mildly, varied. In 1655, although for a time a prisoner in the Bastille, he retained his optimism. Percy Church, a member of Henrietta Maria's household, who as we shall see frequently exerted himself on behalf of royalists in distress, visited him in the Bastille in April and reported to Nicholas that 'Sir Thomas Rokeby I found merry and hopeful of his speedy freedom'. His optimism was justified for a few months later he was free and in England, involved in royalist conspiracy and acting as an agent for Langdale. Back in Brussels by November, Rokeby forwarded to Charles II at Cologne intelligence on English affairs and proposals for a landing in England by a force of exiles. In the aftermath of the suppression of a royalist rising in March, and with England now under the rule of the Major-Generals, proposals to seize ports were totally unrealistic, so Rokeby headed east to try his luck in the Polish army. His luck finally ran out in June 1658 when he was burned to death in an accident near Danzig. Although some royalists suspected Rokeby of being a Cromwellian agent, to the more charitable John Ball, writing from Konigsberg to Nicholas, his death was 'a great loss to the Poles, as also to the King our master, for whom he might have done good service if he had lived'.[7]

The varied career of Sir Robert Stone further illustrates the difficulty of distinguishing genuine exiled Cavaliers from some of the more dubious expatriates among whom they moved. Stone emerges from the scattered references to him in the exiles' correspondence as devious and treacherous, ingratiating or quarrelsome according to circumstances. Like Rokeby, he moved in emigré circles; on 24 August 1655 he was in the company of a number of exiled Cavaliers at a dinner at the Hague, where he toasted the health of Charles II and predicted the King's imminent restoration. This was just six months after he had betrayed to Thurloe the true identity of the so-called merchant Nicholas Wright detained in Dover castle. It was Stone also who confirmed the rumours

circulating in the United Provinces in early September 1658 that the Protector was dead. 'There is no doubt of the truth of the news', reported Hyde to Ormonde from Breda on 10 September. 'Sir Robert Stone saw the carcase, and here are two or three come to this town, who left London since he died, which was on Friday last'.[8] But Stone was no Cavalier. A professional soldier in the Dutch service, variously referred to as major or colonel, and a member of the household of Elizabeth of Bohemia, he was also a correspondent of Thurloe's. Throughout the 1650s Stone travelled apparently freely between Holland and England. Early in 1653 he was even employed by the Dutch as an unofficial go-between with the Commonwealth government during the peace nego-tiations to bring to an end the first Dutch War. Both Hyde and Nicholas suspected that he was carrying 'some private message from the Rebels to the most potent in these provinces', and if they had known of his treachery to his 'friend' Armorer in Dover castle in February 1655, their suspicions that he was 'employed by the Rebels' would have been con-firmed. But despite these suspicions, and notwithstanding his reputa-tion as a quarrelsome duellist, Stone remained in the service of Elizabeth of Bohemia. His treachery was suspected but never proved.[9]

While the exiled Cavaliers were one of a number of groups of English expatriates scattered throughout the continent, they were also, of course, a part of European society in the 1640s and 1650s. Their for-tunes and circumstances were to a great extent determined by their hosts, who were also so often their creditors. The extent of the sympa-thy or support to be expected from the kings of France and Spain, from royal ministers, from German and Italian princes, from ecclesiastical and military authorities and from town councils, were major concerns of the emigrés, prominent themes in the correspondence of men like Hyde, Ormonde and Nicholas. At a more basic level, it was the will-ingness of the local innkeepers, tradesmen and keepers of lodgings to display long-suffering patience and extend indefinite credit that was of most importance to impoverished exiles. The attitudes of local inhabi-tants could range from sympathy and generosity through indifference to outright hostility. When Lord and Lady Newcastle entered Cambrai in the summer of 1648 they were welcomed with a torch-light proces-sion, the governor 'being pleased to send all manner of provisions to My Lord's lodgings', recorded Lady Newcastle complacently, 'and charg-ing our landlord to take no pay for anything we had'.[10] This generous display of hospitality contrasts sharply with the hostility encountered in Antwerp by the one-time royalist general Lord Wentworth, who com-plained to Hyde on 23 October 1659 that 'this morning two or three of

my creditors were with me; threatening me that they would do me an affront if I did not speedily pay them'. Although a privy councillor and a gentleman of the bedchamber to Charles II, Wentworth was unable to attend the court for 'if I should stir an inch out of the town, my creditors would suspect I were quite run away, and then my wife could in no manner appease them'.[11]

It is therefore not possible to consider the exiled Cavaliers in isolation, as a clearly defined and distinctive group, as has been done, for example, with the members of the Long Parliament or the civil service of the English Republic.[12] Rather, they need to be seen as a constantly changing 'crowd of fugitives', their ranks thinning or swelling in responses to alterations either in their own fortunes or in those of the Stuart cause. Their lives in exile were interwoven with those of their hosts, to whom they so often looked for employment, support and, above all else, credit, and with the other English travellers and residents in Europe among whom they lived and moved: the clergy and courtiers, the merchants and Grand Tourists, the adventurers and soldiers of fortune.

So the first problem to overcome in compiling a group biography of the exiled Cavaliers is to be able to distinguish them from the other members of the British expatriate community on the continent. A second problem is caused by the different periods of time royalists passed in exile. Exile could be for a few weeks, even for a few days in the case of the unfortunate Sir Henry Killigrew, or it could last for twenty years. At one extreme were those Cavaliers who remained on the continent until they died – Goring, Hopton, Wilmot and Percy, for example, among a number of others – or until they returned to England with Charles II at the Restoration. At the other were those royalists who quickly gave up trying to survive on inadequate resources in an unfamiliar environment and, as Hyde referred to them derisively in the letter to Lady Dalkeith already quoted, joined the 'multitude of men of honour running to compound'.[13]

The 'short-term' exiles are a problem for the historian as, for obvious reasons, they have left fewer records behind them than did those royalists who remained in Europe for years, who established links with one of the Stuart courts, who corresponded with their fellow emigrés, and whose careers and experiences in exile can consequently be reconstructed from surviving source materials. The existence of these 'short-term' or 'temporary' exiles also complicates any attempt to answer the basic question of how many royalists fled 'beyond the seas' in the first place.

How large exactly was 'the crowd of fugitives'? The evidence is conflicting and fragmentary, derived from a number of different sources. For example, there are several contemporary estimates of the strength of the forces raised by Charles II in Flanders with Spanish support between 1656 and 1660. In all, the King raised six regiments of foot and a small life-guard of about fifty horse commanded by Sir Charles Berkeley. With four Irish regiments, one Scottish and one English, it has been estimated that only about 300 soldiers in Charles's little army, which reached a maximum strength of between 2,000 and 3,000 men in the spring of 1657, were English.[14] As well as genuine exiled royalists, the 300 also included soldiers of fortune and adventurous would-be Cavaliers, such as the 'fifty young blades from England' whom one of Thurloe's spies reported as arriving in Brussels in March 1657, hopeful of military employment.[15]

Other sources support the picture of sudden fluctuations in émigré numbers, with references to royalists in quite large numbers either arriving in Europe or returning to England. Reference has been made above to the seventy gentlemen and attendants who accompanied Newcastle from Scarborough to Hamburg in July 1644, and the 'forty Gentlemen and Officers' who fled with Sir John Marlay and Sir Thomas Glemham from Berwick to Rotterdam in September 1648; while the collapse of royalist hopes after Cromwell's decisive victory at Worcester on 3 September 1651 had caused a flow of traffic the other way.[16] Some of the 'fifty young blades' who arrived so hopefully in Brussels in March 1657, and who it would be rash to assume were all loyal Cavaliers eager to once again draw their swords in the Stuart cause, would probably also have soon drifted back to England after failing to be enlisted in the royalist regiments in Flanders.

This is certainly what happened to two obscure figures who make a brief appearance in Hyde's correspondence during 1657. On 9 July Hyde informed Ormonde that the two brothers, 'Captain' Thomas and Henry Batt, had arrived in Bruges 'a year since in good clothes, believing the King was ready for England, but are now very poor'. After a year hanging around the exiled court at Bruges the Batt brothers were reduced to a condition of 'great necessity' and wished only to return to England. Form the meagre resources available to him, Hyde provided 140 florins to pay for their repatriation; by October they were back in England and we hear nothing more of them.[17] The hard core of 'long-term' emigrés was surrounded by these transient would-be Cavaliers, looking for employment and adventure: temporary and fleeting replacements for those royalists who were unable or unwilling to endure the rigours of

exile and who returned to England to compound for their Delinquency and to conform to the Commonwealth regime.

A group portrait or biography of the Cavaliers in exile therefore has to take into account certain significant divisions within the 'crowd of fugitives'. There is the distinction between genuine exiles and other royalist sympathisers who happened to be living or travelling on the continent: merchants like John Shaw, gentlemen on the Grand Tour like Evelyn and Reresby, religious like Abbess Knatchbull, and soldiers of fortune like Rokeby. Another significant distinction is the one between the 'long-term' and the 'short-term' exiles; between those committed royalists who spent a number of years in Europe rather than submit to Commonwealth or Protectorate, and those who either died in exile within a few weeks or months of leaving England, like Suckling and Henry Killigrew, or were driven to return, either by poverty and lack of employment abroad, like the Batt brothers, or by disillusionment and loss of hope in the success of the Stuart cause. As has been mentioned above, Hyde, a conspicuous and totally committed 'long-term' emigré, with his customary occupation of the moral eminence, had only contempt for 'the multitude of men of honour running to compound'. In his letter from Jersey on 24 October 1646, to Lady Dalkeith, he expressed his horror that 'now all men made haste over, for all were admitted to compound [but] . . . never reckoned how many oaths, and how many lies they paid' above their composition fines.[18]

Any attempt at a group portrait of the exiled Cavaliers that hopes to include the hundreds of 'short-term' exiles, the whole shifting crowd of luke-warm royalists and soldiers of fortune with conveniently professed loyalties to the Stuart cause, must necessarily be very blurred around the edges. If a more rigorous definition of the term 'exiled Cavaliers' is applied, a much more manageable group emerges. The group portrait that occupies the remainder of this chapter focuses on the 'long-term' exiles, those English Cavaliers, sometimes accompanied by families and dependants, whose political or military activities in support of the Stuart cause were responsible for their going into and remaining in exile in Europe for a substantial period of time, a minimum of two years at least.

As well as the 'short-term' exiles, this definition excludes from further examination certain other significant groups of royalist expatriates. The most important are those Anglican clergy who, expelled from their livings, went into exile and maintained, in chapels from Hamburg to Paris, the Anglican communion when it was proscribed in England. The Anglican clergy were a significant group among the emigrés; to mention

only a tiny sample of the more prominent: Hyde's friend and chaplain George Morley; John Bramhall, Bishop of Derry; John Cosin, Dean of Peterborough and the well travelled Isaac Basire and John Bargrave. The clergy were well represented in the various Stuart courts and some of them endured long periods in exile, suffering as much as any Cavalier. Yet many of them were able to reflect on the course of events, to study and to write, and so prepare for the re-establishment of their church after the Restoration.[19] Two Oxford academics, Richard Allestree, Student of Christ Church before the Civil War, and William Beaw, a fellow of New College, temporarily renounced scholarship and theology for more active pursuits during their years in exile. Allestree became a royalist agent, and made several secret journeys to England, while Beaw became an officer in the Swedish army. After the Restoration their careers returned to more orthodox paths; Allestree became Regius Professor of Divinity at Oxford and Beaw ended his days as Bishop of Llandaff.[20]

Although this group portrait is now focused on the 'long-term' English, and some Welsh, Cavaliers, it is not always possible to make a sharp distinction between the English royalist exiles on the one hand and the Scots and Irish on the other. Several Irish and Scottish royalists moved extensively in English exile circles; some, like Daniel O'Neill and the Scot Sir James Hamilton, had fought in England in the Civil War, had places at court, and in general had much stronger links with England than with the country of their birth.

The aggressive and quarrelsome Hamilton, a younger son of the first Earl of Haddington, and a gentleman of the bedchamber to Charles II during the 1650s, was one of a number of Scots who were attached to the court in exile. Some of the others included Sir William Fleming, another younger son of a Scottish peer, the Earl of Wigton. A much more cultivated and worldly figure than Hamilton, he specialised in missions that were doomed from the outset: to the Duke of Hamilton from Henrietta Maria in July 1648 and to the Marquess of Montrose from Charles II in May 1650.[21] According to Thurloe's spy at the exiled court, Henry Manning, Fleming was 'of Middleton and Hyde's party'. As Manning also confirmed, the ex-Covenanter general John Middleton was regarded highly by Hyde who considered him 'as worthy a person as ever that nation bred, of great modesty, courage and judgment'.[22] Sir Alexander Hume, chamberlain to Mary of Orange, and Sir William Keith, whom Hyde described in October 1655 as 'a person who is so much in the care of the King', were two other Scots Cavaliers who moved chiefly in English exile circles. But probably the most Anglicised Scottish emigré was James Livingstone, Viscount Newburgh, who on the

instructions of Charles I was sent as a young man 'to be bred in France'. A gentleman of the bedchamber to Charles I and of the privy chamber to Charles II, he was one of the King's inner circle of companions during the 1650s.[23]

Among the Irish and Anglo-Irish royalists who moved in English exile circles, the dominating figure is that of James Butler, twelfth Earl and first Marquess of Ormonde, the King's Lord Lieutenant of Ireland, who finally abandoned the hopeless struggle against the armies of the Commonwealth and withdrew to France in December 1650. One of the very few great aristocratic and territorial magnates among the exiles, Ormonde's natural authority and prestige were further strengthened both by his dignity and fortitude in adversity and by his high-principled and undeviating adherence to the Stuart cause. Writing to Nicholas on 13 January 1652, after Ormonde had joined Charles II's little court in Paris, Hyde stated that in his life 'he never knew a worthier person than my Lord of Ormonde, nor [one] more impossible to be swayed or guided by any but public and noble rules, and to the best ends'.[24]

Ormonde's close association with Hyde and Secretary Nicholas ensured that some of his followers were also brought into the circle of the English exiled royalists. Three of the most prominent were George Lane, Daniel O'Neill and John Stephens, all of whom had served under him in Ireland and escaped into exile when Ireland was conquered by the armies of the Commonwealth. George Lane, of Tulske, county Roscommon, who is included in the list sent to Thurloe of 'the English with Charles Stuart' that began this chapter, was Ormonde's faithful and long-serving secretary. He was closely identified with the Hyde-Ormonde-Nicholas group in the exiled court, a connection strengthened by his marriage to Susan Nicholas, the Secretary's daughter, in March 1655.[25] Daniel O'Neill also was closely associated with Ormonde for over twenty years. He served under him in several bitter Irish campaigns, was employed on diplomatic missions between the Lord Lieutenant and royalist Oxford during the Civil War, and was a frequent companion of Ormonde in exile. Ormonde's correspondence contains ample evidence of the friendship between them; writing to Lord Digby on 9 July 1644, he referred to 'your good friend and mine, Dan. O'Neill'.[26] Although not so flamboyant a character as O'Neill, John Stephens had similar connections, both to Ormonde and to prominent English exiled royalists. The son of the collector of the customs at Waterford and Ross before the Civil War, Stephens served under Ormonde in Ireland, then accompanied the Lord Lieutenant into exile, being employed by him as a courier during the 1650s. As well as serving his

patron Ormonde, who was only too willing to acknowledge how for 'so long and so faithfully he hath followed my fortune', Stephens also became involved in royalist conspiracy. This involvement brought him into frequent contact not only with other royalist agents like O'Neill and Nicholas Armorer, but also with Hyde, whose correspondence contains numerous references to both O'Neill and Stephens.[27] The fortunes in exile of these three Irish clients and followers of Ormonde are inseparable from those of the English Cavaliers among whom they moved and lived.

Some other Irish exiles, such as Lord Muskerry and the brothers James and George Hamilton, had intermittent contact with the English emigrés, but in at least two more cases the links were more substantial. Murrough O'Brien, sixth Baron Inchiquin, after a turbulent and sometimes ferocious military career in the Irish wars, went into exile in Paris, was admitted to the King's Privy Council and received an earldom from Charles II in May 1654. At first Hyde had a high opinion of Inchiquin, whom he considered 'a gallant gentleman of good parts and great industry, and a temper fit to struggle with the affairs on all sides that we are to contend with'. But when Charles moved to Germany in the summer of 1654, Inchiquin remained in Paris, became a Catholic convert, and moved within the orbit of Henrietta Maria's court at the Louvre.[28] The second case is that of Theobald, Viscount Taaffe, a much more lightweight character than either Inchiquin or Ormonde. More notable as a dancer than a soldier, although he had fought in the Irish wars, Taaffe became a close confidant of Charles; he was at the centre of the exiled court, responsible for maintaining royal morale and keeping up the royal spirits.[29] The formulation of policy was left to graver and more substantial members of the King's following, in particular to Hyde and Ormonde.

A group portrait of the 'long-term' English Cavaliers in exile must therefore also take into account those Scots and Irish royalists who moved principally in English emigré circles and whose presence gave the exiled court a 'British' character. There seem to have been approximately twenty, ranging from Ormonde the dignified grandee to George Arnet, a thuggish Scottish page.[30] A representative group portrait cannot be comprised exclusive of male Cavaliers either. Obviously, the experience of exile was frequently shared by the wives, (like Ann Fanshawe), mistresses, (like the notorious Lucy Walter), children, (like Susan Nicholas, who grew up in exile), and servants, (like the chambermaid to Sir Hugh Cholmley's daughters), of those royalists who fled England. Of course, in the vast majority of cases, women, children and servants

went into exile as the dependants of husbands, fathers or employers, and not as a consequence of their own actions. But, as we shall see, not in all cases.

After excluding from the group portrait of the 'long-term' exiled Cavaliers the various other groups of expatriates so far discussed, we are left with something over 200 male English Cavaliers whose political or military services in the Stuart cause were responsible for their having or choosing to go into exile in Europe for a significant period of time, for at least two years and in many cases much longer than that. A variety of sources make it possible to identify over 220 Cavaliers who spent more than two years in exile. The most useful source material by far is the surviving correspondence of exiled royalists, followed by the papers of John Thurloe, especially the intelligence reports of his agents in Europe. Also very informative are the records of the Committee for Compounding and material in the State Papers Domestic and Foreign in the Public Record Office, in particular royal household lists and accounts. The identity of exiled royalists, as well as valuable accounts of aspects of the experience of exile, are contained in the memoirs of individuals like Clarendon, the Duchess of Newcastle and Lady Fanshawe.

The 'long-term' emigrés who can be identified may not be totally representative of the group as a whole, as the exiled royalists were scattered widely throughout Europe, their arrivals and departures often unrecorded as they moved among the various communities of British expatriates. The group portrait that follows is focused chiefly on those Cavaliers who settled in France, the Netherlands or Germany; who maintained links with the courts of Charles II, Henrietta Maria or Mary of Orange; who had dealings, recorded in their correspondence, with prominent royal counsellors, in particular with Hyde, Ormonde or Nicholas; or who were involved in conspiracy and so attracted the interest of Thurloe's agents. Cavaliers who settled in other countries, or who dropped out of exile circles, are more difficult to trace. As G. E. Aylmer observed about some of the civil servants of the English Republic, after every effort they 'remain obstinately obscure'.[31] The reports of Thurloe's spies or the letters of the exiles sometimes refer with tantalising brevity to such obscure figures as 'Captain Mason . . . an honest man, a soldier of the King and now gets his living as a servant to the merchants at Dort'. He is quite possibly the same Mason listed as among 'the English with Charles Stuart' in the intelligence report to Thurloe quoted at the beginning of this chapter; but he was not a member of the royal household and we never hear of him again.[32] But despite the certain

omissions, the proportion of 'obstinately obscure' figures, and the difficulty in some cases of deciding whether a particular person was a genuine exiled royalist or not, it is safe to claim that the royalists investigated in the remainder of this chapter comprise the greater part of the English Cavaliers who spent a significant portion of the period between the outbreak of the Civil War and the Restoration in exile in Europe.

The dominant social group among the exiled Cavaliers was, not surprisingly, drawn from the landed gentry. The peers among the exiles were predominantly either members of office-holding court families or ex-military commanders, whose titles had been granted for their military services during the Civil War. In the first category were a few elderly relics of the court of Charles I: men like George Goring, Earl of Norwich, John Digby, Earl of Bristol and Francis, Lord Cottington, all with diplomatic experience going back to James I's attempts to improve relations with Spain in the 1620s, and with an accumulation of court appointments acquired over several decades. Norwich, Bristol and Cottington were very much outnumbered by a new generation of courtier peers: Culpepper, Jermyn, the younger Digby and Hatton, for example, with much more recently granted titles. These courtier peers among the exiles were in their turn outnumbered by the swordsmen, the Cavalier generals with peerages granted in recognition of their military services: men like Wentworth, Byron, Hopton, Gerard, the younger Goring and Widdrington. In the case of some peers, like Digby and Jermyn, it is not really possible to make a clear distinction between courtiers and soldiers; they were both.

What is distinctive about the royalist peers in exile is the newness of their titles. Of thirty 'long-term' noble emigrés, not one had a peerage that had been created before 1600; almost all held titles granted since the 1620s. Although the senior peer among the exiles was the flamboyant George Villiers, second Duke of Buckingham, he was not exactly a representative example of the ancient nobility of England. The oldest titles were borne by the Irish peers, James Butler twelfth Earl and first Marquess of Ormonde and Murrough O'Brien, sixth Baron and first Earl of Inchiquin. The lineage of the royalist lords in exile was not nearly as impressive as that of such parliamentary peers as the earls of Northumberland and Pembroke and Lord Saye and Sele.[33]

The comparative absence of aristocratic grandees, apart from Newcastle and Ormonde, and the newness of the exiled peers' titles, meant there was little social distinction between them and the gentry emigrés. Among the latter there were many representatives from substantial landed families: for example, Charles Howard, Viscount Andover;

Charles Lyttelton, son of the royalist High Sheriff of Worcestershire; Oliver Fitzwilliam, son of Viscount Fitzwilliam; Robert Sidney, third son of the Earl of Leicester; Henry Seymour, second son of a baronet; Robert Phelips, son of Sir Robert Phelips of Montacute, Somerset and Edward Stanley, a younger son of the formidable defender of the Lathom House in the Civil War, the Countess of Derby. Although the majority of the 'long-term' exiles were Cavalier ex-officers drawn from the lesser gentry, men like Nicholas Armorer, those families who were the traditional leaders of the royalist party were well represented in exile circles. A surprisingly high proportion, at least a third of the sample of 225 'long-term' exiles, were also eldest or only sons. It is clear that they were not just a rabble of landless adventurers, soldiers of fortune and obscure courtiers, kept in some semblance of order and respectability by a few isolated and towering figures like Ormonde and Hyde.

Although the landed gentry were, not surprisingly, the dominant social group among the exiled Cavaliers, there was a minority of exiles of non-gentry origins who included some well-known figures. Sir John Marlay, a Newcastle merchant, 'hated and abhorred of all', or at least by his many enemies, had been governor of the city during a long and bitter siege in 1644. There were also at least three Londoners with a commercial background: Alderman James Bunce, the silk merchant George Benyon and Captain Silas Titus, the son of a soap maker.[34] Titus was a Presbyterian who had fought for Parliament, but his essential conservatism had pushed him into the King's camp between 1647 and 1649 as the moderate Presbyterians in Parliament lost control of the course of events to the Independents and the senior officers in the New Model army. But the number of 'lapsed' parliamentarians among the exiled royalists remained very small; the soldiers Middleton, Titus and Edward Massey, the one time heroic parliamentarian defender of Gloucester turned daring royalist conspirator, were the most significant.[35] Apart from the exiled Anglican clergy, the middle-class professional men who went into exile usually did so as the employees of more socially or politically prominent royalists. They included some diverse and famous figures: the poet Abraham Cowley, Lord Jermyn's secretary in Paris; Richard Pile, the royal surgeon who became a secret agent; Stephen Fox, the future brilliant financier, who began his career as a servant to Lord Percy; and Charles II's mathematics tutor, the philosopher Thomas Hobbes.

The presence of a scattering of exiled royalists of middle-class background, whether professional or commercial, cannot conceal the predominance of gentry among the 'long-term' emigrés. The characteristic

that they all overwhelmingly had in common was that of having served either or both Charles I or Charles II, although this service could take various forms. Approximately three-quarters of the 'long-term' exiled Cavaliers had fought in the Civil Wars, while almost all the rest had served the Stuarts in various civil capacities, either with positions at court or in the royalist government established at Oxford during the Civil War. A very small group of exiles, like Lady Derby's son Edward Stanley, had taken no part in the Civil Wars at all, generally because they were too young. The military service of the emigrés ranged from the serious and extensive, in the case of army commanders like Goring and Langdale, to the insignificant and shortlived, as illustrated by the brief and obscure military career of Henry Bennet, the future Earl of Arlington.[36]

Of the exiled Cavaliers who had fought in the Civil Wars a significant proportion, about a quarter, had military or naval experience dating from before the war's outbreak. For a few this experience had been in the King's service, as was the case with the sailor Sir John Mennes; for most it had been in the Thirty Years War, either as professional soldiers, like Colonel Sir William Leighton and Colonel Sir William Vavasour, or as gentleman volunteers. Clarendon's comment on Daniel O'Neill, that 'he was very well known in the Court, having spent many years between that and the Low Countries, the winter seasons in the one, and the summer always in the army of the other', could be also applied to several of O'Neill's fellow exiles, like George Goring, Henry Wilmot and John Berkeley. There were also a small number of emigrés – an example is Richard Pile, the army surgeon who became a secret agent – who had served in the royalist armies in a non-military role.[37]

swords in the royalist cause, the other feature common to the background of over a quarter of them was that, like Daniel O'Neill, they were 'very well known in the Court'. Their association with the court of Charles I had taken different forms. There were the placeholders in the royal household: for example, the elegant patron of the arts, Sir Charles Cotterell, Master of Ceremonies to Charles I, and Hyde's friends, Henry Seymour and Richard Harding, grooms of the bedchamber to Prince Charles. Then there were the holders of offices of state. Sir John Culpepper, Master of the Robes, and Christopher, Lord Hatton, Comptroller of the Household, were both members of the King's Privy Council at Oxford during the Civil War. As well, there were a number of exiles with more informal links with the court. Some belonged to families with strong court connections, like the brothers William and Henry Coven-

try, the sons of Charles I's Lord Keeper, and Sir Frederick Cornwallis, Gentleman Usher of the Privy Chamber to the King, whose father, grandfather and uncle had all been courtiers.[38] Stephen Fox began his long and profitable connection with the court as an obscure member of the household of Lord Percy, where he showed great ability in 'the understanding of accounts', a talent that made him indispensable and so took him into exile with his patron.[39]

Several of the courtiers and office holders, and even some of the soldiers, had been prominent in other areas of public life before the Civil War. Twenty-three exiled Cavaliers had sat in the Long Parliament and another five, of whom Secretary Nicholas was the most significant, in one of the earlier parliaments of Charles I. Several, like Berkeley, Jermyn and Wilmot, consistently represented the court interest, but there were others who played a prominent part in the momentous debates in the Long Parliament, most notably Hyde, Culpepper, Hopton and the erratic George Digby. At least a dozen emigrés had also travelled on the continent on diplomatic missions before the Civil War. There was a cosmopolitan element in such men as Montagu, Porter, Fanshawe and Cottington that distinguishes them from most of the other exiled Cavaliers. Endymion Porter, notorious for his admiration of all things Spanish, after he escaped to France in 1646, soon moved with his wife to Brussels, whose environment as the capital of the Spanish Netherlands was presumably more to his taste.[40] This experience in diplomacy of a small but significant group of exiled Cavaliers was of considerable value to Charles II in the complex and frequently frustrating diplomatic relations with his various official hosts during the 1650s. Also, diplomats like Fanshawe and Cottington shared with professional soldiers like Vavasour and courtier-soldiers like O'Neill a familiarity with European customs and conditions that would have made the experience of exile a less daunting ordeal for them than it was for other royalists.

This group portrait of the 'long-term' exiles shows that they were not just a 'crowd of fugitives': socially negligible adventurers, obscure courtiers and broken soldiers. The perhaps surprising strong representation of older and only sons from prominent gentry families, and the wealth of experience in politics, diplomacy and the court possessed by so may exiled Cavaliers, come through strongly in the group portrait. Two other significant features of the emigrés as a group are the not surprising predominance of veterans of the Civil Wars, from generals like Byron and Goring to junior officers like Nicholas Armorer, and the fact that so many of the Cavaliers had already been beyond the seas for one

reason or another before their defeat in the Civil Wars had compelled them to go on their travels again. The royalists who chose exile instead of passive acceptance of the new regime, and who then remained in exile and did not succumb to the temptation to return to England, pay their composition fines and try to pick up the threads of their old existence, were a small minority in the King's party. For the most part the Cavaliers who made this difficult decision were not elderly, worn out men, for whom exile was the final melancholy chapter in their lives. Most of them were still in their prime of life in the 1650s and, as we shall see, more than three-quarters of the 225 'long-term' exiles who can be identified survived to return to England at the Restoration to play an active part in social and political life under the restored monarchy.

Life in exile held little appeal for elderly royalists and few underwent the ordeal. For those who did, exile often was the final melancholy chapter in their lives. Windebank died in Paris in 1646 and Arundel in Padua; Cottington, the Catholic hispanophile, settled in Madrid in 1650 where he died in 1652, the same year in which Hopton died in Bruges. Ormonde's 'good old man' Sir Richard Foster, Keeper of the King's Privy Purse, died in Paris in 1655, as did Hyde's enemy, the Attorney-General Sir Edward Herbert, two years later.[41] These were all elderly men, but they were in a small minority among the emigrés whose median age in 1650 was in the mid-thirties. The number of older emigrés also needs to be balanced against the presence of some very young men among the exiled Cavaliers. On 1 December 1657, Colonel Thomas Blague, a battle hardened Civil War veteran and a groom of the bedchamber to Charles II, while raising troops for his regiment in Flanders, reported to Secretary Nicholas the appointment as his ensign of 'Mr Pooley, son to Sir John Pooley, who hath been in England, Scotland and Ireland in his [the King's] service since he was twelve years old and is now about one and twenty'.[42] As we shall see, failed royalist conspiracies during the 1650s could also drive into exile Cavaliers of a generation too young to have taken part in the Civil War, like Charles Lyttelton, whom Hyde recommended to Ormonde as a 'youth' worthy of the Marquess's protection and patronage, and his younger brother William.[43] The most striking example of a second generation Cavalier in exile is probably Edward Stanley, a younger son of defiantly royalist parents, the Earl and Countess of Derby. 'Young Mr Stanley' was only about seventeen when he was sent to court by his mother to 'be planted in the King's good opinion'; the fact that the King was residing in Bruges at the time was irrelevant to a stout traditionalist like Lady Derby.[44]

This group portrait of 225 identifiable 'long-term' emigrés has emphasised characteristics that many if not most of them had in common: landed gentry social background; service in the King's forces in the Civil Wars; connections with the royal court; political or diplomatic experience as royal counsellors, members of parliament, envoys or ambassadors. It is clear also that the majority of the exiled Cavaliers were between 30 and 40 years old during the 1650s, as exile was not an option attractive to elderly royalists. The comparative youthfulness of the world of the exiles would have been further emphasised by the presence of many families including children. The correspondence of the exiles makes frequent reference to the problem of maintaining families in the harsh conditions of exile, as Nicholas put it, to preventing his 'wife and children starving in the streets'.[45] But if the exiled Cavaliers held a number of characteristics in common, they were also divided by different religious loyalties, often held opposing views on particular issues and policies that confronted Charles II and his advisers, and were further fragmented by a wide variety of personal allegiances or enmities. The divisions were intensified, the quarrels between factions and individuals embittered, by the humiliation of military defeat, the loss of political influence, the sequestration and confiscation of property and all the distressing features of a life in exile. It is not surprising that the correspondence of the exiles, as in Lord Hatton's letter from Paris to Nicholas in January 1655, contains frequent references to such events as 'the divisions and quarrels of Fraiser and Wentworth, Fraiser and Newburgh, Wentworth and Fleming, Newburgh and Taaffe'. As we shall see, feuds and factions were a major feature of the exile experience.[46]

The religious affiliations of the exiled Cavaliers could have an influence on their political views and factional loyalties. Although it is impossible to identify conclusively the religious loyalties of a number of the 'long-term' emigrés, probably between one-quarter and one-fifth were Catholics and fewer than ten were Presbyterians, with the rest being Anglicans of varying degrees of commitment. It is not possible to be precise about the figures as, apart from the 'unknowns', there were also conversions among the exiles. Prominent exiles like Digby, Goring and Inchiquin became Catholic converts while the Scots general Middleton moved steadily from the Presbyterian–Covenanter camp into the Anglican communion and friendship with Hyde.[47] Despite the difficulties in identifying religious affiliations, it seems probable that the proportion of Catholics among the exiles was higher than in the royalist party as a whole; this probability supports the view that the factional groupings, and political and religious allegiances among the exiled

Cavaliers, were not an exact microcosm of the whole body of the King's supporters. It is the plain country gentry, those with no family tradition of office-holding, no court connections and no significant military experience or reputation, who are under-represented among the exiled Cavaliers.

Although no simple stereotype of the exiled Cavalier emerges from this group portrait, certain important features and characteristics can be highlighted. First, the number of Cavaliers who endured a long period of time in exile – anything from two to twenty years – was comparatively small, probably not much more than three hundred men, and many of them returned to England before the Restoration. But around this core of 'long-term' emigrés swirled a shifting and changing 'crowd of fugitives': soldiers of fortune, adventurers, hangers-on about the exiled court and, most numerous of all, those less-committed royalists, Hyde's contemptuously labelled 'men of honour', who soon succumbed to the temptation to compound for their Delinquency and return to the comparative comfort of a quiet life in England. The number of 'short-term' exiles is impossible to estimate exactly, but was certainly much greater, probably over one thousand. It is also impossible to estimate exactly how many exiled Cavaliers shared their life in exile with wives and families, for they too were a constantly shifting group, travelling between husbands or fathers on the continent and England, their movements dictated by various factors but chiefly by the need to raise or save money. For example, early in 1648 Secretary Nicholas sent his wife Jane back to England to attempt to raise money so he could pay the debts he had accumulated at the Hague. Jane Nicholas travelled with 'her two sons, three maidservants, three menservants, two trunks and necessaries'.[48]

Paradoxically, the most striking group characteristic of the exiled Cavaliers is their diversity. Although drawn overwhelmingly from the landowning class, the emigrés were not predominantly plain country gentry. The proportion of exiles who had travelled abroad before the Civil War, who had seen military service in the Thirty Years War, who had been on diplomatic missions in Europe, or who had court connections, was much higher than in the 'King's party' as a whole. Our group portrait certainly needs to include the traditional figure of the exiled royalist existing frugally in miserable conditions, like the Attorney-General Sir Edward Herbert who, according to Hatton, writing to Nicholas from Paris in September 1654, 'lodgeth in a mean lodging with one Colonel Robinson in the same chamber'.[49] But it also needs to take into account such adventurous and enterprising spirits as Sir Richard

Fanshawe and his indomitable wife Ann, the cultured Sir Charles Cotterell and Endymion Porter, the elegant and aristocratic Marquess of Newcastle and the brutal and thuggish Sir James Hamilton, the straightforward and loyal Hopton and the enterprising and resourceful Daniel O'Neill. The exiled Cavaliers, and their long suffering families and dependants, comprised a diverse collection of courtiers, soldiers, diplomats, couriers, conspirators and travellers who, as we shall see, coped with the experience of exile in a variety of different ways.

6
A Long Farewell

Being accused of some Crimes before the Council of State I was
ordered to part the kingdom.

(Colonel Oliver Fitzwilliam)

Among the scores of petitions from hopeful loyalists that flooded into
the office of Secretary Nicholas at the Restoration is one from one
George Cock who requested a position in the customs office at Newcastle. Cock claimed that 'In pursuant of his loyalty he left this kingdom
and hath for eleven years remained abroad'.[1] Unfortunately, George
Cock and his alleged eleven years in exile remain totally obscure, so his
claim that it was his loyalty to the Stuart cause that made him abandon
his native country cannot be checked. But having in the previous
chapter attempted a group portrait of those royalists who went into
exile, and remained there for long periods, it is now necessary to determine why they made the decision, with all its unpleasant implications
and consequences. To what extent was the choice of exile a matter
of principle, as George Cock claimed, or were other motives also
significant?

It is possible to make a broad, but not always helpful, distinction
between those Cavaliers who chose voluntarily, for whatever reasons,
to go into exile and those who had no choice, who were compelled to
leave England because they had been formally banished, or excepted
from pardon, or had seen their estates forfeited to the Commonwealth
under such legislation as the Treason Act of 16 July 1651.[2] Of the
approximately 220 English 'long-term' exiles whose identity, backgrounds and careers were the subject of the the previous chapter, 31
were denied the right to compound and so forfeited their estates under
the 1651 Treason Act. Fourteen of the same names appear in the Com-

mittee for Compounding's list of 25 Delinquents who were proposed for 'perpetual banishment and confiscation'.[3] The obvious and expected names are there: Charles I's principal councillors and advisers, like Hyde, Culpepper and Nicholas, and generals like Langdale, Hopton, Grenville and Byron. Also included were royalists who for different reasons had made themselves particularly obnoxious to Parliament: courtiers who had been particularly close to either Charles I or Henrietta Maria, like Digby and Winter; prominent papists like the Marquess of Worcester and Colonel Thomas Leveson; and Cavalier officers whose behaviour during the Civil War had been exceptionally brutal or ruthless, notably the 'intransigent and bullying' Colonel Sir Francis Doddington, notorious for his practice of hanging prisoners of war. Although not a particularly prominent Cavalier, Doddington's evil reputation ensured his inclusion in all lists of royalist leaders marked for especially severe punishment. He was included in Parliament's list, drawn up on 21 November 1648, of the seven persons to be absolutely excepted from pardon, and was also on the list of royalist exiles required to leave France in 1656 under the terms of the Protectorate's treaty with that country.[4]

The royalists named in the Treason Act whose estates were 'forfeited to the Commonwealth for Treason' were not the only Cavaliers compelled to go into exile. To this list can be added the Scots and Irish Delinquents who were also banished and excepted from pardon, four of whom are included among the 'long-term' exiles who were the subject of the group portrait in the previous chapter: Ormonde, Inchiquin, Middleton and, inevitably, Daniel O'Neill. Other royalists might also be banished in a variety of circumstances, and sometimes apparently quite arbitrarily. Some, like Endymion Porter, at his first attempt, and the Earl of Bristol, were refused permission to return to England to compound despite their attempts to do so.[5] The Staffordshire Cavalier Colonel Oliver Fitzwilliam, who had withdrawn into exile in Holland in 1647, returned to England in 1649 and applied to compound; instead, 'being accused of some Crimes before the Council of State I was ordered to part the kingdom before such time as anything was done in my being in way of composition'. The fact that Fitzwilliam was both a Catholic and a veteran of the Irish wars may have told against him.[6]

Throughout the duration of the Commonwealth royalist prisoners of war, either captured during the 1648 risings or during the Worcester campaign, as well as arrested conspirators, were sometimes released on condition they went into exile. For example, John Villiers, Viscount Grandison, the somewhat unstable younger brother of a brilliant cavalry

officer killed at the storming of Bristol in 1643, spent four years in the Tower after being captured at Worcester, before being freed at last in November 1654 on condition that he 'go beyond sea from Portsmouth within a month . . . having engaged under hand and seal 30 August last to go, and not to act against his Highness or the Commonwealth'.[7] Similarly, Henry Seymour, whose activities as a trusted agent and courier are discussed in Chapter 9, spent more than one period in prison during the 1650s as a consequence of his money-collecting activities on the King's behalf. Partly on the grounds of ill-health, he was released from the Tower in February 1657 'on security to go beyond seas, not to return without leave, and to act nothing prejudicial to [the] government'.[8]

In addition to the royalists excepted from pardon and formally banished, either by legislation or in the special circumstances encountered by prisoners like Grandison and Seymour, or simply because their applications to return to England were rejected, as happened to Fitzwilliam and others, there were also the fugitives on the run. They fled into exile for the simple reason that if they remained in England to be captured they expected at the least to face long periods of imprisonment, as was the fate of the Scottish generals Leslie and Lauderdale captured at Worcester. At the worst, they feared death on the scaffold, the fate suffered by Hamilton, Holland, Capel and half a dozen other captured Cavaliers after the second Civil War and by the Earl of Derby and two of his officers after Worcester. If prominent royalist commanders like Langdale, Middleton and Massey had not been so adept at evading capture after various military disasters until they could be 'safely transported into France', they might have followed Hamilton to the scaffold. Two other notorious Malignants, Buckingham and O'Neill, on the run after the battle of Worcester, might also have suffered Derby's fate if they had been captured.[9]

Some of those royalists who assisted Charles to escape back to France after Worcester, in their turn also faced the necessity of going into exile in order to avoid worse punishment. Colonel Robert Phelips, whose resourcefulness and familiarity with south-west England were both equally valuable, accompanied Charles for some of his adventurous journey. Three years later, after a period of imprisonment in the Tower, he was a member of the King's exiled court in Germany. But the most famous example is Jane Lane, one of the very few examples of a woman going into exile as a consequence of her own actions, and not as a wife, daughter or servant of a male Cavalier. Under suspicion for her part in assisting the King to escape, Jane Lane, escorted by her Cavalier brother Colonel John Lane, fled to France from Yarmouth at the end of October

1651. The Colonel returned to England, and was promptly arrested, but Jane Lane was given a place in the household of Mary of Orange, where she remained until the Restoration.[10] There is at least one other case of a woman who escaped into exile as a result of her own actions. Philippa Mohun, a younger sister of the Cornish Cavalier, Lord Mohun of Boconnoc, turned up at the Hague in September 1654, escorted by her cousin, the royalist agent Jonathan Trelawney. Philippa Mohun, who is one of the royalist women ridiculed, and their morals disparaged, in the contemporary tract *The Commonwealth of Ladies*, was clearly too rash and outspoken for her own safety. According to Nicholas's correspondent, the Cornish exile Joseph Jane, 'she has so exasperated Cromwell by the scorns she had put on his daughter' that she had found it necessary to 'come into Holland, flying the fury of Cromwell'.[11]

Any estimate of the number of royalists who felt they had no alternative but to go into exile must take into account both those who were formally banished or who were deprived, by confiscation of their estates, of their means of existence, and those who fled England for fear of losing their liberty or their lives. Once again we are looking at a drawn-out process that began with the 'clauses of exception' from pardon proposed by the Long Parliament in 1642 and extended right through the 1650s to the suppression of Booth's Rising in August 1659. Any attempt to estimate the number of royalists affected by these measures is complicated by the fact that some prominent Cavaliers, despite being excepted from pardon, somehow managed to remain in England. Sir Philip Musgrave was an intransigent Cavalier who held important commands in Cumberland during the Civil War, seized Carlisle for the King in 1648 and then fought in Hamilton's inglorious campaign. Undeterred by this disaster, he joined Charles II in Scotland in 1650 and even after the 'fatal day' of Worcester continued to hold out for a couple more months on the Isle of Man. Not surprisingly, he was excepted from pardon in 1649 and his estates were confiscated under the 1651 Treason Act. Yet he remained in exile only for about a year after the execution of Charles I. Throughout the 1650s he lived quietly in England, although occasionally harassed by government officials who suspected, understandably considering his record, that Musgrave was likely to be drawn into royalist conspiracy.[12] Endymion Porter was another notorious Delinquent whose name appears regularly on the various lists of royalists excepted from pardon. Although his first attempts in 1647 to compound were rejected, in November 1648 Porter and his wife were permitted to return to England from Brussels and he was admitted to composition in April 1649.[13]

The elements of inconsistency and unpredictability apparent in the policies of different Commonwealth regimes to prominent Delinquents stem largely from one central dilemma that was never solved. On the one hand there was the view that royalists, Delinquents and Malignants that they were, had to be suppressed and rendered powerless or they would undermine the great and godly works in hand. So they had to be excluded from eligibility for office from the local to the national level, to be harassed by a range of restrictions on their movements and social activities and to be subject to special fines, taxes and sequestrations of property. They were required both to subscribe to humiliating engagements to be loyal to the regime while at the same time seeing the ministers of their church ejected and its services proscribed. The succession of risings and conspiracies that were engineered by incorrigible Cavaliers seemed to justify the continuation of these policies. On the other hand there was the different view, to which the Lord Protector fundamentally subscribed, that if there was ever to be a final settlement to the revolutionary upheavals generated by the Civil War, if the Commonwealth were to survive, then somehow at least the bulk of moderate royalists would have to be reconciled to it. A policy of 'healing and settling' rather than one of repression was most likely to achieve this much sought after final settlement. The failure to solve this dilemma, the swings between one policy and the other, the economic dependence of Commonwealth regimes on the revenue generated by composition fines and sales of crown, church and royalist lands, all contributed to the political instability of the 1650s and meant that the two-way traffic of royalists into exile and back into England continued unevenly throughout the entire period of the Commonwealth.

Those Cavaliers who were formally banished or excepted from pardon, or who fled England in the reasonable fear that if they remained they faced the likelihood of execution or at least imprisonment, were in a minority among the exiles. Of the 225 'long-term' exiles who were the subject of the group portrait in the previous chapter, between 60 and 70 had no alternative but to live outside England during the Interregnum. The majority of the 'long-term' emigrés chose not to return to England when they could have safely done so, although a distinction between 'voluntary' and 'compulsory' exiles is not very helpful. It is quite certain that many of those Cavaliers who were formally banished or excepted from pardon would have gone into exile anyway, and for one or more of a variety of reasons, of which loyalty to the Stuart cause is only one.

John Page, a widely travelled but otherwise obscure Cavalier, chose to spend the nine years before the Restoration tracing 'foreign countries, as being unwilling to draw in the air of my own native soil, lest I should be tainted (amongst the rest) with disloyalty'.[14] By its very nature, the importance of this particular motive, stated in such melodramatic language by Page, is difficult to evaluate. Of all the exiled royalists, it was Hyde who, not surprisingly, articulated most forcefully the argument that exile was a matter of principle. 'I cannot be sorry that thou art out of England', he wrote from Madrid on 25 March 1650 to his long-suffering wife, left behind in Antwerp with very little money, 'and I hope thy father and mother are not sorry for following thee, for truly methinks their abode in that cursed climate could not have been pleasant for them . . . The distresses we submit to, proceed from our integrity to Him, or rather for not doing that which cannot consist with our integrity towards Him. If this madness in England cease not, no man can live innocently there'.[15]

Hyde's correspondence shows his rigid opposition to any compromise with a regime tainted irrevocably by the terrible crime of regicide. To compound was 'an acknowledgment of delinquency', a rejection of 'the obligation of natural allegiance'; returning to England would be 'putting yourself into the hands of those devils'; it 'would be as bad as starving'.[16] Whenever Nicholas was tempted to cut his losses and considered trying to return to England with his unfortunate family, he was brought back into line by Hyde. 'All discourse of submitting or compounding with those rogues in England, hath so little of sense or excuse in it, that there needs no reply to it', responded Hyde sharply to the Secretary in December 1650. 'You and I must die in the streets first of hunger'; a high minded sentiment but perhaps not one with which Lady Nicholas would have been much in sympathy. For Hyde rejected contemptuously all proposals of 'submitting or compounding', declaring that 'no temptations can make us decline the severe principles we have professed'.[17]

To Hyde the principle of 'natural allegiance' and a horror of regicide carried out by an unconstitutional regime justified his decision to remain in exile with his family. Although other royalists, as we have seen with George Cock and John Page, might also claim legitimately that loyalty to the lawful king had impelled them to leave England, there is evidence that the decision to go into exile could be motivated by other more mundane factors. The defeat of the royalists in the Civil Wars, followed by the crushing of the subsequent invasions, risings and conspiracies, had devastating effects on the employment opportunities

of many supporters of the Stuart cause. Given the disintegration of the elegant and opulent court of Charles I, the collapse of the patronage networks of the royalist nobility, the end of the Caroline policy of *de facto* toleration of Catholics, and the harassing of Delinquents and Malignants by a naturally suspicious government, it is no wonder that, to many Cavaliers, to remain in England, as Sir John Reresby put it, 'appeared worse than banishment'.[18] For certain groups of the King's adherents, Catholics and ex-soldiers for example, and especially for those who looked traditionally either to the royal court for places and offices, or to the nobility for patronage, the prospects in England from 1646 onwards looked bleak. The choice for many was either to endure an uncomfortable life, encumbered with restrictions and disabilities, under the cold surveillance of the officials of a hostile regime, and with no future prospects – or to go beyond the seas. Having made that decision, in many cases Cavaliers discovered that other people were also profoundly affected by it. Just as Lady Hyde's parents followed their daughter to Antwerp, so the wives and children of Cavaliers, their servants and those attendants who still clung to the shrunken royal court, also faced the prospect of going beyond the seas.[19]

For exile offered opportunities – of a sort. There was the chance of a place, hopefully with modest board wages, if not at the shrunken court of Charles II then possibly in one of the other Stuart households on the continent. For old soldiers there were several possibilities for employment; the Franco-Spanish war was still dragging on, Venice was fighting to hold Crete against a massive Turkish onslaught, Denmark and Sweden were moving towards war with each other, and there were always the Dutch with their tradition of employing English troops. And if the traditional sources of patronage had collapsed in England, then would-be clients had to follow potential patrons abroad; in the service of such royalist magnates as Prince Rupert or the Duke of York, Ormonde or Hyde, Newcastle or Buckingham, there were opportunities for both action and, if the King ever came into his own again, reward. The opportunity to attach oneself to a patron was certainly a major motive behind the decision of Captain Thomas Paulden, one of the garrison of Pontefract castle in its long siege during the second Civil War, to go into exile. He justified his decision to his father on 3 October 1652.

I am promised from a person of great quality (whom I cannot name now) to have a particular care taken of me & now in order to it I am providing myself for France. I hope I shall be there within a month at furthest if you please to give me your leave, which I hope you will not

deny me when I tell you it is a fortune which many men of far greater condition than myself would be glad to meet with, & besides I know of no other way of living by which I can possibly subsist myself above half a year longer, & this which is offered me will plentifully support me for ye present and not without hopes of a raise in fortune.[20]

There were others like Paulden who sought in exile the opportunities that no longer existed for them in republican England. A number of young exiled Cavaliers, including several who were to make prominent careers for themselves after the Restoration, maintained themselves abroad as the followers or clients of patrons. Stephen Fox, the future successful financier, as 'a young man [was] bred under the severe discipline of the lord Percy'; Henry Bennet, later Earl of Arlington, was 'full of duty and Integrity' to the Duke of York; the dashing admiral of the Dutch Wars in the 1660s and 1670s, 'Bonfire' Robert Holmes, was a page of Rupert's in 1647 and a trusted officer of the Prince's by 1654; Daniel O'Neill was so devoted to Ormonde that he showed 'himself at every turn passionately your Excellency's'; the resourceful agent Nicholas Armorer was 'bound by great obligation and affection to Secretary Nicholas'.[21] The list can easily be extended.

The different reasons why royalists went into exile therefore reflect the variations in character and circumstances among the members of 'the King's party'. It is also necessary to be aware of those royalists who went into exile for non-political reasons, debtors escaping their creditors for example, or for other offences, like manslaughter. This last was the motive for the flight of Philip Stanhope, second Earl of Chesterfield, who as well as being an active royalist was also a notable duellist. In January 1660 Chesterfield, according to an unpublished draft of his memoirs, 'had the great misfortune of killing Mr Woolly in a duel, which a servant of his seeing, clapped a Pistol to my head, but missing me [how?] I went to France and from thence to Holland and waited on the King at Breda where I had his Majesty's pardon'.[22]

One feels that the greater misfortune was Mr Woolly's, but in any case Chesterfield's hurried journey to France was in a very different category from that of those Cavaliers who were either compelled or found it necessary, as a result of their political or military activities, to leave England. Foremost among these genuine political exiles were the leaders of the 'King's party', both civilian and military, who, excepted from pardon and with their estates confiscated, had no alternative but to 'go beyond seas'. Then there were the courtiers, a significant group among the 'long-term' exiles, who, when the court of Charles I crumbled and

disintegrated, sought places in the household of his successor. 'The old Court flies begin to flock about him from all parts', reported a Commonwealth agent in Paris where Charles established his court after his escape from Worcester.[23] To some royalists, exile was a question of principle, the inevitable consequence of uncompromising loyalty to monarchy and church, for only in exile could one's allegiance to the King be proclaimed and the Anglican or Catholic religion be practised openly. But the greatest stimulus to the emigration of Cavaliers was quite certainly the bleak prospects that confronted them if they remained in a republican England. The political and economic restrictions and disabilities imposed by successive parliamentarian and commonwealth regimes on the King's followers drove many of them to look abroad for the opportunities, even for the prospects of a reasonable livelihood, that no longer existed at home.

These reasons are sufficient to explain why, although they were not compelled to, many royalists chose to go into exile. There was no need for the spur of a Terror. The mass emigration of French royalists after 1790 or of White Russians after 1917 has no equivalent in Commonwealth England. Although Clarendon in his *History of the Rebellion* praised Cromwell for opposing what 'was more than once proposed (by the council of officers) that there might be a general massacre of the royal party', there is no firm evidence that fear of a reign of terror was ever a significant motive in driving Cavaliers into exile.[24] The winter of 1648–49, when not only was Charles I executed but also several other captured royalist officers including three peers, was probably the time when fear of 'a general massacre of the royal party' was most likely to have influenced the decision of some royalists to flee from England. Rumours that a 'general massacre' of royalists was intended are occasionally mentioned in the correspondence of the emigrés during the 1650s, but such mentions are rare. On 21 December 1655, during the period of the rule of the Major-Generals, the old Earl of Norwich reported to Secretary Nicholas from Antwerp that 'in England it is feared yt [sic] the Cavalier party, being disarmed will be suddenly massacred. If it had not been for Lawrence, now president of ye Council [of State], it had been done before, and then it was only carried to the contrary by one single voice'.[25] But such rumours do not seem to have been taken seriously. The steady drift of Cavaliers back to England, only too willing to compound and conform, is sufficient evidence to reject fear of a Terror as a reason for the flight of royalists into exile.

Those Cavaliers who chose flight and who remained in exile, and they numbered many of the most ambitious, enterprising and adventurous

of the King's supporters, were then faced with the important decisions of where to live and how to live. If they had dependant families, if they were reliant on money reaching them from England, if they needed employment of some kind on the continent, then the choice of where to spend one's time in exile was of considerable importance. It is the subject of the next chapter.

Part II
The Experience of Exile

7
Travels and Retreats

> Mirth makes them not mad,
> Nor sobriety sad;
> But of that they are seldom in danger;
> At Paris, at Rome,
> At the Hague, they're at home;
> The good fellow is nowhere a stranger.
>
> (Sir John Denham, from
> *On Mr Thomas Killigrew's return from Venice*)[1]

Having made the decision to 'fly from their native country as from a place infected with the plague', and having either resisted the temptation to return to England after the disasters of the second Civil War and Worcester or having no alternative but to stay abroad, those Cavaliers who remained in exile were confronted with two closely connected problems. They had to decide both where to live and how to live until their fortunes, or the fortunes of the royal cause, improved. The exiles' movements – the reasons why they chose to settle in particular towns or regions, or decided to move from one place to another, or even in some cases declined to stay put anywhere but engaged instead in restless wandering – were determined by a number of important considerations. They had to take into account the possibility of obtaining a place either in the reduced court of Charles II, or in the household of one of the other members of the Stuart family. They also had to assess the importance of proximity to England and the ability to communicate with the family or friends, preferably ones with money, they had left behind. The comparative cost of living and the attitude of potential creditors, in particular landlords, in different towns and regions had also to be considered. Opportunities for employment, preferably

military in many cases, and the religious and political sympathies and allegiances of one's hosts, from innkeepers to princes, also helped to direct the movements of the exiles. Personal factors – friendships and enmities, the ties between patrons and clients – could also shape the shifting groupings and gatherings of the exiled Cavaliers.

Northern France and the Low Countries saw the greatest concentrations of royalist emigrés. There were two obvious reasons, namely their proximity to England and the presence in Paris and the Hague of Stuart courts or households. During the years immediately following the Civil Wars, many exiles were unwilling to move far from the towns along the Channel and Netherlands coasts – Calais and Boulogne, Antwerp and Rotterdam – hoping, as Secretary Nicholas had vainly hoped in his letter to Dr Isaac Basire in June 1647 already quoted, that a negotiated settlement would enable 'honest men [to] return with comfort to their homes'. As the prospects of either a negotiated peaceful settlement or a spectacular royalist military victory faded and died, many of the exiled Cavaliers turned to one or other of the Stuart courts or households to obtain employment or at least a means of subsistence. As well as the court of Charles II, established in Paris at the end of 1651, the other principal Stuart households were those of Queen Henrietta Maria, either at the Louvre or St Germain, and the King's aunt Elizabeth of Bohemia and sister Mary of Orange, the Princess Royal, at the Hague. Of less significance as magnets to attract the exiles were the households of the Palatine princes, the parsimonious Elector Charles Louis restored to a devastated Heidelberg at the end of the Thirty Years War, and his brother Rupert, and of Charles's brothers, the royal dukes James of York and young Henry of Gloucester.

As we have seen, a significant number of 'long-term' exiles had court backgrounds, having had places in the household of either Charles I or of the Prince of Wales. But it was not until Charles returned to Paris in October 1651, after his six weeks on the run following the 'fatal day' at Worcester, that he remained settled in one place long enough for a reasonably substantial court to gather around him. 'The old Court flies begin now to flock about him from all parts', a hostile observer reported in December 1651. 'Some of them are come to the Louvre already out of Flanders, as Hyde – a man of dignity too, that calls himself [Ex]chequer Chancellor. Here also is [bishop] Bramhall out of Londonderry, Dan. O'Neill, Fraser, a physician, and one Lloyd, a chaplain. These bring word that Buckingham and Nicholas would have come along too but that they wanted gelt. And the rest of his Majesty's black-

guard and retinue that wander in the Low countries, if they were sure of daily bread for their attendance.'[2]

Shortage of money does not seem to have been the real reason for the reluctance of Secretary Nicholas to join the court that was assembling in Paris. On 4 November Charles instructed Lord Gerard to communicate to Nicholas the King's wish that the Secretary join him in Paris, but not even Gerard's superscription on the letter 'Haste Haste post haste' succeeding in dislodging Nicholas from the Hague. There were further letters in the same vein, including one from Ormonde, who was disappointed not to meet Nicholas when he arrived in Paris from Caen in November, and who referred to 'the Gracious mention the King makes of you on all occasions', another from Gerard, and several from Hyde, who entreated the Secretary to 'make haste hither, and then the Marquis of Ormonde and Sir Edward Hyde will be able to do more good'.

This flood of letters failed to persuade Nicholas to leave the Hague for Paris, a city which possessed for him the considerable disadvantage of containing Queen Henrietta Maria, who 'hath several times of late to several persons expressed her high displeasure against me'. As a positive consequence of Nicholas's stubbornness and his fear that Charles would be unable to 'protect an honest man in his honest ways from his mother's unjust displeasure', we have his enormously rich and detailed correspondence, especially with his friends Hyde and Ormonde, but with other emigrés also, in particular his two regular 'intelligencers' and sources of gossip in Paris, Lord Hatton and Percy Church.[3] Historians of the period should be very grateful that Nicholas remained at the Hague and did not join the court until it moved to Cologne in 1654.

The most prominent of the exiled royalists who gathered in Paris to reconstitute a royal court were the King's surviving councillors and senior members of the household, in particular, Ormonde and Hyde, back in favour after the disastrous collapse of the policy of a Scottish alliance; the soldiers Rupert (only between April 1653 and May 1654), Wilmot and Gerard; courtier survivors of the previous generation like the earls of Bristol and Norwich; the Irish royalist leader Lord Inchiquin, and the Lord Keeper, Sir Edward Herbert. If we also include less important crown officials like Robert Long, Secretary to the Council, the permanent members of the royal household, from equerries like William Armorer to chaplains like Dr Lloyd, and those gentlemen who 'go along with the court and are not of the bedchamber or the stables', for example, Charles's cronies, the chosen companions of his leisure hours, the lords Taaffe, Newburgh and Crofts, we have a total of about forty

persons.[4] The notable 'Louvrians' in the Queen's household, which was established sometimes in close and uncomfortable proximity to Charles's own quarters in the Louvre but was more usually just outside Paris at St Germain, were Jermyn, Berkeley and Percy. But factional divisions among the courtiers were not clear-cut. The 'Louvrian' Sir John Berkeley had once been a close friend of Hyde's. Culpepper, another of Hyde's friends whom he had also managed to alienate, had no lasting allegiance to any faction. Hatton maintained close links both with Henrietta Maria and with Hyde and Nicholas, as did Percy Church, who, despite being a long-standing member of the Queen Mother's household, was also one of the Secretary's main 'intelligencers' in Paris during the 1650s.[5]

The other Stuart households in Paris were more modest, providing few employment opportunities for exiled Cavaliers. The Duke of York's household was small (23 servants were dismissed in November 1648 as an economy measure), impoverished and quarrelsome; according to Hyde it was characterised by 'disorder and faction'.[6] The self-interested struggles for influence over James by Berkeley, Jermyn, Sir Edward Herbert, Sir George Radcliffe and Lord Byron, with the Queen constantly and generally ineffectually interfering and criticising from the sidelines, horrified observers like Hyde and Hatton, not to mention Charles himself. Eventually the influence of Jermyn and Berkeley became paramount. Byron died in 1652 and gradually they triumphed over their other rivals, leaving, according to Hatton, the Duke 'totally charmed by Lo. Jermyn and Sir Jo. Berkeley'. This triumph was consolidated by James's friendship with their respective nephews, Charles Berkeley and Harry Jermyn. When James first was permitted to join the French army under Marshal Turenne in April 1652, he was accompanied only by Sir John Berkeley and Colonel Robert Werden, a Cavalier who enjoyed a fairly dubious career both as soldier and conspirator, and half a dozen servants.[7] Clearly, for several reasons, the household of the Duke of York had only limited appeal to exiled Cavaliers looking for employment.

The household of Henry, Duke of Gloucester, who, accompanied by his tutor Richard Lovell, joined Charles in Paris in May 1653, having been expelled from England by the Commonwealth government, was even more modest. At first it comprised no more than half a dozen gentlemen of the chamber and other attendants but when, after the failure of the attempt by Henrietta Maria to bring about Gloucester's conversion to Catholicism, the Duke left Paris to join his elder brother in Cologne, his household was augmented by the impressive addition of Sir Charles Cotterell. Once Master of Ceremonies to Charles I,

Cotterell had been one of the more cultured members of that cultured court, a friend of Endymion Porter and both friend and patron of the artist William Dobson. Cotterell went into exile in Antwerp in 1649, before becoming Steward in the household of Elizabeth of Bohemia and then, in 1656, Secretary to the Duke of Gloucester. Apart from Cotterell, Gloucester's household remained restricted to Lovell the chaplain, two gentlemen of the chamber, and four 'inferior household officers'. Distressed Cavaliers hopeful of employment needed to look elsewhere.[8]

Around these Stuart households in Paris moved a fluctuating crowd of royalist exiles. Some obtained official positions of one kind or another; others just went 'along with the court'. Some became attached to one or other of the court factions, or to particular patrons, but others remained uncommitted. While some of the exiles, like Jermyn and Hatton, became long-term residents of Paris, others, like Newcastle and his fellow officer in the old royalist northern army, Lord Widdrington, moved on fairly quickly to other destinations, in their case, to Antwerp.[9] And although some royalists, like Nicholas and his friend Hopton, avoided Paris completely, most of the 'long-term' exiles, in particular the veterans of the Civil Wars, seemed to have spent at least some time in Paris during the 1650s. Some, like Byron, Percy and Herbert, died there.

The bitterness and frustration of these exiled commanders and officers from the defeated royalist armies is very evident in their correspondence, with frequent references to quarrels, disputes, duels and shortage of money. In one duel in the Bois de Boulogne in January 1647 between four Cavaliers, two were killed, 'Colonel Ambrose Jennings, second to the said [Colonel Sir Thomas] Sandys, and Mr Wittfield, Scotchman, gentleman of the horse to Prince Rupert', while Sandys was seriously wounded.[10] Rupert, Digby, Wilmot, O'Neill, Wentworth, Crofts, Bennet, Gerard – to name only some of the better known exiles – all fought duels during their years in Paris. Typically, O'Neill retained his sense of humour when describing to Ormonde the duel between Digby and Wilmot, in which the seconds, including himself and Wentworth, also joined in: 'whereupon out flew bilboes [and] to work we went a la mode de France'.[11]

When they were not quarrelling and fighting with each other, the ex-generals complained bitterly about the 'ill condition' in which they found themselves and about their lack of influence in the King's counsels, but they were still better off than most of the other Cavalier officers who drifted to Paris. When the complaints of Sir Marmaduke Langdale to the King in May 1652 could draw only an apologetic letter

from Charles regretting 'the impossibility of relieving such persons as you are', there was not much hope of supplying the wants of the equally discontented Lord Keeper Herbert, living in 'a mean lodging with one Colonel Robinson in the same chamber', or of the Northumbrian Captain Thomas Carnaby, who was 'in danger to perish for want of bread and lodging, being destitute of friends in this place'.[12]

Despite the prospect of a spartan existence in 'a mean lodging', until 1654 Paris remained the principal place of exile for many Cavaliers. The presence of the court of Charles II, of the household of Henrietta Maria, of the royal princes, of the King's principal councillors Ormonde and Hyde, and of other prominent royalists like Jermyn and Digby, Byron and Gerard, is sufficient to explain the presence also of the less well-known figures: Sandys, Robinson, Carnaby and others.

Paris also attracted some emigrés who avoided all contact with the exiled court or with the various royalist magnates living in the city. Richard Symonds served in the King's Lifeguard under Lord Bernard Stuart during the Civil War. The *Diary of the Marches of the Royal Army* that he kept during this period reveals his antiquarian interests, his respect for ancient lineage and his strong religious beliefs. Having paid his composition fine in 1647, nevertheless he went into exile in January 1649, arriving in Paris in February and remaining in the city until August when he departed for Italy. Symonds, who clearly had wide-ranging intellectual and cultural interests, compiled extensive notes of his travels: accounts of religious services; descriptions of dress, manners and customs; sketches of churches and palaces, works of art and coats of arms. While in Rome, he met the artist Nicolas Poussin, but, although he visited the Louvre, there is no mention in his notebooks of his paying his respects either to Henrietta Maria or to any of the other royalist leaders in Paris in 1649.[13] Symonds was a battle-hardened veteran of the Civil War who fought at the second battle of Newbury, Lostwithiel, Cropredy Bridge, Naseby and Rowton Heath, but he has more in common with the cultivated gentlemen making a leisurely study of antiquities while on the Grand Tour than he has with the quarrelsome swordsmen hanging around the ante-rooms of the Louvre and fighting duels in the Bois de Boulogne.

The attraction of Paris as a destination for exiled Cavaliers was greatly reduced by two related events, the departure of Charles II and the exiled court to the Rhineland in July 1654 and the alliance negotiated between Protectorate England and France which came into effect the following year. One condition of the alliance was the expulsion from France of a number of named prominent Cavaliers and it was partly in order to

avoid this humiliation that Charles and his court left Paris before the treaty of alliance was confirmed.[14] Sir George Radcliffe, one of the defeated rivals of Jermyn and Berkeley in the struggle for control of the person and affairs of the Duke of York, wrote from Paris on 14 November 1655 to his friend Ormonde, at Cologne with the King, to express the dilemma of the exiles. He deplored how 'the peace between England and France puts the cavaliers here into some doubt, not knowing who may stay and who must be sent away'.[15] In the event a number did remain, especially members of the Queen's circle like Jermyn and Percy, and some other royalists who were notorious for their hostility to Hyde and their opposition to his position as the King's chief counsellor. For example, Sir Edward Herbert, who resigned his office of Lord Keeper in disgust when he learned he was not to accompany the court, remained in Paris, as did the disgraced secretary to the Council Robert Long and the discredited general Sir Richard Grenville. But many other Cavaliers gradually left Paris, either to follow the court or, like Radcliffe himself, who left Paris in mid 1656 and died at Flushing in the Netherlands in May 1657, to find another place of refuge.[16]

Groups of exiled royalists can be found in other regions of France as well as in Paris, notably in the Channel ports, Normandy and the Loire valley, and also, until 1651, in Jersey. The French Channel ports, especially Calais and Boulogne, were familiar mainly to Cavaliers either going into exile or returning to England, or to agents and couriers like Henry Seymour, Nicholas Armorer and the Paulden brothers, passing backwards and forwards on secret missions. Although some 'short-term' exiles seem to have got no further into the continent than the Channel coast, there only occasional references to royalists settling permanently in Boulogne or Calais, where Sir Robert Heath, once Charles I's Chief Justice, died in 1649.[17] But Charles II did maintain permanent agents at some of the Channel ports, as registrars of his so-called 'High Court of Admiralty'. Their principal responsibility was to supervise privateers operating out of the Channel ports under royal licence to prey on shipping flying the Commonwealth flag, with the thankless task of trying to ensure the crown received its share of any prizes taken. In his last intelligence report on 30 November 1655 from the court at Cologne, intercepted by suspicious royal agents and so preserved in the Nicholas and not the Thurloe papers, Thurloe's spy Henry Manning identified these 'registrars'. 'I pray [you] remember Wyndham and Lovinge at Boulogne,' he advised Thurloe in a letter his employer never received, 'Booth and Col. Whitley, a crafty man, at Calais, Holder at Brest, now employed by the King in France'. When Evelyn passed through Calais

on his way back to England in 1652 he recorded meeting 'Mr Booth (his Majesty's agent here) . . . and divers of our banished company', including Sir Robert Heath's son John and the Welsh Cavalier Sir Richard Lloyd.[18]

If the French Channel ports offered some refuge to a few exiled Cavaliers, by the end of 1651 the once-welcoming island of Jersey, with its loyal and hospitable Lieutenant Governor Sir George Carteret, could no longer offer any. Despite a spirited resistance by the local royalists, the authority of the Commonwealth was established in Jersey by an invading force under the redoubtable Admiral Robert Blake. The days when Ann Fanshawe recalled how Carteret had 'endeavoured with all his power to entertain his highness and court with all plenty and kindness possible' were over and Carteret himself had begun eight years of exile in France.[19]

To those exiles who chose to remain in France, but preferred for various reasons to avoid Paris, Normandy and the Loire valley became the favoured regions in which to live while waiting for the fortunes of the King's party to improve. In the years following the end of the Civil War a number of Cavaliers, in many cases accompanied by their families, settled in either Caen or Rouen. Cholmley, Nicholas, Ormonde, Cottington, Bristol, Hopton, Radcliffe and others all lived for a few months or in some cases years in these quiet provincial towns until either they received the royal summons to present themselves at court (Ormonde), or decided to return to England and apply to compound (Cholmley), or were sent on a diplomatic or other mission (Cottington).[20] These two Norman towns retained their popularity among some emigrés throughout the 1650s. General John Digby, who had served in the west country under Prince Maurice, lived in Caen for some time before he renounced his warrior past to become a seminary priest. As late as 1655, Thomas Mompesson and Lieutenant Colonel Thomas Hunt, two fugitives from the Protectorate government's hunt for conspirators involved in Penruddock's rising in March, also found refuge in the same town and remained there until the eve of the Restoration.[21]

The towns of Normandy, with their proximity to England, were obvious refuges for exiled Cavaliers; the choice of the Loire valley is more curious. In the late 1640s and early 1650s Angers, Tours, Blois and Saumur sheltered several little groups of royalist exiles, ex-parliamentarians and 'neutrals', men who had become disenchanted with the course of events in England. Sir Ralph Verney, John Stoye's 'perplexed knight of the sorrowful countenance', with his talent for being in opposition to whatever regime was in power in England, settled

in Blois in 1645 with his wife Mary, two of their children and two English maids, having previously been living in Rouen.[22] Although Mary Verney returned briefly to England in 1646 to attempt to raise money and to deal with the financial problems caused by Parliament's sequestration of their estate – a not unusual responsibility assumed by the wives and trusted servants of the exiles – the rest of the family remained in Blois. In the correspondence of Verney and of Sir Richard Browne, the King's resident ambassador in Paris, there are references to a number of royalist exiles, living in quiet and often scholarly retirement in small towns along the Loire. Among them were the youthful Lord Falkland and Henry Coventry, sons of prominent adherents to Charles I, Sir Thomas Glemham, the last royalist governor of Oxford and the disillusioned Welsh Cavalier, Sir Thomas Hanmer. Verney recorded that at Christmas 1650 a 'party of thirty English exiles met at dinner'. These exiles moved in a circle which also included young men of royalist sympathies and their tutors on the Grand Tour, like Lord Willoughby, Sir John Reresby, Sir George Savile and Joseph Williamson, as well as men of moderate parliamentarian backgrounds, like Lord Mandeville, and the tutor Thomas Cordell, who gave lessons at Blois to boys from royalist families whose parents could not bear to send them to purged and Puritan Oxford and Cambridge.[23]

There are several explanations for this concentration of exiled Cavaliers in the Loire valley. Saumur had a reputation, which it retained until the French Revolution, of being a desirable place of education for aristocratic English youth. The Verneys, and young aristocrats like Willoughby, Falkland and Savile, seem to have been influenced by this factor in their choice of a retreat. Also, several of the Loire towns were old Huguenot strongholds and so had an attraction for Protestants that was conspicuously lacking in courtly and Catholic Paris. Finally, when the cost of living was always a matter of the deepest concern to the exiles, the Loire valley towns, as well as being situated in one of the most beautiful regions of France and surrounded by vineyards, were cheaper to live in than Paris. 'We pass the time indifferently well here', Hanmer informed Sir Richard Browne from Angers on 4 December 1647, 'but we want not good wine'.[24]

The appeal of the Loire valley as a refuge was primarily to 'moderate' Cavaliers, not to courtiers or 'Swordsmen' and not to Catholics. The little groups of exiles in Blois, Angers and Saumur dwindled during the early 1650s. Glemham died in 1649 and Mary Verney at Blois the following year. Most of the rest, like Hanmer and Verney, gradually drifted back to England to compound and make their peace with

Commonwealth or Protector. In Verney's case this was a leisurely process, involving an extensive tour through Italy, Germany and the Netherlands, accompanied by his son Edmund and Thomas Cordell as a tutor. He finally returned to England in January 1653. Those royalists who remained by the banks of the Loire lived quietly and unobtrusively. 'We are very dead as to any news here,' wrote the Herefordshire royalist James Scudamore to Browne from Angers on 15 August 1656.[25]

The major alternative to France as a place of refuge for exiled Cavaliers were the Low Countries. When the Catholic sympathiser Secretary Windebank fled to France at the end of 1640, the Protestant Lord Keeper Finch escaped to Holland. Throughout the 1650s there were significant communities of emigrés in Bruges, Brussels and Antwerp in the Spanish Netherlands and in Breda, the Hague and Rotterdam in the United Provinces. But as many Cavaliers moved frequently from one town to another, either in search of cheaper lodgings and more easily available credit, or because of changes in the attitudes of a host country to its uninvited guests, or as a consequence of the movements and policies of the exiled court, the groupings of exiles were constantly changing.

The travels in exile of Lord Hopton, a close friend and ally of Nicholas and Hyde, illustrate all of these influences on the movements of the exiles. Hopton, who was on all the various parliamentary lists of royalists 'who shall expect no pardon', had sailed to Jersey with the Prince of Wales in April 1646, moved to Rouen in early 1647 after the Prince went to Paris, and then continued on to Calais in 1648. When the parliamentary fleet in the Downs mutinied and a number of ships went over to the royalists, Hopton left France to join Charles at Breda. Early in 1649 he was off the coast of Cornwall with a small fleet, calling on the gentlemen of Cornwall to acknowledge Charles II as their king. Forced to withdraw to the Netherlands, Hopton found himself on the losing side in the intense dispute in Charles's Council over the projected alliance with the Scottish Covenanters; with Nicholas and Hyde he was excluded from the King's counsels. 'Finding little business and less contentment in Breda', he withdrew to Utrecht in May 1650. Further wanderings followed, first to Brussels then back to Utrecht. During this lowest point in royalist hopes Hopton seriously considered returning to England and attempting to compound for his estates. Instead, he finally settled in Bruges, where his travels ended. Nicholas reported to Hyde in Paris the death on 8 October 1652 of 'gallant and virtuous Lord Hopton'.[26] Hopton's wanderings in France and the Netherlands can be reconstructed as he was an important figure among the exiles, with his movements recorded in the correspondence of Nicholas and other

emigrés. The travels of other exiled Cavaliers may have been at least as extensive as Hopton's but, as they were not prominent leaders of the King's party, they are much more difficult to trace.

One valuable source for tracking the movements of the exiled Cavaliers is the reports of Thurloe's agents. For example, on 16 June 1654 John Addams, having first listed the 'violent malignants', principally merchants, present in Rotterdam and Amsterdam, then informed Thurloe which Cavaliers were at the Hague:

At the Hague is
Sir John Culpepper, going for France
Humphrey Bosville (Boswell)
Sir Edward Nicholas
Sir Francis Mackworth
Sir Edward Brett
Sir Miles Hubbard (Hobart)
Mr Jane
Sir Marmaduke Langdale, gone for Antwerp
Sir Charles Lloyd
Sir John Sayers, major to the earl of Oxford
Captain Morton, and many other officers in these states service[27]

The list is a mixture of royalists with different backgrounds: ex-officers, from a senior commander like Langdale to regimental officers like Sayers and Morton; court office-holders like Culpepper and Nicholas, and plain country gentry, like Hobart and the Cornish MP, Joseph Jane.[28] But lists of this kind are of limited value, especially when one takes into account the constantly shifting population of exiles, the occasional deaths, like Hopton's in 1652 and Joseph Jane's in 1658, and the irritating tendency of some Cavaliers simply to disappear from the records. Major Humphrey Bosville (or Boswell) was an active agent and courier until 1655, entrusted with many missions, then nothing more is heard of him; the references to him in the correspondence of the exiles or the reports of Thurloe's agents just stop.[29] One episode illustrates the difficulty in assessing the number of exiles in any one place at any particular time. During the winter of 1655–56 Elizabeth of Bohemia wrote several letters from the Hague to Charles at Cologne which dealt partly with the dismissal from her household of a Mrs Grenville. Some of Mrs Grenville's compatriots objected to her treatment and threatened Elizabeth with a delegation of 'forty English gentlemen' to protest on the injured lady's behalf. Elizabeth ridiculed this threat: 'I assure your majesty, there are

not half so many of this nation in our town.' This estimate of only twenty English gentlemen in the Hague in March 1656 does seem low, although the delegation when it arrived consisted of merely two Cavaliers, Lord Grandison, only recently released from the Tower and banished from England and so hardly likely to be very well-informed on the details of Mrs Grenville's treatment, and Colonel Cromwell.[30]

The attraction of the Hague and other Dutch towns like Rotterdam and Breda, apart from their relative proximity to England and their Protestantism, can largely be explained by the presence at the Hague of the sympathetic courts of Charles's widowed sister Mary of Orange and that authority on the experience of exile, his aunt Elizabeth of Bohemia. Around these two Stuart princesses gathered a considerable circle of royalist exiles who were in varying degrees dependent on these patrons for employment and maintenance: Secretary Nicholas and his family; Lady Hyde and her children who lived rent-free in a house provided for them in Breda while Anne Hyde became a maid of honour to Mary; Sir Charles Cotterell, Elizabeth's steward before he was summoned to join the household of the Duke of Gloucester; the Scots Balcarres, Middleton and Mary's chamberlain, Sir Alexander Hume; Colonel Thomas Howard, Master of the Horse to Mary but also an ex-lover of Lucy Walter and, as we shall see, suspected by some of 'corresponding with the Rebels and giving them intelligence'. Along with Anne Hyde, Mary also found a place in her household for other young women who found themselves in exile: Jane Lane, when she fled to the continent after helping Charles escape from Worcester, and Honora Harding, the daughter of Richard Harding, a groom of the bedchamber to the King.[31]

Two Cavaliers who were to play a prominent role in the organisation of royalist conspiracy also belonged to the circle of emigrés around Mary of Orange. Nicholas Armorer turned up at the Hague in the aftermath of the battle of Worcester, although he had possibly come from Ireland not England. Secretary Nicholas reported that Armorer fought a duel with the professional soldier Colonel Sir William Leighton on 3 June 1652 and just over a year later Nicholas referred to him as 'a servant of the Princess Royal': the same information that Sir Robert Stone passed on to Thurloe when Armorer was detained in Dover castle in February 1655.[32] When not in attendance on either the King or Ormonde, Daniel O'Neill also was a welcome presence at the court of Mary of Orange. Nicholas always had his doubts about O'Neill. On 20 November 1650 he wrote to Hatton in Paris that 'the great governors here in the Princess Royal's family and business are the Lady Stanhope and her Husband; and the great men with them are Lord Percy and Dan. O'Neill'. The

close relationship between O'Neill and Mary's companion Katherine, Lady Heenvliet, who was also known as Lady Stanhope, the English title derived from her first marriage, aroused comment among the exiles at the Hague. 'I believe O'Neill to be a very honest man', Nicholas admitted to Hyde on 9 October 1653, 'only I have heard he hath much passion for Mrs Heenvliet'. O'Neill was also famous among the exiles for his ability, drawn on his experience as an old campaigner, to live comfortably in all circumstances. In February 1656 Nicholas confided to his friend Joseph Jane that he did not believe 'Mr O'Neill will leave Holland till the Lady Stanhope goes for France [in attendance on Mary of Orange], whatever he says to you, for he finds great ease in here at a good table, and at no cost to him. You will find he is like his name, subtle [a reference to O'Neill's nickname – Infallible Subtle].' O'Neill was certainly a 'devotee of Lady Heenvliet' – after the Restoration he became her third husband – but whether it was her charms, or the 'good table' provided by Mary of Orange, that were the main attraction for him of Mary's court at the Hague, we do not know. Probably it was a combination of both.[33]

Apart from the two Stuart courts at the Hague, the United Provinces also had other attractions to exiled Cavaliers: the presence of a substantial English community, including merchants sympathetic to the royalist cause, and a tradition of Englishmen being employed in the Dutch service. Among the English Cavaliers living in Rotterdam in the 1650s was the Lincolnshire Colonel Gervase Holles, MP for Grimsby in 1640, governor of Lyme Regis in 1644, veteran of several battles in the first Civil War and of the siege of Colchester in the second.[34] A strong Protestant and a friend of Hyde and Nicholas, Holles belonged to a family with military links with Holland extending back two generations. A Thomas Holles had been a captain in the Dutch service in 1622 and another relative, Ensign George Holles, died at Maastricht in the service of the United Provinces in March 1655. For these reasons it is not surprising that Holles found Rotterdam a suitable retreat in which to spend his years of exile, lodging in the home of an English widow Mrs Kilvert, from where he corresponded fairly regularly with other exiles, in particular with the courtier Thomas Ross, Hyde and Radcliffe. From this busy port it was also not too difficult to communicate with his wife Elizabeth who remained in Lincolnshire, apart from the occasional visit to her husband.[35]

The combined advantages of their Protestantism, the presence of two Stuart courts, their geographical convenience, and the existence of a comparatively large and well-established community of English

expatriates, explain the appeal of towns like Rotterdam, the Hague and Breda to exiled Cavaliers. The number of emigrés who settled in towns in the Spanish Netherlands, like Antwerp and Brussels, was not so large, although Lord and Lady Newcastle enjoyed a prolonged and elegant residence in Antwerp and Langdale, a Catholic, disappointed at not being brought fully into Charles's confidence when the King was in Paris, eventually settled in Flanders. He was living in Antwerp in 1654 and in Brussels a year later.[36] In April 1656 the appeal of the Spanish Netherlands to royalist exiles was transformed by the arrival of Charles and his court in Bruges. From mid 1656 until the Restoration Bruges, Brussels and Antwerp became increasingly more popular as places of residence for royalists. As early as 7 April the Venetian resident in England reported to the Doge and Senate that many royalists were 'making ready to cross to Flanders to join their natural prince'.[37] Charles's alliance with Spain in the Treaty of Brussels and his raising of royalist regiments in Flanders made the Spanish Netherlands an obvious destination, not just for genuine English Cavaliers and for Irish and Scottish exiles, but for soldiers of fortune from all over Europe. The end of the first Dutch War and the Protector's peace treaty with the Dutch republic in 1654, followed by his alliance with the French monarchy in the following year, served to reduce the appeal of both the United Provinces and France to many of the exiles who from 1656 began to gather instead in the towns and military camps of Flanders.

It is clear that the great majority of exiled Cavaliers confined their travelling and their choice of retreats to France and the Low Countries, although the various concentrations of emigrés were neither stable nor lasting. Apart from the influence of those permanent features of an exile's life – shortage of money and homesickness – his travels and sojourns were determined by changes in the policies of his hosts, by the fluctuating fortunes of the Stuart cause, and by the movements of the court of Charles II. But not all exiled Cavaliers remained in France or the Netherlands. Some settled in towns or regions in other parts of Europe and some, the restless wanderers, never settled anywhere, but spent most of their time travelling, sometimes going well beyond the traditional limits of seventeenth century 'English travellers abroad'.

Spain and Portugal seem to have attracted a fairly small number of exiled Cavaliers. There were occasional official envoys from Charles II; in 1650 Cottington and Hyde were sent to Spain, and Thomas Elliot, one of the grooms of the bedchamber, to Portugal. It is significant that Cottington and Hyde both opposed the alliance with the Scots Covenanters that was being negotiated in the early months of 1650,

which made their presence in the King's Council in Breda an embarrassment. Nor was Thomas Elliot popular in Breda at this time. According to Hyde, he was 'a loud and a bold talker', whose 'bluntness (as he was no polite man)', not surprisingly had made him many enemies, in particular Wilmot, one of the strongest supporters of the projected Scots alliance.[38] Arriving in Madrid in March, Hyde encountered the well-travelled diplomat Sir Richard Fanshawe, accompanied, to Hyde's disapproval, by his indomitable and once again pregnant wife Ann and his growing family. One consequence of Charles's alliance with Spain was the five-year embassy of Sir Henry Bennet to Madrid, which began in March 1657.[39]

Apart from occasional exceptions like the Fanshawes, the exiled royalists who settled in Spain were Catholics. When his embassy with Hyde ended, the elderly Cottington, who was familiar with Spain from diplomatic missions stretching back to the reign of James I, retired to the house of the English Jesuits at Valladolid, where he died in June 1652. A more spectacular and controversial Cavalier also ended his days in Spain. Abandoning his command in the west country Lord Goring had gone into exile in France at the end of 1645. Suspected of treachery (almost certainly wrongly), and condemned for his negligence, recklessness and indiscipline (probably justifiably), Goring was severely criticised by Clarendon in his *History of the Rebellion* for leaving behind a 'dissolute and odious army to the mercy of the enemy, and to a country more justly incensed, and consequently more merciless, than they'. Being blamed by some of the King's councillors, notably Hyde, for contributing significantly to the collapse of royalist resistance in the west country during 1645, Goring naturally avoided Paris. In 1646 he entered the Dutch service, but within a year moved on to Spain, where he obtained the rank of Lieutenant General and where Ann Fanshawe met him in Madrid in 1650. Although at first impressed by Goring's wit, civility and dashing appearance, she considered 'his debauchery beyond all precedents, and that country not admitting his constant drinking, he fell sick of a hectic fever, in which he turned his religion'. Goring died in Madrid in 1657.[40]

Along with these prominent emigrés, like Goring and the Fanshawes, whose activities and travels are reasonably well recorded in correspondence and memoirs, there also existed a shadowy and often disreputable world of mysterious and indistinct figures who usually remain, in Dr Aylmer's words, 'obstinately obscure'. The assassination in Madrid on 6 June 1650 of Anthony Ascham, the newly appointed envoy from the Commonwealth, turned the spotlight briefly onto some of these

shadowy figures. Both Hyde and Ann Fanshawe were in Madrid at the time and have left accounts of 'how some young men meeting in the street with Mr Progers, a gentleman belonging to the Lord Ambassador Cottington, and Mr Sparkes, an English merchant . . . began to speak of the impudence of this As[cham] to come a public Minister from rebels to a court where there were two ambassadors from his king'. Having reached the decision 'to go immediately into his lodging and kill him' they did not waste time. 'They came to his chamber door and finding it open, and he set at his dinner, seized him and killed him, and went their several ways.'[41]

Ascham's six murderers represent some common types among the shady and shadowy exiled Cavaliers who normally remain 'obstinately obscure'. William Sparkes, a 'merchant' – which could mean almost anything – was not an exile, was the only one not a Catholic and, although all the assassins were arrested and imprisoned, was also the only one to be executed for the murder. Of the others, all five subsequently either escaped or were quietly released. The two Progers brothers involved in the assassination, Henry, in Cottington's service, and James, 'who came into this kingdom shortly after the wars were done in England', belonged to a strongly royalist Monmouthshire family with court connections. A third brother, Edward, a groom of the bedchamber and a close companion of Charles II, was one of the King's attendants who was expelled from Scotland in 1650. The other three assassins – Edward Halsall, George Arnet and John Williams – were swordsmen and adventurers like James Progers. In 1650 they were all 'soldiers in the king of Spain's service'.[42] Major Edward Halsall, who had been one of the garrison in the Lathom House during its long siege in the Civil War, was a younger brother of James Halsall, an active royalist agent and conspirator during the 1650s. After eventually escaping from Madrid Halsall returned to England, possibly in the company of Arnet. According to the statement under interrogation of Thurloe's not very reliable spy Henry Manning, he and Arnet 'were in England and came over to kill Cromwell'. Having disposed of Ascham so efficiently, they were perhaps now setting their sights considerably higher. He was certainly involved in royalist conspiracy in his native Lancashire but, after the suppression of the royalist rising in March, Halsall escaped back into exile and turned up at Bruges in 1656, looking for a position in the exiled court.[43] George Arnet, 'a Scotch man who was the earl of Crawford's trumpeter', comes across as a good representative of the stereotype of the loud-mouthed and quarrelsome Cavalier. After also disappearing from Spain, and possibly visiting England with Halsall, Arnet reappeared in

Cologne, where he was for a time a page in the exiled court, until, in October 1655, he was 'banished from the court for beating [William] Armorer', an equerry, in the King's presence.[44] Captain John Williams, who according to Hyde was 'the actual murderer of Ascham', is an even more obscure figure. Apart from the fact that he also either escaped or was quietly released from prison in Madrid, only to turn up at Cologne in June 1655, practically nothing is known of him.[45]

Apart from the occasional diplomatic embassy or residence, and the limited opportunities for a military career as 'soldiers in the King of Spain's service', open to a few senior officers like Goring and obscure soldiers of fortune like Arnet and Williams, Spain and Portugal seem to have attracted few exiled Cavaliers. Italy had a much wider cultural appeal than Spain enjoyed and was seen as more accessible, while the variety of Italian principalities and republics seemed to offer wider opportunities for employment. The traditional 'Grand Tour' itinerary was emerging during the 1630s, and *The Voyage of Italy* (the title of Richard Lassels's guidebook, published in 1670, in which the term 'Grand Tour' is used), was an essential part of that itinerary.[46] Many future royalists had travelled in Italy before the Civil War so it is not surprising that a number of exiled Cavaliers, by no means exclusively Catholics, were able to alleviate the hardships of exile with the pleasures of something approaching the Grand Tour.

One of the first exiled royalists to return to an Italy he had first visited with the architect Inigo Jones in a more peaceful age was the patron and collector Lord Arundel. With the country slipping into civil war, Arundel, accompanied by his wife, left England in February 1642, and travelled slowly through France to northern Italy, to the same region he had explored with Inigo Jones thirty years earlier. The Arundels eventually settled in Padua, where he died in 1646, leaving behind his unfortunate Countess Alathaea, 'so clogged with her husband's debts that [even] if her age would permit, she cannot return to her native country'. Lady Arundel died in Rotterdam in May 1654.[47]

Other cultivated royalists who withdrew to Italy were more fortunate. After leaving Paris in August 1649, Richard Symonds made a leisurely progress southwards to Venice and Rome, recording in his notebooks the palaces, churches and artists' studios he visited.[48] Sir Ralph Verney, who left his quiet retreat at Blois after the death of his wife Mary in 1650, was in Florence in October 1651, spent Christmas in Rome after a quick visit to Naples, then moved north to Venice, and finally reached Antwerp on his way back to England after travelling down the Rhine. Of the Cavalier poets in exile, Richard Crashaw died in Italy shortly

before Verney arrived, while Edmund Waller, who had been in Padua, returned to England at the end of 1651. Edward Sherburne, an artillery officer during the Civil War, but in addition a poet and classical scholar, was also in Italy during the 1650s, as was the widely travelled and perennially intellectually curious Sir Kenelm Digby. As well as these genuine exiled Cavaliers, Italy also attracted young men of royalist sympathies on the Grand Tour who moved in emigré circles. For example, Peter Wyche, son of a gentleman of the privy chamber to Charles I, after taking his degree at Cambridge in 1648, went 'beyond the seas'. Before going to Italy, he requested a pass not from the Protectorate government but from Charles II, so that 'he may not be thought one of the rebels'. Wyche, knighted by Charles at the Hague on the eve of the Restoration, was to become one of the founders of the Royal Society. It is clear that many of the most intellectually distinguished and culturally aware of the exiled royalists spent at least some of their period of exile in Italy.[49]

Some of the Cavaliers in Italy were not exiles 'doom'd to wander', as one of them expressed it, but accredited diplomatic agents.[50] In Rome, Sir Kenelm Digby was Henrietta Maria's agent in the late 1640s while from 1652 Charles II was represented by Charles Howard, Viscount Andover. A Catholic, Andover had been MP for Oxford in the Long Parliament, before Charles I raised him to the peerage, and then governor of Salisbury during the Civil War.[51] But easily the most controversial and turbulent embassy in Italy was that of Thomas Killigrew, appointed as Charles's resident in Venice on 26 August 1649. Killigrew's instructions required him to try and persuade not just the Signoria of the serene republic but also the dukes of Savoy and Tuscany both to favour royalist merchants and to 'discountenance those that are of the Rebels Faction'; he was also to oppose 'the admittance of any Minister from the Rebels'. Killigrew was a man of varied talents, with strong court connections stretching back to 1633 when he had been a page to Charles I. Cultured and cosmopolitan, he had travelled widely in western Europe before the Civil War, including to Italy, but his embassy in Venice ended in humiliation and disgrace. After a series of complaints that Killigrew had 'made his house an asylum for prohibited goods as well as for outlaws and rogues, to the detriment of the Signory, who frequently warned him', on 22 June 1652 his embassy was abruptly terminated. 'As he has not chosen to heed the warnings received from the state on several occasions, the Senate has resolved to dismiss him, and accordingly . . . [orders] that he shall depart speedily'.[52]

Poor Tom Killigrew, protesting his innocence, returned to Paris in

disgrace, to be greeted by the derisive doggerel of another exiled Cavalier poet, Sir John Denham: 'Our resident Tom/ from Venice is come/ And hath left the statesman behind him'. But to some extent Killigrew was the innocent victim of a shift in Venetian diplomatic alliances. In the aftermath of Worcester, the Stuart cause seemed finally to have collapsed while friendly relations with the Commonwealth, a strong naval and commercial power in the Mediterranean, were now essential. If Charles raised the question of a replacement for Killigrew, the Venetian ambassadors in France were instructed in a despatch from the Senate to 'evade the subject . . . with such cautious address as your own prudence will suggest to you'. Less than a month after Killigrew's ignominious recall, on 6 July, another despatch from the Senate, this time to the Captain General of the Sea, informed him 'that some beginning has been made for instituting confidential relations with the parliament of England, and a minister of ours has been despatched to that country'. The order was given that at the residence of the English minister in Venice the royal arms should be replaced by those of the Commonwealth.[53]

The attractions of Italy to exiled royalists were not solely cultural, religious and diplomatic. The conclusion of the Thirty Years War in 1648 had removed one possible field of employment for Cavaliers who hoped to live by their swords, but the principalities and republics of Italy offered some military opportunities. In particular, the Venetian republic was at war with the Ottoman Turks, the long drawn-out War of Crete 1645–70, and was recruiting mercenaries. Two Catholic Cavaliers, Colonel Sir John Mayney, who had served under both Newcastle in the north and Goring in the south-west, and Colonel Edward Stamford, a veteran of the campaigns in the midlands, were in Venice in the late 1640s, negotiating to take service under the banner of St Mark against the Turks. Mayney soon moved on to Naples, where he commanded a regiment in the Spanish service for a time, before returning to England. Stamford was also back in England by 1654.[54]

After 1651, the Venetian Signoria was more interested in recruiting Scots and Irish mercenaries than in hiring wandering Cavaliers, although at least one other English royalist turned up in Venice in the mid 1650s, with fatal consequences for himself. Colonel Alexander Keynes, of Radipole, Dorset, played an active part during 1650 in the attempt to organise a royalist rising in the west country to coincide with Charles II's invasion from Scotland. A wave of arrests in early 1651 destroyed the western royalists' plans for a rising and Keynes, with his estate sequestered and his financial affairs in chaos, fled into exile in Paris, leaving behind his wife Sarah to look after the children. Rashly

but understandably, on 22 September 1652 Sarah Keynes requested from the Committee for Compounding an authorisation that she receive an income of one-fifth the value of the sequestered estate, as her husband 'is lately dead' and she and her six small children 'ready to perish'. The discovery that Keynes was not dead led to the arrest of his wife and the sale of his estate by the Treason Trustees. Sarah Keynes survived these misfortunes and shortly after the Restoration presented another desperate petition for relief, this time to Secretary Nicholas, a much more sympathetic audience. In this second petition she claimed that she was still 'ready to perish', that Keynes had served Charles II in Flanders, then had a command in the Venetian army and had been killed fighting the Turks. She received a grant of £1,000, but the whole episode, including the activities and eventual fate of Colonel Keynes, remains mysterious.[55]

Another Catholic Cavalier, Colonel Sir Theophilus Gilby, had a more successful and somewhat longer military career in Italy. Gilby had served under Lord Belasyse in Yorkshire during the Civil War, and then attempted unsuccessfully to join Charles II in Scotland in 1650; but when most of Charles's closest attendants and companions were being despatched ignominiously back to Holland there was no chance that a popish Cavalier would be allowed anywhere near the young king. After taking part in the Worcester campaign Gilby went into exile and took service under the Grand Duke Cosimo III of Tuscany. Gilby served Cosimo for over four years, being joined in Tuscany by his wife and children. When, after negotiating the Spanish alliance, Charles began to raise his own regiments in Flanders in early 1657, approaches were made 'to the Great Duke' to persuade him to release this experienced veteran from his service. 'For sure', Hyde maintained to Langdale on 10 April 1657, 'if there were ever reason to send for him it holds still'. The approaches were successful – Thurloe was kept informed of them by one of his agents in Livorno – and during 1657 Gilby and his family moved from Tuscany to Flanders. In fact, the demands of Gilby's military duties in Flanders do not seem to have been particularly onerous and by 1659 he was also involved in royalist conspiracy in England.[56]

If the opportunities for a military career in Germany and Italy were limited, some Cavaliers were prepared to travel further afield. For example, two Scots professional soldiers, James King, Lord Eythin and Sir John Henderson, both veterans of the Thirty Years War, resumed the careers that had been interrupted by their participation in the English Civil War. Eythin, who acquired a German wife and a Swedish peerage, returned to the service of the King of Sweden, while Henderson was employed for a time by the Emperor.[57] Another Civil War veteran, Sir

William Vavasour, once the energetic Colonel-General of Gloucester-shire and a strong adherent of Prince Rupert, also took up in exile the career of professional soldier and joined the Swedish service. His travels are recorded fitfully in the correspondence of the exiles and in the reports of Thurloe's agents. He was in Holland in 1648, attempting to raise troops but lacking the money to pay them; a prisoner in Ostend in March 1657 'with other officers that came from Swedeland'; then in northern Germany in January 1658, marching to Kiel with three hundred men. 'I fear he will lose them this cold weather', reported Thurloe's agent in Hamburg. Vavasour was in Zealand in February, commanding Swedish infantry in the invasion of Denmark. His exploits, which have a *Mother Courage* ring about them, came to an abrupt end under the walls of Copenhagen. In a letter on 18 March 1659 to Lady Mordaunt, the wife of the royalist conspirator, Charles referred to the casualties in the unsuccessful Swedish assault on the city, 'whereof honest Sir Wm. Vavasour was one'.[58]

Two Scots Cavaliers, who escaped back to the continent after the suppression during 1654 of the royalist rising in the highlands led by Middleton and the Earl of Glencairn, travelled further than Gilby or Vavasour in search of military employment. In August 1655 Thurloe received a report from one of his agents that 'Colonel Dalyell and Drummond are long since gone to Moscow'. Thomas Dalyell and William Drummond remained in the service of Tsar Alexis for approximately ten years, both rising to high military rank and not returning to Scotland until 1665.[59]

Consideration of the travels of men like Gilby and Vavasour, Dalyell and Drummond, leads us to identify the restless wanderers among the exiled Cavaliers: those inveterate travellers who never settled in one place for long and who had little in common with the rather forlorn groups of homesick emigrés in Angers or Blois, Rotterdam or Bruges.

The restless wanderers need to be distinguished from those emigrés whose travels were motivated by the search for employment, as with the professional soldiers Gilby and Vavasour, or by the movements of Charles II and his court and the loyal courtiers who followed it, or by the demands of royalist diplomacy and the endless search for money. Examples of the last are Cottington and Hyde's embassy to Madrid and Culpepper and Crofts's journey to Russia and Poland in 1650, when they obtained £10,000 for the King.[60] Pragmatic motives of this kind do not fully explain the travels of someone like Tom Killigrew, who first visited the continent in the 1630s and who keeps appearing in different places (Paris, Rome, Venice, the Hague, Madrid, Cologne), or John Bargrave, a

young fellow of Peterhouse, who was ejected from his college in 1643 and then for the next seventeen years travelled extensively in Europe.[61] Although an Anglican clergyman and not a lay Cavalier, Bargrave is difficult to ignore, partly because his extensive travels are fairly well documented. Bargrave was in Italy between 1646 and 1647, where he met John Evelyn and made the first of four visits to Rome. He returned to Rome in 1650 as a tutor to Philip, Lord Stanhope, the future duellist and royalist conspirator, whom he collected in Leyden. He was back in Rome in 1654 and again in 1660 when the news of the Restoration sent him hurrying home to England. In between his four Italian journeys Bargrave travelled widely in France, visiting Lyons, Saumur, La Rochelle and Toulouse, in the Netherlands and in the Holy Roman Empire, where he visited Nuremberg, Augsburg, Innsbruck, Vienna and Prague.[62]

Some royalist exiles travelled well beyond western Europe. Another adventurous Anglican clergyman, Dr Isaac Basire, a friend of Hyde and Nicholas, as a result of his royalist allegiance during the Civil War was 'sequestered, plundered, and forced to fly; having been thrice shut up in the sieges of Carlisle and Oxford, and in confinement in Stockton castle'. Leaving Mrs Basire in England with four children, and pregnant with another, Basire went into exile, at first in France, and then in Italy. He stayed with Killigrew in Venice in June 1650, then travelled through the Turkish territories in the Levant in the early 1650s, before coming to rest in Transylvania where the reigning prince George Rakoczi in 1654 offered him the chair of theology at the university of Weissemburg. After first obtaining the approval of Charles II, he accepted.[63] Colonel Sir Henry Bard, the son of a clergyman but a fighting Cavalier during the Civil War, travelled even further afield than Basire. As a young man in the late 1630s, like Killigrew and several other future emigrés, he had travelled widely in western Europe but had also visited Palestine and Egypt. Raised to the Irish peerage as Viscount Ballamont by Charles I in 1645 in recognition of his military services, Bard was in exile in Holland by 1649 and took part in the Worcester campaign in 1651, eventually escaping back to the continent. Appointed ambassador to Persia by Charles II, presumably partly because of his reputation as an intrepid traveller, he died there in 1660, his health broken by the privations he had endured during his remarkable journeys.[64]

The most well travelled exiled Cavalier of them all is surely the irritatingly obscure John Page. As one of the garrison of Arundel castle, during the brief time it was in royalist hands, his contribution to the royalist war effort was negligible, but he compounded for Delinquency, paid a fine of £55, and then went into exile in 1652. In October 1662,

safely back in London in his chamber in Fetter Lane, he sent Lord Chancellor Hyde an account of his extensive travels.

> For this nine years last past I have traced foreign countries, as being unwilling to draw in the air of my own native soil, least I should be tainted (amongst the rest) with disloyalty. I first steered my course to the occidental parts of the world, and after two or three years traversing several countries resolved . . . to visit the oriental and have for this six years spent my time there, to inform my judgements of the nature and fertility of the soils, the habits and religion of the peoples, their policy in governing their kingdoms, and subduing their enemies. . . . I have ranged Madagascar, Johanna [*sic*], Ceylon, all the coast of Coromandel, the Bay of Bengal, Pegu, Siam, Malacca, Sumatra, Java . . . Timor and several other Islands, with some parts of China . . . all the coast of India from the Cape Cumoxin to the river Indus, as well Bombay as Goa.

Page claimed to have returned to Europe 'by land through Coximania, Persia, Parthia, Media, Kurdistan, Assyria, Mesopotamia and Syria', sailing from Cyprus to Leghorn in order to visit 'all the famous cities of Italy, and so came through France for England to triumph with others for the happy restoration of our most dread sovereign Lord the King'.[65]

Page concluded this remarkable letter with the offer to 'be serviceable to his majesty, by discovering what I know', promising to 'be prompt to make response to all questions' on the places he had visited. In the context of England's recent acquisition of Bombay as part of the dowry of Catherine of Braganza, this offer is understandable. Two more letters to the Chancellor, written within a couple of days of the first, contain a description of Bombay, which Page claimed to have visited in August 1660, with an emphasis on the harbour and the facilities for shipbuilding; but the letters also stress Page's poverty and his desire for a position, no matter how menial, at court.[66] These three letters exist in splendid isolation in the Clarendon MSS in the Bodleian with no apparent surviving evidence of any follow-up to Page's offers and claims. It means that as far as we know the veracity of Page's impressive display of exotic name-dropping was never tested and no more detailed account of his travels apparently exists.

Can any conclusions be drawn from this survey of the travels of the exiled Cavaliers? First, it is clear that a significant number of the 'long-term' exiles had travelled in Europe before the Civil War. Some had been on diplomatic missions in the 1620s and 1630s: Montagu,

Arundel, Cottington, Jermyn, Porter, Bristol and Fanshawe, for example. Clarendon's observation on Culpepper, that he had 'spent some years of his youth in foreign parts and especially in armies', could be applied to a number of Culpepper's companions in exile. Some had either served as professional soldiers in the Thirty Years War, as had Leighton, Massey and Vavasour, for example, or had at least some experience of campaigns in Germany or the Netherlands, as was the case with Goring, Langdale, Wilmot, Hopton, and O'Neill.[67] Then there were those royalists, like Arundel, Bard, Buckingham and Killigrew, who returned as exiles to the regions they had visited for pleasure in the peaceful days before they were swept into the Civil Wars.

These men, with in some cases years of experience of the difficulties and unfamiliar features of life in a foreign land, were unlikely to be overwhelmed by the hardships of exile. The majority of seventeenth century English men and women are often considered to have had an ingrained hatred of 'popery' and to have been hostile to foreign fashions and innovations; their occasional outbursts of intense anti-Spanish or anti-French feeling, have given them the reputation of being extremely xenophobic and insular. By contrast many, although certainly not all, of the exiled Cavaliers come across as remarkably adaptable and cosmopolitan. This is true not only of the cultured connoisseurs like Toby Mathew, Endymion Porter and Sir Charles Cotterell, it is equally the case with some of the professional soldiers like Daniel O'Neill, Sir Theophilus Gilby and Lord Goring. As we shall see in a later chapter, the Scots Cavaliers William Drummond and Thomas Dalyell were clearly in no hurry to return from Russia to Scotland after the Restoration. Sir Richard Fanshawe, secretary to the English ambassador to Spain in 1635, was appointed ambassador to Portugal in 1664. Lord Jermyn, who had lived comfortably in Paris throughout the 1650s in close – according to his enemies, very close – contact with Henrietta Maria, returned to that city as English ambassador after the Restoration. John Bargrave, although he did not travel abroad before the Civil War, seems to have developed a taste for travel in general and a love of Italy in particular. In 1662 he was chosen by Charles II's government to go on a delicate and dangerous mission to Algiers to redeem, with money collected by the Church of England, 300 British slaves.[68]

The Cavaliers who found the hardships of exile extremely difficult to endure, and who were most likely to succumb to the constant temptation to return quietly to England, tended to settle as close as possible to the English Channel. They were often royalists with families left behind in England, with complicated legal processes in progress that

were intended to try and preserve portions of their estate from sequestration or confiscation; and they were often too the more 'moderate' members of the King's party. Their numbers include a strong representation of peers and propertied gentry. Royalist peers and landowners like the earls of Berkshire, Peterborough and Lindsey and Lord Hatton were all back in England by 1656. So were Sir Ralph Verney and Sir Thomas Hanmer, who had withdrawn to the Loire valley in the late 1640s but did not stay the distance to the Restoration. Their various submissions to the Committee for Compounding express their resolve to conform to and live peaceably under the Commonwealth. For example, Lady Hatton's petition to the Committee on 14 February 1654 claimed that her husband 'went abroad to lead a retired life and pay his great debts, and has since done nothing against the state'. The petition was successful and Hatton's estate was discharged from sequestration. After remaining for a while in Paris after the King and the court had left for the Rhineland, Hatton then quietly returned to England.[69]

If opportunities for communication with family and friends in England, for both personal and economic reasons, were a major factor that determined both the choice of place of exile and the duration of the ordeal, other elements were also important. As is clear from the experiences of many exiles, from Charles II deciding to leave Paris for the Rhineland, to Tom Killigrew being ignominiously expelled from Venice, the wandering Cavaliers in search of either a refuge or employment were at the mercy of frequently changing attitudes and unpredictable developments in their host countries. The course of military campaigns from Flanders to Crete; the changes in attitudes towards either the Commonwealth or the Stuart cause of governments from Madrid to Venice; the policies towards the royalists of a succession of republican regimes in England, constantly veering between repression and 'healing and settling'; the movements of the exiled court: all these factors could influence a Cavalier's choice of a place of residence in exile.

Finally, there were the personal circumstances and allegiances of the exiles themselves: the presence or absence of their families, their religious and political affiliations, their factional or patron–client loyalties. All these factors helped to determine their shifting groupings and movements. There were the 'Louvrians' around Henrietta Maria in Paris and the Protestant group centred on the households of Mary of Orange and Elizabeth of Bohemia at the Hague. There was Charles II's 'retinue that wander in the Low countries' and that became the nucleus of his impoverished, faction-ridden court; they make a sharp contrast both to the unobtrusive little groups of scholarly exiles at Caen and Blois and to the

soldiers of fortune in camps and garrisons in Flanders. The Catholic desperadoes who murdered the Commonwealth's envoy Ascham in Madrid had only their religion and their royalist loyalties in common with the cultured and well-travelled Catholics who gathered at the English College in Rome. The scattered diplomats, courtiers, travellers, scholars and soldiers, so often accompanied by wives and families, make up an extraordinary diversity of human character and experience; this is the dominant theme that emerges from an examination of the travels of the exiled Cavaliers.

8
Nothing so Rare as Money

Nothing was so rare as money.

(James, Duke of York)[1]

Material and intellectual poverty, suffering, frustration, unhappiness, grinding penury, homesickness, disappointment, uncertainty, sterile faction fighting, enervating sloth: the experience of exile has not been highly regarded by historians.[2] Was poverty, or 'grinding penury' a major feature of the lives of the exiled Cavaliers and their families? How did they manage to survive, in many cases for years, deprived of their normal sources of income? Many were also burdened with composition fines and during the Civil War had already made considerable financial contributions to the Stuart cause. They faced life in exile with their estates either sequestered or confiscated outright and without the incomes that office in a large royal court or in a department of the government had once provided.

Among the various lists that historians have compiled of the disabilities of exile, poverty seems to take pride of place. Certainly it is a constant theme in the correspondence of the emigrés. 'Nothing', wrote James, Duke of York on the first page of his memoirs, 'was so rare as money'. Some royalists even worried about the possibility of dying of hunger, of being 'like to starve in Paris', as Lord Taaffe complained to a fellow Irish refugee Lord Clanricarde in January 1651. Indeed, in June 1653 Hyde expressed some surprise that he did 'not know that any man is yet dead for want of bread, which really I wonder at'.[3] Was it possible for a royalist exile to die 'for want of bread'? Did it ever actually happen? An assessment of the severity of the ordeal of exile involves examination not only of how the emigrés coped, or in some case failed to cope, with their physical poverty,

but also of how they were affected by the other negative aspects of life in exile.

There is ample evidence that the exiled Cavaliers suffered from poverty in a range of degrees and forms, from the merely inconvenient to the life threatening. One can find many examples of 'grinding penury' in their correspondence, most easily perhaps in Hyde's letters, which portray his agonised concern that his life in exile had both fragmented and brought financial disaster to his family. 'I have not had a Crown these two months but borrow, that is Edgman [Hyde's secretary] borrows', complained Hyde to Nicholas in November 1652. 'For so God help me I have no credit, every week two crowns to fetch my letters from the post . . . and to buy paper and ink, and my wife is in the meantime in as sad a condition as can be imagined.'[4] The cost of maintaining his large correspondence, essential to his role as the King's chief counsellor, and his worries about his family, from whom he was frequently separated for long periods, are two recurring themes in Hyde's letters. Both themes are apparent in his letter to Nicholas from Paris on 14 December 1652:

> I cannot avoid the constant expense of 7 or 8 livres the week for postage of letters, which I borrow scandalously out of my friends' pockets, or else the letters must more scandalously lie at the post house. I am sure all those that concern my private affairs would be received for ten sous a week, so that all the rest are for the King, from whom I have not received one penny since I came hither. And yet it is no purpose to complain, though I have not been master of a crown these many months, and cold for want of clothes and fire, and owe for all the meat which I have eaten these three months, and to a poor woman that is no longer able to trust [me]. My poor family at Antwerp – which breaks my heart – is in as sad a state, and the King as either of us, being in these very personal distresses.[5]

It is clear that, for those Cavaliers who shared the experience of exile with their families, the problems of poverty and the frustration at being unable to relieve the condition of their dependants were felt acutely. 'My wife and children . . . are in very ill case through want', wrote Hyde from Madrid to his friend in Henrietta Maria's household, Anne, Countess of Morton (previously Lady Dalkeith), on 21 June 1650. 'And I am as far from a present power of relieving them as ever I was in my life, having never in my life known so absolute a want of money as I have done since I came hither.'[6]

It is tempting to draw heavily on Hyde's accounts of the hardships of exile, both because of his prominent position among the exiled royalists and for the quantity and richness of the material that he has left for historians. But Hyde's experiences were shared by many other exiles. Sir Hugh Cholmley, in exile in Rouen after the surrender of Scarborough castle, found himself unable to maintain his family with him, and regretfully sent them back to England: 'my money falling short, my dear wife, with her two daughters, resolved for England', sailing from Dieppe in February 1649.[7] According to Hyde, in July 1652 even the Marquess of Ormonde, perhaps the greatest magnate among the exiles, 'hath not a pistole in the world'. If he were still in this impoverished condition three and a half years later, it would explain his inability to help his secretary George Lane, who complained to his father-in-law Nicholas on 4 January 1656 of being 'never in greater distress than at this instant, having no more than will feed my family this day, and which adds to my affliction, my little Ormond is brought so low with his teeth, and my wife [Nicholas's daughter Susan] so tired out with watching and looking to him herself since the falling sick of her maid, that I fear [for] his life and that she may contract a sickness likewise with taking over-much pains.'[8] One feels sympathy for the Lanes. Poverty and exile are enough to cope with, without a teething baby and a sick maid as well. But one also feels sympathy for Nicholas on receipt of this letter. What was he, in Cologne with Charles, meant to do to help his daughter and son-in-law, who at this time were in Antwerp with Ormonde? One also wonders about the anonymous sick maid. How well fed and regularly paid was she?

Although responsibility for a family greatly intensified the problem of how to survive in exile for royalists like Hyde, Nicholas, Lane and others, the rarity of money is also a frequent theme in the correspondence of those exiled Cavaliers who had no dependants. In June 1657 the brothers Henry and Thomas Batt, the 'short-term' exiles whose fortunes were discussed in Chapter 4, were reported as living 'in great necessity' in Bruges, while in Paris Major Thomas Carnaby was 'in danger to perish from want of bread and clothing'. Even the resourceful agent Nicholas Armorer, after escaping back to the continent in September 1659 following the suppression of Booth's rising, found himself stranded in Calais. He claimed in a letter to Hyde that he would have starved but for money sent from London by a friend, so he would 'not press Hyde for money for himself while others are more necessitous'.[9]

There are also several cases of Cavaliers who dared not leave their lodgings in case they were accosted by their creditors. Sir John Marlay,

governor of Newcastle during the Civil War, who with Sir Thomas Glemham had led the 'forty Gentlemen and Officers' who arrived in Rotterdam in September 1648, was in desperate circumstances in Antwerp by early 1658, unable to 'stir without forty pounds to pay his landlady'. In a similar case was Lord Wentworth, who wrote urgently to Hyde on 23 October 1659:

> This morning two or three of my creditors were with me; threatening me, that they would do me an affront if I did not very speedily pay them, and truly my Lord I shall be quite undone now if your Lordship do not find some way to help me; for over and above the affront I shall infallibly receive, my Credit will be utterly lost for the future. . . . I would have come in the place of the letter, but that if I should stir an inch out of the town, my Creditors would suspect I were quite run away, and then my wife could in no manner appease them.[10]

Examples of this kind, of distressed Cavaliers living 'in great necessity' and harassed by their creditors, are scattered throughout the correspondence of the exiles and the reports of Thurloe's agents. But these examples should not be taken as indicating a permanent condition of 'grinding penury'. After all, Hyde, despite his frequent complaints of poverty, used the opportunities of residence in a series of foreign towns to make regular additions to his library, even commissioning Nicholas's son John to buy books for him in Holland, promising that 'whatever directions you send for payment shall be punctually & at a minute observed'. Carnaby, despite being 'in danger to perish from want of bread and clothing', had found the means during 1658 to travel from the Netherlands to Paris; and Armorer, in danger of starving in Calais in September 1659, was, as we shall see in chapter 10, able to afford to travel with all possible speed to Charles II in the Pyrenees in October with the dramatic news of General Lambert's expulsion of the Rump.[11] Wentworth may have been seriously in debt by the end of 1659, but he did not spend his years in exile huddled in mean lodgings and haggling with his creditors. A gentleman of the bedchamber to Charles II and a privy councillor, Wentworth accompanied the court on its travels, from Paris to the Rhineland to the Spanish Netherlands. In April 1653 he and Henry Coventry were sent by the King on a diplomatic mission to Denmark and two of the north German courts, Oldenburg and Holstein, to encourage them to support openly the Stuart cause and to ask for financial aid.[12] But even taking into account possible exaggerations in

the accounts and variations in the circumstances of the exiles, the fact of their widespread poverty is overwhelming. How then did they, and their families and dependants, survive?

One answer to this question is that the exiled Cavaliers borrowed extensively and lived on credit. They borrowed from each other, from friends and neighbours back in England, from tradesmen and landlords, from sympathetic English merchants and other expatriates, from foreign princes, from anyone prepared to extend credit. 'Thou must not be ashamed to be indebted', Hyde insructed his wife from Madrid on 13 May 1650, 'but thou must write into England to anybody that thou thinkest will lend; at least let our friends there know the necessities you are all in, and if that moves them not they will live to be ashamed of it.'[13] Hyde himself borrowed from fellow exiles, including 100 rix dollars from the equally impoverished Richard Harding, in April 1656; 1,000 livres from his friend Sir Richard Browne, the King's resident in Paris, in December 1653; and various sums from the generous and long-suffering Antwerp merchant John Shaw. His concern for his family even drove Hyde to swallow his pride and attempt to borrow money from, of all people, Prince Rupert. On 19 October 1650 Hyde, at this time in Spain, wrote to the Prince, who was at Toulon refitting his little fleet of royalist privateers, to ask him to remit money to Lady Hyde at Antwerp, 'which may supply her for four or five months, in which time I hope to make provision for her. Nor do I know any way under heaven to prevent them from starving, since returning into England would be as bad for them as starving, except by Your Highness's favour.'[14]

There are examples of exiles swallowing their pride and attempting to borrow from outside the circle of their friends and relatives. Even the flamboyant George Digby, who inherited the earldom of Bristol in 1653, but whose long friendship with Hyde was gradually crumbling during the 1650s, was reduced to approaching the Chancellor in a condition of 'uncertainty and disorder' which could only be alleviated by a loan of 'ten pounds, [or] God knows what Courses I shall be reduced into'. But friends and relatives were obviously the best source of loans, as Charles appreciated when he turned to his sister Mary in November 1657. 'I know you are without money, and cannot very easily borrow it, at least upon so little warning; but if you would send me any jewel that I may pawn for $1,500 sterling, I do promise you, you shall have the jewel in your hands again before Christmas.'[15]

One can continue at some length giving examples of exiled Cavaliers, sometimes also supporting families and sometimes not, who survived by borrowing – from friends, relatives or other sympathetic lenders –

and who lived on credit, staggering from one financial crisis to the next. This not uncommom state of affairs raises the question of the avail- ability of credit to persons whose ability to repay their loans must often have seemed extremely dubious. Surprisingly, there are examples of exiles who contrived to live, if not extravagantly at least in reasonable comfort and dignity, their life-style maintained by loans and indefinite credit, extended by patient and long-suffering merchants and trades- men, by friends and relatives, or by sympathetic princes. Hyde on occa- sion referred waspishly to Lord Jermyn, comfortably maintained by Henrietta Maria, whose pension of 8,000 pistoles a year from the French crown was augmented by generous loans from Cardinal Mazarin. According to Hyde, Jermyn 'kept an excellent table for those who courted him, and had a coach of his own, and all other accommodations incident to the most full fortunes', while Ormonde and the Chancellor lodged with 'a poor English woman, the wife of one of the King's ser- vants' and had 'to walk the streets on foot, which was no honourable custom in Paris'.[16]

The Cavalier who was most successful in avoiding anything remotely approaching 'grinding penury' during his sixteen years in exile, and who developed the art of living on credit to a level of refinement never approached by his fellow emigrés, was not Jermyn but William Cavendish, first Marquess of Newcastle. Withdrawing into exile after Marston Moor, Newcastle at first settled in Hamburg, but in April 1645 he joined Henrietta Maria's court at St Germain, where he met and married in the same year Margaret Lucas, a member of a prominent and strongly royalist Essex family, and a maid of honour to the Queen.[17] The *Life of the Duke of Newcastle*, written by the Duchess after the Restora- tion, gives a vivid account of the Newcastles' years in exile and shows how remarkably successful they were in maintaining an appropriately dignified and elegant aristocratic lifestyle in extremely unfavourable circumstances.

When Newcastle married Margaret Lucas, 'having no estate or means left him to maintain himself or his family', all his extensive lands in England having been confiscated by the Commonwealth government, 'he was necessitated to seek for credit, and live upon the courtesies of those that were pleased to trust him'. On one occasion the trust of these obliging creditors seemed to be in danger of wearing thin, but Lady Newcastle, when requested by her husband, was prepared to make her own sacrifices.

I must of necessity pawn my clothes to make so much money as would procure a dinner. I answered my clothes would be but of small

value, and therefore desired my waiting maid [Elizabeth Chaplain] to pawn some small toys, which I had formerly given her, which she willingly did. The same day in the afternoon, My Lord spoke himself to his creditors, and both by his civil deportment, and persuasive arguments, obtained so much that they did not only trust him for more necessaries, but lent him money besides to redeem those toys that were pawned. Hereupon I sent my waiting maid into England to my brother, the Lord Lucas, for that small portion which was left me, and My Lord also immediately after dispatched one of his servants who was then governor to his sons, to some of his friends, to try what means he could procure for his subsistence.[18]

This passage illustrates a number of the methods used by the exiles to overcome the constant rarity of money. As well as borrowing from whoever would lend, they pawned or sold possessions: a jewel worth $1,500 in the case of Charles II, handed down 'toys' in the case of the lady's maid Elizabeth Chaplain, paintings and other treasures in the case of the Duke of Buckingham. They employed wives, other relatives or, in the Newcastles' case, trusted servants to trace assets in England: marriage portions, in some cases, or what remained of the income from estates after sequestration or after composition fines had been paid. For example, Hyde's brother-in-law William Aylesbury, as well as being Buckingham's financial agent, was also entrusted with the task, which he seems to have failed to perform, of selling land in England belonging to Lady Hyde.[19]

In the summer of 1648 Newcastle and his household left Paris, Henrietta Maria having given the Marquess $2,000 and accepted responsibility for his debts. The members of Newcastle's household were transported in one coach 'which he had newly caused to be made', containing six gentlemen and attendants including Elizabeth Chaplain, one small chariot 'that would hold only My Lord and myself', and three wagons, 'beside an indifferent number of servants on horseback'. On the day when Newcastle and his entourage left Paris, 'the creditors coming to say farewell to My Lord, expressed so great a love and kindness for him, accompanied with so many hearty prayers and wishes, that he could not but prosper on his journey'.[20]

'Having put off most of his train', Newcastle settled in Antwerp, leasing the splendid house 'that belonged to the widow of a famous picture drawer, Van Ruben'. There the Newcastles remained until the Restoration, with the Marquess supervising his equestrian school for young aristocrats, buying pedigree horses and writing a work on horsemanship, *La Methode Nouvelle et Invention Extraordinaire de Dresser les*

Chevaux, that was published at great expense in Antwerp in 1658.[21] While maintaining this elegant life-style, Newcastle managed to keep his numerous creditors at bay, mainly by borrowing from friends and sympathetic merchants, including that generous benefactor of distressed Cavaliers, John Shaw of Antwerp. Lady Newcastle and her brother-in-law Sir Charles Cavendish were also sent on money-raising visits to England, from where an irregular supply of funds was extracted from certain estates that had either avoided or been recovered from sequestration and were being administered by sympathetic relatives. On Lady Newcastle's return to Antwerp early in 1653 from one not particularly fruitful fund-raising visit to England, 'the creditors, supposing I had brought great store of money with me, came all to My Lord to solicit the payment of their debts', but when they learned the depressing truth of the situation they agreed to allow Newcastle more time and 'to credit him for the future, and to supply him with such necessaries as he should desire of them'.[22]

During the second half of 1659, as the Commonwealth began to disintegrate, Newcastle gradually found it easier to obtain money from England. 'Some time before the restoration of His Majesty . . . My Lord, partly with the remainder of his brother's estate', for Sir Charles Cavendish had died in 1654, 'and the credit which his sons had got, which amounted in all to $2,400 a year, sprinkled something amongst his creditors.'[23]

By successfully raising money from many sources, and then falling back on gracious and confident reassurances to his faithful creditors when all else failed, Newcastle survived for almost sixteen years without succumbing to the 'grinding penury' or the 'paralysing unhappiness' that feature so prominently in the traditional picture of the existence of the exiled Cavalier. When Charles visited Antwerp in February 1658, Newcastle was able to entertain the King in a style appropriate to a royal visit. On 19 February Sir Edward Walker, the pedantic Garter King-at-Arms, wrote to Nicholas to describe how 'the entertainment was at Lord Newcastle's ushered in by a speech penned by my Lord, and spoken by Major Mohun; then followed French dances . . . and a great banquet brought in by sixteen gentlemen of quality in the King's retinue'. Walker could not resist the gloomy conclusion. 'So however melancholy you are at Bruges, we are merry here, but I fear faction will ensue.'[24]

Newcastle, in his Antwerp mansion, with his attendants and servants, and his stable of pedigree horses, could always obtain credit. But this aristocratic magnate's experience of exile was as unusual as it was distinctive; his settled and elegant life in Antwerp, when so many exiled

Cavaliers, from Charles II downwards, were impoverished wanderers, sets him apart from his fellow emigrés. Newcastle's circumstances were very different from those of the anonymous member of the exiled court, writing from Paris in May 1654 to a friend in London, who declared that 'my credit and bank is exhausted' and although 'with infinite industry and trouble, I have hitherto, without much incommodating my mistress, sustained myself . . . hereafter I must live upon her, for there is no other way'.[25]

The great majority of exiled Cavaliers did not have Newcastle's capacity to survive indefinitely upon 'the courtesies of those that were pleased to trust him', nor had they generous and compliant mistresses to turn to when their financial resources were exhausted. It was to the court that Cavaliers living 'in great necessity' often turned, hoping, if not for a permanent place, then at least for financial help.

As we have seen, the shrunken court of Charles II, and the households of the other Stuart princes and princesses on the continent, were obviously not capable of providing places for large numbers of exiles, but they offered status and a certain degree of financial security to a fortunate few. The courtiers were the King's 'Family', a term for the royal household which possesses considerable poignancy in the circumstances of exile; they were dependants for whose welfare Charles was meant to accept some responsibility.

The exiled court received money from a variety of sources. When the court was in Paris in the early 1650s Charles received a pension from the French crown of 6,000 livres a month, the equivalent approximately of $6,000 a year. Payments were irregular and unreliable. Mazarin promised to continue payment of this pension after Charles withdrew from Paris to the Rhineland in July 1654 but when the King signed the treaty of alliance with Spain in April 1656, the meagre flow of funds from France was replaced by an equally irregularly paid Spanish pension. Between August 1656 and November 1658 Charles received six separate payments from Spain totalling 145,000 florins.[26] There were also occasional contributions from some German princes, from Mary of Orange, from English royalists and other sympathisers like John Shaw the Antwerp merchant. The expectations of windfalls, for example, of prize money from privateers operating in the Channel under letters of marque from the king, or of generous contributions from royalists in England, collected by agents like Henry Seymour, never remotely matched the reality.[27]

During the early 1650s responsibility for the administration and distribution of the money received by the court belonged to the elderly Sir

Richard Foster, Keeper of the King's Privy Purse. Foster had been one of the 'court papists' around Henrietta Maria in the late 1630s; an associate of Windebank and Cottington, he was one of the first royalists to go into exile, early in 1641, when the Queen's circle was shattered. Foster, with his 'good words and promises', was quite unfitted to cope with the chaotic nature of court finances; complaints from Hyde, for example, that he had not been reimbursed for postal expenses incurred on the King's business were met with vague promises that he 'will pay me when he can'. Fortunately for the management of court finances, this 'good old man', as Ormonde generously called Foster, died early in 1655.[28]

Even more fortunately for the management of court finances, Foster had in effect already been replaced by Stephen Fox. Of very modest social origins, Fox early showed his ability 'in the understanding of accounts', first in the service of the Earl of Northumberland and then as a dependant and client of Northumberland's brother, the 'Louvrian' courtier Lord Percy. Having returned to England in 1651, and accepted the position of Keeper of the Privy Purse to the Earl of Devonshire, Fox resigned his position in early 1653 and returned to France, taking his new wife with him. At a time when the fortunes of the Stuart cause seemed to be in ruins, this was a remarkably courageous even rash action. But Fox's allegiance now was to Hyde and the King, not to Percy and the Queen. When the court moved from Paris to the Rhineland, Fox, as the new Clerk of the Kitchen, was 'given the task of governing the expenses of the family, and of payment of the wages of the servants, and indeed, of issuing out all moneys, as well as in journeys, as when the court resided anywhere'.[29] Fox's success in this task formed the basis for his impressive and successful career after the Restoration, in the course of which he founded an aristocratic dynasty as well as being the grandfather of the great Whig leader with the impeccable but, in his case fairly inappropriate, Stuart Christian names: Charles James Fox.

Household accounts and the correspondence of the exiles reveal the magnitude and frustration of the task confronting Fox when, in co-operation with Hyde, he attempted to establish some degree of order and method in the finances of the exiled court. In his *History of the Rebellion* Clarendon presents a glowing picture of Fox's achievement, stressing how 'his great industry, modesty, and prudence did very much contribute to bringing the family, which for so many years had been under no government, into very good order; by which his majesty, in the pinching straits of his condition, enjoyed very much ease from the time he left Paris'.[30]

The *History of the Rebellion*'s cheerful and optimistic picture is contradicted by Hyde's own correspondence at the time. 'The King hath not money enough to provide meat for himself for the next ten days', reported Hyde to Nicholas on 29 June 1655. 'Nor have I, at any time, seen the Court in greater want, save that there is not any importunity from the inhabitants of this place [Cologne] for the money due to them. And yet of 2,000 dollars borrowed from one person to enable the King to make his last journey [to Middleburg] there remain still 1,200 unpaid. Add to this three months arrear for board wages to the Family and the extreme necessity many honest men are in who came lately and indeed come every day from England and Scotland.' In this crisis the court looked with increasing urgency and frustration to the German princes for aid. 'There is nothing to support all these pressures but the expectation of the money from the German Princes who are so slow in paying, though they multiply their promises and give new hopes every day'.[31]

Yet despite its permanent condition of financial crisis, the court somehow kept afloat financially, with Fox having frequent opportunities to demonstrate his flair for producing urgently needed funds at the last minute. 'The King leaves for Brussels tomorrow at 4 a.m.', Fox informed Nicholas on 25 February 1658, at the conclusion of the royal visit to Antwerp during which the court had enjoyed the lavish entertainment provided by Newcastle. 'We could not have got from hence if Mr Shaw had not lent us 1,500 florins, which is all the money I have had since we left Bruges. We have fair promises when we get to Brussels; meantime it will go hard with our menage.'[32]

Of course, Hyde and Fox were chiefly concerned to meet the costs incurred by the King and his 'family'. An examination of the records of payments authorised by Fox shows that they were most often made to the holders of household positions, whose allowances were fixed, according to their rank and office. For example Hyde, Chancellor and member of the Privy Council, was meant to receive 140 guilders a month while Fox himself, in the third rank of the household, was to receive 40 guilders. Payments also had to be made to those who supplied the court with provisions and to those who incurred expenses in the King's service. In January 1660, on Fox's authority, a total of 2,454 florins was paid to a butcher, poultry woman, fishmonger, baker, caterer and herb woman, and to meet different 'small debts'. A further 1,000 florins were paid to 'several merchants', plus 1,000 florins each to Culpepper and Dorothy Chiffinch, the 'seamstress and laundress to His Majesty's person', in part payment of various debts. Agents and

couriers, like Nicholas Armorer and John Stephens, also feature fairly regularly in the lists of recipients of money, as do royalists employed on diplomatic missions, such as Richard Bellings and Colonel John Marsh, who received 450 and 400 guilders respectively during 1654 to help meet the cost of their money raising missions to various German princes.[33]

Although the court clearly had acute difficulty in finding enough money to meet its own expenses, it is clear that exiled Cavaliers with no court connections also looked to the King to help them cope with the demands from their creditors. Included in the series of payments mentioned above, authorised by Fox in January 1660, were 1,000 florins to the Irish royalist Lord Castlehaven, 700 to Sir Theophilus Gilby, the professional soldier released from the service of the Grand Duke of Tuscany, 170 to Lord Grandison and 120 to a Mr Gibson. None of these exiles belonged to the King's 'family', although Gilby had the legitimate complaint that, having terminated at Charles's request his employment by the Duke of Tuscany, for which he had been paid $400 per annum, he had received no pay since 1657 when he and his family had moved from Tuscany to Flanders.[34] Other similar examples can be found in the accounts of money received and expenses incurred by the court. For example, between August and November 1656 the debt-ridden Sir Richard Page received 200 and Sir Marmaduke Langdale 50 guilders, although neither was a courtier.[35]

Hyde, by the nature of his position, was the inevitable recipient of appeals and petitions from impoverished exiles. On 3 June 1657, when the court was established in Bruges, he pointed out to Charles the 'very miserable condition your poor servants are in here. Barlow is in danger to be arrested and some others in such pressing necessities it grieves me exceedingly to see them.' Hyde proposed that he draw a 'bill of 1,000 guilders upon Mr Fox' and distribute the money among deserving cases.[36] One thousand guilders were duly distributed among 'many poor men', including 300 to 'Mr Barlow', probably Lieutenant Colonel John Barlow, and 200 to the brothers Thomas and Henry Batt – whose short and disastrous experience of exile has been referred to above – to pay the cost of their voyage back to England and into the obscurity from which they had so briefly emerged. Nothing was left for Hyde's friend 'poor Dick Harding', a groom of the bedchamber, who had already pawned 'every little thing' he possessed.[37] Wentworth was more fortunate than Harding. His desperate complaint to Hyde on 23 October 1659 than he and his wife were trapped in their lodgings by aggressive creditors resulted three days later in 'a letter from Mr Fox with a bill of

exchange for 416 guilders'. Wentworth thanked Hyde, while at the same time expressing his hope that 'the rest of the hundred pounds assigned me by his Majesty at his parting from Brussels' would soon follow. In the meantime 'this sum hath stopped my creditors' mouths for the present'.[38]

There are a number of other examples in the Clarendon MSS of Hyde responding to appeals for financial help from exiled royalists, including several who had no connections with the court. The desperate condition of Captain Thomas Carnaby, stranded in Paris and in 'want of bread and clothing', has already been mentioned. In the autumn of 1658 the kind-hearted Percy Church, a member of the household of Henrietta Maria, referred to Carnaby's plight in several of the letters he sent regularly to Hyde and Nicholas. Church claimed that he had done 'his uttermost to keep him alive with victuals but to clothe him my credit cannot do it, though really his wants is almost beyond my expression'. In response to Church's appeals Hyde sent money to Carnaby, who wrote on 15 October to thank the Chancellor for 'your unmerited kindness for me'.[39]

Speaking to us through their own correspondence and memoirs, the exiles reveal to us the nature and extent of their poverty. But it is clear that the actual degrees of hardship they suffered varied enormously; the range was from 'grinding penury' to occasional periods of financial embarrassment. It is also clear that the capacity of the exiled Cavaliers to overcome their poverty was determined by certain key, but often changeable, factors. Probably the most important was their ability to raise loans and to live on credit. Many were also dependent on the receipt of funds from England, either gifts or loans from friends and relatives or money raised from property they or their wives still controlled. Some exiles looked for employment, especially military, or for a place in a Stuart household; in the latter situation they were more likely to be able to benefit from the occasional distribution of money by the court to royalists in special need. Poverty, that permanent rarity of money complained of by the Duke of York, was probably the worst aspect of the ordeal of exile; it is certainly the problem most frequently complained of in the correspondence of the emigrés. But it was by no means the only bitter and melancholy feature of the experience.

One of the most bitter features of the experience of exile was the division of families; the separation of husbands from their wives, of fathers from their children. 'Thy kind letters do much comfort my sad troubles', wrote the Cornish royalist Jonathan Rashleigh in 1646 to his wife from London, where he was forced to remain for two years before his

application to compound was accepted and he was permitted to return to Cornwall. In a similar vein, Mary Verney declared that 'I cannot be any longer from you, therefore I am resolved to stand or fall with you', before leaving England to join her husband at Blois.[40]

Unless an exile's wife showed the courage and determination of a Mary Verney, such separations could last for years, with perhaps infrequent and fleeting reunions, that were sometimes accomplished only with difficulty and even danger. Thomas Ross, a courtier and royalist conspirator, occasionally employed by Charles II on delicate missions, wrote to his friend Colonel Gervase Holles at Rotterdam to inform him that he had just returned to Antwerp from Zealand, where he had been 'to fetch a shipwrecked wife, who was in the last great storm'.[41] Hatton, remaining behind in Paris after the court had left that city for Cologne, recounted in September 1654 to his friend Nicholas one such 'gipsy visit of a mother and her children, bag and baggage, that came to visit me and are here with me, and my eldest daughter very ill ever since her journey'. It is perhaps significant that it was not long after this visit that Hatton made his peace with the Protectorate, settled the outstanding issues regarding his composition assessment, and returned quietly to England.[42] Wentworth received a similar 'gipsy visit' to Brussels in September 1658, when he excused himself from attendance at court, not on this occasion because of harassment by his creditors, but as a consequence of 'the sudden and unexpected coming of my wife'. As Lady Wentworth had 'come over in so private a way and in so unfit a condition to wait on Your Majesty publicly . . . she hopes you will pardon her for not coming to kiss your Majesty's hand'. Wentworth also apologised for his continued absence from court. 'I hope your Majesty will pardon my keeping her company after so long an absence.'[43]

The unhappiness that resulted from separation was not confined to those exiled Cavaliers who had left their wives behind them in England. Some wives accompanied or followed their husbands into exile only to discover that they were suffering the worst of both worlds. They had to endure the poverty and the other hardships of exile but still sometimes experienced long periods of separation from their husbands who were occupied on those various activities covered by that blanket term 'the King's business'.

Not all the wives who had joined their husbands in exile were prepared to accept the necessity of long periods of separation from them with the Christian resignation shown by, for example, ladies Ormonde, Hyde and Nicholas. Elizabeth Elliot, the wife of Thomas Elliot, one of Charles II's grooms of the bedchamber, certainly was not. Elliot, whom

Hyde described as a 'loud and bold talker' and an 'insolent and over-active man', had been the rather odd choice to head a diplomatic mission to Portugal in 1650. He was no friend to Hyde and neither was his father-in-law, Colonel Edmund Wyndham, also in exile, an associate of Prince Rupert and the 'Swordsmen' faction.[44] Elliot's was another case where the hardships of poverty and disappointment were aggravated by the presence of his wife Elizabeth and their children, including a daughter born in Paris in September 1652, especially when his duties in the King's service led to frequent absences from his family. Elizabeth Elliot was one exiled wife who was not prepared to accept this situation with quiet and docile resignation. On 26 November 1657 she wrote an angry letter to her father from Bruges, to which she had just returned after a fruitless visit to the exiled court in Brussels.

> When I came to Brussels I did go to the King in hopes to get something to have removed my Children, but I find he has not the least good nature left either for you or yours, for with all I could say to him I was able to get but 100 gilders, which I intend to go back with and live upon as long as I can. He pretends poverty – but I never in my life saw more bravery, so I see it is only for me he is poor and for nobody else. Pray be pleased to write to him and in your letter take notice how unkind he is to let me lie so long at Bruges alone and give me nothing to bring me away, for it may be that will work.[45]

Elizabeth Elliot believed that she had a special claim on the King's favour as her mother, 'the beautiful and bossy' Christabella Wyndham, who died in exile, had been Prince Charles's wet-nurse. Having once been 'His Majesty's foster sister' she expected better treatment, as she was to remind the King in a petition presented after the Restoration when she claimed that it was 'the greatest happiness that could befall her to suck the same breast with so great a monarch'.[46] Elizabeth Elliot was clearly a formidable lady, unwilling to accept quietly the disabilities of exile. Twenty years after the Restoration, and three years after Elliot's death, Ormonde recollected to the diplomat Sir William Temple: 'I remember my old friend Thomas Elliot valued himself much upon the absolute government of his wife; and yet lookers on thought she governed him.'[47]

Aggravated by the unhappiness caused by separation from loved ones, one of the greatest hardships endured by the exiled royalists was an intense homesickness for England. There are frequent nostalgic references to England in the correspondence of the exiles, especially of those

whose backgrounds were less cosmopolitan and who were less well travelled, along with hopeful anticipations of the return home. Most royalists who fled into exile did not expect their ordeal to last very long; they hoped, as Nicholas expressed it to Richard Harding in July 1651, that, although he was uncertain where to fix his 'winter station', he prayed 'it might be peacefully in England'.[48] Hatton, writing to the ejected Anglican divine Peter Gunning from Paris on 23 June 1649, longed to 'suppose myself in full possession of my estate as ever; to be settled at home in peace and quiet'. This nostalgic longing that 'better days' might come again and, as Hyde hopefully expressed it to Sir Richard Browne, they might survive to 'eat cherries at Deptford again,' comes through strongly in the Chancellor's correspondence. After travelling from the Hague to Paris in the summer of 1649, Hyde confessed to his wife, who had been left behind in the Netherlands, that he was 'not at all taken with the delights of it [France], and on my word, for all I have yet seen, give me old England, for meat, drink, and lodging, and even for wine too'.[49] To prefer England over France for wine illustrates the depth of the homesickness into which some exiled royalists sank.

Royalists confronted with the disadvantages of exile – poverty, separation from one's family and homesickness for England – reacted in different ways. For those who could not cope with the rigours of exile, the most obvious response, and certainly the most common, was to return to England. The flow of exiles back to England began, as we have seen, almost before the Civil War had ended and continued unevenly, increasing to a flood during periods when the Stuart cause sank to new depths, until the eve of the Restoration. The list of exiles who returned to England before the Restoration includes not only muddled adventurers, like the poor Batt brothers, and those whose adherence to the Stuart cause was probably fairly lukewarm to begin with, like the Earl of Peterborough, but also many Cavaliers whose loyalty and commitment could not be questioned, and whose sacrifices on behalf of Charles I or Charles II had been enormous. Soldiers like Sir Hugh Cholmley, the heroic defender of Scarborough castle, and Sir Lewis Dyves, famous for his escapes from prison, were back in England well before the Restoration. So were such close companions of the King in his early years of exile as the Duke of Buckingham and Edward Progers.

Most of the well-known literary figures among the exiles also trailed back to England during the 1650s. Thomas Hobbes, one of the first to go into exile in Paris, was also among the first to return, in 1651. Sir William Davenant's return was under duress, when the ship on which

he was travelling to America was intercepted near Cowes in 1650 and escorted into an English port. Sir John Denham claimed to be penniless when he returned to England in 1653. Abraham Cowley, who was Jermyn's secretary in Paris, lasted somewhat longer. Occasionally employed by Jermyn or the Queen as a courier, Cowley was sent into England in 1656, was arrested but released on bail, and decided to remain on the English side of the Channel.[50] It is certain that the majority of Cavaliers who went into exile returned to England before the Restoration. Despite the penalties and disabilities waiting for them – the humiliating requirements to sign Engagements, Covenants and Negative Oaths, the harassing by parliamentary committees and major-generals, the composition fines and decimation taxes, the proscription of the Anglican service, the restrictions on movements and exclusions from eligibility for offices – the exiles steadily drifted back to England. This fact alone is the strongest piece of evidence in support of the argument that to remain in exile meant years of poverty and unhappiness.

Most Cavaliers who were unable or unwilling to endure the rigours of life in exile therefore returned, some much earlier than others, to England. But many, for various reasons, remained in exile. Either they were too closely identified with the Stuart cause, or they had been excepted from pardon or banished, or their loyalty or pride did not allow them to submit to the authority of those they regarded as rebels and regicides. The other major reason, as we have seen, why committed royalists remained in exile was that there were no prospects for them in Commonwealth or Cromwellian England. What happened to those royalists who were unable or unwilling to return to England but who then failed to cope with the poverty and other hardships of exile? Some probably sank into obscurity and their fates were not recorded. Some, as we shall see, abandoned their royalist principles and turned traitor. Some, the ultimate casualties, did die almost literally 'for want of bread'. We are dealing here with a small but tragic minority among the emigrés, those who were broken, demoralised, corrupted or even destroyed by the experience of exile.

For obvious reasons, the fates of those exiles who lost touch with their companions and families and gradually sank into obscurity are the hardest of all to discover. Like the 'Captain Knight', who was among the group of exiles who received a payment of money authorised by Hyde in September 1659, or the Captain Mason, 'an honest man, a soldier for the King, and now gets his living as a servant to the merchants at Dort', they flit in and out of the correspondence of the exiles and the intelligence reports of Thurloe's agents, leaving few traces

behind.[51] We do not know how many exiled royalists dropped into a lower social group or disappeared into the ranks of a continental army. If we define the term 'exiled royalist' narrowly, then the number is probably fairly small; if we apply it more loosely to embrace the drifting adventurers and soldiers of fortune, like the 'fifty young blades' who arrived in Bruges from England in March 1657, then the number possibly becomes much larger.

Certainly, some emigrés did succumb to the 'grinding penury' and other hardships of exile. There is a clear distinction between those royalists who failed to survive the experience of exile and those who were destroyed by it. In the first category are those who died in exile, perhaps in poverty but not literally 'for want of bread', perhaps separated from wives and families, but not reduced to a desperate or destitute condition. Men like Hopton and Wilmot, Joseph Jane and Richard Harding are in this group. They are melancholy figures, their 'last years tinged with the sadness of defeat', but they died respected by their fellow exiles, retaining their principles and dignity.[52] In the second category are men like Sir Richard Page and John Villiers, Viscount Grandison.

The tragic fate of Sir Richard Page aroused sympathy and concern among his fellow exiles. Like Stephen Fox, Page was of modest social status but rose to command a regiment during the Civil War, being knighted and receiving a grant of arms for his part in the storming of Leicester in May 1645. In exile in Holland in the late 1640s, Page soon became active in royalist conspiracy. He was in East Anglia in 1650 as an agent of Charles II, escaping back to the continent when the details of the conspiracy were betrayed by Thomas Coke. He returned to England early in 1655 at the time of Penruddock's rising and escaped back to Holland with Nicholas Armorer in May when the scattered royalist risings were suppressed.[53] But gradually Page was overwhelmed by his debts, his increasingly desperate situation aggravated by the erratic and devious behaviour of his turbulent wife. Lady Page, 'a lewd creature' according to Gilbert Burnet, specialised in plots, intrigues and character assassinations. Early in 1654 she joined with the dubious Colonel Bampfield, a one-time royalist who had become a spy for Thurloe, in a plot to discredit with the King two prominent Scots Cavaliers, William Murray, Lord Dysart – allegedly Lady Page's ex-lover – and Sir Robert Moray, the future first president of the Royal Society. The complicated intrigue, which involved the stealing of letters from Dysart's lodging by Lady Page, culminated in accusations of treason against Dysart and Moray, which were quickly dismissed by Charles and Hyde as unsubstantiated, despite an embarrassed defence by Page of his

wife's allegations. Undeterred by this setback, a few months later Lady Page became involved in one of the abortive plots to assassinate the Lord Protector.[54]

Page might have been better off to remain in England in 1655 and try to make his peace with the Protectorate regime. For two months after landing in Holland with Armorer, he was arrested for debt and imprisoned. 'His condition is very sad', reported Joseph Jane to Nicholas from the Hague on 23 July. 'The imprisonment of Sir R. Page is for his own and such debts as his wife contracted, who, if she continue with him, will most certainly render his condition miserable . . . which is very sad in a man of so much use.'[55] But Page's usefulness to the royal cause was over. Although eventually released from prison, he was no longer employed as an agent and in September 1657 he died in poverty in Bruges. The cost of Page's funeral was paid by Nicholas, until the resourceful Stephen Fox could scratch together the money to reimburse him. As Lady Page had by this time vanished from the scene, the fate of the Page children became another concern of Hyde's, who hoped 'some way could be found to bring up Sir Richard Page's little children here, instead of sending them to England, and would contribute all he could to it, that it might be seen that good men are not presently forgotten'. One problem in the way of sending Page's unfortunate two small sons to England was that Sir Richard's brother Thomas seems to have had some doubts about the paternity of his two reputed nephews and so may have been reluctant to assume responsibility for them. The fate of the two children remains a mystery, as Hyde does not seem to have mentioned them again.[56]

Page, who clearly was a brave and energetic man highly regarded by his fellow exiles, is a sad example of a Cavalier who was broken and ultimately destroyed by the physical hardships of exile, although in his case his wife may also have had something to do with it. The decline and fall of Lord Grandison was even more complete than that of Sir Richard Page. John Villiers succeeded his brother William to the Grandison viscountcy when the latter was mortally wounded at the storming of Bristol in July 1643. Like other members of the widespread Villiers family, he was active on the royalist side in the Civil War, serving under Prince Rupert. Grandison then made the mistake of accompanying Charles II's army in its disastrous invasion of England in the summer of 1651, was captured at Worcester and, along with a number of other distinguished royalist captives, was imprisoned in the Tower.[57]

In the immediate aftermath of Worcester, the Council of State was in favour of the prisoners in the Tower, who included several returned

exiles who had accompanied Charles from Scotland (Fanshawe, Middleton, Fleming, Colonel Thomas Blague), being 'proceeded against as enemies of the Commonwealth', arguing that they were guilty of 'high treason in adhering to Charles Stuart'. Fortunately for Grandison and his fellow prisoners, this original decision that they 'should be made examples of justice' in a series of show trials was soon quietly abandoned. Grandison remained a prisoner, permitted 'to have the liberty of the Tower', with his wife being given permission 'to abide with him'.[58]

Grandison endured over four years of imprisonment in the Tower and on the Isle of Wight. Then, on 22 November 1655, the Council of State ordered that he and a fellow prisoner captured at Worcester, the Scots Earl of Kellie, be banished, ordering them 'to go beyond sea from Portsmouth within a month, they having engaged . . . to go, and not to act against his Highness and the Commonwealth'. By this time Grandison was so impoverished that the Council had to provide the money to pay both his prison expenses and his passage across the Channel; Lady Grandison does not seem to have accompanied her husband into exile.[59]

Grandison seems to have lacked the inner resources that enabled other Cavaliers, whether cloak and dagger types like O'Neill and Armorer or more serious and weighty figures like Ormonde and Hyde, to rise above the hardships of exile. In Holland in 1656, he was soon in trouble. In his begging letters to Hyde, Grandison asked the Chancellor to write to his mother to request an allowance that would at least enable him to buy some clothes. Hyde, who through his first wife was distantly related to Grandison by marriage, responded with reassuring comments and typically measured reproofs, encouraging Grandison to continue 'the retreat he has made from that licence to which he had been too much and too long indulgent'. An attempt by Hyde, through an intermediary in London, 'to persuade Lady Villiers to send somewhat hither to Grandison, to pay his debts and buy him two suits of clothes', seems to have been fruitless. Grandison's difficulties continued to increase. In September 1657 he was imprisoned in Dunkirk, where he was stranded without a passport and without money. On his release, he somehow made his way to Paris where several fellow exiles attempted to assist him. On 28 September 1658 Dr Leybourne wrote to Hyde that 'Abbot Montagu hath taken the Lord Grandison to his care, giving him a competent allowance, and if his lordship shall persist in his good resolutions he will be happier in himself, and in his friends'. But neither the care of Wat Montagu, Benedictine Abbot of St Martin's at Pontoise, nor

a payment of 170 florins authorised by Fox, was able to save him. On 4 November 1659 Percy Church informed Hyde that 'the Lord Grandison sunday last died a most miserable creature in the Charity Hospital and was buried ye Monday night following'.[60]

We know of the fates of Page and Grandison because, for different reasons, they were reasonably prominent figures among the exiles. Page was clearly capable and highly regarded; Grandison was a Villiers and a viscount. Their fortunes were recorded by men like Joseph Jane and Percy Church, regular correspondents of Hyde and Nicholas, who preserved the letters they received. We do not know how many 'obstinately obscure' exiles were finally overwhelmed by their privations and suffered similar fates, without any Joseph Jane or Percy Church at hand to record their deaths.

It is certain that, for a great many exiled Cavaliers, irrespective of whether they were peers and privy councillors, or obscure junior officers, exile was a grim experience. Poverty was pervasive, its effects aggravated by the pains of homesickness and separation from families, leading to frustration and disappointment that, as we shall see, found an outlet in sterile intrigues, bitter quarrels and even in some cases a transfer of allegiances. It does not seem to matter whether we consider those royalists who endured the ordeal and survived it, their moral and political principles remaining intact, like Hyde, Ormonde and many others, or those who swallowed their pride, compromised their loyalties and returned prematurely to England, like Verney, Cholmley, Peterborough and dozens more, or those who died in exile, either mourned and respected like Hopton, or broken and destitute, like Grandison. The picture of life in exile as being an overwhelming and negative experience remains very compelling.

Yet this negative picture is not the complete picture. Exile meant poverty and neglect, isolation and misery; but it also provided for some opportunities to acquire patronage and occasions for displays of energy and resourcefulness. While some exiles decayed in miserable lodgings, scared to go out of doors in case they encountered their creditors, others travelled ceaselessly. Whereas fruitless quarrels and complaints exhausted the energies and abilities of some exiles, others looked optimistically to the future when the King would come into his own again, and, like Henry Bennet, Charles Berkeley, Stephen Fox and others, prepared the ground for that future by establishing connections with influential patrons. So against the negative features of the experience of exile, and we have certainly not yet considered them all, must be set the qualities of loyalty and endurance, as shown by Ormonde, Nicholas and

many less well-known men and women. We should not overlook the resourcefulness and optimism displayed by Fox and Bennet; the fortitude and devotion of the long-suffering wives, for example Lady Wentworth and Mrs Ross, making their difficult and dangerous 'gipsy' visits across the Channel; and the energy and daring of the conspirators and agents, like O'Neill and Armorer. The exiled Cavaliers were a very mixed 'crowd of fugitives', and that diversity is no more apparent than in their responses to the demands and privations of exile.

9
Feuds, Factions and Fornication

> The [royal] party is divided into factions; but some labour to
> reconcile all differences.
>
> (Report of one of Thurloe's agents, Aachen,
> 22 August, 1654)[1]

Survival was the main concern of exiled Cavaliers; how to overcome the
constant nagging shortage of money and the emotional distress of
separation from one's family and absence from one's home. To cope
with these problems and hardships and not be overwhelmed or demoralised by them was probably the most challenging task facing the exiles.
But if, by resorting to one or more of the various measures discussed in
the previous chapter, physical survival could be made reasonably
certain, then another major problem emerged. How were those royalists who remained on the continent to occupy their time in exile? The
enforced idleness of an emigré's life was not the kind of existence with
which royalists of the kind who remained in exile were familiar. After
all, the majority of the exiled Cavaliers were in the prime of life, in their
thirties. If it had not been for the long series of defeats suffered by the
royalists in the civil wars, they would have been enjoying the full and
satisfying careers and activities traditionally available to men of their
social background: positions of influence and prestige at court, seats in
Parliament, the management of estates, the opportunity to play a part
in government administration at national or local level, the social round
of county communities, even the traditional recreations like hunting.
All those activities which normally occupied so much of the time and
energy of the royalist aristocracy and gentry were suddenly no longer
available; instead, the combination of poverty and exile severely limited
the options that were open.

The enforced idleness that resulted, once the original expectation that their period in exile would be short had failed to materialise, has been blamed for the 'endless, sterile faction fighting', the 'tedious triviality of court intrigue' and the 'personal feuds' that absorbed the frustrated energies of the exiles.[2] But these were not, at least to begin with, feuds and quarrels created by the conditions of exile; rather, they were quarrels and grievances already ripe and full-blown and just waiting to erupt when they were carried across the Channel by royalist fugitives. The duels fought in Paris in the autumn of 1647, described by O'Neill in his lively letters to Ormonde, had very little to do with royalists venting their anger and frustration at the conditions of exile and almost everything to do with old personal quarrels and disputes in the royalist party over the conduct of the war against Parliament. In particular, the feuds stemmed largely from controversial decisions and appointments made during the Civil War and the equally controversial behaviour and the ignominious dismissals of certain commanders: Rupert's resentment at Digby's influence over Charles I; Wilmot's anger at the men whose intrigues had brought about his public arrest at the head of his troops in August 1644, and other similar grievances of that kind. The intrigues and manoeuvres that swirled in war-time Oxford around Charles I, his Council and his advisers, and in the royalist armies around his generals, were fundamentally responsible for the quarrels at St Germain that sometimes became duels in the Bois de Boulogne between Prince Rupert and Digby, Wilmot and Digby, Digby and Jermyn, Rupert and Percy, and so on. Other exiles, like O'Neill, Gerard and Wentworth, were sometimes drawn into the duels as well, as enthusiastically participating seconds.[3] The bitterness caused by the military defeat of the King's armies and disputes over whose mistakes, negligence, rashness or incompetence had contributed to this defeat were major causes for the feuds and factions that divided the exiled Cavaliers.

These disputes and divisions, which accompanied so many of those royalists who went into exile, were intensified by the conditions of exile, and by new divisive conflicts over policies and personalities, but they were not created by them. The divisive and disruptive influence of factions among the exiles became most intense between the arrival of Prince Charles in Jersey in the spring of 1646 and the departure of the exiled court from Paris to the Rhineland in the summer of 1654. Certainly, some of the 'divisions and quarrels', the phrase is Lord Hatton's, that set the exiles against each other were over significant and not sterile issues. The arguments in Jersey in June 1646, in Paris between 1646 and 1649 and in Breda in the spring of 1650 over the rival merits of Ireland

or Scotland as spring-boards for royalist invasions of England, or over the opposing claims to support of 'Montrosians' or Covenanters, were arguments over what was the best way to reverse the results of Marston Moor and Naseby. These arguments set those exiles with the pragmatic desire to follow a policy they believed most likely to achieve results against those with the determination not to sacrifice the principles and beliefs for which so many royalists had sacrificed so much. In the course of these frequently bitter debates the conventional division of the exiles into three factions – 'Old Royalists', 'Louvrians' and 'Swordsmen' – broke down. The 'Louvrian' Sir John Berkeley, writing to his former friend Hyde on 22 March 1650, referred critically to a 'cabal' of 'Herbert, Wyndham, Elliot, Progers, Lovinge or those that are lately in all appearance joined with them, Gerard, Nicholas, Hopton & c.'[4] This so-called 'cabal' of exiles opposed to an alliance with the Scots Covenanters brought together 'Old Royalist' friends of Hyde, like Hopton and Nicholas, with his bitter enemies, like Herbert, Wyndham and Gerard, who were all friends and clients of Prince Rupert, the leader of the 'Swordsmen' faction. But this short-lived 'cabal' lasted no longer than the royal policy of alliance with the Scots Covenanters. Along with several hundred soldiers, both the 'cabal' and the alliance died on the battlefield of Worcester.

Unstable alliances and sudden enmities constantly appear and disappear among the shifting 'crowd of fugitives'. Hyde, in his more gloomy letters to his sympathetic friends Ormonde and Nicholas, bewailed the demoralisation apparent among the King's followers. 'Oh, Mr Secretary', he wrote from Paris on 15 August 1652, 'the weakness, credulity and vanity of our friends trouble us little less than the vices of our enemies.' Despairing comments in this vein, inspired both by a sense of the moral disintegration of the court as well as dismay at the factional feuding, seem to have been most frequent during the years Hyde and the court were in Paris. This is not surprising as it was during this period that Hyde's influence over the King was under the most sustained assault, and from several directions; from the Queen and Jermyn at the Louvre and St Germain, from councillors and close associates of Charles, notably Wilmot (now Earl of Rochester) and Lord Keeper Herbert, and from a mixed crowd of embittered 'Swordsmen' and ex-generals, like Grenville and Gerard. Grenville's intense dislike of Hyde had its origins in bitter disputes with the Prince's Council during the last disastrous royalist campaign in the west country, while the Chancellor described Gerard to Nicholas on 27 February 1653 as 'mad and good for nothing'.[5]

The campaign to destroy Hyde's influence over the King came to a head late in 1653 with the absurd accusation of Robert Long, the recently dismissed secretary to the Council, that the Chancellor was in secret communication with Cromwell. Hyde was at first disposed to dismiss Long with contempt as being 'as much fool as knave', but Long was supported in his accusation by a broad but inherently fragile alliance of the Chancellor's enemies. In January 1654 Richard Lovell, the Duke of Gloucester's tutor, stressed to Nicholas the unstable and contradictory nature of the anti-Hyde faction:

> I believe you cannot but wonder with me that Lord Keeper [Herbert], Lord Gerard, Sir John Berkeley, Sir Richard Grenville, Mr Long, Dr Fraiser, Col. Bamfield, and c., persons of so heterogeneous humours and inclinations, and who formerly neither had kindness each for other nor scarce agreed in any one particular, should thus combine in prosecution of Sir Edward Hyde, and make that the cement of their friendship.[6]

Although Hyde, as he confided to Nicholas, was appalled by the extent to which 'the Queen, Lord Keeper, Jermyn and the duke of Buckingham are concerned for him [Long]', and by the 'foul malice the Lord Keeper and Jermyn have expressed against Sir Edward Hyde', this unnatural combination of enemies rapidly fell apart.[7] After being debated before the Privy Council, the charges against Hyde, who conspicuously retained the support of the King, were dismissed. The 'Swordsmen' faction disintegrated. Prince Rupert resigned his position as Master of the Horse and left Paris for Heidelberg, soon followed into Germany by Gerard, although he later rejoined the court. Herbert also resigned his office as Lord Keeper and, with Grenville and Long, sank into obscurity, being no longer welcome at court. Both Grenville and Herbert died in exile without being reinstated in royal favour. The departure of Charles and a somewhat depleted court for the Rhineland in July 1654, to avoid the humiliating embarrassment of a possible expulsion as a consequence of the alliance between France and the Cromwellian Protectorate, meant that physical distance was now added to the considerable problems Henrietta Maria and her followers already were encountering in their attempts to influence the actions of the King and undermine the influence of Hyde. Two major causes of factional divisions and rivalries – the struggle over which group or faction would control royal policy and the series of attempts by the Chancellor's enemies to destroy

him – seemed to have been eliminated by the triumph of Hyde and his friends in the royal counsels.[8]

Unfortunately, this was not the end of 'divisions and quarrels' among the exiled Cavaliers. As one of Thurloe's agents reported from Aachen, a stopping place on the court's journey to Cologne, the court remained 'divided into factions'. The letters of correspondents with a taste for malicious gossip, like Thurloe's spy Henry Manning or Nicholas's friend Lord Hatton, continue to contain frequent references to quarrels among the exiles. In January 1655, for example, Hatton in Paris relayed to Nicholas, still at the Hague, the latest gossip 'at rebound out of letters from Cologne', informing him of the 'the divisions and quarrels of Fraiser and Wentworth, Fraiser and Newburgh, Wentworth and Fleming, Newburgh and Taaffe'.[9] The removal of the court from Paris to the Rhineland in 1654, followed by Charles's alliance with Spain, confirmed by the treaty of Brussels in April 1656, understandably caused considerable anger at the Louvre and St Germain. The natural hostility of Henrietta Maria to the Spanish alliance and the extreme reluctance of the Duke of York to change sides, leaving the French army under Marshal Turenne in which he had spent probably the happiest years of his life, to take service under Spain, against whom he had just been fighting, not surprisingly caused 'divisions and quarrels' between the exiled court at Cologne and Henrietta Maria's and York's households in Paris.[10] But although disputes over the policies to be followed by the exiled court continued to break out at intervals throughout the 1650s, the feuds and quarrels that divided the exiles increasingly take on a more personal and even trivial character.

The distinctive characteristics of the exiled court contributed in several ways to the frequency of disputes and quarrels among the King's 'family'. The enforced idleness, in which tennis became a much cheaper substitute for the hunting that was no longer possible, the constant struggle for places or positions of influence close to the King, a permanent shortage of money, and the sudden fluctuations of mood between wild optimism and despairing pessimism at the likelihood of an end to the exile: all these factors shaped the character of the exiled court. The court also constantly swelled and shrank as it moved around the cities of northern France, the Netherlands and the Rhineland. The frequent absences of certain courtiers on 'the King's business', on missions to attempt to raise money from sympathetic princes or from supporters in England, or to further royalist conspiracy, sometimes led to confusion as to who exactly, at any given time, comprised the King's 'family' and

were entitled to draw board wages.[11] When we take into account the personality of Charles II, the nomadic character and changing personnel of his court, the permanent gnawing shortage of money, and the inadequate and crowded lodgings available for the members of the royal household, it is not surprising that the formal barriers between monarch and courtier and the traditional forms of custom and deference occasionally broke down. When Charles and his household arrived in Bruges from Cologne in April 1656, they encountered a situation where, according to Ormonde 'houses, lodging and furniture are had with more difficulty than at Cologne'. Ormonde described to Nicholas how the King had to be accommodated in the home of the elderly Irish expatriate Lord Tara, 'with trouble to the Lord and some great inconvenience to himself. I am lodged at Mr. Robinson's a good half mile from him, and so are my Lord of Rochester, Mr. O'Neill and Mr. Bennet. His horses are under [William] Armorer's care at an inn, not much nearer and at great expense.'[12]

Charles II's nomadic court in the 1650s normally comprised between about fifty and eighty persons, but constant fluctuations in numbers make an accurate assessment impossible. As Thurloe's spy Manning reported on 29 June 1655: 'this court does increase daily by the arrival of divers [persons]. Wilmot is at length come hither a few days hence. So is general Middleton with some Scottish officers.'[13] The 'family' of Charles II in exile was a shrunken shadow of his father's establishment in the 1630s, when the household below stairs alone numbered almost 200, the chamber and its offshoots included another 263 courtiers, with another 60 under the Master of the Great Wardrobe and further separate establishments for the Queen and the royal children.[14] 'The king's train is not great, but in very good equipage', reported one of Thurloe's spies on 11 August 1654, partly contradicting himself later on in the same letter when he stated that most of the courtiers were 'content to wander up and down in a present subsisting posture'. The departments of the household – the bedchamber, the privy chamber and the stables – contained between 35 and 45 courtiers. We need also to include the Privy Councillors and other office-holders, and a miscellaneous collection of chaplains, secretaries and clerks. There was also a lawyer, John Heath, who had accompanied his father, Charles I's Chief Justice Sir Robert Heath, into exile in Calais, where the father died. There were also normally about 15 to 20 inferior household officers: physicians, cupbearers, pages, a musician ('Gervase the Trumpet'), postilions, grooms and footmen. The 20 or so servants ranged from Dorothy Chiffinch, 'Seamstress and Laundress to his Majesty's person' and

Matthew Clarke, the king's coachman, down to Giles Rose, the 'Child of the Kitchen'.[15]

As well as the official members of the various departments of the King's household, and the varying number of servants in more or less menial positions, there was also a fluctuating number of followers and hangers-on of one kind or another. Household lists sometimes conclude with the names of 'those that go along with the court' or, rather more complimentary, the 'Lords and Gentlemen that follow the Court'.[16] It was among these followers of the court, including those who were too obscure or disreputable to be included in any lists, that disputes and quarrels were most likely to occur.

Another distinctive characteristic of the exiled court that contributed to the likelihood of disputes and quarrels was the marked absence of men of authority and prestige to occupy the great court offices. Ormonde, the Lord Steward, had both authority and prestige, but his wide ranging concerns – diplomatic, military and even the management of royalist conspiracy – meant that he was frequently absent from court. Charles had inherited and recognised as Lord Chamberlain the elderly Scottish professional soldier Alexander Ruthven, Earl of Brentford, whose familiarity with battlefields was much more extensive than his knowledge of courts. In 1650 Brentford accompanied Charles to Scotland, where he died the following year.[17] His successor as Lord Chamberlain was the 'Louvrian' Lord Percy, his appointment a concession to Henrietta Maria that was not regarded favourably by Hyde or Nicholas. Percy had little influence or authority in the exiled court and remained in Paris when Charles and the court moved to Cologne. His name is not even included in the household lists drawn up between 1654 and the Restoration, although he retained his titular office until his death in Paris at the end of 1659.[18] The fate of the office of Groom of the Stole and first Gentleman of the Bedchamber at the exiled court was in some ways similar, but even more drastic. Henry Rich, Earl of Holland, a prominent member of the Queen's circle, was appointed Groom of the Stole in 1636. After a complex series of changes of allegiance, Holland's final commitment to the Stuart cause in 1648 was both ineffective militarily and fatal personally. After his execution in 1649 the office lapsed, not to be revived until the Restoration, when it was bestowed on the prominent royalist conspirator, Sir John Grenville.[19] Grandees of distinguished lineage who also held high office were therefore conspicuously lacking in the exiled court of Charles II; in consequence; there were few courtiers with the authority and prestige to impose order and restraint on the disorderly and quarrelsome

'lords and gentlemen that follow the court'. The periodic disputes and squabbles that occupied the frustrated energies of a number of Charles's followers during the second half of the 1650s reflect this lack of authority and control from the top.

This combination of lax discipline, idleness, poverty and frustration contributed to the tensions and feuds within the court, although the big issues of policy and the confirmation of its direction by the Hyde-Ormonde-Nicholas group had been, at least for the time being, settled. On 30 October 1655 an intelligence report to Thurloe from Manning described how 'one Arnet, a Scot, son to Sir James, is banished the court for beating Armorer. The equerry breeds daily quarrels with those of that nation, of which there are many here.' Arnet, a page, has featured already as one of the murderers of the Commonwealth's envoy Anthony Ascham in Madrid in 1650. William Armorer, the equerry, should not be confused with his younger brother, Nicholas, the royalist agent who had been a prisoner in Dover castle in February of the same year.[20] William Armorer, unlike his younger brother, seems to have had both a savage temper and a pronounced dislike of Scotsmen, perhaps dating back to September 1651 when, during the royalists' flight after the battle of Worcester, according to Clarendon, he denounced to his face General David Leslie, accusing him of 'having betrayed the King and the army all the time'.[21]

The quarrel between Arnet and Armorer reflects another cause of tensions and feuds at the exiled court: the presence of a number of Scots and Irish courtiers. Arnet's version of the dispute was supported by eyewitness accounts by Major Robert Hamilton, an Irishman, and Lord Napier and Sir William Fleming, both Scots. According to their version, an earlier quarrel between Arnet and Armorer broke out, also in the King's presence, when Armorer struck Arnet. 'Arnet bade him forbear, as it added to his infamy to strike in such a place and left the room, going backwards, and Armorer following and striking at him.'[22] Although Arnet and Armorer were both men prone to violence, an Anglo–Scottish antipathy was clearly a factor in this dispute, as it was in other feuds among Charles's easily irritated followers, most notably after the court moved from Cologne to the Spanish Netherlands in the spring of 1656.

'The swordsmen increase here and so do the divisions' reported Manning to Thurloe in May 1655.[23] There is a connection between these two developments. The exiled court, particularly after its departure from Cologne, first to Bruges and then Brussels, as a consequence of the royalist alliance with Spain, attracted both genuine Cavaliers who hoped once again to draw their swords in the royal cause and adventurers and

soldiers of fortune looking for employment and adventure. 'The king of England is not far from this city,' reported an agent in Antwerp of the Venetian resident in May 1656, 'and many English do flock to him from all parts.'[24] The alliance with Spain, which enabled Charles to begin to raise his own small army, and the attempts by royalist conspirators, despite endless discouragements and repeated failures, to bring about a large scale rising in England, encouraged the would-be 'swordsmen', who swelled the numbers of hangers-on about the court, to believe that a royalist descent on England was imminent. The failure of either a Spanish–royalist invasion to be launched or a successful rising in England to eventuate naturally increased the frustration and irritation of the exiles, feelings that were expressed in a depressing series of personal quarrels and even duels.

According to Ronald Hutton, 'the court at Bruges and Brussels was disorderly as it had not been before'.[25] The same names often recur among the references to troublemakers: two of the King's companions and 'men of pleasure', lords Taaffe and Newburgh; the equerry William Armorer; Sir James Hamilton, a Scottish gentleman of the privy chamber; and the young Edward Stanley, whose mother, the formidable countess of Derby, misguidedly had sent to court to 'be planted in the King's good opinion'. While the court was at Bruges George Barker, the avenor or administrator of the stables to the King, had a dispute with William Armorer over their respective responsibilities. The squabble almost became violent for, according to Barker's petition to Charles on 14 November 1657, Armorer attempted to eject him from his position and threatened to cudgel him, 'language never before used to your servants in execution of their places'.[26] Exactly three months later it was Armorer's turn to present a deposition to the King, in which he denounced Sir James Hamilton for having said that, as he had 'always endeavoured to serve his Majesty', he thought 'he could not do his Majesty better service than to kill the Lord Chancellor'. Hamilton, using the excuse that he was drunk at the time, humbly requested a pardon and the restoration of the King's 'favour and protection', at the same time hoping that Charles might be 'graciously pleased to reconcile him to my Lord Chancellor'.[27] Charles apparently saw no problem in retaining Hamilton as one of his gentlemen of the privy chamber until after the Restoration. One sympathises with the King in having to devote time and energy to these petty squabbles of under-employed and violent men, but even more so with Hyde and Ormonde, attempting to maintain the dignity and prestige of the royal court while surrounded by drunken and disorderly intriguers and ruffians.

Far worse than squabbles in the stables and the wild threats of a drunken Scotsman were the duels that suddenly became much more frequent, recalling the rash of encounters between Cavaliers just arrived in exile in Paris over ten years earlier, but this time fought over much more trivial differences. Sir Charles Cotterell, who accompanied the court on the royal visit to Antwerp in February 1658, when the King was lavishly entertained by the Newcastles, related to Nicholas, left behind in Bruges, the latest gossip, how 'Lord Newburgh has not appeared since he fought a duel with and hurt Captain Breame'. As well as this encounter, according to Cotterell, 'there have been challenges between Mr Stanley and Sir James Hamilton about a jest, and between [George] Benion and [Gabriel] Silvius about an old play debt, but both prevented'.[28] Six months later, in Brussels, another duel involving some of the same participants as the affairs in Antwerp had fatal consequences. In a triple fight between three pairs of duellists, with seconds also involved, Sir William Keith, a Scottish veteran of the Worcester campaign, was killed by Taaffe. The cause of the dispute was an unpaid bet of seven sovereigns on a game of tennis. Taffe, protesting the harshness of his treatment, was (temporarily) banished from the court. This spate of duels, fought over trivial disputes, and sometimes with fatal consequences, led Charles to decree banishment from court as the punishment for duellists.[29]

This royal decree may have been effective in discouraging touchy courtiers from drawing their swords at the slightest provocation, but it did not end their propensity to resort to violence. In Brussels in April 1659 a trivial squabble broke out among some observers of a game of tennis between Charles and his brothers. The squabble degenerated into a brawl between, once again, the Scots Lord Newburgh and, once again, young Edward Stanley. The brawl, which had to be broken up by York and Gloucester, polarised the whole court. Thomas Ross, Stanley's ineffectual governor, informed Gervase Holles in Rotterdam that 'all the great ones being for Newburgh, as Ormonde, Taaffe and c. of that gang, but the two Dukes, Gerard and the good old Secretary with the lord Berkeley and I think Langdale, for us'. Although Charles enforced a reconciliation, Ross believed 'this business discovered the inclinations of our whole court, the Irish and Scots (all but honest Will Erskine [the King's Cupbearer]) adhering to Newburgh, but all the English (except D. [Marmaduke] Darcy and two or three sacrifices to Moloch) came and offered their service to Mr Stanley'.[30] What is significant about this otherwise depressingly trivial incident, apart from its value in indicating the depths of irritability and frustration into which some of the

exiles had sunk, is that it shows the court dividing on national and not factional lines: Secretary Nicholas joining with such strange allies as the 'Swordsman' Gerard and the 'Louvrian' Berkeley against his old friend Ormonde.

It is depressingly clear that 'personal feuds' and 'sterile faction fighting' did occupy much of the time of some exiled Cavaliers, in particular, of certain groups and individuals associated with the different Stuart courts and households. There is a pattern to these quarrels and intrigues, an overlapping sequence of different causes of division and dispute that needs to be seen against the permanent setting of poverty, bitterness at the circumstances that had caused the royalists to flee from England in the first place, and frustration at their apparent inability to bring the period of exile to an end. The early feuds had their origin in the quarrels and enmities that emerged during the Civil War itself. They were followed by the prolonged series of disagreements among the royal counsellors, complicated by frequent and often unwelcome interventions by Henrietta Maria, over which policy was most likely to restore Charles to his father's throne. These arguments saw the emergence of recognisable factions among the exiles – 'Louvrians', 'Old Royalists' and 'Swordsmen' – although the structure and even membership of these factions was loose and fluid. The eventual triumph of the 'Old Royalist' faction, dominated by Hyde, Ormonde and Nicholas, in the royal counsels then led to a series of attempts by angry and envious rivals to destroy the Chancellor's position. With the King's support and protection, the Chancellor retained his pre-eminent position, but he never felt entirely secure, as Charles remained accessible to other interests and points of view among his courtiers, to the opinions of Digby and Wilmot, for example. There were also the constant tensions between Hyde and Ormonde, with their elevated and as it turned out unachievable expectations of what was appropriate behaviour for an exiled monarch, and the very different values of the King's preferred companions, 'the men of pleasure', like Taaffe, Newburgh and Crofts. 'Oh! Mr Secretary, this last act of the King's, in making Mr Crofts a gentleman of the bedchamber, so contrary to what he assured me, makes me weary of my life,' complained Hyde despairingly to Nicholas on 13 April 1652.[31] But whatever their feelings on the matter, Hyde and Ormonde had to share access to the King with favourites like Taaffe and Crofts and the proponents of other viewpoints like Digby and Wilmot.

In the second half of the 1650s, after the court settled in Cologne, and more particularly after it moved to the Spanish Netherlands in 1656, the pattern of feuds and disputes gradually changed. Private

quarrels replaced to a great extent divisions over significant issues of policy. Several factors, along with the always present shortage of money, contributed to this development. Probably most important was the inability of the King to impose and enforce the standards of dignified and restrained behaviour that Hyde thought appropriate for a royal court, a problem made more difficult by the rapid swelling in the numbers of hangers-on, mainly young men hopeful of military action in the forces Charles was raising in Flanders. The reports of Thurloe's agents frequently refer to how 'Charles Stuart's court groweth very numerous', how it 'waxeth every day', being constantly augmented by such additions as the sudden arrival of '50 young blades from England'.[32] As well as creating an administrative and financial night-mare for the royalist commanders and their Spanish paymasters, this concentration of would-be Cavaliers added to the disorderly atmosphere of the court, already very noticeable as a consequence of tensions among English, Scottish and Irish emigrés and the presence of aggres-sive pickers of quarrels, like William Armorer and Edward Stanley, and easily provoked duellists, such as lords Newburgh and Taaffe.

The feuds and the factions that occupied so much of the energies of some of Charles's followers have also been seen, both by observers at the time – from Hyde to English government agents – and by some his-torians since, as evidence of a wider moral decay that characterised the experience of exile. Duelling and debauchery, feuds and fornication; apart from alliterative neatness, were these activities associated and widespread among the exiled Cavaliers? Writing from Paris to Nicholas at the Hague on 26 October 1652, Hyde deplored 'the general corrup-tion and licence of the Court, and indeed of our nation, who here with us, and there with you, have shaken off all those obligations and respects they have been formerly liable to'.[33] This opinion, that the experience of exile had demoralised in a literal sense the King's sup-porters, was expressed at a time when Hyde's correspondence suggests he was extremely depressed. This verdict has been accepted by some his-torians since and questioned by others. To Eva Scott, an early but very detailed biographer of Charles II in exile, 'the saddest aspect of the exile is seen in the moral ruin that it wrought, not in the King alone, but also in many of his followers'. Sir Keith Feiling, the historian of the Tory party, also expressed the view that one of the distinctive marks of the 'brand of the emigré' was the 'depravity of public and private morals'.[34] In their biographies of Charles II, both Antonia Fraser and Ronald Hutton discuss the extent to which the exiled court in Flanders was characterised by debauchery. Dr T. C. Barnard has no doubts on the

subject, referring in an article to a negative response of the Protestant interest in Ireland to the news from Catholic Europe, 'where, throughout the 1650s, Charles II and his courtiers lounged and fornicated'.[35]

Hyde's pessimistic picture of a corrupt and licentious court is supported by some of the reports of Thurloe's agents, who, of course, had sound reasons to present Charles and his followers in as unfavourable a light as possible. One agent, writing from Flushing on 22 November 1656, expressed his horror at the 'abominations' practised by courtiers; they included both plundering churches and presenting plays! As well, 'fornication, drunkenness and adultery are esteemed no sins among them'.[36] The view that exile corrupted morally the royalists who endured the experience has drawn heavily on two examples: an allegedly licentious court and the sexual adventures of the young Charles II. The King was nineteen when his father was executed and he found solace in the arms of Lucy Walter, famously described by John Evelyn, who travelled in Wilmot's coach to St Germain in August 1649, with 'Mrs Barlow, the King's Mistress and mother to the Duke of Monmouth, a brown, beautiful, bold, but insipid, creature'.[37] Some accounts of Charles II's life in exile tend to present it as a series of transfers of affections from one mistress to the next, accompanied by various scandals, like the various attempts to remove from Lucy Walter her child by the King, all accomplished with the connivance and assistance of certain debauched courtiers, who provided both the women and the wine and song to go with them.

To determine the extent to which the experience of exile exposed Cavaliers to 'moral ruin' is difficult. The exiles' correspondence is full of complaints of their poverty and a lifestyle devoted to the enjoyment of wine, women and song is traditionally regarded as requiring plenty of money if it is to be pursued successfully. There are also many accounts, in the correspondence and memoirs of the emigrés and in the reports of English government agents, of the feuds and factions that divided the exiled followers of Charles II. Although these divisions and quarrels seem to have been most prevalent among the 'lords and gentlemen that follow the court', they were not confined exclusively to them. That enterprising agent Nicholas Armorer was a totally obscure exile in Holland in June 1652 when he first appears in the correspondence of Secretary Nicholas. Writing to his friend Hatton in Paris, Nicholas related how 'Major Armorer and Leighton met and fought their duel in Brabant. They both passed with good resolution on each other without any hurt, and so closing Armorer had Leighton under him, and thereupon their seconds parted them.' Although we do not

know the reason for the duel or the identity of the seconds, Armorer's opponent can be identified fairly confidently as Lieutenant-Colonel Sir William Leighton, a professional soldier in the 1630s and a field officer in the royalist army during the first Civil war. After being in the royalist garrison in Colchester in the second Civil War, Leighton had gone into exile in Holland. In both military rank and experience, Leighton at this time was a more senior and prominent figure in exile circles than Armorer, but neither was connected to the court.[38]

So, although complaints about poverty are a constant element in the exiles' correspondence – which is also peppered with accounts of quarrels and duels, feuds and factions – references to sexual immorality and debauchery, in any but the most general terms, are much harder to find. Accounts of the problems of maintaining wives and families in exile, of the misery of separation of married couples, of long-awaited reunions and unhappy partings, are much more common. To illustrate this problem, it is instructive to examine the career in exile of one Cavalier whose name has occasionally appeared above: Edward Progers. In so far as Progers has an historical reputation, it is a dubious one. According to the historian of the post-Restoration House of Commons, Progers accompanied into exile the future Charles II, 'whom he helped to debauch'. To the editors of Samuel Pepys's diary, he was 'Groom of the Bedchamber (and pimp) to the King'. Anthony Hamilton, the real author of Count Grammont's *Memoirs of the Court of Charles II*, called Progers 'the confidant of his [the King's] intrigues' at the Restoration court, while Samuel Pepys on 22 February 1664 deplored that Charles was 'led away by half a dozen men' – naming Progers as one of them – so 'that none of his serious friends can come at him'.[39] Progers's name has also been linked with such dubious episodes as Charles's alleged secret marriage with Lucy Walter in the Netherlands in 1649 and the later attempts to remove by force or guile her child by the King, the future Duke of Monmouth.[40] If we want an example of an exiled Cavalier exhibiting the 'depravity of public and private morals' that Sir Keith Feiling saw as so characteristic of the exiles as a group, then Ned Progers would seem to be a most suitable candidate.

Progers belonged to a well-established and strongly royalist Monmouthshire family. Born in 1621, he was the third son of Colonel Philip Progers, a royal equerry, who died at Oxford in 1644. Although many of his family, including at least two of his four brothers, seem to have been Catholic, Progers 'was baptised and buried in the Anglican communion'. Brought up at court, he was a page to Charles I from 1632 until 1646 when he was appointed a groom of the bedchamber to the

Prince of Wales. This appointment determined the course of Progers's career, as for the next five years he accompanied Charles on his travels. He was one of the large group of royalists and their dependants who fled with the Prince from Cornwall in the spring of 1646, first to the Scilly islands and then to Jersey, then continuing on to Paris before the end of the year. Further journeys followed, either in attendance on Charles or as a royal courier: to Holland, where Progers's position as a groom of the bedchamber was confirmed, back to Jersey in early 1650, to Paris again and then once more to Holland, to the negotiations with the Scots commissioners at Breda.[41]

During the first experience of exile a close and informal relationship developed between Progers and Charles. In surviving letters Charles addressed 'Poge' as 'your very loving friend' and 'your affectionate friend', but his requests seem to have been more for the supply of clothes than of women. 'Progers, I would have you (beside the embroidered suit) bring me a plain riding suit with an innocent coat', instructed the King from Jersey on 14 January 1650, when he was planning his journey to Holland and Progers was due to return from a mission to Paris: 'the suits I have for horse-back being so spotted and spoil'd that they are not to be seen out of this Island'.[42] The surviving letters suggest that at least at this stage in their relationship Progers was more concerned with Charles's wardrobe than with his morals; whether he had the scope, the means or the inclination to 'debauch' the young king remains a mystery.

Progers had a wide circle of acquaintances among the exiled Cavaliers, corresponding in 1650 with Montrose in Orkney, Prince Rupert at Toulon and Cottington in Madrid.[43] As has been discussed above, Progers's older brother Henry was a member of Cottington's household and, along with another brother James, took part in the murder of the Commonwealth's envoy Anthony Ascham in June 1650. Progers's friendship with Montrose and Cottington, and a hostile reference to him by the 'Louvrian' Berkeley, indicate that he belonged to the 'cabal' (Berkeley's term) of exiles who opposed the alliance with the Scots Covenanters.[44] Whatever his misgivings about the Scots alliance, Progers was one of the group of household servants and other royalists who accompanied Charles to Scotland in June 1650. Not surprisingly, his presence was unwelcome to the dour lords and ministers of the Kirk who surrounded the King. One major reason why Progers rapidly incurred official disfavour was his involvement in 'the Start', Charles's desperate and unsuccessful attempt in October to escape from the stifling surveillance of the Marquess of Argyll and the ministers of the

Kirk and instead attempt to rally the Highland clans to his side. Progers accompanied Charles on his secret flight and was one of the very few companions who remained with the King to the bitter and humiliating end of this hopeless venture.[45] On 18 November Abraham Cowley in Paris wrote to Henry Bennet that 'Mr Long, Mr Progers, Mr Seymour and Dr Fraiser are again banished for having a hand in this Business'. Two weeks later Nicholas reported to Hatton the arrival of Fraiser and Progers at the Hague, 'being both banished out of Scotland'.[46]

Progers returned to Paris early in 1651, where he seems to have remained, despite receiving a letter from the Duke of Hamilton encouraging him to join the royal army as it approached the English border, it being the King's 'positive pleasure that you make all the haste you can to him'. Charles added a postscript to Hamilton's letter: 'the army being on the march I could not write to you myself, pray make all the haste you can hither'.[47] Despite this pressing royal command, which in any case Progers may have been lucky enough to receive too late to act upon, he did not join the royalist army as it plunged southwards to its decisive defeat at Worcester. On the contrary, the 'fatal day' at Worcester seems to have caused Progers to sever for several years his connection with the exiled court. He probably returned unobtrusively from exile during 1652, one of Nicholas's 'abundance of royalists gone for England from these parts and many more are going, as having little hopes left them'.[48]

For the remainder of the 1650s Progers lived quietly in England, principally in London. He was arrested at least twice, in December 1652 when the Council of State discussed whether or not he should be banished, and again in June 1655, during the roundup of notorious Delinquents and Malignants after the suppression of Penruddock's rising. But, as he does not seem to have been involved in royalist conspiracy, on both occasions he was soon released. In December 1657 Progers was still in London and exchanging letters with that indefatigable royalist correspondent in Paris, Percy Church.[49] Like many other emigrés he exchanged the precarious life of loyal but impoverished exile for an inglorious but relatively secure existence of obscure conformity in Protectorate England. He did not reappear at court until the Commonwealth was on the point of collapse.

Ned Progers's dubious reputation as an immoral influence on the young king, whom allegedly he 'helped to debauch', is difficult to substantiate from this survey of his activities in exile. His was clearly no stay-put life, spent eking out a miserable existence in lodgings in Paris or in a town in the Netherlands, or hanging about the court picking

quarrels with other courtiers, drinking, gambling and fornicating. On the contrary, he seems to have been employed principally as a trusted courier, constantly on the move between England, Jersey, France, the Netherlands and Scotland, with little time left for fornicating, much less lounging. Although Charles may have appreciated Progers's company as one of his 'men of pleasure' and 'the confidant of his intrigues', it can be argued that he may equally have valued him for his conspicuous loyalty, as it was displayed, for example, during the desperate fiasco of 'the Start' in October 1650. The claim by some historians that, on the King's orders, Progers abducted Charles's son James from the child's mother Lucy Walter cannot be sustained. Progers had been back in England for at least five years before the winter of 1657–58, when the sordid wrangle over the possession of the future Duke of Monmouth was taking place.[50]

As an example of how the experience of exile contributed to the 'depravity of public and private morals', Progers is not very convincing. If he pimped for the King, this was only one of several ways by which he won Charles's friendship and favour; nor does he seem to have been prone to quarrels and feuds or associated with any particular faction. In fact, Progers seems to have been on friendly terms with a number of royalist leaders, including such different figures as Queen Henrietta Maria, Prince Rupert, Montrose, Hamilton and Cottington. On the eve of the Restoration he defended the characters of the King and Hyde to Mrs Monck, the suspicious wife of the general, but he does not otherwise seem to have been close to the Lord Chancellor.[51]

The 'prevalence of fornication, drunkenness and adultery' among the exiled Cavaliers, especially among those who frequented the court, remains a charge whose accuracy is difficult to assess. We are concerned here not particularly with the behaviour of Charles II, but with his exiled followers. Clearly, and most notably when it was established in the Spanish Netherlands, the court included a number of short-tempered pickers of quarrels, like Edward Stanley and William Armorer, violent heavy drinkers like Sir James Hamilton, incorrigible duellists like lords Newburgh and Taaffe, and even the occasional murderous ruffian, like the page George Arnet. But just as Ned Progers was much more than 'groom of the bedchamber (and pimp) to the King', so men like Armorer, a royal servant since 1641, and Taaffe were more than just squabblers and bullies. There were also cultivated and cosmopolitan courtiers, like Sir Charles Cotterell and Tom Killigrew, who point a nice contrast to men like Stanley and Hamilton. As well, the King's 'family' contained several men of energy and resourcefulness, like the grooms of the

bedchamber Daniel O'Neill and Henry Seymour, who, as we shall see, did not spend their time in exile quarrelling over unpaid gambling debts or over wagers on games of tennis.

The presence in Flanders, from 1656 onwards, of 'great numbers of English and Irish', anxious to join one of the regiments being raised to serve the King, but in the meantime unemployed and unpaid, also contributed to the disorderly and licentious reputation that gathered about the court. In the absence of other restraints and sanctions, shortage of money probably had the most effect in limiting the would-be Cavaliers' opportunities for 'fornication, drunkenness and adultery'.

The prevalence of feuds, factions and fornication as significant characteristics of the royalists' experience of exile, therefore, needs to be considered in the context of what life in exile could involve. There is an enormous difference between exile as it was experienced in the royal court in Bruges or Brussels, in army camps and garrisons in Flanders, in modest family lodgings in Paris or Rotterdam, or in quiet communities of emigrés in Caen or Blois. Similarly, just as exposure to the ordeal of poverty ultimately destroyed men like Sir Richard Page and Lord Grandison, so also the bitter factional struggles had their victims, like Lord Keeper Sir Edward Herbert and Secretary to the Council Robert Long. The personal quarrels and disputes, when they led to violence, also had their casualties; in some cases fatal, as in the case of Sir William Keith, one of Taaffe's victims, in other cases leading to loss of royal favour and position, as when George Arnet was banished from the court.

These negative and destructive activities, which absorbed the energies and occupied the time of ambitious would-be advisers to the king, frustrated and idle courtiers, and short-tempered swordsmen were not common to all or even most exiled Cavaliers. There were some exiles who were not prepared to waste their time on sterile intrigues and futile personal feuds while they waited for the Commonwealth to collapse and for the King to come into his own again. Instead, they hoped, by helping to further preparations for royalist risings, to hasten by their own endeavours the arrival of that day. But for those exiles who involved themselves in conspiracy, as Nicholas Armorer would have been vividly aware when the cell door closed on him in Dover castle on 4 February 1655, the penalties of failure could be just as severe as those suffered by Lord Grandison or Sir William Keith.

10
Losing the Plot: Agents, Spies and Traitors

> Long, dangerous and expensive journeys.
> (Daniel O'Neill to Sir Edward Hyde)[1]

The biographer of Sir George Carteret, the generous host to Charles and his followers during their two separate sojourns on the island of Jersey, claimed that when it came to Carteret's turn to go into exile in France, in his case for eight years, 'unlike most of his fellow exiles, he did not idle about doing nothing'. A similarly harsh judgement, quoted in the previous chapter, refers to how 'Charles II and his courtiers lounged and fornicated' their way through the 1650s.[2] While these opinions may be justified in the case of some of the courtiers whose experience of exile was considered in the previous chapter, they certainly cannot be applied to the Cavaliers, most of whom were courtiers, who are the subject of this chapter. Some of the exiled Cavaliers were men of infinite resource and energy; they were both anxious to contribute in some way to the overthrow of the Commonwealth and the restoration of the monarchy and ambitious to win the approval and patronage of the King and his principal counsellors. To these men exile was not necessarily a barren and bitter experience; on the contrary, it offered opportunities for adventure, advancement and rewards.

Daniel O'Neill, Nicholas Armorer, John Stephens, Gregory and Thomas Paulden, Robert Phelips, Henry Seymour and others 'did not idle about doing nothing' during their years in exile, except perhaps when they were in prison; on the contrary, they seem to have been almost constantly travelling. Employed as couriers and agents, they maintained lines of communication between the courts of Charles II, Henrietta Maria and Mary of Orange, between frequently scattered royalist leaders like Ormonde, Hyde and Nicholas, and between the

exiled court and the organisers of conspiracy in England or the leaders of a rising in Scotland. They carried letters, collected money, distributed warrants, commissions and instructions and gathered and passed on intelligence.

The life of a courier and agent could be both dangerous and arduous. For those who ventured into England on the King's business, and who then became involved in conspiracy and even in insurrections, there was the constant fear of detection by government officials, of arrest and imprisonment, which could be for years, and even of death on the scaffold. As well as government officials, like the governor of Dover castle, being on the lookout for suspicious characters, there was also the network of Thurloe's agents on the continent. The court of Charles II was not exactly a model of tight security and the comings and goings of agents were constantly reported back to Cromwell's vigilant Secretary of State. 'Armorer and Albert Morton are to go into Holland this week', reported Henry Manning, the Protectorate's principal spy at Cologne, on 4 September 1655. 'Henry Moore, servant to Wentworth, a tall fair young man, is sent hence into England with letters and commissions.'[3] As we shall see, Thurloe's network of agents included some men, originally genuine royalists, who for different reasons, usually either poverty or a perceived neglect by the King and his principal advisers, became informers, reporting on the activities of their companions. Men like O'Neill and Armorer had to survive in a world that attracted mercenary traitors like Henry Manning and dubious adventurers like Sir Robert Stone, who betrayed his 'friend' Armorer when the latter was a prisoner in Dover castle.

As well as the dangers of betrayal and discovery, inseparable from their profession, the agents and couriers were exposed, as were all the exiles, to the various hazards and difficulties of seventeenth century travel. Travelling between the Low Countries and France or Germany, they occasionally crossed the routes of hostile armies on the march. In a letter to his wife, whom he had left in Antwerp while he travelled to Paris in the summer of 1649, Hyde recorded his relief at avoiding the attentions of soldiers on the march. 'We are, I thank God, got safe to this town, whither we came the last night, and conceive ourselves now past the danger of both armies, one of which, the Spanish, we had the pleasure to see march by us.' When Henry Seymour attempted to leave Paris in June 1652 on a mission to England to raise money, he had to take a roundabout route to avoid Fronde and royalist forces skirmishing in the suburbs.[4] The Channel crossing could also involve more hazards than simply avoiding the suspicious scrutiny of government

officials. The great storm that accompanied the death of the Lord Protector also sank off the Flanders coast the ship carrying the agent Charles Davison, to the concern of Stephen Fox who feared that Davison had drowned before repaying John Shaw 1,000 florins as he had been instructed. All this travelling was undertaken by Cavaliers who were perpetually short of money, being sometimes in danger of being stranded without the means to continue a journey, as happened briefly to Armorer at Calais in September 1659.[5]

Fortunately, and unlike some of the Cavaliers whose life in exile was discussed in the previous chapter, those emigrés who were prepared to risk their lives as couriers and agents were for the most part extremely resourceful. This was especially the case with Daniel O'Neill whose reputation for being able to live well despite the adversities of exile was legendary. His skill in this area was utilised by Charles, Hyde and Ormonde on numerous occasions. When the King moved his possessions from Cologne to Bruges in the spring of 1656, he sought O'Neill's advice: 'It is Mr. O'Neill's opinion that the best way for my things to come from Cologne is, that when they come to port they go directly into Zealand, and so to Bruges by Sluys.' Similarly, when Charles made his journey in September 1659 to the Franco–Spanish peace negotiations at Fuentarrabia in the Pyrenees, he appointed 'Daniel O'Neale to take care that they always fared well in their lodgings, for which province no man was fitter'. O'Neill clearly had a way with landlords and landladies. When Hyde was having difficulties with his new landlady in Bruges, he turned to O'Neill, whose 'subtlety would be very useful in ordering her'. Hyde's letters contain a number of references to O'Neill's ability – which may have been first developed during his campaigns in the Netherlands in the 1630s – to live comfortably in all circumstances. For example, in June 1657 the Chancellor referred to O'Neill's claim to have access to 'a cellar of bottles to be filled with the wine de Bone', while in November he asked Ormonde to 'remind O'Neale to make a good provision of sherry and to send a hogshead of pippins'.[6] A reputation for limitless resourcefulness in all situations was a desirable attribute for an exile who intended going on dangerous missions to England on the King's business.

Ranking with O'Neill as one of the most resourceful and highly trusted couriers, as well as one of the first exiles to be employed in this role, was Henry Seymour. Born in 1612, the second son of Sir Edward Seymour Bt. and his wife Dorothy, daughter of Sir Henry Killigrew, it is not surprising that Seymour, with that family background, became a courtier. Appointed a groom of the bedchamber to the Prince of Wales,

Seymour was one of that large group of royalists whose journey into exile was by way of Cornwall and Jersey. Early in 1646 Seymour carried letters from Prince Charles and Hyde in the west country to the Queen in Paris. Two years later, he was with Charles in Holland in 1648 when the exiled court was trying to exploit the mutiny in the parliamentary fleet in the Channel. Entrusted with the Prince's invitation to the parliamentary admiral the Earl of Warwick 'to return to his allegiance', he returned with Warwick's discouraging reply which 'besought his highness to put himself in the hands of Parliament'.[7] In January 1649 Seymour carried Prince Charles's last letter to his father. He saw Charles I (the last Cavalier to do so?) at St James's on the evening of 28 January. Sir Thomas Herbert, who witnessed the meeting, wrote that 'Mr Seymour, at his entrance, fell into a passion, having formerly seen his Majesty in a glorious state, and now in a dolorous; and having kissed the King's hand, clasped about his legs, lamentably mourning.'[8]

Seymour's travels continued. Having returned to Holland, where his appointment as a groom of the bedchamber to the new king was confirmed, he then accompanied Charles II to Jersey. From Jersey he was sent on a hazardous mission to Ireland in October to gain 'a true account of affairs', returning in December with a realistically pessimistic assessment of Ormonde's capacity to resist the relentless advance of the Commonwealth's armies.[9] All ideas of Charles sailing to Ireland to join Ormonde were abandoned; instead, the King returned to Holland to embrace reluctantly the alliance with the Scots Covenanters. Seymour was among the Cavaliers who sailed with Charles to Scotland in June 1650 and, along with O'Neill, Progers, and most of Charles's other attendants and followers, soon discovered his presence was unacceptable to the Kirk's leader. Banned from attendance on the King in August, by October Seymour was at Aberdeen with Progers and other banished Cavaliers, waiting for a ship to return them to the continent. Once more in exile, for the next eighteen months Seymour was based in Paris. During this period he was employed by Henrietta Maria on a number of missions, being sent first to invite the young Duke of York, who was living with his sister Mary in Holland after his escape from London, and then Ormonde, who had settled in Caen after his withdrawal from Ireland, to join the Queen in Paris. 'I find by Mr Seymour that her Majesty is prepared to receive his Royal Highness [York] with great kindness', reported Ormonde to Nicholas from Caen on 15 June 1651, 'and I hope the French will do as much.' Then, when Charles arrived in the

French capital after his escape from Worcester, Seymour was sent to Antwerp to invite Hyde also to attend the King in Paris.[10]

In June 1652 Seymour returned to England, on the first of a series of clandestine visits to raise money for the King, chiefly from royalist sympathisers in the west country, where the Seymour territorial influence was greatest. Seymour was not the first exile to return to England on a mission for the court. The unfortunate Sir Richard Page and Colonel Thomas Blague, a tough veteran of the Civil War when he had been governor of Wallingford, one of the last royalist strongholds to fall, had both been involved in an abortive attempt to organise royalist conspiracy in East Anglia during 1650. Luckily for Page and Blague, they had both returned to the continent before the plans for a rising were discovered, followed by wholesale arrests of the royalists implicated in the plot.[11] But Seymour's money-raising mission did show that Charles and his advisers, slowly recovering from the paralysing impact of Worcester, saw the need to re-establish contact with committed royalists in England. They realised that reliable and resourceful men like Seymour could be entrusted with more important missions than just carrying letters backwards and forwards between Paris, Caen, the Hague and Antwerp.

During 1653 other exiles as well as Seymour also made hazardous journeys into England on the king's business. Two of the most resourceful and courageous were, not surprisingly, Daniel O'Neill, with his history of daring exploits going back to the Army plots, and Nicholas Armorer, who, until September, was an obscure exile living at the Hague, totally unknown to Hyde and the King. Fifteen months after his escape from Worcester, O'Neill returned to England, to spend the winter of 1652–53 in London. One of the most active government spies and informers, the Anglican clergyman turned royalist soldier turned traitor Francis Corker, reported to Thurloe that 'the concealed person, that we have heard to act privately in London for this long time is Mr. Daniel O'Neale', but he once again evaded capture. Safely back in Paris by March, O'Neill presented Hyde with his intelligence report: 'a brief Relation of the Affairs of England as they stand at present'.[12]

Nicholas Armorer began his rise to a modest prominence in exile circles when he offered his services as a courier to Nicholas in September 1653. The Secretary reported the offer to Hyde in Paris: 'Mr Nich. Armorer, a servant of the Princess Royal, going to England in a fortnight upon some particulars of his own, would be glad to receive his Majesty's commands, being well known to, and well beloved by, all the King's

party, not only in the north where he was born, but in Shropshire, Staffordshire, and those parts, and resolved to correspond with Sir Edw. Nicholas.'[13]

For someone who commanded the modest garrison in Lord Newport's small and fairly obscure fortified house at High Ercall in Shropshire during the Civil War, this seems a rather excessive endorsement, but Armorer certainly enjoyed the confidence and patronage of Nicholas, although the Secretary feared that 'he is not for Negotiations'. Armorer arrived in England in October 1653 and remained there for about ten months, spending some of the time in London but also travelling to Shropshire, his old campaigning country, and Yorkshire, making contact with prominent local royalists. He sent his intelligence reports to Nicholas, who forwarded selections from them on to Hyde, with supportive comments: 'Nic. Armorer, I believe, does his Majesty good service in England'. Armorer's most significant letter to Nicholas was the one written on 14 November in which he recommended that the King 'fix on one or two of the most prudent' royalist leaders to 'attend his affairs, and to put them in a form that there may be no clashing'. Within three months of this letter, the Sealed Knot, the secret committee formed to direct royalist conspiracy, and answerable directly to the King and his principal advisers, Ormonde and Hyde, was in existence.[14]

At first Hyde had his doubts about Armorer, wrongly suspecting that 'he acts all by and for Sir Marm. Langdale', for the agents and conspirators also had their factional allegiances and client–patron relationships, but gradually he came to appreciate his energy and resourcefulness. In April 1654 the Chancellor requested Nicholas to 'let Mr Armorer know that the King very well likes all he hath done'. Charles for his part was writing to his sister to request another three months' leave of absence for Armorer from his presumably not very demanding duties as a member of her household.[15] In his turn, Armorer gradually abandoned Nicholas as an intermediary between himself and the court and began to communicate directly with either Hyde or Ormonde. When Armorer finally returned to the continent in the summer of 1654, he did not linger at the Hague but continued on to the court at Aachen. 'One Mr Armorer, whom I formerly advised you was in England, is lately come from the north, where he says Charles Stuart hath many friends', reported Manning to Thurloe from Aachen on 10 September. 'I see the marquis of Ormonde take him from court, to discourse privately with him.' Nicholas, who took offence easily, was irritated by this development, but was consoled by his friend Thomas Ross: 'I know that Armorer is in frequent commerce with Sir Edw. Hyde, but he said it was the King's

command, or he would not have relinquished you, to whom he is bound by great obligation and affection.'[16]

The transfer of Armorer's primary loyalties to his new patrons Ormonde and Hyde was a minor concern of the Secretary's compared to his developing suspicion and disapproval of O'Neill's prominent role in Charles's counsels. Indeed his role was far too prominent according to Nicholas, still sulking at the Hague and clearly nettled by letters like the one from Sir Alexander Hume on 27 November 1654, who claimed to be 'not a little amazed to hear that Sec. Nicholas is so much a stranger to all advertisements that come from our Court, that correspondence being wholly managed by Dan O'Neill and Mr. Chancellor'. O'Neill's alleged influence and his quasi-diplomatic activities, although diplomatic functions were traditionally associated with holders of offices in the bedchamber, were a constant worry to Nicholas. 'Is Mr. O'Neill there now at the Hague?' enquired the Secretary, by this time in Cologne, of Joseph Jane on 4 March 1656. 'For there is a report that he is gone into Flanders, which I cannot believe, though he is more of the secret council than I am, being a great confidant of Hyde's. I wish he may prove worthy of the trust reposed in him, but it's no wisdom to make those who are not sworn to be secret privy to the secrets of state.'[17]

Friendship between the flamboyant and adventurous Irishman, with his past record of involvement in such dubious affairs as the Army plots, and the sober and conservative Chancellor seems unlikely at first sight. But the evidence of their correspondence reveals a mutual trust and respect which flourished despite their different temperaments, values and backgrounds. On several occasions Hyde defended O'Neill to Nicholas, claiming that 'you will find him ingenious and reasonable in all things, and he is honest and kind to the Marquis of Ormond and me, and sufficiently odious to Jermyn and c.', as well as being one 'who cannot be corrupted or overwitted.'[18] Although O'Neill might refer disrespectfully to the 'fat fellow' in an intelligence report sent to the King from England, which he certainly knew Hyde would read, and the Chancellor in his turn request Ormonde to 'send that fool O'Neale to me', the frequency and informality of their correspondence – including Hyde's use of O'Neill's nickname 'Infallible Subtle' – indicate the presence of a strong relationship of mutual respect beneath the surface banter.[19]

To flourish or even survive in the dangerous world of espionage and conspiracy agents like O'Neill, Armorer and Seymour needed the protection and support of powerful patrons at court. The Sealed Knot was created to organise a successful royalist rising; it was intended to be

the instrument by which the Hyde–Ormonde group of 'Old Royalists' directed the activities of the King's supporters in England. Agents and couriers like O'Neill, Armorer, Seymour, the brothers Thomas and Gregory Paulden, and Ormonde's loyal officer, Colonel John Stephens, operated within this clientage network and were associated with this faction, although the Paulden brothers were also occasionally employed by Langdale, no friend of the Chancellor. Just as one of O'Neill's merits for Hyde was that he was 'odious to Jermyn', so, according to the informer Francis Corker, an important characteristic of John Stephens, noted when he was in London on a secret mission in March 1658, was that 'he belongs to Ormond'.[20] For the Sealed Knot was not the only organiser of royalist conspiracy. In competition with the Knot, and its controllers Hyde and Ormonde, other prominent exiles, notably Gerard and Langdale, sponsored their own irresponsible and hare-brained schemes to assassinate the Protector or to seize particular towns and fortresses. They were in touch with different groups of activists in England, and employed agents like Charles Davison who were outside Hyde's control. The rash actions of these 'small factors', as Armorer contemptuously called them, damaged both the money-collecting prospects of agents like Seymour and the more cautious and prudent preparations by the Sealed Knot for a rising.[21]

Despite the divisions among the different groups of conspirators, and the efficient crushing by the government of some half-baked schemes during 1654 followed by wide-scale arrests of known activists, a royalist rising, organised by the Sealed Knot in uneasy and unenthusiastic cooperation with the more recently created and more enterprising 'Action party', finally broke out in March 1655. Penruddock's rising, named after the ill-fated Cavalier whose small force briefly occupied Salisbury, was responsible for a number of exiles returning secretly to England. Appointed to the military command of the royalist forces, until hopefully Charles himself arrived, was the hard-drinking Henry Wilmot, Earl of Rochester. While waiting in Dunkirk for the opportunity to cross the Channel, Rochester encountered Sir Joseph Wagstaffe, an equally hard-drinking professional soldier who had risen to the rank of major-general while serving under Prince Maurice and Goring in the Civil War. According to Clarendon, Wagstaffe 'had a great companionableness in his nature' and he cheerfully accepted Rochester's invitation to take command of the royalists expected to rise in the west country. Experienced and trusted agents like O'Neill, Armorer and Stephens had the responsibility of coordinating the various elements in the insurrection and communicating between the scattered leaders of projected

risings in different counties. Other exiles with particular roles to play, as agents or couriers, also slipped quietly back into England, while, as rumours spread that a royalist rising was imminent, a crowd of emigrés drifted towards the Channel ports, hopeful that their swords were about to be required. 'There is a great gathering of English gallants at Bruges, Ostend and Dunkirk, and some have gone to Calais', reported Thurloe's agent in Bruges on 13 March; 'at least 150 have passed through within ten days; some great plot is intended'.[22]

Those exiles with parts to play in the March rising returned to England by different routes. Armorer, travelling as Mr Wright, and O'Neill, as Mr Bryan, were among a number of suspicious characters detained in Dover castle. Despite the best efforts of Stone and Thurloe, Armorer, as we know, was released, thanks to the intervention on his behalf of Robert Day, the Clerk of the Passage, and the incompetence of Captain Thomas Wilson, the Lieutenant Governor of the castle. The security arrangements at Dover seem to have been extraordinarily lax, especially when it was apparently common knowledge that 'a great plot' was about to explode. O'Neill was able both to conceal his identity and successfully to send a letter to Mary of Orange informing her of his imprisonment but reassuring her that his papers were safe. The hand of the mysterious Robert Day seems evident here. Ormonde heard on 9 March that 'Mr Boswell was also restrained at Dover, but escaped with his usual dexterity'; he was optimistic that O'Neill would soon achieve a similar escape. This optimism was justified as a few days later the King received a letter from the agent Robert Phelips with 'the news of Bryan's [O'Neill's] escape out of Dover castle on Thursday sennight. . . . I must confess', Charles wrote to Hyde, 'that the escape of that lucky fellow Bryan pleases me very well.'[23] O'Neill followed Armorer on the road to London and to another disaster for the royalist cause.

The royalist rising in March, which had aroused such wild hopes and expectations among the exiles, was a dismal flop. Apart from Colonel John Penruddock's local and short-lived success in Wiltshire, it consisted of several fairly insignificant and easily scattered gatherings of small groups of jumpy Cavaliers, their morale undermined by the obvious security precautions of an alert regime and the large-scale arrests of known or suspected conspirators that had occurred during the previous weeks. Within weeks of their arrival in England, Rochester, Wagstaffe, O'Neill, Armorer and the rest were scrambling to escape back across the Channel. In their return to the continent they were joined by a new wave of Cavaliers fleeing into exile, men who were understandably anxious to avoid following the unfortunate Penruddock and some of

his followers to the scaffold. This new wave of fugitives included both royalists who had taken part in the March rising, like the Yorkshire Cavaliers Sir Richard Mauleverer and Marmaduke Darcy who had joined Rochester on Marston Moor for the attack on York that never took place, and agents and couriers employed by either the Sealed Knot or the Action party, but based in England rather than on the continent, such as James Halsall and Jonathan Trelawney.

The letters of Henry Manning to Thurloe at this time show his increasing frustration and understandable anger at the government's failure to round up these fugitives. Manning certainly did his best to make sure they never crossed the Channel. 'Now I conceive you ought to use all care that may be to apprehend Wilmott, Dan O'Neile and one major Armerer', he adjured Thurloe, 'who when your last post came were all in London, and as near as I can guess, you may find them at one Mr Markham's house in the Savoy, the lord Lumley's, or some of those places, which I know to be their haunts.'[24] Despite the government's measures and the information provided by Manning, the great majority of exiles who had returned to England to take part in the March rising were able to make their escape back to the continent. For some it was a close thing. Fleeing southwards from the fiasco of the insignificant rally on Marston Moor, Rochester and Armorer were both apprehended at Aylesbury by a curious magistrate 'appropriately named Henn'. A provincial comedy of errors followed, as responsibility for the two suspicious travellers and their two servants, one of whom was 'a poor countryman' and the other French, was passed between the magistrate, the constable and the local innkeeper until a military escort for the prisoners could be obtained. Before this happened Rochester and Armorer had disappeared into the night, having bribed the innkeeper entrusted with their care to let them escape 'and take all their rich apparel with them', but leaving behind their horses and their two servants, including the unfortunate Frenchman. In June an exiled royalist, Captain Peter Mews, wrote to Nicholas an account of the affair: 'Earl Rochester's escape at Aylesbury cost him dear, being compelled to part with his gold chain; better that than his head.'[25]

Other Cavaliers on the run had similarly narrow escapes. Mauleverer and the agent John Walters were both captured in Cheshire but both escaped. The commander in Chester castle, Captain Griffiths, on 27 March was left in the embarrassing position of having to inform Thurloe of these unfortunate events: 'I formerly gave you account of the taking of Sir Richard Mauleverer, and securing him a prisoner. I must now give

you an account of his escape.' Coming within a couple of weeks of Captain Wilson allowing O'Neill and Armorer to slip through his fingers at Dover, this news is unlikely to have been well received. Arrested in Shrewsbury, Major Thomas Hunt was convicted of high treason and sentenced to death but also escaped from prison and 'fled beyond seas to preserve his life'. Hunt eventually settled in Caen, where he was joined by Thomas Mompesson of Salisbury, 'a principal actor in the rebellion in the west', according to Captain Unton Croke, the officer who pursued and defeated Penruddock's little force at South Molton in Devon. Both Mompesson and Hunt remained in Caen until the eve of the Restoration. Mauleverer also eventually escaped to the continent where he joined the exiled court.[26]

As the royalist fugitives turned up in ones and twos, over a period of some months, in the ports of France, Holland and Flanders, Manning's increasing irritation at these escapes comes through strongly in the letters he was rashly continuing to send to Thurloe. 'Many you name in your last are with us, Mauleverer, Darcy, Edgworth, and much rejoicing there is for major Robert Walters' escape.' O'Neill arrived at the Hague at the beginning of May and Charles was immediately informed that 'O'Neill is safe in this town by his usual good luck in avoiding being hanged.' Rochester and Armorer eventually escaped from London, where they had been hiding, via Gravesend and landed at Antwerp. One of Thurloe's agents wrote on 7 May that 'Wilmot, whose servants have arrived, and Armorer are daily expected at the Hague'. Presumably the servants were replacements for the two unfortunates left behind during the necessarily hurried and secret departure from Aylesbury. Rochester, even when he was on the run and wanted for high treason, was not one to allow himself to be discommoded for long by the absence of servants. Manning's letters list the arrival of most of the other agents and conspirators involved in the March rising: Wagstaffe, Thomas Ross, James Halsall, Jonathan Trelawney and others. 'Mr Phelips is escaped and at Antwerp; col. Worden at the Hague'. His conclusion is understandably bitter: 'you must have more care of your prisoners'.[27]

One prominent and highly regarded agent among the exiles did not make it back to the continent. Henry Seymour was too well known and perhaps too open in his activities to remain undetected. His movements were also disclosed to Thurloe by the government's principal informer in Paris, the treacherous Colonel Bampfield. After being detained for short periods in both 1652 and 1654, when he was interrogated by Cromwell in person, Seymour was arrested again in June 1655 during

the same round up of notorious Malignants that gathered in Ned Progers. Unlike with Progers, this time there was no early release for Seymour and he remained in the Tower until early in 1657.[28] His career as a money collector and courier was over. According to Hatton, Seymour was 'not yet well recovered of his last imprisonment', and when he petitioned for his liberty in February 1657 he referred to 'the injury of health and fortune, both of which are ruined by restraint'. The Council of State responded sympathetically and Seymour's release was ordered in the same month, 'on security to go beyond seas, not to return without leave, and to act nothing prejudicial to the government'. Perhaps because of ill health, perhaps for more complex reasons, Seymour did not return into exile. In June 1657 Hyde wrote to a correspondent in London that he longed to hear from Seymour; he was reported as being still in the capital in December. Apparently without suffering further harassment from the government, Seymour remained in England and did not rejoin the court or resume his office as a groom of the bedchamber until the Restoration.[29]

The flight into exile of Cavaliers involved in Penruddock's rising can be traced through the stream of reports sent to Thurloe from his agents and informers at the exiled court, in Paris and in various towns in the United Provinces and Flanders. Some of Thurloe's 'intelligencers' in his elaborate network of agents, like John Addams at Rotterdam, were genuine 'Commonwealthsmen', but some had an equally authentic royalist background. The traitors are the reverse of the exiles-as-agents coin. While men like Seymour, O'Neill, Armorer, the Pauldens, Stephens, Phelips, Trelawney, Ross and others risked their lives in a series of attempts to bring Charles II back to England, the royalist turncoats equally risked theirs to ensure that he remained in exile.

The traitors are a mixed lot among the royalist emigrés. They include Sir John Marlay, mayor and governor of Newcastle during the Civil War; probably Charles Davison, the agent and courier who was drowned off the coast of Flanders in September 1658; Colonel Sir John Henderson, a Scots professional soldier who was briefly governor of Newark between 1642 and 1643; Colonel Thomas Howard, Master of Horse to Mary of Orange and at one time a lover of Lucy Walter; Peter Massonet, clerk to Charles II's Council; the unscrupulous Irish adventurer Colonel Joseph Bampfield and Henry Manning, Thurloe's prolific and imaginative correspondent at the exiled court. The Thurloe papers contain letters to Cromwell's Secretary from all of these exiled royalists, some much more personally incriminating than others.[30] With the exception of the wretched Henry Manning, none of them seems to have provided

Thurloe with significant or valuable information; the dubious activities of most of them were eventually at least suspected if not discovered by their fellow exiles.

Poverty was the main reason why these exiled Cavaliers became informers for Thurloe; poverty aggravated by bitterness and frustration at what they considered ingratitude for their services and neglect of their talents by the King and his principal advisers, Chancellor Hyde in particular. These motives explain the behaviour of Sir John Marlay, who had stubbornly defended Newcastle during its long siege by the Scots army in 1644, and had then rallied again to the royalist cause in the second Civil War. In October 1648 he fled from Berwick to Rotterdam, where he was eventually joined by his family. As Marlay was on the list of notorious Delinquents and Malignants formally banished and excepted from pardon, his estates were confiscated under the Treason Act of 16 July 1651. When Charles and the exiled court moved from Paris to the Rhineland in the summer of 1654, Marlay travelled to Aachen to meet the King, but his requests for financial aid, a place at court or some other employment were all unsuccessful. An acrimonious correspondence with Hyde followed – ('Sir John Marlay's angry letter', the Chancellor called one epistle) – until eventually Marlay withdrew to Antwerp. From there he wrote bitterly to Hyde on 28 December, declaring that as employment for himself and his son had been denied 'while granted to others' and that as 'he is cast off as an useless servant', he 'will trouble Hyde no more'.[31]

By May 1658 Marlay was in touch with George Downing, the Protectorate's resident ambassador at the Hague. Using his son as an intermediary, he offered to betray 'Charles Stuart's designs' for £100, a pardon, and a pass to return with his family to England. According to Downing, who recommended to Thurloe that the proposal be accepted, Marlay's condition was desperate; he was unable to 'stir without forty pounds to pay his landlady' while his 'Lady and children' were also in great distress. Marlay's career as a government informer was both brief and ineffectual; he was in no position to be privy to inside knowledge of 'Charles Stuart's designs', and during August he returned to England with his family. Hyde, in any case, seems to have had some knowledge of these approaches to Downing, as in a letter to Langdale on 23 July he advised him to have nothing to do with Marlay.[32]

A combination of poverty and alleged neglect by the court drove Marlay briefly to abandon his loyalty to the Stuart cause. The case of the Scottish professional soldier Colonel Sir John Henderson is similar. His fortunes from the end of the Civil War had been mixed: Charles I's

ambassador to Denmark in 1645, followed by a brief period of imprisonment when he returned to England. On his release he had returned to Denmark and then, as a soldier of fortune, had gone into Imperial service for a time. In the winter of 1654–55 he turned up at Cologne, like Marlay looking for employment at court but, also like Marlay, fated to be disappointed. In January he complained bitterly of neglect, 'never having been noticed by the King', and of being overlooked for a command in Middleton's expedition to Scotland, where the Highlanders under the Earl of Glencairn were in revolt against the occupying English army. Shortly afterwards he offered his services to Thurloe, claiming to have also won over the Council's clerk, Peter Massonet, another bitter enemy of the Chancellor, with the promise in Thurloe's name of 'an honourable maintenance'.[33] Henderson, again like Marlay, was in no position to acquire intelligence likely to be of interest, much less of value, to the English government; he and Massonet were feeble acquisitions to Thurloe's network of agents. In any case, Henderson died in 1658.

Colonel Thomas Howard, although a much more colourful character than either Henderson or Massonet, was also quite insignificant as an informer. In his dealings with Downing he seems to have been more indiscreet than treacherous, passing on to the ambassador in May 1659 such important intelligence as the news from the court at Brussels, which was that 'Charles Stuart is very merry'. Discretion was probably not a prominent quality in a married man who was having a public and tumultuous affair with the notorious Lucy Walter. The King refused to take seriously the rumours of Howard's treachery although Nicholas Armorer, who presumably knew quite well his fellow member of Mary of Orange's household, did not trust him.[34]

Those Cavaliers who became informers for Thurloe in return for 'an honourable maintenance', a pardon or some other benefit, were the real moral casualties of the experience of exile; their loyalties were undermined and their reputations compromised by a combination of poverty, bitterness and frustration. In a couple of cases at least, those of the Irish Colonel Joseph Bampfield and Henry Manning, there seems also to have been the further ingredient of deliberate malice, a genuine hope that the information they provided would bring imprisonment and even death to the agents and couriers whose movements they betrayed. Bampfield, who was described as 'of an active and insinuating nature', had an indifferent war record but had gained the favour and protection of the Queen's circle at the Louvre after the notable part he played in

the escape into exile of the young Duke of York, disguised as a girl, from St James's palace in 1647. From early in the 1650s he was in touch with Thurloe, and his intelligence reports are knowledgeable both on the factional struggles within the court, especially when it was in Paris, and on the movements of agents like Henry Seymour.[35] Bampfield was always actively distrusted by both Hyde and Charles who, being well aware of what Clarendon called 'his foul practices', were determined to destroy his influence over the Duke of York. On 13 July 1654 Charles wrote to James ordering him not to 'employ or trust Bampfield in anything, since I am resolved to have nothing to do with him, and to forbid all my Friends to give Credit to him in any thing that concerns me'. Yet somehow Bampfield, whose value to Thurloe as an 'intelligencer' was now effectively over, still retained friends at the Louvre. As late as 20 August 1657 Jermyn recommended Bampfield to Prince Rupert's favour and protection, he being entitled to all 'the reliefs and supports that innocently may be afforded him'.[36]

Henry Manning is the most well known example of an exiled Cavalier who betrayed the royalist cause, who flooded Thurloe with letters, some of which conveyed genuine intelligence while others contained a strong element of fantasy, and who finally came to a miserable end. A member of a Catholic Wiltshire family, Manning had fought in the Civil War, in which both his father and brother had been killed. He compounded for the very modest sum of £3/6/8, and then in late 1654 turned up at Cologne, where, according to Clarendon, he became a drinking companion of Wilmot and other 'good fellows' who hung about the court.[37] Throughout 1655 Manning kept Thurloe supplied with a steady flow of reports on the gossip of the court, the intrigues and quarrels among the factions, and the movements of couriers and agents. Eventually he fell under suspicion, partly because he always seemed to have plenty of money; his dispatches were intercepted, his possessions searched and his treachery proved conclusively. Over a period of about two weeks in December he was interrogated and then 'tried' before an improvised court presided over by Ormonde, Nicholas and Culpepper and, despite his hysterical letters of remorse and desperate pleas for mercy, sentenced to death. The neighbouring prince, Philip William, Count of Pfalz-Neuburg, Duke of Berg and Julich, with whom Charles was on friendly terms, made no objection to the 'execution' taking place on his territory; and so Manning was 'pistolled in a wood near Cologne' by two of the most brutal and violent members of the household, Sir James Hamilton and William Armorer. Although

they certainly disliked each other, Armorer's antipathy towards the Scots being well known, they were apparently prepared to cooperate together to dispose of the wretched turncoat.[38]

Manning had claimed in his letters to be one of Charles's inner circle of companions, privy to the conversations of the King with his intimates. His dispatch to Thurloe on 17 November is a typical example of his style: 'Charles Stuart daily tells us in private, "have patience a little, and you will not fail of action both in England and Scotland, or else adieu Ormonde and Hyde".' He also claimed knowledge of the thoughts and feelings of Charles's advisers – 'Hyde is very fearful of being laid aside' – and expressed satisfaction to Thurloe at the news of the arrests of royalist conspirators in England: 'I am glad you lay about you'.[39] But Manning was never more than a hanger-on about the court; he had no official position in the royal household and was not one of Charles's circle of intimate friends. The rewards of his treachery were modest, perhaps commensurate with his status but hardly justifying the risks he took. Preserved in the Nicholas papers is the inventory of Manning's goods, forfeit to the crown as a consequence of his treason. It tells us something of the modest material possessions of the exiles: one drugget suit and hat, one pair of boots, three or four pairs of stockings, one nightbag and one pair of pistols.[40]

The treacherous activities of Manning and the other turncoats were just one of the perils faced by the loyal agents and couriers as they made what O'Neill called their 'long, dangerous and expensive journeys' on the King's behalf during the 1650s.[41] The resilience and courage of what one may call the 'professional' agents is very impressive. Although they must have known that Thurloe was well-informed of their identities and activities, the willingness of men like O'Neill, Armorer, Stephens, Robert Walters and others to return to England after the fiasco of Penruddock's rising is a refreshing contrast to the anger and bitterness of Marlay and Henderson and the self-serving treachery of Bampfield and Manning. As well as the 'professional' agents, other exiled Cavaliers also made occasional dangerous journeys into England, to attempt to raise money, to deliver letters and dispatches, to engage in conspiracy and to make contact with families and friends. Trusted servants were also used as couriers, although as the use of false names was commonplace, it is sometimes difficult to identify the royalist behind the pseudonym. Ormonde made frequent use of his servant Maurice as a courier, including during the dangerous mission of the Marquess to London at the beginning of 1658, when he requested Hyde to take notice of Maurice's services as he 'does not know an honester or more useful creature'.

Another example of a trusted servant employed in this dangerous role is Henry Moore, 'a man of the Lord Wentworth,' who was included by Manning in his lists of agents travelling on missions between England and the court.[42]

The wives of exiled Cavaliers were also sometimes employed as couriers, especially during times of heightened security precautions in England, as in the aftermath of Penruddock's rising when, as Manning warned Thurloe on 23 June, 'they dare not send men being the ports are so narrowly looked to'.[43] Passports were necessary in order to make the passage across the Channel, and the scrutiny of the port officials or 'Searchers' had to be undergone. According to a dispatch from the Venetian ambassador to the Doge and Senate on 7 April 1656, this procedure was not just a formality. 'Thus even when a passport was granted to a lady of rank who wished to cross the sea, when she reached Gravesend, where all passports are inspected, she was searched and completely stripped by the officials there to see whether she carried letters or anything else prejudicial to the state.' The Venetian ambassador is possibly referring to Lady Margaret Lee, wife of the prominent royalist Sir Richard Lee, who was granted a pass to Holland on 6 March.[44]

The wives who acted as couriers therefore faced at least the same dangers and threats as their husbands, including the attempts by Thurloe's informers to bring about their capture. In October 1655 Charles wrote to thank Thomas Ross's wife for her willingness to travel to England on behalf of her kinsman Sir William Keith 'who cannot safely make the journey'. One wonders how safe it was for Mrs Ross. 'Dr Earles's wife and Mr Elliot's, who is easily known by her red eyes, are to come over', reported Manning, 'and by who [sic] is reported letters of much concernment'. It would have been a brave port official who tangled with the formidable Mrs Elliot. On the other side of the Channel, in London, Francis Corker was Thurloe's chief source for information on the clandestine arrival of the wives of exiled royalists. 'There came several persons over in the last Dutch fleet', he informed Thurloe on 1 March 1658. 'Several of the wives of those that are with Charles Stuart come also in this fleet, expecting their husbands to follow with the army.'[45]

The misguided optimism of these wives of exiled Cavaliers was based on the belief that, as a consequence of the alliance between Charles and Spain concluded by the treaty of Brussels in April 1656, a Spanish supported invasion of England by the royalist regiments raised in Flanders was imminent. For such an invasion to be feasible, royalist conspiracy, shattered and demoralised by the dismal fiasco of Penruddock's rising,

needed to be revived. So gradually the Sealed Knot, still as cautious ever under its old leaders, and the Action party, a much looser group of conspirators with mainly new leaders, began to prepare for another rising.

As the King's Spanish allies would not act without concrete assurances of decisive royalist action in England, Ormonde made a secret visit to London in January 1658 to assess the prospects for a successful rising. He was either accompanied or joined in London by that most resourceful trio of agents, O'Neill, Armorer and Stephens, as well as his faithful servant Maurice. Negotiations and secret meetings with different groups of enthusiastic or reluctant conspirators, uncommitted neutrals, Presbyterian magnates and others took place against a background of narrow escapes as Thurloe attempted to lay hands on Ormonde and his associates. Ormonde was not by temperament or background equipped to survive for long in this cloak and dagger world of spies and informers. His amateurish attempts at disguise included 'a green case over his hat and a nightcap on his head' when he rode into London; he also dyed his hair but the colour ran when it rained. Somehow Ormonde escaped detection, although he stayed in London for little more that a week, shifting his lodging every night, before making his escape through Sussex to Shoreham and then by a hired shallop to Dieppe. O'Neill and Armorer remained in London until April. They continued to try to patch together some kind of commitment to common and united action by the hopelessly divided royalist conspirators, but, against a background of arrests and obvious government alertness, without success. Stephens and Maurice were employed as couriers and were back on the continent in March, in Stephens's case delivering to Hyde and Ormonde 'a long and particular account from O'Neale, who is full of negotiations and had set many treaties on foot'. He and Armorer only returned with great reluctance early in May, by which time Hyde had heard rumours that they were both prisoners.[46]

The plans for a royalist rising early in 1658, to be combined with a Spanish supported landing in England by the King's newly raised regiments of exiles, collapsed in the usual welter of recriminations and accusations, arrests and imprisonments, trials and executions. As usual, O'Neill and his companions were safe on the continent when on 15 May government troops seized most of the conspirators who remained at large in London. Once again, royalist plans to overthrow the Protectorate and enable Charles II and his exiled followers to return to England in triumph lay in ruins. For all their energy and daring, their courage and resourcefulness, those royalist emigrés who had risked their lives for years as couriers and agents were by this time either in prison,

like some minor figures arrested in connections with the plans for a rising in 1658, or had withdrawn from the struggle and were living quietly in England, like Henry Seymour, or had no alternative but to continue to endure the hardships of exile, the fate of O'Neill, Armorer, Stephens, the Pauldens and others.

11

Failed Hopes and Fresh Prospects

My condition appears to me so desperately that I have nothing
to support me, from being very melancholy.
(Honora Harding to Sir Edward Hyde, the Hague,
17 January 1659)[1]

The collapse of the plans for a rising early in 1658, timed to coincide
with a Spanish assisted royalist landing in southern England, ushered
in a prolonged period of bitterness, frustration and disappointment for
the exiled Cavaliers. Once again their hopes of an imminent end to their
lives in exile had been raised to unreal heights, and once again crushed.
With hindsight, it seems obvious that the divided and disorganised
groups of conspirators, with no clear objectives and with their counsels
betrayed to Thurloe by Sir Richard Willys, one of the directing committee of the Sealed Knot, had no chance of success against the military power of the Protectorate. It is also very difficult to believe that a
landing by Charles II at Yarmouth, accompanied by a few thousand
Spanish soldiers and poorly equipped, newly raised and untested regiments of exiles, would have immediately rallied the nation to overthrow
Oliver Cromwell's regime. It is a measure of the exiles' desperation and
impatience that they were willing to believe that this would happen.
The ever optimistic O'Neill claimed that 'the country never was in such
a temper to receive them'. Even the cautious and normally realistic Hyde
argued that 'the conjuncture seems as favourable as could be wished,
nor can it ever be presumed that the king can be in a greater readiness
than he is at present'.[2] In the long term, while this was a view that was
understandably difficult for the impatient exiles to take, it was to the
great advantage of the royalist cause that the restoration of the monarchy was not attempted by Charles II at the head of a Spanish army.

It was in the short term that the collapse of all their plans, the rumours of treachery, the accusations of negligence or incompetence hurled by frustrated conspirators at each other, intensified the disappointment and frustration experienced by the exiles during the remainder of 1658 and for much of 1659. For most of this time morale among the exiled Cavaliers was low. Many of the 'long-term' exiles had now not seen England for over ten years. Some never would again. The older generation of exiled royalists was dying off; prominent emigrés like Arundel, Windebank, Cottington, Hopton, Byron, Radcliffe, Foster and Herbert had all died by the end of 1657. Some younger exiles were now joining them. As we have seen, death by violence, either in duels or in battle, brought down some exiles like Sir William Keith and Sir William Vavasour. But sickness was a greater danger than combat to soldiers in the seventeenth century and one place where sickness spread rapidly was in the overcrowded, poorly equipped and unhealthy quarters of the King's little army in Flanders. One of the victims was Rochester, who commanded the English regiment in Charles's army. Charles's companion during the King's escape to France after Worcester, and, more at the level of farce than of high drama, Nicholas Armorer's during their flight from the aborted rendezvous of conspirators at Marston Moor in March 1655, fell ill in October 1657. While Ormonde was slipping secretly out of London, leaving O'Neill behind to try and hold together the disintegrating plans for a royalist rising, Rochester was dying in Ghent.[3]

Weakened by sickness and hopelessly ill equipped, the King's Flanders regiments were in no condition to meet the advance of the French army and their English allies when the campaigning season opened in the spring of 1658. Thomas Blague, an experienced soldier who with Sir Richard Page had been involved in conspiracy in East Anglia in 1650, succeeded to Rochester's command when the Earl became seriously ill. For the next few months Blague, a groom of the bedchamber to Charles II although he was much more a soldier than a courtier, worked feverishly to organise and equip his regiment. 'We have not one wagon, cart, horse or cloak to take the field withall,' he complained bitterly to Nicholas from Furnes near Dunkirk on 25 May. Nine days later, in the battle of the Dunes, the Spaniards and their English royalist allies were crushingly defeated by the French army and their English Cromwellian allies. Casualties among the King's Guards were heavy, although 'none of the King's officers were killed but Slaughter and Curtis', reported Sir Charles Cotterell to Nicholas from Nieuport, to which town the battered remnant of the Flanders regiments had retired. 'Col. Blagge [*sic*]

is here in town and as well as a man can be with a shot in at his cheek and out of the middle of his neck.'[4] Blague recovered from his wound but the decisive defeat of Charles's small army and his Spanish allies at the battle of the Dunes, coming so soon after the collapse of the plans for a royalist rising in England, was a further blow to the morale of the exiled Cavaliers.

The much longed for death of the Protector on 3 September brought only a temporary break to the general mood of melancholy and gloom afflicting the exiles. The news was brought by several travellers from England including Sir Robert Stone, still trying to keep in with both parties, who, as Hyde informed Ormonde, 'saw the carcase, and here are two or three come to this town, who left London since he died, which was on Friday last'.[5] But as Clarendon observed in his *History of the Rebellion*, 'contrary to all expectation both at home and abroad, this earthquake was attended with no signal alteration' in the state of affairs in England. Oliver's eldest son Richard succeeded peacefully to the office of Lord Protector. The people and, more importantly, the generals and the Army, seemed to be accepting calmly if not enthusiastically the continuation of the Cromwellian regime. Faced by this situation, Clarendon considered that 'the King's condition never appeared so hopeless, so desperate'. To the exiled Cavaliers, their hopes blasted once again, the apparent stability of the Protectorate, evidently unshaken by Oliver's death, 'confirmed their utmost despair'.[6]

It is against this background of gloom and despair that some of the more negative aspects of the exiled royalists' behaviour can best be understood. The petty quarrels and disputes over gambling debts and wagers on tennis matches, the rash of duels, the alleged licentious behaviour of the court, the scandals involving Lucy Walter and the attempts to dispossess her of her young son; these episodes and patterns of behaviour, indications of demoralisation among both Charles and his followers, are most apparent during this period when the Stuart cause appeared to be failing. It is during this time that concern at the frivolous behaviour of the King is a feature of the correspondence of Charles's more serious minded advisers. It was in January 1658 that Ormonde expressed to Hyde his fear that the King's 'immoderate delight in empty, effeminate and vulgar conversations, is become an irresistible part of his nature, and will never suffer him to animate his own designs and others' actions with that spirit which is requisite for his quality and much more to his fortune'.[7] Underlying these concerns, the real cause of the expressions of gloom and despair, was the fear that the monarchy would never be restored and the years of exile would stretch forward indefinitely.

The toll – moral, financial and emotional – exacted by the failure to bring the years of exile to an end was confined not only to the King and his close companions and followers. One can find other examples of royalists gradually worn down by the ordeal of exile until they no longer saw any prospect of an improvement in their condition. One such case is that of Richard Harding, who has been mentioned already in these pages, and his daughter Honora. Richard Harding, a younger son from a minor gentry family in Wiltshire, as a young man had what must have seemed at the time the good fortune to obtain the patronage of William Seymour, Earl of Hertford, the most prominent local magnate. With Seymour support, Harding was elected to represent the borough of Great Bedwin in the Long Parliament, where he was one of the brave minority of 59 MPs who voted against the attainder of Strafford. In July 1641, probably also as a result of Seymour patronage, he was appointed a groom of the bedchamber to the Prince of Wales and found himself committed for the rest of his life to the royalist cause.[8]

Harding became a courtier just when the court of Charles I was on the point of foundering and fragmenting. Like his fellow 'bedchambermen' Seymour, Progers and O'Neill, he attached himself to the fluctuating fortunes of Charles I's eldest son, whom he accompanied into exile, to Jersey, Holland and then to Scotland, where he was forced to leave him and return to the continent when most of the King's attendants were banished by the stern and rigid leaders of the Kirk. An Anglican, Harding was one of the Protestant exiles who originally gathered at the Hague in the circles around Elizabeth of Bohemia and Mary of Orange. To the adventurous Anne Murray, who encountered him in Scotland, he was a 'good old gentleman'; while Elizabeth of Bohemia always referred to him affectionately as the 'reverent Dick Harding'. He accompanied Hyde on his journey from Antwerp to Paris in December 1651 and then for the rest of his life was a member of the exiled court during its wanderings from Paris to the Rhineland to the Spanish Netherlands.[9]

The repeated failures of all the attempts to bring the royalist emigration to an end must have been particularly distressing to Harding. His wife, who seems to have remained in England, predeceased him and his unmarried daughter Honora joined him in exile. His modest estates were sequestered and he made no attempt to compound and save something from the wreckage. By 1657 his poverty was acute. 'Poor Dick Harding . . . hath pawned every little thing he hath', Hyde informed Ormonde sadly on 18 July 1657, 'the cup which the Prince [of Orange] gave him and every spoon, and hath not a shirt to his back'.[10] He was

about 65 when he died in Brussels in June 1658, that melancholy year of failed hopes and expectations for the exiles. Nicholas, Cotterell and O'Neill all received mourning rings from Honora.[11]

In his will, written in Bruges in November 1657, Harding commended his daughter Honora to Hyde's guardianship; it was to the Chancellor that Honora, who had a place in the household of Mary of Orange, turned for guidance and assistance after her father's death. She expressed her gratitude for Hyde's letters of advice – he was good at letters of advice – which were 'no little comfort in the distressed condition I am left in' as she attempted the unpleasant task of recovering the debts owed to her father. 'Mr Elliott [*sic*] indeed, acknowledges his fifty guilders to be due, and says he will pay it, as soon as he can: but Mr Armorer and his wife both deny theirs, as your lordship will see by these letters, which I have sent you.' The reference is to William not Nicholas Armorer. Why Harding, in his circumstances, should have lent money to the violent and quarrelsome William Armorer is difficult to understand. 'Truly I cannot but wonder, she can be so unworthy to outface a truth, though I did not expect any better from him.' Honora seems to have been more perceptive than her father.[12]

Hyde advised Honora Harding on how to recover her debts (without apparently a great deal of success). He also agreed to ask the King to take Harding's servant Tom Bococke into royal service, but recommended that Honora remain in Holland in the household of Mary of Orange; she should not 'desert an honourable employment for a meaner condition'. As well, the Chancellor helped her in her correspondence with her uncle in England – who was generously prepared to give her an annuity of ten pounds! Bococke was given a place in the royal household and on 5 October Honora expressed her gratitude to Hyde that 'his majesty has been so gracious to take Tom into his service, and truly I shall ever acknowledge the part your lordship has had in this business'. Although nearly four months later Honora, doubtless lonely after the loss of both parents and clearly unmarried, complained to Hyde that 'my condition appears to me so desperately that I have nothing to support me, from being very melancholy', she seems to have remained in exile in the service of Mary of Orange.[13]

So by the second half of 1658 it was clearly not only the condition of Charles II that appeared hopeless and desperate. The melancholy example of Harding and his daughter illustrates the desperate circumstances into which, by this time, some exiles had sunk. Yet Harding, who as a groom of the bedchamber was entitled to board wages, and Honora, with a place in Mary of Orange's household, should have been

better off than many exiles. Although a courtier, Harding, an elderly and nor particularly prominent exile, was very different from the frivolous and debauched 'men of pleasure', like Crofts and Newburgh, or the quarrelsome gamblers and duellists, like Taaffe and Stanley, who have traditionally established the character of the exiled court. He was not a soldier like Wentworth and Gerard, or a risk-taking agent involved in conspiracy, like Seymour and O'Neill. He was certainly not a lounger or a fornicator. Harding was an elderly widower with a dependent unmarried daughter whose loyalty and commitment to the Stuart cause brought him and his family intense hardship and distress. He could certainly have compounded and avoided going into exile in 1646, for his connection with the Stuart court was quite recent; he was no Wat Montagu or Endymion Porter. Instead, he chose to accompany Price Charles to Jersey and then to remain with him through the lean years that followed, although he lacked the wealth and aristocratic connections of a Seymour or a Cavendish that might have helped to soften the rigours of exile. But by the end of 1657, when he wrote his will and nominated Hyde and not a relative in England as his daughter's guardian, he must have known that death in exile and in poverty was going to be the reward for his loyalty and self-sacrifice.

To sink into depression and despair was a real possibility for those Cavaliers and their families who were still enduring the hardships and disappointments of exile in 1658. In order to overcome any fatalistic acceptance of the desperate and apparently hopeless condition of the royalist cause, and to maintain, in discouraging circumstances, what Mordaunt called the 'habit of loyalty', it was necessary for the King's more active adherents to generate a new attempt to overthrow the Protectorate, now in the inexperienced and not very secure hands of Richard Cromwell.[14] Not surprisingly, it was some months before the royalist resistance movement, if that is not too flattering a term for it, could recover from the collapse of the plans for a rising in the spring, a collapse accompanied by wholesale arrests and imprisonments and followed in the summer by trials and selective executions. The revival of royalist conspiracy was hastened by the forceful and vigorous leadership of John Mordaunt, the younger brother of that very indecisive royalist, Henry, Earl of Peterborough. Mordaunt had been one of the ringleaders in the plans for a rising early in 1658, and had been in touch with Ormonde and O'Neill during their secret visit to London. Swept up in the wave of arrests in April he had been tried for his life before the feared High Court of Justice but, thanks partly to some judicious lobbying by his enterprising wife Elizabeth, was acquitted on the casting

vote of the president of the court. Undeterred by this narrow escape, Mordaunt informed the King in November that he was ready to attempt to create a new and more effective network to plan another royalist insurrection. His offer was accepted. By March 1659 Mordaunt had received both his instructions to communicate exclusively with the Chancellor and the royal commission to create a new body to organise conspiracy: the 'Plenepotentiary or Great Trust and Commission'. In her turn, Elizabeth Mordaunt received a blank warrant for a viscountcy; in the appropriate space she wrote her husband's name.[15]

The revival of royalist conspiracy at the beginning of 1659 meant, once again, a revival of the hopes of the exiled Cavaliers. The emigrés were further encouraged by the emergence of signs that Richard Cromwell's regime was under threat from more than one direction: from senior officers in the Army, the 'grandees', on one side, and from republicans, who had never forgiven Oliver for his expulsion of the purged remnant of the Long Parliament, the Rump, in 1653 or become reconciled to the Protectorate, on the other. This hopeful situation, as well as reanimating the dejected spirits of the exiles, also meant employment for the some of the more energetic and indefatigable among them, in particular, the agents and couriers. It is not surprising that 'professional' agents like Armorer and Stephens, long since disillusioned with the inactivity and excessive caution of the Sealed Knot, should have willingly transferred their services to Mordaunt and the Great Trust. Mordaunt also developed his own network of loyal agents and couriers – Hartgill Baron was probably the most important and certainly the most devoted to Mordaunt's interests – but they were mostly based in England and not on the continent. Apart from Armorer and Stephens, other exiles employed as couriers by Mordaunt included the clergyman Richard Allestree and Charles Lyttelton. A member of a strongly royalist Worcestershire family, Lyttelton had been arrested in January 1655 as part of the roundup of Cavaliers that helped destroy any chance of success for the March rising. On his release he had gone into exile and obtained a place in the household of Elizabeth of Bohemia, where he was later joined by his younger brother William. Hyde thought highly of Charles Lyttelton and in March 1657 reminded Ormonde of 'his promise to the writer and Nic. Armorer to take Mr Littleton into his service'. Hyde considered that 'the youth is the soberest and best amongst them', (Lyttelton was about 27 in 1657!), and so deserving of the Marquess's protection and patronage.[16]

That the Lyttelton brothers were only in their twenties when they went into exile in the mid 1650s illustrates one aspect of a gradual

change that was taking place in the demographic character of the royalist exiles as a group. On the one hand, as we have seen, a number of the older exiles had died by 1658. Also, by 1658, most of the Cavaliers who had fled into exile after the first or second civil wars had long since returned to England and made their peace with the republican regime, although the process was often both expensive and humiliating. This was particularly the case with plain country gentry Cavaliers, men like Cholmley and Verney, although the returners also included royalists with close links to the court, such as Buckingham and Hatton, and even personally to Charles II, as was the case with two of the grooms of the bedchamber, Progers and Seymour. Those Cavaliers who remained in exile tended to have strong court connections, usually having places in one of the Stuart households; or they were experienced soldiers who could always find some employment for their swords. In many cases their loyalty and their services to the royal cause had been too notable to permit their quiet withdrawal to England, even if they had been willing to return. This last group included not only the King's principal counsellors, like Hyde and Ormonde, but also the other royalists formally banished and excepted from pardon for a variety of reasons that ranged from their participation in the various plots and risings of the 1650s right back to decisions made by the Long Parliament before the Civil War broke out.

As many emigrés returned to England and some died before they could return, the number of Cavaliers remaining in exile was partly maintained by the fresh waves of fugitives from the failed plots and risings of the 1650s. Although some of these fugitives were veterans of the Civil War others, like the Lyttelton brothers and of course Mordaunt himself, were part of a new generation of Cavaliers, too young to have fought in the Civil War, but now old enough to become involved in conspiracy, and when a particular conspiracy inevitably failed, old enough too for the equally inevitable flight 'beyond the seas'. Although the Lyttelton brothers had an impeccably royalist greater gentry background, some of the other recruits to the Struart cause at this time, who were eventually to find themselves in exile, had rather more controversial or unorthodox past histories. Richard Hopton, a younger son of Sir Richard Hopton of Canon Frome, Herefordshire, had a parliamentarian background but converted to royalism; in December 1655 he travelled to Paris and began to move in emigré circles. During 1656 he was drawn into royalist conspiracy and, at first using Armorer as an intermediary, was in touch with both Nicholas and Hyde, to whom he sent reports when he returned to England. Hopton was valuable for his links

with prominent Presbyterians whom Mordaunt, who was working to broaden the base of royalist conspiracy, hoped to win over. But the various disasters that befell the conspirators' plans during 1657 and 1658 only brought him first a brief spell of imprisonment then a period in exile.[17]

If Richard Hopton was a fairly unorthodox recruit to the ranks of the exiled royalists, his friend George Colt was an even more unusual, even dubious, addition. On 1 March 1658 Thomas Ross wrote to Nicholas from Brussels that 'Mr Hopton is gone to Rotterdam to fetch two friends of his, the Colts, from England.' George Colt (his younger brother Thomas remains totally obscure), claimed to have fought on the royalist side in both the second Civil War and at Worcester, although this claim seems to lack supporting evidence. For a committed Cavalier he had some unusual friends. As well as the parliamentarian Richard Hopton, he was also acquainted with the regicide Colonel Richard Ingoldsby, on whose behalf he went on a mission to Ireland in August 1655. Along with the fiery Philippa Mohun, Colt is mentioned in Henry Neville's mildly pornographic and anti-royalist tract *The Commonwealth of Ladies*, where he is listed as the lover of one of the ladies 'whose re-creation lies very much upon the New Exchange about 6 a clock at night'. This colourful figure duly turned up at Rotterdam in March 1658. For nearly a year he was employed as a courier by prominent exiles like Thomas Ross and Gervase Holles until, as Henry Coventry informed Hyde in January 1659, 'George Colt, his man, and Herbert Price's son, were cast away' and drowned while sailing from Dort to Gertrudenberg.[18]

During the first half of 1659 the fears and hopes of the exiles fluctuated wildly as Mordaunt and his supporters developed their plans for a large scale rising to be supported by both royalists and moderate parliamentarians or Presbyterians. Among the exiles employed by Mordaunt as couriers, Armorer, whom Hyde acknowledged 'is specially trusted', was particularly active.

Undeterred by the narrowness of his various escapes in the past, he returned to London in April, carrying letters from Charles to various notables, for example lords Chesterfield and Willoughby, on whose support the King was relying. Typically, Armorer did not restrict his activities to delivering letters but also became involved in Charles Lyttelton's plan to seize Shrewsbury. 'Nic. Armorer sends me word by Maurice that Shrewsbury will be ours', wrote Hyde to Ormonde, adding somewhat dubiously, 'I know not his ground'.[19] Armorer was back in Brussels early in May with letters for Hyde from Mordaunt and other

conspirators but seems to have returned almost immediately to England.[20]

Once again the unrealistically optimistic hopes and expectations of both conspirators and exiles were fated to be shattered. The insurrection that broke out in August was ambitious in its scope but poorly coordinated in its organisation and implementation. The small gatherings of activists in different parts of Kent and Surrey, and in the neighbourhoods of Shrewsbury and Gloucester, were easily scattered. The ex-parliamentarian Cheshire magnate Sir George Booth, who has given his name to the rising, after some local successes including the occupation of Chester, was defeated decisively by General John Lambert at Winnington Bridge. As Lambert's army suffered only one fatal casualty the encounter hardly deserves to be called a battle. Recognised and seized as he fled south in female clothes, Booth's humiliating capture was an appropriate end to a disastrous episode. One of Hyde's correspondents in London, Dr Moore, gave the Chancellor his harsh but understandable verdict on the whole sorry affair, writing that Booth's 'glorious pretext of a free Parliament and the subjects' liberty, is all ended under a wench's petticoat; which makes many conclude him to be rather a fool, knave or coward'.[21]

It took some time for the exiles to appreciate that their hopes that this time they would finally be returning home had once again been crushed. As had happened on several occasions in the past, reliable intelligence of what was happening in England was buried in a host of contradictory and often absurdly optimistic rumours. It was variously reported that Lambert's forces had mutinied, that 'Booth is so strong that Lambert sends daily for more forces', and that Lambert 'is said to have retreated ten miles after viewing Booth's forces'. Booth was also reported to have defeated Lambert after the timely arrival of '1,000 fresh horses from [Sir Thomas] Myddelton' at a critical stage of the battle.[22] The exiles also received rumours of 'a rising in Cumberland', that 'Bristol is believed to be theirs and Massey to be in Gloucester or Hereford', that London had 'shut its gates in the face of three regiments' sent to garrison the city, that 'Exeter and Poole have declared for the King', that 'Cornwall has risen' and, the story carried by ships from Scotland, that 'the Earl of Glencairn and Lord Didupe [sic] have taken up arms'.[23] It was reported from Dort that 'the Duke of York has for certain arrived in the North' but another source claimed that the fleet under Admiral Montagu had declared for the King and York had joined it.[24] Given this flood of positive rumours, it is not surprising that the exiles clung to the hope that the King's fortunes at last were rising,

even while the unfortunate, but in the long run very lucky, Sir George Booth was disappearing into the Tower.

A principal reason for the lack of reliable intelligence reaching the exiles was, as Hyde complained to O'Neill, that 'the best correspondents have left town or are in prison'.[25] Some of these correspondents had departed from London in a hurry and were themselves now fugitives and, with other royalists involved in Booth's rising, were searching urgently for a ship to take them across the Channel. Almost nineteen years after Secretary Windebank had made his hazardous passage across the Channel in an open boat in order to avoid following Strafford into the Tower, the last wave of royalists fleeing into exile was flowing. Richard Allestree reached Rouen by late August, but it was in Calais where most fugitives from the failed rising gathered during late August and September, although Lyttelton did not arrive until October. The forlorn group at Calais included Armorer and two of Mordaunt's most faithful supporters, Hartgill Baron and the Presbyterian agent Captain Silas Titus. Mordaunt, on the run with a warrant out for his arrest, and another royalist conspirator, the Earl of Lichfield, 'came disguised by water in the common barge from Chertsey to London, and got privately to Alderman Robinson's house, where they were for a while concealed', until Mordaunt also succeeded in making his escape and reached Calais on 7 September. It was from these fugitives that the exiles finally learned, as Hyde expressed it in a letter of impressive restraint to Ormonde, that 'our hopes in England are quashed for the present'.[26]

To the exiled Cavaliers 'the fatal news ... of the defeat of sir George Booth' was followed by the usual recriminations among the disappointed conspirators, including criticism by some of Mordaunt's 'vanity and ambition'. The revelation of the treachery of the Sealed Knot's Sir Richard Willys only intensified the bitterness and anger among those royalists who had been active in planning and participating in the insurrection.[27] 'There is no doubt but all our hopes in England are by all possible arts rendered there as desperate as may be', wrote Hyde to Mordaunt on 17 September, 'and there is no question, the failing of our friends in this season of advantage hath made them less valued than they ought to be.'[28] Despairing of the English Cavaliers' ability to bring about his restoration, Charles and Ormonde left the coast of Brittany, where they had been waiting for the opportunity that never came to sail for the west of England, and instead headed for Fuentarrabia on the Pyrenees frontier, where France and Spain were finally negotiating an end to the war that had begun far back in 1636. They took with them only a few companions, notably George Digby, now Earl of Bristol,

(Hyde did not approve of his presence), a couple of servants including the reliable Maurice, and the indispensable O'Neill 'to take care that they fared well in their lodging, for which province no man was fitter'.[29]

In the event Charles, was premature in despairing of the ability of Englishmen to bring about his restoration, although he was justified in feeling pessimistic about the ability of his faithful Cavaliers on their own to accomplish this much desired outcome. It is not surprising that the King failed to foresee how events would unfold, for the months between the crushing of Booth's rising in August 1659 and the restoration of the monarchy in May 1660 are among the most confused and turbulent in England's political history. Even before the rising broke out, Richard Cromwell's Protectorate, and the parliament he had summoned, had already fallen victim to the developing power struggle between the Army and the republican 'commonwealthsmen'. In May the General Council of the Army restored the Rump, but only 42 MPs, the survivors of the series of purges, withdrawals and ejections suffered by the Long Parliament, actually assembled. The constitutional legitimacy of this 'rump of a rump', (the phrase is N. H. Keeble's), was at its best dubious and at its worst non-existent. Both its restoration and its continued existence were dependent on the will of the Army, which had already demonstrated that what it could raise it could also demolish.[30] In these circumstances, it is not surprising that General Lambert's efficient and vigorous suppression of Booth's rising was not observed by the restored Rump with unalloyed satisfaction.

If Charles was unnecessarily pessimistic about the prospects for the Stuart cause in England, he was also over optimistic to expect any effective assistance from the Spanish and French ministers and diplomats at Fuentarrabia. For while Charles and his attendants were engaging in fruitless courtesies and diplomatic exchanges in the Pyrenees, events were moving fast in England. The struggle over who should control the Army, the Rump or the military grandees, culminated in Lambert's coup on 13 October. Once again the Rump was expelled, with no clear alternative to its authority waiting to replace it. 'We are', wrote Dr John Barwick, one of Hyde's London correspondents, 'yet at gaze, what government we shall have.'[31]

Armorer was still stranded in Calais when the news of Lambert's expulsion of the Rump reached the port. Immediately he was ordered by Mordaunt to carry the news to Charles at Fuentarrabia. 'I am tomorrow resolved to venture for England', wrote the irrepressible Mordaunt. 'N. Armorer will inform your Majesty of all particulars I have not time to write.' The indefatigable Armorer, who, although only three weeks

previously had been stranded in Calais and dependent for his survival on money from a friend in London, immediately set off for the south of France. He reached Fuentarrabia on 27 October where his news was well received by Charles and his followers, who by this time also included Culpepper. Within a few days of his arrival, Armorer's years of dangerous and arduous service to the Stuart cause were rewarded with his appointment as Equerry in Ordinary of the Hunting Stable, to take possession of his wages, fees and allowances 'as soon as it shall please God to restore us and that we can settle Our family'. On 4 November O'Neill wrote to the Chancellor that 'your friend Nic. Armorer . . . yesterday proceeded [e]querry and this day as busy as a new broom that I doubt he has not the leisure to give you thanks for your favour in advancing him'. In fact, Armorer had already written to Hyde on the day of his appointment to express his gratitude and his hopes for further patronage: 'I hope I shall not only have your lordship's approbation, but your protection in my master's service.'[32]

Armorer obviously did have a clear understanding of the importance of the role of patronage in his rise from obscurity to a place at court and into the good opinion of powerful persons. Three days later he found the time to write to another patron, Lady Mordaunt, informing her that 'his Majesty has been pleased since my coming here to take me into his service, which, though I have long had the promise, yet I owe the immediate thing to my lord and your ladyship's great kindness to me in employing me hither at this time, which till the last of my breath I will never fail to own with as much gratitude as any servant either of you did oblige'.[33] After many long years of exile, with all the inevitable hardships, and having survived the dangers and disappointments attendant on being in the centre of several failed plots and risings, at last Nicholas Armorer's fortunes were improving. So, although they did not yet realise it, were the prospects of his fellow exiled Cavaliers.

'The good news of the dissolution of the rogues that sit at Westminster', as O'Neill expressed it to Hyde, brought Charles and his small group of attendants hurrying back from the Pyrenees. The King and his companions travelled through France to Paris, where there was a general if superficial reconciliation with Henrietta Maria and her 'Louvrian' courtiers, and where the Fanshawes, once more back in exile, were waiting to meet Charles. Since his capture at Worcester, and eventual release from the Tower on parole, Fanshawe had been subjected to various forms of house arrest and travel restrictions, his 'fetters in which he had been seven years'; but as the authority of the Commonwealth began to fragment the devotedly loyal Fanshawes had seized the oppor-

tunity to rejoin the King in exile.[34] But while the power struggle among the generals and junior officers of the Army, the republican Rumpers and Cromwellians, raged in an England in danger of slipping into anarchy, it was not at first clear how the exiles could profit from this surely promising state of affairs. The formulation of policy was made more difficult by the lack of reliable intelligence as to what exactly was happening across the Channel. 'This is the second week that we have received no letters from England', complained Hyde in a letter on 30 October to Ormonde, still of course languishing in the Pyrenees. 'Nor have the packet boats, which have been sent from Ostend, been suffered to go to Dover, but have been sent back by the ships in the Downs to Ostend, where there are now three weeks packets of these countries together. All that we know is from Dunkirk, where they say that the confusions in England are extraordinarily great, and such as must involve that nation in a new and bloody war.'[35]

In the meantime, as Charles and his followers returned from Paris to Brussels, the exiles contemplated gloomily the prospect of another winter of poverty and discontent in shabby lodgings in Brussels and in the other towns in northern France and the Netherlands where they were largely concentrated. According to Clarendon, the King 'had not been long at Bruxells before he discerned the same melancholy and despair in the countenances of most men which he had left there'.[36] The belief that 'the King's hopes' had been 'totally destroyed', first by the suppression of Booth's rising and then by the apparent reluctance of either France or Spain to provide any effective aid to the royalists, was held by a number of emigrés. Thinking that, at least for the time being, his brother's cause seemed hopeless, the Duke of York, with his remarkable capacity for failing to recognise which way the political wind was blowing, accepted in March 1660 the offer of the position of admiral in the Spanish fleet being prepared for action against Portugal.[37]

Not all Cavaliers, either in England or in exile, were so pessimistic. Mordaunt, although his reputation had been damaged by the failure of Booth's rising and the consequent recriminations among the conspirators, continued to bombard Charles and his advisers with exhortations not to lose faith in the Cavaliers' capacity to bring about the overthrow of the Commonwealth. Several prominent exiles seem gradually to have been persuaded that, as Nicholas wrote to Ormonde in October, Charles should be 'ready to make his best advantage of any changes that may happen in England, where (if we hear truth) his Majesty's business stands still very fair and many of his good subjects are still ready to rise for him'. Hyde's correspondence during this period does not present the

same picture of despair and gloom among the exiles that is conveyed by his *History of the Rebellion*. Also writing to Ormonde, he refers to 'many hopes yet remaining in England . . . [where] the good humour is still in the people generally, and not abated upon these last misfortunes, nor the rebels in any degree united'. The Jersey Cavalier Sir George Carteret, writing to Hyde in December from Paris, also expressed what was clearly the widely held opinion that 'most people think he [Charles] ought to be where he may be ready to set foot in a boat', especially as 'little help can be expected from this nation [France]'. Then, on 1 January 1660, General George Monck's army of occupation in Scotland crossed the Tweed, entered England and began its slow and inexorable march south towards London.[38]

In this situation of intense uncertainty and confusion, with Monck's intentions unknown, including quite possibly to himself, with Lambert marching north to confront him, and with the discredited and widely despised Rump restored again by the Army grandees whose political and even military authority was rapidly crumbling, the exiled Cavaliers could only observe and speculate, torn by conflicting hopes and apprehensions. 'Monck is so dark a man, no perspective can look through him, and it will be like the last scene of some excellent play, which the most judicious cannot positively say how it will end,' wrote Mordaunt, with impressive detachment considering his circumstances, to Henrietta Maria in late January.[39]

One attempt by the exiled court in January to influence events in England ended in failure. Colonel John Dixwell, the efficient successor to the unfortunate Captain Wilson as governor of Dover castle, having been warned by Sir William Lockhart, the Commonwealth commander at Dunkirk, about 'dangerous persons frequently passing and repassing between England and Flanders', actually managed to capture three of them. Colonel James Bovey remains an obscure figure, but Richard Allestree and Sir John Stephens, who had been knighted in March 1658 on his return from his dangerous mission to London with Ormonde, were experienced even 'professional' agents and were both carrying letters from Charles. Having returned unscathed from so many dangerous missions during the 1650s, it was an irony that Allestree and Stephens could not be expected to appreciate that they were finally captured just as the Commonwealth was crumbling. His arrest must have been particularly irritating for Stephens in that his wife had preceded him to England only two months earlier. But the network of royalist sympathisers was clearly still operating at Dover, as Nicholas was informed that 'Mr Allestree's letters and c., were taken care of and safely

delivered into a good hand there . . . to be sent express to London.' Under escort, the prisoners were also dispatched to London; Allestree was imprisoned in the Tower but Stephens was held in Lambeth House.[40]

While Stephens remained confined in Lambeth House, 'used then as a prison for many of the King's friends', dramatic and decisive events were occurring outside its walls. With Lambert's unpaid and demoralised army having disintegrated, on 3 February Monck made an unopposed entry into London. Despite all the efforts to discover his intentions, they remained impenetrable, although he had been bombarded on his march through England with petitions and speeches demanding a full and free parliament. After a week of extreme tension and uncertainty, with the Rump desperate to assert its authority over Monck, and the City of London itself, from the Common Council to the apprentices, on the point of open revolt, the general finally made his intentions (partially) clear. On 11 February a letter signed by Monck and his senior officers, and read to the House that same day, required the Rump to dissolve itself and to arrange for the election of a full and free parliament to succeed it.

News of Monck's action, and of the spontaneous outburst of popular enthusiasm and excitement that it immediately provoked, recorded vividly by Samuel Pepys and other observers, was carried rapidly to the exiled court by a courier despatched by Stephens, with orders to 'make all possible haste to Bruxells that the King might be informed of it'. Not surprisingly, the news was first delivered to Ormonde, Stephens's patron, and then to Hyde and the King by a courier almost incoherent with excitement and exhaustion. As Hyde immediately wrote to Mordaunt, the account of Monck's action and events in London 'turned their heads'.[41]

Events now moved rapidly towards the restoration of the monarchy. First, the Rump reluctantly admitted the MPs expelled by Pride's Purge back in 1648, then finally the Long Parliament dissolved itself to clear the way for the election of a new assembly, the Convention. As an illustration of a world turned suddenly upside down, General Lambert, the victor at Winnington Bridge only a few months earlier, was arrested and sent to the Tower, from which Sir George Booth was released. Unlike the unfortunate Penruddock, Booth could now look forward not to the headsman's axe, but to a peerage. In the middle of March, between the dissolution of the Long Parliament and the meeting of the Convention, Monck finally, but still secretly, established contact with Charles and committed himself to work for a restoration. The Cornish Cavalier Sir

John Grenville and Mordaunt, now very much Grenville's associate rather than his superior in the world of royalist conspiracy, were the secret intermediaries between the general and the king. Their hasty journeys between London and Brussels culminated in both the Declaration of Breda and letters from the King being read by Grenville to the newly assembled Convention on 1 May. The House then enthusiastically and unanimously approved the motion that, 'according to the ancient and fundamental laws', the government of the kingdom resided in King, Lords and Commons.[42]

This rapid sequence of events transformed the mood of the exiled Cavaliers from the dejection and despair described by Clarendon in his *History*, through the stage of a 'new dawning of hope' to the almost unbelievable realisation that the long years of exile were finally over. Some exiles found it difficult to express their feelings in words. On 27 February Thomas Ross in Antwerp sent to Gervase Holles at Rotterdam a confused and excited account of events in London, ending with an apology: 'I am so much overjoyed that you must pardon my method, and all my other faults.' Charles's journey through the United Provinces from Breda to the Hague turned into a triumphal progress. To Elizabeth of Bohemia it was 'a great miracle to see so sudden a change'. Writing to her son Charles Louis at Heidelberg, she stated that 'it is not to be imagined how all are joyed at this . . . the very common people are as hot for the king as any of us'.[43] In this hectic atmosphere of excitement and celebration, the exiled Cavaliers had to come to terms with this sudden transformation in their fortunes. It was now time not only to plan the return home but also to consider how they might be rewarded for the long years of deprivation and hardship they had undergone through their loyal sharing of the King's exile.

Part III
Return

12
Gone for England

'I returned home to meet Sir Richard Browne – who came not till the 8th June – after a nineteen years exile during which he had yet kept up, in his chapel, the liturgy and offices of the Church of England – to his no small honour'.

(Diary of John Evelyn)[1]

On 25 May 1660 the royalist exile ended officially with the landing of King Charles II and his brothers at Dover, to be welcomed by General Monck, the Mayor of Dover, and a vast crowd of enthusiastic spectators. To the accompaniment of the continuous thunder of cannon, the braying of trumpets and the acclamation of the huge crowds, Charles made his leisurely way though Kent to London, delivering gracious speeches and bestowing titles and awards as he went. At Canterbury Monck was presented with the Garter while Mordaunt and Massey were among the recipients of knighthoods. The triumphant return of Charles II from exile was described vividly by many contemporary observers; Evelyn's account is probably the most famous and the most frequently quoted. 'The shouting and the joy expressed by all' that surrounded the King on his progress from Dover to London was followed by the spectacular and triumphal entry into the capital on 29 May, Charles's thirtieth birthday, 'after a sad and long exile ... with a triumph of above 20,000 horse and foot, brandishing their swords and shouting with unexpressable joy: the ways strew'd with flowers, the bells ringing, the streets hung with tapestry, fountains running with wine ... chains of gold, banners; lords and nobles ... everybody clad in cloth of silver, gold, and velvet.' Evelyn 'stood in the Strand, and beheld it, and blessed God'.[2] The return to England of the other exiled royalists is not so well documented, nor, apart from the experience of those who

accompanied Charles on his entry into London, was it so spectacular and colourful.

Many of the more prominent exiled Cavaliers accompanied Charles across the Channel in Admiral Montagu's fleet of hastily and tactfully renamed ships. The *Naseby*, the *Richard*, the *Speaker*, the *Dunbar* and the *Cheriton* became respectively the *Royal Charles*, the *James*, the *Mary*, the *Henry* and the *Henrietta*, a process accompanied by a hurried replacement of republican flags, coats of arms and other symbols of the Commonwealth with suitably royalist images and decorations. Samuel Pepys, who made the journey to bring back the King in the entourage of his patron Montagu, records the cramped and crowded conditions as 'many of the King's servants came on board', determined not to be left behind.[3]

In fact, the return of the exiles had already begun, weeks before Montagu's fleet set sail for England carrying Charles, his brothers and a crowd of royal servants and attendants. As the Commonwealth crumbled during the early months of 1660, many emigrés, lacking the pessimism of the Duke of York, began to anticipate an imminent restoration of the monarchy. Consequently, they saw no reason to endure the discomforts of exile any longer while they waited for this much longed for event to take place formally; from early March there was a steadily increasing flow of Cavaliers and their families back into England. Thomas Ross, writing to Gervase Holles from Antwerp on 11 March, reported that 'many are gone this week for England and I believe many to go the next, among others Dr Morley, and Sir Hugh Cartwright'. Hyde's close friend, Dr George Morley, soon to be the Bishop of Worcester, was despatched to England to hold preliminary discussions with both prominent Anglicans and Presbyterians, hopefully to prepare for an amicable religious settlement, while Cartwright had spent most of his years of exile in Antwerp as one of Newcastle's circle.[4] The Wiltshire Cavalier, Thomas Mompesson of Salisbury, who had lived in Caen since his flight into exile in 1655 as a consequence of his involvement in Penruddock's rising, was also back in London in March. At the end of that month he wrote cheerfully to Nicholas that 'we have now our freedom, the council of State granting passes to any that endeavour to get them, which contains liberty of going into the country or staying in the town. I saw Mr John Heath and diverse others have them, so I have now gotten one myself.' Mompesson was already beginning a law suit to recover his sequestered estate.[5]

Mompesson and Heath, Charles II's 'Counsel at Law' in the exiled court and an active royalist agent in the 1650s, were only two of a

number of prominent exiles who were back in London by early 1660, and apparently moving around freely. Several of Heath's fellow agents and conspirators among the exiles – Nicholas Armorer, Edward Massey, Roger Whitley and Silas Titus – were also in London in March, only about six months after having fled England as fugitives, all of them having been involved in Booth's rising in the previous August. It was appropriate also that Sir John Stephens, whose confinement in Lambeth House seems to have been fairly brief, was once again being employed as a courier, this time carrying letters between Morley and Hyde. But Stephens's days for making hasty and clandestine journeys between the exiled court and royalist sympathisers in England were almost over, and when he crossed the Channel in April on his way to Breda he would have had the company of plenty of royalists going the same way.[6]

For, as had happened on several other occasions during the twenty years of the royalist emigration, the traffic across the Channel was not entirely one way. On the one hand, men like Mompesson, Heath and others were 'gone for England', impatient to pick up the threads of lives broken by the years of exile. But during the last hectic weeks before the Restoration numbers of royalists were leaving England, travelling either to Charles's court at Breda or else directly to the Hague, where the King arrived to an enthusiastic reception on 15 May. As Sir William Denny observed with some embarrassment to Hyde, when in April he resumed a long neglected correspondence with the Chancellor, loyalty was beginning again to be fashionable. Not only fashionable but also, as some of those crossing the Channel to Holland clearly hoped, profitable; it was reported that by May 'Breda swarmed with English'.[7]

It was a mixed crowd of royalist well-wishers who waited on the King. Some were Cavaliers on serious business, trusted conspirators like Grenville and Mordaunt, communicating between the King and his advisers in Holland and Monck and other influential figures in England. In these important but still fairly secret communications there was still a role for experienced couriers like Stephens. Then there were the ex-courtiers, including those who had been in exile but who had returned to England during the 1650s and were now hurrying across to Breda to pay their respects to Charles and to renew their court connections. Lord Hatton was one who decided in April that it was desirable to leave London and 'hasten over to the King', and Ned Progers was another. Charles had not forgotten his old companion and Progers immediately resumed his position as a groom of the bedchamber. Hatton and Progers were genuine Cavaliers who had endured long periods of exile and who were entitled to hope that their appearance would be welcome and their

sufferings rewarded. But at Breda and the Hague, during those tumultuous weeks in April and May, the presence of the 'long-term' exiled Cavaliers would have been swamped in the crowd of enterprising and importunate well-wishers, petitioners and suppliants who crowded around the King on the lookout for rewards and favours, in recognition of their now loudly espoused, but until very recently well-hidden, loyalties. Among the crowd of enthusiastic and hopeful royalists who paid their respects to Charles at Breda was one Roger Palmer and his new young wife Barbara, the niece of the Viscount Grandison who had died in miserable circumstances in a charity hospital in Paris only a few months previously. Despite the crowds, Barbara Palmer seems to have been successful in attracting the King's attention.[8]

While many exiles were already back in London to welcome the King when the arrived, others were still scattered through a number of foreign countries. As the long hoped for but almost unbelievable news of the collapse of the Commonwealth and the restoration of the monarchy spread from the Netherlands, so the widely scattered exiles began to adjust to the new situation and to disentangle themselves from their various commitments and responsibilities. For several exiled Cavaliers an immediate return to England was not possible. For the disgraced secretary to the Council, Robert Long, living in obscure poverty in Rouen, the necessary preliminary to a return to England and the gradual reconstruction of his political career was a 'free pardon for past offences', humbly and successfully requested in a submissive letter to the King. It was not until the spring of 1661 that Sir Henry Bennet was released from his embassy in Madrid. He arrived back in England about the same time as that enterprising traveller Dr Isaac Basire, who, as was mentioned above in Chapter 6, had been appointed by Prince George II Rakoczi of Transylvania to the chair of Theology at the University of Weissenbourg in 1654, and was apparently in no hurry to return to his long-suffering wife and family. The timing of Basire's eventual return to England seems to have been determined as much by the ravages of a Turkish invasion of Transylvania as by the restoration of Charles II. That other well travelled exile, John Page, according to his letters to the Chancellor, was still in India in 1660, arriving in Bombay in August. He also did not return to England for another year. The emigrés whose return from exile was the most delayed seem to have been the two Scottish Cavaliers William Drummond and Thomas Dalyell, who had both risen to high rank in the army and administration of Tsar Alexis of Russia, who did not permit their return to Scotland until 1665.[9]

Some exiled Cavaliers, who were still on the continent when the

monarchy was restored, probably never returned. We cannot know how many exiles gradually adapted to life in a foreign country, perhaps converted to the religious denomination practised in that country, married and had a family, and eventually dropped out of royalist exile circles. The most well-known example of an exile who did something like this, although without the marriage, is Wat Montagu. As one of Henrietta Maria's circle of 'court papists', he had been one of the very first royalists hastily to 'go beyond the seas' back in the early months of 1641. Since then he had become comfortably established as abbot of St Martin's Abbey at Pontoise, which was convenient to Paris and the court, and he saw no reason to uproot himself again in 1660. Montagu remained at Pontoise until his death in 1677. We know what happened to Montagu as he was a prominent figure, with close links to the French court. But it is unlikely that he was the only exiled royalist who decided to remain on the continent and not return to England when the King came into his own again.

The various floods and trickles of Cavaliers into exile had been a complex movement, a series of waves and surges over a period of almost twenty years, beginning with the flight of Windebank and the 'court papists' and ending with the equally hasty passage across the Channel of Mordaunt and other royalists involved in Booth's rising. The return of the exiles also had its own distinctive pattern. An uneven flow of returning royalists began almost as soon as the Civil War ended, Hyde's 'men of honour running to compound', and continued unevenly throughout the 1650s, peaking at times when the royal cause seemed most hopeless, in 1649, after the second Civil War and the execution of Charles I, and again in 1651, after the battle of Worcester. This uneven flow became a major flood during the first half of 1660, with a further trickle of stragglers continuing fitfully for another three or four years. As we have seen, on several occasions during this twenty-year period, a major military defeat for the royalists, or the discovery and suppression of a conspiracy or rising, would result in a simultaneous two-way traffic of large numbers of royalists crossing the Channel. After the total defeat of the royal army at Worcester, fugitives 'who made their escapes arrived every day in France, Flanders and Holland'. At the same time, Nicholas described how the news of 'the fatal day' was responsible for 'an abundance of royalists gone for England from these parts and many more are going, as having little hopes left them'.[10] But before 1660 those Cavaliers who returned to England did so as defeated and submissive Malignants and Delinquents, their decision to return often enormously influenced by the need to make some kind of settlement

with different government committees which would enable them to provide for their families. The Cavaliers who returned from exile at the Restoration did so in triumph, their sufferings at last vindicated and their loyalty, as they hoped or even expected, about to be rewarded. In blunt and simple terms, from long-term losers the exiled Cavaliers believed they had suddenly become winners. To what prospects and positions then did they return; and what values and attitudes did they bring back with them, after their years of enduring the many and various hardships of exile?

13
Rewards and Favours

Appointment of John Sawyer, chief Master Cook, in consideration of ye faithful service he has done us during this time of
Our being in foreign parts.

(One of a series of appointments to places in the
royal household, Breda, 9 April 1660)[1]

After so many months, even years in many cases, of poverty, deprivation, separation from one's family and exclusion from political and
social life, the time had come when the returned exiles could expect to
be rewarded for their suffering and their loyalty. But for some of the
survivors of exile the Restoration had come almost too late. A small
number of the returned emigrés can be viewed as the out of touch relics
of an older generation, the survivors of out-dated conflicts and causes:
the old Cavaliers of Charles I who had no role to play in the new court
and administration of his son. Once prominent figures from the years
of the Personal Rule of Charles I, like ex-Lord Keeper Finch, or of the
early days of the Long Parliament, like Lord Culpepper, having survived
the years of exile to witness the Restoration, could now retire gracefully
and thankfully to their manor houses to die, as both Finch and
Culpepper did before the end of 1660.

This retirement from public life was not always gracious or welcomed
with relief. Although awarded a peerage in 1658 and appointed Lord
Lieutenant of Yorkshire at the Restoration, Sir Marmaduke Langdale had
been left permanently angered, principally by his exclusion from the
inner circle of Charles's advisers during the 1650s but also by the reluctance of the organisers of royalist conspiracy, first the Sealed Knot and
then Mordaunt, to take advantage of his influence among royalists in
the north of England. There is a distinct note of bitterness in his letter

177

to Nicholas from Yorkshire on 7 April 1661 in which he hoped 'the King will excuse his non-attendance at the Coronation'. Langdale pointed out that he was 'too poor to bear [the cost of] the journey and can neither borrow money nor sell land to obtain it'.[2] Nicholas himself, who was 67 at the Restoration and in poor health, still needed to be exposed to a combination of powerful pressure and financial incentives before he was persuaded in October 1662 to vacate with great reluctance the office of Secretary of State, to which he had first been appointed by Charles I back in 1641. While Nicholas withdrew into retirement in his native Wiltshire, the career of his successor as Secretary, Sir Henry Bennet, was now taking off.[3]

Although some returned emigrés may have been prepared go to into retirement, either willingly or because they had no alternative, most were not. The departure of ex-Secretary Nicholas from the scene was widely recognised as a victory for Bennet and his political allies, George Digby, Earl of Bristol, Henry Jermyn, now Earl of St Albans and the rapidly rising new royal favourite, Sir Charles Berkeley, all of whom had spent years in exile. For men like these the Restoration meant not the culmination of their careers, but the moment, long hoped for and long delayed, when their expectations and ambitions were at last to be fulfilled. But according to Dr Seaward, 'the seemingly bright dawning of royalists' hopes and prospects after the long night of banishment and deprivation proved little more than a trick of the light: royalists failed to inherit the earth; some had difficulty enough in inheriting their own estates'.[4]

The view that the legitimate interests and expectations of the Cavaliers were neglected in the Restoration settlement has a long history and has been much examined by historians.[5] The *Act of Free and General Pardon, Indemnity and Oblivion*, which established as law one of the key promises of the Declaration of Breda, was finally passed by the Convention Parliament on 29 August 1660. It inspired the bitter joke of disappointed Cavaliers that 'the king had passed an act of oblivion for his friends and of indemnity for his enemies.'[6] Different explanations have been given for this alleged neglect of the Cavaliers: the selfish ingratitude of the King; the sheer financial impossibility of rewarding adequately all the 'indigent' and deserving royalists; the government's policy of reconciliation which made it impolitic to favour one side in the distribution of favours and offices; and the practical necessity of rewarding Monck and his military, naval and Presbyterian allies, especially given the particular circumstances of 1660. Our concern is with the hopes and prospects of those Cavaliers who had been in exile, and

who according to Clarendon 'had the keener appetites and the stronger presumption', as distinct from those of the royalist party as a whole.[7]

The variety of rewards and favours available for distribution by Charles II and his ministers, although nowhere nearly adequate to satisfy the flood of requests from the petitioners who besieged them, was extensive in both range and value. The most desirable and probably most intensely competed for offices, and over which the King and his ministers had the greatest control, were places at court, followed by positions in various government departments and commissions in the armed forces. There was also a wide range of favours and rewards within the patronage of the King and his ministers: titles, pensions, demonstrations of support in contests for places ranging from a seat in Parliament to a university fellowship, monopolies and grants of one kind or another. 'Favour' is an elastic term. It can embrace both the titles, offices and grants showered on a court favourite like Sir Charles Berkeley and the more indirect support given to someone like Sir Robert Moray, whose services to the royalist cause during his years in exile made him an ideal intermediary between Charles and the Royal Society when the granting of its Royal Charter was being negotiated.[8] Royal favour could be extended, directly and visibly, to close associates of the King like Daniel O'Neill and Ned Progers but it could also be exercised more indirectly, for example to encourage the activities of the theatre managers Thomas Killigrew and Sir John Davenant as they restored a vigorous theatrical life to the London scene. Berkeley, Moray, O'Neill, Progers, Killigrew and Davenant were all Cavaliers returned from exile; they were all in different ways prominent figures in Restoration London, and they were all recipients of royal favour, but it came in a variety of forms.

When considering the extent to which royalists who had gone into exile were rewarded for their sufferings and their loyalty, the obvious place to begin is the court. Here especially, Charles had the best opportunity to reward his faithful companions and followers in exile, but the court also was where the competition for places was most intense. How well represented were the returned exiles in the royal household? In Chapter 4 a distinction was made between the 'short-term' and 'long-term' exiles, the latter group comprising those royalists who either chose voluntarily or were compelled to leave England and then remained in exile for at least two years. Of the 225 'long-term' exiles who were the subject of the group portrait in Chapter 4, at least 38 died in exile before 1660, six died after their return to England (or Scotland) but before the Restoration, while attempts to discover the place and date of death of 17 of the more obscure exiles have been unsuccessful. This leaves at

least 170 'long-term' exiles, many, but by no means all, of whose names have cropped up in the course of this history, who survived until the Restoration.

How many of these names can be recognised among the place holders in the post-restoration court? A *List of the department of the Lord Chamberlain of the Household*, which in fact includes members of both the Chamber 'above stairs' and the Household 'below stairs', was drawn up in the autumn of 1663.[9] It can be compared with surviving lists of the royal household compiled at different times during the royalist exile: in Holland in May 1649 'according to the last reduction in February', in the Rhineland in August 1654 as part of an attempt to calculate who exactly among the King's impecunious followers were entitled to board wages, in Bruges in December 1657 in response to a request from Don Juan, the governor of the Spanish Netherlands, and by Secretary Nicholas at the time of the Restoration in May 1660.[10] If we include not only those returned emigrés whose names occur in the 1663 list of the royal household but also those who had places in the household of the Duke of York (for example, Richard Talbot and Robert Werden) or of the Queen Mother Henrietta Maria (for example, Percy Church), then 83 of the surviving 'long-term' exiles had places at court after the Restoration.[11] To this number must be added the holders of menial offices in the royal household, men and women whose names feature in the various lists of the exiled court compiled at different times, but who were not included in the group portrait of 225 'long-term' exiled Cavaliers discussed above in Chapter 4.

If we consider first the principal officers of the royal household in 1663; of the 18 gentlemen of the bedchamber, a number increased from only four in 1657, nine were returned exiles. They comprised a mixture of aristocratic magnates, Privy Councillors and current royal favourites: Ormonde (also the Lord Steward), Buckingham, Newcastle, Gerard, Crofts, Wentworth, Fitzhardinge (Charles Berkeley), Carteret and Denham. There were 12 grooms of the bedchamber in 1663, compared to the years of exile when the number never rose above six and was sometimes less. Of the 12 bedchambermen, nine had spent at least some of the 1650s in exile. There were some familiar names among them. Henry Seymour, Edward Progers, Thomas Elliot and Daniel O'Neill retained the positions they had occupied during their time in exile, but they were now joined by, among others, Silas Titus and Robert Phelips, who had both been active agents and conspirators in the 1650s, and Tom Killigrew, a man of many talents, although in the light of his experiences in Venice in 1651, diplomacy was not one of them.[12] Similar

proportions of returned exiles exist among the holders of other Chamber offices: three of the six pages of the bedchamber, three of the four gentleman ushers of the privy chamber, and so on. From Thomas Ross, a groom of the privy chamber and Keeper of the Library to Charles Lyttelton, Cupbearer in Ordinary, returned emigrés are scattered through the different departments of the enlarged royal household.[13]

An examination of the names of the holders of less prestigious positions in the household reveals also an impressive number of returned exiles. Among the strongly royalist Progers family, Edward, as we have seen, was a groom of the bedchamber. His three brothers, Henry and James, who had taken part in the murder of the Commonwealth's envoy to Madrid in 1650, and Charles also had positions in the household. Henry, who like Nicholas Armorer was an equerry in 1660, was eventually knighted and succeeded another returned exile, Sir Edward Brett, as Serjeant Porter.[14] At a slightly lower social level, the Chiffinches were another well-represented court family. Thomas Chiffinch, a Page of the Bedchamber, and his wife Dorothy, the 'seamstress and laundress to his Majesty's person', had belonged to the shrunken little court that formed around Charles in Holland in 1649 and had accompanied the King on his travels through all the years of exile. When the court had left Cologne in 1656, Dorothy, 'the most loving poor wretch in the world' according to Hyde, successfully resisted the attempt to leave her behind on the grounds that there was inadequate accommodation for all the King's 'family' in Bruges. The Chiffinches survived the years of exile and retained their positions in the household until 1666 when Thomas died and was succeeded as a Page of the Bedchamber by his brother William. As guardian of the Privy Stairs to the King's bedchamber, Will Chiffinch was to become notorious as the trusted confidant of Charles in his more secret and dubious amorous activities. Memorably praised by David Ogg as having done 'a great and honourable service to the Stuarts by *not* writing his memoirs', Will Chiffinch, with his shady reputation, has made a significant contribution to the image of the Restoration court, overshadowing any record of the loyal and devoted service of his brother and sister-in-law during the royalist exile.[15]

The Chiffinches were not the only household servants to survive long periods in exile, retaining their positions in Charles's little court despite the permanent lack of money with which to pay their wages, and instead hanging on in the hope that eventually their loyalty would be rewarded. James Jack was Yeoman of the Bows in Charles's reduced court in Holland in 1649, but seven years later, in Bruges, he was listed as a porter, an office he still held at the Restoration. Matthew Clarke, the King's

coachman, 'who waited on him in exile', also survived to the Restoration, when he was confirmed in his office, although this did not prevent him from petitioning for further rewards for his loyalty. The names of these holders of menial offices in the exiled court occasionally surface in household lists and accounts, or they are the subject of passing references in correspondence: Jack Forbes the footman, who was accidentally shot and wounded when Charles was making a ceremonial entry into Damme in the summer of 1657; Mr Lisle and Mr Foliard, the king's barbers; Thomas Hethwaite (Hutwayet and Outhwaite) the 'Serjeant of the Wine Cellar'; Richard Ides the falconer; even Giles Rose, the 'Child of the Kitchen'. The endurance, the capacity to survive the 'grinding penury' of years in exile, of humble persons like Dorothy Chiffinch and Jemmy Jack is very impressive, especially when it is compared with that of certain royalist grandees like Buckingham and Peterborough.[16]

The hope of these servants at the exiled court that their endurance and loyalty would be rewarded seems to have been in most cases justified. For example, an intelligence report to Thurloe from Cologne in July 1655 lists among the more obscure members of Charles's household one 'Gervase the Trumpet'. This is certainly a reference to Gervase Price, Sergeant Trumpeter to the King, who survived to the Restoration, when his position as Sergeant Trumpeter was confirmed and he was also appointed Yeoman of the Bows and Guns. By March 1661 he had seventeen court trumpeters under his authority, had a salary of £100 a year, and was also the recipient of occasional gifts from the King. On 20 February 1667, when, with the war against the Dutch going badly and Clarendon's enemies gathering for the final assault on the Lord Chancellor, one would have thought Charles II had other matters to occupy him, a royal warrant ordered the presentation to Price of 'one gilt trumpet, weighing forty ounces or therabouts, as a gift from his Majesty'.[17] This must have finally made 'Gervase the Trumpet's' years of poverty in Cologne, Bruges and Brussels worthwhile.

Royal servants during the years of exile, including recent appointments like Nicholas Armorer, who was 'taken into his [the King's] service' at Fuentarrabia, and Tom Bococke, who was appointed a page of the Presence Chamber as a result of Honora Harding's pleas to Hyde, were in a strong position to have their appointments confirmed or even improved upon when in the early months of 1660 the pressure on places suddenly increased and the court began to expend. Armorer wisely had his appointment as an equerry at Fuentarrabia on 3 November 1659 confirmed on 5 March 1660, when he was authorised in a royal warrant to take possession of all his fees and allowances 'as soon as it shall please

God to restore us and that we can settle Our family'. His example is merely one of many: John Cooper as carver in ordinary on 3 March, Sir Edward Brett as Serjeant Porter on 24 March; Thomas Outhwaite as 'Serjeant of our Wine Cellar' on 22 April, Ralph Folliard as a barber, Maurice Deladale and Hugh Griffith as pages, and Gervase Price as 'Yeoman of our Bows and Guns', all on 5 May and John Sawyer as chief Master Cook, 'in consideration of ye faithful service he has done us during this time of Our being in foreign parts'.[18] These are a mere handful of the new appointments and confirmations of previous appointments that make up a considerable portion of the papers of Secretary Nicholas during the hectic weeks at Breda and the Hague between March and May 1660. Before Charles II even stepped ashore at Dover the exiles, from the Marquess soon to be Duke of Ormonde, as Lord Steward, down to Giles Rose, the Child of the Kitchen, had in many cases already moved quickly to establish a presence in the royal household out of all proportion to their numbers among the royalist party as a whole.

A strong representation of returned exiles in the Restoration court is not particularly surprising when we take into account the significant proportion of courtiers among the royalist emigrés. A suddenly enlarged court provided Charles with a convenient means of rewarding his companions in exile, although he soon discovered that it was not quite that simple as survivors from the court of Charles I emerged from obscurity to reclaim their offices. For example, Sir Henry Herbert attempted to resume his position as Master of the Revels, to which he had been appointed way back in 1623, but he came up against the conflicting grants made by the King to the returned exile Sir William Davenant and to members of that strongly royalist family, well represented both at court and in exile, the Killigrews.[19]

The need to satisfy also the demands for rewards from the powerful figures with parliamentary or Cromwellian backgrounds who had played such an important role in bringing about the Restoration explains the appointment of the Presbyterian Earl of Manchester as Lord Chamberlain and George Monck, Duke of Albemarle as Master of the Horse. In the uncertain and unstable conditions that existed in 1660, with the ever present background fear of some violent attempt by Cromwellians, discontented soldiers, commonwealthsmen, fifth monarchists or other 'fanatics', to send the restored monarchy the same way as the Rump, many interests needed to be satisfied and balanced against each other.[20] So the distribution of offices in the administration, the appointment of military commanders, and the finding of seats in Parliament for trusted supporters of the government were issues of

major importance, going beyond simply a desire to distribute rewards and favours to deserving royalists. To secure the security and stability of the regime was the immediate and most urgent concern of those who were responsible for the Restoration settlement.

The various methods used to establish securely the restored monarchy open up the question of the part played by the returned Cavaliers in the political life of Restoration England. As we have seen, at least 170 'long-term' exiles from the original group of 225 survived to welcome the Restoration. Forty-eight of these returned exiles sat in the House of Commons in one or more of the parliaments of Charles II and James II. These were men who had returned to England not to an obscure retirement but to play a part in the political life of the nation; they obviously had a strong personal vested interest in ensuring the survival of the restored monarchy. They represented the diversity of background and experience that was such a noticeable characteristic of the exiled Cavaliers. Among them were men who were to become some of the most prominent politicians and administrators of the reign of Charles II: Sir Henry Bennet, Henry and Sir William Coventry, Sir Stephen Fox and Sir George Carteret, for example. Courtiers who had been in exile were also strongly represented in Parliament. They included Ned Progers, Sir Charles Cotterell, Sir John Denham and Sir Gilbert Talbot. The cultivated, well-travelled diplomat Sir Richard Fanshawe was MP for Cambridge University while Edward Stanley, the quarrelsome hanger on at the exiled court in Brussels, with his powerful local family interest, represented Lancashire. Sitting in the Cavalier Parliament were ex-conspirators and agents like Daniel O'Neill, Sir Edward Massey and John Heath, as well as plain country gentry like Sir Ralph Verney and Thomas Mompesson.[21]

Different factional allegiances and different generations were also represented by the returned exiles who sat in the Commons after the Restoration. Supporters of the Lord Chancellor, with friendships established during the grim days of exile, for example Henry Seymour and Gervase Holles, were present at Westminster, but so were some of his most bitter enemies among the emigrés, including Sir John Marlay, MP for Newcastle, and the two 'Swordsmen' Sir Charles Wheeler and Edmund Wyndham. The younger generation of the exiles, including several sons who had accompanied or joined their fathers in exile, were also represented in the Cavalier Parliament: two of Ormonde's sons, the Earl of Ossory and Lord Richard Butler; two sons of the Chancellor, Henry and Lawrence Hyde; and the Secretary's two sons, Edward and John Nicholas.[22]

Of course, the returned exiles were also represented in the House of Lords. There were 31 peers among the 'long-term' exiles if we include those who were granted peerages by Charles II during the 1650s.[23] Twenty-one of them survived their years in exile to take their seats in the House of Lords after the Restoration, although in a couple of cases, those of lords Culpepper and Finch, not for long. Several of these noblemen, notably Buckingham, Bristol, St Albans and Gerard, were to play a significant, not to say turbulent, part in the political events of the reign of Charles II. But an assessment of how the years in exile influenced the political activities of those returned exiles who sat in post-restoration parliaments must wait until the next chapter.

In addition to being extremely well represented both at court and in Parliament, the returned exiles can also be found occupying a wide range of government offices while at the same time benefiting from a variety of grants, pensions and annuities of different kinds. Not surprisingly, Daniel O'Neill was very well rewarded for his twenty years of arduous and often dangerous service to the Stuarts. As well as being a groom of the bedchamber and MP for St Ives in the Cavalier Parliament, in March 1663 he was appointed Postmaster General, an office that carried with it various monopolies, for example on the carrying of letters to the colonies, and was potentially extremely profitable. There is an appropriate irony in O'Neill becoming Postmaster General, the office recently held by John Thurloe, the man who had tried so hard over a number of years to frustrate O'Neill's letter-carrying activities. Other appointments and grants were also showered on O'Neill: a commission in the King's troop in the Royal Regiment of Horse, a share in the coveted monopoly on the manufacture of gunpowder, an annuity of £500 drawn on the Irish treasury, grants of land and other property in London, the custody of St James's Palace and Park, as well as interests in activities as diverse as digging for mines north of the Trent and in Wales to the regulation of ale-houses. O'Neill married Catherine Wotton, his close friend of the days of exile in Holland. He was her third husband, she having been at different times Lady Stanhope, Madame Heenvliet and finally Countess of Chesterfield. Together they built Belsize House at Hampstead, 'at vast expense', according to Evelyn, while she also inherited a country estate in Kent. With his duties at court and in Parliament, and his wide range of entrepreneurial activities, by the early 1660s the 'Great O'Neill', as Pepys called him, was one of the most prominent, and possibly wealthiest, men in London. It remains strange, especially considering Charles II's generosity in this area, that he never received a title.[24]

Along with O'Neill, who was both Postmaster General and a captain in one of the King's regiments of guards, other returned exiles can also be found occupying a wide range of government offices and military and naval positions. The most important probably was the remarkable Sir Stephen Fox, who used his office as Paymaster of the Forces from 1661 to 1676, and again by proxy in 1679–80, to establish the foundation of his great fortune. Fox was a genuinely self-made man, whose ability and energy enabled him to become immensely wealthy while at the same time he managed to preserve his reputation for probity and decency. According to Evelyn, his wealth was 'honestly got and unenvied, which is a near miracle'.[25]

One very important government department which provided employment for a number of returned exiles was the Navy Office. Samuel Pepys was surrounded, sometimes to his discomfort and irritation, by Cavaliers who had been in exile in the 1650s. At the top were James, Duke of York, the Lord Admiral, and Prince Rupert, whose privateering adventures in exile in the early 1650s were the basis for his new career as an admiral in the Dutch wars. The Treasurer was Sir George Carteret, who returned from exile in Paris not to Jersey but to England, where he could better take advantage of the King's gratitude for his loyalty and services. The Comptroller was the elderly Sir John Mennes, who had sailed under Rupert in the Mediterranean in 1650; he was highly educated and cultured, although Pepys deplored his incompetence. The commissioners included Hyde's old friend turned enemy, Lord Berkeley and the very capable Sir William Coventry. In addition to being represented strongly in the administration of the navy, returned exiles were also present among the naval officers with whom Pepys had to deal. Prominent among them were the Duke of York's protegé Richard Nicolls, who captured New Amsterdam in 1664 but was killed in the battle of Sole Bay eight years later, and the redoubtable Sir Robert Holmes, who had sailed with Rupert on his privateering voyage to the West Indies in 1652, and who caused Pepys considerable anxiety 'because of the old business he attempted upon my wife'.[26]

As so many of the exiled Cavaliers had fought in the civil wars, and then maintained themselves in exile by service in various continental armies or in the King's Flanders regiments, it is not surprising that many of them considered some form of military or naval employment after the Restoration to be the most appropriate reward for their loyalty and sacrifices. Of our 170 returned 'long-term' exiles, at least 29 and probably more received some kind of military or naval post within two or three years of the Restoration. Some of the appointments can be seen

purely as rewards, commissions that were decorative and prestigious, sources of income and opportunities for patronage rather than intended to advance a professional career. O'Neill's captaincy of the King's troop in the Royal Regiment of Horse is in this category, as by 1660 his military career was really over. Other examples of appointments of this kind are Wentworth's commission as colonel of the Royal Regiment of Guards and Gerard's as colonel of the first troop of Lifeguards.[27] But to professional naval men like Sir Robert Holmes or soldiers like Sir William Leighton and Sir John Skelton, the commissions they received were the basis for their careers after 1660. After fighting a duel with Nicholas Armorer in Holland in 1652, Colonel Leighton, a professional soldier, had briefly entered the Swedish service. He was one of a number of Cavaliers who returned to England early in 1658 in anticipation of the royalist rising being planned to break out in the spring of that year, only to be arrested and imprisoned for some months. Claiming to be an 'indigent officer' at the Restoration, Leighton was rewarded for his loyalty and hardships with a commission as captain in the King's Foot Guards. Captain John Skelton was another in the crowd of obscure royalist officers in exile in the Netherlands in the 1650s. Although never achieving the prominence of an Armorer or a Stephens, he was occasionally employed as a courier during the 1650s, communicating between Sir John Grenville, who was generally accepted as the most influential royalist conspirator in the west country, and the exiled court. In March 1658 one of Thurloe's informers reported that 'Captain Skelton, an officer in Breda' was active in planning the insurrection that, as we know, disintegrated into arrests, reprisals and the hasty flight of agents and conspirators back to the continent. After the Restoration, and probably partly thanks to his patron Grenville, now Earl of Bath, Groom of the Stole, and a great man at court, Skelton received his reward: a knighthood and, doing a little better than Leighton, a commission as major in the Foot Guards.[28]

The newly ordered and restructured English regiments were not the only potential source of commissions for returned exiles with military experience. There was also Ireland. To Ormonde, that most distinguished – in all senses of the word – of the exiled Cavaliers fell some of the greatest rewards: a dukedom, the Lord Lieutenancy of Ireland, several court offices including that of Lord Steward and compensation in land and money for his huge losses in the royalist cause. The creation and organisation of a loyal Irish army was one of the Lord Lieutenant's responsibilities, a duty that carried with it considerable opportunities for patronage. In the distribution of commissions and

appointments, those two faithful agents and clients of Ormonde, Stephens and Armorer, were not overlooked. Sir John Stephens was appointed Governor of Dublin castle, a major in the Irish Guards and 'Customer and Collector' for the ports of Waterford and Ross, an office once held by his father. Stephens also received several grants of confiscated land in different counties. This was partly a consequence of Ormonde's generosity, but he also benefited from being one of the '1649 Officers', those Irish Protestants who had adhered to the royalist cause after the execution of Charles I and who were rewarded for their loyalty by grants of confiscated land in Donegal.[29] Armorer's prospects also seem to have become increasingly centred on Ireland, as he moved steadily further into Ormonde's extensive clientage network. As well as being knighted in 1662, he was granted confiscated land to the value of £200 a year, and was appointed both to a captaincy in the Irish Guards and to the post of Lieutenant Governor of Duncannon fort, which guarded the entrance to the Passage, the estuary that led to Waterford.[30]

The rewards bestowed on Armorer are a minor illustration of the belief held by Charles II and some of his English courtiers that Ireland provided almost limitless opportunities for the King to meet his obligations to his companions in exile. Titles, offices and grants of land were bestowed generously on both Irish and English returned exiles, in particular on companions of Charles and clients of Ormonde. Lord Taaffe, one of the 'men of pleasure' about the King whose influence Hyde had so much deplored, was created Earl of Carlingford in June 1661, with his new dignity supported by lavish land grants, partly of confiscated estates. Sir George Lane, Ormonde's secretary, who with his wife and child had endured acute poverty and distress during their time in exile, rose to become Secretary of War and Secretary of State for Ireland and ended his days as Viscount Lanesborough. As well as his annuity drawn on the Irish Treasury, Daniel O'Neill also received land grants in Ulster, ironically of estates confiscated from branches of the O'Neills who had taken part in the 1641 rebellion. In his instruction to the Irish Lords Justices to authorise the grants, Charles stressed that O'Neill had 'merited our consideration by his loyalty to King Charles I and his service to us abroad'.[31]

Not all the returned exiles who benefited from Charles II's generosity in distributing the resources of Ireland had the links with that country enjoyed by men like Lane and Taaffe, Stephens and Armorer. Prominent among the beneficiaries of grants drawn on the Irish establishment, sometimes to the despair of the Lord Lieutenant, were some of the

King's closest companions, including certain of the bedchamber men. In December 1663 Ormonde received an order from the King that lands to the value of £2,000 a year should be 'set out' for the royal favourite Charles Berkeley, Lord Fitzhardinge. Nicholas's successor as Secretary of State, Sir Henry Bennet received a land grant in January 1664 which, according to his friend Ormonde, was 'worth much more than £10,000 if it prove good'. In the same month Charles ordered that his old companion from Jersey and Scotland, Ned Progers, should receive £5,000 to be 'taken from the sums paid in by adventurers and soldiers in consideration of confirmation of their estates'. Similar grants, either of land or of revenue drawn on the Irish customs, were made to other courtiers, for example, to Marmaduke Darcy, Henry Coventry and the bedchamberman William Legge. The grant to Legge illustrates the optimistic and unrealistic belief in the limitless resources of Ireland that was current at Whitehall; the royal instruction was that Legge should be given '3,000 acres of profitable land in Connaught'![32]

Ireland did not provide much in the way of governorships, another form of reward presented to some returned exiles, although there were some places available. Armorer's appointment as Lieutenant Governor of Duncannon fort has been mentioned above. Sir Faithful Fortescue, whose principal if not only claim to fame was his dramatic defection from the parliamentary to the royalist side at the head of his troop of cavalry at the beginning of the battle of Edgehill, was an English Cavalier with strong connections with Ireland. He served in the Irish wars under Ormonde's command, then joined Charles II in Scotland in 1651, fought at Worcester and escaped from that 'fatal day' to France. He then spent most of the 1650s in exile in the Netherlands. His rewards after the Restoration included a grant of £1,000 in 1664 and the governorship of Carrickfergus castle in Ulster.[33]

Other governorships, more valuable than Duncannon or Carrickfergus, were awarded to returned exiles more prominent than Armorer or Fortescue. General Sir Edward Massey appropriately became Governor of Gloucester, the town he had defended heroically for Parliament during the Civil War and plotted unsuccessfully to seize for the King on several occasions during the 1650s. He also represented Gloucester in the Cavalier Parliament. Sir Edward Brett, a professional soldier, was a veteran of both the first and second civil wars and spent the 1650s principally in Holland. Appointed to the household position of Serjeant Porter in 1660, he then became Governor of York in 1664, in the aftermath of the Derwentdale plot when the government was taking seriously rumours of a republican rising being planned to break

out in the north. In contrast to these two governorships, highly appropriate in Massey's case and understandable from a military point of view in Brett's, Lord Hatton's appointment in May 1662 as Governor of Guernsey, an island with which he had no connection and had possibly never visited, can be seen purely as a reward. It was a dignity, both prestigious and profitable, presented to a royalist of high rank; his peerage may have been of more relevance to his receiving this appointment than his years of exile in Paris.[34]

Diplomatic appointments would seem to have been a very appropriate way of rewarding Cavaliers whose time in exile had forced them to acquire at least some familiarity with foreign values and customs. Either as resident ambassadors or as envoys on specific missions, a number of royalists did return to the countries in which they had spent some of their exile. Years of travelling and living in foreign countries had left them well suited to diplomatic careers. So Henry Jermyn, Earl of St Albans, returned to Paris, a city which he knew extremely well, within a year of the Restoration. Sir Richard Fanshawe, who was appointed Master of Requests at the Restoration but did not receive the Secretaryship for which he had hoped, returned to Lisbon as ambassador to Portugal in 1662 and was then transferred to Madrid in 1664 as ambassador to Spain. Both Jermyn and Fanshawe had developed strong cultural attachments to those countries that had received them as exiles, and they were not the only ones. Sir William Swan had spent much of the 1650s in Hamburg and had served on several of Charles's money raising missions to different German princes. Made a gentleman of the privy chamber in the enlarged court at the Restoration, during the 1660s Swan returned to Germany as envoy to Hamburg and other north German towns. The cultivated Sir Charles Cotterell, Master of Ceremonies at both the courts of Charles I and Charles II, also had the opportunity in 1663 to renew his familiarity with Brussels when he was appointed ambassador to the Spanish Netherlands.[35]

Partly as a consequence of the tortuous foreign policy of Charles II, there were several specific diplomatic missions entrusted to Cavaliers who had been in exile. Henry Coventry, who had accompanied Lord Wentworth to Denmark back in 1654, was employed on several of these embassies. When he undertook his diplomatic mission to Sweden in 1664, he took his fellow returned exile Thomas Ross with him as his secretary. Three years later he accompanied Lord Holles to the peace negotiations at Breda in 1667 which concluded the second Dutch War before returning to Sweden on another embassy in 1671. The Anglican divine, John Bargrave, one of the most widely travelled of all royalists,

especially in the Mediterranean countries, was sent to Algiers in 1662 to negotiate the freeing of English slaves held by the corsairs. Those two other trusted and well rewarded Cavaliers, Daniel O'Neill and Sir Nicholas Armorer, both returned to Holland on several occasions during the 1660s on personal or semi-diplomatic missions for Charles II or Clarendon.[36]

The evidence therefore is overwhelming that very many Cavaliers who went into exile after the civil wars and survived until the Restoration were rewarded by Charles II's government for their loyalty and their sacrifices. The rewards took a variety of forms: places in the enlarged Stuart households or in different government or administrative departments, commissions in the armed forces, diplomatic postings and governorships, knighthoods and peerages and a wide range of grants, pensions and annuities. Although one can argue that some returned exiles, like Charles Berkeley, were grossly over rewarded, the needs of some deserving cases, which could easily have been overlooked, did in fact receive some recognition. For example, Colonel Thomas Blague, the soldier, part-time conspirator and Groom of the Bedchamber, who was seriously wounded at the battle of the Dunes, did not live long enough to enjoy the rewards of his loyalty, dying only a few months after the Restoration. However, in March 1661 his widow Mary was awarded an annuity of £500. In a similar situation, the children of the Cornish royalist Joseph Jane, who died in exile in Holland in 1658, his wife having previously died in England, were granted in August 1660 the lease of a small estate in Liskeard, the borough in Cornwall which Jane had represented in the Long Parliament. In February 1661, another orphan from a royalist family divided by exile, the unhappy Honora Harding, was granted an annuity of £300.[37]

Among the enormous number of petitions and grants that comprise such a substantial portion of the state papers during the early 1660s, it is easy to lose sight of these modest awards to fairly insignificant persons like Mary Blague or Honora Harding. This is especially likely when the focus, both of contemporaries then and of historians since, tends to be on excessively well rewarded royal favourites in contrast to neglected 'poor Cavaliers'. Of course, pensions and annuities, not to mention wages, were not paid regularly in the England of Charles II, while the official estimates of the income likely to be derived from the various grants of land awarded to royalists in Ireland also need to be viewed with a certain healthy scepticism.

Although it is clear that many returned exiles were well rewarded for their loyalty, some were much more generously rewarded than others

and some missed out completely. It is apparent that those who did well when the prizes of power and office were distributed belonged predominantly to one or more of three groups. The first group of principal beneficiaries from the Restoration were the courtiers, especially those who had been companions of the King on his travels or who had acquired influential and powerful patrons, notably York and Rupert, Clarendon and Ormonde. The courtiers, apart from the official emoluments of their particular offices in the household, were well placed to benefit from occasional further displays of royal generosity or gratitude. One hopes that the hard to please Elizabeth Elliot was gratified when her husband Thomas, one of the grooms of the bedchamber, acquired the additional office of Master of the Privy Harriers with its salary of £500 a year. Another beneficiary of royal generosity was the quarrelsome equerry William Armorer, who received a knighthood, an unsolicited gift of £500 from the King in November 1670 and appointment to the bench of magistrates in Reading, where he could satisfy his aggressive and violent temperament in vindictive harassing of the local nonconformists.[38] Of course, the various gifts, grants and titles showered on certain favoured courtiers, one thinks in particular of men like O'Neill, Progers and Berkeley, were not simply the rewards of a grateful monarch for their loyal endurance of the difficult and sometimes dangerous years of exile; the most generous rewards tended to go to the courtiers whose company Charles most enjoyed.

Those exiled Cavaliers who belonged to prominent aristocratic landed families were a second group of notable beneficiaries of the Restoration. As a number of them were also members of traditional court families, there is some overlap between the two groups. The dukedoms awarded to Ormonde and Newcastle were appropriate rewards to two totally loyal royalist grandees who endured long periods in exile. Various Seymours, Howards, Berties, Berkeleys and Villiers who had been in exile also feature prominently among the holders of court and administrative offices under Charles II. Some have been mentioned already in this chapter, like John, Lord Berkeley, the navy commissioner, and his nephew Charles. Henry Seymour, who resumed his post as a groom of the bedchamber at the Restoration, also acquired in 1660 the additional office of Clerk of the Hanaper. Montagu Bertie, Earl of Lindsey, who had been one of the group of exiled royalists who gathered in the Loire valley in the late 1640s, was confirmed as a Privy Councillor and became Lord Lieutenant of Lincolnshire in 1660. Examples of this kind can easily be multiplied. They reflect the concern of the new regime to con-

solidate the support of the great aristocratic families as much as the desire to reward those royalists who had been in exile.[39]

The third group of returned emigrés who were particularly well rewarded at the King's return were those whose services to the royalist cause during the years of exile had been particularly noteworthy. Obviously, there is again some overlap between groups. Daniel O'Neill, for example, was a courtier, soldier, conspirator, diplomat, courier, general 'fixer' and close personal friend of both Charles II and Ormonde. The most striking example of someone in this group is Stephen Fox, whose efficient management of the extraordinarily difficult financial affairs of the exiled court provided the foundation on which he built his spectacular career after the Restoration. During their years in exile Henry Bennet and Henry Coventry, Ormonde's secretary George Lane, and the agents Nicholas Armorer and John Stephens all in different ways won the approval of the King, Ormonde or Hyde, and then used the practical demonstrations of this regard to further their careers when they returned to England.

Who then among the returned exiles received no reward for their loyalty and their sacrifices? The Cavaliers whose hopes and expectations were most likely to be overlooked were the 'short-term' exiles, or those who had avoided the court and so failed to attract the notice and patronage of the King and his principal advisers. Those who did not become involved in conspiracy, or join the royalist forces raised in Flanders, or who were hostile to the predominance of Hyde and Ormonde in the royal councils were also likely to miss out when the rewards and favours were distributed. There are some obscure figures, like George Cock of Newcastle, who stated in his apparently unsuccessful petition on 25 June 1660 that 'in pursuant of his loyalty he left this kingdom and hath for eleven years remained abroad', but who seems to have left no surviving evidence of his activities in exile during those eleven years. The adventurous traveller John Page, who claimed in his letters to Hyde that his travels had reduced him to acute poverty, also seems to have been unsuccessful in his request for a menial position in the royal household.[40]

It is useful in this context to compare the very different treatment received at the Restoration by six junior or middle ranking ex-officers in the royalist forces during the Civil War: George Barnes, Thomas Carnaby, Thomas Paulden, William Leighton, John Skelton and Nicholas Armorer. None of them had aristocratic or court connections and they all turned up in Holland in the late 1640s and early 1650s.

George Barnes had served under Prince Maurice in the west country in the Civil War, rising to the rank of colonel of foot. Claiming to have lived 13 years in exile in Holland and Italy, he petitioned in August 1660 for the place of Bailiff and Verger of Sandwich. Apparently unsuccessful in this request, in December he addressed another petition to General Monck for a foot company in a new regiment, at a time when Monck was hard pressed to find posts for his own officers. Major Thomas Carnaby was one of a strongly royalist Catholic family established in Northumberland. He rode with the Northern Horse under Langdale and also fought at Naseby. In exile in the 1650s, when as we have seen, he was at one time stranded in Paris 'in danger to perish from want of bread and clothing', he was employed by Langdale in various royalist plots in northern England, and also seems to have obtained a commission in one of the King's Flanders regiments. Despite this impressive record of royalist activity over a long period, he does not seem to have received any rewards at the Restoration. Instead he returned to the north of England, only to be killed in a duel in York in 1665. Like Carnaby, Thomas Paulden also belonged to a strongly royalist family from northern England, Yorkshire in his case. Two of his brothers died during the second Civil War in 1648, while Thomas and another brother Gregory, who were both in the garrison at Pontefract, went into exile. Thomas's letter to his father, justifying his decision, in which he refers to the promise of 'a person of great quality' to take a particular care of him, with the hope of a future 'raise in fortune', has already been quoted in Chapter 5. Again like Carnaby, Paulden and his brother were employed as couriers within the royalist resistance movement. In a letter written to a friend in his old age Paulden related how he had 'followed the fortune of King Charles in his exile, and was sent into England on several occasions for his majesty's service'. This letter refers to the Duke of Buckingham as having been Paulden's patron but there is no evidence of that erratic nobleman having done anything for his client. As with Carnaby, he seems to have been unrewarded for his services at the Restoration, although his brother Gregory's petition in 1662 to be given the fee liable to 'the making of a Baronet' was granted.[41]

Lieutenant Colonel Sir William Leighton's war record was probably the most impressive of these six officers and his treatment at the Restoration was a little more generous. He fought in a number of campaigns throughout the Civil War, from Edgehill to Naseby, and was knighted by Charles I in September 1645. Leighton was in the garrison of Colchester in 1648 but in exile in Holland by 1650. In the late 1650s

he resumed his old career as a professional soldier, joining the Swedish service like his fellow exile William Vavasour. More fortunate than Vavasour, he survived to return to England and was commissioned, but only as a captain, in the King's Foot Guards in 1660. In striking contrast to Barnes, Carnaby, Paulden and to a lesser extent Leighton, their fellow exiles Armorer and Skelton, whose social class backgrounds, military records in the civil wars and experiences in exile were similar, were rewarded with knighthoods and various offices and military posts, and, in Armorer's case, a place in the royal household. One possible explanation for the differences in the treatment of these exiled Cavaliers is the role, impossible now to assess, of character and personality. Nicholas Armorer certainly seems to have been very good at getting on with people. He was also clearly both ambitious and resourceful. Although a Northumbrian, unlike Carnaby and Paulden he did not quietly go back to the north country on his return from exile but instead successfully established his career at court and in Ireland.

The differences in the treatment of these royalist ex-officers can also largely be explained by the extent to which they were favoured by influential patrons. Barnes seems to have had none. His Civil War commander Prince Maurice was dead and he seems not to have attracted the notice of any of the leading exiled royalists. The fortunes of the north countrymen Carnaby and Paulden were to some extent linked to those of Langdale, who was himself out of favour with the powerful figures at court, and in any case died in 1661. To what extent Buckingham actually promised to bring about a 'raise in fortune' for Tom Paulden we cannot know, but that unstable and erratic nobleman was notorious for failing to deliver on his promises. In any case, neither Langdale nor Buckingham seems to have exercised effective patronage in Paulden or Carnaby's interests. By contrast, John Skelton seems to have enjoyed the support of Sir John Grenville, Earl of Bath, Groom of the Stole and holder of many other offices both at court and in the west country, while Armorer, during his adventurous career, acquired a series of influential patrons. As an obscure captain in Holland in 1653 he first attracted the favourable notice of Nicholas, then switched patrons in favour of Hyde, for a time worked also for Mordaunt, and eventually finished his career within Ormonde's extensive clientage network.

It was therefore quite possible for returned exiles who were already alienated from an administration dominated by Hyde, Ormonde and their allies, or who were obscure and lacking in influential patrons, to be overlooked in the distribution of rewards and favours at the Restoration. But the examples of returned exiles who were unrewarded need to

be set against the very large number whose interests and expectations were cared for, in a wide variety of ways, as part of the Restoration settlement. In the distribution of rewards and favours, Cavaliers who went into exile seem to have, on the whole, done significantly better than those who remained in England and conformed peacefully to the different Commonwealth regimes.

14

The Brand of the Emigré

> The brand of the emigré is stamped on the generation after 1660.
>
> (Sir Keith Feiling)[1]

The view of the early twentieth century historian of the Tory party, that Restoration political life was characterised by 'a fierce un-English bitterness towards opponents . . . [by] personal feuds in the royal party [and by] the depravity of public as of private morals' is still widely held, although perhaps with reservations about this behaviour being particularly 'un-English'. To Sir Keith Feiling 'the brand of the emigré is stamped on the generation after 1660' and these evils were the direct consequence of the royalist emigration. They were the result of 'a dozen years of starved dependence upon foreign courts, of political schemes divorced from any contact with political reality, of the eternal temptations besetting a party in exile, which sees its women and children hungry, and its homes in others' hands'.[2]

Is it possible to identify a distinctive emigré group in the England of the 1660s, a group holding particular ideas and values that were shaped by their experience of exile? To answer this question we have to determine whether any sense of a group identity, any acceptance of common sets of values, attitudes or loyalties, existed among the returned exiles. There are several possible lines of approach. By examining political groupings at court or in the Cavalier Parliament we may be able to determine whether there were any noticeable concentrations of returned exiles within particular factions or in support of particular policies. A study of clientage networks may show the existence of patterns of friendship or alliance that linked together royalists who had shared the experience of exile. Can one see any evidence of the existence of a sense

197

of group loyalty among those royalists who had refused to acknowledge the authority of Commonwealth or Protector, but had chosen instead to share the rigours and discomforts of exile? Finally, is there any evidence that the returned exiles were a particularly intolerant and dissolute group of men and women, embittered and coarsened by their experiences, and consequently significant contributors to the 'intense factional intrigues' of the 'profane, irreverent and hedonistic court over which Charles presided'?[3]

The evidence on which answers to these questions can be based is fragmentary and partial but a number of conclusions can be drawn. As far as determining the political loyalties and factional allegiances of the returned exiles is concerned, it is clear that the great majority of those who went into Parliament or who obtained positions in the government were identified with the court interest, irrespective of whether or not they occupied places in the royal household. From the Restoration to the Exclusion Crisis, returned exiles who sat in the various parliaments of Charles II are consistently listed as 'court dependants'. Although death removed some of them, like O'Neill suddenly in 1664, many of the familiar names of returned exiles who were elected to the Cavalier Parliament in 1661 were still there during the crisis years 1679–81, categorised on the voting lists of the Whig Earl of Shaftesbury as 'vile' for their opposition to the bills to exclude James, Duke of York from the succession to the throne. Some even stood against the tide of anti-Catholic hysteria generated by the Popish Plot. Ned Progers opposed the impeachment of the embattled Lord Treasurer, the Earl of Danby in 1679 and then ended his parliamentary career with a speech in defence of Sir George Jeffreys, the Recorder of London, who had made the unpopular decision to respite the execution of three convicted Jesuits.[4]

There were, of course, some exceptions to this pattern of a close relationship between the returned exiles and the court. Knighted in 1662, Sir Thomas Mompesson, who during his years of exile in Caen had been a regular correspondent of Secretary Nicholas, was MP first for Wilton and then for Salisbury. A close friend of the Nicholas family – Sir Edward's son John also represented Wilton – Mompesson seems to have cut his links with the court when the Secretary was forced to retire.[5] The best-known example of a returned exile, prominent courtier and royal favourite who moved eventually into opposition is the flamboyant, witty but essentially unstable and ultimately unreliable George Villiers, Duke of Buckingham. The most unusual example is surely Captain Silas Titus, who was a client of Buckingham's during one phase of his extremely varied career. After fighting for Parliament in the Civil War,

Titus, a Presbyterian, became a royalist in the late 1640s. In exile in the 1650s he was active in a series of conspiracies, frequently as an associate of his fellow Presbyterian and ex-parliamentarian Edward Massey, although he was also employed as an agent by Mordaunt. Rewarded with the much coveted post of Groom of the Bedchamber at the Restoration, Titus resigned from this position in 1675, an extremely unusual action, and by 1679 had joined the ranks of the exclusionists. But Buckingham and Titus were both very unusual men and very unorthodox royalists. The allegiance of the great majority of Cavaliers who had been in exile and who were active in political life after 1660 was to the court.[6]

This identification with the court interest by the majority of returned exiles in the Cavalier Parliament was underlined by the dependence of many of them on the places, pensions, grants and titles that flowed from the royal bounty. This close connection between the emigrés and the court certainly contributed to fears of the possible consequences of an unconditional restoration of the monarchy; a fear expressed by Pepys on his visit to the Hague in May 1660 when he observed that the courtiers were 'growing high' with nothing now 'to hinder them and the king from doing what they have a mind'.[7] The journalist Marchamont Nedham's pamphlet, *News from Brussels*, which appeared in March 1660 and purported to be a letter from 'a near Attendant on his Majesty's Person' to a friend in London, played on the fear of an unrestrained campaign for revenge by bloodthirsty Cavaliers. *News from Brussels* ridiculed the notion of any prospect of a genuine reconciliation, promised that traitors would 'feel the scourge that loyal hearts lash rebels with', rejected the idea of mercy for parliamentarians as 'more hateful . . . than hell', and looked forward to cutting 'a passage to the throne through traitors' blood'. Not surprisingly, this lurid picture of an imminent Cavalier terror prompted not only a hunt for the author and printer of the pamphlet but also outraged rebuttals that strongly rejected the idea that the royalists were looking forward to a bloody revenge on their old opponents. For example, in *The Declaration of the Nobility, Knights and Gentry of Oxford* the signatories, headed by the Earl of Lindsey, himself a returned exile, disowned 'all purposes of private revenge' and swore 'to forget all names of difference' in the interest of achieving a general reconciliation.[8]

Although a gross exaggeration, written as a last desperate attempt to derail the apparently irresistible rush towards a restoration of the monarchy, Nedham's *News from Brussels* attempted to dramatise and emphasise the views of the 'high prerogative men' within the royalist party, while at the same time ignoring those who supported the

moderate and constitutional settlement envisaged in the Declaration of Breda. On the controversial issues of defining limits to the royal prerogative or establishing the exact nature of the relationship between monarch and parliament there was no view common to the returned exiles as a group. In so far as it is possible to make any useful distinction between the 'high prerogative men' who favoured strengthening the powers of the crown, the constitutional royalists who supported the principles contained in the Declaration of Breda and the King's favoured companions, the essentially non-political 'men of pleasure', Cavaliers who had been in exile can be found in all three groups. Despite the concern of some contemporaries, it is difficult to believe that Charles II was surrounded by courtiers committed to making him an absolute monarch.[9] Those who surrounded the King tended to be disapproved of for other reasons. On the evening of 22 February 1664 Pepys and 'Mr Alsopp the King's Brewer' spent an hour together 'talking and bewailing the posture of things at present'. In particular they were concerned that 'the King is led away by half a dozen men, that none of his serious servants and friends can come at him. These are Lodderdale [*sic*], Buckingham, Hamilton, Fitzharding . . . Projers [*sic*] is another, and Sir H. Bennet.'[10]

The concern of Pepys and Mr Alsopp is not so much over the political views that might have been expressed by Charles's chosen companions but that they were not suitably 'serious' company for a monarch. But what Pepys does not mention is that, with the exception of the Scottish John Maitland, Duke of Lauderdale, who spent most of the 1650s in prison following his capture after the battle of Worcester, all of these companions of the King in 1664 had also been his companions in exile. There are many reasons, as well as their capacity for witty and indecent conversation, why Charles may have valued their company.[11]

The most spectacular division among the MPs who had been in exile was not over the political and constitutional implications of the monarchy having been restored without conditions but over the dismissal and impeachment in 1667 of the greatest royalist emigré of them all, Edward Hyde, Earl of Clarendon. Although the Lord Chancellor had loyal friends among the returned exiles in the Cavalier Parliament, notably Henry Coventry, Sir George Carteret, Sir Stephen Fox and Henry Seymour, this group also included some of his most bitter enemies. Prominent among them were Henry Bennet, created Earl of Arlington in 1663, and the Duke of Buckingham in the Lords, and Sir William Coventry, Edmund Wyndham and Sir Charles Wheeler in the Commons.[12] The fall of Clarendon was caused by a number of factors,

ranging from holding him responsible for the humiliating reverses suffered in the Dutch war to the intrigues of the King's mistress Lady Castlemaine, none of which had anything to do with the royalist emigration. But the nature of a particular MP's experience of exile certainly did help determine in some cases whether he either stood by or turned on the Chancellor as his power crumbled. Stephen Fox, whose own position in 1667 was not all that secure and who had no great landed or aristocratic interest behind him, remained loyal to the man who had done so much to lift him from obscurity. On the other hand, 'Swordsmen' followers of Prince Rupert, like Thomas Elliot's father-in-law Colonel Edmund Wyndham and Colonel Sir Charles Wheeler, an officer in one of the royalist regiments in Flanders in the 1650s, now had the opportunity for revenge on the man they held responsible for their exclusion from the royal councils for so many years.

A significant element in the fall of Clarendon was his disdain for the business of 'managing' Parliament and his failure to develop his own extensive patronage network. Hyde's personal history during his years in exile is studded with broken friendships, for example with John Berkeley and George Digby, and with the alienation of able and potential allies like William Coventry and Henry Bennet. In 1655, in exile in Paris, Bennet had been so 'happy that by Marquis of Ormonde's and Sir Edward Hyde's sudden favour he is so well with the King', but by the early 1660s he had become a bitter enemy of the Chancellor. Ann Fanshawe also blamed Clarendon, 'that false man', for the failure of her husband to become a Secretary of State at the Restoration, being appointed Master of Requests and ambassador to Portugal instead. This disappointment at not receiving the Secretaryship, which he believed he had been promised, turned Fanshawe against his old patron. Even the way Clarendon let a comparatively minor figure like Nicholas Armorer, who had looked to the Chancellor for patronage and protection in the late 1650s, drift into Ormonde's clientage network by the Restoration, further illustrates his neglect of this essential element of political life in the reign of Charles II.[13]

The Duke of Ormonde, with his royal household office of Lord Steward and his Lord Lieutenancy of Ireland, was, as we have seen already in his relationship with some of his clients like Lane and Stephens, well placed to develop extensive patronage ties among those Cavaliers who had shared his exile. It was natural for many of them to look to him for 'fortune and favour', as did the well travelled diplomat and soldier Sir Gilbert Talbot, for example, who owed his court office of Master of the Jewel House to Ormonde's patronage, although 'not

202 The Cavaliers in Exile

without strong opposition from Lord Chancellor Hyde who had showed himself his enemy upon other occasions'.[14] Ormonde's patronage network did not rest only on his power to distribute 'fortune and favour'; it was extended and strengthened by other ties also: friendship, marriage, the memories of shared dangers and ordeals. Ormonde's bonds to men like O'Neill and Stephens, who had fought under him in Ireland in the 1640s and dodged with him Thurloe's informers and Protectorate soldiers in the back streets of London in 1658, had a strength that went well beyond what was customary between a patron and his clients.

The extensive ties of Ormonde's clientage network linked together a varied collection of returned exiles while at the same time cutting across the divisions of factional allegiance. As has been discussed in Chapter 7, Ormonde's faithful secretary Sir George Lane, knighted at Bruges in 1657 and finally awarded a peerage in 1676, had married in March 1655 Susan Nicholas, the daughter of Ormonde's friend and ally Secretary Nicholas. In a letter to the under Secretary of State, Sir Joseph Williamson, on 2 July 1667, Lane referred to 'your good friend and mine Sir Nicholas Armorer'. Returned exiles like Lane, Nicholas, O'Neill, Bennet, Stephens, Armorer and Henry Coventry were all in different ways attached to Ormonde. O'Neill was a regular correspondent of Ormonde's, sending him the latest court gossip and scandal, but also sometimes acting as a broker or intermediary between the Duke and the King, on at least one occasion over an appointment to an Irish office requested by Bennet.[15] Despite his replacement of Lane's father-in-law Nicholas as Secretary of State and his active role in the downfall of Ormonde's old friend Clarendon, Bennet, or Earl of Arlington as he became in 1663, seems to have maintained friendly relations with Ormonde and his following. 'I must again thank you for the favours shown to me whilst I was at court,' wrote Lane to Arlington on 26 August 1665, 'and assure you of my affection and respect on all occasions.' The private letters among these returned exiles and with Williamson suggest that their ties with each other as well as with Ormonde were stronger than the conventional links between a patron who disbursed offices and favours and a dependant client who received them. 'I have spent all this buckhunting season with your brother Secretary [Henry] Coventry at his lodge in Envile chase', wrote Armorer to Williamson on 23 September 1673. 'I hope he will do well, for he is a worthy and pleasant man. My Lord Arlington and he are very well together, and serve their master as they ought; they are both Lord Ormonde's friends and he theirs.'[16]

Nicholas Armorer was clearly a cheerful and convivial fellow – one of Williamson's correspondents refers to his 'fluency of drollery' – and his letters convey something of the flavour of life, both at court and in the vice-regal world in Ireland. As a royal equerry Armorer sometimes attended on Charles II, who was notorious for his capacity to rise early despite the demands of the previous night. One note to Williamson, hastily scrawled at Newmarket, begins: 'It is 4 a.m. and the King is going into his coach a-foxhunting.' Armorer had a cynical view of 'the crowd, hurry and business' of the court, 'one week making private friendships, and before the month ends, breaking them like glass never to be patched up again'. But his picture of his life in Ireland as a trusted follower of Ormonde is free of this cynicism. His correspondence is full of enthusiastic references to horse racing, theatrical performances, wine, women and song. 'We have here . . . cheerful company; ill wine and not bad women', he wrote to Williamson from Dublin on 9 May 1663. 'If you distrust, come and see.' He refers to dining with his old friend and fellow agent Stephens and spending Christmas at Kilkenny castle with the Ormonde family, whom obviously he admired greatly. 'I came from thence [Kilkenny] on Friday to wait upon the best woman in this world', wrote Armorer to Arlington on 11 September 1665, 'the excellent lady of Ossory, who with some of her infantry goes tomorrow to join with that great and good family.' The same note of familiarity and friendship is apparent in the letters of O'Neill, Lane, Arlington and Henry Coventry, both to Ormonde and to each other.[17] In this correspondence there is little sense of bitterness, whether 'un-English' or otherwise, or evidence of personal feuding; rather, there is a cheerful appreciation of some of the pleasures of life and of the value of friendship.

After the court, the Cavalier Parliament and probably the household of the Duke of York, Ormonde's patronage network contained the largest concentration of returned royalist exiles. The various ties that held Ormonde's network together were not constantly threatening to snap under the pressure of intense personal and factional intrigues, unlike the situation both at court and in Parliament. Although not as impressive as York's or Ormonde's, other networks of patronage and friendship that were developed during the years of exile also survived into Restoration England. As well as being related by marriage to Ormonde's eldest son Lord Ossory, Arlington was similarly connected to Lord Crofts, whose close friendship with Charles when the exiled court was in Paris had so distressed Hyde. Among the inter-related royalist gentry of Suffolk, the Crofts, Cornwallis and Pooley (or Poley) families were particularly prominent. These three families were all

represented among the Cavaliers who went into exile in Paris or Jersey at the end of the Civil War. Sir Frederick Cornwallis, who belonged to a traditional court family and had had both diplomatic and military experience, married Crofts's half-sister Elizabeth in Paris in 1647. A friend of both Cornwallis and Crofts was that other close companion of Charles, Edward Progers. By 1649 Progers, the courtier Sir John Pooley and the Cornwallises were with Charles in Jersey, where Lady Cornwallis became godmother to the daughter of the island's governor, Sir George Carteret. While Crofts remained with the exiled court, and was a constant companion of the King on his travels, Progers, as we have seen, returned to England some time after the news of Worcester reached Paris. Pooley and the Cornwallises must have also returned to England during this period when royalist hopes were at their lowest, although Pooley's son remained in exile and later served under Thomas Blague in Flanders. In June 1655, during the roundup of notorious Malignants that followed the suppression of Penruddock's rising, Cornwallis and Progers were both arrested and imprisoned in the Tower. Despite the vicissitudes and separations of exile the Crofts/Cornwallis/Progers connection was maintained and, along with Pooley, the four families were well rewarded with offices in the restored court of Charles II. Although the Progers family estates were in Monmouthshire, in the 1680s Edward Progers acquired an estate in Suffolk as executor and residuary legatee of the will of Crofts' sister-in-law.[18]

This survey of the careers of Cavaliers who had been in exile partly supports the view that there were identifiable emigré groups in Restoration England. In the households of Charles II and his brother the Duke of York, in the Cavalier Parliament, in the armed forces, in some government departments, in the clientage network of a magnate like Ormonde, there were impressively large concentrations of returned exiles. These Cavaliers had shared the varied experiences of the royalist emigration. They had followed the shrunken and impoverished court on its wanderings and hidden from creditors in shabby lodgings. Some of them had risked their lives, whether on dangerous missions to England, on arduous journeys as couriers, by serving in foreign armies or in the royalist regiments in Flanders. These ordeals and adventures could all serve to bring together exiles and their families into friendships, marriages or patron–client relationships that continued after the Restoration.

Under close scrutiny, however, the view that there was an identifiable 'brand of the emigré' breaks down. There are too many variables, too many distinctions that need to be made between royalist leaders and

followers, between 'long-term' and 'short-term' exiles, between soldiers and civilians, between courtiers and plain country gentry, between members of prominent landed and aristocratic families and obscure adventurers, between those who were rewarded at the Restoration for their loyalty and sacrifices and those who were not. The returned exiles are so varied in their backgrounds and experiences, and exhibited so many different patterns of behaviour, that they cannot be categorised neatly under one label. The self-seeking, frantic hunger for offices and favours displayed by many returned exiles, that so disconcerted Charles II and Clarendon, needs to be set against the relationships of genuine friendship and mutual concern that emerge so strongly from the correspondence of Ormonde's 'clients'. The ferocity and bitterness of Restoration politics is well illustrated by the savage pulling down of Clarendon by enemies like Buckingham, St Albans and Wyndham in 1667. In one sense this was merely the final successful conclusion to their intermittent campaign to destroy the Chancellor which can be traced back at least as far as Paris in 1653. But the vindictiveness of Clarendon's enemies among some of the returned exiles needs to be balanced against the loyalty and support of others, like Stephen Fox and Henry Coventry.

Among both contemporaries like Pepys, Burnet and Evelyn, and historians since, the court of Charles II has been portrayed as corrupt and dissolute, the festering centre of a 'culture of indulgence and licence'. It is always difficult to know how seriously to take the criticisms of court morality voiced by someone like Pepys, who relied heavily on gossip from his friends like Mr Alsopp and was not exactly himself a paragon of the domestic virtues, or even John Evelyn, whose disapproval of the 'wicked folly, vanity and monstrous excess of passion' of the circle around the King features so prominently in his diary. In a letter to his friend Pepys, Evelyn complained that 'never was this Nation ... so atheistical, false and unsteady; covetous, self interested, impudently detracting and uncharitable; ungrateful, lewd, and luxurious; in sum, so universally vicious, dissolute and perverted.' Marvellous stuff, but this letter, in which Evelyn is deploring the effects on England of the long war against Louis XIV, was written on 10 December 1701, towards the end of the reign of the dour and single minded William III, whose fairly dull court has never attracted the wealth of criticism and disapproval showered on the court presided over by his uncle.[19]

To what extent did those courtiers who had been in exile and been literally and in all senses demoralised by the experience contribute to forming what a modern historian has called the 'sybaritic world' of the

court, where 'many of the king's companions decayed around him, rotting in the luxurious atmosphere'?[20] In most cases, the more notoriously debauched and dissolute of the King's companions, especially the so-called 'Wits' like John Wilmot, second Earl of Rochester, Charles Sackville, Lord Buckhurst, John Sheffield, Earl of Mulgrave, and Sir Charles Sedley, were too young to have been in exile, although certainly some had, most notably the Duke of Buckingham and younger men like Charles Berkeley and Harry Jermyn. To some extent, the poet and rake Rochester, whose father died in exile in Ghent, can be seen as a victim of the upheavals and family dislocations caused by the Civil War and the royalist emigration and so perhaps can several of Charles's mistresses during his years in exile, notably Lucy Walter, Elizabeth Killigrew and Catherine Pegge. After the King himself, the most prominent representative of the court's 'culture of indulgence and licence' was probably the principal royal mistress of the 1660s, Barbara, Lady Castlemaine. In some ways her disrupted upbringing was similar to Rochester's. Her father William, the second Viscount Grandison, was mortally wounded at the storming of Bristol in 1643. One uncle, the third viscount, as has been recounted in Chapter 7, died in poverty in a charity hospital in Paris in 1659 and another, Colonel Edward Villiers, returned from exile in 1652, became a member of the Sealed Knot and in consequence was in and out of prison during the 1650s.[21]

How far this pattern of war, exile and poverty, interspersed with separations and untimely deaths within one's family, which had been the experience of so many active royalists, contributed to shape the hedonistic culture of the court of Charles II cannot now be determined. There is no simple answer to this question. Charles had other companions as well as rakes like Buckingham and Rochester and mistresses like Castlemaine and Nell Gwyn. The complexity and diversity of a court which also included cultivated scholars like Fanshawe and Sir Robert Moray of the Royal Society can be illustrated by the examination of one group of courtiers who were traditionally very close to the King, his grooms of the bedchamber. Between 1649 and 1660 Charles II was attended by six grooms of the bedchamber, the names of all of whom have appeared in these pages: Daniel O'Neill, Henry Seymour, Edward Progers, Thomas Elliot, Richard Harding and Thomas Blague. At the Restoration, when the number of bedchambermen was increased, two more returned exiles were appointed: Robert Phelips and Silas Titus.

These eight men, all 'long-term' exiles and courtiers, cannot be categorised simply as decadent sybarites. In fact, in their backgrounds, activities and characters, they were a remarkably diverse group. Socially, they

ranged from Seymour, the second son of a baronet and a cousin of the Marquess of Hertford, and Phelips, the second son of Sir Robert Phelips of Montacute, head of one of the most influential gentry families in Somerset, to Titus, whose grandfather was an Italian immigrant and whose father was a soap maker in London.[22] During their years in exile O'Neill, Seymour, Phelips, Titus and Blague repeatedly ran the risk of death on the battlefield or on the scaffold, which Harding, who was elderly, and Elliot, who was not, never did. Blague was seriously wounded in the battle of the Dunes, while Seymour and Progers both suffered periods of imprisonment during the 1650s. Although they did not all risk their lives, they were all familiar with those two most common and most unpleasant features of an exile's life: poverty and the division of families. Harding, a widower, died in exile leaving behind a distraught daughter, while Blague died within a year of the Restoration, leaving his widow to petition for a pension. Elizabeth Elliot's complaints on being separated from her husband when he was absent on the King's business have already been noted above in Chapter 7.

There is diversity also in the factional and confessional allegiances of the bedchambermen who had been in exile. O'Neill, Harding and Seymour were all on good terms with Hyde, but Elliot can certainly, and Blague probably, be associated with the Swordsmen faction, two of whose leaders were Elliot's father-in-law Edmund Wyndham and Blague's friend Lord Gerard, both of whom were bitter enemies of the Chancellor.[23] Progers seems to have had the quality, rare among many of his companions in exile, of being able to get on with everybody. They all seem to have been Protestants, although both O'Neill and Progers belonged to families who were predominantly Catholic. Of the six grooms who had been in exile and survived until 1661, only Elliot did not have a seat in the Cavalier Parliament. Their careers after the Restoration were therefore not restricted to indulgence in the extravagant and licentious amusements of the court. In any case, most of them were married. Although, as both Charles and Buckingham forcefully demonstrated, marriage does not preclude a life of sexual self-indulgence, O'Neill's devotion to Katherine Stanhope/Heenvliet, whom he married as soon as he had the opportunity, had been notorious in exile circles for years, while it is difficult to imagine Elizabeth Elliot tolerating any irregular behaviour from her husband.

Any attempt therefore to evaluate the effects of exile on those royalists who returned to England must take into account both the range and nature of their individual experiences and the wide differences in their backgrounds, circumstances and characters. There is no valid and

simple stereotype of the exiled Cavalier, no widespread and recognisable 'stamp of the emigré'. On the contrary, the emigrés represented a fascinating and varied cross-section of English society, up-rooted from their previous existence and scattered among a dozen countries for periods of time ranging from few weeks to twenty years. In the alien soil to which they were transplanted some withered and died, some hung on grimly and survived, and some even flourished. All of them, noblemen and generals, courtiers and country gentry, scholars and adventurers, wives and mistresses, soldiers and civilians, children and servants, would have been variously and individually influenced by their experience of exile.

Much of the interest in the fortunes of the 'crowd of fugitives' who either chose or were compelled to go beyond the seas lies precisely in the diversity of behaviour they exhibited in response to the unfamiliar and difficult situations with which they were confronted. There is the contrast between those who survived the ordeal and those who were crushed by it: between the dignified and indomitable Ormonde and the broken and pathetic Grandison. There are the long-suffering and patient wives, like Ann Fanshawe, Mary Verney and Dorothy Chiffinch, determined despite all discouragements to share their husbands' fortunes, and in some cases, like Mrs Ross and Mrs Stephens, to share the dangers of their husbands' activities as couriers. They can be contrasted with those wives who remained in England separated from their husbands, like the wives of Joseph Jane and Richard Harding, or made only rare and fleeting visits to the continent, as was the cases with ladies Ormonde and Hatton. The families of plain gentry, the Verneys at Blois and the Cholmleys at Rouen, had a very different experience of exile to the cosmopolitan travellers like Tom Killigrew and Richard Symonds. The treacherous Henry Manning and the bullying William Armorer, who progressed from provoking brawls in the exiled court in Cologne to persecuting harmless dissenters in Reading, can be set against the reliable and competent Stephen Fox and the scholar and soldier Gervase Holles, who from his retreat in Rotterdam observed that 'banished men find very little business besides books'.[24] Baptist May, the 'odious "Bab" May' as one historian has called him, who was a page to the Duke of York in Holland in 1649 and Keeper of the Privy Purse to the King from 1665, acquired a dubious reputation as Charles's 'toady' and 'court pimp'. This reputation is in marked contrast to that of his cousin, who was also in exile in the early 1650s, the architect Hugh May, appointed Paymaster and Comptroller of the King's Works after the Restoration, and who, as well as his work for the King at Windsor castle, also

designed residences for a series of royalist clients, including Clarendon, Fox, Shaw and Lord Scudamore.[25]

There are many other examples of striking contrasts in both the character and response to their situation of the royalist exiles. Although they were both living in the Hague in the 1650s, the turbulent Philippa Mohun, 'flying the fury of Cromwell', does not seem to have had much in common with the lonely and distracted Honora Harding. There was little in common too between Lord Newcastle, maintaining on apparently endless credit the style of a great magnate in his mansion in Antwerp, and Thomas Carnaby, starving in a garret in Paris; or between Sir Theophilus Gilby, living comfortably in Florence with his family in the service of the Grand Duke of Tuscany, and Sir William Vavasour, dying under the walls of Copenhagen in the service of the King of Sweden. Nor should the loyal and presumably rarely paid servants be overlooked: Lady Newcastle's 'waiting maid' Elizabeth Chaplain and the Hardings' Tom Bococke, or the attendants entrusted with dangerous missions to England, for example, Henry Moore, 'a man of the Lord Wentworth's' and Ormonde's trusted Maurice, and not forgetting the more humble members of the wandering court, like Gervase the Trumpet and Giles of the Kitchen.

Then there is the indefatigably cheerful and endlessly resourceful 'Infallible Subtle' Daniel O'Neill, who for over twenty years demonstrated his courage in many theatres, including being prepared to criticise Charles personally when he thought he deserved it. 'Now I leave your majesty to judge, whether you are not a little to blame,' was O'Neill's conclusion to a letter to the King in December 1655, blaming him for mismanaging the decision on whether to approve a visit to Paris by Mary of Orange.[26] The frankness of the letters O'Neill wrote from London after the Restoration to his friend and patron Ormonde also show that he cannot be fitted into the conventional stereotype of a licentious and sycophantic courtier. 'The King has abandoned himself to his lust and his ministers to their passions against one another', written on 15 May 1664, five months before his death, gives the flavour of some of this correspondence.[27] In a letter to his sister Minette, the Duchess of Orleans, written on 24 October, Charles regretted the death of this loyal and entertaining companion of the years of exile: 'Poor Oneale [*sic*] died this afternoon of an ulcer in his guts; I am sure I have lost a very good servant by it.' In his will O'Neill left his share of the lease of a property, Wallrood House, to his 'dear friend' Edward Progers.[28]

Certainly, for the Cavaliers and their families and servants who endured it, exile was an unpleasant ordeal, generally characterised by

poverty and bitterness, frustration and melancholy. As we have seen, both the poverty and the homesickness come through strongly in their correspondence, in Hyde's nostalgic desire to 'eat cherries at Deptford again' with his friend Sir Richard Browne and in Hatton's longing to once again be 'in full possession of my estate as ever; to be settled at home in peace and quiet'. For some exiles this homesickness was aggravated by the separation of husbands and wives, fathers and children, a separation made even more of an ordeal by the difficulties in the way of receiving visits or even letters from friends or families. This lack of reliable and up to date intelligence on conditions in England is also an important explanation for one of the most noticeable characteristics of the behaviour of the Cavaliers in exile: the way in which their moods swung violently between unrealistically optimistic expectations of the chances of success of enterprises like Charles II's invasion from Scotland in 1651 or Booth's rising in 1659 and the deepest depths of despair when these hopes were crushed.

Certainly, the hardships of exile of far outweighed the positive aspects of the experience, but these positive aspects should not be overlooked. Although some Cavaliers rarely ventured far from their modest lodgings in case they encountered angry creditors or disagreeable foreigners, and almost certainly none could compete with John Page's claim to have 'ranged . . . the coast of Choromandel [sic]' and visited many other Asian countries, the prolonged residence abroad of so many members of a traditionally insular gentry class would certainly have hastened the development of at least upper-class English familiarity with the countries of western Europe. To have travelled abroad was increasingly expected of an educated gentleman. Pepys recorded in 1661 the observation 'that there was none fit to be courtiers, but such as have been abroad and know fashion'. Even Clarendon acknowledged how 'we can all remember when very few Men travelled beyond the seas, except to be a Soldier, which is a Profession we have learnt too much of without travel: now very few stay at Home, or think they are fit for good company, if they have not been beyond the Seas.' To go 'beyond the seas'; from a sentence of banishment it had become an essential requirement for an educated gentleman.[29]

The main significance of the emigration of the Cavaliers and their triumphant return at the Restoration is not, however, the influence of these events on the growing popularity of the Grand Tour, a term that seems to have been coming into use during the 1670s. The royalist emigration was one aspect, distinctive and dramatic but still only one element, in an interest in foreign travel that was already growing among upper-class

Englishmen during the first half of the seventeenth century. The Cavaliers fleeing into exile were part of a much larger movement of travellers and expatriates coming and going across the Channel. As John Stoye has demonstrated in his excellent *English Travellers Abroad 1604–1667*, in the first half of the seventeenth century there was in western Europe a large English expatriate community of merchants, professional soldiers, priests, diplomats and assorted adventurers. To this community can be added the travellers for pleasure, increasingly numerous from at least the 1630s.[30] A striking feature of the exiled royalists as a group is how many of them had already visited the continent on diplomatic missions, as soldiers in the Thirty Years War or purely as travellers for pleasure before the upheavals of the Civil War forced them to return to the continent, only this time as fugitives. In many cases they settled as exiles in countries with which they were already familiar. But unlike the travellers making a leisurely Grand Tour 'who to an extraordinary degree . . . shared a common experience', the exiled Cavaliers encountered a wide variety of circumstances and situations. They were not confined to the already well established itinerary of the 'tour of Italy' but could be found from Copenhagen to Crete, and from Lisbon to Jersey.[31]

The history of the exiled Cavaliers and their families deserves to be studied in its own right. Its interest goes well beyond its influence on the development of the custom of the Grand Tour or even for the ways in which the returning royalists hastened the introduction of European ideas and attitudes into England: in literature especially drama, in architecture, in manners and in the ephemeral world of fashion. As we have seen, the men and women whose experiences have been recorded in these pages chose to go into exile, or to remain in exile when they could have returned to England, for many reasons: poverty, a search for employment, adventure, or to escape imprisonment or worse. But one of the most important of their motives was what Hyde called their 'natural allegiance' to the monarchy, to the church, to the law and to the idea of constitutional government.[32] Although allegiance to some of these ideas and institutions may have been incomprehensible to, or even rejected, by a tough old soldier like Gerard or a sycophantic courtier like Bab May, they prevailed in the terms of the Declaration of Breda and the Restoration settlement. Those Cavaliers who went into exile did so at least partly as a matter of principle, 'being unwilling', as John Page rather melodramatically expressed it, 'to draw in the air of [their] native soil, lest [they] be tainted . . . with disloyalty'.

By enduring the hardships when they could in many cases have avoided them the exiles helped in one significant way to sit Charles II

on his throne in Whitehall. Despite the energy and effort of conspirators like Mordaunt, Massey and Grenville, and the daring and courage of agents like O'Neill, Armorer, Stephens, the Pauldens, Phelips and others, all the attempts to overthrow the different republican regimes during the 1650s ended in ignominious failure. Despite this series of disasters and disappointments a significant number of royalists remained in exile, did not give up, did not drift quietly back to England and conform to the authority of Commonwealth of Protector. Instead, they managed, often in the face of serious obstacles, to maintain a court and an alternative administration and to preserve what Mordaunt called 'the habit of loyalty'. Charles II, with his Privy Council, his court and his Flanders regiments did not dwindle, as eventually was to happen to his great nephew Charles Edward, the Young Pretender, into a shadowy prince living obscurely in a shabby residence dependant on a modest pension from some sympathetic potentate. If the Commonwealth ran into difficulties, Charles II and his followers in exile were always there across the Channel, waiting for the opportunity to replace it. Even Thurloe's spies, perhaps unconsciously, recognised the legitimacy of Charles's claims. Although in their intelligence reports Charles customarily was referred to as plain 'Charles Stuart' or occasionally as the 'king of Scots', sometimes they forgot and recognised his royal title. 'The king's train is not great, but in very good equipage', reported one of Thurloe's intelligencers from the Rhineland in August 1654.[33] The maintenance of this train 'in very good equipage' strengthened his claim to be recognised as king.

The Cavaliers and their families who survived to return to England did so for the most part not as vengeful and dissolute reactionaries, looking forward to the prospect of a white terror at the expense of the former parliamentarians or to erecting an absolutist monarchy on the continental pattern. The majority of returned exiles demonstrated their willingness to cooperate in a moderate constitutional settlement. Nor, with certain notable exceptions who have already been mentioned, did they return in search of a quiet retirement in which to end their days. They returned, in most cases, young enough and sufficiently determined to play an active part in the social, political and cultural life of Restoration England. For some of them this was eventually to bring disaster. Two dominant figures in the royalist emigration who returned in triumph in 1660, Edward Hyde, Earl of Clarendon, and James, Duke of York and then King of England, were both fated to die in exile. So were some of James's followers. The dashing young Harry Jermyn of the 1650s, nephew of the Earl of St Albans, a close companion of York in

exile and one of the more notorious rakes in the court of Charles II, died once more in exile in Flanders, having withdrawn from St Germain after quarrelling with his old friend and master whose fortunes he had followed loyally for over forty years.[34]

Most returned exiles were spared this ironically melancholy end to their adventurous lives. They remained in Britain to contribute to the political history of the reign of Charles II and his successors, to the affairs of court and Parliament, to wars and diplomacy, to literature and the theatre of Killigrew and Davenant and to architecture and science, including the creation and development of the Royal Society. In different ways all of these activities and institutions were shaped and influenced by the Cavaliers who fled beyond the seas – and who survived to return home. If they were lucky they lived long enough to enjoy the benefits of being finally on the winning side and of not being forced to go on their travels again. Nicholas Armorer was one of these lucky ones. In Dublin on 15 February 1686 the Earl of Longford wrote to a friend to inform him that 'Sir Nicholas Armorer died in his chair this afternoon.'[35] It was almost exactly 31 years to the day since Armorer had contrived to escape from Dover castle.

Notes

Prologue: Escape from Dover Castle

1. Bod. L. Rawlinson MS 23, fols. 93, 107, 165, 207. They are printed, not completely accurately, in *A Collection of the State Papers of John Thurloe*, ed. Thomas Birch, (London, 1742), 7 vols.
2. Bod. L. Rawlinson MS 23, f. 207; (*TSP*, iii, 164), (Wilson to Thurloe, 11 February 1655).
3. Ibid.
4. Bod. L. Rawlinson MS 23, f. 93; (*TSP*, iii, 137–38), (Armorer to Stone, 4 February 1655).
5. Bod. L. Rawlinson MS 23, fols. 107, 165. (Stone to Thurloe, 5 February 1655).
6. Bod. L. Rawlinson MS 23, f. 207; (*TSP*, iii, 164), (Wilson to Thurloe, 11 February 1655).

1 A Sad and Long Exile

1. *Calendar of State Papers, Domestic Series 1640–1641*, ed. M. A. E. Green, (London, 1876–1886), pp. 299–300, 312–33; *Journal of Sir Symonds D'Ewes*, ed. Wallace Notestein, (New Haven, 1923), pp. 89–91. See also Caroline Hibbard, *Charles I and the Popish Plot*, (University of North Carolina, 1983), pp. 175–6.
2. *HMC, Portland*, i, 684–85; *The Clarke Papers*, ed. C. H. Firth, Camden Society, (London, 1891–1901), vol. 4, 47–8, 293; *CSPD 1659–60*, pp. 157, 219, 224; D. Underdown, *Royalist Conspiracy in England, 1649–1660.* (New Haven, 1960), pp. 281–85.
3. Eva Scott, *The King in Exile 1646–1655*, (London, 1905), p. 1; P. I. Hardacre, 'The Royalists in Exile During the Puritan Revolution 1642–1660', *Huntington Library Quarterly*, 1952, xvi, 353.
4. D. Underdown, 'Cavaliers in Exile,' *History of the English Speaking Peoples*, (London, 1970), No. 53, 1692; John Miller, *James II: a Study in Kingship*, (London, 1978), p. 5.
5. K. Feiling, *A History of the Tory Party 1640–1714*, (Oxford, 1924), p. 78.
6. G. R. Balleine, *All For the King: the Life Story of Sir George Carteret*, (Jersey, 1976), p. 1.
7. Henry Norwood, 'A Voyage to Virginia,' in *Tracts and Other Papers*, ed. Peter Force (Washington, 1836–46), iii, No. 10. See also Underdown, *Royalist Conspiracy*, pp. 13–14.
8. *HMC Bath MSS*, ii, 101, (Radcliffe to Holles, 21 Feb 1652).
9. Bod. L. *Clarendon MS 59*, fols. 56–7.

2 Court Papists and Army Plotters

1. Hibbard, *Charles I and the Popish Plot*, pp. 168–70.
2. Ibid, pp. 174–5; Anthony Fletcher, *The Outbreak of the English Civil War*, (London, 1981), pp. 3–5; C. V. Wedgwood, *The King's Peace 1637–1641*, (London, 1955), pp. 373, 375–6; *Dictionary of National Biography (DNB)*.
3. *Calendar of State Papers Domestic (CSPD) 1640–1641*, pp. 299–300; *D'Ewes Journal*, pp. 89–91.
4. *CSPD, 1640–41*, pp. 314, 435, 437; *DNB*.
5. *Journals of the House of Lords, 1578–1714*, 19 vols., (London, 1742–), vii, 331; John Stoye, *English Travellers Abroad, 1604–1667*, Revised Edition, (New Haven and London, 1989), p. 178; Wedgwood, *King's Peace*, pp. 379–81; *DNB*.
6. Wedgwood, *King's Peace*, p. 381.
7. Hibbard, *Charles I and the Popish Plot*, pp. 36, 51–3, 62–3, 85, 122–3; Wedgwood, *King's Peace*, pp. 122–3; *DNB*.
8. Gervas Huxley, *Endymion Porter: the Life of a Courtier, 1587–1649*, (London, 1959); Hibbard, *Charles I and the Popish Plot*, pp. 55–6; *DNB*.
9. Stoye, *English Travellers*, pp. 10, 33–4, 76–7, 159, 208–9, 249–52, 263, 312–13, 315–16.
10. Quoted in Stoye, *English Travellers*, p. 79.
11. E. Chaney, *The Grand Tour and the Great Rebellion*, (Geneva, 1985), p. 303; Hibbard, *Charles I and the Popish Plot*, pp. 184–6, 191–2; Fletcher, *Outbreak of the Civil War*, pp. 5–6.
12. Conrad Russell, *The Fall of the British Monarchies 1637–1642*, (Oxford, 1991), pp. 292–4, 350; Donal F. Cregan, 'An Irish Cavalier: Daniel O'Neill', *Studia Hibernica*, iii, (1963), pp. 85–8.
13. Edward Hyde, Earl of Clarendon, *The History of the Rebellion and Civil Wars in England*, ed. W. D. Macray, 6 vols., (Oxford, 1888), 111, 182, 223; Fletcher, *Outbreak of the Civil War*, pp. 26–7, 85; Wedgwood, *King's Peace*, pp. 389, 408–10; Ronald Hutton. 'The Structure of the Royalist Party', *Historical Journal*, 24, 1981, pp. 554–5.
14. Clarendon, *Rebellion*, iii, 182.
15. *CSPD, 1641–1643*, p. 28; Cregan, 'Daniel O'Neill', pp. 89, 92–5.
16. Cregan, 'Daniel O'Neill', pp. 60, 64–71.
17. Clarendon, *Rebellion*, viii, 268.
18. Ibid, viii, 269; Sir Philip Warwick, *Memoirs of the Reign of King Charles I*, (Edinburgh, 1813), pp. 28, 145–6; Cregan, 'Daniel O'Neill', pp. 79–80.
19. Ibid, pp. 96–8; Clarendon, *Rebellion*, viii, 269; *Historical Manuscripts Commission (HMC), 4th Report*, pp. 74, 107; *5th Report*, pp. 4, 21, 147; *12th Report*; p. 494.
20. Cregan, 'Daniel O'Neill', pp. 99–100.

3 To Go Beyond the Seas

1. R. Bosher, *The Making of the Restoration Settlement*, (London, 1951), p. 284; Chaney, *Grand Tour and Rebellion*, pp. 283–314; R. Hutton, *The Royalist War Effort 1642–1646*, (London, 1984), pp. 100–02; P. R. Newman, *Royalist Officers in England and Wales*, (New York, 1981), p. 231; *John Evelyn's Diary*, ed. Philip Francis, (London, 1963), p. 14.

2. John Kenyon, *The Civil Wars of England*, (London, 1988), pp. 90–2, 94–6, 104–10; B. E. G. Warburton, *Memoirs of Prince Rupert and the Cavaliers*, (London, 1849), iii, 467–8; Geoffrey Trease, *Portrait of a Cavalier: William Cavendish, First Duke of Newcastle*, (London, 1979), pp. 140–2.
3. *Richard Symonds's Diary of the Marches of the Royal Army*, ed. C. E. Long, (Cambridge, 1997), pp. 172, 249, 256; *CSPD, 1645–47*, p. 456; W. J. Farrow, *The Great Civil War in Shropshire 1642–1649*, (Shrewsbury, 1926), pp. 85, 88, 91–2.
4. Donal F. Cregan, 'An Irish Cavalier: Daniel O'Neill in the Civil Wars 1642–51', *Studia Hibernica*, iv, (1964), pp. 120–6.
5. Huxley, *Endymion Porter*, pp. 290–92; *State Papers Collected by Edward, Earl of Clarendon*, ed. R. Scrope and T. Monkhouse, 3 vols., (Oxford, 1767–1786), ii, 200–01. For Ronald Hutton on Digby see his *Charles the Second King of England, Scotland and Ireland*, (Oxford, 1989) p. 17. For Robinson see *DNB*.
6. *The Memoirs of Sir Hugh Cholmley, Knt. and Bart.*, (privately printed, 1787), pp. 71–4.
7. British Library (BL), *Egerton MS 2451*, f. 338; Donald Nicholas, *Mr Secretary Nicholas 1593–1669*, (London, 1955), p. 224.
8. *CSPD 1645–1647*, p. 456.
9. Clarendon, *Rebellion*, ix, 54, 55, 56, 100, 101, 102; Mary Coate, *Cornwall in the Great Civil War and Interregnum, 1642–1660*, (Oxford, 1933), pp. 142–3, 166–80, 193–200.
10. *The Memoirs of Anne, Lady Halkett and Ann, Lady Fanshawe*, ed. John Loftis, (Oxford, 1979), pp. 117–18.
11. *Halkett and Fanshawe Memoirs*, p. 118; Coate, *Cornwall in the Civil War*, pp. 213–14.
12. Clarendon, *Rebellion*, x, 73–7; Coate, *Cornwall in the Civil War*, pp. 215–20.

4 The Road to Worcester

1. *The Correspondence of Isaac Basire, D. D.*, ed. W. N. Darnell, (London, 1831), p. 63.
2. *A Collection of Original Letters and Papers Concerning the Affairs of England 1641–1660, found among the Duke of Ormond's Papers*, 2 vols., ed. Thomas Carte, (London, 1739), i, 163, 179–80; Underdown, *Royalist Conspiracy*, pp. 13–14.
3. *ClSP*, ii, 309.
4. PRO, *SP 23/181*/fols. 624, 642 (Committee for Compounding); *ClSP*, ii, 284–5, 480.
5. *Cholmley Memoirs*, pp. 74–5; *CCC*, p. 2062.
6. Huxley, *Endymion Porter*, pp. 300–3; *CSPD 1649–1650*, pp. 39, 294–5, 443, 546; *Calendar of the Proceedings of the Committee for Compounding*, ed. M. A. E. Green, 5 vols., (London, 1889–92), i, 138–9, 1804; *DNB*.
7. Clarendon, *Rebellion*, x, 3–5; *Halkett and Fanshawe Memoirs*, pp. 118–19.
8. *ClSP*, ii, 499–500.
9. *Halkett and Fanshawe Memoirs*, pp. 118–19; Richard Ollard, *Clarendon and His Friends*, (Oxford, 1988), pp. 105–8, 113–16, 119–22.

10. For discussions of factions in the exiled court see Underdown, *Royalist Conspiracy*, pp. 10–12; Hutton, *Charles II*, pp. 40–1.
11. *CCISP*, ii, 28, 32, 38; S. R. Gardiner, *History of the Commonwealth and Protectorate*, 4 vols., (London, 1903), i, 160, 207.
12. HMC, *Ormonde MSS*, 1902, N. S. pp. 231, 251.
13. Donal. F. Cregan, 'An Irish Cavalier: Daniel O'Neill in the Civil Wars', *Studia Hibernica*, iv, (1964), 129; *NP*, i, 303.
14. HMC, *Report 55: Various Collections*, (Harford MSS), v. 2, 349.
15. Hutton, *Charles II*, pp. 34–5, 470–1.
16. *CISP*, ii, 530.
17. *NP*, i, 187; F. T. R. Edgar, *Sir Ralph Hopton*, (Oxford, 1968), pp. 194–5.
18. HMC, *Bath MSS*, ii, 89.
19. Clarendon, *Rebellion*, xiii, 3; *CCISP*, ii, 74; Cregan, 'Daniel O'Neill in the Civil Wars', 131.
20. *Miscellanea Aulica*, ed. T. Brown, (London, 1702), pp. 152–3; *NP*, i, 206–8.
21. Ibid, i, 238, 254; Carte, *Letters and Papers*, ii, 13.
22. *NP*, i, 238, 261–2; Edgar, *Hopton*, p. 196.
23. *NP*, i, 204; Carte, *Letters and Papers*, ii, 31–2; Cregan, 'Daniel O'Neill in the Civil Wars', p. 132.
24. HMC, *Report 10*, v. 4, 148–9.
25. Clarendon, *Rebellion*, xiii, 83; HMC, *Ormonde MSS*, N. S., v. 1, 200.
26. HMC, *Ormonde MSS*, N. S., v. 1, 230; Hutton, *Charles II*, pp. 66–7.
27. Clarendon, *Rebellion*, xiii, 83; *NP*, i, 278; Edgar, *Hopton*, pp. 196–8.
28. *NP*, i, 276.

5   The Crowd of Fugitives

1. *Thurloe State Papers*, (*TSP*) v, 84.
2. *DNB*.
3. Stoye, *English Travellers*, pp. 4–5.
4. *Calendar of the Clarendon State Papers*, (*CCISP*), ed. O. Ogle, W. H. Bliss, W. D. Macray and F. J. Routledge, 4 vols., (Oxford, 1869–1932), iv, 69, 70, 73, 81, 98, 126–7, 134, 143, and passim. For Shaw see B. D. Henning, *The House of Commons 1660–1690*, 3 vols., (London, 1985), iii, 429–30.
5. Margaret Cavendish, Duchess of Newcastle, *The Life of William Cavendish, Duke of Newcastle*, (London, 1915), pp. 67, 88; *CCISP*, iv, 8, 32, 59, 66, 88, 99, 133, 401.
6. *Diary of John Evelyn*, ed. W. Bray and H. B. Wheatley, (London, 1879), ii, 7–28; *The Travels and Memoirs of Sir John Reresby, Bart.*, ed. A. Browning, (Glasgow, 1936), p. 1. For a discussion of the appeal of the Grand Tour during this period to young men of royalist families see Chaney, *The Grand Tour and the Great Rebellion*, (Geneva, 1985).
7. *CCISP*, iii, 71, 88–9, 125, 147; *The Nicholas Papers: the Correspondence of Sir Edward Nicholas Secretary of State*, (*NP*), ed. G. F. Warner, Camden Society, 4 vols., (London, 1886–1920), ii, 72, 256; iii, 135, 137, 202; iv, 42.
8. Ibid, iii, 36; *CISP*, iii, 409.
9. Bod. L., *Rawlinson MS 23*, fols. 107, 165; *TSP*, i, 171, 384, 671–4; *CSPD 1651–52*, p. 577; *1655*, p. 121; *Addenda, 1660–70*, p. 622; *NP*, ii, 2; *CCISP*, ii, 171, 268; Carola Oman, *Elizabeth of Bohemia*, (London, 1938), p. 419; Herbert

H. Rowen, *John de Witt, Grand Pensionary of Holland 1625–1672*, (Princeton, 1978), p. 73.

10. Cavendish, *Life of Newcastle*, p. 67.
11. Bod. L., *Clarendon MS 66*, f. 20.
12. See for example M. F. Keeler, *The Long Parliament 1640–1642*, (Philadelphia, 1954) and G. E. Aylmer, *The State's Servants: the Civil Service of the English Republic 1649–1660*, (London, 1973).
13. *ClSP*, ii, 284–5.
14. *TSP*, v, 479, 694; C. H. Firth, 'Royalist and Cromwellian Armies in Flanders 1657–1662', *Transaction of the Royal Historical Society*, New Series, 17, (1903), 68–9, 73–5, 100.
15. *TSP*, vi, 151.
16. *NP*, i, 178.
17. Bod. L. *Clarendon MS 55*, fols. 164, 169; *CCISP*, iii, 309, 320, 328, 374. It is perhaps significant that 'Captain' Thomas Batt is not listed in Newman, *Royalist Officers*.
18. *ClSP*, ii, 284–85.
19. Clarendon, *Rebellion*, xiii, 44; *Basire Correspondence; The Works of John Cosin, Lord Bishop of Durham*, ed. J. Sansom, (Oxford, 1843–1855); Bosher, *Restoration Settlement*; Richard Ollard, *Clarendon and His Friends*, (Oxford, 1987), pp. 142, 204; Hardacre, 'Royalists in Exile', *HLQ*, xvi, 363–70.
20. *DNB* (Allestree); Newman, *Royalist Officers*, p. 20 (Beaw).
21. PRO. *State Papers Domestic 1660*, 29/26/78; *CSPD 1657–58*, pp. 292, 310; *TSP*, iii, 429; iv, 718; Newman, *Royalist Officers*, p. 174; S. R. Gardiner, *History of the Great Civil War*, (London, 1987), iv, 166; Edward J. Cowan, *Montrose: for Covenant and King*, (London, 1977), pp. 294–5.
22. *CSPD 1655*, p. 225; *ClSP*, iii, 91; *DNB*.
23. *NP*, iii, 137, 179, 196, 204, 227, 231; *CCISP*, iii, 62, 184; Clarendon, *Rebellion*, iii, 396; iv, 478–9; *DNB* (Newburgh).
24. *ClSP*, iii, 42. See Sir Robert Southwell's judgment on Ormonde after the Restoration: 'I think his whole life was a straight line, if ever a man's in the world were so.' Thomas Carte, *Life of James, Duke of Ormond*, 6 vols., (Oxford, 1851) i, x; quoted in Richard Ollard, *Clarendon and His Friends*, p. 148.
25. *TSP*, V, 84; vi, 136; vii, 247–8; *NP*, iii, 127; Carte, *Life of Ormond*, passim; Nicholas, *Secretary Nicholas*, p. 275.
26. Carte, *Letters and Papers*, i, 146–48; ii, 32; Carte, *Life of Ormond*, v, 6; vi, 42–6, 92, 149, 154, 165–6, 188–91, 202–05, 265–77.
27. *CSP, Ireland, 1660–1662*, p. 334; HMC, *Ormonde MSS*, 1895, i, 183, 186, 190–91; 1899, ii, 99–102; 1902, N.S., i, 231; *CCISP*, iv, passim; Underdown, *Royalist Conspiracy*, pp. 104, 106–7, 115.
28. *ClSP*, iii, 67; *DNB*.
29. Antonia Fraser, *King Charles II*, (London, 1979), pp. 137–8, 154–6.
30. For Arnet see *CSPD 1655*, pp. 220, 390; *TSP*, i, 149, 151; iv, 122; *CCISP*, iii, 29, 65; *NP*, i, 158.
31. G. E. Aylmer, *The State's Servants*, p. 172.
32. *CCISP*, iii, 297, (Langdale to Hyde, Bruges, 30 May 1657). A Major Thomas Mason, claiming at the Restoration to be indigent, petitioned to be admitted as a Poor Knight of Windsor. *CSPD 1660–1670*, Addenda, pp. 622, 688; Newman, *Royalist Officers*, p. 248.

33. A special case is Thomas Howard, second Earl of Arundel, who went into exile in France early in 1642. Howard had been restored by James I to the dignity of Arundel, forfeited by his father; he remained prospective heir to the Norfolk dukedom. *DNB*; Kevin Sharpe, The Earl of Arundel: his Circle and the Opposition to the Duke of Buckingham 1618–1628', *Faction and Parliament: Essays on Early Stuart History*, ed. Kevin Sharpe, (London, 1978), pp. 209–11.
34. For Marlay see Henning, *House of Commons*, ii, 21–22; Newman, *Royalist Officers*, pp. 246–47. For Bunce see *CCISP*, iii, 35, 65, 221, 242, 407; *TSP*, 11, 373, 568–9. For Benyon see Clarendon, *Rebellion*, ii, 27–8; *NP*, ii, 157; iii, 244. For Titus see *DNB*; Henning, *House of Commons*, iii, 570–74.
35. For Massey see *DNB*; Henning, *House of Commons*, iii, 29–31; Newman, *Royalist Officers*, p. 248; Underdown, *Royalist Conspiracy*, pp. 14, 55, 236, 242.
36. Violet Barbour, *Henry Bennet, Earl of Arlington*, (Washington, 1914), pp. 7–10.
37. *HMC, Pepys MSS*, 70, pp. 255–56; Underdown, *Royalist Conspiracy*, p. 28.
38. *HMC, 2nd Report (Cotterell Dormer MSS)*, Appendix pp. 82–83; Clarendon, *Rebellion*, iii, 395; vi, 382, 396; *CSPD 1635–36*, p. 433; *1636–37*, p. 303; Carte, *Letters and Papers*, i, 155; *DNB*; M. F. Keeler, *The Long Parliament 1640–1641*, (Philadelphia, 1954), pp. 208, 292–3, 337; Henning, *House of Commons*, ii, 134–35.
39. *Memoirs of Sir Stephen Fox*, (London, 1717), pp. 5–6; Clarendon, *Rebellion*, xiv, 89.
40. Huxley, *Endymion Porter*, pp. 292–301.
41. *CCISP*, iii, 10, 24; *NP*, i, 284; ii, 170; Clarendon, *Rebellion*, xiii, 30; *DNB*.
42. *NP*, iv, 20. Sir John Pooley, of a prominent royalist Suffolk family, was a gentleman usher of the privy chamber to Charles II and had accompanied the King to Jersey, to Holland and to Scotland in 1650.
43. *CISP*, iii, 335; *CCISP, iii, 255; The Letter-book of John Viscount Mordaunt 1658–1660, (LBM)*, ed. Mary Coate, Camden Society, (London, 1945), pp. 93–4, 161–62.
44. *CCISP*, ii, 391; *CSPD 1657–1658*, pp. 310–11; HMC, *Bath MSS*, ii, 122, 124, 127–30, 139.
45. *NP*, i, 234, 277.
46. Ibid, ii, 156–7.
47. *CISP*, iii, 91.
48. BL. *Egerton MS 2558*, fols. 4, 6. Quoted in Nicholas, *Secretary Nicholas*, p. 236.
49. *NP*, iii, 91.

6 A Long Farewell

1. PRO. *SP/29/5/7*, (25 June 1660).
2. *Acts and Ordinances of the Interregnum*, ed. C. H. Firth and R. S. Rait, (London, 1911), ii, 520–1.
3. Ibid, ii, 520–1; *CCC*, ii, 138–39.
4. BL. *Egerton MS. 2542*, f. 6; *Lords Journals*, x, 587, 595, 599; *CISP*, iii, 288.
5. *Acts and Ordinances*, ii, 598–600 (Act for the Settling of Ireland 12 August 1652); *CCC*, i, 138–39; iii, 2168–9; Huxley, *Endymion Porter*, p. 300; *DNB*, (for Bristol).
6. PRO. *SP/23/86/1030*, (Committee for Compounding). For Fitzwilliam see Newman, *Royalist Officers*, p. 133.

7. *CSPD 1651*, pp. 432, 478; *1654*, p. 273; *1655*, p. 307; *1655–1656*, p. 576.
8. *CSPSD 1654*, p. 273; *1655*, p. 204; *1656–1657*, pp. 260–61.
9. Clarendon, *Rebellion*, xiii, 136, 137; *DNB*.
10. *HMC, Appendix to Sixth Report*, p. 473; *TSP*, i, 674; ii, 602; v, 84; *DNB*; Richard Ollard, *The Ecape of Charles II*, (London, 1986), pp. 97–105, 143, 145; Allan Fea, *The Flight of the King*, (London, 1887), p. 104.
11. Henry Neville, *The Commonwealth of Ladies*. (London, 1649), (Thomason Tracts), p. 20; *NP*, ii, 85–6, 88.
12. *Acts and Ordinances*, ii, 520; *CCC*, iv, 2308; *CSPD 1649–1650*, p. 39; Newman, *Royalist Officers*, p. 269; Underdown, *Royalist Conspiracy*, pp. 46, 114–15, 167.
13. *CCC*, i, 747; *Commons Journals*, iv, 501, 523; Huxley, *Endymion Porter*, pp. 300–03.
14. Bod. L. *Clarendon MS 78*, f. 173. For Page see below Chapter 6.
15. HMC, *Bath MSS*, ii, 88–9.
16. *CISP*, ii, 309, 480; T. H. Lister, *Life and Administration of Edward, First Earl of Clarendon*, (London, 1837–38), 3 vols., iii, 61.
17. Lister, *Life of Clarendon*, i, 363; *CISP*, ii, 23–4.
18. Reresby, *Travels and Memoirs*, p. 1.
19. For a discussion of the restrictions and disabilities imposed on the royalist gentry under the Commonwealth see P. H. Hardacre, *The Royalists During the Puritan Revolution*, (Hague, 1956), pp. 65–107; Underdown, *Royalist Conspiracy*, pp. 7–8.
20. Bod. L. *Fairfax MS 32*, f. 182. Paulden's prospective patron was probably the Duke of Buckingham. *Somers Tracts*, ed. Sir W. Scott, (London, 1812), vii, 8–9. For Thomas and his brother and fellow exile Gregory Paulden see *CCISP*, iv, passim; Underdown, *Royalist Conspiracy*, pp. 9, 86n, 145, 207–8, 234.
21. For Fox see Clarendon, *Rebellion*, xiv, 89; *Fox Memoirs*, pp. 5–6. For Bennet see *Miscellanea Aulica*, p. 109 (Charles to York); Violet Barbour, *Henry Bennet, Earl of Arlington*, (American Historical Association, 1914), pp. 17–14. For Holmes see BL. *Add MS 1892*, f. 242; Warburton, *Memoirs of Prince Rupert and the* Cavaliers, iii, 241; Richard Ollard, *Man of War: A Life of Sir Robert Holmes*, (London, 1969), pp. 21, 54–6. For O'Neill see Carte, *Letters and Papers*, ii, 32 (Fanshawe to Ormonde). For Armorer see *CSPD 1655–1656*, p. 263 (Ross to Nicholas.)
22. B. L. *Add MS 19253* (Draft of Chesterfield's autobiography). For Chesterfield's involvement in royalist conspiracy see Underdown, *Royalist Conspiracy*, pp. 242, 278, 287, 296–98.
23. Government newsletter December 1651. Quoted in Eva Scott, *The Travels of the King*, (London, 1905), p. 438.
24. Clarendon, *Rebellion*, xv, 156.
25. *NP*, iii, 218.

7   Travels and Retreats

1. *The Poetical Works of Edmund Waller and Sir John Denham*, ed. G. Gilfillan, (Edinburgh, 1857), p. 247.

2. From a government newspaper, December 1651, quoted in E. Scott, *The King in Exile*, p. 438.
3. BL. *Egerton MS 2534*, fols. 117, 119, 127; *CISP*, iii, 65; *NP*, i, 156, 277, 283, 285.
4. Bod. L. *Clarendon MS 49*, f. 107; *CISP*, iii, 59, 67, 82–4; Warburton, *Memoirs*, iii, 418–20.
5. For Hyde's relationship with Berkeley and Culpepper see Ollard, *Clarendon and His Friends*, pp. 85–6, 128–9, 151–2, 200–1. For Church see *The Letter-Book of John Viscount Mordaunt, 1658–1660*, ed. Mary Coate, Camden Society, (London, 1945), p. 36; *CSPD, 1660–1661*, p. 254.
6. *CCISP*, i, 445 (list of Duke of York's household in November 1648); Clarendon, *Rebellion*, xiii, 122; John Miller, *James II: a Study in Kingship*, (London, 1978), pp. 10–20.
7. *NP*, iii, 4; *TSP*, ii, 312; *The Memoirs of James II: his Campaigns as Duke of York 1652–1660*, ed. A. Lytton Sells, (London, 1962), pp. 57–8; H. Hartmann, *The King's Friend: a Life of Charles Berkeley, Viscount Fitzhardinge, Earl of Falmouth*, (London, 1951), pp. 5–20; Miller, *James II, pp. 13–17*. For Werden see Newman, *Royalist Officers*, p. 405.
8. *CSPD 1657–1658*, p. 201; *Archeologia*, xxxv, 344; Scott, *Travels of the King*, pp. 273–4. For Cotterell see *HMC, 2nd Report, (Cotterell MSS)*, pp. 82–3; *DNB*; Malcolm Rogers, *William Dobson 1611–46*, (National Portrait Gallery, London), 1984, pp. 72–3, 88.
9. Margaret Newcastle, *Life*, p. 86; *TSP*, i, 80; *CSPD 1649–1650*, p. 39. For Widdrington see Newman, *Royalist Officers*, p. 411.
10. *HMC, 10th Report*, Appendix, Pt. II, *(Portland MSS)*, iii, (1894), 150. For Jennings and Sandys see Newman, *Royalist Officers*, pp. 210, 329.
11. Carte, *Letters and Papers*, i, 148, 152, 154, 155, 157–9; *CISP*, iii, 80.
12. *HMC, Report 55, (Harford MSS)*, ii, 350; *CISP*, iii, 81; *NP*, iii, 91; Bod. L. *Clarendon MS 59*, fols. 56–7.
13. BL. *Harley MS 943*, fols. 1, 16, 21–3, 34, 37–40, 60–2, 71; *Harley MS 1278*, (Symonds's notes on public buildings and churches in Paris); Symonds, *Diary of the Marches of the Royal Army*.
14. Bod. L. *Clarendon MS 47*, f. 187; BL. *Egerton MS 2542*, f. 6; *CISP*, iii, 288 (list of royalists to be expelled under terms of the treaty).
15. *TSP*, iv, 196.
16 *CISP*, iii, 112–13, 164, 191; *TSP*, i, 312; ii, 312; v, 145, vi, 325–6; *NP*, iii, 91; *CSPD 1657–1658*, p. 232; T. H. Lister, *Life and Administration of Edward, First Earl of Clarendon*, 3 vols., (London, 1837–8), ii, 379–84; iii, 63, 69–93.
17. PRO. SP 18/92/518 (Committee for Compounding), fols. 291–2.
18. *NP*, iii, 166, 170; *Diary of John Evelyn*, ed. E. S. de Beer, (Oxford, 1955), 6 vols., iii, 55. For Lloyd [Floyd] see Newman, *Royalist Officers*, p. 138.
19. Loftis, *Halkett and Fanshawe Memoirs*, p. 118. For Carteret see Balleine, *All for the King*.
20. Bod. L. *Carte MS 29*, passim (frequent letters from Ormonde in Caen 1650–1); *NP*, i, 276; Carte, *Letters and Papers*, i, 20–1; Clarendon, *Rebellion*, xi, 23; *Basire Correspondence*, pp. 49, 76; Edgar, *Hopton*, p. 189.

21. Thomas Carte, *Life of James, Duke of Ormond*, 6 vols., (Oxford, 18510), vi, 606; PRO. *SP Foreign (France)* 78/114/fols. 5, 102, 110, 137. For Digby and Hunt see Newman, *Royalist Officers*, pp. 109, 206.

22. Stoye, *English Travellers Abroad* pp. 291–2; *Memoirs of the Verney Family*, ed. Frances Verney, 3 vols., (London, 1970), ii, 391–2.

23. BL. *Add. MS 15858*, fols. 11, 13, 14, 17 (Browne's correspondence with Hanmer); *Verney Memoirs*, ii, 391–3, 411; iii, 4–5, 16–21; Stoye, *English Travellers Abroad*, pp. 291–2.

24. BL. *Add. MS 15858*, f. 11; *Verney Memoirs*, iii, 5, 16–7; Stoye, *English Travellers Abroad*, pp. 43–4, 290.

25. BL. *Add MS 15858*, f. 135; *CCC*, i, 541–2; *TSP*, iv, 294, 319; *Verney Memoirs*, ii, 414; iii, 40–9.

26. PRO. *SP 18/9/25; CCISP*, i, 444, 446; ii, 61–2; *NP*, i, 268–8, 284; Edgar, *Hopton*, pp. 187–98.

27. *TSP*, ii, 373. See also Ibid, iii, 429, 457; iv, 10; *CCISP*, iii, 13–14.

28. For Boswell, Brett, Mackworth, Morton and Sayers see Newman, *Royalist Officers*, pp. 38, 41–2, 243, 265, 333.

29. *CSPD 1648–1649*, pp. 157, 320; *1650*, p. 265; *1651–1652*, p. 488; *CCISP*, iii, 22; *NP*, iii, 211–2, 224; *TSP*, ii, 373.

30. *TSP, (Lambeth MSS)*, i, 671–3. There were several Cavalier Cromwells, the discendants of Sir Oliver Cromwell of Hinchinbrooke. A Colonel John Cromwell, who was in Utrecht in 1655, is perhaps the most likely companion for Grandison in their meeting with Elizabeth of Bohemia. *CSPD 1655*, p. 598.

31. Bod. L. *Clarendon MS 58*, fols. 374–5; *MS 59*, fols. 75, 175, 436; *CISP*, iii, 198; *TSP*, iv, 169, 700, 709; v, 160, 169, 178, vii, 428, 444; *CCISP*, ii, 336; iv, 223; Lister, *Life of Clarendon*, i, 392; A. E. Green, *Lives of the Princesses of England*, 6 vols., (London, 1854), vi, 188, 203, 210, 234–7, 242, 276.

32. *NP*, i, 303; ii, 22.

33. BL. *Add MS 4180*, f. 104; *NP*, i, 203; *CSPD 1655–1656*, p. 159.

34. HMC, *Bath MSS*, ii, 79–80; Gervase Holles, *Memorials of the Holles Family 1493–1656*, Camden Society, (London, 1937); pp. viii–ix; Newman, *Royalist Officers*, p. 193.

35. *Holles Memorials*, pp. 84, 87; HMC, *Bath MSS*, ii, 103–11, 113.

36. For the Newcastles in Antwerp see below Chapter 7. For Langdale see BL. *Egerton MS 1535*, f. 611; *TSP*, ii, 373.

37. *CSP Venetian 1655–1656*, p. 201.

38. *NP*, i, 123–5, 182–5; HMC, *Bath MSS*, ii, 84–8; HMC, *Hodgkin MSS*, pp. 120–1; Clarendon, *Rebellion*, v, 212, 214; viii, 96.

39. Loftis, *Halkett and Fanshawe Memoirs*, pp. 128–30; HMC, *Bath MSS*, ii, 89; Violet Barbour, *Henry Bennet, Earl of Arlington*, (Washington, 1914), pp. 31–45.

40. Clarendon, *Rebellion*, ix, 100–2; xiii, 29–30; Loftis, *Halkett and Fanshawe Memoirs*, p. 130.

41. Ibid, pp. 129–30. For Clarendon's account of Ascham's murder see *Rebellion*, xiii, 9–11, and Lister, *Life of Clarendon*, iii, 56–9, (Hyde and Cottington to Robert Long, 7 June 1650).

42. Clarendon, *Rebellion*, xiii, 11; Lister, *Life of Clarendon*, i, 352–3; iii, 56–8; *TSP*, i, 149–51, 204; *Archeologia*, xxxv, 341.
43. BL. *Egerton MS 2542*, f. 138; *TSP*, i, 151, 204; *CCISP*, ii, 220, iii, 16; *NP*, iii, 158–9 (interrogation of Henry Manning); Warburton, *Memoirs*, i, 429; Lister, *Life of Clarendon*, iii, 56–8. For James Halsall see Underdown, *Royalist Conspiracy*, pp. 65, 115, 118, 132–3, 170–3.
44. *TSP*, iv, 122; *CSPD 1655*, p. 390; *CCISP*, iii, 29, 65.
45. *TSP*, i, 149–51; iii, 458, 532; Lister, *Life of Clarendon*, i, 352–3; iii, 56–8. Newman, in *Royalist Officers*, pp. 413–4, lists several officers named Williams, but none can be identified confidently with Ascham's murderer.
46. Chaney, *The Grand Tour and the Great Rebellion*, passim; Stoye, *English Travellers Abroad*, pp. 118, 134, 136.
47. *CCC*, iv, 2461–4; Chaney, *Grand Tour and Great Rebellion*, pp. 303–4; *DNB*.
48. BL. *Egerton MS 1635*, passim; *Add. MS 1719*, passim.
49. *Verney Memoirs*, iii, 40–9; BL, *Add. MS 24121*, fols. 353, 355, 456; *CCISP*, iii, 119; Hardacre, 'Royalists in Exile', pp. 353–70. See also entries in *DNB* for Crashaw, Digby, Sherburne and Wyche.
50. Chaney, *Grand Tour and Great Rebellion*, p. 50.
51. *NP*, i, 296; *CISP*, iii, 65; Newman, *Royalist Officers*, p. 199.
52. BL. *Add MS 20032 (Killigrew Papers)*, fols. 3, 4, 26; *CSP Venetian 1647–1652*, xxviii, 189, 196–8, 215–6, 247–50; *CCISP*, ii, 143.
53. *Poetical Works of Waller and Denham*. From Denham's 'On Mr Thomas Killigrew's Return from Venice', p. 246. *CSP Venetian 1647–1652*, xxviii, 250, 254, 254, 262, 268.
54. *CSPD 1650*, pp. 159, 517; 1651, 203, 527; *CCC*, ii, 1192; iii, 1831. For Mayney and Stamford see Newman, *Royalist Officers*, pp. 250–1, 354.
55. *CCC*, v. 3, 1652, 1654–5; v. 96, 453; v. 152, 513; *CCISP*, ii, 259, 296; *CSPD 1650*, pp. 57, 89, 152–6; *1660–1661*, p. 564; *1661–1662*, p. 54; Newman, *Royalist Officers*, p. 214.
56. *HMC, Report 13*, Appendix 1, p. 614; *HMC, Report 55*, ii, 355; *TSP*, vi, 331, 356; *CCISP*, iv, 430, 449, 451; Newman, *Royalist Officers*, pp. 156–7; Underdown, *Royalist Conspiracy*, p. 276.
57. *CCISP*, iii, 10; *CSPD 1625–1649*, pp. 629–30; Warburton, *Memoirs*, ii, 392; Newman, *Royalist Officers*, pp. 186, 215; *DNB*, (for King).
58. BL. *Add. MS 1892*, fols. 122, 128; *Add. MS 4158*, f. 206; *TSP*, vi, 151, 672, 743, 816; vii, 628; Newman, *Royalist Officers*, pp. 388–9.
59. *TSP*, iv, 718; *NP*, ii, 188. *DNB* (for Drummond).
60. For Culpepper's mission to Moscow and Crofts's to Poland see *CCISP*, ii, 71, 124; *NP*, i, 182–5; *Poetical Works of Waller and Denham*, pp. 203, 244–6, (Denham's account of his 'journey into Poland' with Crofts); Clarendon, *Rebellion*, xv, 131.
61. For Killigrew's travels see BL. *Add. MS 20032*; *TSP*, ii, 602; vii, 27; *CCISP*, ii, 143; Chaney, *Grand Tour and Great Rebellion*, pp. 280–1; *DNB*.
62. John Bargrave, *Pope Alexander VII and the College of Cardinals*, ed. J. C. Robinson, Camden Society, (London, 1867), pp. v, ix–xiii, 11, 30–3, 68–70, 92, 127–35; Bod. L. *Rawlinson MS C799*, fols. 163, 181 (account of Bargrave's travels in Italy); Chaney, *Grand Tour and Great Rebellion*, p. 297; Stoye, *English Travellers Abroad*, pp. 161–3.

63. *Basire Correspondence*, pp. iv, 79–84, 105–6, 115–20, 127–31; *DNB*.
64. *CSPD 1660–1661*, p. 300; Newman, *Royalist Officers*, p. 16; *DNB*.
65. *CCC*, iii, 1652; v, 196, 726; Bod. L. *Clarendon MS 78*, fols. 173–4.
66. Ibid, *MS 78*, fols. 177–8, 179–82.
67. For Clarendon's comment on Culpepper see Ollard, *Clarendon and His Friends*, p. 64.
68. Bargrave, *Alexander VII*, pp. xiii–xvii. Diplomatic appointments made to returned royalist exiles after 1660 are discussed below in Chapter 12.
69. *CCC*, ii, 1579–80.

8 Nothing so Rare as Money

1. *The Memoirs of James II; his Campaigns as Duke of York*. p. 57.
2. Scott, *King in Exile*, p. 1; Hardacre, 'Royalists in Exile', *HLQ*, 1952, xvi, 353; Underdown, 'Cavaliers in Exile', *History of the English Speaking Peoples*, no. 53, p. 1692; Feiling, *History of the Tory Party*, p. 78; Miller, *James II*, p. 5.
3. Taaffe quoted in Scott *King in Exile*, p. 3; *CISP*, iii, 179.
4. Ibid, iii, 120.
5. Ibid, iii, 124.
6. Ibid, ii, 543–4.
7. *Cholmley Memoirs*, p. 74.
8. *CISP*, iii, 81; BL. *Egerton MS 2536*, f. 4.
9. Bod. L. *Clarendon MS 59*, fols. 56–7; *CCISP*, iii, 309; iv, 358, 382.
10. *TSP*, vii, 252; Bod. L. *Clarendon MS 66*, f. 20.
11. *CSPD 1657–1658*, p. 296; *LBM*, p. 105; *NP*, iv, 188.
12. Bod. L. *MS 46*, f. 365; *MS 55*, fols. 306–8; *CCISP*, ii, 192–3, 205; *DNB*; Ollard, *Clarendon and His Friends*, pp. 174–5.
13. *HMC, Bath MSS*, ii, 91.
14. Bod. L. *Clarendon MS 52*, fols. 374–6; *CCISP*, iii, 17; Lister, *Life of Clarendon*, ii, 376; iii, 61.
15. Bod. L. *Clarendon MS 64*, f. 336; Lister, *Life of Clarendon*, ii, 446.
16. Clarendon, *Rebellion*, xiii, 129; *CISP*, iii, 120; R. W. Harris, *Clarendon and the English Revolution*, (Stanford, California, 1983), pp. 220–1.
17. Margaret Newcastle, *Life*, pp. 62–4; *DNB*; Geoffrey Trease, *Portrait of a Cavalier: William Cavendish, First Duke of Newcastle*, (London, 1979), pp. 142–3.
18. Margaret Newcastle, *Life*, p. 64.
19. *HMC, Bath MSS*, ii, 87–8, 90. For Aylesbury's activities see Stoye, *English Travellers*, pp. 212–30.
20. Margaret Newcastle, *Life*, pp. 66–7.
21. Ibid, p. 70; Trease, *Portrait of a Cavalier*, pp. 174–6; *DNB*.
22. Margaret Newcastle, *Life*, pp. 75–9, 88.
23. Ibid, p. 85.
24. *CSPD 1657–1658*, pp. 296–7.
25. *TSP*, ii, 312.

26. Bod. L. *Clarendon MS 49*, fols. 4, 100–09; *CISP*, iii, 46; *NP*, iv, 264; Lister, *Life of Clarendon*, i, 367; ii, 417, 442; Scott, *King in Exile*, pp. 430–2; Harris, *Clarendon and English Revolution*, pp. 220–1.
27. PRO. *SP Foreign (German States)*, 81/54 fols. 93, 101–4, 112–3, 138–40; Bod. L. *Clarendon MS 48*, f. 42; Lister, *Life of Clarendon*, ii, 372–4; *CISP*, iii, 69–70; BL. *Add MS 37047*, fols. 219, 240; *CCISP*, ii, 297, 361–2.
28. *CCISP*, ii, 220; iii, 10, 24; *NP*, ii, 160; *CISP*, iii, 165, 171, 174–5; Hibbard, *Charles I and the Popish Plot*, pp. 178, 185, 289.
29. *Fox Memoirs*, pp. 2, 4–5, 8–9; Clarendon, *Rebellion*, xiv, 89; Clay, *Private Finance and Public Wealth*, pp. 1–2, 8–12.
30. Clarendon, *Rebellion*, xiv, 89.
31. Bod. L. *Clarendon MS 50*, f. 77.
32. *CSPD 1657–1658*, p. 304.
33. Bod. L. *Clarendon MS 49*, f. 108; *MS 64*, f. 352; *MS 68*, f. 206; *CCISP*, ii, 286–7; PRO. *SP Foreign (German States)* 81/54/104; Clay, *Private Finance and Public Wealth*, pp. 12–3.
34. Bod. L. *Clarendon MS 68*, f. 206; Newman, *Royalist Officers*, pp. 156–7. Newman lists three royalist officers named Gibson. It is not clear which 'Mr Gibson' was the recipient of Fox's bounty in January 1660. Ibid, pp. 154–5.
35. Bod. L. *Clarendon MS 52*, fols. 374–6. See also the distribution of 7,000 florins, received in July 1659 from Shaw, to over 20 exiles, ranging from prominent figures like Ormonde, Langdale and O'Neill, to the totally obscure 'Captain Knight'. Ibid, *MS 64*, f. 352.
36. Bod. L. *Clarendon MS 55*, f. 4.
37. Ibid, fols. 164, 169; *CCISP*, iii, 309, 320, 328, 374. For Barlow see Newman, *Royalist Officers*, pp. 16–7.
38. Bod. L. *Clarendon MS 66*, fols. 49–50.
39. Ibid, *MS 59*, fols. 56–7, 93–4, 119.
40. Coate, *Cornwall in the Civil War*, p. 358; *Verney Memoirs*, ii, 391; Felicity Heal and Clive Holmes, *The Gentry in England and Wales 1500–1700*, (Macmillan – now Palgrave Macmillan, 1994), pp. 71–2.
41. *HMC, Bath MSS*, ii, 136.
42. *NP*, iii, 89; *CCC*, ii, 1580.
43. Bod. L. *Clarendon MS 59*, fols. 36–7.
44. Clarendon, *Rebellion*, v, 212, 214; xii, 60, 61; Lister, *Life of Clarendon*, ii, 381–4; iii. 69–83; *CCISP*, ii, 251.
45. Bod. L. *Clarendon MS 59*, f. 236. Elizabeth Elliot's letter was intercepted by de Marce', the royalist agent in the Post Office, who made the copy which is preserved in the Clarendon MSS.
46. Fraser, *Charles II*, p. 84; *CSPD 1657–1658*, p. 378; *1661–1662*, p. 221.
47. Carte, *Life of Ormond*, v, 147.
48. *NP*, i. 261–2.
49. *Evelyn's Diary*, iv, 320; *HMC, Bath MSS*, ii, 81–2.
50. Chaney, *Grand Tour and Great Rebellion*, pp. 51–2 (Hobbes); *CSPD 1650*, pp. 167, 220; *Miscellanea Aulica*, ed. T. Brown, (London, 1702), p. 137 (Davenant); Gilfillan, *Poetical Works of Waller and Denham*, p. 207 (Denham); Brown, *Miscellanea Aulica*, pp. 130–60. (Cowley). See also entries in *DNB*.
51. Bod. L. *Clarendon MS 64*, f. 352; *CCISP*, iii, 297.
52. The quotation is from Edgar, *Sir Ralph Hopton*, p. 187.

53. *HMC, 13th Report, Portland MSS*, i, 584, 586, 598–9; *NP*, ii, 104; *TSP*, iii, 37, 43; *CSPD 1654–1655*, pp. 192–3; *Letters Illustrating the Relations between Charles II and Scotland in 1650*, ed. S. R. Gardiner, Scottish History Society, (Edinburgh, 1894), p. 154; Newman, *Royalist Officers*, pp. 283–4.
54. B. L. *Egerton MS 2534*, fols. 142–3; Bod. L. *Clarendon MS 48*, f. 35; *CClSP*, ii, 288; *NP*, iii, 21, 28, 56–8; A. Robertson, *The Life of Sir Robert Moray 1608–1673*, (London, 1922), pp. 92–4.
55. *CSPD 1654–1655*, p. 193; *NP*, iii, 21.
56. *CClSP*, iii, 360, 361, 364. For Sir Thomas Page's attitude to the 'sons or reputed sons' of his brother see G. E. Aylmer, *The Crown's Servants; Government and Civil Service under Charles II, 1660–1685*, (Oxford, 2002), pp. 197–8.
57. Warburton, *Memoirs*, ii, 395, 464–5; *CClSP*, ii, 69; *CSPD 1651*, pp. 432, 478–9, 502.
58. Ibid, pp. 426, 478–9.
59. Ibid, *1655–1656*, pp. 63, 576.
60. Bod. L. *Clarendon MS 59*, f. 42; *MS 66*, f. 156; *MS 68*, f. 206; *CClSP*, iii, 104, 339, 359.

9   Feuds, Factions and Fornication

1. *TSP*, ii, 546.
2. Scott, *King in Exile*, pp. 4, 458–9; Feiling, *Tory Party*, p. 78; Underdown, 'Cavaliers in Exile', p. 1692; Miller, *James II*, p. 5.
3. Carte, *Letters and Papers*, i, 148, 152, 154–9. See also Nicholas's account of the quarrel between Rupert and Culpepper at the Hague in October 1648, that led to Culpepper being attacked by one of Rupert's followers, Sir Robert Walsh. Ibid, i, 192.
4. *ClSP*, ii, 530.
5. Ibid, iii, 141. For Hyde's relations with Grenville see Hutton, *Charles II*, pp. 9–13.
6. BL. *Egerton MS 2534*, f. 155.
7. *ClSP*, iii, 211.
8. *NP*, ii, 19, 35, 37–40, 49–50; Lister, *Life of Clarendon*, ii, 381–4; Hutton, *Charles II*, pp. 85–6.
9. *ClSP*, iii, 88; *NP*, ii, 156–7.
10. *Memoirs of James II*, pp. 222–3; Miller, *James II*, p. 5; Hutton, *Charles II*, p. 103.
11. For an example of this confusion, see the household list drawn up by Nicholas at Bruges in 1657 where five names, including Langdale's, have been crossed out. PRO. *SP 18/158/10*.
12. BL. *Egerton MS 2536*, f. 83.
13. *TSP*, iii, 561.
14. G. E. Aylmer, *The King's Servants*, (London, 1974), pp. 472–5.
15. *TSP*, ii, 534; iii, 425, 428, 458–9; PRO. *SP 18/138/10*; Bod. L. *Clarendon MS 49*, f. 107; BL. *Egerton MS 2542*, fols. 330–2, 342–4, 347–8, 352.
16. For examples see Bod. L. *Clarendon MS 49*, f. 107; PRO. *SP 18/158/10*; *29/26/78*.

17. For Brentford see *HMC, Pepys MSS*, 70, p. 255; *DNB*; Newman, *Royalist Officers*, p. 322.
18. *CISP*, iii, 67, 77, 86–8, 106; *NP*, i, 283, 285–6, 298, 304.
19. *The English Court: from the Wars of the Roses to the Civil War*, ed. David Starkey, (London, 1987), p. 256 (for Holland); Underdown, *Royalist Conspiracy*, p. 334 (for Grenville).
20. *TSP*, iv, 122; *CCISP*, iii, 65. For example, Hester Chapman, *The Tragedy of Charles II*, combines Nicholas and William Armorer into one person.
21. Clarendon, *Rebellion*, xiii, 80.
22. *CSPD 1655*, pp. 390–1.
23. Ibid, pp. 192–3.
24. *TSP*, v, 36.
25. Hutton, *Charles II*, pp. 122–3.
26. *CSPD 1657–1658*, p. 165. Barker retained his position as avenor and Armorer his as an equerry. PRO. *SP 29/26/78*.
27. PRO. *SP 18/179/*fols. 78, 79.
28. *CSPD 1657–1658*, pp. 310–1. Benion and Silvius were both courtiers, Benion being a gentleman of the bedchamber. *NP*, iii, 244.
29. *Archeologia*, xxxv, 347; *CCISP*, iv, 61, 63; BL. *Egerton MS 2542*, f. 278.
30. *CCISP*, ii, 391; HMC, *Bath MSS*, ii, 129–31:
31. *CISP*, iii, 59.
32. *TSP*, v, 315, 645–6; vi, 151, 254.
33. *CISP*, iii, 108.
34. Scott, *King in Exile*, p. 7; Feiling, *History of the Tory Party*, p. 78.
35. Fraser, *King Charles II*, pp. 153–5; Hutton, *Charles II*, pp. 122–6; T. C. Barnard 'The Protestant Interest, 1641–1660', in Jane H. Ohlmeyer, ed., *Ireland from Independence to Occupation 1641–1660*, (Cambridge, 1995), p. 226. The theme of Hester Chapman's *The Tragedy of Charles II in the years 1630–1660* is essentially the same as Eva Scott's, that, as a consequence of the experiences of civil war and exile, Charles II's moral qualities were 'corrupted and destroyed'.
36. *TSP*, v, 645–6.
37. *Diary of John Evelyn*, ed. E. S. de Beer, (Oxford, 1955). 6 vols., ii, 561–2.
38. *NP*, i, 303. For Leighton see Newman, *Royalist Officers*, p. 230.
39. B. D. Henning, *The History of Parliament: the House of Commons 1660–1690*, 3 vols., (London, 1983), iii, 293; Count Grammont, *Memoirs of the Court of Charles II*, (London, 1853), p. 217; *The Diary of Samuel Pepys*, eds. R. Latham and W. Matthews, 11 vols., (London, 1976–1983), v, 56; x, 347.
40. E. D'Oyley, *James, Duke of Monmouth*, (London, 1938), pp. 13, 25; Chapman, *The Tragedy of Charles II*, pp. 148, 330.
41. J. A. Bradney, *A History of Monmouthshire*, (London, 1914), pp. 196–7; Henning, *Commons 1660–1690*, iii, 293; HMC, *Report 10 (Story Maskelyne MSS)*, iv, 146–8; HMC, *Pepys MSS*, 70, pp. 238, 255; BL. *Add. MS 14,858*, f. 58; Clarendon, *Rebellion*, x, 5.
42. HMC, *Report 10*, iv, 147, 148.
43. Ibid, iv, 147.
44. *CISP*, ii, 530.
45. *Letters and Papers Illustrating relations between Charles II and Scotland*, p. 151; Scott, *King in Exile*, pp. 189–90; Chapman, *Tragedy of Charles II*, pp. 176–7.

46. *Miscellaneas Aulica*, pp. 152–3; *NP*, i, 206–8.
47. *HMC, Report 10*, iv, 148.
48. *NP*, i, 278.
49. *CSPSD 1652–1653*, pp. 25, 28, 94; *1655*, pp. 204, 588; *1655–1656*, p. 149; *NP*, iv, 31.
50. For the claim that 'Edward Prodgers was then sent by Charles to Brussels to kidnap James', see Chapman, *Tragedy of Charles II*, p. 330 and D'Oyley, *James Duke of Monmouth*, p. 25. Although still a groom of the bedchamber, Progers was not included in the list of the royal household drawn up by Nicholas in 1657 and he was certainly in London in December of that year. *CSPD 1657–1658*, p. 201; *NP*, iv, 31.
51. *CClSP*, v, 31.

10   Losing the Plot: Agents, Spies and Traitors

1. Bod. L. *Clarendon MS 67*, f. 191. [O'Neill to Hyde, Paris, 9 December 1659].
2. Balleine, *All for the King*, p. 1; Barnard, 'The Protestant Interest', p. 226.
3. *TSP*, iv, 10.
4. *HMC, Bath MSS*, ii, 81–2; *ClSP*, iii, 69–70.
5. *CClSP*, iv, 69, 71–2, 358, 382.
6. *ClSP*, iii, 150, 181, 304, 379; Clarendon, *Rebellion*, xvi, 58.
7. Ibid, vii, 185; xi, 69; *CCC*, ii, 1543. For Seymour see *DNB*; Henning, *House of Commons 1660–1690*, iii, 421.
8. *Sir Thomas Herbert's Narrative*, ed. R. Lockyer, (Folio Society), (London, 1959), p. 122.
9. *CClSP*, ii, 28, 32, 38; S. R. Gardiner, *History of the Commonwealth and Protectorate*, 4 vols., (London, 1903), i, 160, 207.
10. *CClSP*, ii, 69, 77, 85, 116; *Miscellanea Aulica*, pp. 152–3; *CSPD 1650*, p. 324; Carte, *Letters and Papers*, ii, 11, 20, 21; Clarendon, *Rebellion*, xiii, 108.
11. *Charles II and Scotland*, ed. Gardiner, pp. 4, 133, 154–6; Underdown, *Royalist Conspiracy*, pp. 36, 40–1. For Blague see Newman, *Royalist Officers*, p. 31.
12. *TSP*, i, 710; *CClSP*, ii, 181. '*A brief Relation of the Affairs of England as they stand at present. March 1653*', printed in C. H. Firth, 'Cromwell and the Expulsion of the Long Parliament', *English Historical Review*, (1893), viii, 526–31. For Corker see Underdown, *Royalist Conspiracy*, pp. 175–6.
13. BL. *Add. MS 4180*, f. 104.
14. Ibid, fols. 104, 108, 122; BL. *Egerton MS 2550*, f. 14; *CClSP*, ii, 282, 335–6, 340, 356. For Armorer's role in the formation of the Sealed Knot see Underdown, *Royalist Conspiracy*, pp. 73–75; A. H. Woolrych, *Penruddock's Rising 1655*, (Historical Association, 1955), pp. 4–5.
15. *ClSP*, iii, 100, 224, 229, 234–5; *CClSP*, ii, 340.
16. *TSP*, ii, 599; *CSPD 1655–1656*, p. 263.
17. *NP*, ii, 141; *CSPD 1655–1656*, p. 209. Manning's letters to Thurloe at this time, which refer to Armorer's presence in England, show that Cromwell's Secretary already knew quite a lot about the real identity and activities of the prisoner in Dover castle in February 1655 whom Captain Wilson allowed to slip through his fingers.
18. *ClSP*, iii, 200, 202; *CClSP*, ii, 278, 283.

19. BL. *Add. MS 4180*, f. 74; *CCISP*, iii, 114, 268, 318; iv, passim.
20. *TSP*, iv, 834.
21. *CCISP*, ii, 149, 323, 335–6; Underdown, *Royalist Conspiracy*, pp. 97–104, 322.
22. *CCISP*, iii, 23, Clarendon, *Rebellion*, xiv, 127, 130, 131. For Penruddock's rising see Underdown, *Royalist Conspiracy*, pp. 127–58; Woolrych, *Penruddock's Rising*. For Wagstaffe see Newman, *Royalist Officers*, p. 394; *DNB*.
23. *CCISP*, iii, 21, 22, 23; Bod. L. *Clarendon MS 49*, f. 387. The evidence is fairly conclusive that Robert Day was a royalist agent. 'Mr Day of Dover' is included in one of Nicholas's cipher keys with the pseudonym 'Mr Darke': *Egerton MS 2550*, f. 83. Bradshaw, Thurloe's agent at Hamburg, reported that he had heard that 'one Day, clerk of the passage at Dover, hath permitted many dangerous persons to pass into England': *TSP*, iii, 198. See also Underdown, *Royalist Conspiracy*, pp. 133–4.
24. *TSP*, iii, 358.
25. Bod. L. *Rawlinson MS 25*, f. 29 [*TSP*, iii, 335–6]; *NP*, ii, 327. The observation on the appropriateness of the magistrate's name is David Underdown's: *Royalist Conspiracy*, p. 161.
26. PRO. *SP Foreign (France) 78/114/*fols. 5, 102, 110, 137; *TSP*, iii, 273, 304, 308, 453; iv, 10; *HMC, 7th Report*, Appendix, p. 123; *CCC*, i, 747.
27. *TSP*, iii, 190, 344, 428–9, 455, 458; *CSPD 1655*, pp. 174, 212, 245; *CCISP*, iii, 34, 36.
28. *NP*, ii, 100; iii, 5; *TSP*, ii, 321, 510–1; *CSPD 1654*, pp. 273–4; *1655*, pp. 204, 588.
29. *NP*, ii, 100, 221, 222; iii, 5; *CSPD 1656–1657*, pp. 260–1; *CCISP*, iii, 222, 339.
30. For examples see *TSP*, ii, 405, 510–1, 534, 546, 556, 599, 601–2; iii, 457–9, 510–4, 532–3, 561; iv, 10, 51, 88, 122, 169, 370, 388, 407, 414; vi, 160, 169, 178; vii, 150, 181, 203, 312–3, 346–7, 428, 529.
31. Carte, *Letters and Papers*, i, 179–80; Firth and Rait, *Acts and Ordinances*, ii, 521; Bod. L. *Clarendon MS 49*, f. 153; *CCISP*, iii, 7; *TSP*, ii, 546; Newman, *Royalist Officers*, pp. 246–7; Henning, *House of Commons*, iii, 21–2. For Marlay's defence of Newcastle during the Civil War see Wedgwood, *King's War*, p. 378.
32. *TSP*, vii, 150, 181, 203, 229, 252, 312–3, 333, 346–7; *HMC, Report 55*, Various Collections, ii, 360.
33. *CCISP*, iii, 10, 13–4, 15–6; *TSP*, iv, 370, 407; Newman, *Royalist Officers*, p. 186. Massonet had been involved in the different 'Swordsmen' plots in Paris in 1652–3 to destroy Hyde: Bod. L. *Carte MS 30*, f. 182; Lister, *Life of Clarendon*, iii, 62, 69–83.
34. *CCISP*, ii, 336; iii, 240; iv, 223, *TSP*, v, 160, 169, 178; vii, 428, 444. For Howard's relationship with Lucy Walter see Hutton, *Charles II*, pp. 97, 125–6.
35. PRO. *SP Foreign (France) 78/113/*fols. 198, 202, 227, 233, 282; *TSP*, ii, 510–1; iii, 510–4, 533; iv, 51; Newman, *Royalist Officers*, pp. 15–6. For insights into the character and personal behaviour of Bampfield see Loftis, *Halkett and Fanshawe Memoirs*, passim; Alan Marshall, *Intelligence and Espionage in the Reign of Charles II, 1660–1685*, (Cambridge, 1994), pp. 169–74.
36. *Miscellanea Aulica*, p. 108; PRO. *SP Foreign (Flanders) 77/31/*f. 504; Clarendon, *Rebellion*, xi, 141.
37. *CCC*, iv, 2649; Clarendon, *Rebellion*, xiv, 138.

38. BL. *Egerton MS 2542*, fols. 129–38, 176–7, 210, 216, 221; *TSP*, iv, 290, 313, 718; *CClSP*, iii, 77; Clarendon, *Rebellion*, xiv, 140–5.
39. *TSP*, iv, 122, 169; *CSPSD 1655*, pp. 192–3.
40. BL. *Egerton MS 2542*, f. 221.
41. Bod. L. *Clarendon MS 67*, fols. 191–2. [O'Neill to Hyde, 9 December 1659].
42. *CClSP*, iv, 7, 9, 13, 15, 22–3, and passim [Maurice]; *TSP*, ii, 568–9; iv, 10 [Moore].
43. PRO. *SP Domestic Interregnum 1655, 18/98/f*. 45.
44. *CSP Venetian 1655–1656*, p. 201; *CSPD 1655–1656*, p. 579.
45. *SP Domestic Interregnum 1655, 18/98/f*. 45; *CClSP*, iii, 62; *TSP*, iv, 835.
46. Carte, *Life of Ormond*, iii, 660–6; *CClSP*, iv, 8, 9, 11–2, 13–4, 15, 20–1, 23, 26, 39; Carte, *Letters and Papers*, ii, 132–3. For Ormonde's secret mission to London and the plans for a royalist rising early in 1658 see Underdown, *Royalist Conspiracy*, pp. 214–29.

11 Failed Hopes and Fresh Prospects

1. Bod. L. *Clarendon MS 59*, fols. 436–7.
2. Cited in Underdown, *Royalist Conspiracy*, p. 216. For O'Neill's and other optimistic assessments on the prospects of a successful royalist rising see *CClSP*, iv, 18–24, 28–36.
3. Hutton, *Charles II*, p. 111; Newman, *Royalist Conspiracy*, p. 416; *DNB*.
4. BL. *Egerton MS 22536*, f. 159; *CClSP*, iii, 279, 368, 401; *NP*, iv, 20, 36–9, 50; C. H. Firth, 'Royalist and Cromwellian Armies in Flanders 1657–1662', *Transactions of the Royal Historical Society*, new series, v. 17, (1903), pp. 67–119. For Major Thomas Curtis and Colonel William Slaughter see Newman, *Royalist Conspiracy*, pp. 97, 344.
5. *ClSP*, iii, 49.
6. Clarendon, *Rebellion*, xvi, 1, 2.
7. *ClSP*, iii, 387; *NP*, iii, 13, 15. See also Hutton, *Charles II*, pp. 123–5; Ollard, *Clarendon and his Friends*, pp. 196–7.
8. M. F. Keeler, *The Long Parliament 1640–1641*, (Philadelphia, 1954), p. 202.
9. *NP*, i, 238, 261–2, ii, 91; *CClSP*, ii, 110–2; iii, 29; Bray, *Evelyn's Diary*, iv, 213, 219, 221; Loftis, *Halkett and Fanshawe Memoirs*, p. 53.
10. Bod. L. *Clarendon MS 50*, f. 77.
11. Ibid, *MS 58*, fols. 374–5.
12. Ibid, *MS 59*, f. 75.
13. Ibid, *MS 58*, fols. 374–5; *MS 59*, fols. 75, 175, 436–7.
14. *HMC, 10th Report, Braye MSS*, Appendix vi, (London, 1887), p. 211.
15. *Mordaunt Letter-Book*, pp. 2–4; *HMC, 7th Report, House of Lords Calendar*, Appendix, (London, 1879), p. 103; *10th Report, Braye MSS*, Appendix, pp. 189–90; *CClSP*, iv, 34–5, 127, 136; *DNB*.
16. *Mordaunt Letter-Book*, pp. 93–4, 161–2; *CSPD 1655*, p. 575; *ClSP*, iii, 335, [Hyde to Ormonde, 9 March 1657]; T. R. Nash, *Collections for the History of Worcestershire*, (London, 1781), ii, 493–500. There are several inaccuracies in the *DNB* entry on Lyttelton. For Hartgill Baron see *Mordaunt Letter-Book*, passim and Underdown, *Royalist Conspiracy*, pp. 210, 253, 280, 303, 316.
17. *CSPD 1655–1656*, p. 576; *1656–1657*, pp. 17, 347–8; *Mordaunt Letter-Book*,

p. 8n.; *CCISP*, iii, 107–8, 130, 132, 311; Underdown, *Royalist Conspiracy*, pp. 205, 211.

18. Neville, *The Commonwealth of Ladies*, [Thomason Tracts], pp. 20–1; *CSPD 1655*, p. 595; *1657–1658*, p. 311; *HMC, Bath MS*, ii, 122, 125; *TSP*, vii, 255; *CCISP*, iv, 138, 139; Henning, *House of Commons*, ii, 111. Colonel Sir Herbert Price was a veteran of the Civil War who was excepted from pardon in 1650. He had strong court connections and was a close friend of Rochester. His son was a page to the Duke of York.

19. *CCISP*, iv, 147, 165, 169, 173, 178; Carte, *Letters and Papers*, ii, 129.

20. *CCISP*, iv, 201, 202; *HMC, 10th Report, Braye MSS*, p. 209.

21. *CCISP*, iv, 355, [Moore to Hyde, 2 September 1659]. For a full and excellent account of Booth's rising see Underdown, *Royalist Conspiracy*, pp. 254–285.

22. *CCISP*, iv, 328, 331.

23. Ibid, iv, 331, 332, 334, 336, 338.

24. Ibid, iv, 336, 339.

25. Ibid, iv, 343.

26. *CISP*, iii, 570; Sir Richard Baker, *A Chronicle of the Kings of England*, continuation by E. Phillips, (London, 1679), pp. 573, 650; *CCISP*, iv, 327, 334, 358, 413, 414; Carte, *Letters and Papers*, ii, 205.

27. Clarendon, *Rebellion*, xvi, 45, 46; *CCISP*, iv, 336, 406; Underdown *Royalist Conspiracy*, pp. 288–90.

28. *Mordaunt Letter-Book*, p. 40.

29. Clarendon, *Rebellion*, xvi, 58; Hutton, *Charles II*, pp. 116–17.

30. N. H. Keeble, *The Restoration: England in the 1660s*, (Blackwell, 2002), pp. 5–14.

31. Quoted in Keeble, *Restoration*, p.13.

32. *Mordaunt Letter-Book*, p. 105; BL. *Egerton MS 2542*, f. 331; Bod. L. *Clarendon MS 66*, fols. 134–5, 147; *NP*, iv, 188.

33. *Mordaunt Letter-Book*, p. 105.

34. Bod. L. *Clarendon MS 66*, fols. 95, 147; Loftis, *Halkett and Fanshawe Memoirs*, pp. 135–40.

35. Carte, *Letters and Papers*, ii, 258.

36. Clarendon, *Rebellion*, xvi, 74.

37. Ibid, xvi, 75, 76; Miller, *James II*, p. 24.

38. *Mordaunt Letter-Book*, pp. 38–9; Carte, *Letters and Papers*, ii, 205, 214–5, 217; *CCISP*, iv, 414; Bod. L. *Clarendon MS 67*, f. 169.

39. Quoted in Keeble, *Restoration*, p. 19. For other contemporary expressions on Monck's impenetrability and the difficulties of determining his intentions see Ibid, pp. 17–18.

40. *CSPD 1657–1658*, p. 346; *1659–1660*, pp. 305, 311, 316, 324, 332–4, 338, 342; *CCISP*, iv, 439, 523, 531, 549, 551.

41. Clarendon, *Rebellion*, xvi, 138–40; *CCISP*, iv, 568; Hutton, *Charles II*, p. 127; Keeble, *Restoration*, pp. p. 22.

42. For full accounts of events during this period see Hutton, *The Restoration*, pp. 85–118 and Keeble, *Restoration*, pp. 17–31. For the rise of Grenville's influence and the relative decline of Mordaunt's see Underdown, *Royalist Conspiracy*, pp. 300–4, 312–3.

43. Clarendon, *Rebellion*, xvi, 137, 141; *HMC, Bath MSS*, ii, 142; *Letters of Elizabeth, Queen of Bohemia*, ed. L. M. Baker, (London, 1953), p. 303, quoted in Alison Plowden, *The Stuart Princesses*, (London, 1997), p. 115.

12   Gone For England

1. Sir Richard Browne, resident ambassador in Paris to both Charles I and Charles II in the 1640s and 1650s, was John Evelyn's father-in-law.
2. Baker, *Chronicle of the Kings of England*, p. 771 (for knighthoods to Mordaunt and Massey); *Evelyn's Diary*, iv, 320. For accounts of Charles II's return to England see Hutton, *Restoration*, pp. 125–6; Fraser, *Charles* II, pp. 179–82; Keeble, *Restoration*, pp. 40–6.
3. *Pepys' Diary*, i, 153–4 (22 and 23 May 1660). See also Claire Tomalin, *Samuel Pepys: the Unequalled Self*, (London, 2002), pp. 104, 107, 108.
4. *HMC, Bath MSS*, ii, 144; *CCISP*, iv, 432, 654, 664; Ollard, *Clarendon and his Friends*, p. 216; Trease, *Portrait of a Cavalier*, p. 176.
5. *NP*, iv, 206–7; *CCC*, i, 747.
6. *NP*, iv, 190, 193, 204; *CCISP*, iv, 573, 581, 586, 589, 612–4, 631, 641, 654.
7. Ibid, iv, 680. For 'Breda swarmed with English' see Keeble, *Restoration*, p. 40.
8. *CCISP*, iv, 635, 654, 673; v, 13; PRO. *SP 29/26/78*; Keeble, *Restoration*, p. 97.
9. *CCISP*, iv, 676; Barbour, *Arlington*, pp. 40, 45; *Basire Correspondence*, pp. 127–31, 202; Bod. L. *Clarendon MS 78*, fols. 173–4, 179–82; *DNB* (Long and Drummond).
10. Clarendon, *Rebellion*, xiii, 83; *NP*, i, 278.

13   Rewards and Favours

1. B.L. *Egerton MS 2542*, f. 347.
2. *CSPD 1660–1661*, pp. 654–5; Newman, *Royalist Officers*, p. 223.
3. Clarendon, *life*, i, 584–604; Lister, *Life of Clarendon*, ii, 228–9; Paul Seaward, *The Cavalier Parliament and the Reconstruction of the Old Regime 1661–1667*, (Cambridge, 1989), p. 220.
4. Ibid, pp. 214, 220. The quotation of course refers to the royalist party as a whole and not just to the returned exiles.
5. For valuable discussions of the treatment of royalists in the Restoration settlement see Hardacre, *Royalists during the Puritan Revolution*, pp. 145–51; Hutton, *Restoration*, pp. 126–35 and *Charles* II, pp. 142–51; Seaward, *Cavalier Parliament*, pp. 196–24; Keeble, *Restoration*, pp. 81–4.
6. Ibid, pp. 71, 83. Burnet quoted in Keeble, p. 83.
7. Clarendon, *Life*, i, 269.
8. Robertson, *Sir Robert Moray*, pp. 75–6, 96–9, 150–3; Douglas McKie, 'The Origins and Foundation of the Royal Society of London', in *The Royal Society: Its Origins and Founders'*, ed. H. Hartley, (London, 1960), pp. 32–5.
9. Printed in the *Bulletin of the Institute of Historical Research*, (henceforward *BIHR*), (London, 1942–3), vol. 19, 13–21.
10. *HMC, Pepys MSS*, 70, pp. 255–6; *CCISP*, ii, 386–7; *CSPD 1657–1658*. p. 201; PRO. SP 29/26/78; *Archeologia*, pp. 335–6.
11. Colonel Richard Talbot was a gentleman of the bedchamber and Colonel Robert Werden a groom of the bedchamber to the Duke of York. See *DNB* for Talbot and Newman, *Royalist Officers*, p. 405 for Werden. In a petition of 3 September 1660 Church is described as a servant to Queen Henrietta Maria. *CSPD 1660–1661*, p. 254.

12. *BIHR*, pp. 14–5. Of Charles II's other grooms of the bedchamber in the 1650s, Richard Harding died in exile in 1658 and Thomas Blague a few months after the Restoration.

13. The three pages of the bedchamber were Thomas Chiffinch, Hugh Griffith and Maurice Deladale. Sir John Pooley, Sir William Fleming and Marmaduke Darcy were the gentleman ushers of the privy chamber. *BIHR*, p. 15.

14. Ibid, p. 16; *SP 29/26/78*; *HMC, Ormonde MSS*, 36 N.S., vii, 205; *Archeologia*, xxxv, 341.

15. *HMC, Pepys MSS*, 70, pp. 255–6; *ClSP*, iii, 296–7; *BIHR*, 19, 31; David Ogg, *England in the Reign of Charles II*, (Oxford, 1967), p. 331.

16. *HMC, Pepys MSS*, 70, pp. 255–6; PRO. *SP 18/158/10/*; *29/26/78/*; Bod. L. *Clarendon MS 66*, fols. 88–9; BL. *Egerton MS 2542*, fols. 331, 348; *Archeologia*, xxxv, 342–3; *CClSP*, ii, 384, 387; *CSPD 1661–1662*, p. 271.

17. *TSP*, iii, 532; BL. *Egerton MS 2542*, f. 352; H. C. de Lafontaine, *The King's Musick: a Transcript of Records Relating to Music and Musicians 1460–1700*, (London, 1909), pp. 114, 119–20, 137, 192.

18. Bod. L. *Clarendon MS 66*, fols. 134–5; BL. *Egerton MS 2542*, fols. 330, 331, 332, 342, 343, 344, 347, 348, 352 and passim.

19. For a discussion of both Herbert's and other cases, see G. E. Aylmer, *The Crown's Servants: Government and Civil Service Under Charles II, 1660–1685*, (Oxford, 2002), pp. 70–2.

20. For a discussion of perceived threats to the restored monarchy see Marshall, *Intelligence and Espionage in the Reign of Charles II, 1660–1685*, passim.

21. Henning, *House of Commons*, 3 vols., passim.

22. Ibid, i, 755–7; ii, 626–30; iii, 21–1, 141–3, 702, 774.

23. Between 1650 and 1660 Charles II conferred peerages on the following English exiles: Henry, Lord Wilmot, Earl of Rochester (1652); Sir John Berkeley, Baron Berkeley (1658); William Crofts, Baron Crofts (1658); Sir Marmaduke Langdale, Baron Langdale (1658); Henry, Lord Jermyn, Earl of St Albans (1660). John Mordaunt received a viscountcy in 1659 and earldoms were also conferred on the Irish Lord Inchiquin and the Scots Lord Newburgh and John Middleton in 1660.

24. Cregan, 'An Irish Cavalier: Daniel O'Neill in Exile and Restoration 1651–64', *Studia Hibernica*, v, 64–6; Aylmer, *The Crown's Servants*, pp. 39, 86; *DNB*; Henning, *House of Commons*, iii, 172–4; *Evelyn's Diary*, ed. Bray, ii, 106; *Pepys Diary*, 24 October 1664.

25. Quotation from Aylmer, *The Crowns's Servants*, accompanying illustration No. 18. See also Ibid, pp. 45, 71, 177, 213; Clay, *Public Finance and Private Wealth*, passim.

26. Tomalin, *Samuel Pepys*, pp. 133–4; *Pepys Diary*, 22 December 1661; For Nicolls see *Mordaunt Letter-Book*, p. 7; *DNB*. For Holmes see Richard Ollard, *Man of War: Sir Robert Holmes and the Restoration Navy*, (London, 1969).

27. Newman, *Royalist Officers*, pp. 151, 278, 404.

28. For Skelton's activities see *TSP*, iv, 835; *ClSP*, iii, 364, *CCLSP*, iii, 125, 199, 210, 374, 409; iv, 101, 135; *HMC, Bath MSS*, ii, 86–7; *NP*, iii, 178; *CSPD 1656–1657*, p. 585; Clay, *Public Finance and Private Wealth*, p. 33; Underdown, *Royalist Conspiracy*, pp. 179, 206. For Leighton see Newman, *Royalist Officers*, p. 230.

29. *CSP Ireland, 1660–1662*, 334, 354, 367, 469, 531, 645–6; *1663–1665*, 244, 267; *HMC, Ormonde MSS*, i 239, 256. For the '1649 Officers' see Kevin McKenny, 'Charles II's Irish Cavaliers: the 1649 officers and the Restoration land settlement', *Irish Historical Studies*, 28, (November, 1993), pp. 409–25.
30. *CSPD 1661–1662*, p. 458; *CSP Ireland 1663–1665*, pp. 499–500, 640; *1666–1669*, p. 308; *HMC Ormonde MSS*, ii, 186.
31. *CSP Ireland 1660–1662*, pp. 295, 356, 399, 451, 467, 552; Carte, *Life of Ormonde*, passim.
32. *CSP Ireland 1660–1662*, p. 586; *1663–1665*, pp. 320–1, 351, 354, 355, 357; *1666–1669*, p. 752.
33. *CSPD, 1664–1665*, p. 73. For Fortescue see *DNB*; Newman, *Royalist Officers*, p. 142.
34. *TSP*, ii, 373; iii, 457; BL. *Egerton MS 2542*, f. 343; *DNB* (Massey and Hatton); Newman, *Royalist Officers*, pp. 41–2 (Brett); Henning, *House of Commons*, iii, 29–31 (Massey).
35. *Halkett and Fanshawe Memoirs*, pp. 140, 145–9, 154–84; *HMC 2nd Report, Cotterell MSS*, pp. 82–3; Henning, *House of Commons*, ii, 138, 298–9; *BIHR*, p. 16; Aylmer, *Crown's Servants*, p. 188.
36. Bargrave, *Pope Alexander VII and the College of Cardinals*, pp. xiii–xvii; *CSPD 1660–1661*, p. 259; *1661–1662*, pp. 276, 284; *1663–1664*, pp. 67, 354; *Private Correspondence and Miscellaneous Papers of Samuel Pepys, 1679–1703*, ed. J. R. Tanner, 2 vols., (London, 1926), i, 116; H. H. Rowen, *John de Witt, Grand Pensionary of Holland, 1625–1672*, (Princeton, 1978), pp. 519, 542–3; *DNB* (Ross and Coventry).
37. *CSPD 1660–1661*, pp. 212, 523, 554.
38. Ibid, pp. 76, 595; *1660–1685, Addenda*, pp. 307–8; *1660–1670, Addenda*, p. 570; *1664–1665*, p. 538; *1671–1672*, p. 328; *1675–1676*, p. 167.
39. Aylmer, *The Crown's Servants*, pp. 158–9; Newman, *Royalist Officers*, p. 26.
40. PRO. *SP/29/5/7*; Bod. L. *Clarendon MS 78*, fols. 175–6, 177–8.
41. *CSPD, 1660–1661*, pp. 240, 443; *1661–1662*, p. 528; Bod. L. *Fairfax MS 32*, f. 182; *Somers Tracts*, vii, 3–8; Newman, *Royalist Officers*, pp. 17, 59, 230; Underdown *Royalist Conspiracy*, pp. 139, 142, 145.

14 The Brand of the Emigré

1. Feiling, *History of the Tory Party*, p. 78.
2. Ibid, pp. 78–9. See also the view of Alan Marshall that the 'exiles . . . had suffered, fought and plotted their way through the 1650s and Charles and his key ministers brought all these experiences into government with them: *Intelligence and Espionage in the Reign of Charles* II, p. 8.
3. Paul Seward, 'The Restoration 1660–1668', in *Stuart England*, ed. Blair Worden, (Oxford, 1986), p. 155.
4. *Commons Journal*, viii, 502. For examples of returned exiles listed as 'court dependants' see Henning, *House of Commons*, i, 750 (Bulteale); ii, 138 (Cotterell); 192 (Darcy); 356 (Fox); 518 (Heath); iii, 30 (Massey); 34 (Mauleverer); 35 (May); 173 (O'Neill); 238 (Phelips); 285 (Price); 294 (Progers); 343 (Robinson); 422 (Seymour); 524 (Talbot); 594 (Trelawney); 702 (Wheeler); 774 (Wyndham).

5. Ibid, iii, 71–2, 142–3.
6. For Buckingham see Hutton, *Charles* II, passim; Hester Chapman, *Great Villiers*, (London, 1949). For Titus see Aylmer, *The Crown's Servants*, pp. 164–5; Henning, *House of Commons*, iii, 570–4; *DNB*.
7. Quoted in Tomalin, *Pepys*, p. 108.
8. *Somers Tracts*, vii, 390–3; *CCISP*, iv, 629–30; Keeble, *Restoration*, pp. 58–9.
9. For recent discussions of this issue see Keeble, *Restoration*, pp. 85–9; Aylmer, *The Crown's Servants*, pp. 264–8.
10. *Pepys Diary*, v, 56. (22 February 1664).
11. Sir Charles Berkeley was created Viscount Fitzhardinge in 1663 and Earl of Falmouth in 1665. 'Hamilton' probably refers to one of the courtier and professional soldier sons of the Irish royalist Sir George Hamilton.
12. For Fox's loyalty to Clarendon see Clay, *Public Finance and Private Wealth*, pp. 11–16, 117–18. For Coventry's see Ollard, *Clarendon and His Friends*, pp. 286, 345.
13. *NP*, ii, 25, 217; Clarendon, *Rebellion*, i, 96, 97, 98; *Life*, i, 615; ii, 191; *Halkett and Fanshawe Memoirs*, p. 140; Ollard, *Clarendon and His Friends*, pp. 171–3; Hutton, *Charles* II, p. 144; Seaward, *Cavalier Parliament*, pp. 84–5, 217–21.
14. BL. *Harleian MS 1843*, fols. 3–7; *CSPD 1663–1664*, p. 2; Henning, *House of Commons*, iii, 524. For numerous examples of petitions to Ormonde for places in the royal household and for offices in Ireland see Bod. L. *Carte MS 31*, passim.
15. Bod. L. *Carte MS 32*, fols. 346–7, and passim. For O'Neill's role as an intermediary between Charles and Ormonde see Alan Marshall, *The Age of Faction: Court Politics 1660–1702*, (Manchester University Press, 1999), p. 39.
16. *CSP Ireland 1663–1665*, pp. 633, 640, 641; *1666–1669*, pp. 391, 456–7; *Letters to Sir Joseph Williamson*, ed. W. D. Christie, Camden Soc., (London, 1874), 2 vols., ii, 24. Arlington and Lord Ossory, Ormonde's eldest son, were married to the daughters of Louis of Orange-Nessau, whom they had met when they were in exile.
17. *CSPD 1661–1662*, pp. 86, 276, 284, 458; *1663–1664*, pp. 67, 343; *1667–1688*, p. 543; *1673–1675*, pp. 108; *CSP Ireland 1663–1665*, pp. 87, 91, 268, 301, 640–1, 654; *1669–1670*, pp. 65, 161, 163, 281. For examples of O'Neill's correspondence with Ormonde see Bod. L. *Carte MS 32*, fols. 3, 9, 23, 26, 312, 405; for Henry Coventry to Ormonde see BL. *Add. MS 25125*, fols. 59, 61, 65.
18. Carte, *Letters and Papers*, i, 155; *HMC, 10th Report*, iv, 147; *CSPD 1655*, pp. 204, 588; *NP*, iii, 5; iv, 20; Keeler, *Long Parliament*, p. 142; Barbour, *Arlington*, p. 7; Balleine, *All for the King*, p. 78; Henning, *House of Commons*, ii, 134–5, 172; iii, 257, 294.
19. *Pepys Papers and Correspondence*, ii, 238.
20. Graham Parry, 'Minds and Manners 1660–1688', in *Stuart England*, ed. Blair Worden, p. 176. See also Keeble, *Restoration*, pp. 171–82.
21. Ibid, pp. 176–8; Fraser, *King Charles* II, pp. 153, 280–4; Underdown, *Royalist Conspiracy*, pp. 59, 75–6, 81–2, 333.
22. Henning, *House of Commons*, iii, 237–8, 421–2, (Phelips and Seymour); Newman, *Royalist Officers*, p. 285 (Phelips); Aylmer, *The Crown's Servants*, p. 164 (Titus).

23. Blague was a friend of Gerard and the correspondence of Nicholas and Hatton sometimes associates him with the group around Gerard who attempted to undermine Hyde's position as the king's chief adviser. *NP*, ii, 151, 157; *CClSP*, iii, 115.

24. *Memorials of the Holles Family*, p. 2.

25. For Bab May see *CClSP*, i, 445, ii, 304; *HMC, Bath MSS*, ii, 97; *CSPD 1651–1652*, p. 143; Aylmer, 'Patronage at the Court of Charles II', in the *Stuart Courts*, ed. Eveline Cruickshanks, (Sutton Publishing, 2000), p. 196; Henning, *The House of Commons*, iii, 35–6; Aylmer, *The Crown's Servants*, p. 25. For Hugh May see *CSPD 1655*, p. 582; *1661–1662*, p. 275; H. M. Colvin, *A Biographical Dictionary of English Architects 1660–1840*, (London, 1954) pp. 382–3.

26. *TSP*, (*Lambeth MSS*), i, 682.

27. Bod. L. *Carte MS 32*, f. 405. See also Ibid, fols. 3, 9, 23, 26, 312.

28. Quotations from Cregan 'Daniel O'Neill in Exile and Restoration', p. 72.

29. Pepys quoted in Hardacre 'Royalists in Exile', p. 370; Edward Hyde, Earl of Clarendon, *A Collection of Several Tracts*, (Oxford, 1727), p. 336.

30. Stoye, *English Travellers Abroad*, especially pp. 323–6.

31. Ibid, p. 323.

32. For a valuable discussion of Clarendon's political thinking at the time of the Restoration see Seaward, *The Cavalier Parliament and the Reconstruction of the Old Regime*, pp. 15–21.

33. *TSP*, ii, 534.

34. Miller, *James II*, pp. 17, 20–1, 43, 227–30.

35. *HMC, Ormonde MSS*, New Series, 36, vol. 7, 410.

References

Manuscript sources

Bodleian Library, Oxford

Carte MSS 29–34 (Ormonde papers)
Clarendon MSS 42–78
Fairfax MSS (Includes Thomas Paulden's letter)
Rawlinson MSS A15–65 (Thurloe papers)
Rawlinson MS C799 (John Bargrave's travel journal)

British Library, London

Additional MSS 4156–8 (Thurloe papers)
Additional MS 4180 (Nicholas papers)
Additional MS 15 858 (Correspondence of Sir Richard Browne)
Additional MSS 18 980–2 (Miscellaneous papers: includes correspondence of Prince Rupert and Lord Digby)
Additional MS 19 253 (Miscellaneous papers: includes autobiography of Lord Chesterfield)
Additional MS 20 032 (Killigrew papers)
Additional MS 21 427 (Long papers)
Additional MS 24 121 (Wyche papers)
Additional MS 25 125 (Henry Coventry papers)
Additional MS 28 875 (Miscellaneous papers: includes correspondence of Nicholas Armorer)
Egerton MS 1635 (Travel notebook of Richard Symonds)
Egerton MSS 2534–7, 2542–3, 2546, 2550 (Nicholas papers)
Harleian MSS 943, 1278 (Travel notebooks of Richard Symonds)
Harleian MSs 986, 6852 (Sir Stephen Hawkins papers)

Public Record Office, London

SP 18 (State Papers, Domestic, Interregnum)
SP 23 (Records of proceedings of Committee for Compounding)
SP 28–9 (State Papers, Domestic, Charles II)
SP 77 (State Papers, Foreign, Flanders)
SP 78 (State Papers, Foreign, France)
SP 81 (State Papers, Foreign, German States)

Printed primary sources

Calendars

Calendar of the Clarendon State Papers, ed. O. Ogle, W. H. Bliss, W. D. Macray and F. J. Routledge, 5 vols. (Oxford, 1869–1970)

Calendar of the Proceedings of the Committee for Compounding, ed. M. A. Green (London, 1889–92)

Calendar of State Papers, Domestic Series, 1640–1675, ed. M. A. E. Green (London, 1875–86)

Calendar of State Papers, Ireland, 1603–1675, ed. C. W. Russell, J. P. Prendergast and R. P. Mahaffy (London, 1870–1910)

Calendar of State Papers . . . relating to English Affairs . . . in the Archives and Collections of Venice, ed. R. Brown (London, 1864–)

Correspondence, diaries and memoirs

Anon., *Memoirs of Sir Stephen Fox* (London, 1717)

Cavendish, Margaret, Duchess of Newcastle, *The Life of . . . William Cavendish, Duke of Newcastle* (London, 1915)

Cholmley, Sir Hugh, *Memoirs of Sir Hugh Cholmley, Bt.* (privately printed, 1787)

A Collection of Original Letters and Papers, Concerning the Affairs of England . . . 1641–1660, Found among the Duke of Ormond's Papers, ed. Thomas Carte, 2 vols. (London, 1739)

A Collection of the Papers of John Thurloe, Esq., ed. Thomas Birch, 7 vols. (London, 1742)

The Diary of John Evelyn, ed. W. Bray and H. B. Wheatley, 4 vols. (London, 1879). (Appendix includes correspondence of Elizabeth of Bohemia, Hyde, Nicholas and other exiles)

The Diary of Samuel Pepys, ed. R. Latham and W. Matthews, 11 vols. (London, 1976–1983)

Hamilton, Anthony, *Memoirs of the Court of Charles II by Count Grammont*, ed. Sir Walter Scott (London, 1853)

Holles, Gervase, *Memorials of the Holles Family, 1493–1656*, Camden Society (London, 1937)

Hyde, Edward, first Earl of Clarendon, *The Life of Edward, Earl of Clarendon*, 2 vols. (Oxford, 1857)

The Letter-Book of John, Viscount Mordaunt, 1658–1660, ed. Mary Coate, Camden Society (London, 1945)

Letters and Papers Illustrating the Relations between Charles II and Scotland in 1650, ed. S. R. Gardiner, Scottish Historical Society (Edinburgh, 1894)

Letters to Sir Joseph Williamson, ed. W. D. Christie, Camden Society, 2 vols. (London, 1874)

The Life and Letters of Sir Lewis Dyve, 1599–1669, ed. H. G. Tibbutt, Bedfordshire Historical Society (Streatley, 1948)

The Memoirs of Anne, Lady Halkett and Ann, Lady Fanshawe, ed. John Loftis (Oxford, 1979)

Memoirs of James II: His Campaigns as Duke of York, 1652–1660, ed. J. S. Clark and A. Lytton Sells (London, 1962)

Memoirs of the Verney Family, ed. Frances Parthenope Verney, 3 vols. (London, 1970)

Miscellanea Aulica, ed. T. Brown (London, 1702), (Includes correspondence of Charles II, Sir Henry Bennet and Abraham Cowley)

The Nicholas Papers: Correspondence of Sir Edward Nicholas, Secretary of State, ed. G. F. Warner, Camden Society, 4 vols. (London, 1886–1920)

Private Correspondence and Miscellaneous Papers of Samuel Pepys, 1679–1703, ed. J. R. Tanner, 2 vols. (London, 1926)
State Papers Collected by Edward, Earl of Clarendon, ed. R. Scrope and T. Monkhouse, 3 vols. (Oxford, 1767–86)
The Travels and Memoirs of Sir John Reresby, Bt., ed. A. Browning (Glasgow, 1936)

Historical manuscript reports

2nd Report, Appendix, Cotterell Dormer MSS (Cotterell papers)
6th Report, Appendix (Letters of Charles II)
7th Report, Appendix (Petition of Major Thomas Hunt)
10th Report, 1V, Story Maskelyne MSS (Letters from Charles II and other exiles to Edward Progers)
10th Report, Appendix V1, Braye MSS (Mordaunt papers)
13th Report, Appendix 1, Duke of Portland MSS (Miscellaneous papers)
45th Report, Duke of Buccleuch MSS (Gervase Holles papers)
55th Report, Various Collections, ii, Mrs Harford MSS (Letters from exiles to Sir Marmaduke Langdale)
Marquess of Both MSS, ii (correspondence of several exiles including Hyde, Holles, Radcliffe and Ross)
Duke of Ormonde MSS, old series, I, ii; new series, iii, vii (Ormonde papers)
Pepys MSS, 70 (List of royal household 1649, pp. 255–6)

Official documents, contemporary histories, pamphlets

Acts and Ordinances of the Interregnum, 1642–1660, ed. C. H. Firth and C. S. Rait, 3 vols. (London, 1911)
Archeologia, xxxv (London, 1853), 335–49.
Army Lists of the Roundheads and Cavaliers, ed. Edward Peacock (London, 1863)
Bargrave, John, *Pope Alexander VII and the College of Cardinals*, ed. J. C. Robertson, Camden Society (London, 1867), (Source for Bargrave's travels in Italy)
Baxter, Sir Richard, *A Chronicle of the Kings of England, Whereunto is Added the Reign of King Charles I and the first Thirteen years of his Sacred Majesty King Charles II* (London, 1679)
Chamberlayne, Edward, *Angliae Notitia or the Present State of England*, 2 vols. (London, 1671), (Contains lists of MPs, members of the royal household and other office holders after 1660)
A Collection of Scarce and Valuable Tracts . . . particularly [those] . . . of the late Lord Somers, ed. Sir Walter Scott, 13 vols. (London, 1809–15)
The English Baronetage . . . and a List of such Persons' Names who were Deemed Fit and Qualified at the Restoration to be made Knights of the Royal Oak (London, 1741)
Hyde, Edward, first Earl of Clarendon, *The History of the Rebellion and Civil Wars in England*, ed. W. D. Macray, 6 vols. (Oxford, 1888)
Journals of the House of Commons (London, 1742–)
The King's Musick: a Transcript of Records relating to Music and Musicians 1460–1700 (Records of the Lord Chamberlain's department), ed. H. C. de Lafontaine (London, 1909)
'A List of the Department of the Lord Chamberlain of the Household, autumn 1663', *Bulletin of the Institute of Historical Research*, vol. 19 (London, 1942–3)

Neville, Henry, *The Commonwealth of Ladies*, Thomason Tract E. 590 (10), (London, 1649)
The Poetical works of Edmund Waller and Sir John Denham, ed. G. Gilfillan (Edinburgh, 1857)

Secondary sources

The standard histories of the period are not included in this bibliography. Nor are those works, in particular county and family histories and studies of campaigns in the Civil Wars, which were useful in identifying the backgrounds and careers of particular Cavaliers before they went into exile. They are cited in the appropriate footnotes.

Aylmer, G. E., *The King's Servants: the Civil Service of Charles I, 1625–1642* (revised edition, London, 1974)
—— *The State's Servants: the Civil Service of the English Republic, 1659–1660* (London, 1973)
—— *The Crown's Servants: Government and Civil Service Under Charles II, 1660–1685* (Oxford, 2000)
Balleine, G. R., *All for the King: the Life Story of Sir George Carteret*, Societe Jersiaise (Jersey, 1976)
Barbour, Violet, *Henry Bennet, Earl of Arlington* (Washington, 1914)
Bosher, R. S., *The Making of the Restoration Settlement: the Influence of the Laudians* (London, 1951)
Carte, Thomas, *The Life of James Duke of Ormond*, 6 vols. (Oxford, 1851)
Chaney, Edward, *The Grand Tour and the Great Rebellion: Richard Lassels and 'The Voyage of Italy' in the Seventeenth Century* (Geneva, 1985)
Chapman, Hester, *The Tragedy of Charles II in the Years 1630–1660* (London, 1964)
The Civil Wars: a Military History of England, Scotland and Ireland, 1638–1660, ed. John Kenyon and Jane Ohlmeyer (Oxford, 1998)
Clay, Christopher, *Public Finance and Private Wealth: the Career of Sir Stephen Fox, 1627–1716* (Oxford, 1978)
Coate, Mary, *Cornwall in the Great Civil War and Interregnum, 1642–1660* (Oxford, 1933)
Cowan, E. J., *Montrose: For Covenant and King* (London, 1977)
Cregan, Donal F., 'An Irish Cavalier: Daniel O'Neill', *Studia Hibernica*, iii (1963), 60–100
—— 'An Irish Cavalier: Daniel O'Neill in the Civil Wars, 1642–51', *Studia Hibernica*, iv (1964), 104–33
—— 'An Irish Cavalier: Daniel O'Neill in Exile and Restoration, 1651–64', *Studia Hibernica*, v (1965), 42–76
Dictionary of National Biography, 22 vols (Oxford, 1885–1901)
Edgar, F. T. R., *Sir Ralph Hopton: the King's Man in the West, 1642–1652* (Oxford, 1968)
The English Court: from the Wars of the Roses to the Civil War, ed. David Starkey et al. (London, 1987)
Feiling, Sir Keith, *A History of the Tory Party, 1640–1714* (Oxford, 1924)
Firth, C. H., 'Royalist and Cromwellian Armies in Flanders, 1657–1662', *Transactions of the Royal Historical Society*, new series, v, 17 (1903), 67–119
Fraser, Antonia, *King Charles II* (London, 1979)

Green, M. A. E., *Lives of the Princesses of England*, 6 vols. (London, 1854–5)

Hardacre, P. H., *The Royalists During the Puritan Revolution* (Hague, 1956)

Hardacre, P. H., 'The Royalists in Exile During the Puritan Revolution', *Huntington Library Quarterly*, xvi (San Marino, California, 1952), 353–70

Hartmann, H., *The King's Friend: A Life of Charles Berkeley, Viscount Fitzhardinge, Earl of Falmouth, 1630–1665* (London, 1951)

Henning, B. D., *The History of Parliament: the House of Commons 1660–1690*, 3 vols. (London, 1983)

Hutton, Ronald, *Charles II: King of England, Scotland and Ireland* (Oxford, 1989)

——*The Restoration, 1658–1667* (Oxford, 1985)

——'The Structure of the Royalist Party', *Historical Journal*, 24 (1981), 553–69

Huxley, Gervas, *Endymion Porter: the Life of a Courtier, 1597–1649* (London, 1959)

Keeble, N. H., *The Restoration: England in the 1660s* (Oxford, 2002)

Keeler, M. F., *The Long Parliament, 1640–1641* (Philadelphia, 1954)

Lister, T. H., *The Life and Administration of Edward, First Earl of Clarendon*, 3 vols. (London, 1837–8)

Marshall, Alan, *The Age of Faction: Court Politics 1660–1702* (Manchester, 1999)

——*Intelligence and Espionage in the Reign of Charles II* (Cambridge, 1994)

Miller, John, *James II: A Study in Kingship* (London, 1989)

Morrah, Patrick, *Prince Rupert of the Rhine* (London, 1974)

Morrill, John, 'The Later Stuarts: A Glorious Restoration', *History Today*, 38 (July, 1988)

Newman, P. R., *Royalist Officers in England and Wales, 1642–1660: A Biographical Dictionary* (New York, 1981)

Nicholas, Donald, *Mr Secretary Nicholas, 1593–1669: His Life and Letters* (London, 1955)

Ollard, Richard, *Clarendon and his Friends* (Oxford, 1988)

——*Man of War: a Life of Sir Robert Holmes* (London, 1969)

Oman, Carola, *Elizabeth of Bohemia* (London, 1938)

Robertson, A., *The Life of Sir Robert Moray, 1608–1673* (London, 1922)

Scott, Eva, *The King in Exile, 1646–1654* (London, 1905)

——*The Travels of King Charles II in Germany and Flanders, 1654–1660* (London, 1907)

Scott, Jonathan, *England's Troubles: Seventeenth-century English Political Instability in European Context* (Cambridge, 2000)

Seaward, Paul, *The Cavalier Parliament and the Reconstruction of the Old Regime, 1661–1667* (Cambridge, 1989)

Smith, David L., *Constitutional Royalism and the Search for Settlement, c.1640–1649* (Cambridge, 1994)

Steinman, G. S., *Althorp Memoirs* (privately printed, 1869)

Stoye, J. W., *English Travellers Abroad, 1604–1667* (revised edition, New Haven and London, 1989)

Underdown, David, *Royalist Conspiracy in England, 1649–1660* (New Haven, 1960)

——'Cavaliers in Exile', *History of the English Speaking People*, ed. M. Wheeler, H. Trevor-Roper and A. J. P. Taylor, no. 53 (London, 1970), pp. 1692–5

Warburton, B. E. G., *Memoirs of Prince Rupert and the Cavaliers*, 3 vols. (London, 1849)

Woolrych, A. H., *Penruddock's Rising 1655* (Historical Association, 1955)

Index